ROUTLEDGE HANDBOOK OF THE SOUTH CHINA SEA

The *Routledge Handbook of the South China Sea* presents a comprehensive and in-depth analysis of South China Sea issues. It evaluates the dynamics of the latest developments and identifies factors that contribute to dispute settlement and a cooperative management regime of one of the most important seas in the world – one which not only contains rich marine resources and distinctive biodiversity but is also a critical sea route for global trade and communications.

The Handbook is divided into six parts, each representing a focused area of enquiry:

- History and geostrategic landscape
- Sovereignty and maritime entitlements
- South China Sea policies of major claimants
- Natural resources and environment
- Cooperation and institutions
- Challenges and prospects

Written by world-renowned experts and scholars, with specialisms from geography to international law, the volume's 25 chapters contribute interdisciplinary perspectives, reflecting the impact of how South China Sea policies are shaped by national governments and international organizations. As such, the Handbook provides an authoritative reference to South China Sea Studies, useful for students and scholars of international relations, history, maritime and Asian studies.

Keyuan Zou is Distinguished Professor, Dalian Maritime University, China and Harris Professor of International Law, University of Central Lancashire, UK. He specializes in international law, in particular, the law of the sea and international environmental law, and has published extensively with over 180 refereed English papers in over 30 international journals and various edited books. His single-authored books include *Law of the Sea in East Asia: Issues and Prospects*, *China's Marine Legal System and the Law of the Sea*, *China's Legal Reform: Towards the Rule of Law* and *China-ASEAN Relations and International Law*. His recent edited volumes include *Global Commons and the Law of the Sea* (2018), *Maritime Cooperation in Semi-Enclosed Seas: Asian and European Experiences* (2019) and *The Belt and Road Initiative and the Law of the Sea* (2020). He is a member of Editorial/Advisory Boards of the *International Journal of Marine and Coastal Law*, *Ocean Development and International Law*, *Journal of International Wildlife Law and Policy*, *Marine Policy*, *Copenhagen Journal of Asian Studies*, *Journal of Territorial and Maritime Studies*, *Chinese Journal of International Law*, *Global Journal of Comparative Law*, *Asia-Pacific Journal of Ocean Law and Policy* and *Korean Journal of International & Comparative Law*.

ROUTLEDGE HANDBOOK OF THE SOUTH CHINA SEA

Edited by Keyuan Zou

Routledge
Taylor & Francis Group
LONDON AND NEW YORK

First published 2021
by Routledge
2 Park Square, Milton Park, Abingdon, Oxon OX14 4RN

and by Routledge
605 Third Avenue, New York, NY 10158

Routledge is an imprint of the Taylor & Francis Group, an informa business

British Library Cataloguing-in-Publication Data
A catalogue record for this book is available from the British Library

Library of Congress Cataloging-in-Publication Data
Names: Zou, Keyuan, editor.
Title: Routledge handbook of the South China Sea / edited by Keyuan Zou.
Description: Milton Park, Abingdon, Oxon; New York, NY: Routledge, 2021. |
Includes bibliographical references and index. |
Contents: The South China Sea: geographical overview / Vivian Louis Forbes — The South China Sea: historical developments / Stein Tønnesson — Sea lines of communication and safety of navigation / Sam Bateman — Maritime security and demilitarization of the South China Sea / Mary George — The territorial sovereignty disputes in the South China Sea / Ted L. McDorman — Competing maritime claims and enduring disputes in the South China Sea / Clive Schofield — The u-shaped line and its legal implications / Keyuan Zou and Qiang Ye — Historic rights and the South China Sea / Sophia Kopela — China's South China Sea policies / Feng Zhu and Lingqun Li — Malaysia and South China Sea disputes: applicability of international law / BA Hamzah — Deciphering Duterte's foreign policy on the South China Sea / Jay L. Batongbacal — Vietnam's South China Sea policy / Nguyen Hong Thao — Fisheries management in the South China Sea / Dustin Kuan-Hsiung Wang — Governance of non-living resources in the South China / SeaYen-Chiang Chang — Biodiversity and conservation / Vu Hai Dang — The South China Sea environment: the need for formalised institutional interaction between science, policy and law / David M. Ong — Semi-enclosed seas cooperation under UNCLOS / Seokwoo Lee and Lowell Bautista — ASEAN and the South China Sea / Robert Beckman and Vu Hai Dang — From DOC to COC: a regional rule-based order / Ramses Amer and Li Jianwei — Mainland China-Taiwan interplay in the South China Sea / Fu-kuo Liu — Cooperation through track II mechanisms / Rommel C. Banlaoi — Dispute settlement mechanisms for South China Sea / Issues J. Ashley Roach — The South China Sea arbitration and its implications / Chris Whomersley — US-China rivalry in the South China Sea / Mingjiang Li and Archana Atmakuri —Struggles for prestige and power: command, contest, and confidence-building in the South China Sea, 1960-2019 / C.J. Jenner. | Summary: "The Routledge Handbook of the South China Sea presents a comprehensive and in-depth analysis of South China Sea issues. It evaluates the dynamics of latest developments and identifying factors that contribute to dispute settlement and cooperative management regime of one of the most important seas in the world, one which not only contains rich marine resources and distinctive biodiversity but is also a critical sea route for global trade and communications. The Handbook is divided into six parts, each representing a focused area of enquiry: History and Geostrategic Landscape Sovereignty and Maritime Entitlements South China Sea Policies of Major Claimants Natural Resources and Environment Cooperation and Institutions Challenges and Prospects Written by world renowned experts and scholars, with specialisms from geography to international law, the volume's twenty-five chapters contribute interdisciplinary perspectives, reflecting the impact of how South China Sea policies are shaped by national governments and international organisations. As such, the Handbook provides an authoritative reference to South China Sea Studies, useful for students and scholars of international relations, history, maritime and Asian studies"— Provided by publisher.
Identifiers: LCCN 2021001199 | ISBN 9780367415556 (hardback) | ISBN 9781032013237 (paperback) | ISBN 9780367822217 (ebk) | ISBN 9781000396133 (adobe pdf) | ISBN 9781000396157 (epub)
Subjects: LCSH: South China Sea—International status. Classification: LCC KZA1692 .R68 2021 | DDC 341.4/480916472—dc23 LC record available at https://lccn.loc.gov/2021001199

ISBN: 978-0-367-41555-6 (hbk)
ISBN: 978-1-032-01323-7 (pbk)
ISBN: 978-0-367-82221-7 (ebk)

Typeset in Bembo
by codeMantra

CONTENTS

FIGURES

TABLES

APPENDICES

ACKNOWLEDGMENTS

It is gratefully acknowledged that this Handbook is an outcome of collective wisdom and intelligence of the renowned contributors from various countries across the world. Without these substantive contributions, a handbook like this is simply impossible to come into being. My sincere gratitude goes to former Judge David Andersen who kindly agreed to write the Foreword. Thanks also go to Mr. Qiang Ye who served as a coordinator for this book project and assisted me during the whole editing process. Finally, I express my big thanks to Ms. Stephanie Rogers, Ms. Emily Pickthall, and others at Routledge who provided considerable assistance in accomplishing this Handbook, in particular Stephanie who initiated this significant project and made it a most influential book on the South China Sea Studies.

EDITOR AND CONTRIBUTORS

Editor:

Keyuan Zou is Distinguished Professor, Dalian Maritime University, China and Harris Professor of International Law, University of Central Lancashire, UK. He specializes in international law, in particular, the law of the sea and international environmental law and published extensively over 180 refereed English papers in over 30 international journals and various edited books. His single-authored books include *Law of the Sea in East Asia: Issues and Prospects*, *China's Marine Legal System and the Law of the Sea*, *China's Legal Reform: Towards the Rule of Law* and *China-ASEAN Relations and International Law*. His recent edited volumes include *Global Commons and the Law of the Sea* (2018), *Maritime Cooperation in Semi-Enclosed Seas: Asian and European Experiences* (2019) and *The Belt and Road Initiative and the Law of the Sea* (2020). He is a member of Editorial/Advisory Boards of *International Journal of Marine and Coastal Law*, *Ocean Development and International Law*, *Journal of International Wildlife Law and Policy*, *Marine Policy*, *Copenhagen Journal of Asian Studies*, *Journal of Territorial and Maritime Studies*, *Chinese Journal of International Law*, *Global Journal of Comparative Law*, *Asia-Pacific Journal of Ocean Law and Policy* and *Korean Journal of International & Comparative Law*.

Contributors (in alphabetical order)

Ramses Amer, formerly Associate Professor and PhD in Peace and Conflict Research from Uppsala University, is an Associated Research Fellow at Institute for Security & Development Policy, Sweden. Amer's major areas of research include (a) security issues and conflict resolution in Southeast Asia and the wider Pacific Asia and (b) the role of the United Nations in the international system. His current research focuses on regional collaboration and conflict management in Pacific Asia, e.g. the conflict situation in the South China Sea and the relationship between China and Vietnam. Amer is the author of "China, Vietnam and the South China Sea: Disputes and Dispute Management", *Ocean Development and International Law* 45:1 (January–March 2014) and "The South China Sea: Achievements and Challenges to Dispute Management", *Asia Survey* 55:3 (2015). He is co-editor with Carlyle A. Thayer of *Vietnamese Foreign Policy in Transition* (1999). He is co-editor, with Keyuan Zou, of *Conflict Management and Dispute Settlement in East Asia* (2011).

David H. Anderson attended many international conferences, including the Vienna Conference on the Law of Treaties and the Third UN Conference on the Law of the Sea, and took part in many maritime boundary negotiations. In 1996, he was elected as an inaugural judge of the *International Tribunal for the Law of the Sea*. He has published extensively about the law of the sea, including maritime boundary issues and the peaceful settlement of international disputes.

Archana Atmakuri is currently a Research Analyst at the Institute of South Asian Studies (ISAS) at the National University of Singapore. Her research interests are India's foreign policy in South Asia, China's foreign policy in the Indian Ocean, great power politics and political communication which deals with fake news and misinformation. She has published several commentaries on these themes. Previously, Archana worked as a visiting research fellow at the China programme at the S. Rajaratnam School of International Studies at Nanyang Technological University where she researched on China's non-traditional security diplomacy in Southeast Asia and soft power strategy in the Pacific.

Rommel C. Banlaoi is a Professorial Lecturer at the Department of International Studies, Miriam College and Adjunct Research Professor at the National Institute for South China Sea Studies. He is currently the President of the Philippine Association for Chinese Studies and Chairman of the Philippine Institute for Peace, Violence and Terrorism Research. He sits as a member of the following: Management Board of the World Association for Chinese Studies, Board of Directors of the China-Southeast Asia Research Center on the South China Sea and International Panel of Experts of the Maritime Awareness Project of the National Bureau of Asian Research. He was a Professor of Political Science at the National Defense College of the Philippines, Assistant Professor of International Studies at De La Salle University, Instructor of Political Science at the University of the Philippines (UP) Los Baños, and University Research Associate at UP Diliman where he obtained his BA and MA in Political Science. He acquired his PhD in International Relations at Jinan University, China.

Sam Bateman retired from the Royal Australian Navy as a Commodore and is now a Senior Fellow and Adviser to the Maritime Security Programme at the S. Rajaratnam School of International Studies (RSIS) at Nanyang Technological University in Singapore, and a Professorial Research Fellow at the Australian National Centre for Ocean Resources and Security (ANCORS) at the University of Wollongong in Australia. His naval service included four ship commands, five years in Papua New Guinea (PNG) and several postings in the force development and strategic policy areas of the Department of Defence in Canberra. He was awarded his PhD from the University of NSW for a dissertation on "The Strategic and Political Aspects of the Law of the Sea in East Asian Seas". He has written extensively on defence and maritime issues in Australia, the Asia-Pacific and the Indian Ocean and edited numerous books on related topics. In 2009, he co-authored a report Sea Change: Advancing Australia's ocean interests for the Australian Strategic Policy Institute (ASPI), and the RSIS Policy Paper Good Order at Sea in Southeast Asia. His co-authored report for ASPI, Our Western Front: Australia and the Indian Ocean, was launched by the Australian Minister for Foreign Affairs in Perth on 31 March 2010.

Jay L. Batongbacal is a lawyer from the Philippines with a Master of Marine Management degree and Doctorate in the Science of Law, both from Dalhousie University in Canada. He has extensive experience in maritime affairs, having acted as a legal advisor to the Government of the Philippines in making a submission for a continental shelf beyond 200 nautical miles in the Benham Rise Region, and for the application for the designation of a Particularly Sensitive Sea Area in the Sulu Sea. He presently serves at the University of the Philippines College of Law as Associate Dean and Chair of the Graduate Studies Program, and concurrently as Director of the Institute for Maritime Affairs and Law of the Sea.

Lowell Bautista is a Senior Lecturer and Head of Students at the School of Law and a Staff Member at the Australian National Centre for Ocean Resources and Security (ANCORS), University of Wollongong. He holds a PhD from the University of Wollongong (Australia), an LLM from Dalhousie University (Canada) and BA and LLB degrees from the University of the Philippines. Dr. Bautista is recognized for his expertise in the law of the sea, particularly for his contributions in the area of territorial and maritime disputes in the Asia-Pacific, especially on the South China Sea. He is a lawyer with over two decades of experience in legal and policy research, litigation and consultancy. He sits on the board of multiple journals, including the *Asia-Pacific Journal of Ocean Law and Policy*, the *Philippine Yearbook of International Law* and the *Korean Journal of International and Comparative Law*, among others. His areas of research include territorial and maritime boundary issues in the Asia-Pacific, the South China Sea, Philippine maritime and territorial issues, public international law, law of the sea and international environmental law, on which topics he has also published.

Robert Beckman is the Head of the Ocean Law and Policy programme of the Centre for International Law (CIL) and was the founding Director of CIL. He is also an Associate Professor at the NUS Faculty of Law, where he taught Ocean Law & Policy for many years. He has taught various courses in international law at the NUS Faculty of Law, and he currently offers courses in International Regulation of Shipping and International Regulation of the Global Commons. Since 2009, he has lectured in the summer programme at the Rhodes Academy of Oceans Law and Policy in Rhodes, Greece, and he is a member of the Governing Board for the Rhodes Academy. He has published widely on ocean law and policy issues. He is also a Senior Advisor to the Maritime Security Programme of the Institute for Defence & Strategic Studies at the S Rajaratnam School of International Studies at Nanyang Technological University.

Yen-Chiang Chang is a Professor of Law, Dalian Maritime University, China. After leaving the Taiwanese Coast Guard, having served as a legal enforcement officer, he accepted a research position at the Centre for Marine Policy Studies, Sun Yat-Sen University, Taiwan. Subsequently, having moved to the UK, whilst carrying out his PhD research, he was retained as a research assistant at the School of Law, University of Dundee. He has also had an internship with the British Institute of International and Comparative Law. In August 2007, he started to work for the Marine Institute, University of Plymouth, UK. His work involved in a European project, which brought together a partnership of 27 investments, strategic public sector and research partners from Belgium, England and France. His role was primarily concerned with promoting and facilitating sustainable port-based development and distribution, focusing on the economic, social and environmental benefits. In 2011, he was promoted as a Full Professor and PhD supervisor at the School of Law, Shandong University, China. His recent research focuses on legal issues relating to the exploration of marine renewable energy, marine acidification and the impact of maritime culture on the marine-related law-making process.

Vivian L. Forbes is presently an Adjunct Research Professor, NISCSS, Haikou, PRC and Adjunct Professor, School of Earth and Environment, UWA. He was a Distinguished Research Fellow and Guest Professor, CIBOS and CICTSMR, Wuhan University (2013–2017) and Guest Professor, Xiamen Universities; Dalian Maritime University and Yunnan University, PRC. He is also a Visiting Research Fellow, Maritime Institute of Malaysia (1993–2018). His research interests are in the disciplines of cartography, marine political geography and maritime studies. He lectures on these topics and has published widely on these themes. The main focus of his research is on maritime boundary delimitation and geopolitical issues. He has specialized in Indian Ocean maritime affairs and international boundary issues of East, South and Southeast and Southwest Asia. He has presented a number of papers at conferences and seminars at national and international fora and conducted workshops on the cartographical concepts and geopolitical concerns in determining maritime boundaries. He is the author of a number of books, atlases and journal articles; has been consulted on matters relating to maritime and terrestrial boundaries; and has appeared as a witness at Joint Standing Committee on Treaties Sessions for the Australian Federal Senate in relation to the delimitation of Australia's maritime boundaries with Indonesia in 1997 and East Timor in 2002. He has lectured on an annual basis (since 1995) to Workshops on maritime boundary and archival research issues at the Maritime Institute of Malaysia in Kuala Lumpur and other cities.

Mary George is currently a Professor of Law at the Faculty of Law, University of Malaya, Kuala Lumpur where she teaches, researches and publishes in the law of the sea and equity and trusts. She was also the Head of the Law and Policy Unit of the Institute of Ocean and Earth Sciences at the University till recently. In 2019, she successfully completed the UN Research Project on Ocean Accounts for Malaysia. Her recent research projects include the Governance of Marine Litter in Malaysia and ASEAN under the SDG 14 Goals. She is also the State Editor of the Malaysian Chapter of the Encyclopedia of International Law in Asia, a Brill publication. Other emerging projects include the ERASMUS project on Migration Law for Post-Graduate Study and the Blue Economy Framework for Malaysia through the Academy of Sciences, Malaysia. She supervises undergraduate and national and international postgraduate students including PhD candidates.

BA Hamzah is currently a Lecturer in the Department of Strategic Studies at the National Defense University, Malaysia. He is a keen student of geopolitics and international law. Dr Hamzah has served, among others, as a Research Fellow with ISIS, Malaysia, consultant to Accenture (US-based consultancy firm) as well as PETRONAS (National Oil Company of Malaysia). He was also the first Director-General of the Maritime Institute of Malaysia (MIMA). His research areas range from issues of geopolitical interests to the region and Malaysia. He has published on regional maritime security, law of the sea as well as on defense-related topics.

C. J. Jenner is an Associate Research Fellow, Corbett Centre for Maritime Policy Studies, King's College London; a Research Fellow, University of Oxford Rothermere American Institute; and a Senior Research Fellow, Institute for China-America Studies. He holds Master of Studies and Doctor of Philosophy degrees in Modern History from the University of Oxford and has held various research fellowships and teaching posts in Asia, Europe and the

United States. Focusing on 20th-century strategic policy engagements in the Indo-Pacific, his interdisciplinary publications incorporate Area Studies, History and International Relations. In addition to his academic work, he undertakes governmental analytical assignments and contributes occasionally to internationally televised documentary series.

Sophia Kopela holds a position as Nature Policy Officer at WWF Greece and is also an honorary researcher at Lancaster University, UK. She holds an LLB from the University of Athens (Greece), an LLM in Public International Law from the University of Nottingham (UK) and a PhD in International Law of the Sea from Bristol University (UK). Her specialization lies in the law of the sea, international environmental law and public international law. She has taught these subjects in universities in the UK and has published articles on these fields in international journals. Her article "2007 Archipelagic Legislation of the Dominican Republic: An Assessment" was awarded the Gerard Mangone Prize for the best article in the *International Journal of Marine and Coastal Law* in 2009. She is the author of a monograph titled "Dependent archipelagos in the law of the sea" published in 2013.

Seokwoo Lee is Professor of International Law, Inha University Law School, Korea (2003–present). He was Chairman of the Foundation for the Development of International Law in Asia (DILA) (2012–2017). He was Vice President of the Korean Society of International Law (2019) (Executive Board Member (2010–), Director of International Relations (2010–2011)) and served as Chairman of Research Committee, SLOC (Sea Lanes of Communication) Study Group-Korea (2010–2013). He is Co-Chair of the International Law Association (ILA) Study Group, Asian State Practice of Domestic Implementation of International Law (ASP-DIIL) (2018–) and a member of the ILA Committee on International Law and Sea Level Rise (2016–). He is General Editor of *Encyclopedia of Public International Law in Asia* (EPILA), Co-Editor-in-Chief of *Asia-Pacific Journal of Ocean Law and Policy* (APJOLP) and *Asian Yearbook of International Law* (Asian YBIL), Executive Editor of *Korean Journal of International and Comparative Law* (KJICL), Co-Series Editor of the book series entitled *Maritime Cooperation in East Asia* and Associate Editor of *Brill Research Perspectives in the Law of the Sea*. He has authored more than 100 publications in English in addition to his more than 80 publications in Korean. His representative recent publications in English are: "Yeo Woon Taek v. New Nippon Steel Corporation", *American Journal of International Law* (Vol.113, No.3)(2019) and *The Making of International Law in Korea: From Colony to Asian Power* (Brill/Nijhoff) (2016). He holds a D.Phil. (Oxford), LL.M. (NYU, Minnesota, and Korea University) and LL.B. (Korea University).

LI Jianwei is a Research Fellow at China's National Institute for the South China Sea Studies (NISCSS) and holds Master's degrees from the University of Wollongong, Australia (MMP, 2008) and London School of Economics, UK (MSc, 2001). Her research interests are marine policy and management in general and dispute management in the South China Sea (SCS) in particular. Her publications include "Closing the Net Against IUU Fishing in the South China Sea: China's Practice and Way Forward", *Journal of International Wildlife Law & Policy* 18 (2015) and "China, the U.S. and Maritime Security in East Asia: A Chinese Perspective", in *China, the U.S. and Maritime Security in East Asia*, edited by Mingjiang Li and Kalyan M. Kemburi (Routledge, 2014). She has also contributed commentaries to newspapers and has written reports on issues of the South China Sea.

Lingqun Li is a Research Fellow at the China Center for Collaborative Studies of the South China Sea, Nanjing University. Dr. Li received her PhD degree in Political Science from the University of Delaware, USA. Her research interests include maritime security in East and Southeast Asia, international marine governance and Chinese foreign policy. She has participated in a number of research projects that focus on maritime cooperation in the South China Sea. In her research, she explores the interaction between international law and international relations, and pays special attention to the development of regionalization and multilateralism in Asia in the maritime space. She is currently an editor of Asia-Pacific Security and Maritime Affairs (a quarterly academic journal published in Chinese). Her recent publications include: a monograph on the South China Sea policy of the PRC, book chapters on the subject of marine governance, and journal articles on international practices of dispute management and marine cooperation.

Mingjiang Li is an Associate Professor at S. Rajaratnam School of International Studies (RSIS), Nanyang Technological University, Singapore. He is also the Coordinator of the China Program at RSIS. He received his Ph.D. in Political Science from Boston University. His main research interests include Chinese foreign policy, Chinese economic statecraft, the Belt and Road Initiative, Chinese politics, China-ASEAN relations, Sino-U.S. relations and Asia-Pacific security. He is the author (including editor and co-editor) of 13 books. His recent books are *China's Economic Statecraft* (2017) and *New Dynamics in US-China Relations: Contending for the Asia Pacific* (Routledge, 2014). He has published papers in various peer-reviewed outlets including *International Affairs, Asian Perspective, Asian Politics & Policy, Asian Security, Oxford Bibliographies, Journal of Asian Security and International Affairs, Journal of Strategic Studies, Global Governance, Cold War History, Journal of Contemporary China, Chinese Journal of International Politics, Chinese Journal of Political Science, China: An International Journal, China Security, Harvard Asia Quarterly, Security Challenges* and *International Spectator.*

Fu-Kuo Liu is a Research Fellow at the Institute of International Relations, National Chengchi University, Taiwan. He is a Professor at the International Doctorate Program in the Asia-Pacific Studies (IDAS), College of Social Science, National Chengchi University. He is also the Director of the Taiwan Center for Security Studies (TCSS). He serves as the chief editor of *Strategic & Security Analyses* (bimonthly published in Chinese) and a bimonthly *Strategic Vision for Taiwan Security* at TCSS. He has widely involved in the Asia-Pacific security dialogues process. His research and teaching focuses on Asia-Pacific security, Asian regionalism, national security and the South China Sea, peace process across the Taiwan Strait, US strategy in Asia, Asian maritime security, and Taiwan foreign and security policy. He received a Ph.D. in Politics from the University of Hull, UK.

Ted L. McDorman is a Law Professor at the Faculty of Law, University of Victoria, Victoria, British Columbia, Canada. He has written widely on ocean law and policy issues having published over 120 articles, chapters in books, etc. From 2002 to 2004 and again from 2011 to 2013, Professor McDorman was "academic-in-residence" in the Legal Affairs Branch of the Canadian Department of Foreign Affairs and International Trade (now Global Affairs Canada) where he was involved in a number of Arctic, law of the sea and environmental matters. For 20 years, he was the Editor-in-Chief of *Ocean Development and International Law.* Since the mid-1980s, Professor McDorman has been an observer, commentator and occasional participant in South China Sea legal and political matters.

NGUYEN Hong Thao is currently a Senior Lecturer at the Diplomacy Academy of Vietnam and the National University of Hanoi. Dr. Nguyen received his LLB and PhD from the

University of Paris I Pantheon – Sorbonne, France in 1996. His main academic specializations are in Public International Law, Law of the Sea, International Organizations, and International Humanitarian and Environmental Law. Dr. Nguyen is the author of a series of works on international law, especially on maritime dispute resolutions. He has had over 40 years of experience in maritime affairs and diplomacy, with Ambassador Postings in Malaysia (2011–2014) and Kuwait (2014–2017). He is also a member of Asian Society of International Law, Vietnam Society of International Law, Editor in Chief of the *Vietnamese Yearbook on International Law*, Member of the Advisory Board of the *Asian Yearbook of International Law AYBIL*, Member of the *Asian Journal of International Law* (AsianJIL), *AALCO Journal of International Law* and *Journal of East Asia*, and International Law Editorial Boards. In 2016, he was elected as a Member of the International Law Commission of the United Nations for the term of 2017–2021. In 2018, he was appointed as 2nd Vice Chairman of the Commission. In 2020, he was nominated by the Vietnamese Government as an arbitrator under Article 2 of Annex VII to the United Nations Convention on the Law of the Sea of 1982.

David M. Ong is a Professor of International and Environmental Law at the Nottingham Law School, Nottingham Trent University, UK. His main research interests are in the International Law of the Sea, particularly on offshore joint development, published in *American Journal of International Law* (1999); and International Environmental Law, published in *European Journal of International Law* (2001), *Irish Yearbook of International Law, 2006* (2008), *Yearbook of International Environmental Law, 2006* (2008), *Nordic Journal of International Law* (2010) and *Netherlands International Law Review* (2011); as well as several edited volumes of essays, three of which he has co-edited. More recent publications in the Law of the Sea are: "Implications of Recent Southeast Asian State Practice for the International Law on Offshore Joint Development", in *Beyond Territorial Disputes in the South China Sea: Legal Frameworks for the Joint Development of Hydrocarbon Resources*, edited by Beckman et al., Edward Elgar (2013) 181–217; "Specifying Procedural Obligations for Joint Development and Alternative Joint Development Models for the South China Sea", in Wu Shicun and Nong Hong (eds.), *Recent Developments in the South China Sea Dispute: The Prospect of a Joint Development Regime*, Routledge (2014) Chapter 7, 99–136; and "Alternative Approaches to Piracy and Armed Robbery in Southeast Asian Waters and off the Horn of Africa: A Comparative Perspective", in *The Law and Practice of Piracy at Sea: European and International Perspectives*, edited by Panos Koutrakos and Achilles Skordas, Hart (2014) Chapter 12, 267–295. He has previously served as a consultant on offshore joint development issues to the Guyana legal team in the Guyana-Suriname maritime boundary delimitation arbitration (2007); and as a technical resource expert on Joint Development at the Second United Nations Development Programme (UNDP) South-South High-Level Meeting on Oil and Gas Producing Developing Countries held in Nairobi, Kenya, 12–15 October 2009.

J. Ashley Roach, JAGC, U.S. Navy (retired) was an attorney-adviser in the Office of the Legal Adviser, U.S. Department of State, from 1988 until he retired at the end of January 2009, responsible for the law of the sea matters. He has taught, advised and published extensively on national maritime claims and other law of the sea issues, including the Arctic. He has negotiated and participated in the negotiation of numerous international agreements involving the law of the sea issues. Since retiring, he has concentrated on piracy, Arctic and island-dispute issues. The third edition of his book (with Dr. Robert W. Smith), Excessive Maritime Claims, was published in 2012. He chairs the International Law Association Committee on Baselines under the International Law of the Sea dealing with straight baselines (2013–2016). He is a

Global Associate and Senior Visiting Scholar (2014–2015), Centre for International Law, National University of Singapore. He received his LL.M. (highest honors in public international law and comparative law) from the George Washington University School of Law in 1971 and his J.D. from the University of Pennsylvania Law School in 1963.

Clive Schofield is the Head of Research at the Global Ocean Institute, World Maritime University in Malmö, Sweden and a Professor with the Australian Centre for Ocean Resources and Security (ANCORS), University of Wollongong (UOW), Australia. He holds a PhD in Geography from the University of Durham, UK and also holds an LLM in International Law from the University of British Columbia. His research interests relate to international boundaries and particularly maritime boundary delimitation and marine jurisdictional issues on which he has published over 200 scholarly publications. Clive is an International Hydrographic Office (IHO)-nominated Observer on the Advisory Board on the Law of the Sea (ABLOS) and is a member of the International Law Association's Committee on International Law and Sea Level Rise. He has also been actively involved in the peaceful settlement of boundary and territory disputes by providing advice to governments engaged in boundary negotiations and in dispute settlement cases before international courts and tribunals. Additionally, he served as an independent expert witness in the international arbitration case between the Philippines and China concerning the South China Sea.

Stein Tønnesson is a Research Professor at the Peace Research Institute Oslo (PRIO). During 2011–2017, he led the East Asian Peace programme at the University of Uppsala, Sweden, which led to the publication of Explaining the East Asian Peace (2017). Tønnesson's recent publications include: "Can China and Vietnam Use International Law to Resolve their Maritime Disputes?" in T. Engelbert, ed., *The South China Sea Conflict after the Arbitration of July 12, 2016* (2020); "Four Aspects of the Crisis in the South China Sea" in L. Buszynski & Do Thanh Hai (eds), *The South China Sea: From a Regional Maritime Dispute to Geo-Strategic Competition* (Routledge, 2020); "The Tonkin Gulf Model of Conflict Resolution" in C.J. Jenner and Tran Trong Thuy, eds. *The South China Sea. Towards Sovereignty Based Conflict or Regional Cooperation?* (2016); "The South China Sea: Law Trumps Power", *Asian Survey* 55(3), 2015; and "China's national interests and the law of the sea: Are they reconcilable?" in Wu Shicun and Nong Hong, eds, *Recent Developments in the South China Sea* (Routledge, 2014).

VU Hai Dang is an Ocean Law and Policy Senior Research Fellow at Centre for International Law, National University of Singapore. His area of expertise includes international law, law of the sea, international environmental law, protection of the marine environment, ocean governance, Southeast Asia and the South China Sea. Dang holds a JSD in international marine environmental law from Dalhousie University and a Master's degree in international trade law from the University of Paris V. He has working experiences in the fields of legal service, civil servant, diplomacy and academic.

Dustin Kuan-Hsiung Wang obtained his PhD degree in International Law from the University of Bristol, UK in 1997. He is a Professor of the Graduate Institute of Political Science, National Taiwan Normal University in Taipei. He is a member of the board of directors of the Chinese (Taiwan) Society of International Law and the Secretary-General of the Institute of Marine Affairs and Policy in Taiwan. Dr. Wang also serves as an editorial board member for *Chinese (Taiwan) Yearbook of International Law and Affairs* (English version),

Chinese (Taiwan) Review of International and Transnational Law (Chinese version), *Korean Journal of International and Comparative Law, Asian Yearbook of International Law* and *Asia-Pacific Journal of Ocean Law and Policy*. Dr. Wang's teaching and research interests are mainly on public international law, law of the sea, East and South China Seas issues, and marine policy. For those research fields, he mainly focuses on the sustainable utilization of fishery resources and pays attention to the feasibility of solving disputes through joint development.

Christopher Whomersley was formerly a Deputy Legal Adviser in the UK's Foreign & Commonwealth Office, his career spanning 36 years and covering many areas of international law. Chris spent a number of years dealing with aviation issues, and he was involved in the Channel Tunnel project since its inception. For the last ten years of his time in the Foreign Office, he was responsible for policy on the international law of the sea. This included dealing with these issues both multilaterally and bilaterally, as well as in the European Union. He led the UK delegations in a number of bilateral negotiations on maritime delimitation. He was also the leader of the UK delegation to the International Seabed Authority and was a member of its Finance Committee. He was responsible for the arrangements relating to the declaration of an Exclusive Economic Zone around the UK, as well as for the law updating UK legislation on deep-sea mining. In June 2014, Chris was honoured by HM The Queen for his services to international law.

Qiang Ye is currently a PhD candidate at the School of Justice, University of Central Lancashire, UK and a Research Associate at National Institute for South China Sea Studies, China. He received LLM from Tsinghua University in 2013. His research interests lie in public international law, particularly international dispute settlement and the law of the sea. His major published works include *The 21st Century Maritime Silk Road: Challenges and Opportunities for Asia and Europe* (Routledge 2019); *Case Study on the Law of the Sea* (2016); "Interpretation and Application of Article 298 of the Law of the Sea Convention in Recent Annex VII Arbitrations: An Appraisal" (48 *Ocean Development and International Law* 2017); "Does China's Position Paper on the South China Sea Arbitration Constitute a Preliminary Objection?" (in: *Arbitration Concerning the South China Sea: the Philippines versus China*, 2016); "A Study on the Advisory Proceedings before the ITLOS as a Full Court" (2014 *China Oceans Law Review*); as well as more than 40 commentary articles in both English and Chinese.

Feng Zhu is currently the Executive Director of China Center for Collaborative Studies of the South China Sea and the Director of Institute of International Relations, Nanjing University. Before joining Nanjing University, he was a Professor at Peking University's School of International Studies and served as the vice president of the Institute of International and Strategic Studies at Peking University. He was a visiting fellow of a number of institutions including the Brookings Institute, Harvard University, CSIS, Durham University, etc. Professor Zhu writes extensively on regional security in East Asia, the nuclear issue in North Korea, China-US military and diplomatic relations and the South China Sea issue. His recent books include *America, China and the Struggle for the World Order* (co-edited with Prof. G. John Ikenbery and Prof. Wang Jisi, 2015) and *Sea Power in the 21st Century: Historical Lessons and the Chinese Discourse* (edited). He sits on a couple of editorial boards of scholarly journals and consults independently for the Chinese government and the private sector. Professor Zhu began his undergraduate studies at the Department of International Politics at Peking University in 1981 and received his PhD from Peking University in 1991.

ABBREVIATIONS

ADIZ	Air Defense Identification Zone
ADMM	ASEAN Defence Ministers Meeting
AIS	Automatic Identification System
AJIL	*American Journal of International Law*
AMM	ASEAN Ministerial Meeting
AMTI	Asia Maritime Transparency Initiative
AOIP	ASEAN Outlook on the Indo-Pacific
APEC	Asia-Pacific Economic Cooperation
APFIC	Asia-Pacific Fishery Commission
ARF	ASEAN Regional Forum
ASEAN	Association of Southeast Asian Nations
BCM	Bilateral Consultation Mechanism
BRI	Belt and Road Initiative
CARAT	Cooperation Readiness and Afloat
CBD	Convention on Biological Diversity
CBMs	confidence-building measures
CFMD	Cooperation for Mutual Development
CIDA	Canadian International Development Agency
CLC	Convention on Civil Liability for Oil Pollution Damage
CLCS	Commission on the Limits of the Continental Shelf
CNOOC	China National Offshore Oil Corporation
CNPC	China National Petroleum Corporation
COBSEA	Coordinating Body for the Seas of East Asia
COC	Code of Conduct in the South China Sea
COLREGs	International Regulations for Preventing Collisions at Sea
CPM	Communist Party of Malaya
CS	continental shelf
CSARC	China-Southeast Asia Research Center on the South China Sea
CSCAP	Council for Security Cooperation in the Asia-Pacific
CSIS	Center for Strategic and International Studies
CTI	Coral Triangle Initiative

CUES	Code of Conduct on Unplanned Encounters at Sea
DAV	Diplomatic Academy of Vietnam
DOC	Declaration on the Conduct of Parties in the South China Sea
DRV	Democratic Republic of Vietnam
EAS	East Asian Summit
ECRL	East Coast Rail Link
EDCA	Enhanced Defense Cooperation Agreement
EEZ	exclusive economic zone
EMSA	European Maritime Safety Agency
EU	European Union
FAO	Food and Agriculture Organization
FDI	foreign direct investment
FONOPs	Freedom of Navigation Operations
FoS	Foot of the Continental Slope
GEF	Global Environment Facility
GIWA	Global International Waters Assessment
GMDSS	Global Maritime Distress Safety System
HNS	hazardous and noxious substances
HWM	High Water Mark
IATA	International Air Transport Association
ICAO	International Civil Aviation Organization
ICM	integrated coastal management
IFALPA	International Federation of Air Line Pilots' Associations
IHL	international humanitarian law
ILC	International Law Commission
IMO	International Maritime Organisation
IPFC	Indo-Pacific Fisheries Council
ISC	Information Sharing Centre
ISPS	International and Port Facility Security
ITLOS	International Tribunal for the Law of the Sea
IUU	Illegal, Unregulated and Unreported
JDA	Joint Development Authority
JMSU	Joint Marine Seismic Undertaking
JOMSRE-SCS	Joint Oceanographic Marine Scientific Expedition in the South China Sea
JWG	Joint Working Group
KIG	Kalayaan Island Group
LADS	Laser Airborne Depth Sounding
LIDAR	Light Detection and Ranging
LME	Large Marine Ecosystem
LMC	Lancang-Mekong Cooperation
LNG	liquefied natural gas
LOE	Letter of Exchange
LOSC	United Nations Convention on the Law of the Sea
LPG	liquefied petroleum gas
LRIT	long-range identification and tracking
LTE	low tide elevation
MARPOL 73/78	International Convention on the Prevention of Pollution from Ships, as modified by the Protocol of 1978

MDA	maritime domain awareness
MDT	Mutual Defense Treaty
MEP	marine environmental protection
MOU	Memorandum of Understanding
MPAs	Marine Protected Areas
MSR	marine scientific research
NAPs	National Action Plans
NISCSS	National Institute for South China Sea Studies
ODA	official development assistance
ODIL	*Ocean Development and International Law*
OPRC	Oil Pollution Preparedness, Response and Co-operation Convention
PCIJ	Permanent Court of International Justice
PEMSEA	Partnerships in Environmental Management for the Seas of East Asia
PLA	People's Liberation Army
PLAN	People's Liberation Army Navy
PRC	People's Republic of China
PSCs	production-sharing contracts
RAC	Regional Activity Center
RCEP	Regional Comprehensive Economic Partnership
RCU	Regional Coordinating Unit
ReCAAP	Regional Cooperation Agreement on Combating Piracy and Armed Robbery against Ships in Asia
RFMO	regional fishery management organization
ROC	Republic of China
RSIS	S. Rajaratnam School of International Studies
SAP	Strategic Action Programme
SAR	search and rescue
SCS	South China Sea
SDGs	Sustainable Development Goals
SDNT	Single Draft Negotiating Text
SDS-EAS	Sustainable Development Strategy for the East Asian Seas
SEACAT	Southeast Asia Cooperation Training
SEAFDEC	Southeast Asia Fisheries Development Center
SLOCs	sea lines of communication
SOLAS	Safety of Life at Sea Convention
SOM	Senior Officials Meeting
SRFC	Sub-Regional Fisheries Commission
SRV	Socialist Republic of Vietnam
SSAS	Ship Security Alert System
SUA	Convention for the Suppression of Unlawful Acts against the Safety of Maritime Navigation
TAC	Treaty of Amity and Cooperation in Southeast Asia
TCA	Trilateral Cooperative Arrangement
TDA	Transboundary Diagnostic Analysis
TPP	Trans-Pacific Partnership
TRS	Tropical Revolving Storm
TWGs	Technical Working Groups
UK	United Kingdom

UN	United Nations
UNCLOS	United Nations Convention on the Law of the Sea
UNCLOS III	Third United Nations Conference on the Law of the Sea
UNEP	UN Environment Programme
UNESCO	United Nations Educational, Scientific and Cultural Organization
UNGA	United Nations General Assembly
USA	United States of America
USIBC	US-India Business Council
USSR	Union of Soviet Socialist Republics
VCG	Vietnam Coast Guard
VCLT	Vienna Convention on the Law of Treaties
VFRSF	Vietnam Fisheries Resources Surveillance Force
VTS	vessel traffic system
WCPFC	Western and Central Pacific Fisheries Commission
WMD	weapons of mass destruction
WPNS	Western Pacific Naval Symposium

FOREWORD

David H. Anderson

The *Routledge Handbook of the South China Sea* contains essays by leading experts from different parts of the world addressing the many geographical, historical, economic, environmental, legal, political, strategic and other aspects of the South China Sea. The publication of the Handbook is timely when the South China Sea features regularly in the news.

The essays bring out the vital importance of the South China Sea as part of the marine environment of the wider Pacific Ocean, as well as a primary source of sustenance for the considerable human populations around its shores. It is also a vitally important maritime highway for global trade and communication. For these and other reasons, the South China Sea is an area of global concern.

The essays bring out the facts that while the coastal States are cooperating with each other on some matters of mutual interest, there is much more that could be done. For instance, there exists no Regional Fisheries Management Agreement and no "regional seas" agreement aimed at protecting the marine environment such as applying day-by-day in other comparable seas like the Mediterranean.[1]

In 2002, the signature by the member States of ASEAN and China of a Declaration on a Code of Conduct[2] marked a measure of progress towards improved relations, but the subsequent negotiations for a legally binding Code have not yet succeeded. In the South China Sea, too many issues remain unresolved or are even openly disputed. Unilateral actions of different kinds have exacerbated differences and raised tensions.

Disputes have arisen for two main reasons: territorial sovereignty over various insular features is disputed, and consequential differences have arisen over maritime rights and obligations around those features.[3] In such contexts, disparities in diplomatic, economic or military power between the protagonists, while apparent, should not be decisive factors. Sovereignty disputes should be handled exclusively by peaceful means following the principles of the UN Charter and the rules of international law governing the acquisition of sovereignty over land territory.[4] Similarly, maritime differences, including title to marine resources, should be approached in the light of the UN Convention on the Law of the Sea, the work of its institutions such as the Commission on the Limits of the Continental Shelf (CLCS)[5] and its mechanisms for resolving differences over its interpretation or application.[6] Asian States are at the forefront of reaping the benefit of this Convention, which represents in the famous words of Ambassador Tommy Koh (Singapore) a "Constitution for the Oceans".[7] Naturally,

States must accept the burdens or obligations as well as enjoying the benefits arising under the Convention.

Strictly speaking, each dispute is factually unique, although there are some common features, notably the claim advanced by China through the United Nations to the so-called "U-shaped line",[8] which has been rejected by several other States. Resolution of these disputes would benefit the Parties as well as the wider international community.

Continuing disputes bring uncertainty and instability which, at worst, could threaten international peace and security, impede economic development in the maritime sector, and delay the necessary concerted efforts to protect the fragile marine environment and fish stocks of the South China Sea.

Given the global concern and the common features, several proposals have been advanced for overall solutions to the outstanding differences. In this perspective, the successful completion of the negotiations and the adoption of a Code of Conduct binding the member States of ASEAN and China would represent a major advance. Further negotiation could lead to an arrangement or *modus vivendi* which would, as it were, put the disputed issues of sovereignty aside and permit cooperation and joint development of some marine resources, all without prejudice to national claims. Here, the Antarctic Treaty of 1959 has been pointed to as one example of what can be achieved.[9] Finally, the practice of some Asian States[10] in creating, developing and managing joint maritime areas has been suggested as a precedent for the South China Sea.[11]

Individual solutions to bilateral disputes always remain available. Sovereignty disputes can be settled at any time by negotiation followed by agreement or by recourse to a body such as the International Court of Justice ("the Court"). Maritime disputes can be resolved through successful talks or recourse to the Court or the International Tribunal for the Law of the Sea or arbitration.[12]

Sensitive maritime disputes such as those in the South China Sea may be suitable for submission to a Conciliation Commission, charged with hearing the rival arguments of the Parties, with examining the respective factual and legal claims, and finally with proposing terms for an amicable settlement between the Parties. This process, outlined in article 284 of the UN Convention on the Law of the Sea, was followed recently in regard to the maritime dispute between Timor Leste and Australia, with positive results for both Parties.[13] Such a Conciliation Commission would work flexibly with States in the South China Sea and could, for example, consider more than one dispute or disputes involving several interests.

The situation in the South China Sea remains a source of concern to the international community. A semi-enclosed sea such as this[14] should be the scene of enhanced cooperation, not unresolved differences that could threaten international peace and security in East Asia.

In this context, the essays in the *Routledge Handbook of the South China Sea* are a significant addition to the literature concerning this trouble spot in international affairs. The essays will provide insights and food for thought on the part of diplomats, politicians, scholars and interested citizens worldwide.

Notes

1 See Agreement for the Establishment of the General Fisheries Commission for the Mediterranean (FAO, 1949) and the Barcelona Convention 1976.
2 Declaration on the Conduct of the Parties (ASEAN States and China) in the South China Sea dated 4 November 2002, available at https://asean.org/?static_post=declaration-on-the-conduct-of-parties-in-the-south-china-sea-2.
3 For details, see Chapters 5 and 6 of this book.

4 For instance, Malaysia and Indonesia submitted their dispute concerning sovereignty over Pulau Ligitan and Pulau Sipadan Islands to the International Court of Justice in 1998. The Court gave its decision in 2002.

5 The CLCS has received two submissions relating to the South China Sea, namely the Joint Submission by Malaysia and Vietnam dated 6 May 2009 and a separate submission from Vietnam dated 7 May 2009. Both submissions have been deferred by the CLCS.

6 These mechanisms include recourse to the International Court of Justice, the International Tribunal for the Law of the Sea or arbitration: see Chapter 22 of this book. The South China Sea Arbitration was instituted by the Philippines, invoking Annex VII to the Convention (see Chapter 23 of this book).

7 Ambassador Koh was speaking as the President of the Third UN Conference on the Law of the Sea at the conclusion of the negotiations in December 1982. See the UN Publication of the Convention and related documents, p. xxxvii.

8 Note Verbale dated 7 May 2009 from the Permanent Mission of the People's Republic of China to the Secretary-General of the United Nations, with map attached. The exact implications of the Note were left unclear (see Chapter 7 of this book).

9 K. J. Keith, Reflections on the South China Sea Arbitration Rulings, 49 *NZ International Review* (2017), p. 5. Judge Sir Kenneth Keith refers to the analogy between the sovereignty disputes in the South China Sea and those in the Antarctic which, having been put aside by the Antarctic Treaty of 1959, has resulted the subsequent extensive scientific cooperation between its States Parties to the general benefit of the international community.

10 For example, Japan and South Korea, and Malaysia and Thailand.

11 A joint area has been created where national claims have overlapped; typically, in each instance, an agreed regime for resource management has been agreed. See D. Ong, *Joint Exploitation Areas* in the Max Planck Encyclopedia of Public International Law (2011).

12 For example, a dispute between Malaysia and Singapore over the latter's programme of land reclamation was referred to arbitration under Annex VII to the Convention. After the International Tribunal for the Law of the Sea had prescribed some provisional measures, the Parties resolved their differences and negotiated a settlement: details at XXVII RIAA (2015), p. 133.

13 Available at https://www.pcacases.com/web/sendAttach/2327. See also Crosato, *Conciliation between Timor Leste and Australia,* in Max Planck Encyclopedia of Public International Law (March 2019).

14 See Chapter 17 of this book.

INTRODUCTION

Keyuan Zou

Introduction

The South China Sea, categorised as a semi-enclosed sea under the 1982 United Nations Convention on the Law of the Sea (LOSC),[1] is one of the most important seas in the world, not only that it contains rich marine resources, distinctive biodiversity, but also a critical sea route for global trade and communications. There are important sea lines of communications (SLOCs) which are vital for the adjacent countries in East Asia and also for the rest of the world. More than half of the world's merchant fleet capacity sails through the straits of Malacca, Sunda and Lombok, and the South China Sea.[2] More than 10,000 vessels of greater than 10,000 dwt move southward through the South China Sea annually, with well over 8,000 proceeding in the opposite direction.[3] In addition, with the rise of China and the fast growth of economy in East Asia, the recent trend to greater intra-Asian trade (relative to trade with Europe and North America) results in more shipping in the littoral waters of Southeast Asia and the South China Sea.[4]

The South China Sea is also known as a flashing spot of territorial and maritime disputes between/among multiple claimants. The complicated political landscape of the South China Sea contains the potential of conflicts with various different national interests. For the status of the four groups of islands, because of their different geographical locations, their political statuses are accordingly different from each other. The Pratas Islands are under the full control of the Taiwanese authorities. No competing claims exist there as China treats Taiwan as its integral part. For the Macclesfield Bank Group, the only claimant is China (including mainland China and Taiwan). Nevertheless, as the Scarborough Reef is considered part of the Macclesfield Group, then the recent developments indicate that the Philippines has also lodged its territorial claim over the Reef, and over the Macclesfield Group. The Paracel Islands are under the control of China, though contested by the Vietnamese. The dispute over the Spratly Islands is most complicated since it has been lingering on for a long time and involves as many as five States and six parties, i.e., China, Chinese Taipei, Malaysia, Vietnam, the Philippines, and Brunei. It is predicted that if the issue of the Spratly Islands is not handled well, it could pose danger or threat to peace and security in the East Asian region and even beyond.

Having said that, we come to know that there are three layers of disputes in the South China Sea. The first and most fundamental are the overlapping claims of sovereignty to the geographic features between/among littoral states; the second are the overlapping claims to the maritime zones generated either from the islands or from the surrounding coasts of the littoral states which are basically in terms of sovereign rights and jurisdiction as stipulated under the LOSC; and the third one are the disputes in relation to the use of the oceans including conflicting uses of marine resources and development between/among littoral states, the use of sea lanes and the conduct of military activities in the name of the freedom of navigation between littoral states and user states. These disputes are entangled one into the other, thus making the South China Sea disputes most complicated of all territorial and maritime disputes in the world.

Structure and contents

This Handbook serves as a reference work on the South China Sea issues in inter-disciplinary perspectives from renowned historians, geographers, international lawyers, and political scientists from around the world. With the aim to present a comprehensive and in-depth analysis, this Handbook covers the main issues and topics in the South China Sea by evaluating the dynamics of the development of the current situation, identifying factors that contribute to a successful settlement of the dispute and cooperative management regime, and drawing lessons that may be useful to other nations and organisations for adopting their South China Sea policies, so as to allow for the inclusion of multiple perspectives and interpretations. The focus of the Handbook is on the origin, evolution, current situation, and prospects of the South China Sea issue, which is divided into six Parts.

The Handbook starts with an overview of history and geostrategic landscape of the South China Sea (Part I). In Chapter 1, Vivian Louis Forbes discusses various aspects relating to the physical and natural environment in the South China Sea. In Chapter 2, Stein Tønnesson accounts for five historical developments in the South China Sea, including the seaborne trade; naval rivalry; competition for ownership to multiple small islands, rocks and reefs; expansion of state-claimed rights to resources in the sea and under the seabed; as well as the depletion of fish stocks and destruction of coral reefs by overfishing, pollution and construction of militarized artificial islands, due to the failure of states to cooperate. In Chapter 3, Sam Bateman focuses on the security of the sea lines of communication across the South China Sea which are among the most important in the world, as well as on a range of international instruments and obligations introduced to ensure the safety of navigation in the sea, including the provision of meteorological and hydrographic services, protection against the threats of piracy and sea robbery, and the maintenance of search and rescue (SAR) services, as well as to protect the marine environment from ship-sourced marine pollution. In Chapter 4, Mary George examines the issues relating to maritime security and demilitarization of the South China Sea, particularly the legality and implications of China's construction of artificial islands and installations for military purposes; and China's possible establishment of a maritime or an air defence identification zone to control navigational and overflight rights in the South China Sea.

Part II discusses the sovereignty and maritime entitlements in the South China Sea. In Chapter 5, Ted L. McDorman discusses the overlapping territorial sovereignty claims of the coastal States of the South China Sea. As he points out, the dynamics of the territorial sovereignty disputes have changed dramatically in the wake of the South China Sea Arbitration. The overall picture is one of the entrenched positions with little room for compromise or flexibility to manage the disputes. Clive Schofield in Chapter 6 highlights the enduring maritime disputes related to the definition of baselines, delineation of maritime limits and delimitation of maritime boundaries among claimants, particularly between China and the Philippines. Keyuan Zou and Qiang Ye in Chapter 7 provide a whole picture in relation to the origin, evolution and most recent developments of China's practice relating to the U-shaped line, review a wide range of interpretations of the legal implications of the line, discuss the definite and potential claims within the line made by China, and conclude that China has not given up maritime claims based on the U-shaped line. The recent practice has demonstrated that China has further consolidated the line and related territorial and maritime claims. In Chapter 8, Sophia Kopela examines three interrelated issues with respect to the existence of historic rights in the South China Sea, including the nature and the type of the historic claims made by China; as well as the two types of historic rights that might be potentially relevant in the South China Sea context, namely historic rights short of sovereignty and historic fishing rights.

Part III focuses on the South China Sea policies of major claimants. In Chapter 9, Feng Zhu and Lingqun Li have reviewed the evolvement of the People's Republic of China's policy towards the South China Sea over the past seven decades. BA Hamzah in Chapter 10 analyses Malaysia's policy on the South China Sea disputes from the perspective of applicability of international law. Jay Batongbacal in Chapter 11 evaluates the Philippines' Policy on the South China Sea, particularly under two administrations of President Benigno Aquino III and President Rodrigo Roa Duterte. Nguyen Hong Thao in Chapter 12 presents the main points of Vietnam's policy on maritime issues in the South China Sea, as well as the Vietnamese legal position on sovereignty, maritime delimitation, cooperation for mutual development and the Code of Conduct in the South China Sea.

Part IV explores issues relating to natural resources and environment in the South China Sea. In Chapter 13, Dustin Kuan-Hsiung Wang discusses the abundance of fishery resources in the South China Sea, the dependency of the littoral communities on such resources, the factors of damage to the sources, and the existing multilateral as well as bilateral fishery management cooperation; and advocates that the resolution of the South China Sea disputes should be initiated by joint management of fishery resources. Yen-Chiang Chang in Chapter 14 explains the dilemma of governing the non-living resources in the South China Sea, by examining the legal basis for the governance of non-living resources and analysing the state practices in the exploration of non-living resources in the South China Sea. Vu Hai Dang in Chapter 15 observes regional activities undertaken by coastal states in the South China Sea to fulfill their duty under international law to conserve the marine biodiversity of the South China Sea, by providing an updated account on the status of the marine biodiversity of the South China Sea, and laying out what the obligations under international law for its coastal states are in terms of conserving marine biodiversity. David Ong in Chapter 16 surveys the conjunction and interaction between the scientific, policy and legal disciplines devoted to protection of the South China Sea's environment, by assessing the state of scientific research on this water body, and exploring the connexon between the results of this scientific research with the policy initiatives and legal instruments designed to address the specific pollution issues and general degradation of this semi-enclosed sea.

Part V analyses the cooperation and institutions in the South China Sea region. In Chapter 17, Seokwoo Lee and Lowell Bautista focus on the semi-enclosed seas cooperation under the LOSC, and analyse the textual and contextual issues within LOSC, and how these dovetail concerns in the South China Sea. In Chapter 18, Robert Beckman and Vu Hai Dang examine the role of ASEAN in the South China Sea disputes, by providing a brief historical background of ASEAN, its institutions, and the principles the organisation follows to achieve its objectives; providing a brief background on the sovereignty and maritime disputes in the South China Sea, and the role of ASEAN in those disputes; giving an overview of the ASEAN and ASEAN-led mechanisms which deal with the disputes in the South China Sea; and examining the history of negotiations between ASEAN and China which led to the adoption of the 2002 DOC and the ongoing negotiations to agree on a Code of Conduct in the South China Sea (COC), as well as the possible impact of the ASEAN Outlook on the Indo-Pacific on ASEAN and the South China Sea disputes. Ramses Amer and Li Jianwei in Chapter 19 examine the progress of establishing a rules-based order in the South China Sea. As they point out, China and the ASEAN countries have made two attempts in this respect. The first was the negotiations process leading to the signing of the DOC in 2002 and the second is the current consultation process to reach a COC. However, further efforts are needed to overcome the existing challenges to reach an effective and substantive COC. Fu-Kuo Liu in Chapter 20 examines the cross-strait interplay between mainland China and Taiwan on the South China Sea issues and envisages future development under the circumstance of worsening the cross-strait relation today. In Chapter 21, Rommel Banlaoi examines the role of Track II diplomacy in promoting cooperation in the South China Sea, by describing the role of Track II diplomacy in the adoption of the 2002 DOC, the on-going negotiation on the COC, and the current bilateral mechanisms among claimants to peacefully manage the South China Sea disputes.

Part VI turns to challenges and prospects of the South China Sea situation. Ashley Roach in Chapter 22 describes the dispute settlement provisions in Part XV of the Law of the Sea Convention and their applicability to South China Sea issues, particularly for the four littoral States - China, the Philippines, Malaysia and Vietnam - as they are parties to the Convention. In Chapter 23, Christopher Whomersley focuses on the South China Sea Arbitration and its implications on the current situation in the South China Sea. In Chapter 24, Mingjiang Li and Archana Atmakuri address the issues of China and the United States interaction in the South China Sea in historical context, major sources of rivalry between the two countries in the contemporary era, prominent policy tools the two powers employ for the pursuit of their respective strategic interests, and important implications for the South China Sea disputes from the perspective of Sino-US strategic rivalry. Finally, in Chapter 25, Christopher John Jenner examines and compares the three governing domains of influence – ASEAN, China and the United States – in the semi-enclosed sea where China is attempting to posture itself as the most prestigious sea power and ASEAN, the United States, and their allies and partners are attempting to defend the rules-based regional order.

Prospects

Since 2012, the situation in the South China Sea has dramatically intensified, and largely unfolded around several hotspot issues, including the arbitration case initiated by the Philippines against China, the large-scale land reclamation and militarization in the South China Sea, fisheries conflicts and marine environmental protection, negotiation and consultation of the COC, as well as the US-led military activities and Freedom of Navigation Operation Programs (FONOPs). According to most leading scholars and analysts who pay close attention to the Asia-Pacific, therefore, the South China Sea has been regarded as a 'regional flashpoint' that has the potential for political and military conflict.

Tensions between China and both the Philippines and Vietnam have recently cooled since late 2016, even as China increased its military activity in the South China Sea by conducting a series of naval maneuvers and exercises in 2018. Meanwhile, China continues to construct military and industrial outposts on the newly reclaimed territories in the South China Sea. The United States has also stepped up its military activity and naval presence in the region in recent years, by conducting at least 25 times freedom of navigation operations against China's claims in the South China Sea during the presidency of Donald Trump by September 2020. The US allies like Japan and Australia have also been intensifying their presence in the region. All are offering support to southeast Asian states interested in strengthening their military capabilities, including Vietnam and Indonesia. The UK's role also seems to be on the rise. In August and September 2018, Royal Navy ships conducted freedom of navigation operations in the South China Sea. There is speculation that the Navy's new aircraft carrier may visit the region soon after it enters service in 2020. There has been some progress on confidence-building measures between China and Southeast Asian states, but it is unclear whether such initiatives are more about buying time for China to create more 'facts on the ground' than about improving stability in the region.

Another significant event is the South China Sea Arbitration (the Philippines v. China) (2013–2016), which has affected and continues to affect the discourse of the resolution of the South China Sea disputes. On 22 January 2013, the Philippines, by a *Note Verbale* with the Notification and Statement of Claim on West Philippine Sea (i.e. South China Sea), instituted the compulsory arbitration procedures stipulated in the 1982 United Nations Convention on the Law of the Sea (UNCLOS) against China, asking the Arbitral Tribunal to: (1) declares that China's rights in regard to maritime areas in the South China Sea, like the rights of the Philippines, are those that are established by UNCLOS, and consist of its rights to a Territorial Sea and Contiguous Zone under Part II of the Convention, to an Exclusive Economic Zone under Part V, and to a Continental Shelf under Part VI, and (2) declares that China's maritime claims in the South China Sea based on its so-called "nine-dash line" (U-shaped line) are contrary to UNCLOS and invalid.[5] On 30 March 2014, the Philippines officially submitted its Memorial to the Arbitral Tribunal which reiterated its statements regarding the U-shaped line contained in its Statement of Claims. Regarding the arbitration case initiated by the Philippines, China stated that it would not participate in the arbitration and accused the Philippines of complicating the issue.[6] China accused the Philippines of distorting "the basic facts underlying the disputes between China and the Philippines. In so doing, the Philippines attempts to deny China's territorial sovereignty and clothes its illegal occupation of China's islands and reefs with a cloak of 'legality.'"[7] China asked the Philippines to go back to the right track of negotiation and consultation to settle the disputes so as to avoid further damages to the bilateral relations between the two countries.[8] However, the case continued despite China's non-participation. In the end, the Philippines obtained a sweeping victory.

This case has opened a Pandora Box of "lawfare" in the South China Sea. The Arbitral Award in fact gives the United States, its allies, and other interested states another leverage to impose pressure on China for advancing their interests in the South China Sea, and broadly in Asia Pacific. The fact that the Award denies maritime entitlement of Exclusive Economic Zone and continental shelf for any feature in the Spratly Islands and its ruling that low-tide elevation (LTE) is not subject to appropriation has maximised American Navy's mobility in the South China Sea. Its ruling that Mischief Reef belongs to the Philippines opens a big possibility of armed conflict, even war in the region. As we know that the current Philippine President Duterte decided to put aside the Award, but this is only temporary. The term of the Philippine presidency is only 6 years and cannot be re-elected afterwards. What if another Aquino III comes to power when Duterte finishes his term in 2022? What if a future Philippine president asks the United States to help expel the Chinese personnel from Mischief Reef based on the arbitral ruling?

Lawfare continues remarkably after the Malaysian Submission of its extended continental shelf to the Commission on the Limits of the Continental Shelf (CLCS) in December 2019. So far there were 21 Notes verbale in response to the Submission from 10 countries including the United States, a non-party to the LOSC.[9] Many of them targeted China by rejecting its claims in the South China Sea and upholding the South China Sea Arbitration ruling. For example, on 16 September 2020, France, Germany and the United Kingdom sent a joint diplomatic letter to the UN, rejecting any claim from China in the South China Sea that are, in their view, inconsistent with the LOSC.[10] This kind of lawfare is unprecedented in the international community and accompanied at the same time with ever-increasing military activities of external powers led by the United States in the South China Sea.

Conclusion

As this Handbook unfolds, we can see that there are many pending issues in and relating to the South China Sea. The South China Sea issues and disputes therefore are no longer regional and have become an international concern of peace and security. It is hoped that the *Routledge Handbook of the South China Sea* will attract particular interest from academics, students, industries and policy makers in all walks across the world as a valuable reference.

Finally, it must be noted that during the editing process we were saddened to know that Dr. Sam Bateman, a key contributor to this book, passed away on 18 October 2020. He was a worldwide known expert in ocean law and maritime security, having published extensively on the oceans, including the South China Sea. We will remember him forever. As a token of our lasting memory, this book is dedicated to him.

Notes

1 The text is reprinted in 21 I.L.M. (1982) 1261.
2 See Stanley B. Weeks, "Sea Lines of Communications (SLOC) Security and Access", in Michael Stankiewicz (ed.), *Maritime Shipping in Northeast Asia: Law of the Sea, Sea Lanes, and Security*, IGCC Policy Paper No. 33 (Institute on Global Conflict and Co-operation, University of California, February 1998), 55.
3 Hal Olson, "Marine Traffic in the South China Sea", *Ocean Yearbook*, Vol. 12, 1996, 137.
4 See Stephen J. Meyrick, "Development in Asian Maritime Trade", in Stankiewicz (ed.), *supra* note 2, 21.
5 The diplomatic note and Philippines' "Notification and Statement of Claim" are available at http://www.gov.ph/downloads/2013/01jan/20130122-Notification-and-Statement-of-Claim-on-West-Philippine-Sea.pdf.
6 See "China: No to UN Arbitration on Sea Row", available at http://www.abs-cbnnews.com/nation/02/01/13/china-no-un-arbitration-sea-row.
7 "Foreign Ministry Spokesperson Hua Chunying's Remarks on the Philippines' Efforts in Pushing for the Establishment of the Arbitral Tribunal in Relation to the Disputes between China and the Philippines in the South China Sea", 26 April 2013, available at http://www.fmprc.gov.cn/eng/xwfw/s2510/2535/t1035577.shtml.
8 "Answers from the Foreign Ministry to the Questions at a Press Conference on the Search of the Disappearing Passenger Airplane of the Malaysian Airlines and the Issue of the South China Sea", 26 March 2014, available at http://world.people.com.cn/n/2014/0326/c1002-24745397.html.
9 All the diplomatic notes are available at https://www.un.org/Depts/los/clcs_new/submissions_files/submission_mys_12_12_2019.html.
10 *Note verbale*, UK NV No. 162/20, 16 September 2020, available at https://www.un.org/Depts/los/clcs_new/submissions_files/mys_12_12_2019/2020_09_16_GBR_NV_UN_001.pdf.

PART I

History and geostrategic landscape

1

THE SOUTH CHINA SEA

Geographical overview

Vivian L. Forbes

Introduction

This study offers a geographical overview of the characteristics of the South China Sea basin. It is a narrative about the important natural factors that brings to the fore the rationale for the international attention given to this body of water since the 1950s and in particular, since the introduction of the new law of the sea embodied in the provisions of the 1982 United Nations Convention on the Law of the Sea (UNCLOS).[1] The narrative includes the topics of the natural continental shelf and slope of the mainland and portion of the Sunda Shelves; the nature of the sedimentation on the sea floor; the tides, tidal streams and surface currents; the geography of the Paracel, Pratas and Spratly Archipelagos in their natural form; and sea-mounts, underwater volcanoes and the marine environment.

It is wise, at this early stage of the narrative to present the definition given for the limits of the semi-enclosed sea which is the geographical focus of this study. Not only has the definition of this sea, as a semi-enclosed body of water, been debated between geographers and oceanographers on the one hand and the legal fraternity on the other hand but also the marine features contained therein have varied interpretations, so that there are calls to change its name.[2] To that end, it is vital to offer a geographical overview of the South China Sea basin in this first chapter of the present volume in order to set the scene for other discussions. The South China Sea basin is surrounded by the coast of the Indo-China/Malay Peninsula to the west, the mainland of China to the northwest, the Strait of Taiwan to the north, the Philippine Archipelago to the east, the island of Borneo to the south and a portion of the Indonesian Archipelago.

The names of States and geographical features used in this chapter will adopt the orthodox English nomenclature as employed, for example, by the International Hydrographic Organisation and the International Hydrographic Chart Series.

Geographical limits of the South China Sea

The geographical limits of the South China Sea basin were defined by the International Hydrographic Bureau (now Organisation) in their *Special Publication* 23 of 1953.[3] However, in a revised draft (as of 17 October 2019) of *Limits of Oceans and Seas*, 4th edition (1986), the

International Hydrographic Organization (IHO) officially recognised the Natuna Sea.[4] The geographical coordinates listed hereunder (in degrees, minutes and seconds of arc value) are given as Latitude North (Lat. N) and Longitude East (Lon. E). The southern limit of the South China Sea, IHO code number 6.1, is revised, northward, from the Bangka Belitung Islands to the Natuna Islands. The limits of this semi-enclosed sea, as defined, are reproduced *verbatim*, as follows:

On the North:

> From Jiaowei Cape (20° 13' 30" N; 109° 55' 15" E), the southwestern extremity of Leizhou Peninsula, eastward, along the coast of China, to the mouth of Hanjiang River (23° 27' 30" N; 116° 52' E); thence a line joining the mouth of Hanjiang River eastward to Changshan Head (23° 25' 50" N; 116° 56' 25" E), the western extremity of Nan'ao Island; thence from Changshan Head eastward, along the southern coast of this island, to the south-eastern extremity thereof (23° 23' 35" N; 117° 07' 15" E); thence a line joining the south-eastern extremity of Nanao Island south-eastward, along the southern banks of this island, to Eluan Cape (21° 53' 45" N; 120° 51' 30" E), the southern extremity of Taiwan Island (*the common limit with the Taiwan Strait, **southern approach** – code number 7.2*).

On the East:

> A line joining Eluan Cape to the eastern extremity of Amianan Island (21° 06' 30" N; 121° 57' 25" E); thence from Amianan Island southward to the eastern point of Balintang Island (19° 57'20" N; 122° 08' 35" E); thence from Cape Engaño (18° 35' N; 122° 08" E), the north-eastern extremity of Luzon Island; thence from Cape Engano southward, through Luzon Island, to Fuego point (14° 08' N; 120° 34' 30" E), the north-western extremity of Lubang Island; thence from Fuego Point south-westward to Palapag Point (13° 51' N; 120° 04' 30" E), the north-western extremity of Lubang Island; thence from Palapag Point south-eastward to Cape Calavite (13° 26' 45" N; 120° 18' E), the north-western extremity of Mindoro Island. (*From Eluan Cape (Taiwan Island) to Cape Calavite (Mindoro Island: the common limit with the Philippine Sea – code number 7.1*); thence from Cape Calavite south-westward to the north-western extremity of Busuanga Island (12°18' 40" N; 119° 51' 45" E), and to the northern extremity of Cabuli Island (11°26' 45" N; 119° 35" E); thence a line joining the southern extremity of Cabuli Island southward to Cabuli Point (11° 25' N; 119° 30' E); thence southward, through this island, to the southern extremity thereof (11° 25' 45" N; 119° 35' E); thence a line joining the southern extremity of Cabuli Island southward to Cabuli Point (11° 25' N; 119°30' E), the north-eastern extremity of Palawan Island; thence from Cabuli Point south-westward, along the western coast of Palawan Island, to Cape Buliluyan (8°20' 30" N; 117° 10' 30" E), the southwestern extremity of this island; thence a line joining Cape Buliluyan south-westward to the north-western extremity of Bancalan Island (8° 14' 50" N; 117° 04' 50" E); thence from the north-western extremity of Bancalan Island south-westward, through the western side of Secam Island reefs (8° 11' 40" N; 116° 59' E), and of the western shoals of Balabac Island (7° 55' N; 116° 49' E), to Cape Sempang Mangayan (7° 02' N; 116° 44' 45" E), the northern extremity of East Malaysia; from Cape Calavite (Mindoro Island) to Cape Sempang Mangayan (east Malaysia): (*the common limit with the Sulu Sea, **western approach**, code number 6.27*); and thence from Cape Semang Mangayan south-westward, along the coasts of East Malaysia and Brunei, to Cape Datu (2° 05' N; 109° 38' 20" E), the south-western extremity of East Malaysia.

On the South:

> A line joining Cape Datu north-westward to Subi Kecil Island (3° 03" N; 108° 51' 30" E), thence to Senua Island (4° 00' 04"; 108° 25' 20" E), and to Sekatung Island (4° 47' 50" N; 108° 01' 25" E), the northern island of Natuna Archipelago; thence from Sekatung Island south-westward to Nanas Reef (3° 19' 50" N; 105° 35' E), and to Damar Island (2° 44' 30" N; 105° 22' 50" E), in the Anambas Archipelago; thence from Damar Island south-westward to cape Berakit (1° 13' 50" N; 104° 34' 10" E), the northern extremity of Bintan Island; *from Cape Datu (east Malaysia) to Cape Berakit (Bintan Island): the common limit with the Natuna Sea, code number 6.4*); and thence from Cape Berakit north-westward to Horsburgh Lighthouse (1° 19' 50" N; 104° 24' 30" E), on the Pedra Branca Rock, and to Cape Penyusop (1° 22' 10" N; 104° 17' 05" E), the south-eastern extremity of West Malaysia (*the common limit with the Singapore Strait,* ***eastern approaches****, code number 6.5*).

On the West:

> From Cape Penyusop north-westward, along the eastern coast of West Malaysia, to the eastern side of the mouth of Kelantan River (6° 13' N; 102° 13' 40" E); thence a line joining the eastern side of the mouth of the Kelantan River north-eastward to Cape Bai Bung (8° 36' 40" N; 104° 43' 15" E); the south-western extremity of Viet Nam (*the common limit with the Gulf of Thailand, code number 6.3*); thence from Cape Bai Bung eastward and northward, along the coast of Vietnam, to Cape Lai (17° 05' N; 107° 07' 15" E); thence a line joining Cape Lai, in Viet Nam, north-eastward to Yingge Cape (18° 30' N; 108° 41' 30" E), the south-western extremity of Hainan Island, China; thence from Cape Yingge Cape north-eastward, *through* (?) Hainan island, to Lingao Cape (20° 00' 30" N; 109° 42' 40" E), on the north-western coast of this island; and thence a line joining Lingao Cape north-eastward to Jiaowei Cape (20° 13' 30" N; 109° 55' 15" E), the south-western extremity of Leizhou Peninsula, China (*the common limit with the Gulf of Tonkin,* ***southern approach****, code number 6.2*). [Emphasis added]

The limits of the basin and its adjacent seas are detailed hereunder. The lengths (in nautical mile (M) and kilometre (km)) of the collective line segments, where applicable, of the limiting lines, as delineated on charts, are listed below. One nautical mile (M), a measurement for distance used by mariners, is equivalent to 1.85 km. The values were obtained by measurement from nautical charts.[5]

Table 1.1 Length of Limit of South China Sea (Code: 6.1)

Geographical Limit	*Km*	*M*	*Adjacent Sea (Code)*
North limit (sector)	407	220	Taiwan Strait (7.2)
East limit (sector)	444	240	Philippine Sea (7.1)
South limit (sector)	944	510	Natuna Sea (6.4)
West limit (sector)	390	210	Gulf of Thailand (6.3)
Northwest limit (sector)	235	127	Gulf of Tonkin (6.2)

Source: Prepared by the author.

In the context of this presentation, these are the limits that are adopted for this narrative. Within the prescribed limits the following littoral states, listed by their common form name, are Brunei, China, Indonesia, Malaysia, the Philippines and Vietnam. Clearly, Cambodia, Indonesia, Singapore and Thailand are excluded from the list; however, these countries are often mentioned as littoral states of the South China Sea in the context of territorial disputes and other cultural, economic and social issues. This chapter intentionally avoids the discussion of the claimant states and their territorial disputes as it is purely geographical in content and not geopolitical in intent. Such arguments may be raised in the later chapters of this volume.

Geography of the basin: the coastline

Any evaluation of the length of the coastline encompassing the South China Sea, in an academic study, as in this instance, will of necessity be an estimate and probably deduced from small- to medium-scale topographic maps or nautical charts. The overall length of the coastlines fronting the South China Sea as suggested in this present discussion is slightly over 7,000 km. Brunei's coastline length is a mere 160 km; China's measures about 1,500 km which comprises the southern and eastern coast of Hainan Island and the southern coast of mainland China to as far north as Nan'ao Island.[6]

The coastline (shoreline), on topographic maps, is generally a representation of the High-Water Mark (level) or the line of mean sea level where there is no appreciable tide or change in water level. In tidal waters where there is a beach, the coastline is the landward limit of the beach and therefore corresponds approximately to the High Water Mark (HWM) of the highest tides (or the Highest Astronomical Tide). On nautical charts, the Low Water level or the Lowest Astronomical Tide level is depicted as the coastline of the coastal State.

Natural topographic features shown on charts are grouped under four headings: relief, land drainage (including ice/glaciers), vegetation and volcanic activity. The types of features charted and the distance inland to which they are shown will vary with chart scale, type of terrain availability of source data and possibly adequacy of aids to navigation. The significance to the mariner must be judged by the requirements of both visual and radar navigation.

The length of Malaysia's coast abutting the South China Sea equates to about 2,000 km. The distance incorporates the eastern coast of Peninsula Malaysia (650 km) and the northern coast of Sabah and all of Sarawak (collectively 1,350 km). The length of Vietnam's coast fronting the South China Sea is approximately 1,500 km, and the length of the coast of the western seaboard of the Philippines' archipelago is about 1,800 km.[7]

The characteristics of the coastline and coastal zone are varied. A brief commentary which is generalised in context, for each of the States, follows: beginning in the north, with China's coast and moving anti-clockwise along the rim of the basin with discussions on Vietnam, Malaysia, Brunei and the Philippines.

The sector of the coastline of China, focused in this narrative, is that portion of the southern coast along the Guangdong and Hainan Provinces and Hong Kong and Macau. The coastline, about 1,450 km, may be termed as irregular and 'indented' and indeed, often 'deeply indented' in some cases and fronted by numerous off-lying islands. Most of these islands and other dangers in this sector lie within the 20 m isobath. Along the coast, mudflats and banks are prevalent.

More than half the coastline, predominantly in the south, is composed of rocks; most of the remainder is sandy. For example, the coastline between Dapeng Jiao and Tung Lung Island, including Hong Kong and Macau, is extremely irregular and indented by numerous bays and coves. With few exceptions, the elevated ground to about 1,200 m – lofty and rugged hills – rise abruptly from a shoreline, whose nearshore areas are largely steep-to.[8]

At the head of many of the large inlets, many wide margins of drying mudflats extend well off the coastline. Offshore, the area is generally deep and largely clear of dangers to navigation. Ports in this vicinity include those at Guangzhou, Shekou, Hong Kong and Yantian.

Further southwestward, Hainan Strait separating Hainan Island from the mainland is encumbered with numerous sandy shoals and banks; however, a deep navigable channel exists between the island and the peninsular projecting from the mainland. The east coast of Hainan Island is reef-fringed in places. The southeast and south coasts are bold, but banks and shoals are known to exist as well as along the southwest coastline. Sand or sand and gravel beaches front most of the coast. These are interrupted by bold, rocky points and low marshy land bordering lagoon and river entrances.

China has a long and diverse coastline with marine ecosystems that are important to the nation's economy if managed in a sustainable manner. However, since the 1950s, China has lost about 57 percent of its coastal wetlands, 73 percent of its mangrove cover and 80 percent of its coral reefs. Most of its seagrass beds have disappeared, two-thirds of its coastline is suffering from erosion and nearshore fishery resources have been severely depleted.[9] The situation is similar in the other littoral states.

The sections of the coastline of Vietnam, about 1,500 km in length, considered here, are the central and southern sectors from about Lat. 17° N to the delta of the Mekong River. The coast is generally low with sand dunes, 20–30 m high, with the exceptions of the mountains near Mui Chon May Dong, in the vicinity of Lat. 10° N. It is, for the most part, mountainous and consists of a succession of jagged cliffs and wind-swept sandhills. There are many bays. Other sections of the coast are low and at times inundated by the sea. The coast is fringed by banks of sand, with depths of 1.8–5.5 m which extend offshore up to 15 M (or about 28 km) off the delta of the Mekong River as is the case with the Zhujiang River at the Pearl Delta.

In this section, a commentary on Malaysia's coast, collectively about 2,000 km, is discussed in two parts. The first is that portion of the coast of the east coast of Peninsula Malaysia from Cape Penyusop to the Kelantan River. The second part offers a discussion on the northern coast of Sabah and the entire length of Sarawak.[10]

The east coast of Peninsula Malaysia is characterised by low swampy areas with numerous rivers discharging into the sea. Coastal ridges and hills extend to the coast at isolated points. In general, the off-lying islands are quite high and wooded. The delta of Kelantan River, low and featureless, is backed by numerous lagoons and waterways. The river has two entrances; one entrance, Tongkong Channel, lies about four miles west of Besar Channel at which is located the port of Tumpat. Numerous shoals exist at the approaches to the port of Kuantan; and many off-lying islands and islets front the east coast of Peninsula Malaysia.

The coasts of Sabah and Sarawak comprise the entire length of the northern coast of Borneo Island, but for a small segment of 160 km which belongs to Brunei, discussed below, and a shorter section which is Indonesian territory. The coast is relatively regular; however, it is indented by large bays, for instance, Brunei Bay. Much of the coast is fronted by tidal mud or sand flats and it is relatively free of fringing reefs. Approaches to the coast are fouled in some places by detached shoals (for example, Luconia and James Shoals) and numerous coral reefs.

A number of rivers, for example, the Rajang, discharge into the sea along this section of the coast. Many of the rivers are navigable for some distance inland by small craft. Tidal streams are often swift.

Much of the coastal plain is low, however, about 50 km inland a mountain range extends in a northeasterly direction. Labuan Island's west coast consists of sandy beaches fronted by rocks and coral reefs; the east coast is rocky with low cliffs. The island is located at the entrance of Brunei Bay.

Brunei's coastline is relatively short, a mere 160 km. The coast extends ENE where the cliffs are about 11 m high. Shoal water, with depths of less than 5.5 m, extends up to 3 km offshore. A range of hills rising to an elevation of just over 100 m and grass-covered is aligned parallel to the coast.[11]

This section describes the geography of the coast of the islands along the western seaboard of the Philippine Archipelago. In the context of this section, the coastline measures about 1,800 km. The large islands fronting the South China Sea are Luzon, Mindoro and Palawan. In addition, there are numerous smaller islands and islets.[12]

The Batan Archipelago situated in the Luzon Strait (northern group of features comprising eight main islands and several small islets) forms a chain of islands and islets extending about 100 km in a north/south alignment. The larger islands are high and of volcanic origin. The smaller islands are low and of coral formation.

The southern group, the Babuyan Archipelago, comprises six main islands and several smaller marine features (islets and rocks). The main islands are high, mountainous and steep-to. Reefs extend from these islands, and the coast of the chain of islands consists mostly of rocky cliffs, undermined by the sea and fringed by a narrow coral reef which is marked by breakers.

The west coast of Luzon Island is prominently indented by Lingayen Gulf, Subic Bay and Manila Bay. Volcanoes are the most conspicuous features of the landscape; however, there is little volcanic activity. The coast is low and rises gently to broken and bare ridges and in places is marked by overhanging, black, coral cliffs, with a grass-covered top. Several small bays indent the coast of Luzon.

Near Lat. 16° 13' N; Lon.120° 03' E, there is a large group of small wooded islets, known as Hundred Islands, extending about 6 km from the mainland. The islands of Mindoro, Marinduque, Buritas, Ticao, Masbate, Negros and Samar are located south of Luzon Island. The coasts are generally fringed by reefs which in some instances extend about 1 km offshore. In the vicinity of Bogio Point (Lat. 13° 29' N), the coast is bordered by a wide sandy beach.

The Calamian Group, Linapacan Island and the Cayo Islands together with Palawan Island group form a major part of Palawan Archipelago and hence Palawan Province as the administrative unit. Shoals, banks and reefs are numerous in the vicinity of the Cayo Islands. Many of the islands in this group are of limestone formations and covered by tall grass.

Palawan Island is the fifth largest in the Philippine Archipelago, and it separates the South China Sea from the Sulu Sea. The island is mountainous. The west coast of the island is generally irregular, especially in the north where there are many small islands and deep bays. Within the 200 m isobath which lies about 60 km offshore, the coastline is fronted by numerous shoals and reefs.

Geology and tectonic evidence

Marine waters around major landmasses are typically shallow, lying over a natural continental shelf, which may extend from a few kilometres to several hundred kilometres wide. The most landward portion is the littoral or inter-tidal zone where the bottom is subject to periodic exposure to the air. Water depth here varies from zero to several metres. Seaward of this the continental shelf slopes gently from the shore to depths of one to several hundred metres, forming the sub-littoral or shelf zone. Waters below the low-tide mark in the continental shelf region are referred to as 'neritic'.

The extent, gradient and superficial geology of the continental shelf areas are determined by many factors, including levels of tectonic activity in the Earth's crust. Every part of the Earth's crust is in a continuous movement as evident in the numerous earthquakes that are experienced and recorded at various monitoring stations around the globe. Four major tectonic plates dominate the region. They are the Eurasian Plate, Philippine Plate, Pacific Plate and Indo-Australian Plate.[13]

From the Eocene (about 64 million years ago [mya]) to Miocene (25 mya), the Pacific oceanic plate subducted northwesterly or westerly along the eastern side of the Kamchatka Peninsula through the Kurile, Japan and Ryukyu chain of islands, and the Philippine Trench, bringing about successively, the opening of marginal sea basins in the southern Okhotsk Trough, the Sea of Japan, the South China Sea and in the Okinawa Sea Trough. After the formation of the marginal seas, there followed the development of the volcanic island arc, with the Miocene era serving as the main period of eruption. The Philippine and Taiwan chain of islands has undergone a complicated tectonic evolution.

In the Oligocene period (36 mya), the Pacific Oceanic Plate subducted westerly along the eastern side of Luzon Island to form an arcuate structure convexing towards the east. Since Miocene, the oceanic crust of the South China Sea has subducted eastward along the Manila Trench and the eastern side of Taiwan Island. The opening of the South China Sea began in the early Tertiary (about 36 mya), whilst Borneo Island parted from the Asian continent due to sea-floor spreading. In the middle-Tertiary, the South China Sea continued opening, thus leading to the formation of the present N70°E striking magnetic lineation.

Three types of plate boundaries exist, with a fourth, mixed type, characterised by the way the plates move relative to each other. They are associated with different types of surface phenomena. The different types of plate boundaries are as follows:

1 *Transform boundaries* (Conservative) occur where plates slide or, perhaps more accurately, grind past each other along transform faults. The relative motion of the two plates is either sinistral (left side toward the observer) or dextral (right side toward the observer). The San Andreas Fault in California is an example of a transform boundary exhibiting dextral motion.
2 *Divergent boundaries* (Constructive) occur where two plates slide apart from each other. Mid-ocean ridges (for example, the Mid-Atlantic Ridge) and active zones of rifting (such as Africa's East African Rift) are both examples of divergent boundaries.
3 *Constructive boundaries* (Destructive) – or *active margins* – occur where two plates slide towards each other commonly forming either a subduction zone (if one plate moves underneath the other) or a continental collision (if the two plates contain continental crust). Deep marine trenches are typically associated with subduction zones, and the basins that develop along the active boundary are often called'foreland basins'. The subducting slab contains many hydrous minerals, which release their water on heating; this water then causes the mantle to melt, producing volcanism. Examples of this are the Andes mountain range in South America and the Japanese island arc.
4 *Plate boundary zones* occur where the effects of the interactions are unclear and the boundaries, usually occurring along a broad belt, are not well defined and may show various types of movements in different episodes.

The spreading stopped post-Pliocene[14] and so far, the South China Sea tends to be changing, indeed, shrinking (both naturally and by human and political interference, as stated above). The entire southeastern Asia block including the island chains of Indonesia, New Guinea and the Philippines has been affected by the subduction of the oceanic crusts of the Indian Ocean from south to north, and of the Pacific Ocean from northeast to southwest. The Southeast Asia domain, which rides on the Eurasian Plate should be regarded as a transitional-type earth crust, that is, the continental crust is now in a process of rapid growth.

The continental margins of the South China Basin to the north and west are considered geologically as passive margins. To the east lies the active Manila Trench system, whilst to the south the Reed Bank and other shoals separate the basin from an extinct subduction zone along the Sunda Shelf, Borneo and Palawan Islands. The Basin has complicated structural characteristics and is on the trend of the Tethyan-Himalayan extension and its intersection with the marginal Pacific domain.[15]

The greater part of the South China Sea can be considered as a platform and is floored by Cambro-Ordovician rocks (Hainan Island) and older rocks Precambrian basement on Paracel Islands. The geological evolution of the region has been investigated by Taylor and Hayes and Holloway.[16] Chen described 11 tectonic provinces[17] based on studies of the distribution of fault blocks by Zhang,[18] the nature of the crust based on seismic studies by Li[19] and magnetic anomalies by Chen and others,[20] as well as sedimentary characteristics.

For the purposes of the present study, 4 of the 11 tectonic provinces are worthy of a brief description. Pratas Fault Swell lies on the continental slope in the northern part of the South China Sea. It is separated from the oceanic basin to the south by a fault striking approximately in an east-west trend and is bounded on one side by the Zhujiang Estuary Depression. Paracel - Macclesfield Bank Uplifts are separated by an intervening small depression and lie in the central part of the South China Sea. Reed Bank Uplift is formed of three fault blocks of intervening depressions. Its basement is believed to be continental and is formed of Precambrian granite. The Central Oceanic Basin is bounded by marginal faults against the Pratas, Paracel and Reed uplifts and the Manila Trench to the east. The accumulated bathymetric, geological and tectonic knowledge of the South China Sea Basin and the world oil crisis of the 1970s precipitated prospecting efforts in this basin.[21]

The South China Sea basin

As stated above, the South China Sea is a partially enclosed body of water of Southeast Asia. It is a partly submerged land bridge joining the Asian and Australian continental landmasses (tectonic plates) at the Sunda Trench and Timor Trough. The geophysical structure in parts of the South China Sea basin is such that it is prone to earthquake and volcanic activity. The South China Sea basin is atop the Asian plate which is adjacent to the Australasian and Pacific plates. The South China Sea forms part of the Pacific Ocean Basin.[22] This Sea is about 80 percent enclosed by land. It spans nearly 21° of Latitude, that is, from about Latitude 1° N to the southern extremity of Taiwan Island, at about Latitude 22° N. and extends from about Longitude 103° to 122° E. It is the largest of the regional seas in the Pacific Ocean Basin.

The Sea attains depths of over 4,000 m.[23] The South China Sea can be divided at the 200 m isobath into a peripheral continental shelf and a central basin. The continental shelf is a generally smooth, relatively featureless surface, sloping very gently towards its outer edge. Since the map scale, size and format dictate the number of individual islands, reefs and other small topographic features that can be labelled; the following prose refers to places that may not be named on the map. The map portrays the approximate alignments of the 200 m, 2,000 m, and 4,000 m isobaths and the coastline of the littoral states and the Mainland Shelf.[24]

The Mainland and Sunda Shelves, which lie between Vietnam and Borneo, slopes gently towards its edge. The Saigon, Conson, Mekong, Sarawak and Yingge Basins are on these shelves. The width of this shelf varies: for example, north of the Natuna Archipelago and north of Point Sirik, Sarawak, it is about 150 M; off Bintulu, Sarawak it narrows to about 60 M; in the vicinity of Lat. 13° N off the east coast of Vietnam it is a mere 40 M in width; whilst southeast of Yulin, southern coast of Hainan Island it is about 45 M.

The continental shelf in other sectors of the South China Sea basin also varies in width. Off the west coast of Luzon Island in the vicinity of Lat. 15° N it is a mere 5 M wide and off the west coast of Palawan Island and north coast of Sabah it is about 50 M in breadth. The northwest Borneo Trough and Palawan Trench lie to the north of Borneo Island. A central basin is encompassed by a well-defined continental slope. Here depths rapidly increase from 200 m at the edge of the shelf to more than 1,000 m, and in the northeastern sector, to values greater than 3,000 m.[25]

The maximum width of the South China Sea basin – east-west extent – in the context of this study is about 950 M which was measured along the parallel of Latitude 8° N from the west coast of Balabac Island to a point just north of Songkla, Thailand. The length, as with the breadth, varies throughout the basin; hence, a good indication of the north-south alignment is along the meridian of Longitude 115° E from Daxingshan Island to the coast of Brunei. The surface area is estimated at 1.09 million sqM. The maximum depth of the basin is 5,248 m at the western approaches on Mindoro Strait at about 13°30'N., 119° 30' E (as depicted on Chart 4508 (INT 108)). Within these geographical confines, the South China Sea includes the bays, gulfs and straits.

The structure of the seabed and that of the littoral makes the region a complex mix of terrestrial and marine features. Chains of high mountain ranges, deep trenches and troughs, deep-sea basins and numerous coral islands form a complexity of phenomena. Nearly 35 percent of the South China Sea basin comprises the Mainland/Sunda Shelf. The width of the sea is along Lat. 15° N is about 700 M. The north-south extent may be considered to commence at the Equator and terminate just south of Taiwan. This large body of water exerts a considerable influence, within this regional sea, upon the climate which is essentially tropical maritime throughout the year.

The Philippine Archipelago along the eastern boundary of the South China Sea provides a physical barrier to the strong current circulation of the Pacific Ocean. Bashi Channel to the north of Luzon Island is the only deep water (about 2,000 m) between the two water bodies. In the south, the South China Sea is connected to the Java Sea by the Karimata (Carimata) Strait, Gasper Strait and Banka Strait. To the north, the South China Sea is connected to the East China Sea by the Taiwan Strait.

The deep-sea basin of the South China Sea with a maximum known depth of 5,030 m lies along the axis of the sea north of a line from Cap Saint Jacques (10°19`N, 107°05`E) to Baram Point (4° 36`N, 113° 58`E). The slope along the northwest boundary of the continental shelf is a gentle one falling to a depth of 1,803 m over a mean distance of 100 M; however, off Luzon and Palawan Islands, the slope is very steep and the shelf drops away to 1,830 m within a distance of about 20 M from the coast. The two large shallow areas within the deep-sea basin, Macclesfield Bank and the Paracel Group of islands and reef systems are in the vicinity of Lat. 16° N., Lon.113°E.

The Palawan Trough, with a mean depth of 2,200 m, lies along the steep-sided continental slope off Palawan Island and northwest Borneo. The western side of the trough borders the extensive reef plateau of the Spratly Group of islands, islets, rocks and cays where there are deep water connections through the reef system to the South China Sea. The Spratly Group – Archipelago of Reefs (*Dangerous Grounds*) – broadly defined, for the purpose of this study, extends some 360 M in an east-west direction and about 270 M in a north/south alignment. The Yitong Canyon located in the vicinity of Lat. 19° 00' N. Lon. 114° 12'E, in the northern part of the basin south of Yitong Ansha, was discovered in 2008. It has a maximum depth of 3,611 m and a total relief of 2,511 m and a distance of about 70 M (140 km).[26]

There are over two hundred named marine features – small islands, islets, reefs and rocks, sand cays, banks and shoals – in the South China Sea. With the exception of those islands situated close to the mainland shores of Borneo, China, the Philippines archipelago and Vietnam, these insular features are virtually all coral reefs, particularly in the Paracel and Spratly Archipelagos.

This archipelago of reefs area, although often presented as a shallow region, is in fact a deep and level plateau. Water depths as indicated on the relevant charts of the region infer that an area of numerous reefs and islands rising form a plateau with depths of between 1,280 and 2,380 m as depicted on the various nautical charts.

On the continental margin region off Luzon, there are a number of relatively steep submarine canyons. These are evenly shaped and have a profile that is typical of mature river beds with a mean depth of 600–1,650 m. The heads of the canyons usually lie within one mile of the coast, with a mean depth of 90 m over them.

Basins adjacent to continental margins of the South China Sea, for example, the Andaman Sea, Sea of Japan and the East China Sea may be filled with several kilometres of continentally derived sediments which generally thin away from the Foot of the Continental Slope (FoS) into the basin. The FoS is considered as the outer limit of the continental margin and/or the natural continental shelf.[27]

Natural continental shelf and continental margin

Shelf regions support the marine communities most familiar to humans, and many of the marine resources of particular value to them. Although mangroves and coral reefs are two of the best known tropical coastal ecosystems, they dominate only a minor part of the world coastline: the former mainly in the deltaic or low-lying coastal plain and the latter only in the shallow waters when terrestrial sedimentation is very low. Soft-bottom habitats with sparse vegetation are probably the most wide-spread coastal marine ecosystem type, and virtually the entire seabed away from the coastline is covered in marine sediments.

The natural continental shelves of the basin are: the Sunda Shelf underlying the western South China Sea and including the Gulf of Thailand, the Java Sea, the Karimata Strait and the Straits of Malacca and Singapore; and includes the Mainland Shelf (off the coast of China) extending from the Taiwan Strait through to the Gulf of Tonkin.

The Mainland Shelf between Hainan Island and Taiwan Island is as much as 150 M wide and is relatively featureless with an even, gentle slope to the edge. Islands and banks (shallower waters) on the outer shelf include, from east to west, the Penghu Islands and Taiwan Bank at the southern approaches to the Taiwan Strait and St. Esprit Shoal, which is about 110 M east of Hainan Island. The channel in the Taiwan Strait is between 60 and 80 m deep, and the Hainan Strait channel is between 20 and 40 m deep.

There are two large shallow areas within the limits of the deep-sea basin, the Macclesfield Bank (Lat. 15° 50' N, Lon 114° 30' E) and the Paracel Islands and reef complex. The Macclesfield Bank, a submerged atoll with a mean depth of 75 m but over which a number of shallower patches exist, has an east-west extent of 85 M and a north-south alignment of about 45 M. The Paracel Archipelago, with an east-west alignment of about 80 M (Pattle Island to Lincoln Island) and a north-south axis of about 90 M (North Reef to Triton Island) has an extensive group of low-lying islands and reefs, about 130 insular features, with deep passages between them.

The shelf to the south of Hainan island is narrow (maximum width about 50 M) with a steep gradient. The mainland shelf narrows along the bulge of southern Vietnam and its gradient steepens considerably. South of Cam Ranh Bay it broadens into the 215 M width Sunda Shelf. Sunda Shelf is the name given to the extension of the Asian continent which connects Asia with the islands of the Indonesia Archipelago; it supports the southern half of the South China Sea. Depths here do not exceed 185 m (about 100 fathoms). The Sunda Shelf is intersected with submerged river valleys similar to those found in the Java Sea. These valleys lead into a mainstream aligned north/south from Natuna Archipelago to Karimata Strait.

The deep-sea basin of the South China Sea, with a maximum known depth of 5,030 m, lies along the axis of this sea north of a line from Mui Vung Tau (Lat. 10° 19'N., Lon. 107° 05' E.) to Baram Point (Lat. 4°36' N., Lon. 113° 38' E.) To the southwest of this line, the entire area is supported on the Sunda Shelf and thus has depths of less than 200 m. To the north of this line, the major portion of the region is contained in the South China Sea basin with depths in excess of 1,800 m. In the northern area, the Sunda Shelf is confined to the coastal regions, its width varying considerably due to the coastal configuration. Off the south coast of Vietnam, the mean width of the shelf is about 15 M, but further north, off the coast of China, the width increases to approximately 150 M.

Most continental shelf areas in the tropics are overlain by sand and mud composed of sediment of terrestrial origin (terrigenous deposits). More than 80 percent of the global volume of river-borne sediment is deposited in the tropics (and an estimated 40 percent of it by just two major river systems: the Yellow River and the Ganges-Brahmaputra). Both river systems are outside the scope of this regional study; however, it is worthy of mention in this context as there are relatively few major river systems that deposit their sediments and water into the South China Sea, for example, the Mekong River system and the Si Kiang.

The deposition of sediment is reflected in the extent of the shelf areas in parts of the tropics, and high turbidity of coastal waters in monsoon regions. The Si Kiang (Pearl Delta) and Mekong River systems and other major rivers from Peninsula Malaya and northern Borneo discharge a vast quantity of sediments into the southern sector of the South China Sea basin. The thickness of the sediments, for example, 10 km off Baram Point, Sarawak; 4 km thickness a mere 60 M southeast off Saigon; 6 km about 100 M southeast of Pearl Delta are good indications of the potential and proven hydrocarbon resources that exist in the substratum of the seabed at the mouths of these river systems.[28]

The continental margin, from 200 to about 4,000 m deep, consists of the continental slope and continental rise, in some places interrupted by flat terraces or benches. Between Hainan and Taiwan, the mainland Shelf descends to a terrace between 200 and 1,000 m. It supports several island groups and shoals such as Pratas Island and Reef complex, Helen Shoal and Verebek Banks. This terrace is bordered by the continental slope and continental rise that slope gradually towards the deep ocean floor. Immediately southwest of Taiwan and south of Hong Kong, a secondary terrace, at between 2,000 and 3,000 m depth east of the Pratas islands occasional pinnacles that reach to within about 1,000 m are present.

South of Hainan Island to about Lat. 15° 30' N., the continental margin consists of a broad terrace at between 200 and 1,500 m depth. Situated on this broad terrace is a shoal area between 200 and 1,000 m deep extending from the coast of Vietnam and supporting the Paracel group; both terraces are almost separated from Hainan Island and the mainland Shelf by a large linear depression.

The Macclesfield Bank is situated southeast of the Paracel Group at the southwest corner of a 2,500 m deep terrace. To the south and east of the terrace, the continental margin drops steeply to the deep ocean floor; a small linear depression separates the bank from a complex topography to the southwest. The margin to the east of the Paracel Group and the north of the Macclesfield Bank consists of a normal slope and rise extending to the deep ocean floor.

Off the central Vietnam coast, the narrow shelf merges with the continental slope, which extends eastward to a 200 M terrace at 2,500 m. This area exhibits irregular bathymetry, with a central depression and small, 2000 m terraces at its eastern extremity. To the east, a narrow continental shelf separates the terrace from the deep seafloor. Immediately to the south are two more terraces, one at 200–1,000 m and another at 1,000–2,500 m, with two peaks off the eastern coast of Vietnam reaching to within 1,000 m of the surface.

Marine features

Spratly archipelago: 'dangerous grounds'

Further south, these terraces are separated from an area, that mariners refer to as '*Dangerous Ground*' – for the mere fact of the existence of numerous reefs, sand cays, islets and islands – by a more normal slope and rise sequence, which in this vicinity of inconsistent bathymetry appears as an indentation of the deep seafloor between two shoal areas.[29] The 'Dangerous Ground' is an area where the eastern rim of the Sunda Shelf gives way to an undulating terrace at about 200 m extending over a 600 M length and 280 m width zone that supports numerous irregular shoals, hills and terraces. The Archipelago may be defined as extending from about Lat. 7°33' to Lat. 12° N, and from Royal Captain Shoal (9° 02' N, 116° 40' E) on an azimuth of 40°/220°.

The shallowest terrace on the eastern rim of the Sunda Shelf supports numerous banks, for example, Alexandra and Prince of Wales; and shoals, including Vanguard Reef. To the southeast, Louisa Shoal is sited on another small terrace protruding from the shelf. An extension of this protrusion along the eastern edge of the Spratly Group supports a number of reef systems and banks. A depression at 1,800–2,000 m separates these shallow terraces from the major shoal area to the north and the east.

The central portion of the 'Dangerous Ground' zone comprises series of small plateaus at about 2,000 m separated by depressions. The high areas support many cays and reefs that include Fiery Cross Reef and Nanshan Island. The extreme north part of the area is a 10,000 sqM plateau at 1,000 m upon which rests two shoals. The northern portion is about 85×65 M in dimension within the 200 m isobath and includes Brown, Reed and Templar Banks. Reed Bank (Lat. 11° 26' N, Lon. 116° 55' E) has an east-west extent of about 35 M and a north-south alignment of about 70 M. It is located about 150 M from the northern tip of Palawan Island.

To the southeast, an elongate, smaller terrace area less than 200 m deep which includes Carnatic Shoal; and Sabrina Shoal sits on a promontory extending to the south of this terrace. The continental slope descends steeply northward from 'Dangerous Ground' to merge with the deep ocean floor.[30]

Pratas group

Pratas Island is composed of sand, covered with scrubby brush and attains a height of about 12 m to the top. A reef, which dries, extends off the west side of the island. Pratas Reef is a classic example of a coral atoll roughly circular and about 13 miles in diameter. The lagoon within the reef is coral-studded with depths of up to about 16 m.[31]

Paracel archipelago

The Paracel Islands comprise the Amphitrite Group, the Crescent Group, and several low-lying islands and coral reefs. The islets are of low elevation; some are covered with trees or vegetation. North Reef is about seven M long and about 2.5 M at its broadest north/south alignment.[32]

The Amphitrite Group is the north-western collection of islands, reefs and shoals, which consists of two parts separated by a deep channel. The southern portion consists of Woody Island, the largest in this group, and Rocky Island which share a common reef complex. Two other prominent features are West Sand, a low sandy cay and Tree Island. Iltis Bank with water depths of more than 10 m over it stretches for three miles in length and 1.5 m width and it is fairly steep-to. The Crescent Group consists of several low sand islets and numerous reefs and lie about 45 M southwest of the Amphitrite Group.

Scarborough shoal

Scarborough Shoal (15° 11'N; 117° 45' E) is a triangular-shaped reef complex, with a perimeter of about 50 km, comprising a few rocks (or small islets) encompassing a lagoon of a surface area of about 150 sqkm. One of the rocks is named South Rock which has an elevation of 1.8 m above sea level at high tide. A channel, approximately 370 m wide and about 10 m deep leads into the lagoon. The lagoon provides some protection to small fishing boats during inclement weather.[33] This marine feature is located about 110 M west of Subic Bay, the Philippines. To the east of the shoal is the 5,000 m deep Manila Trench.

Bathymetric and oceanographic features

The Palawan Trough, with its generally northeast-southwest alignment and a maximum depth of 3,475 m separates the 'Dangerous Ground' from the northwest Borneo continental slope. Further north, off northwest Palawan and the Calamian Islands, the continental margin is indented by several valleys that lead to the broad continental rise; the northwest valleys trend into the Manila Trench. The continental margin off west Luzon is narrow and steep, giving way to the 5,000 m Manila Trench and its narrow northward extension before projecting to the deep seafloor. From central Luzon northward to the southern tip of Taiwan, however, a submarine ridge capped by a series of elongate plateaus shoaling to 1,500 m separates the northward extension of the Manila trench from a prominent northeast-trending tongue of the deep seafloor. The North Luzon Ridge to the east of the trench extension also connects Taiwan Island with the Batan and Luzon Islands.[34]

Along the east coast of Peninsula Malaysia, the seabed is covered by a vast quantity of sand, which extends north from the Bangka Strait. This belt has a mean width of 40 M opening to 100 m northeast of Anambas Archipelago and then tappers to a 10 M strip in the northern sector of the region. Off the east coast of Peninsular Malaya in the vicinity of Lat. 4° N., there is a large mud patch. The outlying islands of the Anambas Archipelago are supported on a sand/mud bed and are bordered by coral. In the Gulf of Thailand the seabed is covered by mud and isolated patches of sand/mud, and sand and stone in the coastal regions.[35]

From the southern tip of the west shore of Vietnam to Lat. 7° 30' N. the coast is fronted by a sand/mud strip varying in width from 5 to 40 M. To the north of this latitude to the head of the Gulf, mud predominates in the coastal region with small isolated patches of sand and coral. In the outer approaches to Bangkok, there is a comparatively large area of sand with a smaller area of sand and shell adjoining it. Along the east shore, bordering the coast of Cambodia, there is an extensive belt of sand/mud of mean width of 40 M, with mud predominant close inshore. Around the islands in the southeast part of the Gulf, sand is the dominant sediment. In the main mud areas, the seabed is generally soft and smooth.[36]

Along the coast of Vietnam, south of Lat. 12° N., the continental shelf is covered by sand which extends southward as a belt of 100 M wide almost to the west coast of Borneo. Inshore of the sand belt, off the low-lying alluvial coast off the east tip of Vietnam, mud is the dominant sediment. In the waters of the Mekong River delta, the bottom is sand/mud. Farther to the north there are isolated patches of mud and stone. Coral surrounds the islands and shallow areas dispersed over the sand belt. To the north of 12° N along the narrow coastal strip, rock is abundant on a mainly mud bottom with narrow sand strips fringing the shore.

On the wide shelf region supporting the Gulf of Tonkin and bordering the south coast of China, mud is the main constituent with sand/mud present in patches along the edge of the shelf. Across the southern entrance to the Gulf of Tonkin is an elongated patch of sand/mud and fronting the south shore of the Gulf are narrow belts of sand and sand/mud. In the outer approaches to Haiphong, sand predominates over the mud and there are large areas of sand and sand/mud. To the north of Hainan Island, the sea-bed is covered by mud, but relatively large areas of sand lie along the edge of the shelf and isolated patches of stone and sand/mud are located on the bottom.

In the deep waters off the Sunda Shelf, the seabed is covered with soft mud or ooze, providing a smooth sedimentary layer on the seafloor. The depth of the layer is not known but is probably similar to that of the Pacific Ocean, which is estimated to be about 300 m. Patches of sand, coral and rock surrounded the reefs and banks in the region. On the shelf, mud is still the dominant sediment but is interspersed with large patches of sand and smaller patches of rock, stone and coral. A belt of sand, about 100 m wide, extends north from Natuna Archipelago to the southern coast of Vietnam.[37]

There is a widening belt of sand and mud off the coast of Sarawak and the northwest extremity of Borneo, The belt of mud and sand extends northwest to the southern group of Natuna Archipelago. There is an extensive mud strip inshore of this belt along the west coast of Sarawak, formed by the discharge of the rivers. Mud is extensive off the coast of West Borneo Island but is replaced in the approaches to Karimata Strait by a predominantly sand bottom.

Mud flooring extends along the northwest of Borneo Island and east through the Balabac Strait with offshore patches of coral and rock. The bottom is sand with frequent outcrops of coral and rocks, along the west coast of Palawan; in Palawan Passage, the seabed is covered in mud. At the entrance to Manila Bay and along the south shore of that bay, sand, stone, and rock are present, but elsewhere mud from the deltaic deposition is found. Mud is also predominant north of Mindoro, but south of that island the bottom is sand, with interspersed patches of coral. The steep coast west of Luzon and north of Manila Bay is fronted by rocky outcrops, islets and occasional coral reefs. The narrow coastal shelf is covered by sand or sand and mud, with mud becoming the dominant sediment.

A seamount, which has more than 500 m local relief, is differentiated from a guyot by the mere fact that the latter has a flat top, whilst the former may have a steep crest. Some seamounts may rise as much as 3,000 m above the adjacent ocean floor. These features are also associated with coral atolls. Both seamounts and guyots originated as volcanoes having erupted beneath the ocean floor. They are generally circular in plan view; their slopes tend to be steeper than land volcanoes owing to the more rapid consolidation of the lava in seawater. The difference between the conical seamount and the flat-topped guyot is due to the

Table 1.2 Geographical Coordinates of Guyots

Geographical	*Coordinates*	*Peak Depth (m)*	*Base Depth (m)*
15° 10'N	116° 20'E	1,456	3,840
15° 15'N	117° 45'E	803	3,658
15° 30'N	116° 10'E	914	3,840
16° 20'N	116° 45'E	73	3,658
17° 10'N	118° 40'E (Stewart Smt)	429	3,000

Source: Prepared by the author.

elevation of the guyot above sea level at some stage in its development during which period it suffered sub-aerial erosion, wave action and marine plankton; the top being truncated.[38]

Typically, seamounts are flat top and may have a diameter of about ten to 12 M and lie between 800 and 1,500 m below the surface. An alternative suggestion for the origin of seamounts is that they represent the submerged remains of coral atolls.

The Table 1.2, above, gives the reported positions and depths of several seamounts in the South China Sea. An additional list of recent discoveries of undersea features – canyons, hills, ridge and seamounts of the South China Sea basin – is presented at Appendix A1.

Marine environment and natural phenomena

The Indonesia and Philippine Archipelagos, located in an area of high seismic activity, partially enclose the southern and eastern sectors of the South China Sea. The only significance of submarine volcanic activity to ships at sea is the resultant tsunami, or seismic sea wave if there is an activity within the volcano. These waves are caused by earthquakes or submarine volcanic activity. When the tsunami's progress is constricted by bottom configuration or shoreline, the height of the wave increases rapidly and considerable damage may be done to ships in the vicinity or to adjoining shore installations and the coastline.

Tides are mainly diurnal throughout the South China Sea. On the west coast of Luzon, north of Port Masinloc, and on the coast of Sarawak and Brunei, between Bintulu and Seria, there are stretches where there is seldom more than one tide a day. Throughout most of the area, the range of the tide is between one to 1.5 m, however, there is a marked increase near the western end of Sarawak, where at the mouth of the Sarawak River, it is as much as 3.6 m.

Tidal Bores may occur in certain rivers in Sarawak, for example, in the vicinity of the offshore reefs, there are local tidal streams which set on to or away from the reefs on all sides. In the narrow channels through the reefs, these streams attain greater rates, but generally, they are weak and during the strength of the seasonal currents they may be inappreciable. Tidal currents in the vicinity of the Batan Archipelago in the Luzon Strait are both strong and confused. Their direction is affected by the configuration of the channels as well as the changing monsoons.[39]

The movement of the surface water over the South China Sea is related, in general, to the monsoons, however, the relationship is complex and not direct. The main southwest setting current during the Northeast Monsoon (November to March) and the northeast setting current in the Southwest Monsoon (May to September) generally flow on the west side of the South China Sea. The direction of the water movement over this latter area is controlled to a large extent by the positions of eddies, which occur in the South China Sea in most months and especially between the Malay Peninsula and Borneo Island. Since these features are themselves controlled by varying oceanographic and meteorological conditions, both within and outside the South China Sea, it follows that the currents of this region display a high degree of variability both in direction and rate.[40]

Over the greater part of the South China Sea, the currents are weak, the mean rates over most regions in most months are less than 0.5 knot (a Knot is a rate of speed; thus 2 knots represent 2 M distance covered in 1 hour). During the months when the monsoons are fully developed (July, August and December to February) the mean rates increase to between 0.5 and 1 knot. Currents of up to two knots may occasionally be experienced in any part of the area in any month and on rare occasions, the current may flow at up to three knots, more especially between the Malay Peninsula and Borneo Island, and at four knots through some of the passages linking the South China Sea and the Sulu Sea.

The prevailing current pattern is affected, sometimes considerably, by the violent winds accompanying the passage of a Tropical Revolving Storm (TRS) (commonly referred to as cyclone or typhoon in this regional context). The current thus produced sets in a generally downward direction but is deflected to an extent which may vary between 20° and 45°. However, since the current is greatly dependent upon the length of time that the wind blows in a particular direction, as well as upon the wind strength, the current in most cases does not have time to become fully developed. It is estimated that at wind speeds of 40 knots and over, the wind needs to blow in the same direction for over 48 hours to produce the maximum current. Thus it is only with slow-moving typhoons/cyclones that strong current, which may exceed 2 knots, are encountered. When a typhoon is located in the vicinity of a coast, still higher speeds may be produced due to the pile-up of water against the adjacent coast.

The salinity of the area is extremely variable and is in direct contrast to the uniform sea surface temperature experienced in the western sector of the South China Sea. In general, water masses of low salinity form at the surface, and high salinity water of oceanic origin is found in deeper water. Excessive rainfall and river run-off result in the formation of oceanic water into the area and provides high salinity masses. Between these two masses, a large area of mixed water is formed. These different water masses are transported by the monsoonal currents to and from such that many regions are alternately filled with waters of different origin resulting in large seasonal variations of salinity. The sources of low salinity in this basin are the mouths of the major rivers: the Mekong in Vietnam is a typical example where the discharge from the river has a greater influence on the salinity than the actual rainfall.[41]

The density of water is computed from temperature and salinity readings with corrections to allow for the effect of pressure. Thus, corrections in either the value or distribution of temperature or salinity will automatically change the density of the water. In the southern half of the South China Sea, south of Lat. 11° N., where the annual variation of sea surface temperature is small, the density of the seawater is largely governed by variation in salinity but in the northern part of the basin, where there is a relatively large variation of sea surface temperature, changes in salinity have little or no influence on the density.[42]

There is little variation in the sea surface temperature. The average sea surface temperature in the central portion of the basin is about 28°C in August and around 26°in November. In the southern sector, the average temperature in February is about 24° C and slightly warmer, around 29° during May.[43]

Average atmospheric pressure, measured in Pascal (Pa or hPa) at mean sea level varies from 1010 in the southern sector to about 1020 in the northern portion of the South China Sea basin.[44] Variations in these values should be expected during the monsoon periods and in the path of a typhoon. Apart from the irregular variations in atmospheric pressure, there is a regular diurnal variation.

In this regional context, most typhoons (tropical revolving storms) originate east of the Philippine Archipelago and take a path across the South China Sea basin; however, some originate farther west within the basin and move generally in a northwesterly direction towards the mainland of China. There is an annual movement of the mean latitude of the zone from six degrees N during March to 16° N in August. There is also a longitudinal movement in the region from about 106° E in January to about 140° E. in June. The source of the typhoons moves northwest in about April and returns southeast in August. The average track has a seasonal variation being farther south in November and farther north in July.[45]

Between 5° and 10° N an average of 7 typhoons may be experienced per annum, whilst between 10° and 15° N about 14 may be expected. Farther north, for example, 15° and 20° N the average total for the year may be as high as 40, with the months of September and October experiencing at least eight or nine per annum. These typhoons – tropical revolving storms – can move erratically and occasionally may even produce a complete loop.[46]

The cyclical variation of atmospheric pressure causes regular seasonal winds and monsoons. The Northeast Monsoon season occurs from October to December and the Southwest Monsoon period is generally from May to September annually. The prevailing wind direction is from the Northeast over most of the area during the northern hemisphere's winter months and southwesterly in the months of summer. Strong winds and gales may be experienced within 20–100 M from the coast.[47]

The area in focus generally receives abundant rainfall, with an annual average of 100–500 cm. Along the coast of China, in the context of this study, the mean annual rainfall will be between 150 and 320 cm. Along the southern coast of Vietnam, the mean annual rainfall is between 200 and less than 100 cm. Further south, along the coast of Peninsular Malaysia the annual total exceeds 300 cm.

Along the north coastal region of Borneo Island, Palawan Island and the west coast of Luzon Island rainfall is generally abundant and ranges between 300 and 400 cm. Large variations occur from year to year. The heaviest falls occur along the coast where the hinterland is mountainous. However, during the period February to April along the coast of China spells of low cloud and a light drizzle with poor visibility may be experienced.[48]

There is seasonal variation in the amount of cloud cover over the South China Sea basin. East of Hainan Island, it is mostly cloudy in February and March and partly cloudy in April and May; however, north of Lat. 20° N overcast conditions with very low cloud base with some drizzle and rain may be experienced. Off the coast of Peninsular Malaysia and along the north coast of Borneo Island the cloud cover varies depending on the season.[49]

Fog and reduced visibility may be experienced during the winter months north of Lat. 20° off the coastline of China. Heavy rain may also reduce visibility below fog limits temporarily. In torrential rain minimal to nil visibility may be experienced. In the southern sector of the basin, visibility may be less than 1 percent.

For most of the year, humidity is high in the region. It is very high off Malaysia with very little seasonal variation. The diurnal cycle of humidity and temperature is more marked than the seasonal change. Average humidity is over 90 percent during the night and decreases slightly during the forenoon. Local land breezes provide a welcome relief to the coastal communities.[50]

Elaboration of bathymetric features

Since the mid-1980s, considerable concern has been expressed at the indiscriminate and unregulated naming of undersea features which often get into print in articles submitted to professional journals, or on ocean maps and charts, without any close scrutiny being made concerning their suitability, or even whether the feature has already been discovered and named.

In order to remedy this situation and to bring the geographical names of undersea features to a better standardization, the IHO, at its 13th I.H. Conference (May 1987) and the IOC, at its 14th Assembly (March 1987) adopted similar motions on this subject. International concern for naming undersea features is limited to those features entirely or mainly (more than 50 percent) outside the external limits of the territorial sea, not exceeding 12 nautical miles from the baselines, in agreement with the 1982 United Nations Convention on the Law of the Sea. "Undersea feature" is a part of the ocean floor or seabed that has measurable relief or is delimited by relief. The IHO and the IOC maintain a record of discoveries of underwater features. For example, on 21 August 2018, proposals for 85 newly discovered undersea features were submitted by the Government of China, via the Undersea Feature Names of China Committee on Geographical Names (CCUFN) for acceptance by IHO/ICO.[51]

By 25 April 2020, the issue came to the fore with the Government of China naming, and effectively claiming, 80 geographical features, many of them underwater in the South China Sea basin. During the preceding days, the Government gave names to 25 islands, shoals, and reefs and 55 undersea mountains and ridges. The last time it took such action was in 1983 when it identified 287 features in the region where several littoral States hold competing territorial claims. The Government of Malaysia has also lodged a proposal for recent discoveries of undersea features in the South China Sea.

South China Sea: approaches to and navigation within

There are many approaches to the South China Sea basin. The channels leading through Luzon Strait are wide and deep. The Luzon Strait contains two groups of islands, the Batan Archipelago and the Babuyan Archipelago. The former is separated from the southern extremity of Taiwan Island by Bashi Channel and from the Babuyan Islands by Balintang Channel. Babuyan Archipelago is separated from Luzon Island by Babuyan Channel.

When approaching the South China Sea from the Sulu Sea, the Balabac Strait and Palawan Passage are the channels to be used. The southwestern entry to the South China Sea is via the Straits of Malacca and Singapore or the Sunda and Karimata Straits. The northern entry to South China Sea basin is via the Taiwan Strait. The width of this entry is about 300 M at about Lat. 20° N. The western half is relatively shallow as the seabed is composed of the Mainland Shelf; however, the eastern half is comparatively deeper.[52] Merchant shipping is required by international regulations to comply with the Load Line Rules.

Within the South China Sea, there are two distinct zones defined with reference to the Load Line Rules. To the south of Lat. 10° N the rules of the Tropical Zone apply; and in the section north of this limiting parallel of latitude the Seasonal Tropical Area rules are enforced. The 'Tropical' takes effect from 21 January to 30 April, and the 'Seasonal' is enforced from 1 May to 20 January.[53]

Conclusion

This narrative focused on the geographical description of the South China Sea basin in the context of the revised limits of the semi-enclosed water body, which has yet to be formally adopted. The chapter offers descriptions of the coast of the littoral states, the bathymetry, and features of the seabed, and the natural environment in the context of sea state, weather, tide, and tidal streams and ocean currents.

Brief discussions also focused on the geology and the tectonics that formed the basin and the sediments on the seabed especially found on the continental shelf. The structure of the seabed and that of the littoral makes the region a complex mix of terrestrial and marine features. Chains of high mountain ranges, deep trenches and troughs, deep-sea basins, and numerous coral islands form a complexity of phenomena.

This chapter offered a setting for further discussion on the varied topics that follow which are so important for an understanding of the geopolitical complexities so that future cooperation in managing and sustainably developing the resources therein could be enhanced and for a peaceful resolution to territorial and sovereignty issues could be achieved without further delay. Clues to find a political will to accomplish the tasks ahead may be contained in the following chapters of this present multi-disciplinary edited volume.

Notes

1 The United Nations Convention on the Law of the Sea, 1982; entered into force in 1994. Full text of the Convention, in a number of languages, is available on the UN's website <un.org/Depts/los/>.

2 See, for instance, Ellen Frost 'Re-naming the Waters: Southeast Asia Sea' or 'South Sea', RSIS *Commentary Series* No. 021, 28 January 2014. Philippines utilises the name of 'West Philippine Sea' for the western half of this water body and Vietnam employs the name of 'East Sea'. The Chinese name is Nanhai (South Sea).

3 The IHO Publication *SP* 23 of 1953 offers these defined limits which are for administrative purposes and are not intended as political statements nor indeed as oceanographic and biogeographic boundaries.

4 Draft of IHO's version of *Limits of Oceans and Seas*, 4th edition (1986), the International Hydrographic Organization (IHO) <accessed online 17 Oct. 2019>. The above comments apply to this reference note. The entire definition is reproduced *verbatim* in this narrative <iho.int>.

5 The measurements were derived from medium-scale nautical charts and the limits are based on the definitions given in the draft noted in 5, above.

6 Reference to Draft S23, mentioned above, note 5. <iho.int/en/iho-publications>.

7 The values are based on the present author's measurements and computations.

8 *Sailing Directions* (Enroute) Publication No. 161, US 'South China Sea and the Gulf of Thailand', National Geospatial Intelligence Agency, 2017. A useful guide for mariners operating in this region. For example, a description of the coastline near Hong Kong can be found at p. 24.

9 Poling, G.B. 2019 'China's Undocumented Fishing Activities', AMTI/CSIS, Washington.

10 *Sailing Directions* Publication No. 162 'Philippine Islands' National Geospatial Intelligence Agency, 2017; see also, Ying Wang and D.G Aubrey 1987 'The Characteristics of the China Coastline', *Coastal Shelf Research*, 7, 4, pp. 329–349.

11 *Sailing Directions* (Enroute) Publication No. 162 'Philippine Islands' National Geospatial Intelligence Agency, 2017. A useful guide for mariners operating in this region.

12 *Sailing Directions* (Enroute) Publication No. 163 'Borneo, Jawa, Sulawesi and Nusa Tenggara', National Geospatial Intelligence Agency, 2015. A useful guide for mariners operating in this region.

13 Plate tectonic is a geological concept that describes the movement of the Earth's lithosphere. See Alfred Wegener 1929 *The Origins of Continents and Oceans* and many others on this topic including Zhen Shao Huang 1997 *Speed of Continental Plates*; see also Chen Chin 1988 'The Geology of the South China Sea', in Nairn, A.E.M. and others (eds.), *The Ocean Basins and Margins*, Plenum Press, New York, 245–252.

14 The Pliocene Epoch is the epoch in the geologic timescale that extends from 5.333 million to 2.58 million years BP (Before Present). It is the second and youngest epoch of the Neogene Period in the Cenozoic Era. The Pliocene follows the Miocene Epoch and is followed by the Pleistocene Epoch.

15 See: Taylor and Hayes 1980 'The Tectonic Evolution of the South China Sea Basin', *Geophysical Monograph* 23, 89; Ren and others 1980 *The Geotectonic Evolution in China*, Science Press, Beijing.

16 Taylor and Hayes (1980, 1984: 23) and Holloway (1982: 1355); see also 'Structural Map of the South China Sea, Scale 1:3 million, 1st Ed, Commission for the Geological Map of the World, 2017.

17 Chen, S.Q. and others 1981 'Features of Gravity and Magnetic Anomalies in Central and Northern Parts of the South China Sea and their Geological Interpretation', *Scientia Sinca*, 24,1271.
18 An excellent study is offered by Zhang, W.Y. (ed.) 1983 *Tectonic Map of China and Adjacent Seas*, Science Press, Beijing. See also Atlas of Geology and Geophysics of the South China Sea, Scale 1:2 million, 2015.
19 A concise explanation is presented by Li, Z.W. 1984 'A Discussion on the Crustal Nature of the Central and Northern Parts of the South China Sea', *Acta. Geophys. Sin.* 27, 153.
20 Explained by Chen and others 1981 'Features of Gravity and Magnetic Anomalies in Central and Northern Parts of the South China Sea and their Geological Interpretation', *Scientia Sinca*, 24, 1271.
21 Suggested by Ji 1996 'Maritime Jurisdiction in the Three China Seas: Options for Equitable Settlement', (cited in <*gopher://gopher-igc...Maritime%Disputes*> printed 11 May 1996, 1–33.
22 Strangely, the concept of the semi-enclosed as defined in the 1982 Convention Articles 122, 123, can be debated and open to interpretation by the legal fraternity if they take the definition too literately. See, for example, Nien-Tsu Alfred Hu 2012 'Semi-enclosed Troubled Waters: A New Thinking on the Application of the 1982 UNCLOS Article 123 to the South China Sea', *Ocean Development and International Law*, 41, 3, 281–314. See also Terry Healy and Kenichi Harada, 'Editorial: Enclosed and Semi-Enclosed Coastal Seas', *Journal of Coastal Research*, 7, 1, pp. i–v.
23 The appropriate nautical charts of the basin reveal this information, for example, the International Chart Series and the General bathymetric Chart Series. See, for example, Chart 4508 (INT 108) and other series produced by other national charting and mapping authorities.
24 Greater detail of depth and isobath alignment will naturally be available on larger scale charts and maps.
25 Deduced from available graphics by the present author.
26 The area of *Dangerous Grounds* is delineated on appropriate charts and aptly described by The Hydrographer, 1982:148. For a true appreciation of the work of the former mariners, hydrographers and cartographers involved in surveying, charting and documentation of the nautical information of the region, see A.G. Findlay 1878 *Indian Archipelago, China and Japan Directory*, Richard, Holmes Laurie, London. For the 19th century, there are works with a more modern outlook. Recommended is Horsburgh (1817). Rosser and Imray (1866) cover the latter part of the 19th century. Descriptions of the marine features in their 'original state' when 'discovered' and first surveyed and documented in the English language. The Yitong Canyon discovered in 2008 is recorded by the IHO.
27 The Foot of the Continental Slope (FoS); see Article 76 of the 1982 LOSC.
28 An excellent series of maps, include the *Tectonic Map of the Circum-Pacific Region*, scale 1: 10 million, illustrate the tectonic characteristics of the basin and sediment thickness off the north coast of Borneo Island; see also Jin Xianglong and others (eds.), 'Marine Geology and Geophysics of the South China Sea', *Proceedings of a Symposium* held in Hangzhou, October 1990, China Ocean Press. *Geological and Structural Map of Eastern Asia* in 4 sheets by J. Letouzey and L. Sage, 1988, Institut Francais du Petrole. Published by American Association of Petroleum Geologists. Scale 1:2 500 000 Mercator at 33° N.
29 Refer to Note 27 above.
30 Numerous nautical charts, at varying map scales, produced by a variety of charting national authorities, over a wide time frame, were consulted by the present author.
31 See, for example, Hydrographer of the Navy (The Hydrographer), *China Sea Pilot*, Vol. I, Taunton, HMSO, Revised 1987 which covers the coast and sea area of the western section of the South China Sea Basin and includes the Paracel Islands and Macclesfield Bank.
32 Hydrographer of the Navy, *China Sea Pilot*, Vol. I, Taunton, HMSO, Revised 1987.
33 Ibid.
34 Hydrographer of the Navy, *China Sea Pilot*, Vol. II, HMSO, Revised 1982, p. 148.
35 Ibid., p. 19.
36 Hydrographer of the Navy, *China Sea Pilot*, Vol. I, HMSO, 1987, p. 16.
37 Hydrographer of the Navy, *China Sea Pilot*, Vol. I, 1987, pp. 126–153.
38 Seamount and guyot, Hydrographer of the Navy, *China Sea Pilot*, Vol. I, 1987, p. 16.
39 The Hydrographer of the Navy, Vol. I, 1987, p. 22; The Hydrographer, Vol. II, HMSO, 1982, p. 22.
40 The Hydrographer of the Navy, Vol. I, 1987, pp. 22–23; The Hydrographer, Vol. II, 1982, p. 22.

41 The Hydrographer of the Navy, Vol. I, 1987, p. 17; The Hydrographer, Vol. II, HMSO, 1982, p. 19.
42 The Hydrographer of the Navy, Vol. I, p. 17.
43 The Hydrographer of the Navy, Vol. I, pp. 30–33; and Vol. II, pp. 30–37, Vol. III.
44 The Hydrographer of the Navy, Vol. I, pp. 34–37; and Vol. II, pp. 29–32., Vol. III.
45 Monsoons and typhoon refer to the above Volumes of the Hydrographer.
46 A series of maps in the above-named volumes best illustrate the typical paths taken by typhoons, for example, especially Vol. II, pp. 32 and 33.
47 The Hydrographer of the Navy, Vol. I, 1987, p. 33.
48 The Hydrographer of the Navy, Vol. I, 1987, pp. 38–44; The Hydrographer, Vol. II, 1982, pp. 42–63.
49 The Hydrographer of the Navy, Vol. I, II and III: offer comprehensive accounts of the weather that may be encountered in the South China Sea. The volumes contain maps and climatic tables.
50 Hydrographer of the Navy, Vol. I, 1987, p. 42, and Hydrographer, Vol. II, 1982, p. 38.
51 Refer to the web site of the International Hydrographic Organisation. The IHO and International Oceanographic Commission at their respective meetings in 1987 agreed to standardise the naming of underwater features. In 2018, The Government of China submitted proposals for the acceptance and recognition of recent discoveries of underwater physical features. See also: *South China Morning Post*, 25 April 2020 and 25 May 2020.
52 See for example, Taiwan Strait Chart 94004, Edition 7 NTM: 201130, 2009.
53 The International Load Line Convention of 1930 established uniform regulations governing how deeply ships could be loaded depending on where they were operating and the season. The Hydrographer of the Navy, 'Ocean Passages for the World', 1973.

Appendix A1: undersea features: recent discoveries in the South China Sea

The geographical coordinate of the summit of the feature is listed as degrees and minutes of arc value.

Generic terms of Canyon (C'yon), Hill, Ridge and Seamount (S'mt) are employed in the tabulation

Name	*Type*	*Lat° ' N*	*Lon° ' E*	*Depth Max*	*Depth Min*	*Total Relief*	*Dimension km*	*Date*	*Proposer Organ.*
Penxi	Ridge	12 46.3	112 10.6	4000	500	3500	300 × 200	1982 2005	CCUEN CGS
Wangheng	Hill	7 20.7	111 21.3	1977	165.3	324	18 × 14	2000/01	"
Mahuan	Hill	7 07.7	111 17.9	1985	1059	925	48 × 25	2000/01	"
Tangjing	Hill	7 12.2	111 26.0	2000	1496	504	20 × 10	2000/01	"
Changjun	S'mt	7 20.5	111 41.8	1988	187	1801	26 × 20	2000/01	"
Shuichuan	Hill	6 30.1	109 52.6	1355	974	381	7.5 × 2.2	2000	"
Baochuan	Hill	6 26.2	109 50.7	1246	991	255	8.7 × 2.4	2000	"
Zhanchuan	Hill	6 19.5	109 48.6	1135	933	207	4.5 × 2.3	2000	"
Longhei	S'mt	14 00	114 52.3	4348	550	3798	48 × 34	1988/05	"
Longnam	S'mt	13 21.8	114 58.5	4471	513	3958	45 × 30	1980/82	"
Zhongnam	S'mt	13 58.0	115 25.7	4355	288	4067	50 × 45	1980/04	"
Shenhu	C'yon	19 43.7	114 48.4	1714	296	1418	126.8 × 36.4	2000/01	"
Qinjiushao	Hill	19 03.5	117 13.6	3733	3153	580	30.2 × 5.9	2000/01	"
Dushi	S'mt	19 06.9	117 00.8	3741	2686	1055	50 × 12.3	2000/01	"

(*Continued*)

Name	*Type*	*Lat° ' N*	*Lon° ' E*	*Depth Max*	*Depth Min*	*Total Relief*	*Dimension km*	*Date*	*Proposer Organ.*
Rafflesia (N)	Hill	6 48,8	111 25.4	1855.79					Malaysia
Rafflesia (S)	Hill	6 40.3	111 07.7	1713.69					RMN
Kadazandusun	Hills	7 13.1	114 04.1						"
Murut	Hill	6 38.9	114 15.5	2027.35					"
Bidayah	Hills	5 31.4	112 32.8						"
Iban (N)	Ridge	6 23.2	111 30.7	1604.03					"
Iban (S)	Ridge	6 14.4	111 18.5	1591.75					"

Source: Prepared by the author.

2

THE SOUTH CHINA SEA

Historical developments

Stein Tønnesson

First development: seaborne trade and mapping

For more than two thousand years, ships have sailed along the coasts of the South China Sea, also known as *Nanyang* (南洋; South Sea), Biển đông (East Sea) and, more recently, *West Philippine Sea*. From the west, ships have entered the sea through the Malacca or Sunda Straits, followed the coast of Indochina up north until getting Hainan in sight, then turned east toward the Chinese coast or through the Luzon or Taiwan Strait in the direction of Okinawa, Korea, Japan and the northern part of the Middle Kingdom (China). The ships followed the patterns of the monsoon, sailing north during May–October, turning back when the wind turned. The ships originated in many countries and called on multiple ports, where they were taxed by shifting regimes, some of which promoted seaborne trade, while others tried to prevent foreigners from entering their realm. Piracy was common. Ship captains always did their best to avoid the middle of the South China Sea, where strong currents pulled ships into shallow waters around perilous rocks and reefs. What came to be known as the Spratlys was previously known as Dangerous Grounds.

Mapmakers based at local courts, notably in the Middle Kingdom, drew maps and wrote pilot guides for the coasts and coastal islands, seen from a sideways perspective, and warned against straying too far away from the coasts. From the 15th century, ships from the Far West began to arrive, first from Portugal and Spain, then Holland, France and Britain, and finally America. They used birds-eye maps, drawn from an imagined perspective in the sky. Just like the Chinese mapmakers, who continued their mapping of the Chinese sea routes, the Europeans described the islands, reefs, banks and shoals in the middle of the sea mainly for the purpose of helping ships to avoid them.

From the 15th to 18th centuries, European mapmakers almost consistently drew a string of non-existing islands or shoals off the coast of Indochina. It took until the Enlightenment in the late 18th century before Europeans realized that these islands did not exist. The Nguyen court in Vietnam's capital Hue produced a map with these non-existing islands as late as 1838.[1] The primary function of this exaggerated maritime peril must have been to keep seafarers close to the coast and prevent them from ending up as a wreck on dangerous grounds.

After modern maps were drawn, with precisely numbered latitudes and longitudes and locations for reefs, rocks, shoals and islands, ships began to sail straight through the South China Sea in the deep-water corridor south of the Paracels and Macclesfield Bank. This turned into a "maritime highway" once ships were provided with engines. In our time, hundreds of tankers, cargo ships, container ships and bulk freighters pass on this maritime highway every single day of the year. One research project has found that in 2016, an estimated 3.4 trillion USD in trade passed through the South China Sea, constituting 64 percent of China's, 42 percent of Japan's and 14 percent of the US maritime trade.[2]

Second development: naval rivalries

Trade and naval power are closely connected. Trading ships were often armed, and state-controlled navies would either protect or threaten them. At the time of the Han dynasty (206 BC–220 AD), when the northern part of today's Vietnam was an integral part of the Middle Kingdom, China dominated maritime trade in the South China Sea and continued to do so under subsequent dynasties. From the 8th to 12th centuries, however, ships from the Southeast Asian maritime state of Sri Vijaya, which controlled both sides of the Malacca Strait, held sway in the region. Vietnam now broke loose from the Middle Kingdom. Then came a new Chinese expansion under the Song dynasty (960–1279), and the Yuan (Mongol) dynasty (1271–1378) made a failed attempt to conquer Vietnam from the sea. China reached the apex of its naval power in the 15th century, when Admiral Zheng He (1371–1433) built a fleet of huge ocean-going warships. Then the Ming dynasty (1368–1644) turned inward and canceled its maritime ambitions. This left the sea open to smaller maritime nations, such as the Ryukyus, Japan, Korea and the countries around the Indian Ocean. Persians and Arabs brought Islam to the region and made the Malay language a lingua franca in long-distance trade, and "China" became the name outsiders would use for the country that was known to itself as the Middle Kingdom (Zhongguo).

From the 16th century, the Europeans arrived. Merchant companies, first from Portugal and Spain, then Holland, later France and Britain took over from the Arabs and used their naval and maritime skills to tap into Asia's regional trade, profit from it, and take control of several ports and cities. The Portuguese took Melaka in 1511 and established themselves in Macao from 1557. In 1571, the Spaniards took Manila. The Dutch took over Melaka in 1612 and dominated the lucrative spice trade during the 17th century, and for a while even occupied Taiwan (Formosa). In 1644, the Ming dynasty succumbed to the onslaught of the Qing (Manchus), who set up a new dynasty in the Middle Kingdom. In the 18th century, the Qing dynasty greatly expanded China's territory on land and built a formidable naval power. This Chinese maritime resurgence, and a concomitant decline of Dutch influence, is often overlooked in historical narratives. There was a China-dominated interlude before the British and French arrived with superior firepower, dealing blows to Qing China in the two Opium Wars of 1839 and 1860. Meanwhile, the Middle Kingdom suffered from the hugely devastating Taiping rebellion (1850–1864). Britain took Hong Kong in 1842 and France established a protectorate over Vietnam in 1884–1885, in connection with a short war with China. France now relieved Vietnam of its obligation to pay tribute to the Middle Kingdom. Then, in 1894–1895, China lost its Beiyang fleet in war with Japan, who seized Taiwan and established itself as a power in the South China Sea. In 1902, Japan became a British ally and, in 1905, defeated Russia in war. By that time, however, the United States had also become a formidable power in the Western Pacific. It enforced an "open door" policy on China and took the Philippines from Spain in the Spanish-American War of 1898.

In the period when the Qing dynasty fell to the 1911 revolution when Europe was weakened by the First World War and the armies of the new Republic of China set out to reunite the Middle Kingdom, the South China Sea was dominated by a condominium of external powers, such as Britain, France, the Netherlands, the United States and Japan. In 1923, the Anglo-Japanese alliance broke up, and the four Western powers enforced restrictions on the size of the Japanese fleet. When Japan took control of Manchuria in 1931 and engaged in a naval build-up in defiance of any restrictions, the Western powers took measures to block Japan's further expansion. This placed them firmly on the side of Chiang Kai-shek's Republic of China under the Sino-Japanese war from 1937, although the main military and financial support to Chiang Kai-shek for his struggle against Japan until 1941 came from the Soviet Union. By 1940–1941, French Indochina came under attack by Japanese forces crossing the border from China, and Vichy France decided to allow Japan to establish itself on Indochinese territory. In 1942, right after its attack on Pearl Harbor, Japan invaded all the countries around the South China Sea. For three years, it was a "Japanese lake," but in January 1945, a heavily armed US fleet arrived to bombard the coasts of Indochina, Hainan and Taiwan.

After the Second World War, the US Navy established its dominance in the Western Pacific, with naval bases at Guam, Okinawa and Subic Bay of the Philippines, and with Japan, the Republic of China on Taiwan, the newly independent Philippines and Thailand as Allies. The US dominance became even more pronounced as France and Britain withdrew militarily from the region in 1957 and 1968, respectively. For almost two decades, the US Navy held sway in the former French base at Cam Ranh Bay, on the Vietnamese coast right inside the Paracel Islands. Then came the US defeat in the Vietnam War, and the new Socialist Republic of Vietnam (SRV) invited the Soviet Navy to use Cam Ranh Bay. During the last phase of the Cold War, following President Richard Nixon's visit to China in 1972, China and the US were de facto Allies against the Soviet Union and Vietnam. In the 1980s–1990s, China seized this chance to methodically build up its naval and air forces. For a long time, this did not cause much worry across the Pacific, not even after the People's Republic of China's suppression of the demonstrations in Beijing 1989, and the 1991 breakup of the Soviet Union, which removed the threat that had forged the Sino-American partnership. The United States had now regained the confidence it had lost in Vietnam. When China tried to sway Taiwan's elections in 1995 through missile exercises, the United States displayed its military superiority by sending a carrier group undetected into the Taiwan Strait. This was a shock for Beijing and inspired it to deploy thousands of precision-guided missiles along its coast and build a stronger navy. This happened at a time when China, Japan and the United States greatly expanded their trade with each other and integrated their economies in complex transnational production and marketing chains. China could use its surplus from exports to America and Europe to finance its military modernization and gain regional influence through trade with and financial support to its neighbor states, including the US Allies. Yet it lasted until the 2010s before the United States developed the open hostility to China that is so evident today. China has built huge numbers of attack submarines and ocean-going ships in many sizes, has docked its first self-built aircraft carrier and acquired a capacity for cyber warfare. As yet, the People's Liberation Army, which suffers from a lack of combat experience, would hardly be able to win either a full-scale confrontation or a limited war with the United States, if such a thing as limited war is possible. In peacetime, however, China may already have become the dominant power in the South China Sea, with a capacity to make its presence felt wherever it wants. The recent Chinese construction of sophisticated military installations in the Paracels as well as on seven reefs in the Spratlys should be seen in this perspective.

The first two developments accounted for in this chapter, increasing maritime trade and great shifts in naval power, will have huge long-term consequences. They also form the context for our third development, a long and complicated process transforming the "dangerous grounds" into subjects of passionate sovereignty disputes.

Third development: disputes over sovereignty to islands

Sovereignty over land is the *sine qua non* of the modern state. States jealously guard their sovereignty to territories, big and small, populated and unpopulated. Even the smallest of islands are shown on maps as part of the national territory. They are marked with stones and flags, named and occupied by nationalist activists or government troops. To keep an island permanently occupied becomes all the more important when it is disputed among several states. Today, the South China Sea is surrounded by the states of China and Taiwan, the Philippines, Malaysia, Brunei, Indonesia and Vietnam. One of them, the Middle Kingdom, can trace its history as an independent state back several thousand years. Chronicles on sea routes written under the Song dynasty in the 12th–13th centuries describe groups of dangerous islands called *Qianli Changsha*, which must be the Paracels, and *Wanli Shitang*, which most likely is the Spratlys. Only when we get to the mid-19th century, however, do we find such chronicles saying that the islands are parts of certain prefectures, i.e., administered by the Middle Kingdom.[3] Around that time, the Vietnamese Nguyen dynasty, which would later succumb to French conquest, also sent expeditions to and declared ownership to the Paracels.

Most legal experts see the pre-20th-century Chinese and Vietnamese claims as *inchoate* (incomplete) since they were not accompanied by permanent administration or occupation. Weather conditions did not permit any constant habitation, although fishermen from around the South China Sea established themselves on a seasonal basis in multiple islands to fish and collect turtle eggs or bird-nests.

The first European claim to sovereignty was made in 1877 when Great Britain officially took possession of two islands in the Spratlys, Spratly and Amboyna Cay, which they approached from Labuan in north Borneo. For many years, the UK government listed the two islands as British but did not pursue the claim when others made rival claims. The British claim was allowed to lapse and could not therefore be taken over by any of Britain's former colonies (Brunei or Malaysia).

In 1909, the Qing dynasty in China formally claimed both the Paracels and Spratlys, without apparently provoking any protests or counterclaims from France, which by now held responsibility for the foreign policy of its protected states in Indochina. However, the Qing dynasty succumbed to a revolution in 1911, and the ensuing internal strife between warlords and political parties prevented China from following up its claim effectively. This gave France an opportunity it did not seize. In spite of admonitions from business interests and mandarins at the Nguyen court, the French colonial authorities showed little interest in the Paracels and Spratlys until the 1930s, when it realized the magnitude of the Japanese threat to French Indochina. Since taking Taiwan in 1895, Japan had been a player in the South China Sea with direct commercial and military interests. In 1931, French ships set up markers on several Spratly islands, and the French government formed the intention to claim all islands within a rectangle it drew on a map. When the British Foreign Office learned about this, it hoped France would take responsibility for stemming the Japanese advance. London notified Paris that its claim would be stronger in international law if it designated specific islands rather than claiming an area marked up with lines on a map. In 1933, France followed the advice, gave up its rectangle, and officially claimed nine islands in the Spratlys. Japan protested. China also prepared a protest letter, although no copy of it has yet been found in French, British or US archives.[4] It should be added that France made the claim on behalf of itself, not on behalf of any part of Indochina, and the French claim was not later formally transferred to Vietnam.[5] After 1957, however, France let it lapse just as Britain was doing with its claim to Spratly and Amboyna Cay.

France also took action to prevent Japan from seizing the Paracels. In 1938, it built a lighthouse on Woody Island and formally claimed sovereignty over the whole island group, this time on behalf of Annam (Vietnam). Japan was not, however, deterred. In February 1939, it conquered Hainan Island and shortly after established a presence in the Paracels. From then until March 1945, a Japanese-Taiwanese garrison lived side by side with a Franco-Vietnamese garrison in Woody Island of the Paracels. In March 1945, after Japan had launched a coup against the French administration in Indochina, it also forced the French and Vietnamese soldiers in Woody Island to leave. In Itu Aba of the Spratlys, Japan had ousted the local French garrison already in October 1940 and built military installations there. They were destroyed at the end of the war, either by the Japanese themselves or by US artillery.[6]

In 1945–1946, the Republic of China (ROC) took over Taiwan from Japan by virtue of an allied agreement made in Cairo in 1943 and was quick to take action with the aim to occupy the Japanese-Taiwanese installations in the Paracels (Xisha) and Spratlys (Nansha). It sent one ship to each of the two island groups and set up garrisons, and built installations in Woody Island (Yongxing) in the Paracels, and Itu Aba (Taiping) in the Spratlys. France also sent ships to reassert its claims, but because it now faced a rebellion in Vietnam, where the communist leader Ho Chi Minh had proclaimed the new Democratic Republic in September 1945, France lost its competition with China. When a French ship arrived in Woody Island in January 1947, a Chinese garrison had already been established. A crisis ensued, but France did not want war with China at a time when it was essential to prevent Chiang Kai-shek from helping Ho Chi Minh's rebel government, so the French sailed away from Woody Island and established a garrison in Pattle Island instead.[7] While Woody Island is the largest island in the eastern part of the Paracels (the Amphitrite group), Pattle is the largest in the western part (the Crescent group). Concerning the Spratlys, France made no attempt to oust the ROC forces from Itu Aba and did not at this stage establish any permanent presence there.

In 1947, as a signal of its claim to all the islands in the South China Sea, the ROC government drew a map with a dashed U-shaped line around the islands. It was first officially published in a 1948 atlas and would later, in slightly altered versions, become standard in the ROC (Taiwan) as well as the People's Republic of China (PRC). The map was drawn on the basis of European cartography, but the mappers do not seem to have been fully familiar with European maritime terms. This led to misunderstandings, such as making Macclesfield Bank into an island group (Zhongsha) although it is actually submerged, and pushing the U-shaped line as far south as James Shoal, which is 30 meters below the sea level.[8] As has been shown in a remarkable doctoral thesis based on archival research in Taipei, the U-shaped line was meant to indicate a claim to the islands inside it and, by implication, their 3-nautical-mile territorial sea.[9] It was not meant as a claim to historical rights in any larger water zone or resources under the seabed. As we shall soon see, however, new developments in the 1970s led the U-shaped line to be reinterpreted as a claim to "maritime territory."

The ROC's actions in 1946–1948 established China as the lead claimant to sovereignty over the largest Paracel and Spratly islands. It had seized Woody and Itu Aba at a time when they were unoccupied and had established a permanent presence. Yet this did not last long.

In 1949–1950, when the new PRC had been proclaimed in Beijing and the ROC withdrew to Taiwan, and a PRC invasion of Taiwan seemed imminent, the ROC government withdrew its garrisons from Woody and Itu Aba islands, and the PRC was not in a position to replace them. Yet France did not use this opportunity to strengthen Vietnam's claim by establishing a permanent presence. France faced a dramatic escalation of its war with Ho Chi Minh's Democratic Republic of Vietnam (DRV), which was officially recognized by the PRC and USSR in January 1950. China provided the DRV with massive military support so that it could carry out regular offensives against the French forces and win a big battle in October 1950. Under these conditions, France refrained from establishing a presence in the islands vacated by the ROC, so Woody and Itu Aba were left unoccupied for the next five to six years, while the Franco-Vietnamese garrison in Pattle Island of the western Paracels remained in place.

This was the situation when the San Francisco conference was convened in 1951 to agree on a peace treaty between Japan and the victorious Allies. The conference set out to settle the fate of Japan's former territories. While the United States, USSR, the United Kingdom, France and also the new French-dominated State of Vietnam (later South Vietnam) took part in the conference, the DRV, PRC and ROC did not. It soon became clear that the most influential parties to the conference saw no need to reach an agreement as to who held sovereignty over the Paracels and Spratlys. Japan surrendered Taiwan and the Penghu (Pescadores) to China and renounced "all rights, title and claim to the Spratly Islands and to the Paracel Islands," but did not concede them to any particular country. In 1952, however, the ROC signed its own bilateral peace treaty with Japan and scored a diplomatic victory by having the South China Sea islands mentioned along with Taiwan and Penghu in its treaty.[10] France worried that this could undermine its claim in the Spratlys and Vietnam's claim to the Paracels, and therefore exchanged letters with Japan to the effect that the ROC-Japan treaty in no way altered the outcome of the San Francisco treaty.[11]

In 1956, a new actor entered the scene. Since the Philippines gained independence from the United States in 1946, its former colonial master had discouraged it from claiming sovereignty to islands outside the perimeter of the Philippines archipelago as defined in the Spanish-US treaty of 1898. In 1956, however, the Filipino mariner and businessman Tomas Cloma proclaimed a new Freedomland *(Kalaya'an)*, encompassing most of the Spratlys but not Spratly Island itself. He set up markers on some islands and published a map of the same type that the French had intended to publish in 1930, and which the ROC had used in 1948 with its U-shaped line. Tomas Cloma drew six straight lines to indicate the maritime boundaries around Freedomland.[12] In terms of the law, he could base his initiative on the assertion that the islands west of the Philippines were *res nullius* (did not belong to any state) since no state had permanently occupied them since 1950. His proclamation led to official diplomatic protests from France, the new Republic of (South) Vietnam, the DRV (North Vietnam), the PRC (China) and the ROC (Taiwan). The ROC now moved to reoccupy Itu Aba, and the PRC had established a presence in Woody Island in late 1955.

In the 1960s, the sovereignty disputes in the Paracels and Spratlys were more or less forgotten, as the Vietnam War caught everyone's attention, China was engulfed in its Cultural Revolution, and Malaya, Sabah and Sarawak joined up to become Malaysia, leaving Singapore on its own. The 1970s, however, marked a turning point in the South China Sea. A scramble began to occupy islands, as a 1969 UN report indicated the likelihood that huge oil deposits might be found under the seabed. In 1971, president Ferdinand Marcos officially claimed Freedomland as a Philippines possession and ordered his forces to occupy a number of islands. In March 1974, the Chinese People's Liberation Army-Navy (PLA-N) defeated the South Vietnamese forces in the western Paracels and took over the Crescent group. By this time, the United States had signed the 1973 Paris Peace Agreement and withdrawn its troops from Vietnam. President Richard Nixon was keen to align China with the United States against the USSR, so Washington did not protest China's use of force. After having lost the Paracels, South Vietnam followed the example of the Philippines and quickly occupied a number of Spratly islands, which were peacefully transferred to North Vietnamese representatives in 1975, as Saigon succumbed to Hanoi's Ho Chi Minh-offensive. In the following year, Vietnam was unified in the SRV, which maintained all of South Vietnam's claims.[13] In 1979, Malaysia joined the scramble for the South China Sea with a continental shelf claim and also occupied a number of features, but not the same ones that Britain had claimed in 1877 (Spratly and Amboyna Cay), which had been occupied by Vietnam. By the end of the 1970s, virtually every naturally formed island in the Spratlys had been occupied by one or another state.

The new SRV, which was established in 1976 through a merger of North and South Vietnam, was soon marginalized in its home region, squeezed as it was between a hostile China and the even more hostile Khmer Rouge in Democratic Kampuchea. Vietnam became dependent on Soviet aid. In the final days of 1978, it invaded Cambodia, where it was embroiled in a protracted counterinsurgency against a coalition of rebel forces. The Vietnamese invasion of Cambodia provoked a five-week punitive Chinese counter-invasion of northern Vietnam, and the two communist party states engaged in a number of deadly artillery exchanges and cross-border raids until 1987. In the first half of the 1980s, Vietnam's position in the South China Sea was bolstered by the Soviet Navy, which took over from the United States in the deep sea harbor at Cam Ranh Bay. Vietnam and the Soviet Union also engaged in profitable offshore oil production through the joint venture Vietsovpetro, which took over oil fields developed by South Vietnam in cooperation with US companies. In 1985, however, the situation changed when Michael Gorbachev took over as Soviet leader. He canceled the expensive aid to Vietnam and forced Hanoi to reorient its policies. While launching market economic reforms at home, Vietnam withdrew its forces from Cambodia and engaged in serious peace talks. This led to a rapprochement with China as well as with the Association of Southeast Asian Nations (ASEAN) and its six member states: Indonesia, Malaysia, the Philippines, Singapore, Thailand and Brunei.

At the 1987–1988 juncture, before Vietnam had established normal relations with its neighbor states, the PRC for the first time established a presence in the Spratlys. It was the only claimant state that did not occupy any Spratly island. In 1987, a Chinese expedition undertook scientific research under the auspices of UNESCO, and in 1988, it established a physical presence on several small reefs and built huge installations on some of them, notably the Fiery Cross Reef. In March 1988, when a contingent of Vietnamese engineering troops tried to forestall a Chinese occupation of a submerged reef, a battle occurred in which China sank a Vietnamese ship and strafed the reef with machine guns, killing the Vietnamese troops who had taken up position there.[14] Until today, the Sino-South Vietnamese battle for the Paracels in January 1974 and the Sino-Vietnamese battle in the Spratlys in March 1988 are the only cases of direct military combat in the South China Sea since the Second World War. It is rumored in China that the PLA Navy planned to forcefully occupy the Vietnamese-held islands in the Spratlys in 1989, but that the operation was canceled in the runup to Soviet leader Gorbachev's visit to Beijing in June 1989, amidst demonstrations on Tiananmen Square.

The dominant trend in the 1990s–2000s, after the Cold War ended, was rapprochement, cooperation and peace around the South China Sea. Vietnam normalized its relations with

China in 1991 and spent the rest of the 1990s negotiating a land border treaty with China, signed in 1999, and a treaty on the delimitation of the maritime boundary in the Gulf of Tonkin, signed in 2000. Meanwhile, in 1995, Vietnam obtained membership in ASEAN and established diplomatic relations with the United States. China welcomed the expansion of ASEAN to include Vietnam, Laos, Cambodia and Myanmar, and improved its economic, diplomatic and cultural relations with the Southeast Asian countries through "good neighbor policies." In that period, the countries around the South China Sea also entered into several fishery agreements, and they took part in the annual Managing Potential Conflict in the South China Sea workshops, hosted by Indonesia.

Amidst all the improvement, however, two incidents provoked tension, foreshadowing the crisis we see today. One was about oil. To put a long story short, from 1992 onward, China and Vietnam have issued concessions for oil exploration in overlapping areas, and China has in various ways sought to disrupt exploration for oil by companies operating under offshore licenses from Vietnam, Malaysia or the Philippines. Vietnam, on its side, has obstructed Chinese exploration in areas it claims as parts of its continental shelf. While these squabbles have not led to any closedown of already producing oilfields, it has effectively prevented exploration for oil and gas in most of the South China Sea. This may be good for the environment.

The other incident in the 1990s concerned a low-tide elevation outside of the Philippines island of Palawan, called Mischief Reef. In 1994, the Philippines discovered that China had carried out construction work there and removed the Chinese buildings. China claimed it had just built a shelter for fishermen, then returned to Mischief Reef and occupied it. This was the first step on the way to what today is a sophisticated Chinese military facility. The Philippines government of president Fidel Ramos was deeply concerned at the time and received support from its ASEAN partners to protest against China's encroachment on what the Philippines considered as its continental shelf. (As a low-tide elevation, Mischief Reef does not qualify as an island under United Nations Convention on the Law of the Sea (UNCLOS) and therefore cannot be the object of a sovereignty claim.) After some hesitation, China accepted to talk with ASEAN about establishing a Code of Conduct (COC), and discuss ASEAN's wish for a prohibition against constructing new features. No legally binding COC was agreed upon. Yet in 2002, China and ASEAN signed a Declaration on the Conduct of Parties (DOC), undertaking to "resolve their territorial and jurisdictional disputes by peaceful means, without resorting to the threat or use of force" and to exercise self-restraint, "refraining from action of inhabiting on the presently uninhabited islands, reefs, shoals, cays, and other features."[15] While China did not give up its construction work on Mischief Reef, the DOC calmed down the South China Sea for the next six years. This was a time when China and Vietnam joined the World Trade Organization, and East Asia took over North America's position as the main driver of global economic growth.

Since 2009, the pacifying effect of the DOC has evaporated. Instead, we have seen an escalating crisis between China and the ASEAN claimants, as well as between China and the United States. While the underlying cause is China's growing military power, which frightens its neighbors as well as the Americans, the crisis also has a lot to do with fish, oil, gas and certain aspects of international law. To understand the crisis that has characterized the last ten-twelve years, we have to take a step back and look at developments within the law of the sea. First, however, we must emphasize that the dispute over sovereignty to islands is not regulated by the law of the sea. Islands are land, not sea. While sovereignty to land is established *historically* by treaty or effective occupation and administration, sovereign rights at sea are established *geographically* by calculating distances from coasts.

Fourth development: expanding economic zones

Through the centuries there has been disagreement among the world's maritime powers concerning the rights of coastal states to interfere with shipping off their coasts. Seafaring nations are always at the same time coastal states but if their navies are sufficiently powerful to deter any encroachment on their homeland from the sea, they see less need than other coastal states for international legislation to protect their coastal waters. Instead, they wish to enjoy full freedom for their fleets to sail wherever they want, and they argue that this is good for global trade. In 1609, at a time when Holland had the world's most powerful fleet and England could not match its power, Hugo Grotius (1583–1645) wrote his seminal treatise *Mare Liberum*, advocating the freedom of navigation and reducing coastal states rights to interfere with shipping to just a narrow band of waters. In 1662, the Englishman John Selden published his counter-treatise, *Mare Clausum: The Rights and Dominions of the Sea*, which sought to protect the interests of coastal states. In the 18th century, when Britain rose to become the world's most powerful maritime power, it adopted the Grotian principles. Today the world's most ardent defender of *Mare Liberum* is the Unites States. The Chinese PLA Navy is not yet sufficiently powerful to overcome its worries for coastal security, so China's national legislation curtails the right of foreign navies to conduct surveillance activities or exercises in China's exclusive economic zone (EEZ) or pass through its territorial sea without prior permission.

The third United Nations Conference on the Law of the Sea, 1973–1982 (UNCLOS III) produced a seminal treaty that has rightly been called a "constitution for the oceans." It widened the allowed limit of a coastal state's territorial sea to 12 nautical miles and created a legal innovation with huge implications for the South China Sea: In addition to a territorial sea, coastal states were allowed to claim sovereign rights to all resources in an EEZ outside of their territorial sea. This zone may extend all the way to 200 nautical miles from the coastal baselines used to measure the breadth of the territorial sea. The EEZ came about as a compromise between a group of maritime powers defending the freedom of navigation and a grand coalition of developing coastal states in Africa, South America and Asia. Before UNCLOS III, some of them had unilaterally proclaimed extensive fishing zones while others had extended their territorial seas much further than international law allowed. The essence of the new EEZ is in its name: coastal states gained *exclusive rights* to marine resources. No other state can claim historical or traditional rights in another country's EEZ. And the rights are just economic. They do not amount to full sovereignty, so states cannot prevent ships from sailing through their EEZ or from laying cables on the seabed. UNCLOS III also made another radical decision: All states would have exclusive rights to resources under the seabed out to 200 nautical miles and, if their continental shelf extended even further out, they could apply to the UN for recognition of a continental shelf beyond 200 nautical miles. These decisions were of great consequence for the South China Sea since they produced a potential for conflicting, overlapping claims.

Just like the 12-nautical-mile territorial sea, the new EEZ was created on the basis of the key principle in the law of the sea that *land dominates the sea*. Sovereignty to land generates sovereign rights to resources in the sea outside it. A state does not need to occupy the sea or set up boundary markers. It is enough to claim rights within a certain distance from its coast. Generally speaking, this makes the law of the sea a recipe for peace. While land borders were established through wars, maritime boundaries are established through map-based calculations. When legitimate zone claims overlap, the state parties use the median line principle to divide the overlapping area equitably between themselves. Unfortunately, this is still rather complicated in an enclosed or semi-enclosed sea with several states around it, above all if it contains disputed islands. Besides the shift of military power from the United States to China, the EEZ principle is a key reason why, since 2009, there has been a crisis in the South China Sea.

Why have no maritime boundaries been agreed upon in the South China Sea, when agreements have been made in nearby waters? Already in 1979, Malaysia and Thailand agreed on their maritime boundary in the Gulf of Thailand, and in 1997, Vietnam and Malaysia agreed on their boundary in the Gulf of Thailand. In 2000, China and Vietnam resolved their maritime boundary in the Tonkin Gulf. In 2003, Vietnam and Indonesia agreed on their continental shelf boundary. In 2009, Brunei and Malaysia made an undisclosed agreement on their maritime boundary and decided to undertake joint development of oil fields straddling it. Yet, for the central part of the South China Sea, there have not even been any talks.

This has several reasons. One is that China remains divided between two states, the PRC and the ROC, which must coordinate their policies if they engage in serious negotiations. Taiwan is situated between mainland China and the Philippines. It occupies Pratas Island in the northern part of the South China Sea as well as the largest of the Spratly Islands, Itu Aba (Taiping). A second reason is that there are so many claimants. A comprehensive solution would require a combination of bilateral and multilateral talks. While difficult, this should not be impossible. A third reason is the ambiguous nature of the regime of islands in Article 121 of UNCLOS, which defines an island as "a naturally formed area of land, surrounded by water, which is above water at high tide" (121.1), and says that "Rocks which cannot sustain human habitation or economic life of their own shall have no exclusive economic zone or continental shelf" (121.3). Article 121.3 has been interpreted differently in various parts of the world, and until 2016, no international tribunal had dared to establish the criteria to be used in order to establish if a feature, whether rock or island, can sustain human habitation or economic life of its own. If the many small features in the Spratlys were given the right to generate EEZs and continental shelves, this would seriously affect maritime delimitation.

The fourth reason is most important: China is geographically disadvantaged in the South China Sea by the fact that the coasts of Vietnam, the Philippines and Taiwan (which it does not control) protrude much closer to the middle of the sea than China's own coast, including the coast of its main asset, Hainan. The logical implications of the EEZ regime thus run up against the idea of China's "national geobody," as visualized by the U-shaped line. Chinese children learn at school that their nation extends south to James Shoal just north of Borneo, and includes four "archipelagos": Xisha Qundao (Paracels), Dongsha Qundao (Pratas), Nansha Qundao (Spratlys) and Zhongsha Qundao (Macclesfield Bank and Scarborough Shoal). This irredentist vision, which has been reinforced by Xi Jinping's China Dream, has made it extremely hard for the Chinese to reconcile themselves to the necessity of conceding the rights that their neighbors have under UNCLOS.

The year 2009 marked a turn from relative calm to a crisis. Some of the background was the financial crisis and the successful Beijing Olympics of 2008. The former struck the West hard but not China. This boosted China's self-confidence and strengthened other nations' fear. In 2009, a number of developments increased the tension. The Philippines adopted new laws to conform its national legislation to UNCLOS. Instead of keeping up its claim to Freedomland, it claimed sovereignty to a number of named features, including Scarborough Shoal. Before the UN's deadline in May 2009, Vietnam and Malaysia submitted a joint calculation for an extended continental shelf beyond 200 nautical miles in the southern part of the South China Sea, and Vietnam submitted a separate claim for the northern part. These claims were made on the assumption that the disputed islands cannot have a continental shelf of their own. Protests followed. China for the first time included its map with the U-shaped line in an official letter of protest to the UN, explaining obliquely that China held sovereignty to the islands in the South China Sea and "the adjacent waters" and also had sovereign rights and jurisdiction over "the relevant waters as well as the seabed and subsoil thereof."[16] This provoked protests from the other claimants. In the same year, an incident occurred when China tried to expel a US military surveillance ship, the *USNS Impeccable*, from an area outside its territorial sea. China does not agree with the United States that the freedom of navigation includes military surveillance. By 2010, the United States expressed a keener interest in the South China Sea than before, not only in the freedom of navigation but also in some aspects of the sovereignty disputes. Washington insisted that they must be resolved peacefully on the basis of the law of the sea. A statement to that effect by Secretary of State Hillary Clinton at an ASEAN Foreign Ministers meeting in Hanoi 2010 caused much consternation in Beijing.

Since 2009, China has developed a legal doctrine that contradicts a growing convergence of views among the Southeast Asian claimants. The Chinese doctrine finds little support in the rest of the world, yet China has followed it up through a number of actions to assert its alleged rights within its U-shaped line. It has sent fishermen to fish in other countries' EEZ, including Indonesian waters, has prevented foreign fishermen from fishing in their EEZs, has taken control of Scarborough Shoal in a dramatic standoff with the Philippines, has disrupted exploration for oil under concessions from other states, has cut cables from seismic exploration ships operating on behalf of Vietnam, has issued oil concessions along the Vietnamese coast, has built new military facilities on seven reefs and low-tide elevations in the Spratlys, and has sought to block the so-called Freedom of Navigation Operations (FONOPs) by the United States and other navies.

What we have seen since 2009 is a polarization between two opposite legal doctrines:

China maintains the U-shaped line as the outer perimeter of its maritime claims. The Southeast Asian claimants no longer use mapped lines to indicate their claims but claim individual island features and their territorial seas.

China considers the four groups of islands as archipelagos (*qundao*), which together constitute a super-archipelago (*zhudao*) with internal Chinese waters within them and a right to a territorial sea, EEZ and a continental shelf around. The Southeast Asian claimants hold states recognized by UNCLOS as archipelagic (such as Indonesia and the Philippines) can draw straight baselines to link up the outermost points of their islands and claim maritime zones outside. No continental state has the right to draw straight baselines around groups of offshore islands.

By contrast, China holds that UNCLOS Article 121.3 allows its archipelagos or islands from generating EEZs and continental shelves of their own. The Southeast Asian states have reached an informal consensus that none of the Spratlys can have more than a 12-nautical-mile territorial sea.

China also holds that it has *historical rights* to fish and, by extension, to exploit mineral resources under the seabed within the U-shaped line. With reference to solid international expertise, the Southeast Asian claimants contend that no country can have such rights in another country's EEZ.[17]

In 2013, after having lost Scarborough Shoal to China, the Philippines asked for compulsory arbitration between itself and China for the purpose of clarifying some of these legal matters. China refused to take part, but the Arbitral Tribunal was established anyway with a Chair from Ghana and four European arbitrators. With secretarial assistance from the Permanent Court of Arbitration in The Hague, it came up with two awards in 2015 and 2016 giving the Philippines right on almost every point. China has no sovereign rights within its U-shaped line that go beyond its entitlements under UNCLOS.[18] China cannot use archipelagic baselines. None of the Spratlys satisfy the requirements for having an EEZ or continental shelf, not even Itu Aba. China's constructions on Mischief Reef and other low-tide elevations are illegal, and China has no historical rights in other countries' EEZs. China immediately declared the Arbitral Tribunal's ruling as null and void, although it is legally binding on China under UNCLOS, which China has signed and ratified. At the same time, China clarified and radicalized its legal position in a governmental statement on its territorial sovereignty and maritime rights and interests:

> i. China has sovereignty over Nanhai Zhudao [South China Sea islands], consisting of Zhongsha Qundao [Macclesfield Bank and Scarborough Shoal], Xisha Qundao [Paracel archipelago], Dongsha Qundao [Pratas archipelago] and Nansha Qundao [Spratly archipelago]; ii. China has internal waters, territorial sea and contiguous zone, based on Nanhai Zhudao; iii. China has exclusive economic zone and continental shelf, based on Nanhai Zhudao; iv. China has historic rights in the South China Sea.[19]

The statement further claimed that the above positions "are consistent with relevant international law and practice." This is clearly not the case. The quoted text, which was repeated verbatim in a Chinese letter of protest to the UN on 12 December 2019, in response to a Malaysian submission claiming an extended continental shelf in the northern part of the South China Sea, must be understood to mean that China claims an EEZ and continental shelf, calculated from archipelagic baselines around the four archipelagos. This would include almost the whole area within the U-shaped line. The statement also seems to define the areas within each archipelago as Chinese internal waters.[20] This is something not even archipelagic states can do; they do not have internal but only "archipelagic" waters, where foreign ships have a right to transit.

In such a polarized situation, there is perhaps little reason to expect any cooperation among the states concerned. Yet China and ASEAN are engaged in negotiations for a COC. A strong reason to cooperate is the dire consequences that the lack of cooperation has had for the marine environment.

Fifth development: environmental degradation

The "dangerous grounds" in the South China Sea were once the habitat for an incredible amount of birds, nesting undisturbed on the rocks and filling them with heavy layers of guano leading businessmen in the 1920s to think they could make fortunes from producing fertilizer for China's rice fields. The huge turtles that used to swim along the shoals are gone. Many coral reefs have been destroyed. Yet there is still a great variety of fish around the Spratlys, the Paracels, Pratas, Macclesfield Bank and Scarborough Shoal. The opportunity to fish there attracts fishing vessels from all over the region, these days notably from China.

Scientists have long sounded the alarm concerning the depletion of fish stocks in a sea that is said to represent 12 percent of the total global fish catch.[21] The depletion is due to overfishing and fishing with illegal methods, such as cyanide, dynamite, and trawls destroying coral reefs. States find it difficult to prevent illegal fishing as long as there is no agreement as to who has jurisdiction. They also find it hard to know the real situation, since there is no one to authorize scientific research. Over the last 25 years, the Norwegian survey ship Fridtjof Nansen has surveyed the waters off the coast of Myanmar. During that time, the fish stocks have been reduced by approximately 80 percent. The same is likely to have happened in the South China Sea, where no systematic surveys have been made.

The total *catch* in the South China Sea increased significantly over the period from 1950 to the mid-1990s. Then it stagnated, and more recently began to decline. Between 2000 and 2010, the total *reported* catch remained stable, while estimates for the unreported catch went down.[22] The fact that the catch has remained almost on the same level since 2000 is actually worrisome. This is due in part to the introduction of large modern vessels, using more effective and destructive fishing methods than before, such as bottom trawling, and partly to what is called "fishing down the food web." Catches consist of smaller and smaller species whose populations have boomed as their natural predators have disappeared.[23] A 2015 report claimed that marine resources had been fished down to 5–30 percent of their 1950s level, and total biomass (quantity of fish) had been even further reduced.[24]

If this development continues, then Asians will no longer get wild fish from the South China Sea, which for centuries has provided healthy protein for the coastal populations. Aquaculture already now covers a huge and growing share of Asia's rising fish demand. Yet this gives little ground for joy since aquaculture represents a threat to marine ecosystems and is likely to contribute to further decimation of the remaining wild fish. Farmed fish escape from fish farms and take their diseases with them. Cultivated fish are fed with fishmeal from the smallest species of wild fish, which in the past were left alone by humans. Now they are caught because they are so easy to harvest and receive good prices from fish farm companies. Hence, even the bottom of the food chain may be depleted.[25]

Fishermen have long complained that they catch less fish than in the past and must move further and further away from their coasts. Yet for some time, there will be fish in the waters of the disputed islands. One long-held but apparently unproven theory says that the main breeding grounds for fish in the whole of the South China Sea are located in the coral reefs around the disputed islands.

What could be done to save the fish and fisheries? Might it be possible to cooperate in fishery management even without resolving any sovereignty disputes? UNCLOS Article 123 prescribes that states bordering a semi-enclosed sea "should cooperate with each other in the exercise of their rights and in the performance of their duties" either directly or through an appropriate regional organization to "coordinate the management, conservation, exploration and exploitation of the living resources of the sea."

One of the Arbitral Tribunal's rulings in its 2016 award in the Philippines v. China case is not much known. The Tribunal ruled that fishermen from China, Taiwan, the Philippines and Vietnam all have historical rights to fish *in the 12-nautical-mile territorial sea* of Scarborough Shoal. This may seem strange since the same tribunal held that no historical rights can exist in the EEZs of other states. However, the laws governing the territorial sea were laid down in the 1958 Convention on the Territorial Sea and Contiguous Zone, which was incorporated almost verbatim in the 1982 Convention. This explains that traditional or historical fishing rights can exist in the territorial sea but not in the EEZ. This is important since there is more fish to catch near coasts than in the open sea. If several countries have a right to fish in the territorial sea of Scarborough Shoal, then China and Vietnam must both have fishing rights in the territorial seas of the Paracels, and all the South China Sea claimants are likely to have traditional rights to fish in the territorial seas of the disputed Spratlys. With rights follow duties, so then they must cooperate in fishery management.

If such shared historical rights were to generate a regional urge to cooperate in saving the fish and other species in a protected marine environment, then the historical developments described in this chapter would finally bring something good.

Notes

1 Stein Tønnesson, "Locating the South China Sea," in Paul Kratoska, ed. *Locating Southeast Asia: Geographies of Knowledge and Politics of Space*, Singapore: Singapore University Press, 2005, 203–233 (213).

2 https://chinapower.csis.org/much-trade-transits-south-china-sea/ (accessed 5 June 2020.)

3 Chris P.C. Chung, *"Since Time Immemorial": China's Historical Claim in the South China Sea*, PhD thesis, University of Calgary, 2019, 14–15.

4 Chung, *op. cit.*, 43, note 126, cites a protest letter in the ROC Ministry of Foreign Affairs file "Nansha Qundao," file series 019.3/0012, files 145. A French Foreign Ministry memo from September 1946 says China did not protest the French claim in 1933. Stein Tønnesson, "The South China Sea in the Age of European Decline," *Modern Asian Studies* 40 (1), 2006, 1–57 (24, note 69).

5 In the 1930s, the Spratly Islands were administratively attached to the directly ruled French colony Cochinchina, but the French archives from the 1949–1957 reveal that when France gave up its sovereignty to Cochinchina and transferred it to Vietnam, it withheld the Spratlys as French territory, on a par with the French colonies in the Pacific. Tønnesson, "The South China Sea in the Age, *op. cit.*, 38.

6 *Ibid.*, 15, 19.

7 *Ibid.*, 27.

8 Bill Hayton, "The Modern Origins of China's South China Sea Claims: Maps, Misunderstandings, and the Maritime Geobody," *Modern China* 45 (2), 2019, 127–170.

9 Chung, *op. cit.* See also Chris P. C. Chung, "Drawing the U-Shaped Line: China's Claim in the South China Sea, 1946–1974," *Modern China* 42 (1), 2016, 38–72.

10 Kimie Hara, *Cold War Frontiers in the Asia-Pacific: Divided Territories in the San Francisco System*, London: Routledge, 2007, 126–154; Nong Hong, "The South China Sea Disputes: A Review of History and Prospects for Dispute Settlement," in Kimie Hara, ed. *The San Francisco System and Its Legacies: Continuation, Transformation, and Historical Reconciliation in the Asia-Pacific*, London: Routledge, 2013, 81; Lin Man-Houng, "A Neglected Treaty for the South China Sea," in Tsu-Sung Hsieh, ed. *The South China Sea Disputes: Historical, Geopolitical and Legal Studies*, Singapore: World Scientific, 2018, 1–24.

11 Tønnesson, "The South China Sea in the Age…", *op. cit.*, 40–43.

12 Stein Tønnesson, "Locating the South China Sea," in Paul Kratoska, ed. *Locating Southeast Asia: Geographies of Knowledge and Politics of Space*, Singapore: Singapore University Press, 2005, 203–233.

13 The DRV in North Vietnam, which had depended on Chinese support during the war, had not issued any official protests against China's actions in the Paracels, and had declared itself in general support of a Chinese law that mentioned the Paracels and Spratlys as Chinese possessions. Legally speaking this may amount to *estoppal* of the Vietnamese sovereignty claims, unless the Socialist Republic of Vietnam (SRV) is seen as having derived from a merger of North and South Vietnam with a right to pursue South Vietnam's claims.

14 Lu Ning, *Flashpoint Spratlys!* Singapore: Dolphin Books, 1995.

15 Christian Schultheiss, "Power in Institutions: Interstate Negotiations of Incremental Agreements for the East and South China Sea Disputes," PhD dissertation, Cambridge University, 2019, 198–208.

16 The Permanent Mission of the People's Republic of China to the UN to Secretary General Ban Ki Moon, CML 17/2009, 7 May 2009.

17 Clive R. Symmons, *Historic Waters and Historic Rights in the Law of the Sea: A Modern Reappraisal*, Leiden: Brill, 2019.

18 "China's claims to historic rights, or other sovereign rights or jurisdiction, with respect to the maritime areas of the South China Sea encompassed by the relevant part of the 'nine-dash line' are contrary to the Convention and without lawful effect to the extent that they exceed the geographic and substantive limits of China's maritime entitlements under the Convention.

The Tribunal concludes that the Convention superseded any historic rights or other sovereign rights or jurisdiction in excess of the limits imposed therein." The South China Sea Arbitration Award of 12 July 2016, para 278.

19 "Statement of the Government of the People's Republic of China on China's Territorial Sovereignty and Maritime Rights and Interests in the South China Sea," 12 July 2016.

20 The Permanent Mission of the PRC to the UN to Secretary-General Guterres, CML/14/2019, 12 December 2019. "Nanhai Zhudao" is normally translated as "South China Sea Islands," but China sees it as *a unit*. In its own official English translations, China thus writes "The Spratlys is…" instead of "The Spratlys are…"

21 Adam Greer, "The South China Sea Is Really a Fishery Dispute: The Hidden Cause of the South China Sea Disputes: There Aren't Enough Fish in the Sea," *The Diplomat*, 2 July 2016.

22 U. Rashid Sumaila and William W. L. Cheung, *Boom or Bust: The Future of Fish in the South China Sea*, Vancouver: University of British Columbia, 2015, 3.

23 Greer, *op. cit.*

24 Sumaila and Cheung, *op. cit.*, 2.

25 Zhang Hongzhou, "Can Aquaculture Solve the Fishing Problems in the South China Sea? China's Example Suggests That Aquaculture Actually Contributes to Diminishing Wild Fish Stocks Worldwide." *The Diplomat*, 26 March 2018.

3

SEA LINES OF COMMUNICATION AND SAFETY OF NAVIGATION

Sam Bateman

Introduction

The South China Sea is the location of some of the world's busiest commercial shipping routes. In 2016, about 21 percent of global trade by value used the sea lines of communication (SLOCs) across the South China Sea.[1] Shipping is the main mode of transport for trade in the region. The free movement of commercial shipping through the seas of East Asia is vital to the economies of regional countries and unlawful restrictions on freedoms of navigation would have a serious impact on regional economies. Ensuring the safety of navigation along these SLOCs in all its dimensions (e.g. ship-tracking services, accurate hydrographic charts, provision of navigational aids), as well as effective search and rescue (SAR) arrangements, is a major requirement for the littoral countries necessitating close coordination between them.

The South China Sea has become the focus of the concern of extra-regional countries for freedoms of navigation in the seas of East Asia. China's widespread claims in the sea, its reclamation of features, and the build-up of military facilities on these features have led to widespread allegations that it is threatening freedoms of navigation in the sea. Freedoms of navigation have relevance for both commercial and military vessels, but calls for a more aggressive regional response to China's activities are typically couched in terms of the alleged threat that Chinese actions pose to commercial shipping. However, China has repeatedly said it poses no such threat.[2]

International trade is carried by sea, air or overland (road, rail and pipeline). By volume, about 90 percent of international trade is carried is by sea but by value, only about 73 percent of trade is carried by sea.[3] Most of the cargo carried by sea is of lower value per tonne (e.g. bulk minerals, grains) or a specialized nature only suited for carriage in large quantities by sea (crude oil, petroleum products, LNG, LPG) although several seaborne trades still involve high-value goods such as those carried in containers (e.g. retail goods, frozen meat and other foodstuffs). Air transportation accounts for only about 0.25 percent of international trade by volume but 13 percent of trade by value. Air transportation typically carries high value to volume cargoes such as mail, electronic goods, fresh fruit and vegetables.

Shipping is a major use of the marine environment but cooperation is required to enhance the commercial efficiency of shipping operations, maintain safety and reduce the impact of these operations on the marine environment. Cooperation is also necessary for the mitigation and prevention of ship-sourced pollution, including arrangements for responding to the major oil spills that may result from maritime accidents and monitoring oil spills in open waters from routine tank cleaning and ballasting operations. Anecdotal information suggests these activities occur undetected in the South China Sea due to the lack of an effective coordinated monitoring system.

Maritime geography

The maritime geography of East Asia with the off-lying island and archipelagic chain stretching from the Kamchatka Peninsula through the Japanese and Philippine archipelagos to Indonesia creates numerous straits, as well as other 'choke points' for shipping. These straits occur both along the coast of mainland Asia where the island chain presses close into the coast (e.g. the Tsushima Strait, the Taiwan Strait and the Straits of Malacca and Singapore), and through the off-lying islands (e.g. the Tsugaru Strait through the Japanese archipelago, the San Bernadino Strait in the Philippines, the Balabac Strait north of Borneo, and the Sunda and Lombok Straits through the Indonesian archipelago). Many of these straits are important SLOCs for international shipping both for the ships making passage along the East coast of Asia between Southeast Asia and Northeast Asia, and for those heading into mainland Asian ports from the Americas and Oceania.

The Indonesian archipelago is a major barrier to sea movement between the Indian and Pacific Oceans. The various straits through and adjacent to this archipelago are of immense strategic importance. The straits through the archipelago between Singapore and Darwin in northern Australia now constitute the most significant shipping 'bottleneck' in the world. Vessels pass through this area carrying the sources of energy (oil, liquefied natural gas and liquefied petroleum gas) and raw materials essential for the maintenance of economic growth and survivability of China, Japan, South Korea and Taiwan, as well the large container ships on the main around the world route linking Europe to East Asia.

The South China Sea is part of the chain of enclosed or semi-enclosed seas in East Asia subject to the regime of enclosed or semi-enclosed seas established by United Nations Convention on the Law of the Sea (UNCLOS) Part IX. From North to South, these seas are: Sea of Okhotsk, Sea of Japan, Yellow Sea, East China Sea, South China Sea, Gulf of Thailand, Java Sea, Sulu Sea, Celebes Sea, and Timor and Arafura Seas. The South China Sea is the largest of these regional seas. It is about 80 percent enclosed by land.

The South China Sea has long been regarded by mariners as an area of considerable navigational danger, particularly in the area around the Spratly Islands commonly referred to on navigational charts and in various nautical publications as 'Dangerous Ground'.[4] Even now there are parts of the sea that are poorly charted and regarded as dangerous to navigation – even for surface navigation let alone submarine navigation. Part of this problem is the very uneven nature of the bottom of large areas of the sea. It may be roughly divided by a line running from the southern tip of Vietnam to Brunei. To the south of this line, the entire area is supported on the Sunda Shelf and has depths of less than 200m. To the north of this line, the major portion of the region is contained in the South China Sea basin with depths in excess of 1,800m. This latter area includes the Spratly and Paracel islands and the Macclesfield Bank, as well as the possibility of uncharted seamounts.

Large areas of the South China Sea have not been systematically surveyed, as well as others that have only had lead-line surveys.[5] Traditionally depth sounding was by hand lead and line but mechanical sounding machines with an ability to sound the greatest depths of the ocean were introduced in the late 19th Century.[6] The coverage of these systems depended on how frequently soundings were taken and the distance apart of lines of soundings. Particularly in the area of uneven bottom topography, potentially dangerous underwater features could easily be missed. Electronic echo-sounding gear was introduced in the 1930s to provide a means of obtaining a sounding under a ship without the use of any form of measuring line and lead or sounding machine. Modern oceanographic and hydrographic survey ships are fitted with multi-beam, wide-angle precision sonar systems that make it possible to chart continuously a broad strip of ocean floor. Light Detection and Ranging (LIDAR) systems, also known as Laser Airborne Depth Sounding (LADS), were developed in the 1970s. These allowed aircraft to carry out depth sounding covering a large survey area in a much shorter period of time than it would be possible with a ship-based system but with limitations regarding the maximum depth achievable.

The safety of navigation across the South China Sea will only be assured when the areas of the sea not well surveyed at present are surveyed using modern systems, such as multi-beam sonar and LIDAR. The need for such surveys is increasing as shipping traffic increases including by ships, such as very large ore carriers and container ships with laden drafts in excess of 20 metres. However, most of the poorly surveyed areas are within the claimed exclusive economic zones (EEZs) of bordering countries and the required surveys are unlikely without a higher level of trust and preparedness to cooperate than exists between these countries at present.

Legal regime

An *enclosed* or *semi-enclosed* sea is defined by UNCLOS Article 122 as

> a gulf, basin or sea surrounded by two or more States and connected to another sea or the ocean by a narrow outlet or consisting entirely or primarily of the territorial seas and exclusive economic zones of two or more coastal States.

The second last 'or' in this definition is important. It provides for a geographical definition of an *enclosed* or *semi-enclosed* sea on the basis of its narrow physical connections with nearby bodies of water, as well as a legal definition that such a sea should consist entirely or primarily of the territorial seas and EEZ of two or more countries. The South China Sea meets this latter criterion as an enclosed or semi-enclosed sea.

The regime established by UNCLOS Part IX is particularly important to the South China Sea. Under it, the bordering countries to this sea have a binding obligation to cooperate specifically with regard to managing marine living resources, protecting the marine environment and conducting marine scientific research.[7] Although the wording of this obligation is not as strong as it might be, it does recognize the fundamental importance of cooperation with these three activities to the effective management of enclosed and semi-enclosed seas.[8]

A question for consideration is whether the responsibility of the littoral States to cooperate extends to coordinating their efforts to provide for the safety of navigation. While some activities mentioned specifically as areas for cooperation, the opening sentence of UNCLOS Article 123 that 'States bordering an enclosed or semi-enclosed sea should cooperate with each other in the exercise of their rights and in the performance of their duties under this Convention' sets a more general obligation to cooperate.[9] That responsibility might be interpreted as including security and maritime safety. The current *Single Draft Code of Conduct in the South China Sea (COC) Negotiating Text* acknowledges this responsibility with references to the responsibility of the parties to cooperate with regard to the safety of navigation and the provision of SAR services, as well as the likely establishment of technical committees to handle the responsibilities.

It is of note that the United States initially opposed the UNCLOS Part IX regime during negotiations on the treaty because it could provide an opening for the bordering States to introduce arrangements restricting other States from exercising high seas freedoms of navigation in these seas.[10] This explains the tendency of American officials to persist in referring to the South China Sea as 'international waters' when of course it is not – except for small areas of high seas, it is comprised largely of the EEZs of the bordering States. Use of the expression 'international waters' allows the United States to persist in referring to the South China Sea as part of the 'global commons' where the freedoms of navigation and overflight are identical with those available on the high seas.[11] This ignores the requirement in UNCLOS Article 58 (3) that these freedoms should be exercised with 'due regard' to the rights and duties of the coastal State. This requirement means that for example, it would be inappropriate for another State to seek to exercise its high seas freedoms in a marine park or marine protected area legitimately declared by the coastal State as part of its duty to preserve and protect the marine environment.

Shipping routes

The South China Sea is entered from the north via either the Luzon Strait between the northern Islands of the Philippines and Taiwan or the Taiwan Strait between Taiwan and mainland China. In the south, the Singapore Strait feeds traffic into the South China Sea from the Strait of Malacca, while the Karimata Strait feeds traffic from the Indian Ocean through the Sunda Strait. In the East, shipping enters mainly through the Balabac Strait between Borneo and Palawan, which is used by shipping traffic that has come up from the Indian Ocean through Lombok Strait and the Macassar Strait. Some of this traffic also goes on from the Macassar Strait up through the Sulu Sea and the Philippines before entering the South China Sea through the Mindoro Strait. These routes through the Lombok and Macassar straits are much used by the bulk carriers carrying iron ore from Western Australia to Northeast Asia. Other shipping traffic comes into the South China Sea through the various straits through the Philippines.

Key SLOCs across the South China Sea connect these entry and exit points. These are shown in Figure 3.1. The most important SLOC is the one leading from the Singapore Strait to the Luzon Strait in the north. This carries the trade through the Malacca and Singapore Straits to Northeast Asia, Korea, Japan and northern China. It has a second leg which splits away about the middle of the South China Sea leading on to Hong Kong and the southern ports of China. It is of note that this route actually passes through the Paracel Islands establishing a regular pattern of traffic through disputed waters claimed by China with notional restrictions on the freedoms of navigation. However, merchant ships of all flags pass freely through the Paracels without interference or disruption.[12]

Another important SLOC into the South China Sea is the one running up from the Lombok and Makassar Straits through the Sulu Sea and the Mindoro Strait into the South China Sea and on to the north. Then there are other coastal SLOCs carrying mainly coastal traffic along the coast of Vietnam or across from Malaya to Borneo and the Philippines.

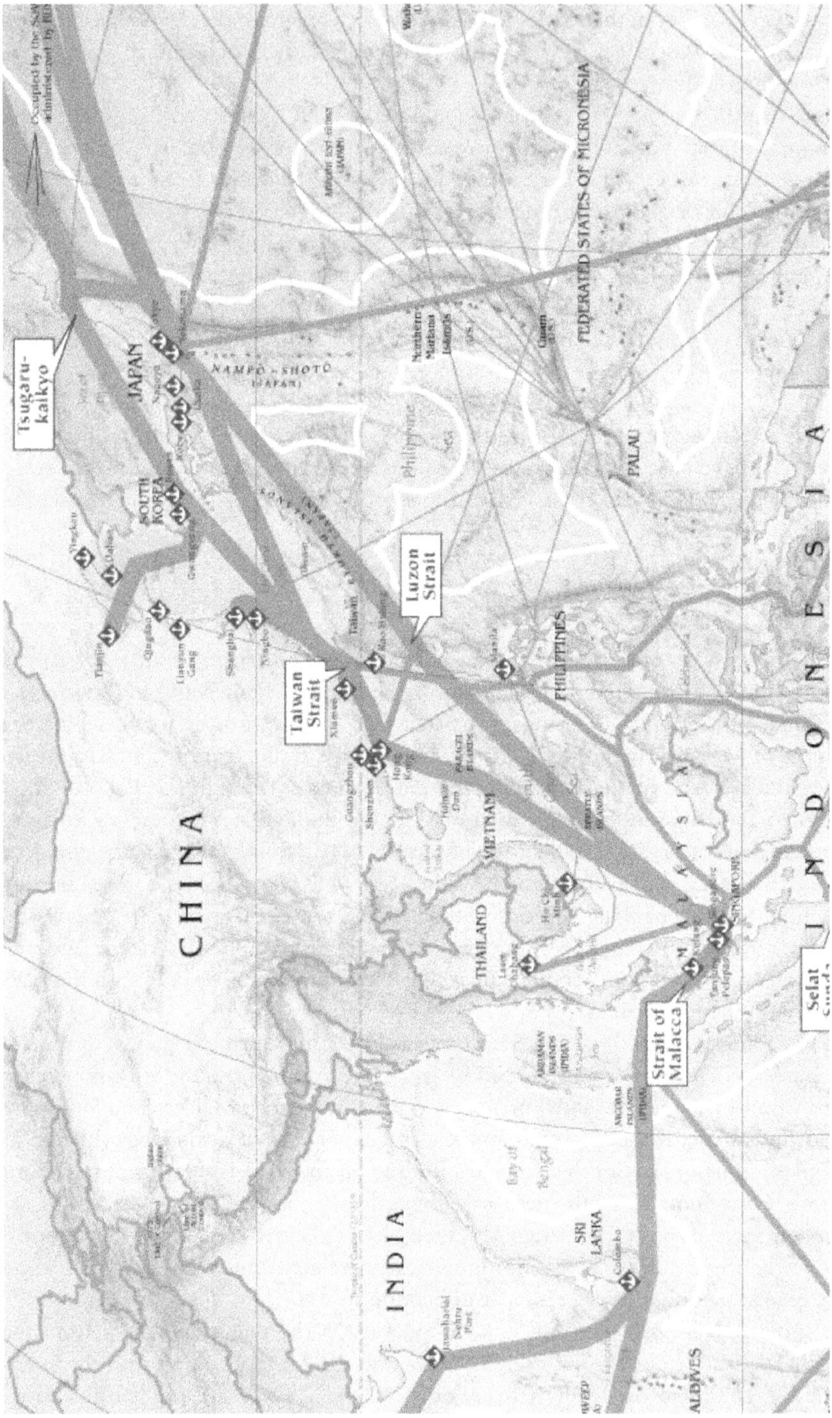

Figure 3.1 SLOCs in the South China Sea.

Source: US Naval Institute, Maritime Security Blog on 15 December 2012.

https://blog.usni.org/posts/2012/12/15/sunday-12-16-12-on-midrats-episode-154-offshore-control-and-asiapacific-with-tx-hammes

Trade dependencies

While the South China Sea includes some very important SLOCs carrying much international seaborne trade, there has been a campaign by extra-regional countries specifically to overstate their importance, particularly with regard to the level of their own dependence on trade across the sea. This is all with the intention of justifying their own strategic interest and involvement in the sea.

The figure that has been often bandied around is that $5.3 trillion dollars of trade by value crosses the sea each year.[13] This figure has its origins in a press briefing in 2011 by Admiral Bob Willard, the then Commander of the US Pacific Command, who claimed that 'The sea lines of communication that crisscross the South China Sea carry $5.3 trillion in bilateral annual trade, of which $1.2 trillion is U.S. trade'.[14] The admiral went on to assert 'that the South China Sea region and the sea lines that it contains is incredibly vital to the region, to our partners and allies, and certainly to the United States'.[15]

Both the $5.3 trillion and $1.2 trillion figures have subsequently been shown to be marked exaggerations. According to a 2018 report from the Washington-based Center for Strategic and International Studies (CSIS), 30 percent of global maritime trade passes through the South China Sea with a total value of approximately US$3.4 trillion.[16] The United States trade that most obviously crosses the South China Sea is that with Association of Southeast Asian Nations (ASEAN), but according to ASEAN trade statistics, America's total trade with ASEAN in 2015 was just over US$212 billion.[17] This figure was later generally confirmed by the CSIS report that found that US$208 billion of US trade passed through the South China Sea in 2016. Additionally, a large proportion of that trade would have been carried by air, and much of that carried by sea would have been with the Philippines and Indonesia, two of ASEAN's biggest members, and may not have passed through the South China Sea.

An analysis of the ASEAN-US trade confirms that much of that trade would have been carried by air rather than by sea. In 2017, the bilateral trade balance was in favour of ASEAN with exports valued at US$142.7 billion and imports from the United States at US$91.6 billion.[18] Much of this two-way trade (perhaps as much as 30 percent) was in high-value goods usually carried by air, such as foodstuffs and electrical and electronic equipment.

In 2016, the value of China's trade transiting the South China Sea was $1.47 trillion, South Korea – $423 billion, Japan – $240 billion, and Indonesia – $239 billion. The South China Sea is a major trade route for crude oil.[19] In 2016, more than 30 percent of global maritime crude oil trade passed through the South China Sea, of which 42 percent was bound for China. About 90 percent of the crude oil supplies for China, Japan and South Korea transited the sea.

Australian sources have also overstated Australia's trade crossing the South China Sea. With much of its seaborne trade passing through the confined archipelagic waters of Indonesia, Papua New Guinea and the Solomon Islands to its north, Australia has a strong interest in the freedoms of navigation.[20] However, Australia can also exaggerate its trade through the South China Sea to justify its strategic interest in the sea.[21] Its 2016 Defence White Paper says a lot about the South China Sea, both directly and indirectly. It noted that territorial disputes between claimants in East China and South China Seas have created uncertainty and tension in Australia's region.[22] It said that Australia does not take sides on competing for territorial claims in the South China Sea, but expressed concern about land reclamation and construction activities by claimants in the sea and about the possible use of artificial structures for military purpose.[23] But in making a big play of the South China Sea, the White Paper falls in line with what Greg Austin has called 'The Pentagon's Big Lie about the South China Sea'.[24] For Austin, the lie is the claim that China's actions in the South China Sea threaten commercial shipping.

The Australian Defence White Paper replays Austin's sentiment. With regard to the free flow of trade through the South China Sea, it claimed that 'nearly two-thirds of Australia's exports pass through the South China Sea, including our major coal, iron ore and liquefied natural gas exports'.[25] However, this figure was an exaggeration.[26] The accurate figure, based on data for Australia's overseas trade,[27] is a little over 20 percent and most of this is trade with China.[28] The White Paper actually disproves its own estimate with its map in Figure 3.2 showing that most of Australia's sea freight does not pass through the South China Sea.[29] Nor does the map show the busy trade route between eastern Australia, Japan and South Korea that passes to the East of the Philippines, rather than the South China Sea.

Australia's overseas trade crossing the South China Sea includes that with China (with a total of 23.9 percent of two-way overseas trade), Thailand (2.8 percent), Taiwan (1.9 percent), Vietnam (1.4 percent) and Hong Kong (1.2 percent). And even these figures overstate Australia's dependence on the South China Sea, as it trades with southern China by sea, and much of its trade is carried out by air. These figures are based on overseas trade by value, which may hide the fact that a significant amount of trade by value is carried out by air. In volume, shipping is the main mode of transport for international trade, accounting for about 90 percent of all the tonnage carried, but this is only about 73 percent of the value of global trade.[30] Thus Australia's trade by volume across the South China Sea could provide a different result to that by value recognising the high volume of Australia's exports (coal, iron ore, LNG, and other minerals) carried by sea, but it would still be nothing like 60 percent.

Freedoms of navigation

The maritime geography of East Asia means that freedoms of navigation are of great importance in the region both for the movement of merchant ships and naval vessels. Freedom of navigation along SLOCs is the leading international concern in the South China Sea. However, fundamentally different perspectives of the freedoms of navigation are evident in the Asia-Pacific region. The need for freedoms of navigation in South China is frequently mentioned in statements from regional forums, but there may be no common understanding of what constitutes a particular freedom of navigation or of the relevant law.[31]

The two extreme views on freedoms of navigation are held by China and the United States. According to China's laws, foreign vessels including warships enjoy the right of freedom of navigation through China's EEZ but only if they comply with relevant Chinese law and regulations and with international law.[32] China's laws also State that while merchant ships enjoy the right of innocent passage through China's territorial sea, foreign warships must seek China's prior permission. The United States hotly disputes these Chinese laws.

Major powers, including ones from outside the region, argue the importance of freedoms of navigation in the sea mainly due to their concern for the free movement of commercial shipping across the sea, but in doing so, they can overstate the significance of their own maritime trade across the sea. Surprisingly, regional countries, with the exception of Japan, appear less concerned about freedoms of navigation for commercial shipping in regional seas, largely because of the extent of their trade with China.

The United States and other extra-regional countries, including France and the United Kingdom, argue that because of China's assertive actions in the South China Sea, it poses a threat to freedoms of navigation in the sea, especially for the free movement of commercial shipping. However, China has repeatedly denied it poses such a threat. And with so much of China's own trade passing through the sea, it is most unlikely that it would.[33]

Piracy and armed robbery

Piracy and armed robbery against ships are often cited as a major threat to SLOCs in and around the South China Sea. However, they are not the same problems that they used to be.[34] Recently, there has been an outbreak of attacks in the Singapore Strait, particularly in the eastbound traffic separation scheme lane. Ships in this area may be proceeding slowly and are vulnerable to hit and run attacks with the robbers stealing anything that is readily available such as engine spares and paint.

The other area of ongoing and recent attacks is in and around the Sulu archipelago off Sabah and between the Sula and Celebes seas. Major SLOCs leading into and from the South China Sea pass through this area, but most of the attacks over the years have been attacks on small vessels, fishing vessels, tugs and barges with crew members being kidnapped and held for ransom. However, one or two larger merchant ships have been attacked in this area. These attacks are largely perpetrated by militants, possibly members of the Abu Sayyaf Group (ASG). The Trilateral Cooperative Agreement (TCA) has been established by Indonesia, Malaysia and the Philippines to provide greater maritime security in this area. It involves enhanced cooperative maritime and air patrols and the establishment of operational hubs in each country.

Attacks also still occur occasionally on ships at anchor or alongside in various ports in and around the South China Sea, particularly in Indonesia, the Philippines and Vietnam. Ships are warned to be vigilant when anchored in these ports.

The largest spike in attacks in the South China Sea itself was back in 2009–2011 when many attacks occurred on ships in the southern part of the South China Sea and the eastern approaches to Singapore Strait.[35] This was a period when many ships were unemployed owing to the Global Financial Crisis with some ships anchored while others remained underway in the area of to the west of the Natuna Islands. These latter ships were loitering waiting for their next job but were probably stopped or proceeding slowly and thus vulnerable to hit and run attacks.

A high level of cooperation now exists around the South China Sea for operational coordination and information sharing to deal with piracy and sea robbery. Relevant activities in addition to the TCA include: the Malacca Straits Patrol (MSP) network, involving Indonesia, Malaysia, Thailand and Singapore, to have oversight of the air and sea patrols of the straits and the exchange of information and intelligence; the Information Sharing Centre (ISC) set up in Singapore by Regional Cooperation Agreement on Combating Piracy and Armed Robbery against Ships in Asia (ReCAAP); the Information Fusion Centre (IFC) at Changi Naval Base with an area of interest covering much of Southeast and South Asia; and the Indonesia-Singapore Coordinated Patrol (ISCP) arrangement that coordinates patrols in Singapore Strait.

Piracy and sea robbery are unlikely ever to be totally eradicated in Asia. Poverty, unemployment and the decline of traditional fishing in the face of over-fishing are major economic causes of piracy. Many pirates are displaced fishermen, who are no longer able to earn a living from their traditional fishing. Piracy and sea robbery are attractive alternative vocations and ships are vulnerable if they don't adopt appropriate security measures.

The improved situation in Asia in recent years can be attributed to two main factors. Firstly, there is a high level of cooperation between countries across the region to counter piracy. Secondly, there is better policing onshore to identify offenders, as well as enhanced coordination between national agencies to prevent and manage the threat. It is a fundamental principle that the fight against piracy begins on land.

International conventions

UNCLOS provides the broad principles and the framework for international regimes and treaties dealing with the safety of navigation.[36] Several UNCLOS articles relate particularly to the safety of navigation including *Article 94 – Duties of the Flag State* which requires that every State shall effectively exercise its jurisdiction and control in administrative, technical and social matters over ships flying its flag, including such matters as the seaworthiness, manning and equipping of ships flying its flag; and *Article 98 – Duty to render assistance* which requires every State to require that ships flying its flag render prompt assistance to persons in distress at sea and that every coastal State shall promote the establishment, operation and maintenance of an adequate and effective SAR service.

In addition to UNCLOS, several key international conventions provide for the safety of navigation. These are:

- SOLAS – the 1974 Safety of Life at Sea (SOLAS) Convention – deals with the safety and security of merchant ships, and includes the ISPS Code. It is the most important of all international treaties concerning the safety of merchant ships. Chapter V identifies certain navigation safety services, which should be provided by contracting governments, including meteorological and hydrographic services for ships; mandatory AIS requirements; routeing of ships; and the maintenance of SAR services.
- SAR – the 1979 International Convention on Maritime SAR Convention – encourages cooperation between parties and SAR organisations with regard to search and rescue operations at sea and requires each party to maintain an SAR organisation.
- SUA – the 1988 Convention for the Suppression of Unlawful Acts against the Safety of Maritime Navigation (SUA), and its Protocol covering offshore facilities, extends coastal State enforcement jurisdiction against acts of violence at sea beyond territorial limits. It was introduced by the International Maritime Organisation (IMO) to overcome the limitations in the piracy provisions of UNCLOS following the 1985 hijacking of the Italian-flag cruise ship *Achille Lauro* by extremists in the Mediterranean Sea.[37]
- SUA 2005 – the SUA 2005 Convention brings together the 1988 Convention and its 2005 Protocol to create measures related to maritime terrorism and shipment of weapons of mass destruction (WMD). This contains significant new provisions relating to when and where ships might be boarded but these were more limited than those sought by the United States in particular demonstrating that the international community is very reluctant to create new exceptions to the principle of flag State jurisdiction on the high seas.
- MARPOL 1973 – the International Convention on the Prevention of Pollution from Ships, as modified by the Protocol of 1978 (MARPOL 73/78) has the objective of preventing pollution of the marine environment by ships caused by operational or accidental causes. It has six annexes covering respectively pollution from ships by oil, noxious liquid substances in bulk, harmful substances carried in packaged form, sewage, garbage and air pollution.
- OPRC Convention 1990 – the Oil Pollution Preparedness, Response and Cooperation (OPRC) Convention requires parties to establish measures for dealing with oil pollution incidents either nationally or in cooperation with other countries. The Convention also extends to floating and fixed offshore platforms engaged in oil exploration, exploitation or production. It involves an obligation to report without delay any event on a ship or offshore unit involving a discharge or probable discharge of oil.

Table 3.1 Status of International Conventions – South China Sea Countries

	SOLAS 1974	*SAR 1979*	*SUA 1988*	*SUA 2005*	*MARPOL*	*OPRC 1990*	*OPRC-HNS 2000*	*COLREGs 1972*
Brunei	X(a)		X		X(a)			X
Cambodia	X		X		X(a)			X
China	X	X	X		X	X		X
Indonesia	X	X			X			X
Malaysia	X				X	X		X
Philippines	X		X		X	X		X
Singapore	X	X	X		X	X		X
Thailand	X(a)				X(a)	X		X
Vietnam	X	X	X		X			X

Source: International Maritime Organisation, Status of Conventions.
Notes: X signifies that the Convention has been ratified, and X(a) denotes that not all protocols and annexes to the Convention have been ratified.

- OPRC-HNS Protocol 2000 – the OPRC-HNS Protocol 2000 aims to provide a global framework for international cooperation in establishing systems for preparedness and response in combating incidents involving HNS (hazardous and noxious substances) at the national, regional and global levels.
- COLREGs – the 1972 International Regulations for Preventing Collisions at Sea set out the 'rules of the road' or navigation rules to be followed by ships and other vessels at sea to prevent collisions between two or more vessels, as well as the lights, shapes, and sound signals to be used by different types of vessel.

Table 3.1 shows the status of these conventions among the countries bordering the South China Sea. Some significant gaps are evident in the level of ratification of some of these instruments. SOLAS is widely accepted although Brunei and Thailand have not yet agreed to all the relevant protocols notably the 1988 Protocol regarding the introduction of the Global Maritime Distress Safety System (GMDSS). The 1988 SUA Convention has not been ratified by Indonesia, Malaysia, and Thailand and no country has yet ratified SUA 2005. MARPOL is generally well supported around the South China Sea except for Brunei, Cambodia and Thailand. The OPRC 1990 Convention has not yet been ratified by Brunei, Cambodia, Indonesia or Vietnam while no regional country has yet ratified the HNS Convention. All regional countries have ratified COLREGs. The SUA and SAR Conventions have not been well ratified because they involve some concession of sovereignty.

Marine environmental protection

Arrangements to protect the marine environment of the South China Sea from pollution by ships and other sources at sea remain embryonic.[38] Two types of pollution are possible: accidental pollution arising for example, from an accident such as a collision involving one of the many laden oil tankers crossing the sea, or from an accidental spill from one of the many offshore oil exploration and production platforms in and around the South China Sea; and of operational or incidental pollution arising from routine ship operations (e.g. ballast water discharge, tank cleaning and bilge pumping).

Operational pollution is the major problem because it likely occurs on a regular basis. Satellite pictures have shown in the past that the sea area northeast of Singapore seems to be a preferred area for discharging oil from ships with heavy areas of pollution off the East coast of Malaysia (near Kuantan) and off the west coast of Sabah (Borneo).[39] Ships are likely to engage in tank cleaning, ballast water discharge or bilge pumping in the southern part of the South China Sea to lighten their draft in preparation for their passage through the Singapore and Malacca straits or prior to entering Singapore for repair or maintenance. Ships are required under the OPRC Convention to report incidents of pollution to coastal authorities but that may not happen. Unfortunately, there are still unscrupulous shipmasters who will pollute at sea rather than pay the costs of disposing of oily waste in port.

The situation is not helped by not all bordering countries being party to the OPRC Convention. This Convention requires its parties to have a national oil spill prevention and response plan, as well as stockpiles of oil spill combating equipment, oil spill combating exercises and the development of detailed plans for dealing with pollution incidents. In November 2018, ASEAN member countries adopted the Regional Oil Spill Contingency Plan.[40] This provides for a mechanism whereby the ASEAN Member States can request for and provide mutual assistance in response to any oil spills.

This ASEAN contingency plan is aimed mainly at controlling a large oil spill in a regional port or harbour, or possibly a major accidental spill at sea. It does not help towards countering the regular incidents of operational pollution that seem to be occurring in the South China Sea. That requires a coordinated programme of surveillance, monitoring and investigation such as the Marine Pollution Surveillance Programme in the United States.[41] Australia and the European Union (EU) have similar programmes.

Search and rescue

The major problem revealed in Table 3.1 is that five of the bordering countries have not yet ratified the SAR Convention. Possible explanations of this are the costs involved in establishing a national SAR organisation and the obligation in the Convention to allow entry into the territorial sea or territory of a State by rescue units from another State for the purpose of SAR. The SAR Convention States that parties should take measures to expedite entry into its territorial waters of rescue units from other parties, but countries may be reluctant to permit this due to a perceived need to protect their sovereignty over their territorial sea. An additional problem in the South China Sea is the lack of any mechanism for SAR cooperation between ASEAN and China.[42]

The risks of a major accident in South China Sea requiring a coordinated SAR operation is relatively high. Apart from the dense shipping traffic, there is much fishing activity and a high volume of air traffic between Southeast Asia and Northeast Asia as well as trans-Pacific flights to North America. Numerous offshore oil and gas installations are also evident with an associated risk of a major accident. The South China Sea is also vulnerable to storms and typhoons with a typhoon season in the northern part of the sea running from May to October each year. Without an agreed coordination plan for SAR in the South China Sea a major SAR operation, such as the loss of a large passenger jet or a major accident involving a cruise liner, could present problems of coordination.

SAR was one of the areas identified for cooperation in the 2002 Declaration on the Conduct of Parties in the South China Sea, Article VI of the DOC provided that all parties would engage in cooperation regarding navigation safety, and SAR before a permanent mechanism is developed. In August 2014, the ASEAN Regional Forum issued a Statement on Strengthening Coordination and Cooperation on Maritime and Aeronautical SAR.[43]

Regional search and rescue exercises (SAREX) are conducted under an agreement between ASEAN countries. These have been conducted involving most ASEAN countries aimed at ensuring that all regional SAR agencies are able to coordinate assistance during major emergencies. There are also various bilateral SAREX arrangements and exercises between ASEAN countries, such as SAREX INDOPURA between Singapore and Indonesia, SAREX MALBRU between Malaysia and Brunei, and SAREX MALSING between Malaysia and Singapore.[44]

ASEAN and China have also been making several first steps towards their SAR cooperation in the South China Sea with China largely taking a lead. These initiatives have included a series of "tabletop" exercises and several hotlines being established between national SAR centres. The first ASEAN- China Maritime Field Training Exercise was held off Zhanjiang, in China's southern Guangdong province in October 2018.[45] The exercise was based on a SAR scenario and was co-organised by Singapore and China, It the first exercise that ASEAN has held with one other country. Ships participated from China, Thailand, Singapore, Philippines, Brunei, and Vietnam. Beijing also claims that its reclaimed islands in the Spratly Islands have a public good utility by providing a base for SAR services. In January 2019, it opened a maritime rescue centre on Fiery Cross Reef.[46]

With current search and rescue regions (SRR), Singapore has accepted SAR responsibility for a large part of the South China Sea (SCS) (see Figure 3.2) and has promulgated the Singapore Plan for SAR Services and Passenger Ships. However, SRR boundaries do not accord with national maritime boundaries, and this along with the lack of ratification of the SAR Convention by some littoral countries, suggests that there could still be problems with mounting a large-scale maritime SAR operation in the region, particularly in disputed waters.

Ship reporting systems

Following the terrorist attacks of 9/11, the IMO introduced several measures to improve the safety and security of merchant ships at sea. These are the AIS, the long-range identification and tracking (LRIT) system, and the Ship Security Alert System (SSAS).[47]

AIS enhances the safety of navigation by providing all ship and shore stations with details of the identification, position, course and speed of all other AIS-equipped ships within range. It is a broadcast system used by ship and vessel traffic services principally for the identification and locating of vessels. It provides a means for ships to electronically exchange ship data at regular intervals with other nearby ships and vessel traffic system (VTS) stations. It helps and allows maritime authorities to track and monitor vessel movements. It is much used by merchant ships to avoid collisions and to pass information from ship to ship regarding what their intended movements are.

There are three types of AIS transponder that all interoperate:[48] Class A AIS transponders, the main type, are mandated for vessels on international voyages over 300 tons, fishing vessels over 15m, passenger-carrying vessels; AIS Class B transponders for yachts and other recreational craft installation and have a transmission power of 2W (range of about 10 miles); and AIS Class B+, more visible than a Class B one because it has the same technology as an AIS Class A transponders thus ensuring that they will always be able to transmit, even in high traffic areas.

AIS may be switched off to hide a vessel's identity. The fact that the American destroyer, USS *McCain*, was not showing AIS data was a major factor in its collision with a merchant

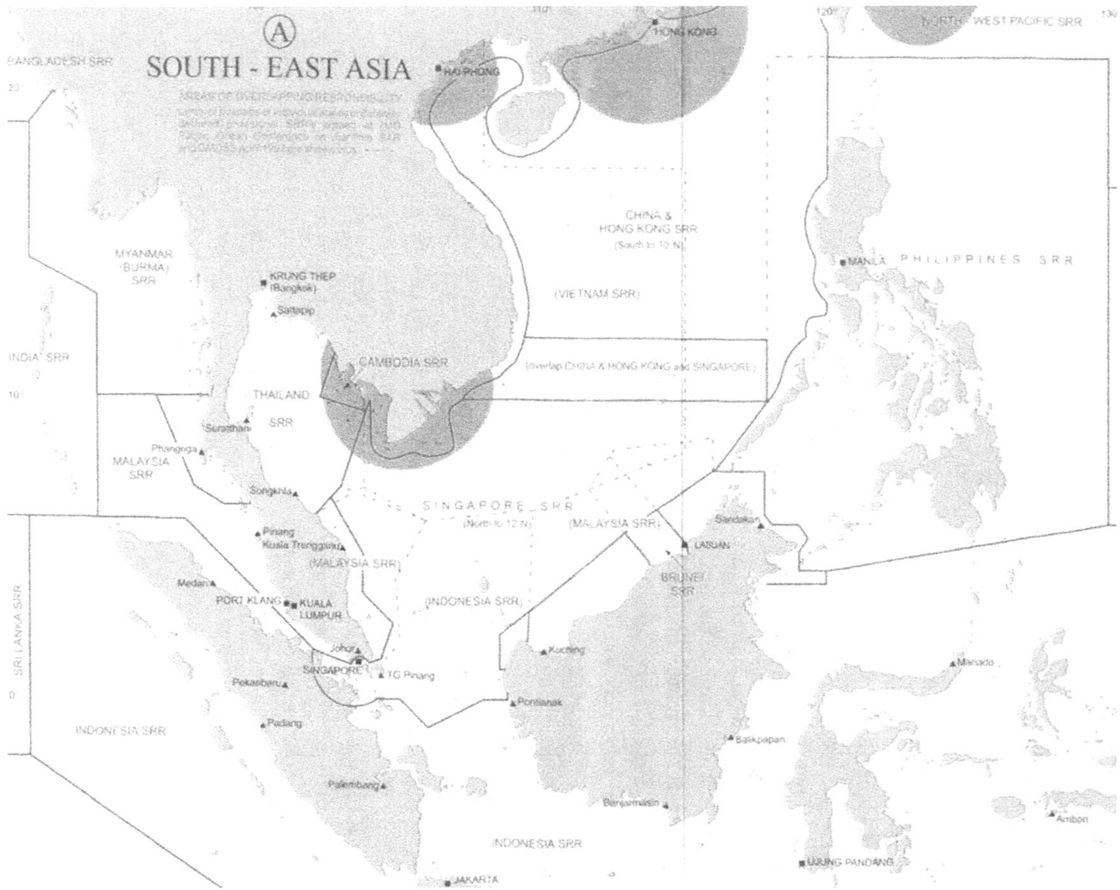

Figure 3.2 Search and Rescue Regions in Southeast Asia.

Source: Maritime and Port Authority of Singapore, "Rescue region (SRR)", SAR Cooperation Plan. Map published by the IMO, and can be found originally on the Maritime Institute of Malaysia (MIMA) website.

https://www.mpa.gov.sg/web/wcm/connect/www/eff1c6fb-320a-44fe-adaa-482aa5a1258b/singapore-srr.jpg?MOD=AJPERES ship in the eastern approaches to Singapore Strait in 2018.[49] As a consequence of this accident and another fatal collision in 2018 involving the destroyer, USS *Fitzgerald*, the United States Navy (USN) now requires all its ships to show AIS data when in busy shipping lanes.[50]

Particularly in areas of high fishing activity such as the South China Sea, it would help the safety of navigation in the area if fishing vessels also carried AIS, if only the Class B transponders that are typically available for less than USD$800. This would assist in helping to avoid collisions between fishing vessels and other ships. However, it is reported that in Southeast Asia, very few fishing vessels have AIS, and the reception quality is poor.[51] Another limitation of AIS is that in areas of dense maritime activity, shipping and fishing, the AIS signals might merge and it will be hard to distinguish between different vessels.

At present, AIS is only a requirement for vessels on international voyages. There is extensive domestic shipping traffic around and across the South China Sea, particularly along the coast of Vietnam and between West and East Malaysia. It would help if these vessels were also required to show AIS data. Singapore made a similar recommendation some years ago that Class B AIS transponders be carried on all small vessels of less than 300 gross tons in the Malacca and Singapore Straits.[52] While a demonstration project was conducted supported by Australia, Japan and South Korea, it is not believed that the plan was implemented.

AIS has also proven useful in allowing intelligence agencies and maritime security 'think tanks' in tracking the activities of vessels engaged in maritime disputes in the South China Sea. A recent months-long standoff over oil and gas operations in the South China Sea was played out between Malaysian, Chinese, and a small number of Vietnamese vessels. The Asia Maritime Transparency Initiative (AMTI) operated by the CSIS in Washington DC tracked the standoff using the vessels' AIS broadcasts along with commercial satellite imagery.[53] This data revealed a dangerous, ongoing game of chicken involving law enforcement, militia, and civilian vessels. However, it was an incomplete picture as it only captured those ships broadcasting AIS or which happened to be in the area when a satellite image was captured. It is also possible that additional naval, air, law enforcement, and militia assets from all sides had been involved for over the previous two months. Equally likely is the possibility that maritime law enforcement vessels choose to show AIS data to show their presence in a disputed area.

This incident shows how AIS contributes to maritime domain awareness (MDA), as well as to the safety of navigation. While both LRIT and AIS contribute to MDA in the South China Sea, the two systems are not to be confused. LRIT is a closed system but AIS is an open one with information on a conforming ship's position and movements publicly available on several ship-tracking websites, such as www.marinetraffic.com.

LRIT provides reliable and persistent global surveillance of maritime traffic for the purpose of detecting, identifying and classifying vessels. It was introduced following concerns mainly held by the United States following the 9/11 attacks that ships could enter port with explosive devices hidden in innocent cargo, and coastal States required information on ships preparing to enter one of their ports or were navigating in their adjacent waters.[54] LRIT data is only available to the following:

- Flag States can receive information on ships flying their flag anywhere in the world.
- Port States can receive information on ships declaring their intentions to enter one of its ports.
- Coastal States can receive information on ships passing within 1000 nautical miles of their coasts.
- SAR authorities.

LRIT is a requirement for the following on international voyages, all passenger ships, cargo ships over 300 tons, and mobile offshore drilling units. A ship is required to transmit its ship identity, location and date and time of its position, which is reported automatically to its flag administration at least four times a day or on demand. Data through the LRIT is available only to recipients who are entitled to receive such data. These include contracting governments so that they receive information about ships, which have indicated their intention to enter a port facility or a place under their jurisdiction and contracting governments to receive information about ships navigating with a distance of 1000 nautical miles from the coast, and also the air SAR services of the contracting governments for the purpose of SAR of ships, and persons in distress at sea.

Introduction of LRIT presented several legal and technical problems.[55] Intense negotiations were required at the IMO on who could have access to LRIT information, including the distance from the shore from which information may be received. There were concerns held by some States that seeking information from ships more than 200 nautical miles offshore was an interference with their high seas freedoms of navigation. Confidentiality considerations were another key concern that was held by flag States and industry in relation to the adoption of LRIT and other vessel tracking systems.

Contracting governments are required to implement a national data centre and comply with the LRIT regulations. However, in view of the costs involved, many coastal States have not implemented a data centre. All bordering countries to the South China Sea are contracting governments to the LRIT system and have implemented national LRIT data centres.

In Europe, European Union Member States have established an EU LRIT Data Centre (EU LRIT DC) through the European Maritime Safety Agency (EMSA), which is in charge of the technical development, operation and maintenance of the EU LRIT DC.[56] The system was initially set up for the purposes of maritime security but was soon extended for use in areas such as SAR, maritime safety and protection of the marine environment. The EU LRIT DC serves as a model for regional cooperation as an example for the rest of the world.

SSAS is part of the ISPS Code. It is intended to allow ships to get urgent security assistance should they fear an attempted or actual piracy or terrorist attack. It is a requirement for merchant ships to allow them to report a ship to shore security alert to a competent authority ashore. It does not raise any alarm on board the ship. There must be at least two activation points or buttons: one must be on the navigation bridge and the other situated in at least one other location on board the ship. Although good in concept, the weakness of the SSAS is that nearby responders may not be the initial parties alerted.[57] The recipient of the alerts is the ship's flag State or an authority designated by the flag State, which is usually in practice the ship owners. These of course may be a long distance from the ship activating the alert. It is also prone to false alarms.

Information sharing

Information sharing between the bordering countries the South China Sea is essential for establishing MDA across the sea. MDA is central to a coastal State's ability to provide for the safety of navigation and SAR services in its adjacent waters, as well as for the provision of these services on a coordinated basis in the South China Sea. It also would help in identifying and tracking ships that have committed an act of wilful pollution of the marine environment.

There are now several national information sharing centres around the South China Sea that contribute to MDA. The IFC operated by the Singapore Navy is the leading one of these. With the assistance of international liaison officers (ILOs) from other regional navies and coast guards, including from China, it provides for regional maritime information sharing cooperation among regional navies and other agencies. It helps cue participating countries to take action to respond early to potential threats and developing situations. At the heart of the IFC is the Regional Maritime Information Exchange System (ReMIX), which is an initiative of the Western Pacific Naval Symposium (WPNS) to share maritime security-related information. There will be a reference database of more than 150,000 vessels that is designed to flag suspicious vessels that warrant closer surveillance.

Other national maritime information systems include Indonesia's multiagency Sea Security Coordination Centre (Badan Keamanan Laut, or BAKAMLA) and the Philippines' National Coast Watch System (NCWS), which includes the National Coast Watch Centre (NCWC), to provide interagency coordination and maritime security across the Philippines archipelago.[58] The Piracy Reporting Centre (PRC) of the International Maritime Bureau (IMB) established in Kuala Lumpur and the ISC set up in Singapore by ReCAAP also collect data relevant to MDA and the safety of navigation at the regional level. The potential exists for greater coordination and cooperation between these various regional and national maritime information systems.

Conclusion

The high intensity of shipping traffic along the SLOCs of South China dictates the need for effective measures to ensure the safety of navigation and protection of the marine environment from ship-sourced pollution. The most fundamental requirement is a higher level of cooperation and coordination between the bordering countries to provide for the safety of navigation and SAR. Unfortunately, this remains unlikely due to several factors. Littoral countries are still not party to all the relevant international conventions. No effective regional organization has been established for managing the South China Sea, and attempts at cooperation have generally shown little progress. It is unfortunate that much of the current commentary on the South China Sea falls within a realist construct of a competing power game and fails to recognize the possibility of a "win win" outcome achieved through cooperation. The consequential lack of trust inhibits cooperation.

Countries bordering the South China Sea tend to be focused on their independence and sovereignty. They are reluctant to engage in cooperative activities because that may compromise their sovereignty claims and national independence. This is often despite enthusiastic rhetoric about the cooperative ideal. States will only cooperate with each other when they perceive that the gains from cooperation will outweigh the costs, particularly the loss of independence or fears of domination by a larger partner in the cooperative framework. Perceptions that cooperation implies some concession on sovereignty claims are a significant obstacle to cooperation.

An agreed Code of Conduct for the South China Sea is key to establishing effective cooperation for the safety of navigation in the South China Sea. Cooperation for the safety of navigation would be facilitated by the technical committee for this activity as recommended in the current draft negotiating text for the South China Sea Code of Conduct. Particular measures that might be considered include the wider adoption of AIS by fishing vessels and vessels on domestic voyages, if only by the fitting of Class B transponders; greater cooperation for maritime SAR and hydrographic surveys; and regional protocols for the handling of LRIT data.

Notes

1 China Power Project, 'How Much Trade Transits the South China Sea', available at https://chinapower.csis.org/much-trade-transits-south-china-sea/.
2 James Laurenceson, 'Economics and Freedom of Navigation in East Asia', *Australian Journal of International Affairs*, 2017, p. 2, available at doi: 10.1080/10357718.2017.1301374.
3 'Modal Shares of World Trade by Volume and Value', 2008, available at https://transportgeography.org/?page_id=3950.
4 A detailed geographic and oceanographic description of the South China Sea is available in: Vivian Louis Forbes, 'Re-framing the South China Sea: Geographical Reality and Historical Fact and Fiction', *Universiti Brunei Darussalam Working Paper No. 33*, Institute of Asian Studies, Universiti Brunei Darussalam Gadong, 2017.
5 Jean-Nicolas Pasquay 'Safety of Modern Shipping and Requirements in Hydrographic Surveying and Nautical Charting', *International Hydrographic Review*, Monaco, Vol. LXIII, No. 2, July 1986, p. 68, and Figure 5, p. 73.
6 This discussion of the science of hydrographic surveying is based on Commander R.J. Hardstaff RAN (Rtd), *Leadline to Laser – The Hydrographic Service Royal Australian Navy 1920–1995*, Sydney, RAN Hydrographic Office, 1995, Technical Notes, pp. 181–213.
7 UNCLOS Article 123.
8 Ian Townsend-Gault, 'Maritime Cooperation in a Functional Perspective' in 'Maritime Energy Resources in Asia - Energy and Geopolitics', *NBR Special Report #35*, edited by Clive Schofield (Seattle: The National Bureau of Asian Research, December, 2011), p. 11, available at http://www.nbr.org/publications/issue.aspx?id=248.
9 CSCAP Memorandum No. 13 – Guidelines for Maritime Cooperation in the Enclosed and Semi-Enclosed Seas of East Asia, July 2008, available at http://www.cscap.org/.
10 Mitja Grbec, *Extension of Coastal State Jurisdiction in Enclosed and Semi-enclosed Seas – A Mediterranean and Adriatic Perspective*, Abingdon: Routledge, 2014, p. 18.
11 Sam Bateman, 'Turning the Clock Back on UNCLOS', *The Strategist*, 20 August 2016, available at https://www.aspistrategist.org.au/turning-back-the-clock-on-unclos/.
12 The author did so himself several years ago when travelling by large container ship from Hong Kong to Port Klang in Malaysia.
13 For example in Ben Blanchard, 'China Says South China Sea Militarization Depends on Threat', *Jakarta Globe*, 20 January 2016, available at https://jakartaglobe.id/context/china-says-south-china-sea-militarization-depends-threat/.
14 White House, Office of the Press Secretary, 'Press Briefing by NSA for Strategic Communications', Ben Rhodes and Admiral Robert Willard, US Pacific Command', Moana Surfrider Hotel, Honolulu, Hawaii, 13 November 2011, available at https://obamawhitehouse.archives.gov/the-press-office/2011/11/13/press-briefing-nsa-strategic-communications-ben-rhodes-and-admiral-rober.
15 Ibid.
16 Linda B. Paul, 'The Need for Open Sea Lines of Communication in the South China Sea', *PacNet #59*, 21 August 2018, available at https://www.csis.org/analysis/pacnet-59-need-open-sea-lines-communication-south-china-sea.
17 ASEAN External Trade Statistics Table 20 - Top Ten ASEAN Trade Partner Countries/Regions, 2015, available at https://asean.org/wp-content/uploads/2016/11/Table20_as-of-6-dec-2016.pdf.
18 *ASEAN Statistical Yearbook 2018*, p. 118, Table 5.52. Top-Ten Traded Goods between USA and ASEAN, 2017, available at https://www.aseanstats.org/publication/asyb-2018/?portfolioCats=56%2C42%2C55%2C33%2C31%2C32%2C50%2C34%2C48%2C49%2C35%2C36%2C66%2C51.
19 AJOT, 'More Than 30% of Global Maritime Crude Oil Trade Moves Through the South China Sea', *American Journal of Transportation*, 27 August 2018, available at https://www.ajot.com/news/more-than-30-of-global-maritime-crude-oil-trade-moves-through-the-south-china-sea.
20 Sam Bateman, 'Some Thoughts on Australia and the Freedoms of Navigation', *Security Challenges*, Vol. 11, No. 2, 2015, pp. 57–66.
21 Sam Bateman, 'Australia's Flawed Position on the South China Sea', *East Asia Forum*, 10 March 2016, available at http://www.eastasiaforum.org/2016/03/10/australias-flawed-position-on-the-south-china-sea/#more-49860.

22 Australian Government, *Defence White Paper 2016*, Canberra: Department of Defence, 2016, paragraph 1.6.
23 *Defence White Paper 2016*, paragraph 2.77.
24 Greg Austin, 'Mountains Out of Molehills: The Pentagon's Big Lie about the South China Sea', *The Diplomat*, 24 February 2016, available at https://thediplomat.com/2016/02/mountains-out-of-molehills-the-pentagons-big-lie-about-the-south-china-sea/.
25 *Defence White Paper 2016*, paragraph 2.72.
26 Sam Bateman, 'What Are Australia's Interests in the South China Sea?', *The Strategist*, 28 May 2015, available at http://www.aspistrategist.org.au/what-are-australias-interests-in-the-south-china-sea/.
27 Department of Foreign Affairs and Trade, Composition of Trade Australia 2013–2014, Table 7, available at http://dfat.gov.au/about-us/publications/Documents/cot-fy-2013-14.pdf.
28 Bateman, 'Australia's Flawed Position on the South China Sea'.
29 *Defence White Paper 2016*, Figure 2, p. 70.
30 Modal shares of world trade by volume in 2008 were 89.8 percent by sea, 10.0 percent overland, and 0.3 percent by air. By value the shares were very different – 72.7 percent by sea, 14.3 percent overland, and 13.0 percent by air. Modal Shares of World Trade by Volume and Value, 2008, *The Geography of Transport Systems*, available at https://transportgeography.org/?page_id=3950.
31 Sam Bateman, *Freedoms of Navigation in the Asia-Pacific Region – Strategic, Political and Legal Factors*, Abingdon: Routledge, 2020, p. 16.
32 Nong Hong, 'Arctic vs. South China Sea: How Coastal States and User States View the Navigation Regime and Security', Chapter 7 in Wu and Zou, *Non-Traditional Security Issues and the South China Sea*, p. 119.
33 Laurenceson, 'Economics and Freedom of Navigation in East Asia'.
34 Sam Bateman, 'Piracy in Asia: A Situation Report – A Little Known Success Story', *Policy Forum*, 11 December 2019, available at https://www.policyforum.net/piracy-in-asia-a-situation-report/.
35 Sam Bateman and Jane Chan, 'Piracy and Armed Robbery against Ships in the South China Sea – Possible Causes and Solutions', Chapter 8 in Shicun Wu and Keyuan Zou, *Non-Traditional Security Issues and the South China Sea – Shaping a New Framework for Cooperation*, Farnham: Ashgate, 2014, pp. 133–143.
36 Cambodia is the only Southeast Asian coastal state that is not a party to UNCLOS.
37 For more information on SUA 1988 and 2005 see Robert C. Beckman, 'The 1988 Convention and 2005 Protocol: Tools to Combat Piracy, Armed Robbery, and Maritime Terrorism', Chapter 12 in Herbert Burns, Bateman and Lehr, *Lloyd's Handbook of Maritime Security*, pp. 187–200.
38 R. M. Warner, 'Stemming the Black Tide: Cooperation on Oil Pollution Preparedness and Response in the South China Sea and East Asian Seas', *Journal of International Wildlife Law and Policy*, Vol. 18, No. 2, 2015, pp. 184–197.
39 ESA Earth online, *Oil Pollution – South China Sea*, available at https://earth.esa.int/web/guest/missions/esa-operational-eo-missions/ers/instruments/sar/applications/tropical/-/asset_publisher/tZ7pAG6SCnM8/content/oil-pollution-south-china-sea.
40 'ASEAN Member States Adopt Regional Oil Spill Contingency Plan', *World Maritime News*, available at https://worldmaritimenews.com/archives/265874/asean-member-states-adopt-regional-oil-spill-contingency-plan/.
41 NOAA, *Marine Pollution Surveillance Program*, available at https://www.ospo.noaa.gov/Products/ocean/mpsp.html.
42 Chen Xiangmiao, 'The South China Sea Needs a Mechanism for Joint Search and Rescue Operations', *China – US Focus*, 27 September 2018, available at https://www.chinausfocus.com/foreign-policy/the-south-china-sea-needs-a-mechanism-for-joint-search-and-rescue-operations.
43 ASEAN Regional Forum Statement on Strengthening Coordination and Cooperation on Maritime and Aeronautical Search and Rescue, 11 August 2014, available at https://www.fmprc.gov.cn/mfa_eng/wjdt_665385/2649_665393/t1181700.shtml.
44 Prashanth Parameswaran, 'Search and Rescue Exercise Highlights Malaysia-Singapore Defense Relations', *The Diplomat*, 15 October 2019, available at https://thediplomat.com/2019/10/search-and-rescue-exercise-highlights-malaysia-singapore-defense-relations/.
45 Lim Min Zhang, 'First Asean-China Maritime Exercise Will Tackle Simulated Collision in Waters off Zhanjiang', *The Straits Times*, 24 October 2018, available at https://www.straitstimes.com/singapore/first-asean-china-maritime-exercise-will-tackle-simulated-collision-in-waters-off.

46 'Beijing Opens Maritime Rescue Base in South China Sea', *ABC News*, 31 January 2019, available at https://www.abc.net.au/news/2019-01-31/beijing-opens-maritime-rescue-base-in-south-china-sea/10768048.
47 A fuller explanation of AIS and LRIT may be found in Martin N. Murphy, 'Lifeline or Pipedream? Origins, Purposes and Benefits of Automatic Identification System, Long-Range Identification and Tracking, and Maritime Domain Awareness', Chapter 2 in Rupert Herbert Burns, Sam Bateman and Peter Lehr, eds., *Lloyd's Handbook of Maritime Security*, London: Lloyd's MIU, 2009, pp. 13–28. However. It should be noted that this chapter was written before the advent of Satellite-based AIS (S-AIS) which allows AIS to be detected from vessels regardless of their location.
48 Digital Yacht, AIS Transponders, https://digitalyachtamerica.com/product-category/ais-transponders/.
49 Sam Bateman, 'The Troubled US Seventh Fleet', *Global Asia*, Vol. 13, No. 1, Spring 2018, pp. 33–35.
50 Sam Bateman, 'Norwegian Frigate Sinking Has Far-Reaching Implications', *The Strategist*, 11 December 2018, available at https://www.aspistrategist.org.au/norwegian-frigate-sinking-has-far-reaching-implications/.
51 Sarah Bladen, 'New Global Atlas on Using Advanced Technology to Monitor Fishing Activity', *Global Fishing Watch*, 19 November 2018, available at https://globalfishingwatch.org/news-views/global-atlas/.
52 Sam Bateman, Joshua Ho and Jane Chan, 'Good Order at Sea in Southeast Asia', *RSIS Policy Paper*, May 2009, p. 31.
53 'Malaysia Picks a Three-Way Fight in the South China Sea', *AMTI Brief*, 21 February 2020, available at https://mailchi.mp/csis.org/reading-between-lines-1911385?e=d8dd0878fe.
54 Murphy, 'Lifeline or Pipedream?' p. 17.
55 Martin Tsamenyi and Mary Ann Palma, 'Long-Range Identification and Tracking Systems for Vessels: Legal and Technical Issues', Chapter 14 in Burns, Bateman and Lehr, *Lloyd's Handbook of Maritime Security*.
56 http://www.emsa.europa.eu/lrit-main/lrit-home.html.
57 Thomas Timlen, 'Ship Security Alert System: A Failed Effort to Protect Coastal Communities', *RSIS Commentary 80/2014*, 19 February 2008, available at https://www.rsis.edu.sg/wp-content/uploads/2014/07/CO08015.pdf.
58 Peter Chalk, 'Boosting Maritime Domain Awareness in Southeast Asia', *The Strategist*, 13 December 2019, available at https://www.aspistrategist.org.au/boosting-maritime-domain-awareness-in-southeast-asia/. More details of these three information fusion centres are in Peter Chalk, 'Augmenting Maritime Domain Awareness in Southeast Asia', *ASPI Special Report*, December 2019, available at https://s3-ap-southeast-2.amazonaws.com/ad-aspi/2019-12/SR%20150%20Maritime%20domain%20awareness_1.pdf?oSJh.esxFRumNPbVt1hYfriTfiQD36K5.

4
MARITIME SECURITY AND DEMILITARISATION OF THE SOUTH CHINA SEA

Mary George

Introduction

In this chapter, the theme "maritime security, militarisation and demilitarisation of the South China Sea" (SCS), a part of the Pacific Ocean, is considered as one inter-related issue,[1] combining traditional security threats such as wars, threats to peace, breaches of peace and acts of aggression. The geographic location of the SCS where tensions escalate is in the highly contested and overlapping 200 nm exclusive economic zones (EEZs) of the claimant SCS States and China. The contested EEZs cover the Paracels and Spratlys. The EEZ claims by Vietnam, the Philippines, Malaysia and Brunei are precipitated under the 1982 Law of the Sea Convention (LOSC). China's claim of sovereignty is based on a 1947 map and historic title as an integral part of China. The Paracels are also claimed by Vietnam since the 17th century. It is estimated that there are 11 billion barrels of untapped oil and 190 trillion cubic feet of natural gas in the contested and overlapping EEZs. The Scarborough Shoal, a 60 square mile (97 km) chain of rocks and reefs is claimed by both China and the Philippines. The Philippines claim is based on geographical proximity and history dating back hundreds of years. In summary, the Spratlys comprise more than 700 reefs, islets, atolls and islands.

Under Article 122 of the 1982 LOSC,[2] the SCS is a semi-enclosed sea that is bordered by mostly all ASEAN Member States and China. The SCS States have not affirmed what the agreed facts of the tensions are and what constitutes the legal disputes of the region.[3] In January 2013, the SCS tensions resulted in an Annex VII Arbitration under the 1982 LOSC filed by the Philippines against China, a legal battle that China lost.[4] The SCS military tensions are traced from the period of UNCLOS III negotiations (1973–1982) to the present. The SCS tensions comprise the military actions of the SCS claimant States and external powers led by the United States. The overlapping and contested EEZs mean that the extraction of the living and non-living resources is a destabilising factor in the region likely to lead to confrontations as the territorial dispute management has been fragile in the SCS. Therefore, it is possible to recognize that the actions, reactions and provocations of the States are all a part of the causation of the tensions. The military actions of the SCS claimant States are tied in with their economic interests in oil, gas and fisheries reserves in the EEZs.

Issues connected with the safety of navigation or cleaner oceans under the IMO/FAO Conventions[5] or under the UNGA Resolution 62/215 on "Oceans and the Law of the Sea"[6] are not examined here.[7]

The SCS tensions

The SCS tensions are considered chronologically over four decades: the eighties, the nineties, first decade of the millennium from 2000 to 2010 and the second decade from 2010 to 2020.

Eighties and nineties

In the eighties and nineties, for reasons undisclosed, China maintained a military presence on Fiery Cross Reef in the Spratlys that Vietnam was closely monitoring from several other reefs, eventually resulting in a confrontation between Vietnam and China on Johnson Reef in the Spratly Archipelago. States believed that there were security threats to the freedom of navigation for warships when the Chinese Law on the Territorial Sea and the Contiguous Zone of February 1992 was passed. Not long thereafter, in 1996, there was a clash between the Philippines and the Chinese military in Mischief Reef in the Spratlys that served to revive the US-Philippine military ties, as the United States has a defence treaty pact with the Philippines. After this incident, whether consequent to or independent of the Mischief Reef clash, the United States and the Philippines began to conduct joint military exercises on Palawan Island. Also, by mid-1996, the Philippines and China signed a non-binding Code of Conduct underscoring the need for a peaceful resolution of their territorial dispute and to promote confidence-building measures. Two years later, in 1998, China and the United States signed the Military Maritime Consultative Agreement, a confidence-building instrument to ease the breakdown in their bilateral relations and to promote a defence dialogue between the blue water naval forces of the two States.[8]

First decade of the millennium: 2000–2010

In the first decade of the millennium, in 2001, a Chinese F-8 interceptor and a US Navy surveillance aircraft collided in mid-air causing a human fatality. To ease the mounting tensions, by 2002, the ASEAN-China Declaration on the Conduct of Parties in the SCS, a non-binding instrument was signed. Then, seven years later, in 2009, a non-military peaceful exercise took place: Malaysia and Vietnam submitted a joint claim to the UN Commission on the Limits of the Continental Shelf to delimit the outer continental shelf in the south of the SCS, under the terms of the 1982 LOSC. The delimitation could not take place as China and the Philippines objected to the exercise saying it was an infringement of their sovereignty over the islands and Sabah (East Malaysia), respectively. Though neither Malaysia nor Vietnam showed their dissatisfaction by a show of force over this objection, it should be noted as part of the fragile territorial dispute management issue of the SCS. By 2010, the United States using non-legal language had affirmed its interest in the "open access to Asia's maritime commons." It is regarded that this affirmation was inimical to China's interests. Between 2010 and 2011, skirmishes took place between the Philippines and China because a Philippine vessel had conducted surveys in the Reed Bank and China's surveillance ships had forced the vessel to leave the area. Days later, Vietnam and China faced a diplomatic standoff when Vietnamese oil exploration ships working with multinationals such as ExxonMobil and Chevron, to develop hydrocarbon assets, were countered by Chinese ships. As a result of this clash, the Philippines renamed the SCS in October 2011 as the West Philippine Sea and that was endorsed by the United States.[9]

Second decade of the millennium: 2011–2020

2011–2013

The second decade of the millennium saw external power tensions escalate further as strategic maritime and trade interests intersected. In 2011, President Barrack Obama in a speech to the Australian Parliament highlighted the strategic interest of the United States in the south of the Asia-Pacific region and renewed US commitments to the region. At that time, the United States also excluded China from the Trans-Pacific Partnership (TPP, a free trade agreement,) talks. In 2012, Japanese Prime Minister Shinzo Abe warned that the SCS was transforming into "Lake Beijing," and proposed a "democratic security diamond" comprising Japan, the United States, India, and Australia to "safeguard the maritime commons stretching from the Indian Ocean region to the Western Pacific." It is to be noted that Japan's statements may have other implications for China as the two nations suffer territorial sovereignty disputes too. At the same time, China's new leaders referred to maritime rights as part of the country's "core interests." By March 2013, Japan joined the TPP to be closely associated with Southeast Asia. Within a few months therefrom, in May 2013, China announced that it might join the TPP negotiations too. Another significant event in the second decade of the millennium was the Scarborough Shoal incident of 8 April 2012, a conflict between the Philippines and China that lasted about two months. China maintained regular patrols there to protect its fishing interests. To counter Chinese presence, the Philippines dispatched a warship. To counter this counter-threat, China sent its surveillance vessels to protect the fishing boats. Diplomatic talks about withdrawal from the Shoal ceased. The Philippines pursued its claim on several fronts: through ASEAN involvement, under the 1982 LOSC, and by an appeal to the United States for a guarantee of assistance in case of a military confrontation. There was no peaceful solution regarding the matter. Then Vietnam passed its Maritime Law in June 2012 and soured Hanoi-Beijing relations for the law proclaimed jurisdiction over the disputed Spratlys and Paracels by demanding notification of any foreign naval ships passing through the area. It remains to be confirmed whether this was an act of enforcement jurisdiction or a mere prescriptive exercise. However, China responded strongly that a new city built on the Paracels would be responsible for the administration of the Paracels, Spratlys, and the Macclesfield Bank. This event was followed by another where Chinese surveillance ships cut the cables of Vietnamese oil and gas survey vessels.

In October 2013, the tensions between Vietnam and China eased when the two States entered into a bilateral agreement for handling maritime disputes. In another non-military event, in 2012, ASEAN failed to issue a Communiqué on China's claims in the SCS after its annual meeting in Cambodia as the Member States had reached an impasse on this matter. The ASEAN failure was attributed to China's influence over Cambodia. By 12 September 2012, China claimed Territorial Sea Baselines over Diaoyu Islands, but it had no implications for Chinese claims in the SCS. By 25 September 2012, China launched its first aircraft carrier for training and national sovereignty protection and embarked on naval modernization. By 16 January 2013, Japan strengthened its relationship with Vietnam, Thailand and Indonesia through friendly visits as Japan was going through a "dynamic change" in the strategic environment of the Asia-Pacific saying closer relations with ASEAN countries was in "Japan's national interest" and contributed to the region's peace and stability. On 22 January 2013, the Philippines sued China in an Annex VII Arbitration under the 1982 LOSC at the PCA over China's Sovereignty Claims in the Spratlys and Scarborough Shoal stemming from the April 2012 clashes and previous conflict resolution failures. China did not participate. On 12 July 2016, the Tribunal ruled against China's SCS claims. On 13 July, the US affirmed the decision of the Annex VII Tribunal that the Chinese claims had no legal basis, and issued a statement that "most of China's claims in the SCS are unlawful. Specifically, Washington rejected all of Beijing's claims that extended beyond 12 nm from Chinese shores, including waters off Indonesia, Malaysia, and Vietnam." China asserted otherwise and accused the US of "stirring up trouble." Earlier in the month, two US aircraft carriers sailed through the disputed waters. To complete the story, after the Philippines won at the Tribunal, on 20 November 2016, the Philippines established a no-fishing zone and marine sanctuary at a lagoon in the Scarborough Shoal. However, despite the win, the Philippines decided to boost economic links with China and resumed bilateral dialogue with China on the disputed territories. Though both States did not give up their respective sovereignty claims, the two countries adopted a more reconciliatory approach. Besides, in the earlier TPP talking engagements, in May 2013, Japan offered military aid to Cambodia and the ASEAN Member States. Further, Japan also considered selling military equipment, including seaplanes, shallow-water submarines, patrol boats to the Philippine Coast Guard in response to maritime threats from China.

For the first time on 23 November 2013, China declared an air defence identification zone, namely, the East China Sea Air Defence Identification Zone that required "all non-commercial air traffic to submit flight plans prior to entering the area, which covers most of the East China Sea and includes the Senkaku/Diaoyu Islands." Naturally, the question looms in one's mind whether an ADIZ will be established over the SCS by any of the claimant States.[10]

2014–2020

The next event in this region was the revival of the old US-Philippine allegiance where the two States signed a new ten-year defence pact on 28 April 2014. Under the Enhanced Defence Cooperation Agreement, the US military has access to the Philippines' bases, ports and airfields. The US said that neither the defence pact nor the SCS Arbitration was meant to isolate China economically or contain its military power. The next month on 4 May 2014, there was a clash between Vietnam and China over the establishment of a Chinese oil rig in contested seas near the Paracels with damaging trade impacts for Chinese businesses in Vietnam. On July 15 of the same year, China's state-owned oil company said it would withdraw the rig a month ahead of schedule. By 2 October 2014, the US allowed Vietnam to purchase maritime security weaponry that was expected to defend its territorial claims and counter China's military in the SCS. A few months later in August 2015, the US Department of Defense reported that China had almost reclaimed 3000 acres of land and engaged in infrastructure development in the Spratlys. It is also said that other claimant States have built up 100 acres over the last 45 years. At the annual 2015 Shangri-La Dialogue in Singapore, the US urged China to stop the building projects, as it was concerned about the further militarization in the SCS. When on 26 October 2015, a US warship sailed within 12 nm of Chinese-built islands to assert its "freedom of navigation" in disputed waters in the SCS, China informed the US that this action was a "serious provocation, politically and militarily." To counter the US freedom of navigation operations in disputed waters, on 14 February 2016, China deployed surface-to-air missiles on Woody Island in the Paracels. The United States warned that this may be interpreted as a "militarization" of the maritime disputes. China's argument was that the installation of missiles was its right to defend its sovereign territory. China has also stationed J-11 fighter aircraft in the Paracels in October 2015. On 15 December 2016, the *USNS Bowditch*, a US Navy underwater drone, which was gathering scientific data in the SCS, was seized by a Chinese warship despite repeated calls to return the drone but it sailed away. Though China agreed to return the drone, it accused the United States of "hyping up" the dispute. The United States classified the action as an "unlawful seizure" that should not be repeated. On 18 May 2018, a Chinese bomber, an H-6 aircraft landed and took off from Woody Island in the Paracels. The implication of this action was that such aircraft "could reach all areas of the SCS and nearly all of the Philippines, according to expert analysis." A few months later, on 30 September 2018, a collision took place between a US destroyer, the *USS Decatur*, and a Chinese destroyer, the *Lanzhou*, near the Spratlys, within 45 yards of each other. The US destroyer was said to be engaged in a routine freedom of navigation exercise. China viewed the US patrol as a threat to its sovereignty. The consequences seemed to be the cancellation of a US trip to China and uncertainty over the two States' friendship. The next incident concerned Thitu Island, which is claimed by both the Philippines and China. From January to March 2019, China sent about 200 ships near the Philippines-occupied Thitu Island. In response, on 5 April 2019, the Philippines warned that it would send troops on a "suicide mission." The Philippines was building a beaching ramp on the island, to ease the delivery of construction equipment and supplies. On 3 July 2019, it was reported that a Chinese survey ship, *Haiyang Dizhi 8*, and several escort ships entered Vietnam's EEZ near an offshore oil block presumably to prevent Vietnam from drilling there. Vietnam wanted China to remove all ships with their aggressive manoeuvres. However, the *Haiyang Dizhi 8* only left in October that year.[11]

In February 2020, it was reported that a Chinese naval ship targeted its weapons control system at a Philippine naval ship in the Spratlys. In March, China established new research stations including defence silos and military-grade runways, on the Fiery Cross and Subi Reefs. In April, Vietnam formally protested China's actions after a Chinese vessel rammed and sank a Vietnamese fishing boat near the Paracels. Soon after, Beijing established two administrative districts that covered the Paracels and Spratlys. The Philippines and Vietnam denounced the move. In April, tensions were high when a Chinese survey ship entered Malaysia's EEZ. The incident prompted the US to send naval ships through the waters and call on China to end its "bullying." On 15 May, after almost six months, the standoff involving Chinese, Malaysian, and Vietnamese ships in the SCS ended when a Malaysian drillship exploring for oil and gas in the disputed area finally left. It was alleged that Chinese Coast Guard ships harassed the vessel.[12]

Summary

Briefly, the main SCS tensions are as follows:

1 Regional tensions between China and the Philippines[13] and Vietnam.[14] Japan is said to have sold military ships and equipment to the Philippines and Vietnam in order to improve their maritime security capacity and to deter Chinese aggression. The United States has a defence treaty with Manila that could draw the United States into the conflict.
2 Disputing SCS claimant States, namely, China. Vietnam, the Philippines and Taiwan have since 2014, pursued militarization of the disputed features in the Spratlys. China constructed seven artificial islands over the impugned reefs in the Spratly group in disputed areas.[15]

3. China's sovereignty claims over the SCS maritime features have been backed up by the Chinese military presence and occupation of these artificial islands. Military occupation here means the deployment of missiles and armed forces on the features. The missiles referred to are the anti-ship missiles, surface-to-air missiles, electronic jammers, and the landing of bomber aircraft at Woody Island, Paracel Islands.[16] It is reported that since 2014, China is equipped with a range of dual-use facilities on seven artificial islands in the Spratly group and the placement of coastal defence cruise missiles and surface-to-air missiles has allowed China to crystallize its control in the region. It is reported that satellite images indicate that China has withdrawn a long-range missile battery, an HQ 9 battery, from Woody Island, perhaps due to unfavourable climatic and weather conditions for storage of the missile system.[17]
4. Military activities by China where it is reported to have conducted a series of naval manoeuvres and exercises in March and April 2018.[18]
5. Construction of ports, military installations and airstrips on artificial islands in the Paracels and Spratlys, where China has piled sand onto existing reefs.
6. China has militarized Woody Island by deploying fighter jets, cruise missiles, and a radar system.
7. Construction of military and industrial outposts on artificial islands by China.[19] Commentators state that China's conversion and subsequent aerial and naval militarization of the six contested Spratlys reefs from an initial length of approximately 5–2000 miles are a manifestation of China's intention to lay claims and to exercise sovereignty over the artificial islands and airspace. When the US conducted its first freedom of navigation operation (FONOP) in the SCS, China reacted by an aerial interception of a US surveillance aircraft in international airspace near Hainan Island.[20] However, the mid-air collision on 1 April 2001 between a United States Navy EP-3E ARIES II signals intelligence aircraft and a People's Liberation Army-Navy (PLAN) J-8II interceptor fighter jet resulted in an international dispute between the United States of America and the People's Republic of China. However, this incident did not take place in the airspace of Fiery Cross Reef (artificial island) but on Hainan Island and is called the Hainan Island incident. During the incident, one Chinese J-8 fighter jet was destroyed, its pilot Lt. Cdr. Wang Wei killed and 24 US aircrews were captured and detained until 11 April 2001.[21]
8. Freedom of navigation exercises and securing sea lines of communication by the United States to counter China's threats on the sea lines of communication vital for international trade and commerce and naval forces.[22]
9. Differences of opinions between China and the United States on the interpretation of the nature of the EEZ and freedom of navigation, with Beijing differentiating between navigational rights for military and civilian vessels. China, additionally, opposes military surveillance activities within its exclusive economic zone.
10. Military activity and naval presence by the United States to bolster support for its Southeast Asian partners.
11. Conduct of several freedom of navigation operations (about six so far) by the United States in January and March 2018.
12. China-US tensions.[23]
13. The China and ASEAN failure to settle the tensions by now.
14. Philippine litigation against China under an Annex VII Arbitration, 1982 LOSC where China did not appear before the Tribunal as it had not withdrawn the Declaration it entered under the 1982 LOSC. China has opposed the Award.

15 Land reclamation by China in the SCS by physically creating artificial islands built over coral reefs for military purposes including the possible establishment of an air defence identification zone over the SCS.
16 At the second annual high-level meeting 2018, the US–China Diplomatic and Security Dialogue, called on China to withdraw its missiles from disputed features in the Spratlys and reaffirmed that all countries should avoid addressing disputes through coercion or intimidation.[24] US Secretary of Defence Jim Mattis pointed out at the Shangri-La Dialogue in 2018 that the reason why China has militarized the SCS, despite China's claims to the contrary, is that the placement of these weapons systems is tied directly to military use for the purposes of intimidation and coercion. The United States moved to disinvite the PLAN from the 2018 iteration of the Rim of the Pacific biennial multilateral naval exercise as a result of Beijing's moves in the SCS. So far China has not withdrawn the impugned missiles.
17 In October 2018, a US guided-missile destroyer, USS *Decatur*, was involved in a near collision with a PLAN Type 052C destroyer, the *Lanzhou*, after it tried to interrupt an innocent passage FONOP near Gaven Reef in the SCS.
18 China and the United States also agreed that they were "committed to support peace and stability in the SCS, the peaceful resolution of disputes, and freedom of navigation and overflight and other lawful uses of the sea in accordance with international law."[25]

Issues

Legality of impugned actions of the States

No State has submitted the matter to the UN whether under Chapter VI "Pacific Settlement of Disputes" or Chapter VII "Action with Respect to Threats to the Peace, Breaches of the Peace, and Acts of Aggression" of the UN Charter;[26] or even under the IHL Conventions and Protocols for breach of peace or threat to breach of peace or act of aggression.[27] The UNGA, responsible for ocean governance under the 1982 LOSC for the peaceful and lawful use of the oceans, has not adopted a resolution condemning the SCS tensions. However, the SCS tensions have led to legal infractions under the UN Charter, the 1982 LOSC and the 1944 Chicago Convention on Civil Aviation.[28] The gold standard in interpreting the term 'peaceful' as including passive aggression still remains as in the *Corfu Channel* Case.[29] Global indifference of the UN administrative structure to the SCS military build-up is very concerning. It is trite that peacetime assets can give rise to wartime liabilities:[30] where a breach of international law of peace occurs, State liability will arise. As war is outlawed under the UN Charter and peaceful dispute settlement is mandatory both under the UN Charter and the 1982 LOSC, the question of the legality of these actions causing war-like tensions in the SCS is in order, namely, the artificial islands and structures build-up of the various claimant States for military purposes, China's alleged militarization of their respective maritime reefs under *jus ad bellum* and under the 1982 LOSC;[31] and the likely establishment of a China air and maritime air defence identification zone over the SCS under the 1944 Chicago Convention and the 1982 LOSC.

One of the constituent ASEAN (1967) instruments is the 1976 ASEAN Treaty of Amity and Cooperation where 18 non-ASEAN States, including China, have acceded to the 1976 Treaty of Amity and Cooperation (Table 4.1).[32] The Treaty strives to settle non-peaceful situations and disputes between the States Parties through the good offices of the High Council, a governance institution under the Treaty. However, it has not been used so far.

Table 4.1 Non-ASEAN Countries That Have Acceded to the Treaty of Amity and Cooperation

Papua New Guinea	5 July 1989
China	8 October 2003
India	8 October 2003
Japan	2 July 2004
Pakistan	2 July 2004
Republic of Korea	27 November 2004
Russian Federation	29 November 2004
Mongolia	28 July 2005
New Zealand	28 July 2005
Australia	10 December 2005
France	13 January 2007
Timor-Leste	13 January 2007
Sri Lanka	30 July 2007
Bangladesh	30 July 2007
DPR Korea	24 July 2008
Colombia	10 November 2020
Cuba	10 November 2020
South Africa	10 November 2020

Source: Prepared by the author.

Several legally binding instruments have been adopted to maintain peace in the SCS such as the Declaration on the Code of Conduct and the imminent Code of Conduct, the –G-7 Joint Communique 2017,[33] the 2016 G-7 Hiroshima ministerial statement on maritime security in 2016,[34] and the 2015 G-7 leaders' statement.[35] The SCS actors include their Allies in a complicated labyrinth of international trade and security relationships. China calls these tensions as "indisputable disputes."[36] The SCS States are party to the Declaration of Conduct of Parties in the South China Sea (DOC) 2002 where two of its principles focus on exercising self-restraint and building trust and confidence.[37] China believes that some parties have deviated from the DOC with no follow-up of a solution. The 17th China-ASEAN Summit raised hopes that the 2015 consensus-based Code of Conduct for the SCS would be adopted but, unfortunately, has not materialized so far.[38] China, a State Party to the 1982 LOSC hopes to engage in a peaceful bilateral dispute resolution process with individual claimant States, as it has opted out of Part XV, 1982 LOSC.[39] China's (The PRC Government) Position Paper in Point 30 issued in December 2014 stated: "With regard to disputes concerning territorial sovereignty and maritime rights, China has always maintained that they should be peacefully resolved through negotiations between the countries directly concerned."[40] As the United States is not a party to the 1982 LOSC, China and the United States have engaged in confidence-building measures such as the April 2014 Code of Unplanned Encounters on the Sea[41] and in September 2015 Presidents Obama and Xi signed an agreement on rules for military air-to-air encounters.[42] China wanted the United States to remain neutral and to work with China based on "non-conflict and non-confrontation, mutual respect, and win-win cooperation." China upholds the principle of freedom of navigation and overflight for all nations under international law, upholds territorial sovereignty and is open to joint development of zones for oil and gas as it has already established a common fisheries zone with Vietnam in 2000.[43]

ASEAN is not a supranational regional organization with its own army, therefore it is not a regional military organization. However, if an SCS nation or external power uses its military power to carry out military or non-military actions in its bilateral or multilateral relationships in the SCS, it could be considered a military State in the SCS tensions. There is also state practice to be considered in the SCS tensions: old and new behaviours, a nation's foreign relations track record, stepping up of defence budgets, upgrading of the military, attempts at solving overlapping territorial claims by the use of force, provocation, territorial defence, movement of a country into the global maritime domain, successes and failures of bilateral trade engagements, different interpretations of international law leading to aggressive results, would, it is submitted, all add up to causing the SCS tensions. It is obvious that the incumbent ASEAN and non-ASEAN States Parties have failed to settle the SCS tensions under the 1976 Treaty attracting state liability for breach of its provisions. The EU are also unhappy with the SCS tensions.[44]

Legality of artificial islands and military equipment

There is an allegation that in the Spratlys, China has built artificial islands for alleged military expansion and sovereign control over Cuarteron Reef, Subi Reef, Mischief Reef, Johnson Reef, Hughes Reef, Gaven Reef and Fiery Cross Reef (floating and submerged installations) and installed airstrips and missile defence systems in violation of international norms.

Military equipment owned by States that are placed on sovereign natural islands or carried on board warships in times of peace are allowed under international law. However, where military equipment is placed on artificial islands and structures built up from reefs in contested foreign or overlapping EEZs, the rules of international law need to be examined. There are allegations that China has placed military equipment on artificial islands built up from reefs in the contested EEZs of the SCS claimant States. Is this action in breach of the UN Charter and the 1982 LOSC? A rule of customary international law,[45] Art. 2(4) of the UN Charter provides, "Members shall refrain in their international relations from the threat or use of force against the territorial integrity or political independence of any state, or in any other manner inconsistent with the purposes of the United Nations." The 1982 LOSC states that it is lawful to build artificial islands in national EEZs under Part V for economic purposes. However, to militarize an artificial island is unlawful under Article 301, 1982 LOSC as would be the conduct of nuclear weapons testing, if any, following the dicta in the *Nuclear Test* Cases.[46] Passive aggressive display of weapons on ships is permitted under the gold standards of the *Corfu Channel* Case, but military equipment is not to be stationed on disputed maritime features/artificial islands under the 1982 LOSC. The purpose of emplacement of military weapons and installations on artificial islands and structures in disputed areas could be interpreted as an intention to violate international law.

Demilitarisation

To promote demilitarisation, five factors need to be considered: (a) the perceived international recognition of the Spratlys after World War II and ensuing gap, (b) lack of a declaration of war in the SCS, (c) rules of war under the *jus ad bellum*, (d) the provisions of the 1982 LOSC, and (e) the Virginia Commentary.

Perceived international recognition of the Spratlys after World War II and ensuing gap

After World War II, following Japan's defeat in 1945 when it was stripped of the area it had occupied in the SCS, the post-war ownership of the islands remains disputed. Both Mainland China and Taiwan were accorded the area that Japan was stripped off based on the Cairo Declaration of 1943[47] and Potsdam Declaration of 1945,[48] where the instruments "adopted the position that rather than creating a 'void,' the areas have been restored to Chinese ownership." The areas here refer to Manchuria, Formosa and the Pescadores.[49] Western powers such as the US have not objected to these claims. In addition, Taiwan has occupied Taiping Island since 1946. Furthermore, the US has repeatedly sought Taiwan's permission to perform aerial surveys in the region between 1957 and 1961.[50] It needs to be determined whether the Pescadores and the Spratlys refer to the same geographical area.

No declaration of war in the SCS

Though there has been no declaration of war in the SCS by an SCS State or its Ally, the question is whether China's militarisation of the seven artificial islands in the SCS Spratlys is tantamount to an act of war, a breach of peace in the region[51] or an act of aggression under the rules of *jus ad bellum* and under the 1982 LOSC. After World War I (1914–1918), the use of force was a common method to solve disputes but not for long. The 1919 Covenant of the League of Nations[52] and the 1928 Treaty of Paris (the Kellogg-Briand Pact)[53] were well-intentioned to settle disputes peacefully but could not prevent World War II.[54] Finally, the 1945 UN Charter stopped the use of force to settle disputes and instead mandated the peaceful settlement of disputes. After World War II, following the new international political order and the establishment of the United Nations, the ICJ was established as the principal judicial organ of the United Nations. It succeeded the Permanent Court of International Justice (PCIJ) which was formally dissolved in April 1946 following the San Francisco Conference decision.[55] It was based on the

> principle of the sovereign equality of all peace-loving States, and open to membership by all such States, large and small, for the maintenance of international peace and security. The SCS States are parties to the UN Charter. The Charter stated that the Statute of the International Court of Justice was based upon that of the PCIJ. At the same time, the necessary steps were taken to transfer as much of the PCIJ's jurisdiction as possible to the International Court of Justice.

The first case decided by the ICJ was the *Corfu Channel* Case (United Kingdom *v.* Albania), Assessment of Compensation.[56] World Wars I and II have shown the world that at best the SCS States, except for Thailand, were drawn into the war as colonized territories and not as aggressors.

Jus ad bellum

The UN Charter or *jus ad bellum* has outlawed war for the settlement of disputes. Member States are mandated to abstain in their international relations from resorting to the threat or use of force. The UN Charter offers two exceptions to the use or threat of force: first, in the right of individual or collective self-defence under Article 51 of the UN Charter or under UN authorization under Chapter VII of the UN Charter, "Action With Respect to Threats to the Peace, Breaches of the Peace and Acts of Aggression," where collective force is allowed to be used.[57] Anticipatory self-defence, generally disallowed, is only permitted under the exigencies of the *SS Caroline Case*. Once war has broken out, international humanitarian law or *jus in bello* operates to regulate the conduct of all parties engaged in an armed conflict by protecting and assisting all victims of armed conflict to the greatest extent possible. Article 301 of the 1982 LOSC mandates the peaceful uses of the oceans. The precursor to the dispute settlement provisions of the 1982 LOSC is the 1958 Geneva Optional Protocol of Signature concerning the Compulsory Settlement of Disputes.[58]

Chapter VI of the UN Charter, "Pacific Settlement of Disputes," Articles 33–38, set out the provisions of dispute settlement. Article 33 states that States Parties to a dispute that endangers international peace and security shall start the peaceful dispute settlement process by negotiations and other forms of alternate dispute resolution such as enquiry, mediation, conciliation, arbitration, judicial settlement, resort to regional agencies or arrangements, or other peaceful means of their own choice. The Security Council will intervene and call upon the parties to settle their disputes peacefully when it deems it necessary. Article 33 is repeated in several other international instruments and conventions.[59] Under Article 34, the Security Council has the option to investigate any dispute or situation that is likely to lead to international friction or give rise to a dispute or endanger international peace and security. Members of the United Nations can draw the attention of the General Assembly or the Security Council to a dispute under Article 34. A similar right is also given to non-Member States under Article 35. Article 35(3) states that "the proceedings of the General Assembly in respect of matters brought to its attention under this Article will be subject to the provisions of Articles 11 and 12." In such scenarios, Article 36 empowers the Security Council to recommend an adjustment or an appropriate procedure for dispute settlement, and refer legal disputes to the International Court of Justice: "If the chosen dispute settlement mechanism fails, then Article 37 provides that the matter shall be referred to the Security Council. Where the Security Council deems that the continuation of the dispute is likely to endanger the maintenance of international peace and security, it shall decide whether to take action under Article 36 or to recommend such terms of settlement as it may consider appropriate." Notwithstanding the provisions of Articles 33–37, the terms of Article 38 states that the Security Council can make recommendations to settle the dispute peacefully.[60]

Articles 92–96 of the UN Charter refer to the establishment of a world court for the peaceful resolution of disputes. Article 95 of the UN Charter has explicitly provided for the freedom of entrustment by States of their differences to other tribunals according to an agreement. Article 66 of the Vienna Convention on the Law of Treaties 1969 deals with procedures for judicial settlement, arbitration and conciliation of issues and refers States to Article 33 of the UN Charter to settle a dispute. Under the terms of Article 66, where no solution has been reached within a 12-month period, any of the parties to a dispute concerning the application or interpretation of Article 53 or 64 of the Vienna Convention 1969, may submit the matter in writing to the ICJ for a decision, unless the parties consent to submit the dispute to arbitration. The other method is for the parties to a dispute concerning the application or interpretation of any other Article in Part V of the Vienna Convention of 1969, according to the procedure specified in the Annex to the Convention, to submit a dispute to the Secretary-General of the UN.

1982 LOSC

The 1982 LOSC is an instrument to promote the peaceful uses of the ocean under Articles 300 and 301 and compulsory peaceful dispute settlement under Part XV. Consequently, there are no dedicated set of provisions addressing security threats.[61] However, the Convention makes several references to the security of a coastal State in the following provisions:

- In the territorial sea in respect of innocent passage which a State may take action – Articles 19 (2), including Article 19 (2) (c), 19 (2) (d) and 19 (2) (l), and Article 25 (3);
- For the exercise of criminal and civil jurisdiction as found in Articles 27 (1) (a – d), 27 (2) – (5), and Article 28 (2), respectively, and (3) and provision on warships as in Article 30;
- In the Contiguous Zone, Article 33 (1);
- In Straits Used For International Navigation: Articles 34 (1) and (2) and for a violation of Articles 39, 42 (1) (a), and 42 (5) whilst being mindful of Article 44;
- Security of an archipelagic State: Article 52(2);
- Security within the EEZ: Articles 56(1)(c), 58, and 73, 79(4);
- Security on the high seas: Articles 87 (2), 94 (2), 94 (7), 97, 98, 99, 100, 105, 107, 108, 109, 110, 111, 113114, 115, and 119 (3);
- Article 105 on universal jurisdiction for piracy;
- Protection of the marine environment: Articles 192–196, 197–201, 202, 204, 206, 207–217, 218, 219, 220 *et al.*;
- Marine Scientific Research: As provided by Part XIII; and
- Security of a State Party: Article 302.

Article 123, 1982 LOSC calls for cooperation of States bordering enclosed or semi-enclosed seas such as the SCS but does not refer to regional security as a collective measure of regional cooperation. This is evident as the Article refers to the coordination of management, conservation, exploration and exploitation of the living resources of the sea; the implementation of their rights and duties with respect to the protection and preservation of the marine environment; the coordination of their scientific research policies and where appropriate joint programmes of scientific research in the area and invitation to other interested States or international organization to cooperate with them in furtherance of the provisions of this Article.

The 1982 LOSC prides itself in the strength of its Part XV Compulsory Dispute Settlement Provisions. Dispute settlement Part XV, Section 1 is an interplay of the 1982 LOSC and the 1945 UN Charter. The thrust of Section 1 is the legal requirement of States to settle their disputes by peaceful means using the means indicated in Article 33 of the UN Charter. In Article 279 of the 1982 LOSC, States Parties are reminded of their legal obligation to settle disputes between them concerning the interpretation or application of this Convention by peaceful means in accordance with Article 2(3), of the UN Charter and, to this end, to seek a solution by the means indicated in Article 33 of the UN Charter. The call of Article 279 is amplified in Article 282 of the 1982 LOSC that gives primacy to a State's obligation to settle disputes under general, regional or bilateral agreements:

> If the States Parties which are parties to a dispute concerning the interpretation or application of this Convention have agreed, through a general, regional or bilateral agreement or otherwise, that such dispute shall, at the request of any party to the dispute, be submitted to a procedure that entails a binding decision, that procedure shall apply in lieu of the procedures provided for in this Part unless the parties to the dispute otherwise agree.

This is a significant step for States bordering a region such as the SCS to adopt as, without the adoption of such a treaty, this legal requirement of the 1982 LOSC cannot be given effect to.

The Virginia Commentary

The Virginia Commentary states that the inspiration for the provisions on artificial islands, installations and structures, and for the establishment of safety zones around them, is found in the 1958 Convention on the Continental Shelf.[62] In the 1982 LOSC, coastal States have jurisdiction in the EEZ with regard to artificial islands, installations and structures, marine scientific research, and the protection and preservation of the marine environment, as well as other rights and duties provided for in the Convention.[63]Articles 60 and 80 provide for jurisdiction on artificial islands, installations and structures in the exclusive economic zone and on the continental shelf, respectively.[64] The rights of landlocked countries to resources beyond the territorial sea were also discussed at UNCLOS III under Item 7 – *Coastal State preferential rights or other non-exclusive jurisdiction over resources beyond the territorial sea.*[65]

7.7 Other rights and obligations

> Several other items in the list were relevant, including the rights and interests of land-locked countries in regard to living resources of the sea (item 9.4); the rights and interests of shelf-locked States and States with narrow shelves or short coastlines with regard to fisheries (item 10.2); artificial islands and installations (item 18); and settlement of disputes (item 21) (see Volume I, at 34).

Articles 58, 59 and 60 deal with the relationship between the rights and jurisdiction of the coastal State and of other States in the EEZ. Article 60 clarifies the authority of the coastal State with regard to artificial islands, installations and structures.[66] The package of the EEZ as discussed in the Second Committee included the establishment and use of artificial islands, installations and structures by coastal States in good faith, military and strategic uses of the zone; and the issue of residual rights in the zone.[67] Disputes regarding historic titles and bays come within the scope of the optional exception of Article 298, paragraph I, with its requirement of compulsory recourse to conciliation under Annex V. That provision leads to a binding third-party settlement in accordance with Part XV, Section 2, or, as an alternative, the conciliation procedure set out in Article 298, paragraph 1(a), and Annex V.[68] Finally, in semi-enclosed seas, the matter is a little more delicate as it is to be noted that in semi-enclosed seas States have tended to limit the extent of their claims to EEZs or exclusive fishery zones; in the Mediterranean Sea no State has yet claimed an EEZ. Where a State does not establish an EEZ or an exclusive fishery zone, all waters outside the territorial sea remain subject to the regime of the high seas. In those circumstances, jurisdiction over the natural resources of the continental shelf is governed by the provisions of Part VI.[69] The Virginia Commentary also offers insights into the evolution of the legal status of the EEZ.[70]

It is submitted that the point of concern is that though an artificial island is not an island under Article 121 of the 1982 LOSC and in public international law and cannot generate a territorial sea or an exclusive economic zone of its own, the maritime feature is still 'territory' that China has occupied regardless of an EEZ argument.[71] The legality of that title under other rules of international law are not assessed here.

Legality of an air defence identification zone

The establishment of a maritime and air defence identification zone during the early years of the Cold War was perceived as illegal.[72] The early origins of an Air Defence Identification Zone show that they have been used during the period of the Cold War by some States for purposes of national security. During this earlier period and extending to the eighties, these zones extended over maritime and aerial spaces whose sovereignty did not belong to the claimant States. By maritime and Air Defence Identification Zones are meant areas of airspace over land and water in which the ready identification, location and control of civil aircraft are required mainly in the interest of national security. They are to be distinguished from aerial buffer zones on land between neighbouring States which are usually within their land boundary. These zones are then listed and delineated geographically. Besides security, other objectives were considered too such as conservation of the resources of the continental shelf and protection from pollution. To attain these objectives, many States had extended limited aspects of their sovereignty seaward.

The customary international law before the 1944 Chicago Convention on Civil Aviation was that States exercised sovereignty over the airspace above their territory – mostly land and territorial waters that extended up to three nautical miles generally from the coastline. An example of such practice is by the United States of America which though it did not ratify the Paris Convention adopted the principle of "Aer Clausum" when Congress asserted sovereignty over US airspace in 1926. The US Air Commerce Act of 1926 states that "The Congress hereby declares that the Government of the United States has, to the exclusion of all foreign nations, complete sovereignty of the airspace over the lands and waters of the United States, including the Canal Zone." Notwithstanding the above, the 1944 Chicago Convention on Civil Aviation in Article 12 does not permit States to enact unilateral regulations effective over the high seas. Article 12 reads: "Over the high seas, the rules in force shall be those established under this Convention." Thus, the establishment and modification of rules of navigation in the airspace over the high seas is the exclusive domain of international regulation.

Since 1950, an increasing number of States have unilaterally asserted their limited right to control the airspace seaward of their shores. These States have established Air Defence Identification Zones extending in some cases several hundred miles seawards, within which aircraft must identify themselves to the coastal State and follow specified procedures. Failure to comply could well result in sanctions ranging from forced landing at an airfield of the coastal State and even to aerial attack. As far back as 1977, about 12–14 States were maintaining ADIZs extending seawards from their shores: they were Burma, Canada, Iceland, India, Japan, Korea, Oman, Philippines, Sweden, Taiwan, the United States, France and Vietnam.

The United States was the first nation to adopt an ADIZ extending over the high seas approximately 300 miles from the coastline. In September 1950, the Congress amended the Civil Aeronautics Act of 1938 to allow the establishment of security provisions regarding civil aircraft whenever the President determined such action to be required in the interest of the national security. Once such a Presidential determination had been made, implementation rested with the Secretary of Commerce. In December 1950, President Truman signed an Executive Order directing the Secretary of Commerce to exercise these powers and seven days later the Secretary adopted the regulations designating certain areas of airspace as ADIZ and prescribed rules applicable within them. The 1950 Regulations replaced an earlier 1938 Act and the 1963 Regulations replaced the 1950 Regulations.[73]

France established its ADIZ in 1956 during the Algerian insurgency against the French Rule.[74] The Zone extended some 70–90 miles from the Algerian Coast over the high seas. The French regulations required filing flight plans that contained information about the purpose of the flight and the identification of passengers and crew aboard the aircraft. Acceptance of the flight plan by French military authorities before the aircraft take-off was required and the regulations expressly authorized French interceptor aircraft to open fire on aircraft entering the zone without having complied with the regulations. Once Algeria gained independence, the zone was abolished. However, there was an incident that took place between France and the USSR before the French ADIZ was abolished. On 9 February 1961, French military aircraft intercepted and fired upon a Soviet civil aircraft carrying the President of the USSR bound for Morocco, while it was over the high seas but within the French ADIZ. The Soviet Statements following the incident clearly challenged the right of States unilaterally to establish identification zones over the high seas.

Canada followed the US example and adopted the Canadian Air Defence Identification Zone (CADIZ) in 1951 which was approximately 100 miles from the coastline. The CADIZ is based upon the statute which limits the powers of the Minister of Transport to the territorial waters of Canada. The Canadian rules too require the filing of flight plans and *en route* position reporting for any aircraft that will operate within the coastal ADIZ. The Canadian rules expressly provided that (1) a violation of these rules will render the pilot of an aircraft liable to in-flight interception by military interception aircraft; (2) the rules are applicable to military aircraft as well as civil aircraft; and (3) the rules apply to all aircraft about to enter the CADIZ so long as the path of flight is "toward the continental landmass of Canada" regardless of whether or not the destination is Canada. There was also a rule of CADIZ, which stated that it did not apply to aircraft below 3000 feet.[75]

Canadian ADIZ is defined as "Airspace of defined dimensions extending upwards from the surface of the earth within which certain rules for the security control of air traffic apply."[76] The main difference between the US ADIZ and the CADIZ was that the American Regulations were applicable only if the civil aircraft had the intention of entering the US territory and the Canadian regulations applied to any aircraft about to enter the path of flight which was towards Canada whether or not the destination was Canada. The legality of ADIZ and CADIZ can be questioned under (1) Article 12 of the 1944 Chicago Convention on Civil Aviation (considered earlier); (2) Article 24 of the 1958 Geneva Convention on the Territorial Sea and the Contiguous Zone (TSC); (3) Article 2 of the 1958 Geneva Convention on the High Seas; (4) Article 3 of the 1958 Geneva Convention on the Continental Shelf; and (5) Articles 87 and 89 of the 1982 LOSC.

Article 24 of the 1958 TSC reads:

1 In a zone of the high seas contiguous to its territorial sea, the coastal State may exercise the control necessary to:

   a prevent infringement of its customs, fiscal, immigration or sanitary regulations within its territory or territorial sea;
   b punish infringement of the above regulations committed within its territory or territorial sea.

2 The Contiguous Zone may not extend beyond 12nms from the baseline from which the breadth of the territorial sea is measured.

3 Where the coasts of two or more States are opposite or adjacent to each other, neither of the two States is entitled, failing agreement between them to the contrary, to extend its Contiguous Zone beyond the median line every point of which is equidistant from the nearest points on the baselines from which the breadth of the territorial seas of the two States is measured.

From the above provision, it is clear that Article 24 makes no mention of and does not include "security" as among the purposes for which the coastal States may exercise control in their contiguous zones. Article 16(3) of the 1958 TSC clearly limits security-related jurisdiction to the territorial sea, where impositions of control must be justified by circumstances in which suspension of innocent passage is "essential for the protection of its security."

Article 2 of the 1958 High Seas Convention provides:

> The high seas being open to all nations, no State may validly purport to subject any part of them to its sovereignty. Freedom of the high seas is exercised under the conditions laid down by these articles and by other rules of international law. It comprises, *inter alia*, both for coastal and non-coastal States:
>
> a Freedom of navigation;
> b Freedom of fishing;
> c Freedom to lay submarine cables and pipelines; and
> d Freedom to fly over the high seas.
>
> These freedoms and others which are recognized by the general principles of international law, shall be exercised by all States with reasonable regard to the interests of other States in their exercise of the freedom of the high seas.

The 1958 Convention on the High Seas is a companion convention to the 1958 TSC which deals with aircraft (freedom to fly over the high seas) and specifically proscribes States from subjecting any part of the airspace over the high seas to their sovereignty.

In Article 3 of the 1958 Continental Shelf Convention, the rights of the coastal States over the continental shelf do not affect the legal status of the superjacent waters as high seas or that of the air space above those waters. Therefore, it could be concluded that the airspace above the continental shelf is free space.

Article 87 of the 1982 LOSC states that the "high seas are open to all States, whether coastal or landlocked. Freedom of the high seas is exercised under the conditions laid down by this Convention and by other rules of international law." It comprises in sub-paragraph 1, *inter alia*, both for coastal and landlocked States: (a) freedom of navigation; (b) freedom of overflight; (c) freedom to lay submarine cables and pipelines subject to Part VI; (d) freedom to construct artificial islands and other installations permitted under international law, subject to Part VI; (e) freedom of fishing, subject to the conditions laid down in Section 2; and (f) freedom of scientific research, subject to Parts VI and XIII. Sub-paragraph 2 provides that

> These freedoms shall be exercised by all States with due regard for the interests of other States in their exercise of the freedom of the high seas and also with due regard for the rights under this Convention with respect to activities in the area.

Further, Article 88 states that the high seas shall be reserved for peaceful purposes and under Article 89 no State may validly purport to subject any part of the high seas to its sovereignty. Article 58 of the EEZ says that though the Convention has provided for an EEZ of 200 nm (measured from the baselines from which the breadth of the territorial sea is measured), it still guarantees the freedom of overflight as provided in Article 87 of the 1982 LOSC. Generally, under Article 38 of the 1982 LOSC aircraft enjoy the right to transit passage in the straits referred to in Article 37. Last but not least, Article 33, 1982 LOSC on the Contiguous Zone makes no mention whatsoever of the legal status of the airspace above its waters.

The above examination reveals two conclusions: first, there seems to be an inescapable conclusion that States are specifically prohibited from any unilateral attempts to adopt ADIZs to regulate air traffic in the airspace beyond their territorial seas and over the high seas for the purpose of "security" where they also ban such traffic and establish no-fly zones in non-territorial areas. Under international law, the question is whether these unilateral claims of limited sovereignty in the airspace over the high seas for special purpose jurisdiction appear to have a basis and whether any source in international law can validate the States' claims to partial jurisdiction in the airspace above the high seas for special purpose jurisdiction for protection under conventional or customary international law. It is therefore submitted that Chapter VII of the UN Charter has not referred to the establishment of an air defence identification zone for the protection of regional security. Neither has the Security Council passed a resolution authorizing such establishment in the SCS. There are no references to an ADIZ or MADIZ in the 1982 LOSC or the 1944 Chicago Convention. Therefore, to use ADIZ/MADIZ as an excuse to expand sovereignty over territory or subject civil aviation to coastal State jurisdiction when not intending to enter the territory of the coastal State is unlawful. Eight years ago, bearing in mind the unprecedented rise in piratical attacks in the SCS and taking into account UNSC resolutions to control piracy in the Gulf of Aden, Somalia,[77] I proposed rather cautiously that a limited purpose maritime and air defence identification zone be established over the SCS through a UNSC Resolution, for the limited purpose of controlling maritime piracy[78] as merchant marine were defenceless against pirates;[79] there were frequent vessel ownership changes with less responsible owners;[80] taking into account the human cost of piracy as seen in the Case of Captain Prem Kumar;[81] and the effects of recession and sub-standard shipping.[82] The limited purpose ADIZ could not be used to extend and legalise State aerial sovereignty over territory and could not be used to infringe the right of overflight under the 1944 Chicago Convention.[83]

Under Article 12 of the 1944 Chicago Convention, ICAO adopts flight rules which are published in Annex 2 – Rules of the Air over the high seas. These rules are to apply without exception, elsewhere they apply to the extent they do not conflict with the rules published by the subjacent State. States that adopt different rules in their sovereign airspace from that prescribed by ICAO are required to report them and they are then appended to Annex 2. Annex 2 is silent on an ADIZ. The ICAO recognize that the establishment of an ADIZ is related to some military or political reasons of national security, as follows:

1.1 Annex 4 – Aeronautical Charts and Annex 15 – Aeronautical Information Services define an air defence identification zone (ADIZ) as "special designated airspace of defined dimensions within which aircraft are required to comply with special identification and/or reporting procedures additional to those related to the provision of air traffic services". Annexes 4 and 15 also include requirements for the publication of information on an ADIZ, if established, in the Aeronautical Information Publication (AIP) and charts, and Annex 2 – Rules of the Air, includes Standards and Recommended Practices (SARPS) relating to the interception of aircraft. However, although the term ADIZ is listed and defined in ICAO documentation, there are no SARPS or procedures written for the establishment and operation of an ADIZ.
1.2 Although the International Air Transport Association (IATA) and the International Federation of Air Line Pilots' Associations (IFALPA) recognize the right of each State to ensure the integrity of its national security, the implementation of an ADIZ should be properly coordinated, and include accurate charting and specific instructions, clearly promulgated to ensure airlines and international civil aviation stakeholders are made aware of the requirements.
1.3 IATA and IFALPA also recognize that often the establishment of an ADIZ is driven by Military or political sensitivities attributed to national security. However, in these

instances, they would urge the applicable civil aviation authorities, to strongly advocate for minimizing the impact to international civil aviation during both the planning and implementation phase of a national ADIZ or any other non-ICAO military requirement or restriction as recommended in ICAO documentation on civil-military cooperation in air traffic management, which is under revision.

3 CONCLUSION 3.1 In light of the above, IATA and IFALPA invite the Conference to urge ICAO to: (a) ensure civil aviation authorities take into account the impact their military security measures may have on civil aviation during the planning phase of any airspace access requirement or procedure; (b) remind States that appropriate charting and the procedures associated with airspace access requirements, must be promulgated in accordance with the Standards and Recommended Practices (SARPs) found in Annexes 4 and 15 to the Convention; and (c) enhance the ICAO guidance on civil-military cooperation to include recommendations regarding rigorous testing of any new ADIZ/ security areas, prior to their effective date, to ensure that the associated procedures actually work.[84]

Conclusion

The war-like SCS tensions originated post-1982 LOSC. As the territorial dispute management framework of the SCS is weak and the dispute resolution framework of the 1976 ASEAN Treaty of Amity and Cooperation, the UN Charter and the 1982 LOSC have not been successfully used to ease the tensions, it could be argued that, *prime facie*, the Heads of States and Governments of the SCS and foreign States have already failed in their international duty to prevent a threat or breach of peace and security in the region. External States seem to offer no definitive solutions to the SCS conundrum. With regards to the three issues, *prima facie*, based on the law and alleged facts, it is probable to conclude that the impugned actions of all the States are in breach of the UN Charter and the 1982 LOSC. Further, China's militarisation of the seven reefs through the construction of artificial islands over the reefs in the high seas and positioning of military outposts there is causing much concern over the peace and stability of the region to the SCS States and external powers (Allies). This is unlawful as some incidents on the use of force have been reported. Likewise, no State is entitled to establish an SCS ADIZ over the EEZ or high seas under international law as States do not have sovereignty over these areas. Extenuating circumstances, if any, have not been demonstrated as suggested by the ICAO Working paper. While the rest of the SCS claimant States perhaps seek a multilateral binding instrument, a Code of Conduct, to control the SCS tensions, China maintains that the future lies in bilateral or multilateral negotiations. Inter-State negotiations are a sharp exercise, compelling experienced leaders and highly seasoned diplomats and negotiators to negotiate with China. Poor negotiations may entail a re-envisioning or withering away of state sovereignty. As China is keen on this process, it could be assumed that it is ready, but are the other SCS claimant States ready?[85] For this exercise, negotiators must equip themselves with knowledge on world war history with the accompanying policies of power, national sovereignty, appeasement and collective security[86] so that nation-building efforts of the SCS States from colonial domination and establishment of permanent sovereignty over their territories and resources are not in vain. Though there is no apparent overt arms race in the SCS for empire-building and enhancing military preparedness, it is possible that there might be a tangled web of clandestine alliances within the SCS States and their Allies who nevertheless intend to promote peace.[87]

Notes

1 At the start of this chapter, I wish to enter a caveat. The veracity of the facts regarding militarisation of the South China Sea, sourced from the internet, is uncertain. However, any errors in the interpretation of the law is mine. All the States bordering the South China Sea have their unique state practices of international law based on their culture and historical evolution. For uniqueness of state practice, see Xue Hanqin, *Chinese Contemporary Perspectives on International Law: History, Culture and International Law* (Hague Academy of International Law: 2012); and Edith Brown Weiss, *Establishing Norms in a Kaleidoscopic World: General Course on Public International Law* (Leiden: Brill, 2018).

2 Montego Bay, 10 December 1982. Entry into force: 16 November 1994, in accordance with Article 308(1). 1833 U.N.T.S. 397. All claimant States are States Parties to the 1982 LOSC. However, the United States has not ratified the Convention but recognizes its provisions as customary international law.

3 Chris Rahman and Martin Tsamenyi, "A Strategic Perspective on Security and Naval Issues in the South China Sea" *ODIL* 41: 315–333, 2010. Other non-traditional security threats, namely, piracy, and criminal activities like international terrorism, illicit drug trafficking, human smuggling and money-laundering, and environmental degradation, and refugee flows are not considered here.

4 [2013–2019] *The South China Sea Arbitration* (The Republic of Philippines v. The People's Republic of China).

5 An example of issues found in the suite of IMO/FAO related conventions are maritime terrorism and illegal, unreported and unregulated fishing respectively.

6 Adopted on 22 December 2007 by the United Nations General Assembly: UN document A/RES/62/215 of 14 March 2008. See also Paragraphs 53–79 therein on Maritime Safety and Security and Flag State Implementation and Preamble.

7 For the extraction of living marine genetic resources and non-living resources in the Common Heritage of Mankind of the SCS, it has been said that some SCS States have engaged in this practice quietly. The *Nauru* and *Tonga* cases have tremendous implications for the SCS States. The *Nauru* Case – *Responsibilities and Obligations of States Sponsoring Persons and Entities with Respect to Activities in the Area*, Advisory Opinion, ITLOS Case No 17, [2011] ITLOS Rep 10; and the *Tonga* Case - *Responsibilities and Obligations of States with Respect to Activities in the Area, 2.1* Advisory Opinion, 1 February 2011, ITLOS Reports 2011, p. 10.

8 Timelines, China's Maritime Disputes, https://www.cfr.org/timeline/chinas-maritime-disputes, 12 October 2020.

9 *Ibid.* Timeline, China's Maritime Disputes, https://www.cfr.org/timeline/chinas-maritime-disputes, 12 October 2020.

10 *Id.* Timelines, China's Maritime Disputes, https://www.cfr.org/timeline/chinas-maritime-disputes, 12 October 2020.

11 *Id.* Timeline: China's Maritime Disputes, https://www.cfr.org/timeline/chinas-maritime-disputes, 12 October 2020.

12 *Id.* Timelines, China's Maritime Disputes, https://www.cfr.org/timeline/chinas-maritime-disputes, 12 October 2020.

13 Associated Press, MARCH 26, 2018, "Philippines to Continue Patrols in the South China Sea"; Reuters, MARCH 9, 2017, "Chinese Ships Survey Philippines' Zone"; AP, NOVEMBER 21, 2016, "Philippines Announces Ban on Fishing in Scarborough Shoal" - Philippine President Rodrigo Duterte announced a ban on fishing in the South China Sea's Scarborough Shoal (AP); https://www.cfr.org/interactives/global-conflict-tracker?_utm_source=1-2-2#!/conflict/territorial-disputes-in-the-south-china-sea, 21 August 2018.

14 Reuters, MARCH 23, 2018, "Vietnam Halts South China Sea Drilling Project," https://www.cfr.org/interactives/global-conflict-tracker?_utm_source=1-2-2#!/conflict/territorial-disputes-in-the-south-china-sea, 21 August 2018.

15 *Associated Press*, Sat 27 June 2015 08.11 BST, China proceeds with building artificial islands on reefs claimed by Philippines, https://www.theguardian.com/world/2015/jun/27/china-proceeds-with-building-artificial-islands-on-reefs-claimed-by-philippines, 21 January 2020; and China / Diplomacy, Beijing to restore coral reefs 'damaged by island building' in South China Sea, Liu Zhen in Beijing, Published: 9:05pm, January 2, 2019, https://www.scmp.com/news/china/diplomacy/article/2180426/beijing-restore-coral-reefs-damaged-island-building-south-china, 21 January 2020.

16 At the 2018 Shangri-La Dialogue, U.S. Secretary of Defense Jim Mattis highlighted China's militarisation of the South China Sea before an audience of Asian security officials and independent defense experts. See U.S. Calls on China to Remove Missiles From South China Sea Artificial Islands By Ankit Panda. November 10, 2018, https://thediplomat.com/2018/11/us-calls-on-china-to-remove-missiles-from-south-china-sea-artificial-islands/, 9 December 2019.

17 Has China Withdrawn A Long-Range Missile Battery From Woody Island? Satellite imagery indicates that a HQ-9 battery was taken off Woody Island on or around July 10. By Franz-Stefan Gady, July 26, 2016. https://thediplomat.com/2016/07/has-china-withdrawn-a-long-range-missile-battery-from-woody-island/, 9 December 2019. See IHS Jane's Defense Weekly, July 21, 2019. For further explanation of China's actions and images on July 8 on HQ 9 air defense system, July 9, July 10, see IHS Jane's Defense Weekly.

18 See also Reuters, MAY 9, 2018, "Vietnam Asks China to Withdraw Military Equipment from South China Sea"; See also MAY 4, 2018, "U.S., Australia Warn China Over Militarizing Islands." "Chinese Navy Shows Strength in South China Sea"; Reuters, MARCH 27, 2018, "Chinese Navy Conducts Large-Scale Drills in South China Sea"; https://www.cfr.org/interactives/global-conflict-tracker?_utm_source=1-2-2#!/conflict/territorial-disputes-in-the-south-china-sea, 21 August 2018.

19 CNN, MAY 21, 2018, "China Lands Bombers on South China Sea Island"; *Wall Street Journal*, December 15, 2016, "Chinese Antiaircraft Weapons Reported on Disputed Islands"; https://www.cfr.org/interactives/global-conflict-tracker?_utm_source=1-2-2#!/conflict/territorial-disputes-in-the-south-china-sea, 21 August 2018.

20 China Protests as G7 Leaders Call for 'Demilitarisation' of East, South China Seas: The G-7 leaders call on parties in the South China Sea to demilitarize features. By Ankit Panda, May 29, 2017, https://thediplomat.com/2017/05/china-protests-as-g7-leaders-call-for-demilitarisation-of-east-south-china-seas/.

21 Source: https://www.youtube.com/watch?v=SE8qx8mNe1M.

22 South China Morning Post, June 27, 2018, 'Mattis in China Amid Tensions Over Waterways, Taiwan'; *NBC News*, May 28, 2018, 'Confrontation Over FONOP in South China Sea'; *Wall Street Journal*, May 24, 2018, "U.S. Rescinds China's Invitation to Join Military Exercise in the Pacific"; Reuters, March 24, 2018, "U.S. Navy Conducts FONOP in South China Sea"; Reuters, August 10, 2017, "United States Conducts Freedom of Navigation Operation in South China Sea"; https://www.cfr.org/interactives/global-conflict-tracker?_utm_source=1-2-2#!/conflict/territorial-disputes-in-the-south-china-sea, 21 August 2018.

23 Bloomberg, March 16, 2018, "Chinese Hackers Target U.S. Firms Doing Business in South China Sea"; see also Asia Times, March 15, 2018, "U.S. Aircraft Carrier and Japanese Navy Conduct Drills in South China Sea"; Channel News Asia, March 5, 2018, "U.S. Aircraft Carrier Visits Vietnam"; Guardian, July 27, 2017, "UK to Sail New Aircraft Carriers in Contested Asian Waters"; Washington Post, July 3, 2017, "China To Increase Patrols in South China Sea"; Wall Street Journal, May 25, 2017, "U.S. Conducts First South China Sea Patrol Under Trump"; *New York Times*, December 20, 2016, "China Returns Captured U.S. Drone"; Reuters, December 14, 2016. "U.S. Ready to 'Confront' China Over Sea, Admiral Says"; https://www.cfr.org/interactives/global-conflict-tracker?_utm_source=1-2-2#!/conflict/territorial-disputes-in-the-south-china-sea, 21 August 2018.

24 US Calls on China to Remove Missiles From South China Sea Artificial Islands By Ankit Panda November 10, 2018, https://thediplomat.com/2018/11/us-calls-on-china-to-remove-missiles-from-south-china-sea-artificial-islands/, 9 December 2019.

25 US Calls on China to Remove Missiles From South China Sea Artificial Islands, Ankit Panda 2018, *The Diplomat*, https://thediplomat.com/2018/11/us-calls-on-china-to-remove-missiles-from-south-china-sea-artificial-islands/, 21 January 2020.

26 San Francisco, 26 June 1945. Entry into force: 24 October 1945, in accordance with Article 110, 557 U.N.T.S. 143.

27 "Geneva I" - Geneva Convention for the Amelioration of the Condition of the Wounded and Sick in Armed Forces in the Field, 12 August 1949, 75 U.N.T.S. 31; "Geneva II" - Geneva Convention for the Amelioration of the Condition of Wounded, Sick and Shipwrecked Members of Armed Forces at Sea, 12 August 1949, 75 U.N.T.S. 85; "Geneva III" - Geneva Convention Relative to the Treatment of Prisoners of War, 12 August 1949, 75 U.N.T.S. 135; "Geneva IV" - Geneva Convention Relative to the Protection of Civilian Persons in Times of War, 12 August 1949, 75 U.N.T.S. 287;

"Protocol I" - Protocol Additions to the Geneva Conventions of 12 August 1949, and Relating to the Protection of Victims of International Armed Conflicts, 8 June 1977, 1125 U.N.T.S. 3; "Protocol II" - Protocol II Additional to the Geneva Conventions of 12 August 1949 and Relating to the Protection of Victims of Non-International Armed Conflicts, 8 June 1977, 1125 U.N.T.S. 609; "Protocol III" - Protocol III Additional to the Geneva Conventions of 12 August 1949, and Relating to the Adoption of an Additional Distinctive Emblem, 8 December 2005, No U.N. T. S. citation; can be found on the ICRC website at: http://www.icrc.org/ihl.nsf/FULL/615.

28 Convention No 102. Chicago, 7 December 1944. 296 U.N.T.S. 1948.

29 1949 ICJ reports at 4.

30 ARGUMENT, China's South China Sea Militarization Has Peaked: Artificial islands are becoming more trouble than they're worth. BY STEVEN STASHWICK | August 19, 2019, 4:12 pm, https://foreignpolicy.com/2019/08/19/chinas-south-china-sea-militarization-has-peaked/ 9 December 2019.

31 ICRC, https://www.icrc.org/en/document/what-are-jus-ad-bellum-and-jus-bello-0, 27 December 2019.

32 Bali, Indonesia, 24 February 1976, 1025 U.N.T.S. 15, 316, http://www.aseansec.org/1217.htm, 30 August 2018.

33 2017 – Following two days of meetings in Taormina, Italy, on 26 and 27 May 2017, the Heads of State and Government from the Group of Seven (G-7) countries issued a joint communiqué that addressed a range of international issues. This year's communiqué, like last year's, drew attention to ongoing maritime tensions in the Asia-Pacific, focusing specifically on the East and South China Seas.

34 This statement called on parties not to engage in land reclamations including large scale ones, building of outposts, as well as their use for military purposes; acknowledged China's completion of the construction of artificial islands and their subsequent conversion into dual-use facilities; and China's dissatisfaction with the G-7's communiqué, according to Chinese Foreign Ministry spokesperson Lu Kan who stressed that Beijing sought to solve disputes through peaceful negotiations.

35 See Articles 13–16 of the 1976 Treaty of Amity and Co-operation in South-East Asia on preventing a dispute from arising and in case, the dispute has arisen, to settle it peacefully and accept offers of assistance where forthcoming through the High Council. Article 15 states direct negotiations are to be followed by the High Council intervention and recommendation to settle through good offices, mediation, inquiry or conciliation. The High Council can also constitute itself into a committee of mediation, inquiry or conciliation. Article 17 refers States to Article 33 (1) of the UN Charter. The 2015 G-7 Leaders Statement mentioned land reclamation in the South China Sea but not military activities.

36 Michael Yahuda, "China's New Assertiveness in the South China Sea", (2013) 22(81) *Journal of Contemporary China* 446–459. Published online: 02 January 2013, doi: 10.1080/10670564.2012.748964.

37 How does China Envisage Management and Resolution of the Disputes in the South China Sea? http://isdp.eu/publication/understanding-chinas-position-south-china-sea-disputes/, 16 December 2019.

38 Saving the China-ASEAN South China Sea Code of Conduct, https://thediplomat.com/2019/06/saving-the-china-asean-south-china-sea-code-of-conduct/, 21 January 2020.

39 China signed the Convention on 10 December 1982 and formally ratified the Convention on 7 June 1996.

40 The South China Sea Issue: Position Paper of the Government of the People's Republic of China on the Matter of Jurisdiction in the South China Sea Arbitration Initiated by the Republic of the Philippines, 7 December 2014, https://www.fmprc.gov.cn/nanhai/eng/snhwtlcwj_1/t1368895.htm, 21 January 2020.

41 USNI News, https://news.usni.org/2014/06/17/document-conduct-unplanned-encounters-sea, 21 January 2020. The document considered non-legally binding was signed by 21 Pacific nations at the 14th Western Pacific Naval Symposium in Qingdao, China to prevent tensions from escalating in the SCS.

42 Reuters, Technology News, 26 September 2015 / 12:30 am / 4 Years Ago. U.S., China agree on rules for air-to-air military encounters by Phil Stewart, https://www.reuters.com/article/us-usa-china-pentagon/u-s-china-agree-on-rules-for-air-to-air-military-encounters-idUSKCN0RP1X520150925, 21 January 2020.

43 Agreement on Fishery Co-operation in the Tonkin Gulf between the Government of the People's Republic of China and the Government of the Socialist Republic of Vietnam. This Agreement was signed in Beijing on 25 December 2000, and written in Chinese and Vietnamese, both of which are equally authentic. http://extwprlegs1.fao.org/docs/pdf/bi-51872.pdf, 21 January 2020.

44 https://chinapower.csis.org/, 16 December 2019; EU criticises 'militarisation' of South China Sea, EURACTIV.com with AFP August 5, 2019, https://www.euractiv.com/section/china/news/eu-criticises-militarisation-of-south-china-sea/, 16 December 2019; South China Morning Post, China / Diplomacy, European militaries 'will do more to counter assertive China' in Indo-Pacific - EU leaders to discuss ten proposals to seek balanced relationship with China, while President Xi Jinping is due to travel to Italy and France, https://www.scmp.com/news/china/diplomacy/article/3002319/european-militaries-will-do-more-counter-assertive-china-indo, 16 December 2019.

45 *Case Concerning Military and Paramilitary Activities in and against Nicaragua* (Merits) (Nicaragua v United States) Judgment, I.C.J. Reports 1986, p. 727.

46 *Nuclear Tests* (Australia v. France), Judgrnent, I.C.J. Reports 1974, p. 253.

47 "The Cairo Declaration," 26 November 1943, History and Public Policy Program Digital Archive, Foreign Relations of the United States, Diplomatic Papers, The Conferences at Cairo and Tehran, 1943 (Washington, DC: United States Government Printing Office, 1961), 448–449. https://digitalarchive.wilsoncenter.org/document/122101, 21 January 2020.

48 Proclamation Defining Terms for Japanese Surrender, Issued, at Potsdam, July 26, 1945, https://www.ndl.go.jp/constitution/e/etc/c06.html, 21 January 2020.

49 Pescadores: In Pinyin Peng·hu - An island group in Taiwan Strait between the western coast of Taiwan and mainland China. The name, meaning "fishermen's islands," was given to the group by the Portuguese in the 1500s. Ceded to Japan in 1895 and returned to China after World War II, the islands have been administered by Taiwan since 1949. https://www.yourdictionary.com/pescadores, 27 December 2019.

50 Source: Institute for Security and Development Policy, Understanding China's Position on the South China Sea Disputes, ISDP, BACKGROUNDER June, 2016, p. 8, http://isdp.eu/publication/understanding-chinas-position-south-china-sea-disputes/, 16 December 2019. See also same article for How Does China View Responsibility for the Escalation of Disputes? How does China Envisage Management and Resolution of the Disputes in the South China Sea?

51 See, for example, the Austro-Hungarian Declaration of War with Serbia dated Vienna, July, 28, 1914 (WWI), and Imperial Germany's Declaration of War against Russia, dated July 19 (August 1), 7.10 pm by F. Pourtales. At the first session of the 65th Congress, House of Representatives, Report No 1, (April 4, 1917) the War with the Imperial German Government was passed.

52 Signed: 28 June 1919, Parties: League of Nations members, Effective: 10 January 1920, Expiration: 20 April 1946.

53 Officially, General Treaty for Renunciation of War as an Instrument of National Policy was signed on 27 August 1928 and effective on 24 July 1929.

54 See Article 14 of the Covenant of the League of Nations.

55 The San Francisco Conference, also known as the United Nations Conference on International Organization took place from 25 April 1945 to 26 June 1945 in San Francisco, California, United States of America. The Conference adopted the Charter of the United Nations, San Francisco, 26 June 1945. EIF: 24 October 1945, in accordance with Article 110.

56 [1949] ICJ Rep. 4.

57 International Committee of the Red Cross, https://www.icrc.org/en/document/what-are-jus-ad-bellum-and-jus-bello-0, 12 December 2019.

58 The Optional Protocol of Signature concerning the Compulsory Settlement of Disputes 1958 was done at Geneva on 29 April 1958. It entered into force on 30 September 1962, 450 U.N.T.S. 169 but did not muster a sufficient number of ratifications to enter into force. This Protocol underscores the settlement of disputes arising under any three of the four 1958 Geneva Conventions on the law of the sea under the compulsory jurisdiction of the ICJ provided the party to the dispute is a party to the Optional Protocol.

59

i Paragraph 15 of the Declaration of Principles Governing the Sea- Bed;
ii Article 65 (3) of the 1969 Vienna Convention on the Law of Treaties;
iii Article 9 of the 1958 Convention on Fishing and Conservation of Living Resources of the High Seas; and
iv Article 4 of the 1947 Treaty between Turkey and Jordan.

60 Without prejudice to the provisions of Articles 33–37, the Security Council may, if all the parties to any dispute so request, make recommendations to the parties with a view to a pacific settlement of the dispute.
61 Stuart Kaye, "Freedom of Navigation in a Post 9/11 World: Security and Creeping Jurisdiction" in David Freestone, Richard Barnes and David Ong (eds.), *The Law of the Sea Progress and Prospects* (Oxford University Press: Oxford; 2006) at pp. 356–361.
62 Virginia Commentary, UNCLOS, University of Virginia, Center for Oceans Law and Policy, p. 505.
63 Virginia Commentary, p. 491.
64 Virginia Commentary, p. 492.
65 Virginia Commentary, V. 10 at pp. 497–498.
66 Virginia Commentary, p. 505.
67 Virginia Commentary, V. 32, pp. 508 and 509.
68 Virginia Commentary, V. 25, p. 507.
69 Virginia Commentary, p. 510.
70 Virginia Commentary, pp. 502–504, fn. 31 for a discussion on the legal status of the EEZ, not as high seas nor territorial sea but as a *sui generis* zone is set out. See 1 *CONF.62/C.21L.89/Rev.1* (1975), paras. 5 and 16, IV Off. Rec. 196 (Rapporteur, Second Committee); p. 502 PART V, for "residual rights" of freedom of navigation and communication enjoyed by other nations and coastal state rights to resources. And paras 35 and 36, for the efforts of the Castaneda Group (on articles 44–47 of the RSNTI Part II).
71 M.N. Shaw, Territory in International Law, Volume 13 December 1982, pp. 61–91; doi: 10.1017/S0167676800003019 Published online by Cambridge University Press: 07 July 2009 for the link between territorialty, a State and international legal personality.
72 See Ian Brownlie, *Principles of Public International Law*, Seventh Edition, (Oxford University Press: New York: 2008) at pp. 197 and 198; Shabtai Rosenne, *The Perplexities of Modern International Law*, The Hague Academy of International Law (Martinus Nijhoff: Leiden: 2004) at pp. 242, 313 and 316; Vaughn Lowe, *International Law* (Oxford University Press: Oxford: 2007) at pp. 151–152; Christian J. Tams, *Enforcing Obligations Erga Omnes in International Law* (Cambridge University Press: Cambridge: 2005) at pp. 225–226; and Malcolm Evans, *International Law*, Second Edition, (Oxford University Press: Oxford; 2006).
73 US ADIZ regulations are found in the Code of Federal Register, Parts 99 and 45. Part 99 - Eff. 03/30/2004. Part 45 Amendment No. 45-22 - Eff. 04/27/2001, Part 45 Amendment No. 45-25 - Eff. 11/13/2007, Site visited on http://rgl.faa.gov/Regulatory_and_Guidance_Library/rgFAR.nsf/MainFrame?OpenFrameSet, 22 January 2020. Sec.99.3-Definitions. *Air defense identification zone* (ADIZ) means an area of airspace over land or water in which the ready identification, location, and control of all aircraft (except for Department of Defense and law enforcement aircraft) is required in the interest of national security. [Doc. No. FAA–2001–10693, 66 FR 49822, September 28, 2001, as amended at 69 FR 16755, March 30, 2004].
74 Peter A. Dutton, "Caelum Liberum: Air Defense Identification Zones Outside Sovereign Airspace", (2009) 103(4) *The American Journal of International Law* 691–709.
75 *ADIZ* 602.145 (1) This section applies in respect of aircraft before entering into and while operating within the ADIZ, the dimensions of which are specified in the *Designated Airspace Handbook. ESCAT Plan* (amended 2002/09/24) 602.146 (1) This section applies in respect of aircraft before entering into and while operating within Canadian domestic airspace or the ADIZ. Source: https://laws-lois.justice.gc.ca/eng/regulations/sor-96-433/page-94.html, accessed on 28 October 2011.
76 See Designated Airspace Handbook, Published under the authority of the Minister of Transport, Issue No 226, effective 0901Z 20 October 2011, (Next Issue: 15 December 2011), Caution –http://www.navcanada.ca/ContentDefinitionFiles/Publications/AeronauticalInfoProducts/DAH/DAH_current_EN.pdf, site accessed on 28 October 2011; current version: Designated Airspace Handbook, Published under the authority of the Minister of Transport, Issue No 280, effective 0901Z 30 January 2020 to 0901Z 26 March 2020, https://www.navcanada.ca/EN/products-and-services/Documents/DAH_Next_En.pdf, site accessed on 22 January 2020 – it is updated every 56 days in its entirety.
77 Mary George, Can a limited ADIZ/MADIZ be established over the SCS? Diplomatic Academy of Vietnam, 2011, Hanoi, Vietnam.
78 See also, Interim guidance on use of privately contracted armed security personnel on board ships agreed by IMO Maritime Safety Meeting, Maritime Safety Committee (MSC), 89th session: 11–20 May 2011, Briefing: 27, 20 May 2011.

79 See Sam Bateman, *The Hijacking of the MV Zirku: A Case Study in Shipping Security*, RSIS Commentaries, No. 58/2011 dated 15 April 2011.

80 *Ibid.*

81 See Sam Bateman, *Sub-standard Ships and Human Costs of Piracy: The Case of Captain Prem Kumar*, RSIS Commentaries No. 130/2011 dated 7 September 2011.

82 See Euan Graham, *Shipping Glut Portends Piracy, Safety Risks*, RSIS Commentaries No. 143/2011 dated 7 October 2011.

83 See, the UNSC Resolutions on Somalian piracy in the Gulf of Aden, namely, Resolutions 1814 (2008), 1816 (2008), 1838 (2008), 1844 (2008), 1846 (2008), and 1851 (2008). For Australia and New Zealand state practices on the establishment of maritime / air defence identification zones and protests from Indonesia and Malaysia, see Gillian Triggs, *International Law: Contemporary Principles and Practices* (LexisNexis Butterworths: Australia: 2006) at p. 329. For Jurisdiction over flags of convenience: see *Molvan* v *AG for Palestine* [1948] AC 351; *Arrest Warrant of 11 April 2000 (Democratic Republic of Congo* v *Belgium*, Preliminary Objections and Merits, Judgment, ICJ Reports 2002 at p. 3. Separate Opinion of Judges Higgins, Kooijmans and Buergenthal, para 61. Separate Opinion of President Guillaume, para 5.

84 International Civil Aviation Organization WORKING PAPER AN-Conf/13-WP/2951 28/9/18, Thirteenth Air Navigation Conference Montréal, Canada, 9 to 19 October 2018, Committee A, Agenda Item 3: Enhancing the global air navigation system 3.4: Civil/military cooperation. Establishment of Military Requirements and Restrictions on International Civil Aviation (Presented by the International Air Transport Association (IATA) and the International Federation of Air Line Pilots' Associations (IFALPA)), https://www.icao.int/Meetings/anconf13/Documents/WP/wp_295_en.pdf, 21 January 2020.

85 The South China Sea Conundrum for the United States: What is left for the United States to do about China's militarization of the South China Sea? By Robert Farley, June 05, 2018, https://thediplomat.com/2018/06/the-south-china-sea-conundrum-for-the-united-states/ 9 December 2019.

86 In the Pacific Ocean, see for example, Japan's bombardment of Pearl Harbor and experience in the Battle of Midway. See Luciano Tosi, "The League of Nations: An International Relations Perspective", (March 2017) 22(1) *Uniform Law Review* 148–157, doi: 10.1093/ulr/unw055. See also Shabtai Rosenne, Note 111 at p. 11.

87 America's history in promoting peace: UNOG Library on League of Nations, https://libraryresources.unog.ch/leagueofnationsarchives, 25 November 2019. It has been said that it is the past actions of the Allied Powers in WWI that triggered reactions within the SCS States, including the reason perhaps why China turned to communism and Japan turned to Hitler.

PART II

Sovereignty and maritime entitlements

5

THE TERRITORIAL SOVEREIGNTY DISPUTES IN THE SOUTH CHINA SEA

Ted L. McDorman

Introduction

The core of the conflict amongst the coastal States of the South China Sea – Brunei, the People's Republic of China/the Republic of China, Malaysia, the Philippines and Viet Nam – involves the overlapping territorial sovereignty claims of these States to the various islets, reefs, and low-tide elevations (insular features) in the region that are estimated to number between 150 and 180.[1] The principal concentration of these features is referred to as the Spratly Islands. A note can also be made of the Paracel Islands, Macclesfield Bank and Scarborough Reef to the north of the Spratlys.

The dynamics of the South China Sea territorial sovereignty disputes have changed dramatically in the wake of the *South China Sea Arbitration*.[2] The pre-*Arbitration* imagery of the barren, disputed insular feature with the two forlorn soldiers ostensibly asserting sovereignty has changed to built-up features with significant populations, airfields, defence facilities, hospitals, etc.[3] Added to this, has been the expansion of the navies and coast guards by the regional States[4] and the continuing issues regarding vessel navigational rights within the South China Sea.[5]

The overall picture is one of the entrenched positions with little room for compromise or flexibility to manage the disputes.

Historically, the Spratlys and adjacent features were of minimal practical importance to the regional States and/or the Colonial powers in residence in the region.[6] This changed in the late 1960s and early 1970s for a combination of reasons that includes: the "cold-war" climate within the South China Sea region which led to an emphasis on military scenarios and defence which might be enhanced by the use of the South China Sea islets, intra-regional rivalry, and growing regional State nationalism.[7]

Of particular importance were the negotiations from the 1960s to the 1980s of the United Nations Convention on the Law of the Sea[8] (LOS) and the consequent legal expansion of exclusive coastal State jurisdiction over both the living and mineral resources (oil and gas) in adjacent waters. As a result of the new law of the sea, territorial sovereignty over small insular features could lead to jurisdictional authority over large areas of the oceans and seafloor and the resources therein.[9] The LOS Convention draws a distinction between an island, that is entitled to an adjacent 12 nm territorial sea, 200 nm exclusive economic zone (EEZ) and continental shelf beyond 200 nm, and a rock, that is only entitled to a 12 nm territorial sea.[10] It was the potential for oil and gas development in South China that is put forward as the major factor underlying the regional States staking out their territorial sovereignty claims to the insular features in the South China Sea.[11]

Efforts by the regional States to peacefully manage the conflict/disputes commenced in the late 1980s. The 2002 Declaration on the Conduct of the Parties in the South China Sea involving the Association of Southeast Asian Nations (ASEAN) and the People's Republic of China[12] was, for a short time, an effective check on the escalation of both the territorial sovereignty and maritime disputes.[13] The 2002 Declaration noted "that the adoption of a code of conduct in the South China Sea would further promote peace and stability in the region."[14] To date, discussions to establish a legally-binding code of conduct (COC) that might contain wording that calms or deals in some manner with the territorial sovereignty disputes have been unsuccessful.[15]

The first section below provides some political and legal context respecting territorial sovereignty and territorial sovereignty disputes. This is followed by a section that sets out the formal statements and claims made in documents submitted by the regional States related to or in response to the 2009 Joint Submission by Malaysia/Viet Nam,[16] the 2009 Partial Submission by Viet Nam regarding the Northern Area,[17] and the 2019 Partial Submission by Malaysia,[18] submitted to, Commission on the Limits of the Continental Shelf (CLCS), a body created pursuant to the LOS Convention.[19] The primary purpose of these submissions was to indicate and provide evidence in support of claimed areas of the continental shelf beyond 200 nm in the South China Sea.

It is acknowledged that the three CLCS Submissions and the consequent diplomatic correspondence does not necessarily provide a full picture of the extent of national territorial sovereignty claims or the evidence supporting the claims of the various States.[20] Nevertheless, as communications to a United Nations body, they have the benefit of unquestioned authority and authenticity. Moreover, it was the 2009 Joint Malaysia/Viet Nam Submission[21] and the 2009 Viet Nam Partial Submission for the Northern Area[22] that triggered China's communication to the United Nations that, for the first time, formally presented to the international community the U-shaped nine-dashed line.[23] The relative calm achieved by the 2002 Joint Declaration[24] was shattered and the seeds of the *South China Sea Arbitration*,[25] which included arguments about territorial sovereignty, were sown.

A reason for care respecting the claims of the States, the supporting evidence and a legal evaluation is highlighted in the 2017 article by historian Bill Hayton, titled: "When Good Lawyers Write Bad History: Unreliable Evidence and the South China Sea Territorial Dispute,"[26] which calls into question the reliability of evidence presented by some international lawyers. Mindful of the above, this contribution is not primarily focused on a legal evaluation of the claims by the South China Sea stakeholders, rather the goal is to provide a picture of the region's territorial sovereignty disputes and their legal and political context.

Territorial sovereignty

Territorial sovereignty is an international law construct. Vaughn Lowe comments that "The concept of the State is rooted in the concept of control of territory" and that "the control over the activities in a territory is captured by the concept of sovereignty."[27] Malcolm Shaw states that "The essence of territorial sovereignty is contained in the notion of title."[28] As indicated by James Crawford, "title prevails over occupation."[29] This proposition is important to counter the idea that "might makes right" such that, just because a piece of land is occupied by State A does not mean State B is not the rightful sovereign.

Not surprisingly States guard and protect their territories from uninvited incursions or challenges by other States. Where incursions or challenges occur, the issue is labelled as a territorial sovereignty dispute which is essentially conflicting claims of title by States to the territory.

Beyond the utilitarian motives of resource wealth and national defence for the competing territorial sovereignty claims, there are most often other motivations that are captured by the term "domestic politics" which, amongst other things, encapsulates the arguments and conviction within a State that the territory in question is unquestionably and rightfully under its sovereignty.[30]

The globe is populated with numerous territorial sovereignty disputes, many of which involve insular features. The nationalistic nature of the disputes makes a negotiated resolution politically difficult, further unhelped by the usual necessity of a winner and a loser. Most States confronted with a territorial sovereignty dispute question why they should negotiate, go to Court or otherwise put in jeopardy their sovereign territory, it is ours.

As will be further detailed below, in situations where there are competing territorial sovereignty claims, States often indicate the basis of their claim and may provide evidence to support their assertions and, frequently at the same time, point out the weaknesses of the other State's claim. It is an interesting phenomenon of international relations that States inevitably resort to legal arguments and supporting evidence, however transparent or untenable, to justify or legitimize their territorial sovereignty claims.

Despite, or perhaps because of, the centrality of territorial sovereignty to States and the international legal and political system, the international law applicable to assess the validity of territorial sovereignty claims is complex with there often being reference to differing modes of acquisition.[31]

Over the years there have been a number of times when States, confronted with a territorial sovereignty dispute, have placed the matter before an international court or tribunal to resolve the matter by applying international law to assess which of the two States has tittle to the territory in question. These cases have helped to develop the law regarding territorial sovereignty. A significant number of the territorial sovereignty cases have involved insular features.[32] Two of the recent cases involving insular features were between South China Sea States: the 2002 *Indonesia/Malaysia Case Concerning Sovereignty over Pulau Ligitan and Pulau Sipadan*[33] and the 2008 *Malaysia/Singapore Case Concerning Sovereignty over Pedra Branca/Pulau Batu Puteh, Middle Rocks and South Ledge.*[34]

It is not the intention here to review the international case law on territorial sovereignty, however, several of the comments and findings by the International Court of Justice in the 2002 *Indonesia/Malaysia Case* and the 2008 *Malaysia/Singapore Case* may have some relevance in the South China Sea. It is important to note that, unlike most of the insular features in the South China Sea, the two *Cases* dealt with insular features located close to shore.

The 2002 Indonesia/Malaysia Case

The two features in question in the 2002 *Case*, Ligitan and Sipadan, located in the Celebes Sea, were described by the Court as being "small" with the larger feature having an area of approximately 0.13 sq. km. and both having trees and vegetation.[35] The two features are close to the Borneo coast.

Each State presented detailed arguments supporting their claimed title to the features. The principal Indonesian argument was that the 1891 Treaty between Great Britain and the Netherlands, which divided islands, included Ligitan and Sipadan on the Netherlands side of the line, even though the features were not specifically named in the 1891 Treaty, and that Indonesia is the successor State to the Netherlands. The Court determined that the 1891 Treaty did not deal with Litgitan and Sipadan.[36] Malaysia argued

> that it acquired sovereignty over the islands of Litgitan and Sipadan further to a series of alleged transfers of title originally held by the former sovereign, the Sultan of Sulu, that title having allegedly passed in turn to Spain, the United States, Great Britain on behalf of the State of Borneo, the United Kingdom … and finally to Malaysia.[37]

The Court did not accept this argument.[38]

Having rejected the successor title arguments of both States, the Court turned to what can be described as the "*res nullius*" approach where what is to be decided is the title to features without a title. In such situations, international courts and tribunals have based their decisions on an evaluation of the exercise by the claiming States of effective authority through sovereign activities. "Precisely what acts of sovereignty are necessary to find title will depend in each instance upon all the relevant circumstances of the case."[39]

The Court observed: "that it can only consider those acts as constituting a relevant display of authority which leave no doubt as to their specific reference to the islands in dispute…."[40] The Court cast doubt on the relevance of maps, echoing the statements made in previous *Cases* that "maps of themselves, and by virtue solely of their existence … cannot constitute territorial title."[41] The Court stated clearly that "activities of private persons," such as traditional fishers, "cannot be seen" as evidence of legal title "because they do not take place on the basis of official regulations or under government authority…."[42]

Note should also be made of the concept of "critical date" described as the date that the dispute crystallized. When it exists, the "acts after that date will not be taken into consideration, unless such acts are a normal continuation of prior acts and are not undertaken for the purpose of improving the legal position of the party relying on them."[43] The critical date also focuses on the question to be answered – to which of the competing States had title to the feature on that date. In the *Indonesia/Malaysia Case*, the International Court determined that the critical date was 1969.[44]

The Court found that Malaysia had title to the two features.[45]

The 2008 Malaysia/Singapore Case

Three different features were involved in this *Case*. The largest was Pedra Branca/Pulau Batu Puteh, described as a "granite island … covering an area of about 8,560 sq. km. at low tide," 24 nm from Singapore and 7.7 nm from Malaysia.[46] Middle Rocks are located.6 km from the above feature and described as "two clusters of small rocks about 250 m apart that, at high tide, are 1.2 m high."[47] South Ledge is 2.2 m from Pedra Branca/Pulau Batu and is only visible at low tide.[48]

The critical date was determined by the Court to be 1980 for the main island in dispute Pedra Branca/Pulau Bath Puteh,[49] and 1993 for the other features.[50]

The Court found that the Sultanate of Johor "had original title" to Pedra Branca/Pulau Batu Puteh.[51] However, the Court concluded that "by 1980 sovereignty over Pedra Branca/ Pulau Batu Puteh had passed to Singapore."[52] The Court based this result on its findings that "the Johor Authorities and their successors took no action at all on Pedra Branca/Pulau Batu Puteh from June 1850 for the whole of the following century;"[53] in 1953 an official of Johor stated that Johor did not claim ownership of the feature;[54] and that the United Kingdom/Singapore had exercised sovereign jurisdiction over the island.[55]

The Court concluded that Middle Rocks were not part of the original title of the Sultanate of Johor and that Singapore had not made the case that the title had passed to the United Kingdom/Singapore as these features had a distinctive history from that of Pedra Branca/Pulau Batu Puteh.[56]

South Ledge, located 1.7 nm from Middle Rocks,[57] was determined to be a low-tide elevation within Malaysia's territorial sea and, therefore, subject to Malaysian sovereignty.[58] The Court, relying on comments made in the 2001 *Qatar-Bahrain Maritime Delimitation Case*,[59] stated that

> It is … not established that in the absence of other rules and legal principles, low-tide elevations can, from the viewpoint of acquisition of sovereignty, to be fully assimilated with islands and other land territory.[60]

Subsequently, the *South China Sea Arbitral Tribunal* determined that "notwithstanding the use of the term 'land' in the physical description pf a low-tide elevation, such low-tide elevations do not form part of the land territory of a State in a legal sense" with the result that low-tide elevations "cannot be appropriated."[61]

Territorial sovereignty claims

As noted above, the 2009 Joint Submission by Malaysia/Viet Nam[62] and the 2009 Vietnam Northern Area Partial Submission[63] indicating their claimed outer limit of the continental shelf beyond 200 nm in the South China Sea to the CLCS led to a flurry of diplomatic communications by the South China Sea States. A similar flurry has taken place in response to Malaysia's 2019 CLCS Partial Submission.[64]

The focus herein is solely on those parts of the diplomatic communications that refer to the territorial sovereignty of the insular features in the South China Sea. Nevertheless, it is interesting to observe that in the above submissions that the outer limits of the 200 nm EEZ and the outer limits of the continental shelf beyond 200 nm were constructed based on the mainland of the States and did not take into account any of the insular features. This has no bearing on the territorial sovereignty of the insular features claimed by Malaysia and Viet Nam but indicates that the insular features within 200 nm of the mainland coasts in the area covered in the submissions are either accepted as being rocks, as opposed to islands, or that the two States have decided politically not to treat the features as islands. The relevance of this to territorial sovereignty will be briefly commented upon below.

China

China's response to the 2009 Malaysia/Viet Nam Joint Submission[65] and the Partial Viet Nam Northern Area Partial Submission[66] stated:

> China has indisputable sovereignty over the islands in the South China Sea and the adjacent waters, and enjoys sovereign rights and jurisdiction over the relevant waters as well as the seabed and subsoil thereof (see attached map). The above position is consistently held by the Chinese Government, and is widely known by the international community.[67]

The attached map portrays the U-shaped dashed line. The dashed lines are near-shore of the Philippines, Malaysia, Brunei and Vietnam and, if connected, encloses virtually the entire South China Sea north of the Natuna Islands.

In subsequent diplomatic notes, China stated that it has "indisputable sovereignty over the islands in the South China Sea;" that "China's sovereignty and related rights ... are supported by abundant historical and legal evidence" and that "Since the 1930s the Chinese Government has given publicity several times the geographical scope of China's Nansha Islands (South China Sea islands) and the names of its components. China's Nansha Islands is therefore clearly defined."[68]

Regarding Malaysia's 2019 CLCS Partial Submission,[69] China stated that it "has sovereignty over Nanhai Zhudao consisting of Dongsha Qundao, Xisha Qundao, Zongsha Qundao and Nansha Qundao" and that this is "known to the international community" and is in compliance with relevant international law and practice.[70]

In an April 2020 communication, China further asserted that it "has sovereignty over Xisha Qundao (Paracels) and Nansha Qundao ..." that its sovereignty is based on

> the long course of historical practice ... and that it has been "upheld by successive Chinese Governments and are consistent with international law".[71] China commented that its "sovereignty is widely recognized by the international community" with an explicit reference made to 1958 communications by the Viet Nam Prime Minister supporting China's view.[72]
>
> Of final note is China's statements that: "The Kalayaan Island Group" claimed by the Philippines is in fact part of China's Nansha Qundao has never been part of the territory of the Philippines

and that "Being part of China's Zhongsha Qundao, Huangyan Dao (Scarborough reef) is China's inherent territory."[73]

The basis of China's South China Sea territorial sovereignty claims is set out in China's December 2014 "Position Paper on the Matter ofJurisdiction in the South China Sea Arbitration."

> China has indisputable sovereignty over the South China Sea Islands (the Dongsha Islands, the Xisha Islands, the Zhongsha Islands and the Nansha China has indisputable sovereignty over the South China Sea Islands (the Islands) and the adjacent waters. Chinese activities in the South China Sea date back to over 2,000 years ago. China was the first country to discover, name, explore and exploit the resources of the South China Sea Islands and the first to continuously exercise sovereign powers over them. From the 1930s to 1940s, Japan illegally seized some parts of the South China Sea Islands during its war of aggression against China. At the end of the Second World War, the Chinese Government resumed exercise of sovereignty over the South China Sea Islands. Military personnel and government officials were sent via naval vessels to hold resumption of authority ceremonies. Commemorative stone markers were erected, garrisons stationed, and geographical surveys conducted. In 1947, China renamed the maritime features of the South China Sea Islands and, in 1948, published an official map which displayed a dotted line in the South China Sea. Since the founding of the People's Republic of China on 1 October 1949, the Chinese Government has been consistently and actively maintaining its sovereignty over the South China Sea Islands. Both the Declaration of the Government of the People's Republic of China on the Territorial Sea of 1958 and

> the Law of the People's Republic of China on the Territorial Sea and the Contiguous Zone of 1992 expressly provide that the territory of the People's Republic of China includes, among others, the Dongsha Islands, the Xisha Islands, the Zhongsha Islands and the Nansha Islands. All those acts affirm China's territorial sovereignty and relevant maritime rights and interests in the South China Sea.[74]

Of note is that Itu Aba, described by the *South China Sea Arbitral Tribunal* as "the largest high tide feature in the Spratly Islands" is "under the control of the Taiwan Authority of China"[75] (the Republic of China). In a 2015 press release, the Republic of China stated:

> whether from the perspective of history, geography or international law, the Nansha (Spratly) Islands (Shisha (Paracels) Islands, Chungsha (Macclesfield Bank) Islands, and Tungsha (Pratas) Islands (together known as the South China Sea Islands) ... are an inherent part of ROC territory ....[76]

Viet Nam

Viet Nam made no direct comment concerning territorial sovereignty in the 2009 Joint Submission with Malaysia[77] or its 2009 Partial Submission.[78] Viet Nam indicated in a 2011 *note verbale* that

> Hoang Sa (Paracels) and Truong (Spratlys) Archipelagoes are integral parts of Vietnamese territory. Viet Nam has sufficient historical evidences and legal to assert sovereignty over these two archipelagoes.[79]

Similar language is in two Vietnamese 2020 diplomatic notes[80] arising from Malaysia's 2019 Partial Submission to the CLCS.[81]

The Philippines

In the Philippine response to 2009 the Malaysia/Vietnam Joint CLCS Submission[82] and Viet Nam's Partial Submission,[83] it was noted that there was "controversy arising the territorial claims on some islands in the area"[84] without elaboration and that the submissions were without prejudice to land disputes.[85]

In the Philippine response to China's *notes verbale* containing the U-shaped dashed line,[86] the Philippines asserted that "the Kalayaan Island Group constitutes an integral part of the Philippines" and that "The Philippines has sovereignty and jurisdiction over the geological features in the KIG."[87] In response to the 2019 Malaysian CLCS Partial Submission,[88] the Philippines communicated that the Submission "covers features within the Kalayaan Island Group over which the Philippines has sovereignty."[89]

The KIG is a box-shaped area established pursuant to a 1978 Presidential Decree.[90] The KIG box includes most, but not all, of the insular formations of the Spratlys area.[91] The Decree asserts that

> by reason of history, indispensable need, and effective occupation and control established in accordance with international law, such areas must now be deemed to belong and subject to the sovereignty of the Philippines.[92]

Malaysia

There is no comment by Malaysia respecting claims of territorial sovereignty of insular features in the 2009 Joint Submission[93] or the 2019 Partial Submission.[94] In *notes verbale* to the CLCS, Malaysia indicated that the two submissions are "without prejudice to the position of States which are parties to a land … dispute."[95]

Malaysia has occupied and claimed a number of insular features in the southeast corner of the Spratly area.[96] The basis of the claim has been attributed to discovery/occupation and proximity.[97] The proximity argument arises from Malaysia's claim in the 1960s to the continental shelf adjacent to its main coast and that the islets were within the area claimed.[98] A map published in 1979 made clear its claim as regards islets and ocean space.[99]

Brunei

Brunei has claims respecting two islets (reefs) and an ocean area within the Spratly area.[100]

Summary

Respecting the Spratlys, China and Vietnam claim territorial sovereignty over all the insular features. The Philippines claims territorial sovereignty over a subset of the Spratlys. Malaysia and Brunei claim several selected features. The sovereignty dispute respecting the Paracels is between China and Vietnam.

The Chemillier-Gendreau analysis

The 2000 book *Sovereignty over the Paracel and Spratly Islands* by Chemillier-Gendreau[101] is currently the leading academic work in English on the history of the territorial sovereignty disputes in the South China Sea. The book is generally dismissive of the territorial claims of South China Sea States other than Vietnam and China.[102]

Respecting the Paracels, the author concludes that Viet Nam's rights "are ancient and well founded" as compared to the claims of title by China.[103]

There is less clarity regarding the Spratly Islands, not surprisingly given their distance from the mainland and their diminutive size. Chemillier-Gendreau notes that France, during the colonial period, treated the two island groups differently.[104] She indicates that in 1930 France notified other States that it had occupied the Spratlys.[105] In the conclusion, she states that France asserted its rights to the Spratlys as the "first occupant" and not on the basis of a successor in title to the historic Viet Nam claim.[106] She notes in italics that the French claim, based on *res nullius*, was not challenged by anyone.[107]

The book notes that the People's Republic of China commenced speaking about the Spratlys in 1951 commenting that "this was an abstract claim, devoid of any trace of effective occupation of these islands remote from the Chinese territory."[108] More pointedly, amidst a sea of uncertainty, Chemillier-Gendreau states that "it is easy to see that China's claim to the Spratlys has no legal basis and is just one aspect of a maritime expansion policy."[109]

The South China Sea Arbitration

China's 2014 "Position Paper"[110] argued that the *South China Sea Arbitral Tribunal* did not have jurisdiction to hear the matter as the "essence of the subject-matter of the arbitration is the territorial sovereignty over several maritime features in the South China Sea," which is beyond the scope of the [Law of the Sea] Convention.[111] The key principle underlying China's position was that the "land dominates the sea,"[112] in effect asserting that rights to ocean space are based on and cannot be divided from the territorial sovereignty of the land features. The Tribunal did not accept this argument.[113]

What the Tribunal did do, however, was diminish or minimize the importance of territorial sovereignty over the insular features in the South China Sea by indicating that all the insular features in the South China Sea were rocks and thus only entitled to a 12 nm territorial sea.[114] As noted above, this is essentially what had been presented in the 2009 Joint Malaysia/Viet Nam Submission[115] and the Viet Nam Partial Submission[116] and accepted by the Philippines and what was supported and advocated by knowledgeable observers.[117]

The effect of "feature isolation" is to change the maritime disputes in the South China Sea from multilateral disputes, for example, China-Malaysia-Viet Nam or China-the Philippines-Viet Nam to primarily bilateral EEZ (continental shelf) overlapping claims derived from the mainland coasts that would be subject to bilateral (rather than multilateral) negotiation.

Whatever the faults of the Arbitral Tribunal, the outcome is a reasonable path forward for the resolution of the South China Sea maritime disputes and is consistent with the primary function of a judicial body which is to resolve the dispute both as between China and the Philippines but also as between the other claimant States in the South China Sea.[118] All of the South China States have successfully concluded bilateral maritime boundary agreements with neighbours.[119] The most notable is the 2000 Agreement between China and Viet Nam[120] and the most recent is the 2014 Philippines-Indonesia EEZ boundary Agreement.[121]

The changing face of the territorial sovereignty disputes

There is little doubt that the *South China Sea Arbitration* has marked a significant change in approach and attitude by China to the territorial sovereignty disputes in the South China Sea.[122] China has expressed clearly its view that both the decision on *Jurisdiction* and on the *Merits* are "unjust and unlawful" and that it "neither accepts or recognizes the awards and will never accept any claim or action based on the awards."[123]

In a direct response to the *Arbitration*, China commenced a programme of construction turning a number of the South China Sea insular features under its control into substantial bases and features.[124] Viet Nam and the Philippines have reportedly followed suit.[125]

These activities have dramatically changed the optics of the territorial sovereignty disputes from involving unpopulated or underpopulated reefs, rocks and sandbars without freshwater into disputes involving military installations and populated features.

From a legal perspective, the LOS Convention indicates that a State cannot, by construction, change the legal status of a feature from a rock or a low-tide elevation to an island.[126] As commented above, wherein a territorial sovereignty dispute there is a critical date, activities undertaken after that date are not relevant in assessing territorial sovereignty.[127] More generally, the international law respecting territorial sovereignty discourages occupancy as being determinative of a legal title.[128]

Critically, however, the substantial construction activities enhancing occupation of insular features by a State, in particular where it involves the creation of military bases, greatly increases the possibility of serious direct confrontation. It also further entrenches the political position of the occupying State and makes a compromise in order to achieve resolution, or even management of the territorial sovereignty disputes, more difficult.

Conclusion

Territorial sovereignty disputes are the most intractable of all international disputes, even between States that are good neighbours, as evidenced by the Canada-US territorial sovereignty dispute over Machias Seal Island, a small islet on the Atlantic coast.[129] Attachment to land physically, emotionally, and politically is universal.

An immediate priority for the South China Sea States is to find a way to reduce the intensity of the territorial sovereignty disputes. Agreeing to halt rock construction activity would be a helpful first step. While at-sea confrontations regarding fisheries and oil and gas activities are not *per se* territorial sovereignty disputes, "peace on the water" would go a long way to desensitizing the territorial sovereignty disputes.

The above is easily stated. The various options for achieving peace and possible resolution of the territorial sovereignty disputes are well known.[130]

The difficulty is political will.

Notes

1 Regarding the uncertainty of the number, see Clive Schofield, "Dangerous Ground: A Geopolitical Overview of the South China Sea," in Sam Bateman and Ralf Emmers (eds.), *Security and International Politics in the South China Sea* (London: Routledge, 2009), at p. 8.
2 *The South China Sea Arbitration (Philippines v. People's Republic of China* (2015) *Award on Jurisdiction and Admissibility* and (2016) *Award,* on the Permanent Court of Arbitration website at www.pca-cpa, visited 20 May 2020. See: Chapter 23 in this collection.
3 See: Centre for Strategic and International Studies, Asia Maritime Transparency Initiative, "Island Tracker," at https://amti.csis.org/island-tracker/, visited 22 May 2020.
4 See: Derek Grossman, "Military Build-Up in the South China Sea," in Leszek Buszynski and Do Than Hai (eds.), *The South China Sea: From a Regional Maritime Dispute to Geo-Strategic Competition* (New York and London: Routledge, 2020), at pp. 182–200.
5 See: Chapter 3 in this collection.
6 See: Monique Chemillier-Gendreau, *Sovereignty Over the Paracel and Spratly Islands* (The Hague: Martinus Nijhof, 2000), at pp. 34–47; Geoffrey Till, "The South China Sea Dispute: An International History" in Bateman and Emmers, *supra* note 1, at pp. 27–31; Bill Hayton, *The South China Sea: The Struggle for Power in Asia* (New Haven, CT: Yale University Press, 2015), at pp. 50–78; and see Chapter 2 in this collection.
7 Till, *supra* note 6, at pp. 33–34 and Ralf Emmers, *Geopolitics and Maritime Territorial Disputes in East Asia* (London: Routledge, 2010), at pp. 68–69.
8 United Nations Convention on the Law of the Sea, done 10 December 1982, entered into force 16 November 1994, 1833 *U.N.T.S.* 397.
9 See: Chapter 6 in this collection.
10 LOS Convention, *supra* note 8, Article 121.
11 See: Mark J. Valencia, Jon M. Van Dyke and Noel A. Ludwig, *Sharing the Resources of the South China Sea* (The Hague: Martinus Nijhoff, 1997), at pp. 9–12 and Hayton, *supra* note 6, at pp. 121–150.
12 Declaration on the Conduct of Parties in the South China Sea, 4 November 2002, available on the website of ASEAN at www.aseansec.org/13163.htm.
13 See: Ted L. McDorman, "The South China Sea after 2009: Clarity of Claims and Enhanced Prospects for Regional Cooperation?" (2010) 24 *Ocean Yearbook*, at pp. 527–529.
14 Declaration on the Conduct of Parties, *supra* note 12, paragraph 10.
15 See Chapter 19 in this collection.
16 "Joint Submission Malaysia/Viet Nam to the Commission on the Limits of the Continental Shelf in respect of the Southern part of the South China Sea," May 2009, available on the website of the Commission on the Limits of the Continental Shelf, at https://www.un.org/Depts/los/clcs_new/clcs_home.htm.
17 "Viet Nam Partial Submission: Northern Area," April 2009, available on the CLCS website, *supra* note 16.

18 "Malaysia Partial Submission to the Commission on the Limits of the Continental Shelf in the South China Sea," December 2019, available on the CLCS website, *supra* note 16.
19 LOS Convention, *supra* note 8, Article 76 (8) and Annex II.
20 See generally, Chemillier-Gendreau, *supra* note 6, at pp. 49–133.
21 "Malaysia/Viet Nam Joint Submission," *supra* note 16.
22 "Viet Nam Partial Submission," *supra* note 17.
23 People's Republic of China, *notes verbal*, CML/17/2009 and CML/18/2009, 7 May 2009, available on the CLCS website, *supra* note 16. For a fulsome discussion of the U-shaped nine-dashed line, see Chapter 7 in this collection.
24 Declaration on the Conduct of Parties, *supra* note 12.
25 *South China Sea Arbitration*, *supra* note 2.
26 Bill Hayton, "When Good Lawyers Write Bad History: Unreliable Evidence and the South China Sea Territorial Dispute," (2017) 48 *Ocean Development and International Law* 17–34.
27 Vaughn Lowe, *International Law* (Oxford: Oxford University Press, 2007), at p. 138.
28 Malcolm Shaw, *International Law* (Cambridge: Cambridge University Press, 8th ed., 2017), at p. 363.
29 James Crawford, *Browlie's Principles of Public International Law* (Oxford: Oxford University Press, 8th ed., 2012), at p. 216.
30 See: Nguyen Hung Son and C.J. Jenner, "Domestic Politics: The Overlooked Undercurrent in the South China Sea," in C.J. Jenner and Tran Truong Thuy (eds.), *The South China Sea: A Crucible of Regional Cooperation or Conflict-Making Sovereignty Claims?* (Cambridge: Cambridge University Press, 2016), at pp. 133–148.
31 See generally: Crawford, *supra* note 29, at pp. 213–239 and Shaw, *supra* note 28, at pp. 372–387.
32 Leading cases include: *Island of Palmas* (Netherlands/United States) (1928), *UN Reports of International Arbitral Awards*, Vol II, 831; *Island of Clipperton* (Mexico v. France) (1931), *UN Reports of International Arbitral Awards* Vol II, 1105; *Legal Status of Eastern Greenland* (Denmark v. Norway) [1933] *P.C.I.J.* Ser. A/B No 53; and *The Minquiers and Ecreho Case* (France/United Kingdom) [1953] *I.C.J. Reports* 47.
33 *Case Concerning Sovereignty over Pulau Ligitan and Pulau Sipadan* (Indonesia/Malaysia) [2002] *I.C.J. Reports* 625.
34 *Case Concerning Sovereignty over Pedra Branca/Pulau Batu Puyeh, Middle Rocks and South Ledge* (Malaysia/Singapore) [2008] *I.C.J. Reports* 12.
35 *Indonesia/Malaysia Case*, *supra* note 33, para.14.
36 *Ibid.*, para. 32.
37 *Ibid.*, para. 97.
38 *Ibid.*, para. 124.
39 Shaw, *supra* note 28, at p. 379 and more generally, at pp. 372–387. For a condensed overview with the South China Sea in mind, see: Valencia, Van Dyke and Ludwig, *supra* note 11, at pp. 17–20.
40 *Indonesia/Malaysia Case*, *supra* note 33, para. 37.
41 *Ibid.*, para. 88.
42 *Ibid.*, para. 140.
43 Shaw, *supra* note 28, at p. 378.
44 *Indonesia/Malaysia Case*, *supra* note 33, paras. 135–136.
45 *Ibid.*, para. 150.
46 *Malaysia/Singapore Case*, *supra* note 34, para. 16.
47 *Ibid.*, para. 17.
48 *Ibid.*
49 *Ibid.*, paras. 33–34.
50 *Ibid.*, para. 35.
51 *Ibid.*, para. 69.
52 *Ibid.*, para. 276.
53 *Ibid.*, para. 275.
54 *Id.*
55 *Ibid.*, paras. 273–274.
56 *Ibid.*, paras. 288–290.
57 *Ibid.*, para. 293.
58 *Ibid.*, paras. 297 and 299.
59 *Maritime Delimitation and Territorial Questions between Qatar and Bahrain, Merits* [2001] *I.C.J. Reports*, at paras, 205–206.

60 *Malaysia/Singapore Case*, *supra* note 34, para. 296.
61 *South China Sea Arbitration*, *Award*, *supra* note 2, para. 309.
62 "Joint Submission Malaysia/Viet Nam," *supra* note 16.
63 "Viet Nam Partial Submission: Northern Area," *supra* note 17.
64 "Malaysia Partial Submission," *supra* note 18.
65 "Joint Submission Malaysia/Viet Nam," *supra* note 16.
66 "Viet Nam Partial Submission: Northern Area," *supra* note 17.
67 People's Republic of China, *notes verbale*, CML/17/2009 and CML/18/2009, *supra* note 23, paragraph 2.
68 People's Republic of China, *note verbale*, CML/8/2011, 14 April 2011, available on the CLCS website, *supra* note 16.
69 "Malaysia Partial Submission", *supra* note 18.
70 People's Republic of China, *note verbale*, CML/14/2019, 12 December 2019, available on the CLCS website, *supra* note 16.
71 People's Republic of China, *note verbale*, CML/11/2020, 23 March 2020, available on the CLCS website, *supra* note 16.
72 *Id.*
73 *Id.*
74 People's Republic of China, Foreign Ministry, "Position Paper of the Government of the People's Republic of China on the Matter of the Jurisdiction in the South China Sea Arbitration Initiated by the Republic of the Philippines," 7 December 2014, para. 4, available at https://www.fmprc.gov.cn/nanhai/eng/snhwtlcwj_1/, accessed 27 24 May 2020.
75 *South China Sea Arbitration*, *Award*, *supra* note 2, at para. 401.
76 Republic of China, "Government Reiterates Its Position on South China Sea Issues," 31 October, 2015 Mo. 240, available at https://www.mofa.gov.tw/en/News_Content.aspx?n=1EADDCFD-4C6EC567&s=F5170FE043DADE98 accessed 20 May 2020.
77 "Joint Submission Malaysia/Viet Nam," *supra* note 16.
78 "Viet Nam Northern Area Partial Submission," *supra* note 17.
79 Viet Nam, *note verbale*, 77/HC-2011, 3 May 2011, available on the CLCS website, *supra* note 16.
80 Viet Nam, *notes verbale*, No.22/HC-2020, 30 March 2020 and No. 25/HC-2020, 10 April 2020, available on the CLCS website, *supra* note 16.
81 "Malaysia Partial Submission," *supra* note 18.
82 "Joint Submission Malaysia/Viet Nam," *supra* note 16.
83 "Viet Nam Northern Area Partial Submission," *supra* note 17.
84 Philippines, *note verbale* 00819, 4 August 2009, on the CLCS website, *supra* note 16.
85 *Ibid.* and Philippines, *note verbale* 00818, 4 August 2009, on the CLCS website, *supra* note 16.
86 People's Republic of China, notes *verbale*, CML/17/2009, 7 May 2009 and CML/18/ 7 May 2009, supra note 23.
87 Philippines, *note verbale* 000228, 5 April 2011, on the CLCS website, *supra* note 16.
88 "Malaysian Partial Submission," *supra* note 18.
89 Philippines, note verbal 000192-2020, 6 March 2020, on the CLCS website, *supra* note 16.
90 Philippines, Presidential Decree No. 1596, s. 1978, Declaring Certain Part of the Philippine Territory and Providing for The Government and Administration, Official Gazette of the Philippines at available at https://www.officialgazette.gov.ph/1978/06/11/presidential-decree-no-1596-s-1978/, accessed 20 May 2020.
91 Valencia, Van Dyke and Ludwig, *supra* note 11, at p. 34.
92 Philippines, Presidential Decree No. 1596, *supra* note 90.
93 "Joint Submission Malaysia/Viet Nam," *supra* note 16.
94 "Malaysia Partial Submission," *supra* note 18.
95 Malaysia, *notes verbale*, HA/24/09, 20 May 2009, HA41/10, 20 August 2009 and HA/59/19, 12 December 2019, available on the CLCS website, supra note 16.
96 See: Valencia, Van Dyke and Ludwig, *supra* note 11, at p. 36.
97 *Id.*
98 *Ibid.*, at p. 36 and more generally, at pp. 36–37.
99 See generally: *ibid.*, at pp. 36–37. Respecting the 1979 Malaysian map, see: R. Haller-Trost, *The Contested Maritime and Territorial Boundaries of Malaysia: An International Law Perspective* (The Hague: Kluwer Law International, 1998), at pp. 13–22.

100 Valencia, Van Dyke and Ludwig, *supra* note 11, at pp. 38–39 and Haller-Trost, *supra* note 99, at pp. 47–49.
101 Chemillier-Gendreau, *supra* note 6.
102 *Ibid.*, at pp. 27–29 regarding geographical contiguity; p. 137, but see also pp. 138–139.
103 *Ibid.*, at pp. 80 and 135–137.
104 *Ibid.*, at p. 137.
105 *Ibid.*, p. 111.
106 Ibid., at p. 137.
107 *Id.*
108 *Id.*
109 *Ibid.*, at p. 139.
110 "Position Paper on the Matter of the Jurisdiction in the South China Sea Arbitration," *supra* note 74.
111 *Ibid.*, at para. 3.
112 *Ibid.*, para. 11.
113 *South China Sea Arbitration (Jurisdiction), supra* note 2, paras. 151–178.
114 *South China Sea Arbitration (Award), supra* note 2, para. 626.
115 "Joint Submission Malaysia/Viet Nam," *supra* note 16.
116 "Viet Nam Northern Area Partial Submission," *supra* note 17.
117 See generally: Valencia, Van Dyke and Ludwig, *supra* note 11.
118 See generally: Ted L. McDorman, "The South China Sea Tribunal Awards: A Dispute Resolution Perspective," (2018) 3 *Asia-Pacific Journal of Ocean Law and Policy* 134–145.
119 See generally, Ted L. McDorman, "Central Pacific and East Asian Maritime Boundaries," in David A. Colson and Robert W. Smith (eds.), *International Maritime Boundaries*, Volume V (Leiden/Boston: Martinus Nijhoff, 2005), at pp. 3442–3447.
120 Agreement between The People's Republic of China and Viet Nam on the Delimitation of the Territorial Sea, Exclusive Economic Zones and Continental Shelves of the two Countries in Beibu Gulf/Bac Bo Gulf, 25 December 2000, 2336 *U.N.T.S.* 179.
121 Agreement between Indonesia and the Philippines concerning the Delimitation of the Exclusive Economic Zone, 23 May 2014, entry into force 1 August 2019, *U.N.T.S.* No. 55946.
122 See: Chapter 23 in this collection.
123 People's Republic of China, *note verbal*, CML/11/2020, 23 March 2020, *supra* note 71.
124 Centre for Strategic and International Studies, Asia Maritime Transparency Initiative, "Island Tracker," *supra* note 3.
125 *Id.*
126 LOS Convention, *supra* note 8, Article 13(1) "A low-tide elevation is a naturally formed area of land" and Article 121(1) refers to an island as "a naturally formed area of land." Note: *South China Sea Arbitration (Award), supra* note 2, at para. 306. See more generally, Tara Davenport, "Island Building in the South China Sea: Legality and Limits," (2018) *Asian Journal of International Law* 76–90.
127 *Indonesia/Malaysia Case, supra* note 33, para. 41 and *Malaysia/Singapore Case, supra* note 34, paras. 47–48.
128 Crawford, *supra* note 29, at p. 216.
129 Ted L. McDorman, *Salt Water Neighbors: International Ocean Law Relations between the United States and Canada* (New York: Oxford University Press, 2009), at pp. 190–195.
130 See Chapters 19, 21 and 22 in this collection.

6

COMPETING MARITIME CLAIMS AND ENDURING DISPUTES IN THE SOUTH CHINA SEA

Clive Schofield

Introduction

Located between the mainland coast of Southeast Asia and the archipelagic island groups of the Philippines, Borneo and Indonesia, the South China Sea is a large tropical ocean space covering an area of over 3 million square kilometres (see Chapter 1 and Figure 6.1).

The South China Sea is vital to the flow of global maritime trade as it provides the critical maritime link between the Indian and Pacific Oceans. Many of the States within the South China Sea region, as well as East and Southeast Asia more generally, tend to be natural resource-poor yet feature dynamic, industrialized economies that are highly dependent on access to such resources which can only be met through imports. Likewise, the manufactured goods produced by countries such as China, Korea and Japan are predominantly exported by sea. Overall, the global economy is heavily dependent on shipping with over 80 percent of global trade by volume and over 70 percent by value being carried by sea.[1] More specifically, approximately one-third of the world's maritime trade passes through the South China Sea equating to an estimated U.S.$3.6 trillion in 2016 (see Chapter 3).[2]

The South China Sea is also an area of globally significant biological diversity, home to reef habitats that help support at least 3,365 known species of marine fishes.[3] This explains why for a relatively small part of the oceans, the South China Sea delivers an astonishing abundance of fish, estimated at 12 percent of the *global* fishing catch, worth over U.S.$21 billion per year.[4] These living resources are worth more than money. They are fundamental to the food security of regional populations numbered in the hundreds of millions.

Additionally, there has long been speculation that the South China Sea may be a major source of seabed energy resources, with United States sources estimating in 2013 there to be approximately 11 billion barrels of oil and 190 trillion cubic feet of gas of "proved and probable" untapped resources located there.[5] Some Chinese estimates are much higher, with the Chinese National Offshore Oil Company in November 2012 estimating 125 billion barrels of oil and 500 trillion cubic feet of natural gas in undiscovered resources.[6] It is impossible to be sure about the potential oil and gas resources underlying disputed waters, as exploration for these resources is constrained precisely because of the existence of competing claims and contentious maritime disputes. Nonetheless, the larger resource estimates for the South China Sea appear to be highly speculative and questionable.[7]

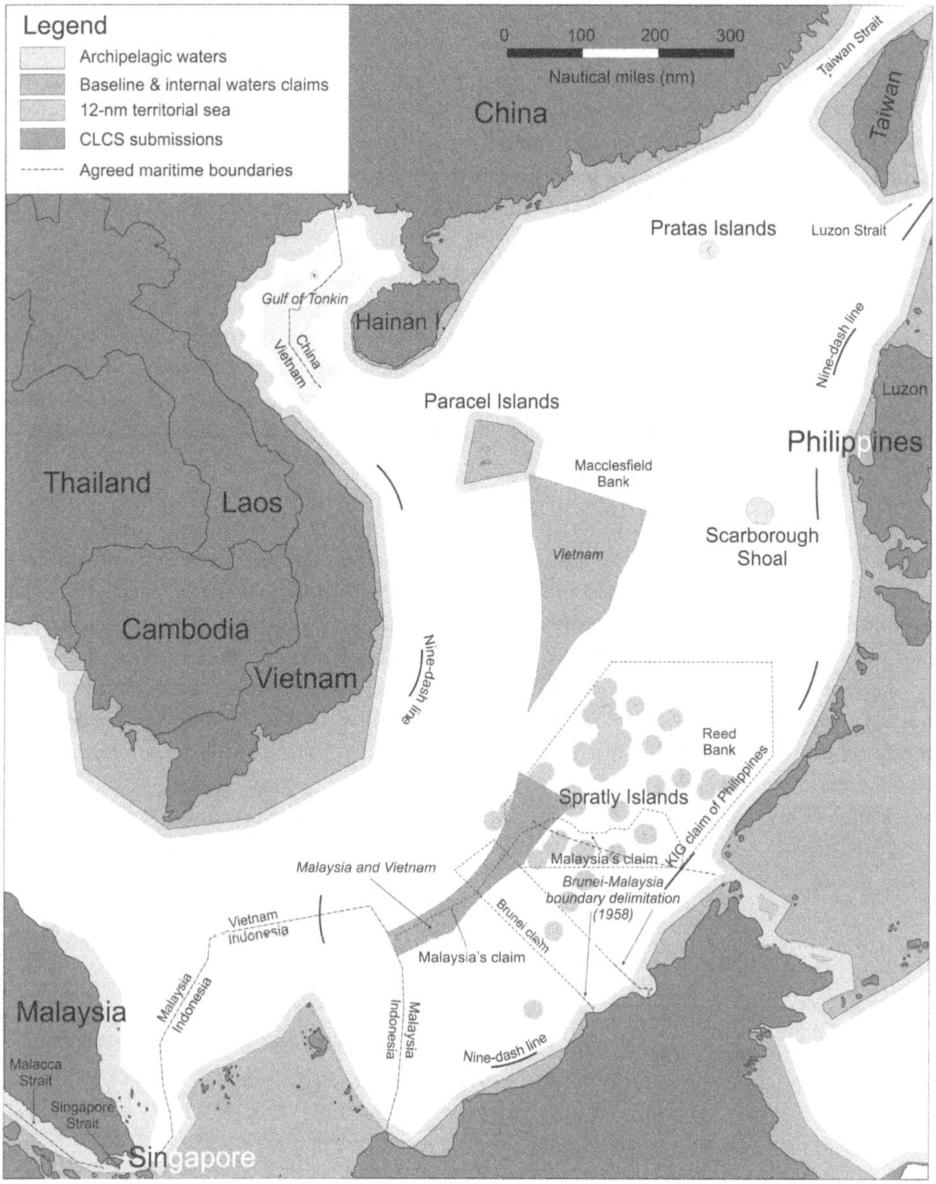

Figure 6.1 Baselines, Maritime Claims and Boundaries in the South China Sea.

Source: Adapted from: C.H. Schofield, "An Incomplete Maritime Map: Progress and Challenges in the Delimitation of Maritime Boundaries in South East Asia," in D. Rothwell D. Letts (eds.), *Law of the Sea in South East Asia: Environmental, Navigational and Security Challenges* (London: Routledge, 2019), 33–36, Figure 3.5, 45.[8]

While the fundamental cause of the South China disputes is disputed sovereignty over multiple island groups (see Chapter 5), it is the multiple overlapping claims to maritime jurisdiction that severely complicate access to and compromise access to and the management of the South China Sea's valuable marine environment and resources. These overlapping claims arise from the fact that numerous States border the South China Sea and their maritime claims tend to converge and overlap.[9] The maritime claims associated with South China Sea islands compounds the problem as these maritime entitlements are often claimed by multiple States as a consequence of their disputes over territorial sovereignty. The picture is further clouded and complicated by ambiguous historic claims to large parts of the South China Sea.

Accordingly, this chapter reviews the South China Sea States status under the international law of the sea before analyzing their practice in relation to baselines along the coast from which their maritime claims are predominantly measured. The discussion then turns to the maritime claims of the South China Sea coastal States, where overlapping claims have been resolved through the delimitation of maritime boundaries or where coastal States have, as it were, "agreed to disagree" and instead entered into joint arrangements to manage overlapping claims areas. This chapter then examines areas of bilateral and multilateral overlaps, especially in light of the 2016 Award of the Arbitral Tribunal in the case between China and the Philippines.[10] This chapter then provides some concluding reflections on the competing visions of jurisdictional rights in the South China Sea which arise from that case and which unfortunately appear to set the scene for further maritime disputes in the South China Sea in the future.

Baselines

All of the South China Sea coastal States are parties to the United Nations Convention on the Law of the Sea (LOSC).[11] The LOSC can be considered to represent the international law applicable to the definition of baselines along the coast, the delineation of the outer limits of maritime zones and the delimitation of maritime boundaries between them.

Baselines along the coast are of fundamental importance to maritime claims and consequently, where baselines are of a questionable or excessive character, they are implicated in maritime disputes. This is because baselines represent the "boundary" between land and sea and therefore provides the, as it were, "starting line" for the measurement of the limits of maritime claims (see Figure 6.2). This is in keeping with the longstanding legal maxim that "the land dominates the sea" and, further, that "it dominates it by the intermediary of the coastal front."[12]

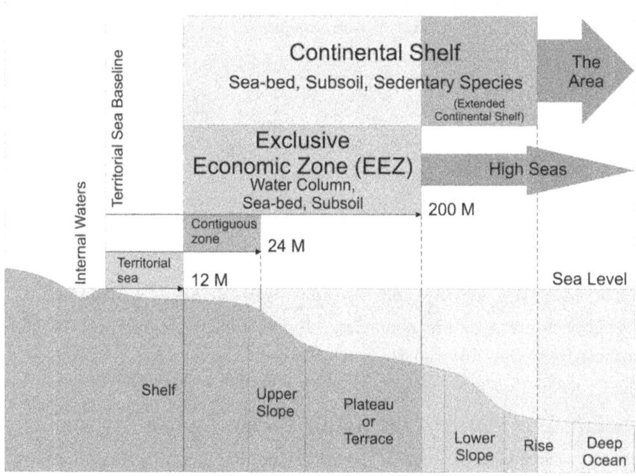

Figure 6.2 Baselines and Zones of Maritime Jurisdiction.

Source: Adapted from: International Hydrographic Bureau and the International Association of Geodesy (IAG), *Manual on Technical Aspects of the Law of the Sea* (TALOS Manual), Special Publication No. 51 (Monaco: International Hydrographic Bureau, 2014), Figure 5.1, Chapter 5, 3.[13]

The LOSC provides for several distinct types of baseline. Of particular interest in the South China Sea context are normal baselines, baselines related to reefs, straight baselines and archipelagic baselines.

Normal baselines

Normal baselines are a coastal State's default baselines. That is, the baselines that it possesses in the absence of other baseline claims. Normal baselines are defined in Article 5 of the LOSC as "the low-water line along the coast as marked on large-scale charts officially recognized by the coastal State."[14] This provision is silent on the choice of low-water line, leaving this up to the coastal State. The low-water line is, in turn, dependent on the choice of vertical datum, which is the level of reference for vertical measurements such as depths and heights of the tide. The lower or more conservative the vertical datum is chosen, the further seaward the normal baseline will lie. This issue is, however, mediated by the fact that coastal States tend to use low-water lines as depicted on nautical charts and chart-makers in any case tend towards low or conservative vertical datums, and thus low-water lines, in view of safety of navigation considerations, rather than for maritime jurisdictional purposes.

Normal baselines also apply to the numerous and often disputed, islands of the South China Sea. Moreover, low-water lines are vital to determining the baselines of reef features. Consistent with Article 6 of the LOSC, where islands are located on atolls or where islands have fringing reefs, baselines are coincident with the "seaward low-water line of the reef, as shown by the appropriate symbol on charts officially recognized by the coastal State." This is important in the South China Sea context where many features are reef features such as Scarborough Reef (or Shoal), the largest atoll in the South China Sea.[15]

As far as the mainland and main island shorelines semi-enclosing the South China Sea, it is notable that with the exception of Brunei's relatively constricted coastal front, extensive systems of straight or archipelagic baselines have been declared.

Straight baselines

Where the coastline is particularly complex, giving rise to "highly irregular" normal baselines,[16] the LOSC provides for coastal States to define straight baselines drawn along selected parts of their coastlines. Article 7(1) of LOSC provides that straight baselines should only be applied in localities "where the coastline is deeply indented and cut into, or if there is a fringe of islands along the coast in its immediate vicinity."[17] Additionally, Article 7(2) allows the drawing of straight baselines "[w]here because of the presence of a delta and other natural conditions, the coastline is highly unstable."[18] Moreover, in accordance with Article 7(3),

> [t]he drawing of straight baselines must not depart to any appreciable extent from the general direction of the coast, and the sea areas lying within the lines must be sufficiently closely linked to the land domain to be subject to the regime of internal waters.[19]

Article 7(4) also stipulates that straight baselines

> shall not be drawn to and from low-tide elevations, unless lighthouses or similar installations which are permanently above sea level have been built on them or except in instances where the drawing of baselines to and from such elevations has received general international recognition.[20]

Furthermore, Article 7(5) allows for account to be taken of "economic interests peculiar to the region concerned, the reality and the importance of which are clearly evidenced by long usage."[21] Finally, Article 7(6) states that a system of straight baselines may not be applied by a coastal State "in such a manner as to cut off the territorial sea of another State from the high seas or an exclusive economic zone."[22]

Key interpretational uncertainties arising from the text of Article 7 of the LOSC include how deep the indentations need to be to constitute a "deeply indented and cut into" coastline, how many and how close islands need to be to one another in order to form a "fringe" of islands and at how far offshore such a fringe of islands may be yet still fulfil the requirement that they be in the coastline's "immediate vicinity," what is meant by the term "highly unstable," and by what means is the "general direction" of the coastline to be determined and what angle represents divergence to an "appreciable extent" from that direction. Article 7 of the LOSC is similarly silent on these issues as well as how to determine whether the sea area enclosed by a particular straight baseline system is "sufficiently closely linked to the land to be considered subject to the regime of internal waters" or not, and it is also unclear how economic interests peculiar to a particular region are to be assessed or what period of time equates to "long usage" of such areas by the coastal State concerned.

These uncertainties led one eminent commentator to observe, apparently with some asperity, that "the imprecise language [of Article 7] would allow any coastal country, anywhere in the world, to draw straight baselines along its coast."[23] As a result, many coastal States have interpreted Article 7 of the LOSC in a liberal or expansive manner, and this applies to several of the South China Sea littoral States. In contrast, the United States adopts a more restrictive or conservative interpretation of the LOSC. Here it can be observed that although the United States is not a party to the LOSC, it generally regards the Convention as being reflective of customary international law and conducts its oceans policy accordingly.[24] Consequently, the United States routinely protests against any practice that it deems to be excessive or contrary to the provisions of LOSC as part of its Freedom of Navigation (FON) programme.[25] Indeed, in 1987 the U.S. Department of State published a set of guidelines for evaluating straight baseline claims for their conformity with international law.[26] It is also worth noting that the International Court of Justice has expressed the view that the definition of straight baselines is "an exception to the normal rules for the determination of baselines" and "must be applied restrictively."[27]

China

In 1996, China claimed a system of straight baselines along most of its mainland coast and around the Paracel group of islands in the South China Sea. A detailed analysis of this baseline system by the U.S. Department of State was highly critical of these claims as most of China's coastline does not meet the LOSC criteria for applying straight baselines either on the basis of being deeply indented or cut into or being fronted by a fringe of islands in its immediate vicinity.[28] Further, a 107.8 nautical mile (M)-long straight baseline segment was critiqued for closing off the Eastern entrance to the Qiongzhou Strait between Hainan and the Chinese mainland, which the U.S. viewed as "an international strait" and because it served to enclose "large areas of high seas and claiming them as internal waters."[29]. In contrast, China has expressed the position that international shipping does not have a right of innocent passage in this strait.[30]

The enclosing of the Paracel Islands by China with apparent straight baselines would seem to be clearly contrary to international law. There is no provision in the LOSC for baselines around mid-ocean archipelagos that are not part of an archipelagic State (as opposed to mainland or continental State such as China).[31] In any case, the Paracels would not qualify for archipelagic status under the LOSC because the ratio of water to land in the group would far exceed the 9:1 ratio prescribed in LOSC Article 47(1).[32] China's action in drawing straight baselines around the Paracels is particularly problematic from Vietnam's perspective which also claims sovereignty over these islands.

The Arbitration Tribunal in the South China Sea case addressed the possibility that China's references to consideration of the Spratly Islands as a whole might signify an assertion on the part of China that the Spratly Islands should be enclosed within a system of archipelagic or straight baselines and therefore be considered as a single unit, concluding that this was not possible.[33] With respect to archipelagic baselines the Tribunal reasoned that their use "is strictly controlled" and "limited" by the Convention to archipelagic States in keeping with Article 46 of the LOSC.[34] As such the Tribunal was explicit in stating that China is "constituted principally by territory on the mainland of Asia and cannot meet the definition of an archipelagic State."[35]

With respect to the application of straight baselines to the Spratly Islands, the Tribunal acknowledged the practice of some coastal States in applying straight baselines "to offshore archipelagos to approximate the effect of archipelagic baselines" but was of the view that "any application of straight baselines to the Spratly Islands in this fashion would be contrary to the Convention."[36] Moreover, the Tribunal indicated that the application of straight baselines "to offshore archipelagos not meeting the criteria for archipelagic baselines...would effectively render the conditions in Articles 7 and 47 meaningless."[37] The Tribunal also made the point that despite the practice of some mainland coastal States concerning straight baselines being applied to dependant archipelagos it "sees no evidence that any deviations from this rule have amounted to the formation of a new rule of customary international law that would permit a departure from the express provisions of the Convention."[38]

Taiwan

Taiwan claimed a system of straight baselines in 1998.[39] Specific baselines were claimed for three areas: the main island of Taiwan and "appurtenance" islands, the Pratas Islands and the Macclesfield Bank.[40] The main system of straight baselines encloses the main island of Taiwan itself, the Penghu or Pescadores Islands and other outlying features. While these baselines appear to have the configuration of archipelagic baselines, they are straight baselines as Taiwan, as the government of Taiwan claims to represent China as a whole.

A detailed analysis of this system by the U.S. State Department concluded that overall "Taiwan uses straight baselines in many areas where the normal baseline, the low-water mark, should be used."[41] Further, while acknowledging that Taiwan's mainland coastline does feature "some indentations", this analysis concluded that "most do not meet the geographic standards, as set forth in the LOS Convention, for using straight baselines."[42] The U.S. Department of State study also noted that the offshore features employed by Taiwan as turning points for its claimed system of straight baselines "are not physically close enough to the mainland to justify incorporation" and that the waters enclosed by the straight baselines "for the most part...do not have the close relationship with the land as needed, but rather reflect the characteristics of the territorial sea or high seas."[43]

Malaysia

Malaysia's baselines claims remain somewhat obscure, at least officially. Malaysia has not formally published the coordinates defining its claimed straight baselines. In previous years it was possible to infer the existence of Malaysian straight baselines from an examination of official maps. In particular, a map issued by the Malaysian Directorate of National Mapping on 21 December 1979 in order to illustrate Malaysia's agreed maritime boundaries and the limits of Malaysia's territorial sea and continental shelf limits was significant in this context.[44] Although no baselines are shown on these maps, the fact that in certain areas the outer limit of the Malaysian territorial sea claim is marked with straight lines allows the conclusion to be drawn that Malaysia has constructed a system of straight baselines. The location of these baselines may then be inferred by drawing lines parallel to the straight line outer limits of the Malaysian territorial sea claim but transposed 12 M to landward.[45] Similarly, Malaysia's maritime boundary agreements with Indonesia in relation to continental shelf rights and territorial sea of 1969 and 1971 respectively are also relevant in this context.[46]

More recently, Malaysia enacted the Baselines of Maritime Zones Act 2006 on 1 May 2007.[47] This legislation provides for the declaration of geographical coordinates of base points for the purpose of determining the territorial sea baselines of Malaysia and for other associated matters. However, geographical coordinates have yet to be specified as anticipated in the Act; and, while most of the Act appears to be unobjectionable, there appears to be a qualification that allows the outer limits of the territorial sea to be arbitrarily declared on the recommendation of the relevant Minister. This would seem to allow the existing situation to be preserved.[48] Further, Malaysia and Vietnam's joint submission with respect to extended continental shelf rights includes a map that features straight baselines fronting the coast of the Malaysian provinces of Sarawak and Sabah on the South China Sea.[49] These straight baselines appear to differ from the baselines "inferred" from the 1979 map.

Vietnam

Vietnam made a claim to straight baselines in 1977,[50] which was implemented in 1982.[51] The system of straight baselines defined by Vietnam in 1982 has been termed particularly "radical".[52] Vietnam's claimed straight baselines start in the north and extend for a distance of approximately 850 M to enclose the entire Vietnamese coast south of the Gulf of Tonkin.[53] The islands used as base points for Vietnam's claimed straight baselines are small, scattered and largely distant from the mainland coast such that of the nine turning points defined, five are more than 50 M offshore. Further, according to the U.S. Department of State analysis, on average 39.4 M offshore and up to 80.7 M offshore and enclosing claimed internal waters of approximately 27,000 M^2 (93,000 km^2).[54] It is therefore difficult to see how these features constitute a "fringe of islands" in the "immediate vicinity" of the coast in keeping with the requirements of LOSC Article 7(1). Vietnam's straight baselines claims have been subject to critical assessment by the U.S. Department of State[55] and have been subject to U.S.[56] and Thai protests.[57]

Archipelagic baselines

The South China Sea is also host to two archipelagic States: Indonesia and the Philippines (see Figure 6.1).[58] Following revisions, both States have now defined archipelagic baselines fronting the South China Sea that are compliant with Article 47 of the LOSC. The archipelagic States may define systems of archipelagic baselines joining "the outermost points of the outermost islands and drying reefs of the archipelago"[59] provided that five key criteria are fulfilled. These are: that the claimant State's "main islands" must be included within the archipelagic baseline system;[60] that the ratio of water to land within the baselines must be between 1:1 and 9:1;[61] that the length of any single baseline segment must not exceed 125

M;[62] that no more than 3 percent of the total number of baseline segments enclosing an archipelago may exceed 100 M;[63] and, that such baselines "shall not depart to any appreciable extent from the general configuration of the archipelago."

Indonesia

Indonesia, the world's largest archipelagic State, composed of over 17,500 islands, was a key pioneer of the archipelagic concept, and it is notable that the provisions governing the drawing of such baselines in LOSC Article 47 appear to a considerable extent to have been inspired by the "prototype" archipelagic baselines claimed by Indonesia in 1960.[64] Indonesia has subsequently revised and refined its claims on several occasions since that date, notably through legislation dating from 1996[65] and regulations of 2002[66] and 2008.[67] The latest version of Indonesia's archipelagic baselines was deposited with the UN Secretary-General on 11 March 2009, accompanied by a map illustrating the baselines, consisting of 195 points.[68] Indonesia's archipelagic baselines, including those enclosing the Natuna Islands group and fronting the South China Sea, can be considered as being compliant with the terms of Article 47 of the LOSC (see Figure 6.1).

The Philippines

The Philippines established baselines through Republic Act No. 3046 of 17 June 1961,[69] and subsequently amended them through Republic Act No. 5446 of 18 September 1968.[70] While this system of baselines certainly appears to be archipelagic in character, enclosing as they do the approximately 7,000 islands that constitute the Philippines, the relevant Philippines legislation referred to "straight baselines."[71] Additionally, it is worth noting that one of the baseline segments defined by the Philippines, that closing the Moro Gulf, measures approximately 141 M – a configuration that would breach the maximum archipelagic baseline segment length limit of 125 M set out in the LOSC Article 47(2).[72]

The Philippines baseline claims are also complicated by its historical claims associated with its 1961 declaration that the territorial sea of the Philippines comprised the waters lying between these baselines and the limits set out in the 1898 Treaty of Paris between the United States and Spain and by which Spain ceded sovereignty over the Philippines to the United States.[73] The limits established through these agreements are often termed the "Treaty Limits" of the Philippines or, more colloquially, as the "Philippines Box." Thus, in accordance with the Philippines Constitution of 1973,[74] the waters landward of these baselines were claimed to be the *internal waters* of the Philippines. However, in 2009 the Philippines revised its baselines and brought them into line with the LOSC.[75] The Philippines now claims archipelagic baselines around its main archipelago and applies the "regime of islands" to outlying islands claimed, such as Scarborough Shoal and those Spratly Islands claimed by the Philippines.[76]

Assessment of claimed baselines

With respect to baselines issues and particularly straight baselines, it seems clear that the claims of the South China Sea States are, as is the case in respect of other law of the sea issues, problematic in a number of ways. Concerning the baselines along the mainland coasts bordering the South China Sea, claimed straight baselines are clearly excessive in character. Arguably this may be a case of excessive practice leading neighbouring States to follow suit in order to "balance" their own position against their neighbours.

Claims to maritime jurisdiction

The South China Sea coastal States have proved to be enthusiastic claimants of the full suite of maritime zones provided for under the Convention, notably territorial seas out to 12 M, continental shelf rights and exclusive economic zones out to 200 M. As noted above, a number of these maritime claims are measured from baselines along the coast that can be considered to be excessive in character.

With respect to the central part of the South China Sea, that is, the area seaward of 200 M limits defined from baselines along the surrounding mainland and main island coastlines rather than the disputed islands of the South China Sea, a number of the South China Sea coastal States have made submissions to the Commission on the Limits of the Continental Shelf (CLCS).[77] In May 2009 Malaysia and Vietnam made a Joint Submission to the CLCS claiming a continental shelf beyond 200 M.[78] Vietnam also made a separate submission for an extended continental shelf further to the north, opposite the Philippines.[79] Brunei-Darussalam, China and the Philippines have either made partial submissions or submitted preliminary information indicating that they also intend to make submissions claiming an extended continental shelf in the South China Sea.[80] More recently, in December 2019, Malaysia made a partial submission concerning the southern central part of the South China Sea seawards of 200 M from surrounding mainland and main island coasts.[81]

The extended continental shelf submissions of Malaysia and Vietnam provoked protests from China which, in turn, prompted counter-protests that also generated responses from Beijing. Indeed, China issued near-identical protest notes including, as noted above, maps showing its nine-dashed line, stating that China has "indisputable sovereignty over the islands in the South China Sea," and that, consequently, Malaysia and Vietnam's joint submission "seriously infringed China's sovereignty."[82] Malaysia and Vietnam countered that their submissions "constitute legitimate undertakings" in the implementation of its obligations as a party to LOSC.[83] Vietnam further stated that the Paracel Islands and Spratly Islands "are parts of Vietnam" over which it has "indisputable sovereignty."[84] Subsequently, communications to the UN Secretary-General were also made by Indonesia[85] and the Philippines,[86] both protesting China's nine-dash line, with the latter's note, in turn, generating a vigorous response from Beijing.[87] The Chinese response, dated 14 April 2011, to the note from the Philippines is especially intriguing as China stated explicitly that "China's Nansha [Spratly] Islands is fully entitled to Territorial Sea, EEZ, and Continental Shelf."[88]

Malaysia's 2019 partial submission lso led to protests on the part of China that it had sovereignty over the Spratly Islands (Nansha Qundao) and Scarborough Reef (Huangyan Dao) and their "adjacent waters" and has sovereign rights and jurisdiction over the "relevant waters as well as the seabed and subsoil thereof" – language that can be taken to correspond to the territorial sea and EEZ/continental shelf rights respectively – as well as "historic rights in the South China Sea."[89] Accordingly, China asserted that Malaysia had "seriously infringed China's sovereignty, sovereign rights and jurisdiction in the South China Sea."[90] Vietnam asserted that China's claims in its notes verbale "seriously violate Viet Nam's sovereignty, sovereign rights and jurisdiction in the East Sea (South China Sea)." It is also notable that in their responses to China's protests, both Indonesia and the Philippines made direct reference to the Arbitral Tribunal's Award concerning its decision that none of the Spratly Islands generate EEZ or continental shelf entitlements.[91]

The implication of these submissions is that, as far as Malaysia and Vietnam are concerned, the disputed islands of the South China Sea are incapable of generating full 200 M EEZ and continental shelf rights. This is significant because if the disputed islands are in fact islands capable of claiming EEZ rights, then any high seas pocket in the central South China Sea as a consequence of 200 M claims as measured from the mainland and main island coastlines disappears. Under such a scenario no extended continental shelf would, in fact, exist in the South China Sea.[92] The diplomatic notes of Indonesia and the Philippines also suggest that as far as these States are concerned, they view the South China Sea Tribunal's Award to be "an authoritative interpretation of the law" concerning maritime claims in the South China Sea.[93]

It is, however, worth emphasizing that the CLCS has a scientific and technical role rather than a legal one. That is, the CLCS lacks the mandate to address areas subject to a sovereignty dispute or to assess the merits of competing claims to overlapping areas of the extended continental shelf. Furthermore, the Commission's recommendations are also specifically without prejudice to the delimitation of maritime boundaries.[94]

Moreover, as explored in Chapter 7, China (and Taiwan) appears to maintain a claim of historic rights within the so-called nine-dashed line which encompasses approximately 80 percent of the South China Sea (see Figure 6.1).

Maritime boundary agreements

The South China Sea is arguably best known as an area hosting intractable maritime and sovereignty disputes, especially relating to islands and a potential arena for maritime conflict. Nonetheless, some incremental progress has been achieved in terms of maritime boundary delimitation towards the margins of this large semi-enclosed sea. For example, the above-mentioned Indonesia and Malaysia boundary agreement of 1969, delimited not only the two States continental shelf rights in the Malacca Strait but also provided for two lateral delimitation lines in the south-western part of the South China Sea.[95] While the western segment between peninsular Malaysia and, principally, Indonesia's Natuna Islands group, is an equidistance boundary line, the eastern segment between Malaysia's Sarawak Province on the island of Borneo and the Natuna Islands is an adjusted equidistance boundary line favouring Malaysia.[96] Again, it is understood that Indonesia accepted an outcome to Malaysia's advantage in return for its support of Indonesia's archipelagic State concept.[97] Negotiations between Indonesia and Vietnam to, essentially, bridge the gap between these two lateral Indonesia-Malaysia continental shelf boundaries were initiated in 1972. However, an agreement was not forthcoming until 2003 (See Figure 6.1).[98]

Although continental shelf boundaries have been agreed upon between Indonesia, Malaysia and Vietnam in the south-western part of the South China Sea, agreement on water column boundaries has yet to be reached. This is because Indonesia has claimed water column jurisdiction beyond the agreed continental shelf boundary lines, that is, to the north of its continental shelf boundary with Vietnam, and to the east of its continental shelf boundary with Malaysia (see Figure 6.1).[99] Here it can be observed that Indonesia, as is made clear by its official mapping, is clearly of the view that seabed and water column boundaries need not coincide.[100] Malaysia and Vietnam would apparently prefer their continental shelf boundaries with Indonesia to be, as it were, 'upgraded' to single EEZ boundaries.

Additionally, China and Vietnam reached an agreement in December 2000 on maritime boundary delimitation through the Gulf of Tonkin (Beibu Gulf in Chinese and Bắc Bộ Gulf in Vietnamese) in conjunction with an agreement on fishery cooperation through which multiple zones straddling the boundary line relating to joint fishing activities were established.[101] In particular, a joint Common Fishery Zone was defined which straddles the maritime delimitation line, 30.5 M on either side of the boundary, from the 20°N parallel of latitude to the closing line of the Gulf.[102] The Common Fishery Zone therefore encompasses approximately 30,000 km^2 (around 8,747 M^2).[103] Additionally, a transitional arrangement zone north of 20° N. was established where the parties aim to gradually reduce the number of fishing vessels operating. A buffer zone on either side of the parties' territorial sea boundary in the immediate vicinity of the terminus of the land boundary on the coast in the north of the Gulf was defined in order to minimize disputes involving small fishing vessels that may have inadvertently trespassed across the boundary line.[104]

Further, Brunei and Malaysia inherited territorial sea boundaries from the United Kingdom[105] and also appear to have clarified their maritime boundary issues through a 16 March 2009 Exchange of Letters (see Figure 6.1).[106] A number of joint oil and gas resources-oriented zones have also been concluded in lieu of maritime boundary agreements in the Gulf of Thailand.[107] Such joint arrangements are consistent with Articles 74(3) and 83(3) of the LOSC which provide in identical terms that pending agreement being reached on the delimitation of the continental shelf or EEZ respectively, "the States concerned, in a spirit of understanding and cooperation, shall make every effort to enter into provisional arrangements of a practical nature."[108] It can be observed that these provisions also contain an obligation on the States involved "not to jeopardize or hamper the reaching of a final agreement."[109]

Competing maritime claims

As noted above, the fundamental dispute, or disputes, between the South China Sea littoral States that prevent maritime delimitation from progressing in the South China Sea relate to sovereignty over islands and island groups (see Chapter 5). In particular, these include the Paracel Islands in the north-west, Pratas Island in the north, Scarborough Reef (or Shoal) in the north-east and the Spratly Islands in the southern part of the South China Sea (see Figure 6.1).[110] Without a resolution on the core question of sovereignty over the disputed insular features of the South China Sea, progress towards maritime boundary delimitation remains profoundly compromised.

Additionally, China's apparent claims to historic rights within the nine-dashed line encompass around 80 percent of the South China Sea – claims which are objectionable to the other South China Sea littoral States and which profoundly complicates if not entirely forestall maritime boundary delimitation in the South China Sea (see Chapter 7). Moreover, a further dimension to the South China Sea disputes relates to the status of insular features. That is, whether they should be classified as islands capable of generating EEZ and continental shelf rights, "rocks" within the meaning of LOSC, Article 121(3) incapable of doing so, low-tide elevations (LTEs), or wholly and permanently submerged components of the seafloor. The status of insular features is important from a maritime delimitation perspective because it impacts on their capacity to generate maritime entitlements, and therefore it has to be noted whether overlapping maritime zones exist that require the delimitation of a maritime boundary. The potential role of insular features as base points influencing the course of a maritime delimitation line will likewise be directly impacted by their status.

The legal basis for any claims on the part of China to historic rights to the waters within the nine-dash line was essentially dismissed by the South China Sea Arbitral Tribunal.[111] This ruling, coupled with the Tribunal's finding that none of the Spratly Islands or Scarborough Reef is capable of generating extended maritime claims has the potential to dramatically curtail the extent of claims to maritime jurisdiction in the South China Sea and thus the extent of areas subject to overlapping maritime claims. Should the Award be implemented China's undisputed EEZ and continental shelf areas would be restricted to the northern part of the South China Sea. The extent of disputed waters in the southern part of the South

China Sea would therefore be reduced from the order of 80 percent of the South China Sea to 12 M pockets of contested territorial sea surrounding islands sovereignty over which is disputed, as well as any disputes between adjacent neighbouring States (see Figure 6.1). The Tribunal's Award, hould it be implemented, therefore both significantly clarifies and dramatically reduces areas of overlapping maritime claims and thereby arguably assists in the resolution of the South China Sea disputes.

The Award necessarily also has implications for the delimitation of maritime boundaries in the South China Sea. This is because the Tribunal's determination that all of the Spratly Islands, as well as Scarborough Reef, are rocks necessarily has significant implications for the scope of entitlements involving these features. This, in turn, impacts on the extent to which such entitlements overlap and therefore the existence of potential maritime boundaries to delimit.

On the basis of the Award, potential territorial sea boundary situations exist between above high-tide rocks of the Spratly Islands group but this ce again depends on the resolution of the sovereignty disputes over these features. Additionally, potential lateral maritime boundaries will exist between the coastal States bordering the South China Sea.[112] Clockwise from the northwest, are situated China and Vietnam,[113] China (Taiwan) and the Philippines, the Philippines and Malaysia,[114] Malaysia and Brunei,[115] Malaysia and Indonesia,[116] and Indonesia and Vietnam[117] as well as between the States bordering the Gulf of Thailand.[118] Additionally, in the eastern part of the Singapore Straits, in the far south-west of the South China Sea Indonesia, Malaysia and Singapore will need to delimit maritime boundaries in the vicinity of Pedra Branca, subsequent to the ICJ's (International Court of Justice) clarification of sovereignty over insular features in 2008.[119]

Conclusions: competing maritime visions and ongoing disputes

The consequence of the Arbitration Award is that the Philippines and, by extension, Malaysia, Brunei-Darussalam and Indonesia, are free to claim rights over the sea to 200 M from their coasts as part of their EEZs. If implemented, the Award also significantly reduces the maritime area in the South China Sea that is under dispute essentially to 12 M pockets of water around the disputed islands (see Figure 6.1).

The key obstacle in this context is that China has consistently and robustly rejected the ruling and there are no mechanisms by which it can be enforced. As a result, there is every indication that the Chinese will maintain not only its claims to sovereignty over all of the disputed South China Sea islands but to maritime areas within the nine-dashed line as well.

While there appeared to be a desire on the part of China to de-escalate regional tensions in the immediate aftermath of the Tribunal handing down its Award, it seems clear that the Award has led to a hardening in China's claims.[120] Indeed, coercive measures and incidents subsequent to the Award suggest that China is likely to continue to pressure other South China Sea coastal States, especially over marine resource issues. This is evidenced by fisheries-related confrontations between China and Indonesia off the Natuna Islands.[121] Additionally, China has either undertaken oil and gas exploration activities of its own or sought to impede those of other South China Sea coastal States in waters proximate to Brunei-Darussalam and Malaysia,[122] as well as to Vietnam.[123]

China has also undertaken fresh acts of administration designed to support its claims in the South China Sea. For example, in April 2020 China unilaterally named 80 geographical features, including 55 submerged ones, in the South China Sea, apparently in order to assert its "sovereignty and sovereign rights".[124] Additionally, the city of Sansha, located in China's Hainan Province, has established two new districts to "administer waters in the South China

Sea" including the Xisha, Zhongsha, and Nansha Islands.[125] While the Xisha Islands correspond in English to the Paracel Islands, the Zhongsha "Islands" comprise the entirely and permanently submerged Macclesfield Bank[126] and the 5–7 "miniscule" coral protrusions that are the only above high-tide features present on Scarborough Reef.[127]

This scenario of competing geographies, or fundamentally opposed spatial visions of the South China Sea, is ominous and sets the scene for ongoing maritime disputes in the South China Sea as China seeks to assert what it views as its historic rights in the South China Sea and other coastal States attempt to use the resources, such as oil and fish, that lie within what they firmly regard as "their" waters. This not only compromises the protection of the region's precious marine biodiversity and management of its abundant fisheries resources but threatens regional stability and freedom of navigation through waterways of global significance.

Notes

1 See United Nations Conference on Trade and Development (UNCTAD) *Review of Maritime Transport 2018* (New York: United Nations, 2018).

2 China Power, Center for Strategic and International Studies (CSIS) 'How Much Trade Transits the South China Sea?', available at <https://chinapower.csis.org/much-trade-transits-south-china-sea/>.

3 *Ibid.*

4 R. Sumalia and W. Cheung, *Boom or Bust: The Future of Fish in the South China Sea* (Vancouver: University of British Columbia, 2016). See also, C.H. Schofield, R. Sumalia and W. Cheung, 'Fishing Not Oil Is at the Heart of the South China Sea Disputes', *The Conversation*, 16 August 2016, available at <https://theconversation.com/fishing-not-oil-is-at-the-heart-of-the-south-china-sea-dispute-63580>

5 See, United States Energy Information Administration (EIA) 'South China Sea', available at <https://www.eia.gov/international/analysis/regions-of-interest/South_China_Sea>.

6 Ibid.

7 See, for example, N.O. Owen and C.H. Schofield, 'Disputed South China Sea Hydrocarbons in Perspective', (2012) 36(3) *Marine Policy* 809–822, at 813–820.

8 See C.H. Schofield, 'An Incomplete Maritime Map: Progress and Challenges in the Delimitation of Maritime Boundaries in South East Asia', in D. Rothwell D. Letts (eds.), *Law of the Sea in South East Asia: Environmental, Navigational and Security Challenges* (London: Routledge, 2019), 33–36, Figure 3.5, 45.

9 This chapter addresses the competing maritime claims and disputes in the South China Sea 'proper', as it were. That is, the maritime issues related to the body of water bordered by, clockwise from the north, China/Taiwan, the Philippines, Malaysia, Brunei-Darussalam, Indonesia and Vietnam. The Gulf of Thailand arm of the South China Sea is therefore not considered in this contribution. For discussion of maritime claims and disputes, as well as maritime boundary agreements and maritime joint development zones, in the Gulf of Thailand, see C.H. Schofield and M. Tan-Mullins 'Claims, Conflicts and Cooperation in the Gulf of Thailand', *Ocean Yearbook*, 22 (Leiden/Boston: Martinus Nijhoff, 2008), 75–116.

10 *South China Sea Arbitration*, Philippines *v* China, Award, PCA Case No. 2013–19, ICGJ 495 (PCA 2016), 12 July 2016, Permanent Court of Arbitration [PCA] [hereinafter the South China Sea case].

11 *United Nations Convention on the Law of the Sea*, 10 December 1982, 1833 UNTS [hereinafter LOSC]. Cambodia is the only country in South East Asia which remains a non-party to LOSC. It can be noted that Taiwan, otherwise known as the Republic of China, as a non-member State of the United Nations is not a party to the LOSC.

12 P. Weil, *The Law of Maritime Delimitation - Reflections* (Cambridge: Grotius, 1989), at 50. See also, *North Sea Continental Shelf Cases (FDR v. Denmark; FDR v. The Netherlands)* [1969] ICJ Reports 3, at para.96.

13 Figure 6.2 was produced by Dr I Made Andi Arsana and the present author for the International Hydrographic Bureau and the International Association of Geodesy (IAG), *Manual on Technical Aspects of the Law of the Sea* (TALOS Manual), Special Publication No. 51 (Monaco: International Hydrographic Bureau, 2014), Figure 5.1, Chapter 5, 3. Material from IHO-IAG publication C-51,

A Manual on Technical Aspects of the United Nations Convention on the Law of the Sea – 1982 (TALOS), Edition 5.0.0 dated June 2014 is reproduced with the permission of Professor Clive Schofield and Dr I Made Andi Arsana, authors of the graphic, and of the Secretariat of the International Hydrographic Organization (IHO) and the Executive Council of the International Association of Geodesy (IAG) (Permission N° 8/2020) acting for the International Hydrographic Organization (IHO) and the International Association of Geodesy (IAG), which do not accept responsibility for the correctness of the material as reproduced: in case of doubt, the IHO-IAG's authentic text shall prevail. The incorporation of material sourced from IHO-IAG shall not be construed as constituting an endorsement by IHO or IAG of this product.

14 It can be observed that this provision is a near verbatim repetition of Article 3 of the 1958 Convention on the Territorial Sea and Contiguous Zone. See, Convention on the Territorial Sea and Contiguous Zone, adopted 29 April 1958, 516 UNTS 205 (entered into force 10 September 1964), Article 3.

15 Scarborough Shoal is described in the relevant British Admiralty Sailing Directions (Pilot) as being "step-to on all sides and consists of a narrow belt of coral enclosing a lagoon of clear blue water." While the reef and associated lagoon are extensive, the majority of the feature is submerged at high tide. South Rock, at 3 m high, is the "tallest rock" located at the southeast extremity of the reef. See United Kingdom Hydrographic Office, *China Sea Pilot*, Vol. 2, 9th edition, Admiralty Sailing Directions (Taunton: UKHO, 2010), 74.

16 TALOS Manual, Chapter 4, at 6.

17 See J.R.V. Prescott and C.H. Schofield, *The Maritime Political Boundaries of the World* (2nd ed., Leiden/Boston: Martinus Nijhoff Publishers, 2005), at 142–147.

18 Article 7(2) does not, however, create a third justification for the drawing of straight baselines in addition to the two laid out in Art 7(1) (namely a deeply indented or cut into coastline or a fringe of islands). See Prescott and Schofield, *ibid.*, at 148–149.

19 See *ibid.*, at 154–156.

20 See *ibid.*, at 157–158.

21 It should be noted, however, that Art 7(5) in isolation does not justify the drawing of straight baselines in the absence of a deeply indented or cut into coastline or the existence of a fringe of islands along the coast. See Prescott and Schofield, *ibid.*, at 158.

22 See Prescott and Schofield, *ibid.*, at 158–159.

23 J.R.V. Prescott, *The Maritime Political Boundaries of the World* (London: Methuen, 1985), at 64. See also Prescott and Schofield, (n 17), at 162–164.

24 See J.A. Roach and R.W. Smith, *Excessive Maritime Claims* (3rd ed., Leiden: Martinus Nijhoff, 2012), at 15.

25 See *ibid.*, at 3–16.

26 U.S. Department of State, Bureau of Oceans and Environmental and Scientific Affairs, 'Developing Standard Guidelines for Evaluating Straight Baselines', *Limits in the Seas, No. 106*, August 1987, available at <http://www.state.gov/documents/organization/59584.pdf>.

27 *Case Concerning Maritime Delimitation and Territorial Questions between Qatar and Bahrain (Qatar v Bahrain)* [2001] Merits, ICJ Rep 40, at 67, para 212. For a useful discussion of these provisions see, CG Lathrop, JA Roach and DR Rothwell (eds), "Baselines under the International Law of the Sea: Reports of the International Law Association (ILA) Committee on Baselines under the International Law of the Sea" (2019) 2(1-2) *Brill Research Perspectives on the Law of the Sea*, at 66-82.

28 U.S. Department of State, Bureau of Oceans and Environmental and Scientific Affairs, 'Straight Baselines Claim: China', *Limits in the Seas, No.117*, 1996, available at <http://www.state.gov/documents/organization/57692.pdf>, 3.

29 *Ibid.*, 8.

30 See D.J. Dzurek, 'The People's Republic of China Straight Baseline Claim', (Summer 1996) 4(2) *Boundary and Security Bulletin* 77–89. See also LOSC, Part III (Articles 34–45), especially Articles 35(a) and 37–38. Article 35(a) has the effect that where straight baselines drawn in accordance with LOSC Article have the effect of enclosing as internal waters areas which had not previously been considered as such, the transit passage regime will continue to apply.

31 In the course of the Third United Nations Conference on the Law of the Sea a number of mainland coastal States did argue that the special rules applicable to archipelagos should also be applicable to their offshore island possessions, these proposals did not prove successful. See Jayewardene, 1990: 140–142 and M.B. Tsamenyi, C.H. Schofield and B. Milligan, 'Navigation through Archipelagos:

Current State Practice', in M.H. Nordquist, T.B. Koh and J.N. Moore (eds.), *Freedom of the Seas, Passage Rights and the 1982 Law of the Sea Convention*, (Leiden/Boston: Martinus Nijhoff, 2009), 413–454.

32 In its analysis of China's straight baseline claims the U.S. Department of State noted that even if hypothetically the Paracel Islands were an independent archipelagic State, the water to land ration within China's declared baselines "would approximate 26.1:1", thus "far exceeding" the maximum limit of 9:1. See U.S. Department of State, 'Straight Baselines Claim: China', *supra* note 27, at 8,

33 South China Sea Arbitration, Award (n 10), para.573.

34 *Ibid.*

35 *Ibid.*

36 *Ibid.*, para.575.

37 *Ibid.*

38 *Ibid.*, para.576. See also, C.H. Schofield, 'The Regime of Islands Reframed: Developments in the Definition of Islands and their Role in the Delimitation of Maritime Boundaries under the International Law of the Sea', *Brill Research Perspectives in the Law of the Sea*, 3(1-2) (2021): 86-88.

39 Law on the Territorial Sea and Contiguous Zone, 25 February 1992, available at Annex II, U.S. Department of State, 'Straight Baselines Claim: China', *supra* note 27, at 11–14.

40 US Department of State, 'Taiwan's Maritime Claims', *Limits in the Seas No. 127*, Washington, DC, 15 November 2005, at 11.

41 *Ibid.*, at 15.

42 *Ibid.*

43 *Ibid.*

44 The *Peta Menunjukkan Sempadan Perairan dan Pelantar Benua Malaysia* or 'Map Showing the Territorial Waters and Continental Shelf Boundaries of Malaysia', often referred to as the *Peta Baru* (new map), published by the Malaysian Directorate of National Mapping in two sheets.

45 See M.J. Valencia, 'Validity of Malaysia's Baselines and Territorial Sea Claim in the Northern Malacca Strait', (2003) 27 *Marine Policy* 367; Schofield and Tan-Mullins, (n 9), at 86–87.

46 See, US Department of State, 'Continental Shelf Boundary: Indonesia-Malaysia', *Limits in the Seas*, No. 1 (US Department of State, Bureau of Intelligence and Research, 21 January 1970), at 2.

47 V.L. Forbes, 'The Territorial Sea Datum of Malaysia', (2007) 14(4) *MIMA Bulletin* 3, at 7–8.

48 *Ibid.*

49 Malaysia and Vietnam, 'Joint Submission to the Commission on the Limits of the Continental Shelf pursuant to Article 76, paragraph 8 of the United Nations Convention on the Law of the Sea 1982 in respect of the southern part of the South China Sea', Executive Summary, 6 May 2009, available at <http://www.un.org/Depts/los/clcs_new/submissions_files/submission_mysvnm_33_2009.htm>.

50 Through Vietnam's *Statement on the Territorial Sea, the Contiguous Zone, the Exclusive Economic Zone and the Continental Shelf* of 12 May 1977, available at <http://www.un.org/Depts/los/LEGISLATIONANDTREATIES/PDFFILES/VNM_1977_Statement.pdf>.

51 *Declaration on Baseline of Territorial Waters* of 12 November 1982, available at <http://www.un.org/Depts/los/LEGISLATIONANDTREATIES/PDFFILES/VNM_1982_Statement.pdf>.

52 See Schofield and Tan-Mullins (n 9), at 89.

53 U.S. Department of State, Straight Baselines: Vietnam, *Limits in the Seas no. 99* (Washington, DC: Bureau of Intelligence and Research, 12 December 1983), at 5.

54 *Ibid.*, at 5–6.

55 *Ibid.* In particular the U.S. analysis highlighted that the longest distance between basepoints is 161.8 M, (the average being 84.6 M), that island basepoints averaged 39.4 M offshore with a maximum of 80.7 M offshore, and that the internal waters claimed total approximately 27,000 M^2 (93,000 km^2).

56 The U.S. note of protest stated that "there is no basis in international law for the system of straight baselines provided in the declaration of November 12, 1982." See Roach and Smith, (n 24), at 99.

57 The Thai note, dated 9 December 1985, stated that between points 0 and A7, Vietnam's claimed straight baselines were "at variance with the well-established rules of international law," referring to both the 1958 and 1982 Conventions, and concluded that "the Government of Thailand reserves all its rights under international law in relation to the sea areas in question and the airspace above them." See *UN Law of the Sea Bulletin* 7 (April 1986): 111.

58 "Archipelagic States" are defined in Article 46 of the LOSC as being States "constituted wholly by one or more archipelagos and may include other islands"
59 LOSC Article 47(1).
60 LOSC Article 47(1).
61 LOSC Article 47(1). Article 47(7) provides clarification as to what may be reasonably regarded as water and land in order to aid in the computation of the water to land ratio, providing that for this purpose

> land areas may include waters lying within the fringing reefs of islands and atolls, including that part of a steep-sided oceanic plateau which is enclosed or nearly enclosed by a chain of limestone islands and drying reefs lying on the perimeter of the plateau.

62 LOSC Article 47(2).
63 *Ibid.*
64 Indonesia, *Act Concerning Indonesian Waters*, 20 January 1960, Article 1. Reproduced in US Department of State, Bureau of Intelligence and Research, 'Straight Baselines: Indonesia', in *Limits in the Seas, No. 35* (Washington, DC, 1971).
65 Indonesia, *Act No 6 of 8 August 1996 Regarding Indonesian Waters*, available at <www.un.org/Depts/los/ LEGISLATIONANDTREATIES/PDFFILES/IDN_1996_Act.pdf>.
66 See *Peraturan Pemerintah* (PP) [Government Regulation] No. 61 of 1998, on the List of Geographical Coordinates of the Base Points of the Archipelagic Baselines of Indonesia in the Natuna Sea, available at <http://www.un.org/Depts/los/LEGISLATION ANDTREATIES/PDFFILES/IDN_1998_Regulation61.pdf>.
67 See C.H. Schofield and I.M.A. Arsana, 'Closing the Loop: Indonesia's Revised Archipelagic Baselines System', (2009) 1(2) *Australian Journal of Marine and Ocean Affairs*, at 57–62.
68 For maritime zone notification and a complete list of the coordinates, available at <http://www.un.org/Depts/los/LEGISLATIONANDTREATIES/STATEFILES/IDN.htm>.
69 See online: <http://www.un.org/Depts/los/LEGISLATIONANDTREATIES/PDFFILES/PHL_1961_Act.pdf>.
70 An Act to Amend Section One of the Republic Act Numbered Thirty Hundred and Forty-Six, Entitled An Act to Define the Baselines of the Territorial Sea of the Philippines', available at <http://www.un.org/Depts/los/LEGISLATIONANDTREATIES/PDFFILES/PHL_1968_Act.pdf>.
71 *Ibid.*
72 The Philippines, Republic Act No. 3046, An Act to Define the Baselines of the Territorial Sea of the Philippines, of 17 June 1961, subsequently amended by through Republic Act No. 5446, An Act to Amend Section One of the Republic Act Numbered Three Hundred and Forty Six Entitled 'An Act to Define the Baselines of the Territorial Sea of the Philippines', of 18 September 1968, available at <http://www.un.org/Depts/los/LEGISLATIONANDTREATIES/STATEFILES/PHL.htm>. See also M.B. Tsamenyi, C.H. Schofield and B. Milligan, 'Navigation through Archipelagos: Current State Practice', in M.H. Nordquist, T.B. Koh and J. Norton Moore (eds.), *Freedom of the Seas, Passage Rights and the 1982 Law of the Sea Convention* (The Hague: Martinus Nijhoff, 2008), at 413–454, at 442–445.
73 *A Treaty of Peace Between the United States and Spain*, US Congress, 55th Cong, 3d Sess, Senate Doc. No. 62, Part 1 (Washington, DC: Government Printing Office, 1899), at 5–11, available at <http://avalon.law.yale.edu/19th_century/sp1898.asp>.
74 The Philippines, Constitution of the Republic (in force since 17 January 1973), Art 1, available at <http://www.un.org/Depts/los/LEGISLATIONANDTREATIES/PDFFILES/PHL_1973_Constitution.pdf>.
75 The Philippines, Republic Act No. 9522, An Act to Amend Certain Provisions of Republic Act No. 3046, As Amended by Republic Act No. 5446, To Define the Archipelagic Baselines of the Philippines, and for Other Purposes, 10 March 2009. See (200) 70 Law of the Sea Bulletin, at 32.
76 *Ibid.*
77 Information on the work of the Commission including its Rules of Procedure and Scientific and Technical Guidelines as well as regarding the Submissions of coastal States and the Recommendations of the Commission are available on the Commission's website at, <https://www.un.org/Depts/los/clcs_new/clcs_home.htm>.
78 Malaysia and Vietnam, 'Outer Limits of the Continental Shelf beyond 200 Nautical Miles from the Baselines: Submissions to the Commission: Joint Submission by Malaysia and Socialist Republic of Viet Nam', (n 49).

79 Vietnam, Outer Limits of the Continental Shelf beyond 200 Nautical Miles from the Baselines: Submission to the Commission: Submission by the Socialist Republic of Viet Nam, Executive Summary, 7 May 2009, available at <http://www.un.org/Depts/los/clcs_new/submissions_files/submission_vnm_37_2009.htm>.

80 Brunei-Darussalam, Brunei-Darussalam's Preliminary Submission concerning the Outer Limits of Its Continental Shelf, 12 May 2009, available at <http://www.un.org/Depts/los/clcs_new/commission_preliminary.htm.>; China, Preliminary Information Indicative of the Outer Limits of the Continental Shelf Beyond 200 Nautical Miles of the People's Republic of China, 11 May 2009, available at <http://www.un.org/depts/los/clcs_new/submissions_files/preliminary/chn2009preliminaryinformation_english.pdf>; The Philippines, Outer Limits of the Continental Shelf beyond 200 Nautical Miles from the Baselines: Submissions to the Commission: Submission by the Republic of the Philippines, 19 July 2012, available at <http://www.un.org/Depts/los/clcs_new/submissions_files/submission_phl_22_2009.htm>; China, Outer Limits of the Continental Shelf beyond 200 Nautical Miles from the Baselines: Submission to the Commission: Submission by the People's Republic of China, 14 December 2012, available at <http://www.un.org/Depts/los/clcs_new/submissions_files/submission_chn_63_2012.htm>.

81 Malaysia, Partial Submission to the Commission on the Limits of the Continental Shelf pursuant to Article 76, paragraph 8 of the United Nations Convention on the Law of the Sea 1982 in the South China Sea, Executive Summary, available at <https://www.un.org/Depts/los/clcs_new/submissions_files/mys85_2019/20171128_MYS_ES_DOC_001_secured.pdf>.

82 See Note from the Permanent Mission of the People's Republic of China addressed to the Secretary General of the United Nations, CML/17/2009, 7 May 2009, available at <http://www.un.org/Depts/los/clcs_new/submissions_files/submission_mysvnm_33_2009.htm>; see also, an English language translation of China's reaction to Vietnam's submission available at <http://www.un.org/depts/los/clcs_new/submissions_files/vnm37_09/chn_2009re_vnm.pdf>.

83 See Note from the Permanent Mission of Malaysia to the United Nations to the Secretary General of the United Nations, HA 24/09, 20 May 2009; and, Note from the Permanent Mission of the Socialist Republic of Vietnam to the United Nations to the Secretary General of the United Nations, 86/HC-2009, 8 May 2009, available at <http://www.un.org/Depts/los/clcs_new/submissions_files/submission_mysvnm_33_2009.htm>; and, <http://www.un.org/depts/los/clcs_new/submissions_files/vnm37_09/vnm_re_chn_2009re_vnm.pdf>.

84 Note from the Permanent Mission of the Socialist Republic of Vietnam to the United Nations to the Secretary General of the United Nations, No. 86/HC-2009, 8 May 2009, available at <http://www.un.org/Depts/los/clcs_new/submissions_files/vnm37_09/vnm_re_chn_2009re_vnm.pdf >.

85 See Note from the Permanent Mission of Indonesian to the United Nations to the Secretary-General of the United Nations, No. 840/POL-703/VII/10, 8 July 2010, available at http://www.un.org/Depts/los/clcs_new/submissions_files/mysvnm33_09/idn_2010re_mys_vnm_e.pdf.

86 See Note from the Permanent Mission of the Republic of the Philippines to the United Nations to the Secretary-General of the United Nations, No. 000228, 5 April 2011, available at <http://www.un.org/Depts/los/clcs_new/submissions_files/mysvnm33_09/phl_re_chn_2011.pdf>.

87 See Note from the Permanent Mission of the People's Republic of China to the United Nations to the Secretary-General of the United Nations, CML/8/2011, 14 April 2011, available at <http://www.un.org/Depts/los/clcs_new/submissions_files/mysvnm33_09/chn_2011_re_phl_e.pdf>.

88 Ibid.

89 China, Note Verbale Received with regards to the submission made by Malaysia, 12 December 2019 and 23 March 2020, available at https://www.un.org/Depts/los/clcs_new/submissions_files/submission_mys_12_12_2019.html.

90 China, Note Verbale Received with regards to the submission made by Malaysia, 12 December 2019, available at https://www.un.org/Depts/los/clcs_new/submissions_files/submission_mys_12_12_2019.html.

91 See the CLCS website at <https://www.un.org/Depts/los/clcs_new/submissions_files/submission_mys_12_12_2019.html>.

92 S. Bateman and C.H. Schofield, 'Outer Shelf Claims in the South China Sea: New Dimension to Old Disputes', *RSIS Commentary* 65/2009 (Singapore: S. Rajaratnam School of International Studies, 1 July 2009), available at <http://www.rsis.edu.sg/publications/Perspective/RSIS0652009.pdf>.

93 R. Beckman, 'US Joins "Lawfare" by Diplomatic Notes Over Chinese Claims in the S. China Sea', *The Straits Times*, 10 June 2020, available at <https://www.straitstimes.com/opinion/us-joins-lawfare-by-diplomatic-notes-over-chinese-claims-in-s-china-sea>.

94 Article 76(10) of UNCLOS explicitly provides that "[t]he provisions of this article are without prejudice to the question of delimitation of the continental shelf between States with opposite or adjacent coasts". See also, Annex II of UNCLOS and the Rules of Procedure of the Commission on the Limits of the Continental Shelf. The current version of the Rules is contained in Doc. CLCS/40/Rev.1 of 17 April 2008, available at <http://www.un.org/Depts/los/clcs_new/commission_documents.htm#Rules%20of%20Procedure>.

95 Indonesia-Malaysia continental shelf agreement, note 33. Note that this section draws on Schofield (n 8).

96 J.I. Charney and L.M. Alexander (eds.) *International Maritime Boundaries*, Vol. I, (Dordrecht/Boston/London: Martinus Nijhoff Publishers, 1993), at 1021.

97 *Ibid.*, at 316.

98 *Agreement between the Government of the Socialist Republic of Vietnam and the Government of the Republic of Indonesia concerning the delimitation of the continental shelf boundary*, 26 June 2003 (entry into force 29 May 2007), reprinted in D.A. Colson and R.W. Smith (eds.) *International Maritime Boundaries*, Vol.VI (Leiden/Boston: Martinus Nijhoff, 2011), at 4301.

99 See, *Peta Negara Kesatuan Republik Indonesia* [Map of the Unitary State of the Republic of Indonesia], Badan Informasi Geospasial [Agency for Geospatial Information] (BIG), Cibinong, 2017.

100 *Ibid.* See also, L. Bernard and C.H. Schofield, 'Separate Lines: Challenges and Opportunities of Differentiated Seabed and Water Column Boundaries' in M.H. Nordquist and J.N. Moore (eds.), *International Marine Economy: Law and Policy* (Leiden/Boston: Martinus Nijhoff, 2017), at 283.

101 See *Agreement between the Socialist Republic of Viet Nam and the People's Republic of China on the Delimitation of the Territorial Sea, Exclusive Economic Zone and Continental Shelf between the Two Countries in in Beibu Bay/Gulf of Tonkin*, 25 December 2000 (entry into force 30 June 2004); and, available at <www.un.org/Depts/los/legislationandtreaties.htm>. See also, Nguyen Hong Thao, 'Maritime Delimitation and Fishery Cooperation in the Tonkin Gulf', (2005) 36 *Ocean Development and International Law* 25.

102 R.W. Smith and D. Colson (eds.) *International Maritime Boundaries*, Vol. V (The Hague: Martinus Nijhoff, 2005), at 3748.

103 Zou Keyuan, 'The Sino-Vietnamese Agreement on Maritime Boundary Delimitation in the Gulf of Tonkin', (2005) 36 *Ocean Development and International Law* 13–24, at 16.

104 Smith and Colson, (n 101) above, at 3749. See also, N.H. Thao, 'Maritime Delimitation and Fishery Cooperation in the Tonkin Gulf', (2005) 36 *Ocean Development and International Law* 25–44.

105 The territorial sea boundaries between Brunei-Darussalam and Malaysia were defined in 1958 out to the 100 fathom isobath through two British Orders in Council. See, Charney and Alexander, (n 95), at 924.

106 See I. Storey, 'Brunei's Contested Sea Border with China', in B. Elleman, S. Kotkin and C.H. Schofield (eds.), *Beijing's Power and China's Borders* (Armonk: M.E. Sharpe Publishers, 2012), 36, 39–41. It is also notable that Brunei's submission of preliminary information to the CLCS further states that maritime boundaries between Brunei and Malaysia have been delimited by virtue of the 1958 Orders in Council and "an Exchange of Letters dated 16 March 2009" which served to delimit territorial sea, EEZ and continental shelf rights "to a distance of 200 nautical miles." See, Brunei (n 79) 'Brunei-Darussalam's Preliminary Submission concerning the Outer Limits of its Continental Shelf'.

107 See Schofield and Tan-Mullins, (n 7).

108 LOSC Articles 74(3) and 83(3).

109 Ibid.

110 See C.H. Schofield 'Adrift on Complex Waters: Geographical, Geopolitical and Legal Dimensions to the South China Sea Disputes', in L. Buszynski and C. Roberts(eds.), *The South China Sea and Australia's Regional Security Environment* (London: Routledge, 2014), at 24–45.

111 South China Sea Arbitration, Award, (n 8), para. 1203(B)(2). See also, for example, R. Beckman, '"Deliberate Ambiguity" and the Demise of China's Claim to Historic Rights in the South China Sea', (2016) 1 *Asia-Pacific Journal of Ocean Law and Policy* 164–182, at 182.

112 See Schofield, (n 9), at 44–48.

113 Partially delimited through a maritime boundary in respect of the Gulf of Tonkin/Beibu Gulf. See, *Agreement between the Socialist Republic of Viet Nam and the People's Republic of China on the Delimitation of the Territorial Sea, Exclusive Economic Zone and Continental Shelf between the Two Countries in the Tonkin Gulf*, 25 December 2000 (entry into force 30 June 2004).

114 Any such delimitation negotiations are likely to be severely impaired on account of Philippines historical and ongoing claims to sovereignty over the Sabah region of northern Borneo.

115 The territorial sea boundaries between Brunei and Malaysia were delimited in 1958 out to the 100 fathom isobath through two British Orders in Council. Additionally, a 16 March 2009 Exchange of Letters, appears to signify agreement on to delimit territorial sea, EEZ and continental shelf rights "to a distance of 200 nautical miles."

116 In respect of which a continental shelf delimitation line has been agreed. See, *Agreement between the Government of Malaysia and the Government of the Republic of Indonesia on the Delimitation of the Continental Shelf between the Two Countries*, 27 October 1969 (entered into force 7 November 1969).

117 In respect of which a continental shelf delimitation line has been agreed. See, *Agreement between the Government of the Socialist Republic of Vietnam and the Government of the Republic of Indonesia Concerning the Delimitation of the Continental Shelf Boundary*, 26 June 2003 (entry into force 29 May 2007).

118 See, Schofield and Tan-Mullins, (n 7), at 75–116.

119 International Court of Justice, *Case Concerning Sovereignty over Pedra Branca/Pulau Batu Puteh, Middle Rocks and South Ledge (Malaysia/Singapore)*, Judgment of 23 May 2008. See also, R. Beckman and C.H. Schofield, 'Moving Beyond Disputes over Island Sovereignty: ICJ Decision Sets Stage for Maritime Boundary Delimitation in the Singapore Strait' (2009) 40 *Ocean Development and International Law* 1–35.

120 See, for example, F. Zhang, 'Assessing China's Response to the South China Sea Arbitration Ruling', (2017) 71(4) *Australian Journal of International Affairs* 440–459, at 447–454.

121 See, for example, D. Grossman, 'Why Is China Pressing Indonesia Again Over Its Maritime Claims', *World Politics Review*, 16 January 2020, available at <https://www.worldpoliticsreview.com/articles/28476/why-is-china-pressing-indonesia-again-over-the-natuna-islands>.

122 See, for example, 'The South China Sea: Chinese Ship Haiyang Dizhi 8 Seen Near Malaysian Waters, Security Sources Say', *South China Morning Post*, 18 April 2020, available at <https://www.scmp.com/news/asia/southeast-asia/article/3080510/south-china-sea-chinese-ship-haiyang-dizhi-8-seen-near>.

123 See, for example, *The Maritime Executive*, 'Chinese Survey Vessel Returns to Disputed Vietnamese Waters', 15 April 2020, available at <https://www.maritime-executive.com/article/chinese-survey-vessel-returns-to-disputed-vietnamese-waters>.

124 See K. Huang, 'Beijing Marks Out Claims in South China Sea by Naming Geographical Features', *South China Morning Post*, 20 April 2020, available at <https://www.scmp.com/news/china/diplomacy/article/3080721/beijing-marks-out-claims-south-china-sea-naming-geographica>.

125 See L. Xin, 'Sansha City Establishes Two Districts for Better Management', *Global Times*, 18 April 2020, available at <https://www.globaltimes.cn/content/1186004.shtml>.

126 See United Kingdom Hydrographic Office (UKHO), *Admiralty Sailing Directions: China Sea Pilot (NP30)*, Vol. 1 (8th ed., Taunton: UKHO, 2010), at 69.

127 South China Sea Arbitration Award (n 8), paras 555–556.

7

THE U-SHAPED LINE AND ITS LEGAL IMPLICATIONS

Keyuan Zou and Qiang Ye

Introduction

The "U-shaped line" (also alternatively called "dotted line" or "nine-dash line") is a unique legal phenomenon in international law and becomes the hottest subject in the discussion of East Asian maritime disputes. The common Chinese term for the "U-shaped line" is "traditional maritime boundary line," which refers to a line with nine segments off the Chinese coast in the South China Sea, as shown mainly on Chinese maps. The U-shaped line originally came into being in 1914 and later gradually expanded in a southerly direction. It was officially confirmed in 1947 after the Second World War (WWII). Since then the line has remained unchanged on all the Chinese maps published either on mainland China or in Taiwan. For a long time, China kept silent and offered no express clarification on the legal nature of this line.

Recently, however, the legality and legal implications of the U-shaped line have become a hot-spot issue subject to discussion and debate at both global and regional levels whenever talking about the South China Sea issues. For example, the US Department of State published a report on *China's Maritime Claims in the South China Sea* on 5 December 2014, focusing on the coordinates of the dashes of the evolving U-shaped line, and on the terminologies regarding to the maritime laws and *Notes verbale* of China. The South China Sea Arbitration (the Philippines v. China) raised important issues regarding the contemporary relevance and validity of the U-shaped line, and the relationship between the 1982 United Nations Convention on the Law of the Sea (LOSC) and China's legal entitlements within this line.

This chapter will first examine the origin and evolution of the U-shaped line in almost the past century, officially published by both the governments of Republic of China (ROC) and the People's Republic of China (PRC); then, it will review a range of practices and declarations by Chinese government in relation to the U-shaped line that may be helpful for the understanding of China's claims within the line; then it will explore other States' responses to the U-shaped line, both from the coastal States of the South China Sea, and from the major powers outside the region; it will also look through some academic accounts of the legal implications of the U-shaped line from different perspectives; and finally, concluding remarks will be given.

China's official actions relating to the legal implications of the U-shaped line

Evolution of the U-shaped line

In the late Qing Dynasty and early ROC period, a series of survey activities and intellectual discussions on China's boundaries had been conducted by a number of government officials as well as private cartographers, following the awareness that parts of the Qing territory had been occupied by foreign powers. Against this background, a line encompassing Pratas (Dongsha) and Paracel (Xisha) Islands, which has been regarded as the earliest analogue to the U-shaped line, was first marked by Hu Jinjie, a Chinese cartographer, in a map entitled Chinese Territorial Map before the Qianlong-Jiaqing Period (前清乾嘉以前中華領域圖, i.e. before 1735–1820) in December 1914.[1] The idea behind this map may have come from the document on the patrol of the Li Zhun fleet around the South China Sea in 1909,[2] and this line was outlined in reaction to the recovery of Pratas Islands from the Japanese. However, the line was later modified due to the cartographer's increased understanding of China's actual claim to the island features in the South China Sea.

It is worth noting that, by 1927 the Zhonghua Book Company's Map of National Humiliation included the so-called Chinese lost territory such as mainland Southeast Asia, northern Borneo and the Sulu Islands within a line which was labelled as the "old national boundary."[3] One explanation for why the map was drawn this way is probably that the cartographer believed that these places which had paid tribute to Chinese emperors in the past, such as the Sultanate of Sulu, should be considered part of the Chinese empire.[4]

However, this idea was not accepted by the ROC government. The period of official cartographic uncertainty began to end after the establishment of a new central government under the Chinese Nationalist Party (Kuomintang) of Chiang Kai-shek in October 1928. Just over a year later, in January 1930, the new government promulgated the Inspection Regulations of Land and Water Maps. The regulations mandated the formation of a Land and Water Maps Review Committee, with representatives of government ministries, to inspect Chinese maps and specify what they could and could not display. The process would, in effect, define China's official geobody. In January 1935, the Committee published the Chinese and English names of 132 insular features in the South China Sea, which were divided into four island groups.[5] The Committee conferred the Chinese name Tuansha (團沙) for the Spratlys. The publication had an annexed map that marked the James Shoal at the location of about 4° north latitude, 112° east longitude, though there was no demarcation of the line on the map.[6] It is believed that the reason for publishing this list was a response to the situation that France and Japan were competing for the grapple of the South China Sea islands starting from the 1920s.

During the following decade, through the turmoil of the late 1930s and the Second World War, new ideas about China's maritime geobody emerged among influential individuals. For example, in 1936, Bai Meichu, a founder of the China Geography Society, published his New Atlas of China's Construction (中華建設新圖) including the new information about China agreed on by the Maps Review Committee and encompassing all the listed maritime features in the South China Sea by another analogue of the U-shaped line.[7]

The ideas of using a U-shaped line to mark the scope of China's sovereign and maritime claims in the South China Sea were then transmitted to State officials who, eventually, developed them into an official territorial claim.[8]

Japan's wartime occupation of the archipelagos and island groups in the South China Sea had suspended a prior contest in the 1930s between France, Japan, and the ROC.[9] By 30

March 1939, Japan had militarily occupied the Pratas, Paracel, and Spratly Islands. On the following day, it formally proclaimed the creation of the Shinnan Guntō (新南群島, New South Archipelago), an administrative area covering a portion of the Spratlys and incorporated into Taiwan province.[10]

In April 1946, just a few months after the Second World War when Japan unconditionally surrendered and China recovered Taiwan and the South China Sea islands from Japan, the new ROC governor of Taiwan, Chen Yi, requested permission from the Executive Yuan to take over Pratas, the Paracels, and the Spratlys, arguing that they had been administered by Taiwan during the Japanese occupation period. Chen asked the government to request the assistance of the American authorities in the Philippines with the takeover. Following a request from the Executive Yuan, the Ministry of the Interior reported that Pratas and the Paracels had been administered by Guangdong province before the war and they had little information about them. In June 1946, due to a temporary failure to relocate the exact position of the Spratlys, the Foreign Ministry actively engaged the Ministry of Military Command and the Ministry of Military Administration to deliberate on the takeover of the Pratas and Paracel Islands.[11]

This may be the essential reason for drawing up the Sketch Map of the South China Sea Islands (南海諸島位置略圖). This task was commissioned for a meeting of representatives from the Ministry of Foreign Affairs, Ministry of the Interior, Ministry of National Defence, and Navy at the ROC Ministry of the Interior on 25 September 1946. Thus, the U-shaped line was first drawn on an official map, marking eight dashes.[12]

In 1947, another two dashes were added to the Gulf of Tonkin, now also known as Beibu Gulf. In October the same year, further improvement was made finally leading to eleven dashes (see Figure 7.1).[13] On 1 December 1947, the Chinese Ministry of Interior renamed the islands in the South China Sea and formally allocated them into the administration of the Hainan Special Region.[14] Meanwhile, the same ministry prepared a location map of the islands in the South China Sea, which was first released for internal use.

In February 1948, the *Atlas of Administrative Areas of the Republic of China* was officially published,[15] in which the above Map of Position of the South China Sea Islands was included.[16] This is the first officially released map with the line in the South China Sea for public use. According to the official explanation, the basis for drawing the line was that

> [t]he southernmost limit of the South China Sea territory should be at the James Shoal. This limit was followed by our governmental departments, schools, and publishers before the anti-Japanese war, and it was also recorded on file in the Ministry of Interior. Accordingly, it should remain unchanged.[17]

After the founding in 1949, the PRC inherited the U-shaped line. Official Chinese government maps published between 1950 and 1956 continued to depict the dashed line from the 1947 map – reduced from eleven to ten dashes, but otherwise unchanged – without explanation of the status of the waters or seabed encompassed by the line.[18] An example can be seen from the Location Map of the South China Sea Islands attached to the 1951 New Map of the PRC.[19]

China did not give a public explanation about the reason why the line underwent a slight change in 1953, in particular, why the two segments in the Gulf of Tonkin were removed from the map. It is believed that this might be related to the transfer of the sovereignty over the Bai Long Wei Island (Bach Long Vi) in the Gulf from China to Vietnam.[20] It is said that the removal of the two segments was approved in 1953 by Zhou Enlai, then Premier of the PRC.[21]

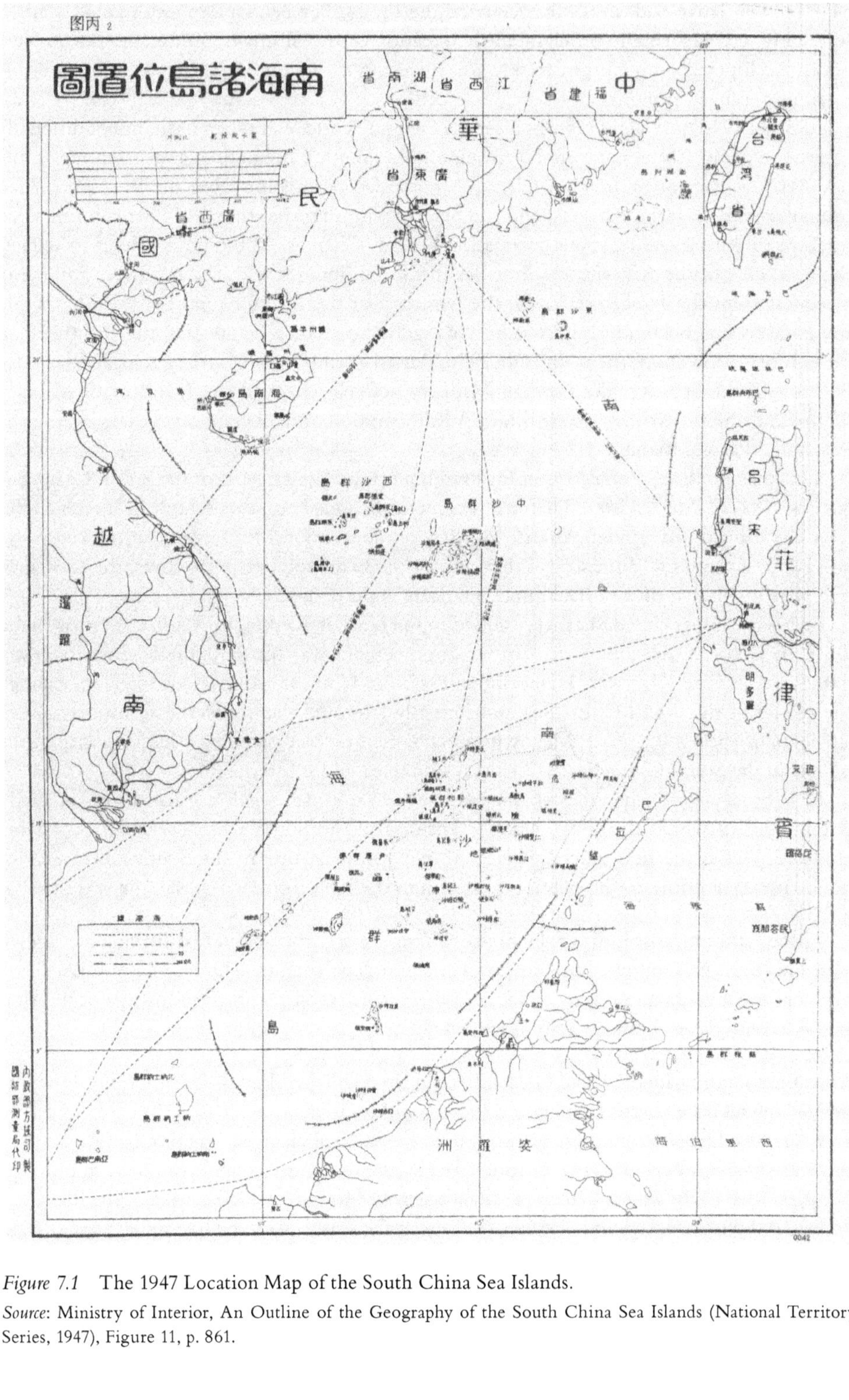

Figure 7.1 The 1947 Location Map of the South China Sea Islands.

Source: Ministry of Interior, An Outline of the Geography of the South China Sea Islands (National Territory Series, 1947), Figure 11, p. 861.

Between the late 1950s and 2000s, the U-shaped line has been continuously left unchanged on all official Chinese maps.[22]

On 7 May 2009, China submitted two *Notes verbale* to the Secretary General of the United Nations. One was in response to the joint submission of Malaysia and Vietnam to the Commission on the Limits of the Continental Shelf (CLCS), the other to a separate submission of Vietnam, in which those States provided information on their continental shelf beyond 200 nautical miles. China's substantively identical *Notes verbale* included a map with the U-shaped line (see Figure 7.2).[23] China declared that it has "indisputable sovereignty over the islands of the South China Sea and the adjacent waters, and enjoys sovereign rights and jurisdiction over the relevant waters as well as the seabed and subsoil thereof (*see attached map*)."[24]

In January 2013, China issued a slightly amended version of the U-shaped line map, which included a tenth dash east of Taiwan. The January 2013 map depicts the ten dashes as marking China's "national boundary." The map's legend states that "China's border on this map is based on the 'Geographical Map of the People's Republic of China' (1:4000 000) published by [China Cartographic Publishing House] in 1989. The administrative district information is as at November 2012."[25]

Official positions of the Chinese government

The domestic laws and policies of China suggest that China asserts a legal basis for its maritime claims that is separate from, and in addition to, the LOSC.

In September 1958, China issued its Declaration on the Territorial Sea, in which it proclaimed a territorial sea of 12 nautical miles extending from all Chinese coasts that

> The breadth of the territorial sea of the People's Republic of China shall be twelve nautical miles. This provision applies to all territories of the People's Republic of China, including the Chinese mainland and its coastal islands, as well as Taiwan and its surrounding islands, the Penghu Islands, the Pratas Islands, the Paracel Islands, Macclesfield Bank, the Spratly Islands, and all other islands belonging to China, which are separated from the mainland and its coastal islands by the high seas.[26]

This statement *per se*, obviously, claimed no more than a 12 nautical miles territorial sea, including for all those island groups in the South China Sea. In addition, it expressly recognized that the South China Sea islands were "separated from the mainland and coastal islands *by the high seas*."[27]

From that year, however, official Chinese claims and protests employed terms such as "adjacent" and "relevant" to characterize the waters surrounding the islands it has claimed. The first case was an official Chinese statement on 11 January 1974, issued five days before China and South Vietnamese forces battled for the control of the southern part of the Paracel Islands (the Crescent Group), and in reaction to South Vietnam's official incorporation of the Spratly Islands on 6 September 1973. It stated that

> the Nansha [Spratly], Xisha [Paracel], Zhongsha [Macclesfield Bank and others], and Dongsha [Pratas] archipelagos are all part of Chinese territory. The People's Republic of China has indisputable sovereignty over these islands and islets. The resources of these islands and their *adjacent seas* also belong entirely to China.
>
> *(Italics added)*[28]

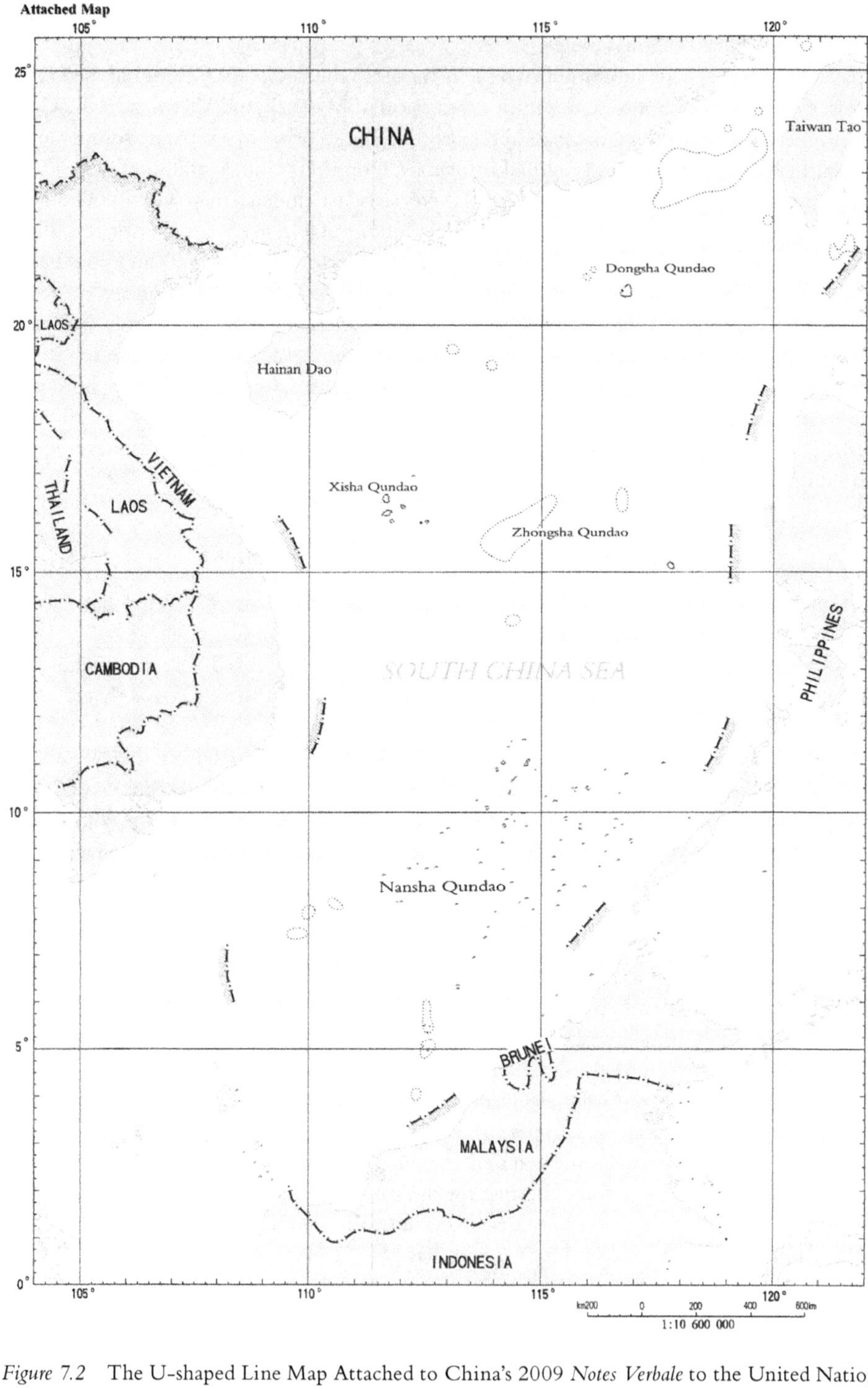

Figure 7.2 The U-shaped Line Map Attached to China's 2009 *Notes Verbale* to the United Nations.
Source: Permanent Mission of the People's Republic of China to the United Nations, Note verbale to the Secretary-General of the United Nations, No. CML/18/2009 (7 May 2009).

This statement did not clarify the geographic extent of these "adjacent" waters.

Another worth noting stance from Chinese official is that, as early as April 1986, Liu Huaqing, the then commander of the Chinese Navy stated that "the sea areas which should be under our jurisdiction are more than three million square kilometres,"[29] which may be based on the following calculation: in the Yellow Sea, an equidistance line for delimitation with the Korean Peninsula; in the East China Sea, a delimitation with Japan the middle line of the Okinawa Trough according to the principle of natural prolongation; and, in the South China Sea, the sea areas within the U-shaped line in addition to the exclusive economic zone east of Taiwan.[30]

The above official stance seems to indicate that the 1958 Declaration does not mean that China confines its maritime rights in the South China Sea to the 12 nautical miles' territorial sea. This can be further confirmed by China's 1992 Law on the Territorial Sea and Contiguous Zone and the 1998 Law on the Exclusive Economic Zone and the Continental Shelf.

In 1992, China's Law on the Territorial Sea and Contiguous Zone reaffirmed the 12 nautical miles territorial sea adjacent to its mainland coast, offshore islands, and South China Sea islands. The 1992 Law added a claim to a 12 nautical miles contiguous zone extending from China's territorial sea limits.

When China ratified the LOSC in June 1996, it seized the occasion to publicly claim "sovereign rights and jurisdiction over an exclusive economic zone of 200 nautical miles and the continental shelf."[31] Two years later, on 26 June 1998, China officially promulgated the Law on the Exclusive Economic Zone and the Continental Shelf. In this law, however, Article 14 provides that "the provisions of this Law shall not affect the historic rights enjoyed by the People's Republic of China."[32] It is generally agreed that this provision is connected to China's claim to the South China Sea within the U-shaped line. However, instead of using the term "historic waters," China wisely chose the more softened term "historic rights."

China's 1999 amended Law on Marine Environmental Protection seemingly follows the 1998 Law and describes its scope of application as covering "internal waters, territorial sea, contiguous zone, exclusive economic zone, continental shelf of the People's Republic of China and *other sea areas under the jurisdiction of the People's Republic of China*."[33] Since coastal State jurisdiction under the LOSC is limited to the aforementioned maritime zones, the phrase "other sea areas" is regarded as referring to areas where China considers that it has historic rights.[34] Similar references to "other sea areas under the jurisdiction of China" can be found in other Chinese laws and regulations, such as Articles 2, 7, 32, 41, and 51 of the 2002 Surveying and Mapping Law[35] and Articles 2, 4, 9, and 10 of the 1996 Provisions on Administration of Foreign-related Marine Scientific Research.[36]

Obviously, according to Chinese domestic legislation, it can be concluded that in addition to sovereignty, sovereign rights and maritime jurisdiction China enjoys under general international law including the LOSC, it is believed by China that the U-shaped line can generate historic rights, which are allowed in international law.

In addition to mainland China's legislation and policy, Taiwan's past attitude seemed more assertive. In 1993, the Taiwanese government adopted the South China Sea Policy Guidelines. Taipei indicated that it regarded the entire area within the U-shaped line as its historic waters by declaring that "the South China Sea area within the *historic water limit* is the maritime area under the jurisdiction of the Republic of China, in which the Republic of China possesses all rights and interests."[37] However, later developments indicate that Taiwan has retreated from its original position. For example, in its draft Territorial Sea Law, the water areas in the South China Sea were regarded as "historic waters" but on the second reading in the Legislative Yuan, this wording was dropped.[38]

In addition to above legislative activities, maritime law enforcement activities and economic activities in the South China Sea, while not directly reflecting clear proposition of the waters within the U-shaped line, have provided shreds of evidence for China's attitude towards its territorial and maritime claims within the line.

In the past two decades, China has intensified its maritime law enforcement patrols in the South China Sea. The South China Sea Brigade of the China Maritime Surveillance increased its patrol journeys from two times in 2001 to 24 times in 2008.[39] In 2008, China Marine Surveillance began to conduct regular maritime patrols in waters (including the South China Sea) under China's jurisdiction within the U-shaped line. According to the *Law Enforcement Bulletin 2008*, China Maritime Surveillance sent 113 vessels/time and 242 aircraft/time, monitoring 285 foreign vessels/time and 43 foreign aircraft/time, including stopping illegal foreign activities in outer continental shelf investigations in 2008,[40] while in 2010, the numbers increased to 188 vessels/time, 523 aircraft/time, monitoring 1303 foreign vessels/time, and 214 foreign aircraft/time.[41] In addition, two China Maritime Surveillance branches were created in 2010 for the South China Sea – the 10th Branch stationed in Haikou and the Law Enforcement Branch for the Paracel, Spratly, and Macclesfield Islands.[42]

Evidence from China's practice in relation to oil exploration and fishery activities in recent years may also be helpful for the understanding of China's stance on the U-shaped line.

As regards oil exploration, a lease of an oil exploratory block in the South China Sea to a foreign oil company may have profound significance for the line. In May 1992, Beijing granted a concession to the Crestone Energy Corporation to explore oil in a 7,347 square-nautical-mile area between Vanguard Bank (*Wan'an Tan*) and the Prince of Wales Bank (*Guangya Tan*), 160 nautical miles from Vietnam's coast within the U-shaped line.[43] Since China had not declared its exclusive economic zone at that time, some scholars assumed that the Crestone concession reflected China's view that it was asserting sovereign authority over the waters and resources within its "nine-interrupted-lines" historic claim.[44] The assumption is plausible since the block is situated around a permanently submerged bank that is difficult to claim independently unless it is claimed as being within the historic rights area or an integral part of the Spratly Islands.

When Vietnam protested China's concession, the reason given by the spokesperson from the Chinese Foreign Ministry was that China had "indisputable sovereignty" over the Nansha and Xisha Islands and the contiguous waters and, as a result, that "[t]he exploitation by China's oil company is irreproachable."[45] There was no express mention of the U-shaped line or historic rights. On the other hand, China protested the Vietnamese concession to foreign oil companies near Vanguard Bank. On 17 April 1996, a spokesperson from the Chinese Foreign Ministry stated that Vietnam's granting of rights to foreign petroleum companies for oil exploration in the sea area of the Nansha Islands was "illegal and invalid" and "an encroachment on China's sovereignty and its maritime rights and interests."[46] The entire area covered by the Vietnamese contract falls within the Wan'an Tan Bei-21 block licensed by Beijing to Crestone Energy Corporation. In 1996, the contract for the Wan'an Tan Bei-21 block was transferred to another US oil company, Harvest Natural Resources, which continued to hold its interest with the license being extended to 31 May 2013.[47]

In 2012, the China National Offshore Oil Corporation (CNOOC) introduced lease blocks opposite to the coast of Vietnam that purport to be within "waters under [the] jurisdiction of the People's Republic of China."[48] It is worth noting that

> portions of two of these blocks (BS16, DW04) extend without explanation to waters that are beyond 200 nautical miles from any Chinese-claimed island (blue hatch). This

> is an assertion of maritime jurisdiction that exceeds what is provided for under the LOS Convention.[49]

With the China Maritime Surveillance (China Coast Guard since 2013) intensifying its patrols in the South China Sea, more incidents have happened in and around Vanguard Bank. The recent incident started in July 2019, when China sent the geological survey ship Haiyang Dizhi 8 and armed coast guard escorts to force an end to Hanoi-sanctioned foreign drilling operations via the Hakuryu-5 oil rig near the Spratly Islands. It is said that in 2018 China forced Vietnam to cancel a $200 million contract with the Spanish energy firm Repsol on exploring the seabed off the southern coast of Vietnam.[50]

As for fishery activities, the most recent incident occurred between late 2019 and early 2020, when dozens of Chinese fishing vessels, along with a coast guard escort, entered waters off the Natuna Islands, which are claimed by Indonesia as its exclusive economic zone but within the U-shaped line. China's Foreign Ministry spokesperson stated unequivocally on 31 December 2019 that

> China has sovereignty over the Nansha Islands and has sovereign rights and jurisdiction over relevant waters near the Nansha Islands. In the meantime, China has historic rights in the South China Sea. Chinese fishermen have long been engaging in fishery activities in relevant waters near the Nansha Islands, which has all along been legal and legitimate. The China Coast Guard were performing their duty by carrying out routine patrol to maintain maritime order and protect our people's legitimate rights and interests in the relevant waters.[51]

The South China Sea Arbitration raised important issues regarding the contemporary relevance and validity of historic claims within the U-shaped line. These issues were triggered by the Philippine Submissions 1 and 2 in its Memorial, which reads:

1 China's maritime entitlements in the South China Sea, like those of the Philippines, may not extend beyond those permitted by the [LOSC];
2 China's claims to sovereign rights and jurisdiction, and to "historic rights," with respect to the maritime areas of the South China Sea encompassed by the so-called "nine-dash line" are contrary to the Convention and without lawful effect to the extent that they exceed the geographic and substantive limits of China's maritime entitlements under the [LOSC].[52]

The arbitral tribunal rendered its final award on 12 July 2016. To respond to the award, China issued the Statement on China's Territorial Sovereignty and Maritime Rights and Interests in the South China Sea (2016 Statement) on the same day. In this statement, China clearly affirmed that it had enjoyed historic rights in the South China Sea:

> China has territorial sovereignty and maritime rights and interests in the South China Sea, including, *inter alia*:
>
> i China has sovereignty over Nanhai Zhudao, consisting of Dongsha Qundao, Xisha Qundao, Zhongsha Qundao, and Nansha Qundao;
> ii China has internal waters, territorial sea, and contiguous zone, based on Nanhai Zhudao;

iii China has an exclusive economic zone and continental shelf, based on Nanhai Zhudao;
iv China has historic rights in the South China Sea.[53]

It is worth noting that in the 2016 Statement, the term "U-shaped line" is only mentioned once at the beginning of the statement:

> To strengthen the administration over Nanhai Zhudao, the Chinese government in 1947 reviewed and updated the geographical names of Nanhai Zhudao, compiled *Nan Hai Zhu Dao Di Li Zhi Lüe* (A Brief Account of the Geography of the South China Sea Islands), and drew *Nan Hai Zhu Dao Wei Zhi Tu* (Location Map of the South China Sea Islands) on which the *dotted line* is marked. This map was officially published and made known to the world by the Chinese government in February 1948.[54]

Thus, some scholars may suppose that the U-shaped line claim has been dropped or de-emphasized by the Chinese government, because

> the Chinese leadership may have realized that the Nine Dash Line has become too much of a diplomatic liability. The Nine-Dash Line is completely *sui generis* and no other state has made a historic maritime claim anything like it. For this reason, the Nine-Dash Line makes China an easy target for foreign criticism in a way that straight baselines around island groups probably will not.[55]

However, according to China's practice, this is not the case. The 2016 Statement has obviously concretized the rights which are included in the U-shaped line. While the geographical scope of the line has been almost unchanged over the years, the content of the rights embraced by them may have evolved, with Chinese practice being informed by the developments in the law of the sea, including its own ratification of the LOSC.[56] This has been further reaffirmed by the latest Chinese official position.

On 9 September 2020, while attending the 10th East Asia Summit Foreign Ministers' Meeting, Foreign Minister Wang Yi pointed out that

> China's sovereignty and sovereign rights over the South China Sea Islands have solid historical and legal grounds. Under international law, UNCLOS included, the historic rights of countries should be respected. China's claims have been consistent. They have not changed, and will not change. They have not expanded, yet nor will they contract. The allegation that China claims all waters within the dotted line as its internal waters and territorial sea is totally unfounded. It is a deliberate attempt to confuse different concepts and distort China's position.[57]

The latest statement by the Chinese Foreign Minister is very significant and at least contains three new legal connotations concerning the U-shaped line. First, he emphasized that China's historic rights in the South China Sea were in conformity with international law and called for other countries to respect; second, the wording "not expand" and "not contract" indicates the scope of China's claims in the South China Sea within the U-shaped line drawn in 1947 and it may mean that China will not expand its claims beyond the U-shaped line, nor will allow other countries to use other means including the LOSC squeezing its original claims within the U-shaped line; and third, he explained that not all waters within the U-shaped line were China's internal waters or territorial sea. That may explain that in addition to internal waters and territorial seas based on the LOSC in the South China Sea, China should enjoy historic jurisdictional waters based on the U-shaped line.

Responses from foreign States

Coastal States of the South China Sea

Vietnam

According to a Vietnamese official, the U-shaped line is exaggerated and legally groundless:

> There is nothing in the international law of the sea that can justify this kind of claim [...] The fact that other countries have carried on their activities in the Bien Dong Sea (South China Sea), the use of the sea and legislative provisions, have disproved neglecting completely the existence of such a line.[58]

Vietnam has also challenged the provision on historic rights in China's EEZ Law. A Vietnamese scholar asked whether

> this article tacitly refers to other interests that China has claimed such as the traditional right of fishing in maritime zones of other countries and the nine broken lines claiming over 80 percent of area of the East Sea.[59]

He further stated that "[a] long time ago, regional countries pursued their normal activities in the East Sea without encountering any Chinese impediment and they have never recognized historical rights of China there."[60] Vietnam officially lodged a protest against China's historic rights in the South China Sea, stating that it will "not recognize any so-called 'historical interests' which are not in consistent with international law and violate the sovereignty, the sovereign rights of Vietnam and Vietnam's legitimate interests in its maritime zones and continental shelf in the eastern Sea as mentioned in article 14" of China's EEZ Law.[61] In response to China's objection to its outer continental shelf claims, Vietnam replied that "China's claim for the nine-dotted line on the map attached to its diplomatic note is null and void as it has no legal, historical and factual ground."[62]

Indonesia

On several occasions, Indonesia has expressed its concern over the publication of Chinese maps showing unclear maritime boundaries between the Natuna and the Spratly Islands. Indonesia was satisfied with China's position that there was no territorial dispute between China and Indonesia regarding the Natuna Islands. In the view of Hasjim Djalal, an Indonesian senior diplomat, the U-shaped line indicates that "the Chinese territorial claims are limited towards the islands and all rights related thereto, and [are] not territorial claims over the South China Sea as a whole."[63] Recently he commented that, since there is no definition of the dashed lines and there are no stated coordinates, the legality and precise location indicated by the lines is not clear.[64] In July 2010, Indonesia sent a diplomatic note to the United

Nations stating that the so-called "nine-dotted lines map" as contained in China's 2009 *Notes verbale* "clearly lacks international legal basis and is tantamount to upsetting" the LOSC;[65] Indonesia reiterated this position in both *Notes verbale* dated 26 May and 12 June in 2020.[66]

Malaysia

For the past decades, Malaysia had been unwilling to express an official stance regarding the U-shaped line.[67] Rather, some views were expressed or implied by personal ways. According to B. A. Hamzah, then Director-General of the Maritime Institute of Malaysia, the line as a claim over the entire South China Sea should be regarded as "frivolous, unreasonable and illogical" as there is no basis in law or history.[68] He further states that the parties concerned should "drop area claims and focus instead on their claim to islands and non-islands." He dismissed the idea that the water areas within the line are historic waters saying that "[b]y no stretch of imagination can the South China Sea be considered by any nation as its internal waters or historic lake as a basis to assert a claim."[69]

Very recently, Malaysia has made its position more clearly. The *Note verbale* to the CLCS submitted by the government of Malaysia on 29 July 2020 expressly rejected

> China's claims to historic rights, or other sovereign rights or jurisdiction, with respect to the maritime areas of the South China Sea encompassed by the relevant part of the 'nine-dash line' as they are contrary to the Convention and without lawful effect to the extent that they exceed the geographic and substantive limits of China's maritime entitlements under the Convention.[70]

The Philippines

In April 2011, the Philippines sent a diplomatic note to the United Nations questioning the validity of the U-shaped line, stating that China's claim to the relevant waters and seabed and subsoil thereof as reflected in the so-called nine-dash line map have no basis in international law, specifically in the LOSC.[71] In January 2013, the then Philippine President Benigno Aquino III decided to initiate an arbitration against China according to Annex VII of the LOSC. One of the Philippine Submissions was to ask the arbitral tribunal to decide the validity of China's historic claims within the U-shaped line. In July 2016, the tribunal issued a ruling rejecting the legal basis for nearly all of China's maritime and territorial claims in the South China Sea. In particular, it determined that China's historic rights claim within the U-shaped line was inconsistent with the LOSC.

Many had believed that President Rodrigo Duterte would put the arbitral award aside and pay much more attention to the Philippines-China friendly relationship. It may have been the case for the early years of the Duterte administration. Recently, however, Duterte has repeatedly reaffirmed that the Philippine lawful rights in the South China Sea had been well defined by the arbitral award.

On 6 March 2020, the Permanent Mission of the Republic of the Philippines to the United Nations presented a *Note verbale* to the CLCS, and reaffirmed that the arbitral tribunal in 2016 had "settled the issue of historic rights and maritime entitlements in the South China Sea."[72] Thus the Philippines expressly rejected China's "claims to historic rights, or other sovereign rights or jurisdiction that exceed the geographic and substantive limits of maritime entitlements under UNCLOS," as they are without lawful effect. It further reiterated that the LOSC "superseded any historic rights, or other sovereign rights or jurisdiction, in excess of the limits imposed therein."[73]

In a pre-recorded speech delivered to the opening of the 75th session of the General Assembly on 22 September 2020, Duterte reaffirmed the outcome of the case:

> The award is now part of international law, beyond compromise and beyond the reach of passing governments to dilute, diminish, or abandon. We firmly reject attempts to undermine it.[74]

Singapore

The debate concerning the legal nature of the line has expanded to non-claimant States.[75] S. Jayakumar, former Senior Minister of Singapore, criticized the ambiguity of China's claims based on the U-shaped line on the occasion of a conference on the South China Sea held in Singapore in June 2011. Jayakumar stated that "China should not continue to leave unaddressed the concerns and questions raised by many over its puzzling and disturbing nine-dotted-lines map."[76] He further warned that

> This ambiguity has led to concerns not just among claimant States, and it is clearly in China's interests to clarify the extent of its claims and thereby dispel any apprehensions over its intentions. Failure to do so could jeopardise the trust essential for any peaceful resolution and undermine all the gains of Chinese diplomacy made in the last two decades.[77]

In response to media queries on the visit of Chinese maritime surveillance vessel *Haixun 31* to Singapore on 20 June 2011, the spokesperson of Singapore's Foreign Ministry commented that "it is in China's own interests to clarify its claims in the SCS with more precision as the current ambiguity as to their extent has caused serious concerns in the international maritime community."[78]

Response from external powers

United States

The United States has not only requested China to clarify its claims in the South China Sea but also denied directly the validity of the U-shaped line in recent years. The then US Secretary of State Hilary Clinton, in June 2011, called on all parties "to clarify their claims in the South China Sea in terms consistent with customary international law, including as reflected in the Law of the Sea Convention."[79] She further stated that "[c]onsistent with international law, claims to maritime space in the South China Sea should be derived solely from legitimate claims to land features."[80] A retired US naval officer recently called for his country to "join Indonesia and Vietnam in protesting China's expansive U-shaped claim of sovereignty in the South China Sea."[81] On 5 December 2014, the US Department of State published the Report on China's Maritime Claims in the South China Sea and stated that China's "dash-line" claim had no legal basis for historic claims. On 13 July 2020, the then US Secretary of State Mike Pompeo issued a formal statement rejecting China's claims to the offshore resources in the South China Sea.[82] He particularly questioned the legal basis of the "Nine-Dashed Line" claim in the South China Sea and pointed out that the arbitral tribunal has in 2016 unanimously rejected China's maritime claims as having no basis in international law. Pompeo concluded that "the world will not allow Beijing to treat the South China Sea as its maritime empire" and said the US stood with its allies and partners in protecting their sovereign rights to offshore resources, consistent with their rights and obligations under international law.[83]

Australia

Australia has long maintained its neutrality with respect to maritime disputes in the South China Sea. However, Australia's submission of a *Note verbale* to the CLCS on 23 July 2020 changed its previous policy and came in the wake of a major change in US policy made by the then Secretary of State Mike Pompeo ten days earlier. Australia followed the United States to support the 2016 Arbitral Award. However, Australia went further and was more precise in its rejection of the legal basis of China's maritime claims in the South China Sea.[84]

Australia's *Note verbale* commenced with a direct rejection of "any claims by China that are inconsistent with the 1982 United Nations Convention on the Law of the Sea" particularly with respect to drawing baselines, delimiting maritime zones, and classifying features. Specifically, Australia argued that China had "no legal basis [...] to draw straight baselines connecting the outermost points of maritime features or 'island groups' in the South China Sea" with specific reference to the entire Pratas Islands, Macclesfield Bank, the Paracel Islands, and the Spratly Islands.[85]

Australia rejected China's assertion that its sovereignty claims over the Paracel and Spratly islands were "widely recognized by the international community." Australia took note of protests by Vietnam and the Philippines to document its case. This is the first time the Paracel Islands had been mentioned in a string of *Notes verbale* submitted to the CLCS since December 2019.

European Union and the United Kingdom

The European Union (EU) has always paid close attention to the developments in the South China Sea. However, while there are many reasons for the EU's interest in the South China Sea, its policies and actions are less visible for a long time.[86] For example, just after the South China Sea Arbitration, the EU issued a statement that "[t]he EU does not take a position on sovereignty aspects relating to claims;" rather, "[i]t expresses the need for the parties to the dispute to resolve it through peaceful means, to clarify their claims and pursue them in respect and in accordance with international law."[87]

In recent years, joining the United States to contain China's rise, the EU has shifted its neutral position leaning more towards the United States. In August 2019, France, Germany, and the United Kingdom (called EU3) released a joint statement showing concerns over the situation in the South China Sea.[88] On 16 September 2020, the EU3 sent a joint diplomatic letter to the UN, rejecting any claim from China in the South China Sea that are, in their view, inconsistent with the LOSC.[89]

Scholarly interpretations of the U-shaped line

Neither the ROC (including the authority of Taiwan after 1949) nor the PRC has officially clarified the legal nature of the line. Over the years there are overall four categories of interpretations about the U-shaped line: a line of maritime features ownership, a line of traditional maritime boundary, a line of historic waters, and a line of historic rights.

Some scholars, such as Li Jinming and Zhao Lihai, argue that the line is an "islands ownership line," which only delimits a claim to the disputed islands, features, and adjacent waters derived from contemporaneous conceptions of international law.[90] Others, such as Fu Kuen-Chen, Huang Wei, Wu Shicun, Gao Zhiguo, and Jia Bingbing, assert that it delimits a "historic rights" waters zone. This confers the sole right to economic exploitation, scientific exploration and research, environmental conservation, and the construction of artificial islands and installations over all of the waters contained within the U-shaped line, on the basis of historic Chinese dominance.[91]

Soon after the enactment of the 1998 EEZ Law, Chinese legal experts began explaining that the "historic rights" China sought to preserve were those within the U-shaped line, beyond the areas covered by its entitlements under the LOSC. One view opines that "[t]he legal definition and implications of [the U-shaped line] are still controversial, but generally the line is regarded as indicating the ownership of islands within the line, although the wording 'historic rights' may imply more than this."[92] This view was shared by Li Jinming and Li Dexia, who wrote that "[t]he [1998] Law does not [...] interpret the precise meaning of the phrase 'historic rights,' but we can imagine that it is related to the historic rights of the region within the dotted line of the South China Sea."[93] In a 2013 article which was co-authored by Gao Zhiguo and Jia Bingbing, described the dashed line as reflecting China's claim that its maritime rights extend beyond those conferred by the LOSC, based on Article 14 of China's 1998 Law.[94] According to Gao and Jia,

> In addition to these rights conferred by UNCLOS, China can assert historic rights within the nine-dash line – under Article 14 of its 1998 law on the EEZ and the continental shelf – in respect of fishing, navigation, and exploration and exploitation of resources.[95]

They explained in this respect that the line has "three meanings":

> First, it represents the title to the island groups that it encloses. In other words, within the nine-dash line in the South China Sea, China has sovereignty over the islands and other insular features, and has sovereignty, sovereign rights, and jurisdiction – in accordance with the LOS Convention – over the waters and seabed and subsoil adjacent to those islands and insular features. Second, it preserves Chinese historic rights in fishing, navigation, and such other marine activities as oil and gas development in the waters and on the continental shelf surrounded by the line. Third, it is likely to allow for such residual functionality as to serve as potential maritime delimitation lines.[96]

Furthermore, a few scholars explained the U-shaped line and argued its function from a natural scientific perspective. For example, as Li Jinming and Li Dexia note, Wang Xiguang, an ROC official who helped formulate the U-shaped line, stated that "the dotted national boundary line was drawn as the median line between China and adjacent states."[97] Thus a line equidistant to the shores of countries claiming the same waters can suggest that it is a maritime boundary line. Such a line was one of many basic methods of compromise between competing spheres of maritime sovereignty at the time. Indeed, the distance of the U-shaped line between the southeasternmost feature of the Spratly Islands and Borneo/Palawan Island is roughly equidistant on maps.

Wang Ying, a senior geologist in China, shares a similar view. In a 2017 article, she, jointly with two other geologists, concluded that "[the U-shaped line] was both connected with, and an extension of, the land boundary of China" and can be seen as "historical and scientific evidence of China's sea boundary in the South China Sea."[98]

It is worth noting that Wang Ying's article may have been seen as a rebuttal to the *Report on the Limits in the Seas* issued by the Bureau of Oceans and International Environmental and Scientific Affairs of the US Department of State in 2014, which also focused on the geographic description of the U-shaped line and represented the views of the US government. This report found that

> The dashes are not uniformly distributed and are separated from one another by between 106 (dashes 7 and 8) and 274 (dashes 3 and 4) nautical miles (nm). The dashes are located in relatively close proximity to the mainland coasts and coastal islands of the littoral States surrounding the South China Sea. Dash 1 is 50 nm from the mainland coast of Vietnam and 36 nm from Vietnam's coastal island of Ly Son. Dash 3 is 75 nm from the closest Indonesian island, Pulau Sekatung. Dash 4 is 24 nm from the coast of Malaysia on the island of Borneo. Dash 5 is 35 nm from the closest point on the Philippines' southeastern island of Balabac. Dash 9 is 26 nm from Y'Ami Island, Philippines' northernmost island in the Luzon Strait.[99]

And that

> A geographic description of China's dashed line is complicated by inconsistencies between China's 2009 map and other Chinese maps, such as the 1947 map. The geographic description above is applicable to the 2009 map, but not to the 1947 map or even contemporary Chinese maps because those maps appear to depict the dashes in varying sizes and locations.[100]

However, it failed to give any reason for the inconsistencies.

The above accounts of the U-shaped line, however, may face factual and legal difficulties. First of all, an obvious fact is that the U-shaped line drawn on maps has been occasionally changing, though slightly, both on the number of segments and the direction of each segment as well as the scope covered by the line. For example, the disappearance of the two segments of the eleven-dash line in the Gulf of Tonkin in 1953 indicates that the U-shaped line is flexible, rather than an iron-fixed "sea boundary." At most, it only serves as a temporary maritime boundary line between China and its neighbours in the South China Sea pending the final settlement of maritime boundary delimitation.

Despite these academic debates, China has kept its official position ambiguous for a long time. However, given the related domestic legislation and national practice, especially the 2016 Statement, we may presume that there have been some definite legal implications and potential legal functions of the U-shaped line. The current prevailing interpretation on the implications of the U-shaped line, from the Chinese perspective, may include three components:

1. a line claiming territorial sovereignty over the island groups that always belonged to China;
2. a line indicating potential maritime delimitation boundaries;
3. a line claiming historic rights to marine resources and traditional maritime jurisdiction.

Further observations of the U-shaped line

Territorial sovereignty and maritime rights conferred by the LOSC within the U-shaped line

The widely recognized function of the U-shaped line is to indicate a scope of claims over the ownership of maritime features within it. As mentioned above, both the ROC and the PRC governments used the line in a way to claim all the features within the line. After 1949, PRC made its first official claim to the islands in 1951, when Premier Zhou Enlai denounced the joint draft for the Treaty of San Francisco by the United States and the United Kingdom that "As a matter of fact, the Paracel Archipelago and Spratly Island, like the entire Nansha, Zhongsha, and Dongsha Archipelagos, have always been Chinese territory."[101]

The view of the "islands ownership line" has been recognized by China's neighbouring States as well. For instance, the Philippines officially admitted in 2014 that the U-shaped line map in 1948 "indicated the islands over which China claimed sovereignty," and asserted that the line "did not then purport to assert sovereignty or sovereign rights to all the waters within it."[102]

However, a difficulty China has been facing since the entry into force of the LOSC is the legal status of the maritime features within the U-shaped line. The legal conundrum is caused by Articles 13 and 121 of the LOSC, which differentiate low-tide elevations and islands (including rocks) among maritime features. A low-tide elevation (LTE), according to Article 13 of the Convention, does not have a territorial sea of its own unless it is wholly situated at a distance within the breadth of the territorial sea from the mainland or an island.[103] In other words, a LTE may be used as a basepoint in drawing a baseline to "bump out" the territorial sea, which makes it different from mid-ocean LTE or non-offshore LTE. Furthermore, as pointed out by the International Court of Justice (ICJ) in the 2001 case on Maritime Delimitation and Territorial Questions between Qatar and Bahrain, that international treaty law is silent on the question of whether LTEs can be considered to be "territory,"[104] and it is not established that low-tide elevations can, from the viewpoint of acquiring sovereignty, be fully assimilated to islands or other land territories.[105] This position is further reinforced by the South China Sea Arbitration Award.[106]

However, China has long been reiterated the position that it enjoys the sovereignty, sovereign rights and maritime jurisdiction over the Xisha, Zhongsha, Dongsha, and Nansha Islands in their entirety, each as a single unit, rather than the individual island or reef or LTE one by one. This position has been very clearly explained not only in its domestic legislation, including the 1992 Territorial Sea Law and the 1998 EEZ Law but also in the *Note verbale* No. CML/8/2011 of 14 April 2011 which reads

> under the relevant provisions of the 1982 [LOSC], as well as the Law of the People's Republic of China on the Territorial Sea and the Contiguous Zone (1992) and the Law on the Exclusive Economic Zone and the Continental Shelf of the People's Republic of China (1998), China's Nansha Islands is fully entitled to Territorial Sea, Exclusive Economic Zone and Continental Shelf.[107]

In the 2016 Statement, the Chinese government reiterated that

> China has territorial sovereignty and maritime rights and interests in the South China Sea, including, inter alia: ...ii. China has internal waters, territorial sea and contiguous zone, based on *Nanhai Zhudao*; iii. China has exclusive economic zone and continental shelf, based on *Nanhai Zhudao*....[108]

From the above, we can see that China would definitely claim the maritime zones conferred by the LOSC for each islands group in the South China Sea within the U-shaped line. This has been reflected by the existing case of Xisha Islands.

In May 1996, China designated straight baselines for the Xisha Islands, in their entirety, by joining several islands and reefs. The issue that whether or not the use of straight baselines to enclose dependent archipelagos is authorized by international law is mentioned in the award of the South China Sea Arbitration. The tribunal concluded that it could be inconsistent with the LOSC or customary international law, but did not explain its rationale in detail.[109]

On the other hand, the fact that neither Article 5 on the normal baseline nor Article 7 on straight baselines explicitly preclude their use to enclose dependent archipelagos, making it possible that the last preambular paragraph of the LOSC applies. That paragraph states that "matters not regulated by the Convention continue to be regulated by the rules and principles of general international law."[110] Furthermore, the considerations of the adoption of a straight baseline include not only the pure geographical factors, but also social/historical factors as well as economic factors, just as the case of the Xisha Islands.[111] The question here is: what is the relationship between the U-shaped line and the straight baselines within the U-shaped line? Our answer is: the drawing of baselines within the U-shaped line means that the U-shaped line is not equivalent to baselines and the waters with the U-shaped line may have different legal statuses.

U-shaped line and historic-related rights on the basis of customary international law

The U-shaped line was officially proclaimed more than a half-century before the adoption of the LOSC and even a decade before the adoption of the 1958 Geneva Conventions. The historic rights derived from or area delineated by this line cannot be ignored. While it is acknowledged that the LOSC is a "constitution for the oceans" being widely recognized and accepted in the international society, and playing an indispensable role in handling international relations concerning the oceans, it has been recognized that it is under the framework of international law, and it is one of the international treaties governing ocean affairs.

It is worth noting that during the period when the U-shaped line was originally drawn and came into being, there was no existing treaty specifically on the law of the sea, thus customary international law playing a key role, and the historic-related doctrines and rules had been essential parts. Given the issue of historic rights in the South China Sea will be discussed in depth in the following chapter, this chapter will not examine it in detail; rather, we observe that China may be able to argue that since ancient times, China has been continuously exercising its legitimate rights and authority in the South China Sea, in particular, the use of marine resources, construction of artificial structures and installations, marine scientific research, maritime law enforcement, navigation, and military uses within the U-shaped line. Another observation is: with the ratification of the LOSC, however, the content of the rights enjoyed by China within the U-shaped line may have evolved. And consequently, the geographical scope where China enjoys historic rights may also have changed.

Concluding remarks

Based on the fact that the evolution of the U-shaped line has taken place in the 20th century, it can be concluded that the legal implications of the U-shaped line should be interpreted within the context of the post-WWII reconstruction of international order and the rebuilding of maritime legal frameworks; and the validity of the U-shaped line has never been disrupted or terminated. It is shown in this chapter that China has never given up the U-shaped line and related sovereignty and maritime claims in the South China Sea. Recent practice has demonstrated that China has further consolidated the effectiveness of the line by carrying out massive land reclamations, intensified law enforcement patrols, and fishery conservation activities within the line.

From China's long-term practice and recent developments, we can see that the legal implications of the U-shaped line may include three components, namely: a line indicating territorial sovereignty over the island groups; a line serving a temporary maritime boundary pending the final delimitation; and a line preserving China's historic rights to marine resources and the exercise of maritime jurisdiction.

Finally, it is worth emphasizing that in the South China Sea Arbitration the arbitral tribunal mentioned the U-shaped line when it deliberated matters relating to historic rights. The arbitral award declared that China's historic rights within the U-shaped line were inconsistent with the LOSC,[112] but it did not touch upon the legal nature of the U-shaped line itself. In this sense, the tribunal at least indirectly helped the maintenance of the integrity and validity of the U-shaped line in international law.

Notes

1 See Han Zhenhua (ed.), *A Compilation of Historical Materials on China's South China Sea Islands*, Beijing: Oriental Press (1988) (in Chinese), p. 355; Zou Keyuan, "South China Sea Studies in China: Achievements, Constraints and Prospects," 11 *Singapore Year Book of International Law* (2007), p. 88; Zou Keyuan, "China's U-Shaped Line in the South China Sea Revisited," 43 *Ocean Development and International Law* (2012), p. 19.

2 Bill Hayton, "The Modern Origins of China's South China Sea Claims: Maps, Misunderstandings, and the Maritime Geobody," 45(2) *Modern China* (2019), p. 143.

3 William A. Callahan, "The Cartography of National Humiliation and the Emergence of China's Geobody," 21(1) *Public Culture* (2009), p. 155.

4 Bill Hayton, supra note 2, p. 144.

5 Institute for Security & Development Policy, "Understanding China's Position on the South China Sea Disputes," ISDP website (June 2016), available at: https://isdp.eu/publication/understanding-chinas-position-south-china-sea-disputes/.

6 See Zou Keyuan, "The Chinese Traditional Maritime Boundary Line in the South China Sea and Its Legal Consequences for the Resolution of the Dispute over the Spratly Islands," 14 *International Journal of Marine and Coastal Law* (1999), p. 33.

7 Zou Keyuan (1999), supra note 6, p. 33.

8 Bill Hayton, supra note 2, p. 158.

9 See Ulises Granados, "Japanese Expansion into the South China Sea: Colonization and Conflict, 1902–1939," 42(2) *Journal of Asian History* (2008), pp. 132–140; Marwyn Samuels, *Contest for the South China Sea*, New York: Metheun (1982), pp. 55–64.

10 Ulises Granados, ibid., p. 138.

11 Qianping Chen, "The Nationalist Government's Efforts to Recover Chinese Sovereignty over the Islands in the South China Sea after the End of World War Two," 11(1) *Journal of Modern Chinese History* (2017), p. 75.

12 Wang Ying, Ge Chendong and Zou Xinqing, "Evidence of China's Sea Boundary in the South China Sea," 36(4) *Acta Oceanol. Sin.* (2017), p. 3.

13 Office of Ocean and Polar Affairs of the Bureau of Oceans and International Environmental and Scientific Affairs of the US Department of State, "China: Maritime Claims in the South China Sea," (5 December 2014) *Limits in the Seas* (No. 143), p. 3. Available at: https://www.state.gov/wp-content/uploads/2019/10/LIS-143.pdf.

14 Ministry of Interior, *An Outline of the Geography of the South China Sea Islands* (National Territory Series, 1947), Figure 11, p. 861.

15 Wang Ying, Ge Chendong and Zou Xinqing, supra note 12, p. 5.
16 Ibid., p. 6.
17 See Han Zhenhua, supra note 1, pp. 181–184.
18 See China Cartographic Publishing House, *Hanging Map of the People's Republic of China* (1950); Ya Guang Yu De Xue She, *Large Map of the People's Republic of China* (1951); Ya Guang Yu De Xue She, *Large Map of the People's Republic of China* (1952); China Cartographic Publishing House, *Hanging Map of the People's Republic of China* (1956). These are official Chinese maps published between 1950 and 1956.
19 Wang Ying, Ge Chendong and Zou Xinqing, supra note 12, pp. 10–11.
20 See Zou Keyuan, *Law of the Sea in East Asia: Issues and Prospects*, London: Routledge (2005), p. 83.
21 Li Jinming and Li Dexia, "The Dotted Line on the Chinese Map of the South China Sea: A Note," 34 *Ocean Development and International Law* (2003), p. 290.
22 See China Cartographic Publishing House, *Map of the People's Republic of China* (1971); China Cartographic Publishing House, *Map of the People's Republic of China* (January 1973); China Cartographic Publishing House, *Map of the People's Republic of China* (May 1973); China Cartographic Publishing House, *Map of the People's Republic of China* (May 1978); China Cartographic Publishing House, *Map of the People's Republic of China* (1980); China Cartographic Publishing House, *Map of the People's Republic of China* (June 1981); China Cartographic Publishing House, *Map of the People's Republic of China* (June 1982); China Cartographic Publishing House, *Map of the People's Republic of China* (June 1984); China Cartographic Publishing House, *Map of the People's Republic of China* (March 1987); China Cartographic Publishing House, *Map of the People's Republic of China* (August 1988); Sino Maps Press, *Map of the People's Republic of China* (1990); China Cartographic Publishing House, *Map of the People's Republic of China* (June 1992).
23 *Note verbale* from the Permanent Mission of the People's Republic of China to the United Nations to the Secretary- General of the United Nations, No. CML/18/2009 (7 May 2009), available at: https://www.un.org/depts/los/clcs_new/submissions_files/vnm37_09/chn_2009re_vnm.pdf.
24 Ibid. See also: *Note verbale* from the Permanent Mission of the People's Republic of China to the United Nations to the Secretary-General of the United Nations, No. CML/17/2009 (7 May 2009).
25 See: J. Michael Cole, "China to Issue New Official Map of 'Full' Territory," *Taipei Times* (15 January 2013), available at: http://www.taipeitimes.com/News/front/archives/2013/01/15/2003552554.
26 People's Republic of China, Declaration of the Government of the People's Republic of China on China's Territorial Sea (4 September 1958), in *Collection of the Sea Laws and Regulations of the People's Republic of China* (3rd ed. 2001), para. 1. "The Declaration Was Approved by the Standing Committee of the People's Congress on September 4, 1958, Thus Making It Part of Chinese law". Z. Gao and B.B. Jia, "The Nine-Dash Line in the South China Sea: History, Status, and Implications," 107(1) *American Journal of International Law* (2013), p. 104.
27 Ibid., para. 1 (emphasis added).
28 "Ministry of Foreign Affairs spokesman issues statement," *People's Daily* (in Chinese), 12 January 1974.
29 As quoted in Ni Jianmin (ed.), *Ocean China*, Beijing: China International Broadcasting (1997), p. 368. See also "The Committee of Propaganda Activities for the International Year of Ocean Established," *People's Daily* (in Chinese), 18 February 1998, p. 3.
30 Zou Keyuan (2012), supra note 1, p. 22.
31 United Nations, Secretary-General, *Multilateral Treaties Deposited with the Secretary-General*, Vol. 3, Part 1, Chapters 12–29, and Part 2, U.N. Doc. ST/LEG/SER.E/26 (1 April 2009), para. 1. MP, Vol. XI, Annex LA-67.
32 See Law on the Exclusive Economic Zone and the Continental Shelf, 26 June 1998, available at: www.un.org/Depts/los.
33 Law on Marine Environmental Protection (1999), Articles 2 and 39.
34 Office of Ocean and Polar Affairs of the Bureau of Oceans and International Environmental and Scientific Affairs of the US Department of State, supra note 13, p. 17.
35 Surveying and Mapping Law of the People's Republic of China, available at: http://www.npc.gov.cn/zgrdw/englishnpc/Law/2007-12/12/content_1383865.htm.
36 Provisions of the People's Republic of China on Administration of Foreign-Related Marine Scientific Research, available at: http://www.lawinfochina.com/display.aspx?lib=law&id=12053&CGid=.
37 The Republic of China, *South China Sea Policy Guidelines*, are attached as an appendix to Kuan-Ming Sun, "Policy of the Republic of China Towards the South China Sea," 19 *Marine Policy* (1995), p. 408.

38 Central News Agency (CAN) Taiwan, 30 December 1997.
39 "Commemorating 10th Anniversary of the Founding of the South China Sea Brigade of the China Maritime Surveillance," 21 September 2009, available at: www.scsb.gov.cn/html/2/13/article-236.html.
40 See *China Maritime Law Enforcement Bulletin 2008*, available at www.soa.gov.cn/soa/hygb/xzgb/webinfo/2009/03/1271382649196436.htm.
41 See *China Maritime Law Enforcement Bulletin 2010*, available at: www.soa.gov.cn/soa/hygbml/xzgb/ten/webinfo/1304230574153971.htm.
42 Ibid.
43 Vanguard Bank lies 22 nautical miles southwest from Prince Consort Bank (Xiwei Tan) at 7°32'N, 109°45'E. The linear crest of this bank is aligned west-east and within the 18.3-meter isobath measures 16 nautical miles long and 3 nautical miles wide. The least recorded depth is 16.5 meters. See David Hancox and Victor Prescott, "A Geographical Description of the Spratly Islands and an Account of Hydrographic Surveys amongst Those Islands," 1(6) *Maritime Briefing* (1995), p. 16.
44 M. J. Valencia, J. M. van Dyke, and N. A. Ludwig, *Sharing the Resources of the South China Sea*, Dordrecht: Martinus Nijhoff (1997), p. 27; Mark J. Valencia, "Spratly Solution Still at Sea," 6(2) *Pacific Review* (1993), p. 158, that "Although the Crestone concession is clearly on Vietnam's geologic continental shelf and within 350 nm of its coast China argues that the area is within its 'historical line' claim."
45 See *Straits Times*, 21 May 1992, p. 7.
46 Xinhua News Agency, Beijing, 17 April 1996.
47 See "China," available at: www.harvestnr.com/operations/china.html.
48 CNOOC, "Notification of Part of Open Blocks in Waters under Jurisdiction of the People's Republic of China Available for Foreign Cooperation in the Year of 2012," available at: http://en.cnooc.com.cn/data/html/news/2012- 06-22/english/322127.html.
49 Office of Ocean and Polar Affairs of the Bureau of Oceans and International Environmental and Scientific Affairs of the US Department of State, supra note 13, p. 17.
50 Derek Grossman, "Why Vanguard Bank and Why Now? Explaining Chinese Behavior in the South China Sea," *Rand Corporation* (19 August 2019), available at: https://www.rand.org/blog/2019/08/why-vanguard-bank-and-why-now-explaining-chinese-behavior.html.
51 "Foreign Ministry Spokesperson Geng Shuang's Regular Press Conference on December 31, 2019," Ministry of Foreign Affairs of the People's Republic of China, available at: https://www.fmprc.gov.cn/mfa_eng/xwfw_665399/s2510_665401/2511_665403/t1729013.shtml.
52 The Philippines' Memorial –Volume I, *The South China Sea Arbitration* (The Republic of Philippines v. The People's Republic of China), p. 271, available at: https://files.pca-cpa.org/pcadocs/Memorial%20of%20the%20Philippines%20Volume%201.pdf.
53 Statement of the Government of the People's Republic of China on China's Territorial Sovereignty and Maritime Rights and Interests in the South China Sea (12 July 2016), available at: https://www.fmprc.gov.cn/nanhai/eng/snhwtlcwj_1/t1379493.htm.
54 Ibid., para. 1.
55 Julian Ku and Chris Mirasola, "The South China Sea and China's 'Four Sha' Claim: New Legal Theory, Same Bad Argument," *Lawfare*, available at: https://www.lawfareblog.com/south-china-sea-and-chinas-four-sha-claim-new-legal-theory-same-bad-argument.
56 Zhiguo Gao and Bing Bing Jia, supra note 26, p. 118.
57 "Wang Yi Laid Out Three Basic Facts of the Issue of the South China Sea," website of the Ministry of Foreign Affairs of the People's Republic of China (9 September 2020), available at: https://www.fmprc.gov.cn/mfa_eng/zxxx_662805/t1814210.shtml.
58 Huynh Minh Chinh, "Sovereignty of Vietnam over Hoang Sa (Paracels) and Truong Sa (Spratlys) and Peaceful Settlement of Disputes in the Bien Dong Sea (South China Sea)," in *Conference Proceedings, ASEAN in the 21st Century: Opportunities and Challenges*, Hanoi: Institute of International Relations (March 1996), pp. 98–99.
59 Nguyen Hong Thao, "China's Maritime Moves Raise Neighbors' Hackles," *Vietnam Law and Legal Forum* (July 1998), p. 21.
60 Ibid., pp. 21–22.
61 Vietnam, "Dispute Regarding the Law on the Exclusive Economic Zone and the Continental Shelf of the People's Republic of China Which Was Passed on 26 June 1998," *Law of the Sea Bulletin*, No. 38 (1998), p. 55.

62 See: "Viet Nam's Submission on Its Outer Limits of the Continental Shelf, Ministry of Foreign Affairs' Spokesman Mr. Le Dzung Answers Question on 08 May 2009," available at: www.mofa.gov.vn/en/tt_baochi/pbnfn/ns090508180346#Z4GcTd019sbm.
63 Hasjim Djalal, "Conflicting Territorial and Jurisdictional Claims in the South China Sea," 7(3) *Indonesian Quarterly* (1979), p. 42.
64 Hasjim Djalal, "The South China Sea: The Long Road Towards Peace and Cooperation," in Sam Bateman and Ralf Emmers (eds.), *Security and International Politics in the South China Sea: Towards a Cooperative Management Regime*, London: Routledge (2009), p. 177.
65 Indonesia, Letter to the U.N. Secretary-General, Doc. 480/POL-703/VII/10 (8 July 2010), available at: www.un.org/los/clcs new/clcs home.htm.
66 See: Indonesia, *Note verbale* (No. 126/POL-703/V/20), available at: https://www.un.org/Depts/los/clcs_new/submissions_files/mys_12_12_2019/2020_05_26_IDN_NV_UN_001_English.pdf; Indonesia, *Note verbale* (No. 148/POL-703/VI/20), available at: https://www.un.org/Depts/los/clcs_new/submissions_files/mys_12_12_2019/2020_06_12_IDN_NV_UN_002_ENG.pdf.
67 Even in response to China's objection to its joint submission of the outer continental shelf in the South China Sea, Malaysia stated only that its act conforms to the LOSC and the submission is made without prejudice to the question of delimitation in the South China Sea. Malaysia, Letter to the U.N. Secretary-General, Doc. HA24/09 (20 May 2009), available at: www.un.org/los/clcs new/clcs home.htm.
68 B. A. Hamzah, "Conflicting Jurisdiction Problems in the Spratlys: Scope for Conflict Resolution," paper presented at the Second Workshop on Managing Potential Conflicts in the South China Sea, Bandung, Indonesia (15–18 July 1991), pp. 199–200.
69 Ibid.
70 Malaysia, *Note verbale* (HA 26/20), available at: https://www.un.org/Depts/los/clcs_new/submissions_files/mys_12_12_2019/2020_07_29_MYS_NV_UN_002_OLA-2020-00373.pdf
71 The Philippines, Letter to the U.N. Secretary General, Doc. No. 000228 (5 April 2011), available at: www.un.org/los/clcs new/clcs home.htm.
72 The Philippines, *Note verbale* (No. 000191-2020), available at: https://www.un.org/Depts/los/clcs_new/submissions_files/mys_12_12_2019/2020_03_06_PHL_NV_UN_001.pdf.
73 Ibid.
74 Sebastian Strangio, "In UN Speech, Duterte Stiffens Philippines' Stance on the South China Sea," *The Diplomat* (23 September 2020), available at: https://thediplomat.com/2020/09/in-un-speech-duterte-stiffens-philippines-stance-on-the-south-china-sea/.
75 Erik Franckx and Marco Benatar, "Dotted Lines in the South China Sea: Fishing for (Legal) Clarity," paper presented at the Second International Workshop on the South China Sea: Cooperation for Regional Security and Development, Hanoi (11–12 November 2010).
76 S. Jayakumar, "Keynote Address," Conference on Joint Development and the South China Sea (16 June 2011), Singapore, available at: cil.nus.edu.sg/wp/wp-content/uploads/2011/06/CIL_Keynote_Address_16_Jun_11_7.45am-pdf.pdf.
77 Ibid.
78 Singapore, "MFA Spokesman's Comments in Responses to Media Queries on the Visit of Chinese Maritime Surveillance Vessel Haixun 31 to Singapore," (20 June 2011), available at: www.mfa.gov.sg/.
79 Hilary Clinton, "The South China Sea," Press Statement of the Secretary of State (22 July 2011), available at: www.state.gov/secretary/rm/2011/07/168989.htm.
80 Ibid.
81 Raul Pedrozo, "Beijing's Coastal Real Estate: A History of Chinese Naval Aggression," (15 November 2010), available at: www.foreignaffairs.com/articles/67007/raul-pedrozo/beijings-coastalreal-estate.
82 Michael R. Pompeo, Secretary of State, "U.S. Position on Maritime Claims in the South China Sea," US Department of State (13 July 2020), available at: https://www.state.gov/u-s-position-on-maritime-claims-in-the-south-china-sea/.
83 Dzirhan Mahadzir, "China Pushes Back against U.S. Statement on South China Sea Claims, ASEAN Stays Silent," *USNI News* (14 July 2020), available at: https://news.usni.org/2020/07/14/china-pushes-back-against-u-s-statement-on-south-china-sea-claims-asean-stays-silent.
84 Carl Thayer, "Australia Abandons Its Neutrality on the South China Sea Maritime Disputes," *The Diplomat* (27 July 2020), available at: https://thediplomat.com/2020/07/australia-abandons-its-neutrality-on-the-south-china-sea-maritime-disputes/.

85 Australia, *Note verbale* (No. 20/026), available at: https://www.un.org/depts/los/clcs_new/submissions_files/mys_12_12_2019/2020_07_23_AUS_NV_UN_001_OLA-2020-00373.pdf.
86 Eva Pejsova, "Between Principles and Pragmatism: The EU and the South China Sea," 14(2) *Global Asia* (June 2019), available at: https://www.globalasia.org/v14no2/focus/between-principles-and-pragmatism-the-eu-and-the-south-china-sea_eva-pejsova.
87 Laurence Norman, "EU Issues South China Sea Statement Ending Discord within Bloc," *The Wall Street Journal* (17 July 2016), available at: https://www.wsj.com/articles/eu-issues-south-china-sea-statement-after-failing-to-agree-common-stance-1468583961.
88 Linh Pham, "UK Joins Choir Defying China's South China Sea Claims," *Hanoi Times* (16 September 2020), available at: http://hanoitimes.vn/uk-joins-choir-defying-chinas-south-china-sea-claims-314227.html.
89 *Note verbale*, UK NV No. 162/20 (16 September 2020), available at: https://www.un.org/Depts/los/clcs_new/submissions_files/mys_12_12_2019/2020_09_16_GBR_NV_UN_001.pdf.
90 Li Jinming, "An Overview of Reviews on the Legal Status of the U-shaped Line in the South China Sea," 2 *Southeast Asian Affairs* (in Chinese) (2011), pp. 60–61; Zhao Lihai, *A Study of the Issue of the Law of the Sea* (in Chinese), Beijing: Peking University Press (1996), p. 38.
91 Fu Kuen-Chen, *Legal Status of the South [China] Sea* (in Chinese), Taipei: 123 Information Co. Ltd (1995), pp. 35–42, 210; Huang Wei, "Discussing the Historical Rights of 'Other Waters' within the U-shaped Line", 3 *Journal of Ocean University of China* (2011) (in Chinese), pp. 36–40; Wu Shicun, *The South China Sea Dispute: Origin and Development* (revised ed.) (in Chinese), Beijing: China Economic Publishing House (2013), pp. 81, 82; Gao and Jia, supra note 26, pp. 108–110, 123–124.
92 Yann-huei Song and Zou Keyuan, "Maritime Legislation of Mainland China and Taiwan: Developments, Comparison, Implications, and Potential Challenges for the United States," 31(4) *Ocean Development and International Law* (2000), p. 318.
93 Li Jinming and Li Dexia, supra note 21, p. 293.
94 Law on the Exclusive Economic Zone and Continental Shelf of the People's Republic of China (26 June 1998), Article 14.
95 Z. Gao and B.B. Jia, supra note 26, pp. 109–110.
96 Ibid., pp. 123–124.
97 Li Jinming and Li Dexia, supra note 21, p. 290.
98 Wang Ying, Ge Chendong and Zou Xinqing, supra note 12, p. 1.
99 Office of Ocean and Polar Affairs of the Bureau of Oceans and International Environmental and Scientific Affairs of the US Department of State, supra note 13, pp. 4–5.
100 Ibid., p. 5.
101 Zhou Enlai, *Selected Works of Zhou Enlai on Foreign Relations* (in Chinese), Volume 1, Beijing: Central Literature Publishing House, p. 41.
102 The Philippines' Memorial, supra note 52, p. 34, para. 2.38.
103 See: UN Convention on the Law of the Sea, available at: http://www.un.org/depts/los/convention_agreements/texts/unclos/unclos_e.pdf.
104 Maritime Delimitation and Territorial Questions Between Qatar and Bahrain (Qatar v. Bahrain), Merits, Judgment, *I.C.J. Reports* 2001, para. 205.
105 Ibid., para. 206.
106 Award, PCA Case No. 2013–19, paras. 378, 646–647, available at: https://www.pcacases.com/web/sendAttach/2086.
107 Position Paper of the Government of the People's Republic of China on the Matter of Jurisdiction in the South China Sea Arbitration Initiated by the Republic of the Philippines (2014/12/7), para. 21, available at: http://www.fmprc.gov.cn/mfa_eng/zxxx_662805/t1217147.shtml.
108 Government of the People's Republic of China, supra note 53.
109 PCA Case No. 2013–19, supra note 106, paras. 575–576.
110 UN Convention on the Law of the Sea, supra note 103
111 Duan Jielong (eds.), *International Law in China: Cases and Practice* (in Chinese), Beijing: China Law Press 2011, pp. 84–85.
112 Award, PCA Case No. 2013–19, para. 1203.

8

HISTORIC RIGHTS AND THE SOUTH CHINA SEA

Sophia Kopela

Introduction

The South China Sea (SCS) has a long and rich history with activities going back to some 2,000 years. Seafarers, tradesmen, government officials in diplomatic missions, local rulers, migrants, pirates, fishermen, and later colonial powers have used this important maritime space, a crucial cross-road between East and West. As noted by Schottenhammer, "the seas were sometimes considered a barrier but above all a contact zone, a medium that despite its dangers and difficulties enabled people to establish and maintain manifold exchange relations."[1] Equally important was this area for the littoral communities. People of coastal nations have depended on the sea and its rich resources for their sustenance and livelihood, and fishermen from various coastal areas have fished in this sea since time immemorial.[2] The sea – albeit distant and remote – has been an important part of their lives and their history.

Tension started rising with the occupation of the islands and the maritime features in the SCS by colonial powers and by the littoral states. Opposing claims over the islands were followed by claims over maritime areas which were also linked to the extension of coastal states' sovereign rights and jurisdiction consolidated by the UN Convention on the Law of the Sea (LOSC).

The dispute concerning the existence of historic rights in the SCS was triggered by China's official pronouncement of the so-called U-shaped line in 2009 as a response to claims to the outer limit of the continental shelf by other states in the region. How China's historic claim relates to the U-shaped line, or to specific waters of the SCS, is not clear. Nonetheless, this issue appears to be – among others - at the core of the dispute between the states in the region. It was one of the central issues examined by the Tribunal in the arbitration between China and the Philippines concerning the Philippines' submission that "China's claims based on its 'nine-dash line' are inconsistent with the Convention and therefore invalid."[3] China's historic claim and the existence and relevance of historic rights in the SCS have also been discussed by many authors both before and in the light of the SCS arbitral Award.

This chapter examines three interrelated issues with respect to the existence of historic rights in the South China Sea in the light of China's historic claim and the Award of the SCS Tribunal. Firstly, it explores the nature and the type of the historic claim raised by China by examining China's statements and pronouncements, their interpretation by authors, and by the Tribunal in the SCS arbitration. It then turns to assess two types of historic rights that might be potentially relevant in the SCS context, namely historic rights short of sovereignty and historic fishing rights. For each of these categories of rights, it examines in turn their post-LOSC existence and relevance (in general and with reference to specific claims in the SCS), and then the requirements for the ascertainment of these rights. Finally, it draws some conclusions regarding the potential existence of historic rights in the SCS.

The nature of China's historic claim in the SCS

The U-shaped line and China's official pronouncements

China's historic claim in the SCS seems to be linked to the so-called U-shaped or nine-dash line.[4] The U-shaped line is named after the shape of a dotted line depicted on a map initially released by the Ministry of Interior of the Republic of China for internal use and then included in the Atlas of Administrative Areas officially published in 1948.[5] The Ministry of Interior had already, in 1947, published a list of the Chinese and English names of 172 maritime features in the SCS.[6] This 11-segment line depicted "the southernmost limit of the South China Sea territory" (at the James Shoal).[7] In 1953, two segments of the line were removed and the new line, as appeared in maps, contained nine segments (and hence the name nine-dash line).[8] In 1984 "the islets, reefs and sea areas of Xisha, Nansha and Zhongsha islands" in the SCS were included in the Hainan Administrative Region by the National People's Congress.[9] Up until this stage, there was no reference to historic rights linked with the map or the U-shaped line.

Explicit reference to historic rights in the light of this map was made in a set of policy guidelines published by the Republic of China in 1995.[10] The People's Republic of China (China hereafter), on the other hand, referred to historic rights – without specifically linking them to the U-shaped line – in 1998 when it enacted its law on the exclusive economic zone (EEZ) and the continental shelf. Article 14 provides that "the provisions of this Act shall not affect the historical rights of the People's Republic of China."[11] Article 2 of the 1999 Law on Marine Environmental Protection provides that "the Law shall apply to internal waters, territorial sea, contiguous zone, EEZ, continental shelf of the PRC and other sea areas under the jurisdiction of the PRC."[12] The scope and extent of these "other sea areas" beyond the maritime zones recognised by the LOSC are not clarified, but it has been argued that they may be related to historic rights and/or the U-shaped line.[13]

The U-shaped line was officially invoked by China in a *note verbale* submitted to the Secretary-General in May 2009 following the joint submission by Malaysia and Vietnam to the Commission on the Limits of the Continental Shelf. Therein, China stated that it

> has indisputable sovereignty over the islands in the South China Sea and the adjacent waters, and enjoys sovereign rights and jurisdiction over the relevant waters as well as the seabed and subsoil thereof (see attached map). The above position is consistently held by the Chinese Government, and is widely known by the international community.[14]

The attached map included the U-shaped line. In a further *note verbale* in 2011, following a protest by the Philippines, China stressed that "China's sovereignty and related rights and jurisdiction in the South China Sea are supported by abundant historical and legal evidence."[15] It further noted that "China's Nansha Islands is fully entitled to Territorial Sea, Exclusive Economic Zone (EEZ) and Continental Shelf."[16]

Within the framework of the arbitration initiated unilaterally by the Philippines, China, which rejected the Tribunal's jurisdiction and did not participate in the proceedings, published a position paper presenting its objections to the Tribunal's jurisdiction.[17] In this paper, it made no direct reference to historic rights, but it referred to the history of China's presence in the SCS: "China has indisputable sovereignty over the South China Sea Islands (the Dongsha Islands, the Xisha Islands, the Zhongsha Islands, and the Nansha Islands) and the adjacent waters. Chinese activities in the South China Sea date back to over 2,000 years ago."[18] It also referred to "relevant maritime rights and interests in the SCS" without however again clarifying what these may entail.[19]

Following the Award of the SCS Tribunal on the jurisdiction, the Ministry of Foreign Affairs stated that "the arbitration is null and void, and has no binding effect on China" and also made some statements related to certain aspects of the SCS dispute making clearer the link between the "relevant rights" and their historic relevance:

> China has indisputable sovereignty over the South China Sea Islands and the adjacent waters. China's sovereignty *and relevant rights in the South China Sea, formed in the long historical course,* are upheld by successive Chinese governments, reaffirmed by China's domestic laws on many occasions, and protected under international law including the UN Convention on the Law of the Sea.
>
> *(Emphasis added)*[20]

Nonetheless, the nature and the extent of these rights have not been clarified, but it seems that they may not be necessarily or entirely linked to the U-shaped line.

Interpretation of Chinese statements regarding the historic claim and the SCS arbitration

Different views have been expressed in the academic literature regarding the scope of the Chinese historic claim and its link to the U-shaped line.[21] It has been argued, for example, that the U-shaped-line-related claim refers only to the sovereignty over maritime features of the Spratly archipelago and not over the waters,[22] or that it concerns a historic claim to a EEZ/continental shelf as historic rights with tempered sovereignty.[23]

The Tribunal in the SCS arbitration examined the nature of the Chinese historic claim within the framework of the Philippines' submission points 1 and 2. The Philippines requested in its notification and statement of claim that the Tribunal "declare that the parties respective rights and obligations in regard to the waters, seabed and maritime features of the SCS are governed by UNCLOS, and that China's claims based on its 'nine-dash line' are inconsistent with the Convention and therefore invalid."[24]

The Tribunal started by noting that "China has never expressly clarified the nature or scope of its claimed historic rights. Nor has it ever clarified its understanding of the meaning of the 'nine-dash line,'"[25] and then proceeded to examine China's legislation, activities, and official statements.[26] A key consideration that played an important role in the Tribunal's conclusion was that China was committed to "respect both freedom of navigation and overflight."[27] The Tribunal found that

> on the basis of China's conduct, the Tribunal understands that China claims rights to the living and non-living resources within the "nine-dash line", but (apart from the territorial sea generated by any islands) does not consider that those waters form part of its territorial sea or internal waters.[28]

Indeed, China has never sought to restrict freedom of navigation in practice[29] which confirms that the historic claim – albeit ambiguous – is not a sovereignty claim to a territorial sea or internal waters. China's historic claim in the SCS was found to be historic rights short of sovereignty.

China's claim, historic rights short of sovereignty and the LOSC

A key issue for assessing the validity of the Chinese historic claim, but also the existence of any historic rights, in the SCS is the relationship between the LOSC and historic rights. The Tribunal observed that "the term 'historic rights' is general in nature and can describe any rights that a state may possess that would not normally arise under the general rules of international law, absent particular historical circumstances."[30] Historic titles, often referred to as historic waters, relate to claims of sovereignty over a maritime area.[31] On the other hand, historic rights short of sovereignty take two distinct forms: historic rights short of sovereignty which have a quasi-territorial or zonal impact beyond the territorial sea, and non-exclusive historic rights (mainly related to fishing rights).[32] The Tribunal examined China's claim in the light of the first category, namely as a zonal historic claim short of sovereignty relying on the exercise of sovereign rights (i.e. exclusive exploitation of resources). It also examined the potential existence of non-exclusive historic fishing rights – albeit refraining from calling them historic – in the framework of the Philippines' argument concerning the Tribunal's jurisdiction regarding activities of Philippine fishermen in the territorial sea of Scarborough Shoal and the infringement of their rights by China.

The following two sections examine these two types of historic rights separately: exclusive quasi-territorial historic rights with a zonal impact and non-exclusive historic fishing rights with an emphasis on their post-LOSC relevance.

Historic rights short of sovereignty and the SCS

The SCS Tribunal posed the question related to the post-LOSC relevance of historic rights as follows:

> does the Convention, and in particular, its rules for the EEZ and continental shelf, allow for the preservation of rights to living and non-living resources that are at variance with the provisions of the Convention and which may have been established prior to the Convention's entry into force by agreement or unilateral act?[33]

The SCS Tribunal concluded that

> upon China's accession to the Convention and its entry into force, any historic rights that China may have had to the living and non-living resources within the 'nine-dash line' were superseded, as a matter of law and as between the Philippines and China, by the limits of the maritime zones provided for by the Convention.[34]

Historic rights short of sovereignty and the LOSC

The Tribunal found that it can be inferred from articles 311 and 293 (1) of the LOSC and article 30 (3) of the Vienna Convention on the Law of Treaties (VCLT) that only those pre-existing rights that are either expressly "permitted or preserved such as in articles 10 and 15" or compatible with the LOSC would be preserved.[35] In this framework, it stressed "the intent of the parties to a convention" as a key to "control its relationship with other instruments."[36] However, article 311, which explicitly regulates the relationship between the LOSC and conventions and international agreements, cannot be analogically applied to the relationship between the LOSC and historic rights as rules of customary international law. Article 30 (3) of the VCLT which refers to "successive treaties relating to the same subject matter" is similarly inapplicable. Furthermore, article 293 concerns dispute settlement and the applicable law and not the relationship between the LOSC and other rules of international law, including historic rights.

The relationship between treaties and customary international law is complex, and it is thought to be regulated by customary international law and general interpretative principles (i.e. *lex posterior, lex specialis*).[37] The LOSC refers to this relationship in its Preamble: "affirming that matters not regulated by this Convention continue to be governed by the rules and principles of general international law. There is no explicit provision in the LOSC prohibiting the preservation of such rights or nullifying them. Historic rights, which are established on the basis of a particularised regime and can thus be regarded as *lex specialis*, cannot be superseded by a general treaty without explicit reference to them.[38]

What is more, the rationale of historic rights is to preserve, and not to disturb, a continuous, long-established, and accepted situation with the view to providing stability. Historic titles/rights in this respect share elements with the concept of historic consolidation which, according to Jennings, relates to the "fundamental interest of the stability of territorial situations from the point of view of order and peace."[39] The desired stability was also noted by the Tribunal in the *Grisbadarna* arbitration: "it is a well-established principle of the law of nations that the state of things that actually exists and has existed for a long time should be changed as little as possible."[40] Historic titles have been thought – admittedly not without controversy – to be related to acquisitive prescription whose rationale is also to "preserve international order and stability."[41] Some authors have stressed the close relationship between concepts such as prescription, customary rights, and historic rights. Fitzmaurice has referred to them as special rights

> different from, and in principle contrary to, the ordinary rules of law applicable,... built up by a particular state or states through a process of prescription – leading to the emergence of a usage or customary or historic rights in favour of such state or states.[42]

McGibbon commenting on the category suggested by Fitzmaurice states that "the concepts of prescription, customary right and historic right overlap."[43] These might be cases of special customary law referring to and regulating a particular and individualised situation. Historic rights should not be perceived to be incompatible with the LOSC but exceptions recognised in general international law. Talmon argues that "the rules on historic legal title and historic rights are quasi-superimposed as a separate layer of normativity over UNCLOS."[44]

Furthermore, the comprehensiveness of the regulatory regime of the LOSC and the intention of the drafters to settle all issues related to the law of the sea and provide stability and order, as invoked by the SCS Tribunal,[45] does not presuppose that any previously-established regimes were eliminated, especially since no explicit provision was included to this effect.[46]

The jurisdictional regime of the LOSC validated rights, which might have been claimed as historic before, but it cannot be inferred from the Convention or its *travaux preparatoires* that states intended or were willing to *generally* waive any pre-established historic rights. Neither can this be inferred *a contrario* from article 15 as this provision relates to the delimitation of the territorial sea and not generally to the preservation of historic rights.

With respect to the EEZ and the continental shelf provisions of the LOSC, the Tribunal found that the recognition of the exclusive right of the coastal state to the resources of these maritime zones should be interpreted as excluding any rights of third states.[47] There is, however, some indication from international jurisprudence that international courts and tribunals have accepted the preservation of historic rights in parallel to the jurisdictional regime established by the LOSC. In the *Tunisia/Libya* case, the International Court of Justice (ICJ) stated that "historic titles must enjoy respect and be reserved as they have always been by long usage."[48] In the *Gulf of Fonseca* case, the ICJ repeated this statement and noted that it was "clearly necessary... to investigate the particular history of the Gulf of Fonseca to discover what is the 'regime' of the Gulf resulting therefrom."[49] In the former case, the ICJ specifically referred to the draft (at that time) Law of the Sea Convention, and noted that

> nor does the draft convention of the Third Conference on the Law of the Sea contain any detailed provisions on the "regime" of historic waters: there is neither a definition of the concept nor an elaboration of the juridical regime of 'historic waters' or 'historic bays'. There are, however, references to 'historic bays' or "historic titles" or historic reasons in a way amounting to a reservation to the rules set forth therein.[50]

And the ICJ continued:

> it seems clear that the matter continues to be governed by general international law which does not provide for a single "regime" for "historic waters" or historic bays but only for a particular regime for each of the concrete recognised cases of "historic waters" or "historic bays".[51]

Referring to this pronouncement, Symmons observes that "the Court thus endorsed a potential particularised regime for each historic claim, and so for some diversity of types of historic regimes."[52] In this respect, the question of supersession of historic rights by the LOSC cannot be answered *in abstracto*.[53] Since historic rights and titles create a special regime related to the specific historic circumstances, it cannot be considered that historic claims can be phased out as a whole, but the history of each individual case needs to be examined taking into consideration the LOSC. This will depend on whether a historic claim meets the requirements for the establishment of historic rights in a specific maritime area.

Special reference needs to be made to the continental shelf, as it has been suggested that no historic rights can be acquired on the continental shelf as this exists *ipso facto* and *ab initio* and therefore cannot be subjected to prescription.[54] This argument is often associated with comments made by the ICJ in the *Tunisia/Libya* case:

> it is clearly the case that, basically the notion of historic rights or waters and that of the continental shelf are governed by distinct legal regimes in customary international law. The first regime is based on acquisition and occupation, while the second is based on the existence of rights "*ipso facto* and ab initio"; No doubt both may sometimes coincide in part or in whole, but such coincidence can only be fortuitous [...].[55]

Interestingly, Tunisia argued that the historic rights it acquired were in line with the natural prolongation aspect of the contemporary concept of the continental shelf:

> the historic titles which Tunisia acquired in the course of centuries have come to anticipate the appearance of the legal concept of natural prolongation, and after the appearance of that concept in international law, those titles have come to be the manifestation of part of the prolongation. So far from contradicting the natural prolongation, they afford the most apt illustration of it… drawn from history.[56]

Despite the fact that its approach has been interpreted as rejecting historic rights in the context of the delimitation of the continental shelf,[57] the ICJ noted the different ways of claiming such rights (juridical and historic) but did not say that historic rights cannot play a role in the delimitation of the continental shelf.[58] A middle position recognising the customary nature of the continental shelf as *ipso facto* and *ab initio* has been expressed by Gioia who noted that "these 'historic rights' might only survive if it were proved that they have in fact continued to be exercised with the acquiescence of the state concerned after the establishment of the customary rules on the continental shelf."[59] A critical issue would be the continuation of relevant activities and acquiescence of other states following the establishment of the customary rule on the continental shelf.

However, it should be noted that in cases of overlapping continental shelves, historic rights do not necessarily contradict the inherent character of the continental shelf, as they determine the extent of the continental shelf and not its existence. A state cannot claim historic rights over the continental shelf of another state, but could potentially claim rights over parts of the overlapping continental shelves vis-à-vis another coastal state. Indeed, the ICJ in the *Tunisia/Libya* case recognised that the historic rights claimed by Tunisia over the seabed "may be relevant in a number of ways," for example, to provide an indication of an established maritime boundary, ensuring that there is no encroachment over these rights by this boundary. Therefore, such historic quasi-territorial claims may be relevant with respect to the existence of a maritime boundary and for maritime delimitation purposes in overlapping EEZs and continental shelves. Tanaka, though generally critical of the relevance of historic rights to the continental shelf, noted that "states will not regard a line disregarding their historic rights as equitable."[60] With respect to the delimitation of the continental shelf and the EEZ, reference to "equitable solution" in articles 74 and 83 could entail acknowledgement of historic rights as circumstances to be taken into account in maritime delimitation. It should however be noted that international courts and Tribunal have not found that historic rights have had effects on maritime delimitation based on the facts of the cases before them, and there is limited state practice where historic rights had an impact upon the maritime boundary.

Whether these observations are also relevant outside the context of maritime delimitation is not clear. In cases of overlapping continental shelves, these rights operate in a bilateral way (vis-à-vis the other littoral state(s)), whereas in the case of non-overlapping zones, the rights would operate *erga omnes*.[61] This outcome might be uncommon but not necessarily impossible. Gioia argues that

> there is in principle no reason why an historic title could not be invoked in order to acquire sovereignty over a wider belt of territorial sea, or even special sovereign rights falling short of full territorial sovereignty beyond the territorial sea,

but admits that

> the recent evolution of the law of the sea – the recognition of a 12-mile belt of territorial waters and the birth of the new institutions of the continental shelf and of the EEZ – appears to have made reliance on exceptional historic titles no longer necessary in order to justify such claims.[62]

The SCS Tribunal has precluded the survival of such rights as a matter of law and not of factual realities. Kolb referring to the *Grisbadarna* case and *Tunisia/Libya* pointed out that for the Court

> historic rights were not an ordinary relevant circumstance, one which must be weighed against other relevant circumstances so that the Court could finally reach a decision. On the contrary, they were the basis of a prescriptive title which in principle might result in the attribution of the area in question to one of the states in dispute. Here one is dealing not with relevant circumstances of a "relative" or "indicative" nature, but with a relevant circumstance that is "absolute" or "dispositive" in its nature.[63]

Taking into account the approach of the ICJ in the *Tunisia/Libya* case which advocated respect for established historic rights, but also the lack of a general theory and the importance of historic particularised regimes, any historic claims should be treated on their own merits according to the historical particularities of the claim.

China's historic claim (rights short of sovereignty) and the LOSC

The Philippines attempted to stress the uniqueness of the Chinese claim to an extensive maritime area to demonstrate that international law had never recognised such expansive maritime claims based on historic reasons.[64] Similar views have been expressed in academic literature.[65] Symmons argues that "the historic 'EEZ-claim' viewpoint also seems to ignore the precedents of history on exaggerated claims in the past where excessive claims such as by Czar Alexander's no-go zone off Alaska were 'stymied at birth by immediate protests from the major powers, [causing it to be almost immediately withdrawn].'"[66] Talmon, on the other hand, suggests that sizeable historic claims were not uncommon; indeed the Philippines had raised a claim of historic rights covering the waters of its archipelago.[67] As noted by Blum "the common feature of all these claims seems to be the belief that a special relationship exists between the water area concerned and the land territory enclosing it," but "the legality of such an historic claim is to be measured, in the words of Jessup, 'not by the size of the area affected, but by the definitiveness and duration of the assertion and the acquiescence of foreign powers.'"[68] The validity of these claims depended on whether the requirements for historic titles could be met, especially the element of acquiescence of other states, as it was unlikely that states would have acquiesced in expansive claims. On the other hand, some authors have acknowledged the "uniqueness" of the Chinese claim but have considered it to be a particularised regime of historic rights, which could be established in customary international law.[69] It has been suggested that "the Chinese claim to sovereignty over the islands in the SCS and the adjacent waters could be regarded as such a 'particular regime.'"[70] As noted above, each case should be examined on its own merits based on the historical circumstances of each claim.

Requirements for the establishment of historic rights short of sovereignty and the SCS

The UN Study on historic waters including historic bays noted that for the determination of the establishment of a historic title to a maritime area the following need to be taken into account: "(1) the exercise of authority over the area by the state claiming the historic right; (2) the continuity of this exercise of authority; (3) the attitude of foreign states."[71] The Tribunal in the SCS arbitration accepted the application of these criteria for the establishment of historic rights short of sovereignty: "the process is the same for claims to rights short of sovereignty."[72] The evidence for the exercise of authority needs to be clear and related to the specific waters. The Tribunal noted that "either party's historical use of the islands of the South China Sea is of no interest with respect to the formation of historic rights"[73] and found that much of the evidence related to the islands (and therefore supporting the sovereignty aspects of the dispute) "has nothing to do with the question of whether China has historically had rights to living and non-living resources beyond the limits of the territorial sea in the South China Sea and therefore is irrelevant to the matters before this Tribunal."[74]

Furthermore, the exercise of authority needs to be exclusive and cannot form part of the exercise of freedoms of the high seas.[75] With respect to activities on the continental shelf related to exploitation of natural resources, the Tribunal argued that it was "theoretically impossible" for such activities to lead to historic rights as "seabed mining was a glimmer of an idea when the Seabed Committee began the negotiations that led to the Convention. Offshore oil extraction was in its infancy and only recently became possible in deep water areas."[76] This does not however preclude activities related to the exploitation of other resources of the continental shelf, especially sedentary species (i.e. sponge or pearl fishing), though admittedly solely one activity may not lead to historic rights over a certain maritime zone.

Finally, acquiescence plays an important role in the formation of historic rights/titles since these rights have been performed in an inconsistent way to general rules, and therefore the acquiescence of the affected states is a necessary element for their establishment.[77]

Historic fishing rights and the SCS

Non-exclusive historic rights, in contrast to the category discussed above, relate to activities performed in a non-exclusive way (i.e. fishing), do not have a zonal impact, and would thus be recognised in the maritime zones of another state. As regards China's claim, there is no clear indication that China has invoked this type of rights; however, these rights may be relevant and important for the SCS. The Philippines invoked such rights (though refraining from calling them historic) to justify their claim concerning the Tribunal's jurisdiction with respect to activities of Philippine fishermen in the territorial sea of Scarborough Shoal and the infringement of their rights by China.[78]

The SCS Tribunal referred approvingly to the dictum of the Eritrea/Yemen Tribunal about the continuation of historic/traditional fishing rights which stated:

> the conditions that prevailed during many centuries with regard to the traditional openness of Southern Red Sea marine resources for fishing, its role as means for unrestricted traffic from one side to the other, together with the common use of the islands by the populations of both coasts, are all important elements capable of creating certain "historic rights" which accrued in favour of both parties through a process of historical consolidation as a sort of "*servitude internationale*" falling short of territorial sovereignty.

> Such historic rights provide a sufficient legal basis for maintaining certain aspects of a *res communis* that has existed for centuries for the benefit of populations on both sides of the Red Sea.[79]

The Tribunal clarified the traditional fishing regime as follows:

> is not an entitlement in common to resources nor is it a shared right in them. Rather, it entitles both Eritrean and Yemeni fishermen to engage in artisanal fishing around the islands which, in its Award on sovereignty, the Tribunal attributed to Yemen.[80]

Reference to "tradition" indicates the relationship between the fishing practices and the traditions and customs of a local community related to their right to pursue their livelihood; however, it is the historical consolidation that provides the legal basis for these rights and therefore, as long as the requirements for the establishment of historic fishing rights are met, the qualitative elements of fishing, such as methods, gears, etc are not relevant for the establishment of the entitlement but only for the ascertainment of its content.[81] In this sense, historic and traditional fishing rights coincide.

Historic fishing rights and the LOSC

The Tribunal in the *Eritrea/Yemen case* found that these fishing rights continue to exist regardless of the maritime zones established by the LOSC, both within and beyond the territorial sea.[82] On the contrary, the Tribunal in the SCS arbitration drew a distinction between the territorial sea and the EEZ and found that traditional fishing rights have been preserved only in the territorial sea and not in the EEZ. This Tribunal distinguished the two arbitrations on the basis of the facts and the applicability of article 293 of the LOSC which, according to its dictum, did not bind the *Eritrea/Yemen* Tribunal to apply only "the Convention and rules of law not incompatible therewith."[83] Regardless of the validity of this argument,[84] the question concerning the potential existence of these rights in the EEZ and the territorial sea should be examined with reference to the LOSC.

The LOSC refers to traditional fishing rights only in article 51 regarding archipelagic waters. The SCS Tribunal found that this reference and the UNCLOS III negotiations on the EEZ demonstrate that traditional/historic fishing rights have been superseded in the EEZ and are only relevant for access to the surplus according to the conditions stipulated in article 62 (3).[85]

On the contrary, in the territorial sea, the Tribunal accepted the Philippines' argument concerning article 2 (3) and the preservation of traditional fishing rights in the territorial sea.[86] However, this provision aimed to ensure that the maximum of state competence, namely sovereignty, is exercised in line with international rules[87] and not as the coastal state unilaterally desires. What is more, the caselaw invoked by the SCS Tribunal, especially related to the nature of the rights as private rights related to the expansion of the territorial sea "equivalent to the adjustment of a boundary or a change in sovereignty,"[88] demonstrates that regionally-established traditional fishing rights should be preserved and guaranteed regardless of the maritime boundary or the legal regime of the waters.[89]

Similarly, there is no reference to traditional or historic fishing rights in the EEZ provisions of the LOSC. Article 62 (3) of the LOSC was the outcome of negotiations on the regulatory and management regime concerning how the coastal state would exercise its sovereign rights to ensure optimum utilisation of the natural resources.[90] The *travaux preparatoires* of this provision cannot be deemed to demonstrate that it was the intention of the drafters to exclude such rights but to regulate access to these waters (with emphasis on the surplus).[91]

The SCS Tribunal argued that the absence of a provision regarding historic fishing rights in the LOSC demonstrates that any such pre-existing rights have been superseded by the LOSC and referred to the *Gulf of Maine* case in support.[92] This case addressed the impact of fishing practices on the maritime delimitation of the EEZ and not the existence of non-exclusive fishing rights and access rights. The Chamber rejected the relevance of this factor to the maritime delimitation. However, there was no claim to access rights (to common fishing grounds) and a crucial issue was that this shared regime was terminated when coastal states' jurisdiction was extended. A similar argument was raised by Barbados in the *Trinidad and Tobago/Barbados* arbitration where it argued that the maritime delimitation should take into account "a centuries-old history of artisanal fishing."[93] The Tribunal found that there was no evidence of any traditional fishing rights as the practice was relatively recent,[94] and, therefore, rejected Barbados's argument for an adjustment of the equidistance line. It however pointed out that it "does not however mean that the argument based upon fishing activities is either without factual foundation or without legal consequences."[95] The Tribunal did not discuss the potential existence of "a right of access for Barbadian fishermen to flying fish within the EEZ of Trinidad and Tobago," as it found that this was outside its jurisdiction.[96]

State practice may demonstrate that regardless of the absence of a relevant provision in the LOSC, historic/traditional fishing rights of neighbouring states in the territorial sea and the EEZ have been recognised in bilateral or regional agreements.[97] Most of these agreements were signed at the time when states extended their maritime zones and their jurisdiction (mainly through declarations of EEZ) regardless of the adoption and entry into force of the LOSC. These agreements are different from transitional agreements to allow fishermen from third states to adjust to the seaward expansion of coastal state jurisdiction, and also different from article 62 (3) access to the surplus arrangements. The state practice reflected in these agreements may demonstrate that the survival of historic fishing rights in the territorial sea and the EEZ of a state will depend on the local circumstances, the fishing history, and the intentions and attitudes of the relevant states.[98]

Regardless of the ownership of the maritime features in the SCS, other states may be able, according to the above, to claim historic fishing rights. This will apply to the maritime zones generated by the maritime features, both the territorial sea and the EEZ. According to the SCS Tribunal, all maritime features in the Spratly group are rocks by virtue of article 121 (3).[99] The assessment of this finding is beyond the scope of the present chapter; however, if this is the case, historic fishing rights would be relevant for the areas of the territorial sea generated by each maritime feature, whereas beyond that, the freedom of the high seas would apply, and no invocation of historic rights would be necessary or applicable. In the opposite case, and considering the objections raised by China regarding the Award, historic fishing rights could be potentially relevant beyond the territorial sea as part of a shared fishing regime evolved based on historic fishing practices in the area as analysed above.

Historic fishing rights and requirements for their ascertainment related to the SCS

In contrast to title-based historic rights, historic fishing rights do not create an entitlement to a maritime area and are based on a shared and non-exclusive use of the sea. Their formation is thus different from historic titles. Historic fishing rights rely on the practice of fishermen in maritime areas often close to the coasts where they live, regardless of the legal status of the maritime zones and of the gradual extension of the jurisdiction of the coastal states. In this respect, the practice may have taken place within the territorial sea of a state, and thus have an adverse element (inconsistent with the legal status of the maritime zone), but also on the high seas (as part of the exercise of freedom of fishing). In both the *Eritrea/Yemen* and *SCS* cases, the development of historic fishing rights related to disputed sovereignty over islands, which created uncertainty concerning which state exercised sovereignty or sovereign rights in the adjacent sea.

The *Eritrea/Yemen* Tribunal described the process for the formation of historic fishing rights with reference to the concept of "historical consolidation."[100] In the *Anglo-Norwegian Fisheries* case, the ICJ referring to this concept found that the straight baseline system applied by Norway to its coasts was "a well-defined and uniform system … which would reap the benefit of general toleration, the basis of an historical consolidation which would make it enforceable as against all States."[101] The formation of special customary international law is also pertinent.[102] The key requirements for the establishment of these rights are: consistent and clearly-defined fishing activities or "common patterns of behaviour,"[103] often linked with local traditions and customs, which are performed uninterrupted and unobjected for a lengthy period of time.

With respect to the length of time, the *Eritrea/Yemen* Tribunal referred to the existence of the fishing regime for centuries and to its continuous exercise "through the ages."[104] The *SCS* Tribunal reiterated this and referred to practice "over an extended period."[105] The Tribunal in the *Barbados/Trinidad and Tobago* arbitration, on the other hand, rejected the existence of a tradition due to the short time of the performance of the practice:

> the practice of long-range Barbadian fishing for flying fish, in waters which then were the high seas essentially began with the introduction of iceboats in the period 1978–1980, that is, some six to eight years before Trinidad and Tobago in 1986 enacted its Archipelagic Waters Act. … Those short years are not sufficient to give rise to a tradition.[106]

Acquiescence, albeit an important element for the ascertainment of historic titles as examined above, cannot be deemed to play an important role for the ascertainment of historic fishing rights, as, apart from cases where the practice was performed in the territorial sea of another state, the fishing practice was part of the freedom of the high seas – at least initially – and was therefore lawful and not adverse. What is important, as noted by the Eritrea/Yemen Tribunal, is unobstructed performance of activities by fishermen "without encountering difficulties of a political or administrative nature"[107] and "without any need to obtain any authorisations from the rulers on either the Asian or the African side of the Red Sea and in the absence of restrictions or regulations exercised by public authorities."[108] The SCS Tribunal did not refer to the acquiescence of any authorities but to "longstanding practice" and "continuous" activities by fishermen in the area.[109]

As regards the necessary evidence, the *Eritrea/Yemen* Tribunal referred to "the most reliable historical and geographical sources, both ancient and modern," to "a variety of sources" supporting these "historical facts" as "submitted in evidence during the arbitral proceedings" and specifically referred to books on the history of the area and the Red Sea evidencing these activities.[110] It also referred to "statements attributed to fishermen from both coasts of the Red Sea, taken as a whole, which have been submitted by both parties."[111] The SCS Tribunal referred generally to the "record before it" supporting that "Scarborough Shoal has been a traditional fishing ground for fishermen of many nationalities."[112] In its assessment of the required evidence, the SCS arbitration took into account the nature of the activities, and noted that "matters of evidence should be approached with sensitivity" and specifically referred to the fact that the stories of these traditional fishermen "have not been the subject of written records" and "that certain livelihoods have not been considered of interest to official record keepers or to the writers of history does not make them less important to those who practise them."[113] Furthermore, the Tribunal relied on the fact that both the Philippines and China claimed to have traditionally fished at Scarborough Shoal, and the Tribunal found that these claims were "accurate and advanced in good faith."[114]

Concluding remarks

The relevance of historic rights in the SCS is complex from various perspectives. First, the exact scope and nature of China's historic claim is not clear, nor has China tried to clarify it, either during or after the SCS arbitration. Its link with the U-shaped line and the sovereign rights and jurisdiction arising from the maritime zones recognised by the LOSC is also unclear. As noted by the SCS Tribunal, China's claim is not a claim to historic waters, namely a claim of sovereignty akin to either internal or territorial waters. China's claim has been found to be historic rights short of sovereignty.

Second, the post-LOSC existence and relevance of historic rights are controversial. Although there is consensus that historic titles may exist with respect to the territorial sea/internal waters (normally referred to as historic waters), the issue of historic rights short of sovereignty is more controversial. Two types of such rights have been identified as potentially relevant for the SCS: historic rights short of sovereignty that have a quasi-territorial or zonal impact beyond the territorial sea, and non-exclusive historic rights.

The SCS Tribunal pronounced that historic rights short of sovereignty have been superseded by the LOSC and the maritime zones recognised therein. However, international courts and tribunals have examined the relevance of such rights in maritime delimitation cases, and even though they have not accepted the specific claims due to lack of evidence, they have not precluded their potential relevance in the law of the sea. In overlapping maritime zones, these rights relate to the location of the maritime boundary and the extent of a state's maritime zones vis-a-vis another coastal state. To what extent, these rights can be accepted outside the framework of maritime delimitation is unclear, and it would relate to the specific circumstances of each situation. Since China has not clarified the scope and extent of its historic claim with respect to the SCS, it is difficult to assess where and whether such rights may be potentially relevant.

Historic fishing rights may also be relevant in the SCS. These rights differ from exclusive historic rights in the sense that they do not have a zonal impact and can be recognised in the maritime zones of other states. They rely on a shared regime of open, non-exclusive access to the fishing grounds by fishermen, developed through a process of historical consolidation over the course of a lengthy period of time, which may also relate to the fishing traditions and customs of the local communities. The SCS Tribunal recognised the existence of traditional fishing rights of fishermen of the littoral states in the territorial sea around the Scarborough Shoal. It has been argued that, based on the *Eritrea/Yemen arbitration* Award, this may also be relevant beyond the territorial sea depending on the location of these shared fishing grounds. However, the relevance of these rights for areas beyond the territorial sea in the SCS will depend on the legal status of the maritime features according to article 121 (3) of the LOSC. The SCS Tribunal found that the features in the Spratly archipelago were rocks and could not thus generate maritime zones beyond the territorial sea. In these areas, the freedom of the high seas would apply (including freedom of fisheries) and therefore historic fishing rights would not be relevant.

Notes

1 A. Schottenhammer, 'The "China Seas" in world history: A general outline of the role of Chinese and East Asian maritime space from its origins to c. 1800' 1 (2) *Journal of Marine and Island Cultures* (2012), p. 64.
2 *The Republic of the Philippines v the People's Republic of China, PCA Case N° 2013–19 in the Matter of the South China Arbitration*, Award of 12 July 2016 (Merits), para. 805.
3 Ibid., para. 28.
4 The official name of this line depicted on the map is 'traditional maritime boundary line' and it has been referred to by the use of various other names such as 'tongue-shaped line', 'dotted line' etc. See K. Zou, 'China's U-shaped line in the South China Sea revisited' 43 *ODIL* (2012), pp. 18–19.
5 See L. Jinming and L. Dexia, 'The dotted line on the Chinese map of the South China Sea: a note' 34 *ODIL* (2003), p. 290.
6 Z. Gao and B.B. Jia, 'The nine-dash line in the South China Sea: History, states and implications' 107 (1) *AJIL* (2013), p. 102.
7 K. Zou, *supra* note 4, p. 19.
8 Gao and Jia, *supra* note 6, p. 103.
9 Ibid., 104.
10 K-M. Sun, 'Policy of the Republic of China towards the South China Sea' 19 *Marine Policy* (1995), p. 408. South China Sea Policy Guidelines (Appendix I); 'the South China Sea area within the historic water limit is the maritime area under the jurisdiction of the Republic of China, in which the Republic of China possesses all rights and interests'.
11 Exclusive Economic Zone and Continental Shelf Act (adopted at the third session of the Standing Committee of the Ninth National People's Congress, 26 June 1998); available at https://www.un.org/Depts/los/LEGISLATIONANDTREATIES/PDFFILES/chn_1998_eez_act.pdf.
12 K. Zou, 'Historic rights in the South China Sea' in S. Wu and M. Valencia (eds.), *UN Convention on the Law of the Sea and the South China Sea* (Routledge, 2015), p. 246.
13 Ibid.
14 Letter from the Permanent Mission of the People's Republic of China to the UN Secretary General, No CML/17/2009, 7 May 2009, available at https://www.un.org/Depts/los/clcs_new/submissions_files/mysvnm33_09/chn_2009re_mys_vnm_e.pdf.
15 Letter from the Permanent Mission of the People's Republic of China to the UN Secretary General, No. CML/8/2011, 14 April 2011, available at https://www.un.org/Depts/los/clcs_new/submissions_files/vnm37_09/chn_2011_re_phl_e.pdf.
16 Ibid.
17 Position Paper of the Government of the People's Republic of China on the Matter of Jurisdiction in the South China Sea Arbitration Initiated by the Republic of the Philippines, 7 December 2014, available at https://www.fmprc.gov.cn/nanhai/eng/snhwtlcwj_1/t1368895.htm.
18 Ibid., para. 4.
19 Ibid.; it also noted the following:

> both the Declaration of the Government of the People's Republic of China on the Territorial Sea of 1958 and the Law of the People's Republic of China on the Territorial Sea and the Contiguous Zone of 1992 expressly provide that the territory of the People's Republic of China includes, among others, the Dongsha Islands, the Xisha Islands, the Zhongsha Islands and the Nansha Islands. All those acts affirm China's territorial sovereignty and relevant maritime rights and interests in the South China Sea.

20 Statement of the Ministry of Foreign Affairs of the People's Republic of China on the Award on Jurisdiction and Admissibility of the South China Sea arbitration by the Arbitral Tribunal Established at the request of the Republic of the Philippines, 30/10/2015, available at https://www.fmprc.gov.cn/mfa_eng/zxxx_662805/t1310474.shtml.
21 See an overview in L. Jinming and L. Dexia, *supra* note 5, p. 291.
22 M. Sheng-Ti Gau, 'Issues of jurisdiction in cases of default of appearance' in S. Talmon and B.B. Jia (eds.), *The South China Sea Arbitration: A Chinese Perspective* (Hart, 2014), pp. 88–89.
23 K. Zou, 'Historic rights in international law and in China's practice' 32 (2) *Ocean Development and International Law* (2001), p. 160; "since it is referable to the EEZ and continental shelf regimes, such a claim involves sovereign rights and jurisdiction but not full sovereignty". Similarly, Z. Gao

and B. Jia, *supra* note 6, p. 108; these authors refer to additional (to the LOSC) 'historical rights of fishing, navigation, and other marine activities (including the exploration and exploitation of resources, mineral or otherwise'.

24 SCS Award (Merits), *supra* note 2, para. 28. This request was further clarified in its memorial during the jurisdictional hearing in the following two points:

> China's maritime entitlements in the South China Sea, like those of the Philippines may not extend beyond those permitted by the LOSC" "China's claims to sovereign rights and jurisdictions and to historic rights with respect to the maritime areas of the South China Sea encompassed by the so-called nine-dash line are contrary to the Convention and without lawful effect to the extent that they exceed the geographic and substantive limits of China's maritime entitlements under LOSC

The Republic of the Philippines v the People's Republic of China, PCA Case N° 2013–19 in the Matter of the South China Arbitration Award on jurisdiction and admissibility of 29 October 2015, para. 101.

25 *South China Sea Arbitration Award (Merits), supra* note 2, para. 180; *South China Sea Arbitration Award on Jurisdiction and Admissibility, supra* note 24, para. 160.

26 *South China Sea Arbitration Award (Merits), supra* note 2, para. 207–214.

27 Ibid., para. 213. See also reference to a statement of the Chinese Ministry of Foreign Affairs regarding an "insightful formulation by China of its claims in the South China Sea", para. 206, footnote 199.

28 Ibid., para. 214.

29 See, for example, the Statement of Chinese Foreign Ministry Spokesman Chen Jian 'News briefing by Chinese Foreign Ministry' cited in Y.H. Song and K. Zou, 'Maritime legislation of mainland China and Taiwan: Developments, comparison, implications and potential challenges for the US' 31 *ODIL* (2000), p. 322.

30 *Award (Merits)*, para. 225. See similarly, F. Dupuy and P.-M. Dupuy, 'A legal analysis of China's historic rights claim in the South China Sea' 107 (1) *AJIL* (2013), pp. 124–141.

31 The Tribunal refers to "claims of sovereignty over maritime areas derived from historical circumstances"; Merits award, *supra* note 24, para. 226. See also Study prepared by the Secretariat, 'Juridical Regime of historic waters, including historic bays' Doc. A/CN.4/143. (March 1962), p. 6, para. 33–34. The ICJ in the *Fisheries case* referred to "historic waters" as 'usually [meaning] waters which are treated as internal waters, but which would not have that character if it were not for the existence of historic title'. *Fisheries case* (United Kingdom v Norway) Judgment of 18 December 1951, ICJ Reports, p. 130. F. Dupuy and P.-M. Dupuy, *supra* note 29: "historic waters can only be an extension of internal or territorial sea" p. 139.

32 S. Kopela, 'Historic titles and historic rights in the law of the sea in the light of the South China Sea arbitration' 48 (2) *ODIL* (2017), p. 188.

33 *South China Sea Arbitration Award (Merits), supra* note 2, para. 234.

34 Ibid., para. 262.

35 Ibid., para. 238 (a).

36 Ibid., para. 237.

37 See H. Thirway, 'The sources of international law' in M.D. Evans (ed.), *International Law* (4th ed., OUP, 2014), p. 109.

38 See similarly M.A. Xinmin, 'Merits Award relating to historic rights in the SCS arbitration: an appraisal' 8 *Asian Journal of International Law* (2018), pp. 15–16.

39 R.Y. Jennings, *The Acquisition of Territory in International Law* (Manchester University Press, 1963), p. 24.

40 *Grisbadarna arbitration* (Norway v Sweden) Award of the Tribunal of 23 October 1909, p. 6.

41 Blum, *infra* note 43, p. 12.

42 G. Fitzmaurice, 'The law and procedure of the ICJ, 1951–54: General principles and sources of law' 30 *British Yearbook of International Law* (1953), p. 68.

43 I.C. McGibbon, 'Customary international law and acquiescence' 33 *British Yearbook of International Law* (1957), p. 122. Blum regards historic rights as a category of special customary rights, Y.Z. Blum, *Historic Titles in International Law* (Nijhoff, 1965). M. Wesley Clark, *Historic Bays and Waters: A Regime of Recent Beginnings and Continued Usage* (Oceana, 1994), pp. 52–57. Thirlway suggests that

> if practice apparently inconsistent with a general rule shows enough internal consistency it may reveal the existence of a local or special custom differing from the general rule; or of an

exception to the general rule where special circumstances exist (e.g. the preferential fishing rights of a coastal state exceptionally dependent on fishing resources).

H.Thirlway, 'The law and procedure of the ICJ: 1960–1989 (Part II)' 61 *British Yearbook of International Law* (1990), p. 82.

44 S. Talmon, 'Possible preliminary objections to the Philippines' claims' in Talmon and Jia (eds.), *supra* note 22, p. 51.

45 See Barbados's argument in *Arbitration between Barbados and the Republic of Trinidad and Tobago, relating to the delimitation of the exclusive economic zone and the continental shelf between them*, decision of 11 April 2006, *RIAW* Vol. XXVII, para. 140:

> it would be contrary to established methods of interpretation of treaties to read into a treaty an intention to extinguish pre-existing rights in the absence of express words to that effect' and that acquired rights such as historic rights 'survive unless explicitly terminated.
>
> (para. 138)

46 See M.A. Xinmin, *supra* note 38, p. 14.

47 *SCS Award* (Merits), supra note 2, paras. 243–244 (on EEZ and continental shelf respectively).

48 *Case concerning the continental shelf* (Tunisia / Libyan Arab Jamahiriya), [1982] *ICJ Reports*, para. 100.

49 *Case concerning land, island and maritime frontier dispute* (El Salvador/Honduras: Nicaragua intervening), [1992] *ICJ Reports*, p. 589, para. 384.

50 *Tunisia/Libya case, supra* note 48, para. 100.

51 Ibid., para. 100.

52 C. Symmons, 'Historic waters and historic rights in the South China Sea: A critical appraisal' in S. Wu and M. Valencia (eds.), *UN Convention on the Law of the Sea and the South China Sea* (Routledge, 2015), p. 200.

53 Cottier in his discussion of the relevance of historic rights in maritime delimitation notes

> the problem cannot be dismissed in summary terms. Neither would predomination or subjection *in abstracto* of such rights provide a satisfactory answer. Conclusive answers have to rely upon the legal nature of the shelf and the EEZ and the doctrine of intertemporal law

T. Cottier, *Equitable Principles of Maritime Boundary Delimitation: The Quest for Distributive Justice in International Law* (CUP, 2015), p. 486.

54 Symmons, *supra* note 52, pp. 203–205. Also K. Zou, *Law of the Sea in East Asia: Issues and Prospects* (Routledge, 2005), p. 150; he notes: "China has to prove that its historic rights existed prior to the establishment of the customary rules on the continental shelf. Otherwise, China's claim is only relevant to the EEZ not continental shelf area."

55 *Libya/Tunisia* case, *supra* note 48, para. 100. Libya had argued that the fishing practice of one state could not "in principle prevail over the inherent and *ab initio* rights of another state in respect of its natural prolongation", p. 72, para. 98.

56 Ibid.

57 Cottier argues that "the fact that the Court suggested that matters may be different in the context of the EEZ (not invoked by the parties) suggests that the majority of the court thought historic rights irrelevant in the context of the self", Cottier, *supra* note 53, p. 486.

58 See also different views expressed by two judges: *Tunisia/Libya* case, *supra* note 48, Dissenting Opinion by Judge Oda, p. 211 para. 88. Separate Opinion by Judge Arechaga, para. 82:

> a new legal concept, consisting in the notion introduced in 1958 that continental shelf rights are inherent or *ab initio* cannot by itself have the effect of abolishing or denying acquired and existing rights. That would be contrary to elementary legal notions and to basic principles of intertemporal law. It would be absurd to contend that the Truman proclamation or the 1958 Convention abolished or disregarded pre-existing rights over the continental shelf, when, on the contrary, they embodied or assimilated those rights into the new doctrine.

See also Cottier, *supra* note 53, pp. 486–487: "From a historic perspective of the shelf, which only emerged in customary law in the early 1960s, it follows that the existence of historical rights cannot be excluded".

59 A. Gioia, 'Tunisia's claim over adjacent seas and the doctrine of "historic rights" 11 *Syracuse Journal of International Law and Commerce* (1984), p. 372.

60 Y.Tanaka, *Predictability and Flexibility in the Law of Maritime Delimitation* (Hart, 2006), p. 301.

61 See C. Symmons, *Historic Waters in the Law of the Sea: A Modern Reappraisal* (Brill/M. Nijhoff, 2008), pp. 243–244 on the issue of "opposability" with respect to the establishment of historic titles.

62 Gioia, *supra* note 59, para. 17.

63 R. Kolb, *Case Law on Equitable Maritime Delimitation: Digest and Commentaries* (Brill/Nijhoff, 2003), p. 185.

64 *South China Sea arbitration*, Merits Pleadings, Day 1, pp. 59–63, available at https://pcacases.com/web/view/7:

> In short, from the time of Grotius through the widespread acceptance of the UN Convention on the Law of the Sea, international law has not preserved, admitted or accepted claims to control vast areas of the sea in derogation or either the freedom of the seas or the rights of the immediately adjacent coastal state.

65 McDorman notes that

> such a claim beyond near-shore waters would be exceptional and inconsistent with the history of the law of the sea where, until recently, what existed were narrow bands of national waters along a coast and wide expanses of high seas with which high seas freedom existed.

T. McDorman, 'Rights and jurisdiction over resources in the South China Sea: UNCLOS and the nine-dash line' in Jayakuman et al. (eds.), *South China Sea Disputes and the Law of the Sea* (Elgar, 2014), p. 155.

66 Symmons, *supra* note 52, p. 206.

67 Talmon, *supra* note 44, pp. 49–50. See also Tonga's claim to a rectangle of sea in the archipelago and comments by O'Connell with respect to its potential validity based on history: "History might validate the claim to the rectangle, as an exception to the law relating to the high seas, but only as a broadening of the area which could be claimed under the standard rules"; D.P. O'Connell, *The Law of the Sea*, Vol. I (OUP, 1982), p. 418.

68 Y.Z. Blum, *supra* note 43. M. Wesley Clark, *Historic Bays and Waters: A Regime of Recent Beginnings and Continued Usage* (Oceana, 1994), p. 256 quoting Jessup, *The Law of Territorial Waters and Maritime Jurisdiction* (1927), p. 382.

69 Zou has noted that

> China has set a precedent in the state practice relating to historic rights. It is not clear whether China's practice establishes a rule in international law, but it may already be influencing the development of the concept of historic rights.

Zou, *supra* note 23, p. 160. Similarly, N. Hong, *UNCLOS and Ocean Dispute Settlement: Law and Politics in the South China Sea* (Routledge, 2012), pp. 70–71.

70 Talmon, *supra* note 44, p. 53. See also M.A. Xinmin, *supra* note 38, pp. 22–23; he refers to Sri Lanka's historic claim beyond 12 n.m. and the agreement with India in this respect.

71 Study prepared by the UN Secretariat, 'Juridical regime of historic waters, including historic bays' Doc. A/CN.4/143. (March 1962), para. 80, p. 13.

72 *SCS Merits* award, *supra* note 24, para. 267.

73 Ibid., para. 267.

74 Ibid., para. 264.

75 Ibid., paras. 268–269.

76 Ibid., para. 270.

77 G. Fitzmaurice, *supra* note 43, pp. 28, 68–69. I.C. McGibbon, *supra* note 43, p. 123. See Blum for an account of the views of international scholars, international bodies and tribunals regarding the prominent role of acquiescence as the juridical basis of historic rights, Y.Z. Blum, *supra* note 43, pp. 60–89.

78 Submission 10 read: 'China has unlawfully prevented Philippine fishermen from pursuing their livelihoods by interfering with traditional fishing activities at Scarborough Shoal' *SCS Merits* award, supra note 2 para. 758.

79 Ibid., para. 126.

80 Second stage of the proceedings between Eritrea and Yemen (Maritime Delimitation) Award of 17 December 1999, RIAW Vol. XXII, para 103.

81 S. Kopela, 'Historic fishing rights in the law of the sea and Brexit' 32 (4) *Leiden Journal of International Law* (2019), pp. 700–701.

82 *Eritrea/Yemen arbitration* (second stage), *supra* note 79, para. 109.
83 SCS arbitration (merits), *supra* note 2, p. 259.
84 On this issue see S. Kopela, 'Historic titles and historic rights in the law of the sea in the light of the SCS arbitration' 48 (2) *ODIL* (2017), p. 194.
85 The Tribunal notes that "the Tribunal considers that the inclusion of this provision – which would be entirely unnecessary if traditional fishing rights were preserved in the EEZ – confirms that the drafters of the Convention did not intend to preserve such rights". See also similar argument with respect to article 51 (1) regarding archipelagic waters; *South China Sea Arbitration Award (Merits), supra* note 24, para. 804 (a). See similarly, C. Symmons, *supra* note 12, pp. 195–196; R. Beckman, 'The UN Convention on the Law of the Sea and the maritime disputes in the South China Sea' 107 *AJIL* (2013), p. 158. A. Proelss (ed.), *UN Convention on the Law of the Sea: A Commentary* (Hart, 2017), p. 550.
86 SCS Arbitration, Hearing Day 4, p. 110; Hearing, Day 2, p. 164. Article 2 para. 3 provides that "the sovereignty over the territorial sea is exercised subject to this Convention and to other rules of international law".
87 The provision was transferred verbatim from article 2 of the Geneva Convention on the Territorial Sea and Contiguous Zone. See M.Nordquist, S.Nandan and A.Rosenne (eds), *UNCLOS 1982: A Commentary* Vol. II (M.Nijhoff, 2002), *supra* note, pp. 72–73.
88 SCS Arbitration (Merits), *supra* note 2, para. 802.
89 For an analysis on this, see S. Kopela, *supra* note 80, p. 705.
90 A. Proelss, *supra* note 84, p. 465.
91 See S. Kopela, *supra* note 80, pp. 706–707.
92 *South China Sea Arbitration Award (Merits), supra* note 2, para. 256. See also similar arguments by C. Symmons, *supra note 60*, p. 28 note 28 and *Limits in the Seas No 143: China: Maritime Claims in the South China Sea* (US Department of State, 2014), p. 20.
93 *Barbados/Trinidad and Tobago Arbitration, supra* note 45, paras. 125–129, also arguments para. 133–142.
94 Ibid., para. 266.
95 Ibid., para. 273.
96 Ibid., para. 283.
97 See for example Agreement between Sri Lanka and India on the Boundary in Historic Waters between the two Countries and Related Matters 26 and 28 June 1974, entry into force: 10 July 1974; this agreement concerns the acknowledgment of traditional fishing rights of fishing vessels from Sri Lanka and India in the historic fishing grounds of Palk Bay; available at http://www.un.org/Depts/los/LEGISLATIONANDTREATIES/PDFFILES/TREATIES/LKA-IND1974BW.PDF; See similarly Treaty between Australia and the Independent State of Papua New Guinea concerning Sovereignty and maritime Boundaries in the area between the two Countries, including the area known as Torres Strait, and related Matters (adopted in 1978, entered into force 1985) Australian Treaty Series 1985 No 4, Department of Foreign Affairs, Canberra, available at http://www.austlii.edu.au/au/other/dfat/treaties/1985/4.html.
98 Bernard argues that "it is clear that although historic/traditional fishing rights of a third State in the EEZ regime continue to exist, the rights are subject to recognition and approval by the coastal States"; L. Bernard, 'The effect of historic fishing rights in maritime boundaries delimitation' in *Proceedings from the 2012 LOSI-KIOST Conference on Securing the Ocean for the Next Generation*, p. 9, available at https://www.law.berkeley.edu/files/Bernard-final.pdf. McDorman referring to the *Eritrea/Yemen arbitration* argues that the award "supports the view that historic fishing rights by a third state in waters otherwise under the jurisdiction of a coastal state are not necessarily extinguished by UNCLOS" and concludes that "as the Eritrea/Yemen arbitration makes clear, historic rights in limited circumstances may exist that, while they do not undermine the sovereignty of the adjacent coastal state, require tolerance and attention to be paid by the coastal state"; this author does not seem to differentiate between the regimes in the territorial sea and EEZ. T. McDorman, 'Rights and jurisdiction over resources in the South China Sea: UNCLOS and the nine-dash line' in Jayakuman et al. (eds.), *South China Sea Disputes and the Law of the Sea* (Elgar, 2014), p. 158.
99 Ibid., para. 643–647.
100 *Territorial Sovereignty and Scope of the Dispute (Eritrea/Yemen)*, Award of 9 October 1998, RIAW Vol. XXII, para. 126.
101 *Fisheries case, supra* note 31, p. 138.

102 The SCS Tribunal referred to "customary rights acquired through long usage"; SCS Tribunal (Merits), *supra* note, para. 806. See also the Rights of Passage case where the ICJ referred to local custom as follows: "The Court sees no reason why long continued practice between two States accepted by them as regulating their relations should not form the basis of mutual rights and obligations between the two States"; *Case Concerning the Right of Passage over Indian Territory* (Portugal v. India, Judgment of 12 April 1960), *ICJ Reports 1960*, p. 39.
103 *Eritrea/Yemen arbitration* (first stage), *supra* note 99, para. 129. Activities might also entail fishing-related activities i.e. the Eritrea/Yemen Tribunal referred to "cross-relationships which are marked by eventual recourse to professional fishermen's arbitrators *(aq 'il) in* charge of settling disputes in accordance with the local customary law".
104 *Eritrea/Yemen case* (second stage), *supra* note 79, para. 104.
105 *SCS arbitration* (merits), *supra* note 2, para. 798.
106 *Barbados/Trinidad and Tobago award, supra* note 45, para. 266.
107 *Eritrea/Yemen* case (first stage), *supra* note 99, para. 128.
108 Ibid., para. 127.
109 *SCS arbitration* (merits), *supra* note 2, para 798. 'The Philippines referred to this practice as "long-standing', 'long', 'deep', peaceful', 'uninterrupted', 'ancient' and having occurred 'since times immemorial', *ibid.*, para. 779.
110 *Eritrea/Yemen arbitration* (first stage), *supra* note 99, para. 127, 129.
111 Ibid., para. 315: "numerous witness statements were submitted by both sides as to the longevity and importance of their respective fishing practices and the significance of fishing in the lives of their people".
112 *SCS arbitration* (merits) *supra* note 2, para. 805.
113 Ibid., para. 805–806.
114 Ibid., para. 805.

PART III

South China Sea policies of major claimants

9
CHINA'S SOUTH CHINA SEA POLICIES

Feng Zhu and Lingqun Li

China's claims to the SCS

The People's Republic of China's (PRC) policy towards the South China Sea (SCS) has two major components. One is China's legal stance, including claims to sovereignty and maritime entitlements. The second component concerns the approach China adopts, in face of conflicting claims asserted by other claimants, to manage the SCS dispute.

When founded in 1949, the PRC inherited its predecessor, the nationalist government's position with regard to the SCS. The basic skeleton of the nationalist government's claims to the SCS was formalized in 1947–1948 in the form of the dotted line.[1] The history and legal implications of the dotted line are well elaborated in Chapter 7, suffice it to say that over the years, while the dotted line remains at the core of the PRC's claims to the SCS, the content and elaboration of China's claims have experienced a series of subtle changes.

1950s–1960s

In 1951, the newly established PRC government revealed for the first time to the international community its official position concerning sovereign claims to the SCS. This move was a direct response to challenges that emerged during the 1951 San Francisco Peace Conference, a conference convened between 48 Allied nations and Japan to negotiate post-war order in Asia. For political reasons, the PRC was not invited to attend this conference. However, the PRC was alerted by the circulation of a Draft Treaty of the Conference which only stipulated that Japan would renounce all its rights to wartime occupation including the SCS islands. Such wording raised the question of whether China could restore sovereignty over the SCS islands as previously expected, to which the PRC responded quickly. On 1 September, a week before the opening of the San Francisco Peace Conference, Zhou Enlai, then Foreign Minister of the PRC, made a public statement in Beijing as follows:

> The Draft Treaty stipulated that Japan should renounce all rights to Nanwei (Spratly) Island and Xisha Islands (Paracels), but again deliberately makes no mention of the problem of restoring sovereignty over them. As a matter of fact, just like all the Nansha Islands (Spratlys), Zhongsha Islands (Macclesfield Bank) and Dongsha Islands (Pratas), Xisha Islands and Nanwei Island have always been China's territory.[2]

During the San Francisco Conference also emerged another challenge from Vietnam. When the Vietnamese delegation asserted claims to sovereignty over the Paracel and Spratly Islands, the Soviet delegation, on behalf of the PRC, conveyed the latter's position that

> Japan recognizes the full sovereignty of the Chinese People's Republic over Manchuria, the Island of Taiwan with all islands adjacent to it, the Penghu Islands, the Dongsha Islands, as well as over the islands of Xisha and Zhongsha, and Nansha Islands including the Spratly, and renounces all right, title and claim to the territories named herein.[3]

The PRC's initial legal claims to the SCS were also expressed in an official document—the *1958 Declaration on Territorial Sea*. Issued on 4 September 1958, the Declaration represents the PRC's first domestic legislation concerning maritime affairs. In this document, the Chinese government laid claims to sovereignty over all the four island groups in the South China Sea—Dongsha, Xisha, Zhongsha and Nansha Islands. A 12-nautical-mile belt of territorial sea surrounding these islands, using a straight baseline system, was also declared. Article 1 of the *1958 Declaration* reads:

> The breadth of the territorial sea of the People's Republic of China shall be twelve nautical miles. This provision applies to all territories of the People's Republic of China, including the Chinese mainland and its coastal islands, as well as Taiwan and its surrounding islands, the Penghu Islands, the Dongsha Islands, the Xisha Islands, the Zhongsha Islands, the Nansha Islands and all other islands belonging to China....[4]

There are two observations we can draw from the PRC's official statements and legislation cited above. First, it seems that from the very beginning, the PRC government viewed the features in the SCS as typical islands and together they formed into four island groups—Dongsha island group, Xisha island group, Zhongsha island group and Nansha island group. The second observation is, the PRC's initial SCS claims focused mainly on the issue of territorial sovereignty. Little was mentioned about maritime entitlements and rights other than the 12-nautical-mile territorial seas.

1970s–1980s

This period starts to witness China's efforts to expand its original SCS claims to sea areas and resources beyond the limit of 12-nautical-mile territorial sea. This was motivated by two events. The first event has to do with a scientific survey conducted in 1969 in the SCS exploring offshore hydrocarbon potentials. The survey was undertaken by a UN-organized committee specialized in prospecting for mineral resources and yielded a quite positive result, estimating potentially large hydrocarbon deposits in the area. The survey result attracted great interest, among SCS countries including China, in vast natural resources in the SCS.

The second event was the convening of the Third UN Conference on the Law of the Sea (UNCLOS III), which started in 1973[5] and ended in 1982 after nine years of marathon-style negotiation, brought about profound changes to the international maritime order. The conference yielded a number of revolutionary regimes, such as exclusive economic zone, archipelagic waters and extended continental shelf, which enabled states to extend their national jurisdiction much further into the seas than previously allowed.

The PRC sent a delegation to the UNCLOS III, participated in the full negotiation process throughout, and signed the final text of the UNCLOS in December 1982. During the

Conference, ongoing debates regarding whether states can expand national jurisdiction over extensive sea areas inspired China to consider that it may expand its SCS claims to cover additional maritime space and entitlements in the SCS far beyond the 12-nautical-mile limit.

Against this background, from 1974 onward, terms related to maritime space and rights, such as "adjacent sea areas," "surrounding sea areas," and "the natural resources," began to appear in official statements and documents. For example, in 1974, to protest against the South Vietnamese government's move to incorporate the Spratly Islands into Phuoc Tuy Province, the Chinese government issued a statement in which it claimed that "...the natural resources in the sea areas (emphasis added)" around the Nansha, Xisha, Zhongsha and Dongsha Islands belong to China.[6] In another statement, China claimed that it enjoyed sovereignty over both the SCS islands and their adjacent seas (emphasis added).[7] These terms reflect China's awareness of potential maritime rights and entitlements beyond territorial seas, although it remained unclear to what natural resources or which sea area China was referring to in those statements.

In the meantime, the Chinese government found itself facing an unexpectedly complicated situation in the SCS. While China embraced the idea of universal expansion of national jurisdiction in the ocean space during the UNCLOS III and applied it to its own SCS claims, it soon came to realize that other bordering states in the SCS were also encouraged by this legal development and started to stake/modify their respective maritime claims, creating a number of overlapping and conflicting claims in the SCS. This situation prompted the Chinese leadership to seriously consider "joint development" as a potentially promising solution. The idea of "joint development" was first endorsed in 1984 by the late Chinese leader Deng Xiaoping when he was visiting the Center for Strategic and International Studies of Georgetown University in the United States. In 1988, Deng Xiaoping again shared with Filipino president Aquino his thoughts on joint development during the latter's state visit to Beijing that "for the sake of a cordial relationship between the two countries, we could shelve the disputes and adopt a joint development approach instead."[8]

1990s

In this period, two legal advancements took place in regard to the PRC's claims to the SCS. First, the PRC government passed three important pieces of national maritime legislation in the 1990s. The first piece of legislation is related to the 1982 UNCLOS. The UNCLOS officially entered into force on 16 November 1994, a year after Guyana became the 60th nation to ratify the treaty. On 15 May 1996, the Standing Committee of the Eighth National People's Congress issued a declaration approving the ratification of the Convention. The other two pieces of legislation are the *Law on the Territorial Sea and the Contiguous Zone* and the *Law on the Exclusive Economic Zone and Continental Shelf*. The promulgation of these two laws brought China's SCS claims under the legal framework of the UNCLOS.

The *Law on the Territorial Sea and the Contiguous Zone* was enacted in 1992. In this law China reasserted its sovereignty to features in the SCS: "the PRC's territorial land includes ...Dongsha Islands, Xisha Islands, Nansha Islands and other islands that belong to the People's Republic of China."[9] Besides 12-nautical-mile territorial seas, this law also proclaimed China's rights to exercise control over additional 12-nautical-mile contiguous zones outside of, but adjacent to, its territorial seas.

In 1998, the Chinese government promulgated the *Law on the Exclusive Economic Zone and Continental Shelf*, which entered into force on the same day of promulgation. This law aimed at establishing at the domestic level the legal regimes of the exclusive economic zone and the continental shelf. The text adopted very similar wording as that in the 1982 UNCLOS. Article 2 reads:

> The exclusive economic zone of the People's Republic of China is an area beyond and adjacent to the territorial sea of the People's Republic of China extending to a distance of 200 nautical miles from the baseline from which the breadth of the territorial sea is measured;
>
> The continental shelf of the PRC "comprises the seabed and subsoil of the submarine areas that extend beyond its territorial sea throughout the natural prolongation of its land territory to the outer edge of the continental margin, or to a distance of 200 nautical miles from the baselines from which the breadth of the territorial sea is measured where the outer edge of the continental margin does not extend up to that distance.[10]

What is worth highlighting here is Article 14 of the *Law on the Exclusive Economic Zone and Continental Shelf*, which stipulates that the establishment of exclusive economic zones and continental shelves shall not affect the historical rights enjoyed by China. The insertion of Article 14 reflects China's shifting attitude towards the role of the concept of historic rights in defending its maritime interests, in particular with regard to its claims to the SCS.

In the 1970s and 1980s, confronted by an escalating dispute over the delimitation of the Gulf of Tonkin, the Vietnamese government tested the waters by proposing that the Gulf of Tonkin be viewed as historic waters. This idea was rejected by the Chinese government at that time. Negative attitude towards historic rights began to change in the mid-1990s when the issue of ratifying the 1982 UNCLOS was given serious consideration by the Chinese leadership. Critical voices emerged in the domestic discourse, requesting a full assessment of the impact of the Convention on China's maritime interests and practices before official accession.

During the Eighth National People's Congress, Li Zhaoxing, then Chinese Vice Foreign Minister, elaborated on four issues that may affect adversely China's maritime rights and interests, a major concern of which was that the legal regimes of the exclusive economic zone (EEZ) and CS established by the Convention may bring about challenges to China's dotted line/nine-dash line claim and potentially undermine China's maritime interests in the SCS.[11] Li also suggested to the Congress that once acceded to the Convention, the government would take the additional policy to cope with some of these issues. Consequently, China came to value the role of historic rights in mitigating the side-effect associated with the application of the Convention to its SCS claims.

The second legal advancement related to the PRC's SCS claims is China's *Declaration on the Baselines of the Territorial Sea* issued in 1996.[12] Besides the base points delimiting the territorial sea adjacent to the mainland coast, this declaration also listed 28 base points encircling the territorial sea of Xisha Islands using a straight baseline system. It was also declared that the remaining baselines of the territorial sea would be announced at another time. This declaration has two legal implications: (1) it implicates that China views Xisha Islands as a single unit for generating maritime entitlements, and (2) it implicates the possibility that China would draw basepoints of other SCS island groups using similar delimiting method as that used for the Xisha Islands.

2000s

In the 2000s, a major legal move made by China was related to its submission to the UN in 2009 a map of the SCS marked by the dotted line/nine-dash line. On 6 May 2009, Malaysia and Vietnam jointly submitted an application for defining a portion of the continental shelf between the two states in the southern part of the SCS to the Commission on the Limits of the Continental Shelf (CLCS), a body established by the Convention concerning the delimitation of outer limits of the continental shelf in areas beyond 200 nautical miles.[13] The next day, Vietnam made a separate submission to the CLCS concerning the area north of its joint submission with Malaysia.[14] Since these two submissions involved areas in dispute, the Chinese government lodged two *notes vervale* to the UN Secretary-General dated 7 May 2009, protesting against Vietnam and Malaysia's submissions, in which China attached the dotted line/nine-dash line map.

The two Notes were quite similar in wording, in which China asserted that

> China has indisputable sovereignty over the islands in the South China Sea and the adjacent waters, and enjoys sovereign rights and jurisdiction over the relevant waters as well as the seabed and subsoil thereof (see attached map).[15]

The enclosure of the dotted line map in the PRC's diplomatic notes to the UN marked the first time China had officially reaffirmed the line to elaborate its claims in the SCS. This move, similar to its embrace of the concept of historic rights in the 1990s, was motivated by China's intention to defend and advance its SCS claims in face of potential legal challenges posed by the UNCLOS. Previously, although the dotted line/nine-dash line map was regularly circulated in numerous Chinese maps and atlases, the PRC government never publicly used the line to reaffirm its SCS claims. Part of the reason is that up to the early 1990s China's SCS claims focused mainly on island features in the SCS. When China and Vietnam engaged in an intermittent legal battle in the 1970s and 1980s, each side publicized organized archives and other historical materials to prove the legitimacy of their respective claims to sovereignty over the SCS features. At that time, China was confident in the strength of its own historical evidence vis-à-vis that of Vietnam and did not feel the need to reaffirm the dotted line to reinforce its claims.

Entering the 1990s, however, the Chinese leadership started to feel the pressure imposed by the universal application of the UNCLOS, which unexpectedly provided a powerful legal ground enabling other SCS countries to expand their claims over much more extensive areas further deep into the coverage of the dotted line. This situation prompted China to make a two-step adjustment to its claims. The first step, as discussed earlier, was coined in Article 14 of the 1998 Law on the EEZ and CS indicating China's endorsement of the concept of historic rights, implying that China viewed part of its SCS claims as related to historic rights and independent from its EEZ and CS entitlements. In 2009, when responding to the challenge mounted by Malaysia and Vietnam's CS applications to the CLCS, China took the second step, connecting the dotted line with its SCS claims. In absence of China's clarification of the legal status of the line, such connection led to speculation that China's claims to historic rights in the SCS might apply to the water areas (including the seabed and subsoil thereof) encompassed by the dotted line.

From 2010 onward

China's assertation of historic rights with its potential connection with the dotted line raised concerns among other SCS claimants. On 5 April 2011, the Philippine government issued a diplomatic note to the UN to respond to China's 2009 note verbale. In its note, the Philippines particularly targeted on China's unspecified claims associated with the dotted line/nine-dash line, challenging that the PRC's claims on "relevant waters as well as the seabed and subsoil thereof (as reflected in the so-called nine-dash line)... would have no basis under international law, specifically UNCLOS."[16] A few days later, China responded in its note verbale dated 14 April 2011 that "China's sovereignty and related rights and jurisdiction in the South China Sea are supported by abundant historical and legal evidence (emphasis added)," reaffirming its intention to use the dotted line/nine-dash line to justify some kind of historic rights.

At this point, China's legal claims to the SCS, after going through six decades of development and adjustment, were getting very close to what we see a three-layered claims to sovereignty and maritime rights and interests expounded in the *Statement of the Government of the People's Republic of China on China's Territorial Sovereignty and Maritime Rights and Interests in the SCS* (the SCS Statement) published on 12 July 2016. This statement was released in the background of the 2013 SCS Arbitration case. The SCS Arbitration case was initiated by the Philippines against China in 2013. In the Philippines' written statements, the Philippines brought up the matter of the nine-dash line and requested that the arbitral Tribunal adjudge three matters:

1 China is not entitled to exercise "historic rights" over the waters, seabed and subsoil beyond the limits of its entitlements under the Convention in the areas encompassed within its so-called "nine-dash line";
2 Various maritime features relied on by China as a basis upon which to assert its claims in the SCS are not islands that generate entitlement to an "EEZ" or continental shelf, but rather are "rocks" within the meaning of UNCLOS Article 121(3), or are low-tide elevations or submerged banks incapable of generating such entitlements; and
3 China has unlawfully interfered with the exercise of the Philippines' sovereign rights and freedoms under UNCLOS and other rules of international law not incompatible with the Convention.[17]

While it was made clear in the *Position Paper of the Government of the People's Republic of China on the Matter of Jurisdiction in the SCS Arbitration* (the Position Paper) that China would "neither accept nor participate in the arbitration thus initiated by the Philippines,"[18] China found it necessary to make an official clarification on, and respond to, some of the issues which emerged during the arbitration process and attracted many speculations in the international community. Hence, on 12 July 2016, the same day the Tribunal rendered the final award, the Chinese government published the South China Sea statement, in which it laid down a three-layered claim to the SCS:

> Based on the practice of the Chinese people and the Chinese government in the long course of history and the position consistently upheld by successive Chinese governments, and in accordance with national law and international law, including the United Nations Convention on the Law of the Sea, China has territorial sovereignty and maritime rights and interests in the South China Sea, including, inter alia:
>
> 1 China has sovereignty over Nanhai Zhudao, consisting of Dongsha Qundao, Xisha Qundao, Zhongsha Qundao and Nansha Qundao;
> 2 China has internal waters, territorial sea and contiguous zone, based on Nanhai Zhudao;
> 3 China has an EEZ and continental shelf, based on Nanhai Zhudao;
> 4 China has historic rights in the SCS.

The first layer of China's SCS claims (no. 1 of the Statement cited above) focuses on sovereignty over all the SCS features (grouped by China into four archipelagos—Dongsha Qundao, Xisha Qundao, Zhongsha Qundao and Nansha Qundao). As noted earlier, from the very beginning, the PRC considered the SCS features as typical islands/land territory qualified for state appropriation. This is a rather consistent view that China upholds throughout all these years. In addition, by reaffirming its sovereignty claims in the Statement, China intended to argue against the ruling by Tribunal's award that the nine maritime features identified by the Philippines' submission were not islands but rocks or low-tide elevations.[19]

The second layer of China's claims to the SCS set out in the Statement (no. 2 and no. 3 of the Statement cited above) is related to maritime entitlements generated by the land features in the SCS. From China's standpoint, the SCS features form four offshore archipelagos that, according to the UNCLOS, can generate internal waters, territorial seas, EEZ as well as the continental shelf. This position of treating each island group/archipelago as an integral entity to generate maritime entitlements was already reflected in the *Declaration on the Baselines of the Territorial Sea* in 1996 where the China government treated Xisha Islands as an offshore archipelago and used a straight baseline system, connected by 28 base points encircling the archipelago as a whole, to measure its territorial sea and other maritime entitlements. The waters encircled inside the straight baseline are hence internal waters. This view was also echoed in China's 2014 Position Paper, paragraph 21 of which reads:

> It is plain that, in order to determine China's maritime entitlements based on the Nansha Islands under the Convention, all maritime features comprising the Nansha Islands must be taken into account (emphasis added).[20]

The third layer of China's claims to the SCS concerns historic rights (no. 4 of the Statement cited above). In this Statement, China did not make further clarification on this matter. What type of historic rights does China deem itself to enjoy? What areas in the SCS do China's historic claims apply? What is the relationship between China's historic claims and the dotted line? Questions in this regard remain unanswered. However, China seems to allude to the connection between its legal claims and the dotted line in some other occasions. For example, on 12 May 2016, the Director-General of the Chinese Department of Treaty and Law of the Chinese Ministry of Foreign Affairs, Xu Hong, gave a "Briefing on the South China Sea Arbitration Initiated by the Philippines." During the press conference, when asked about the nine-dash line issue in the context of the arbitration case, Xu responded that

> ...I want to stress that China's sovereignty and relevant rights in the South China Sea were formed throughout the long course of history...Early in 1948, the dotted line was mapped on China's official map. It was a confirmation of China's rights in the South China Sea formed throughout the history.... On the other hand, we have to note that the dotted line came into existence much earlier than the UNCLOS, which does not cover all aspects of the law of the sea (emphasis added).[21]

In his speech quoted above, Xu Hong suggested two legal implications of the dotted line: (1) The dotted line map fixated China's claims of maritime rights which had been formed throughout history, and (2) China's claims supported by the dotted line were independent of the UNCLOS, as the latter came into being much later than the former.

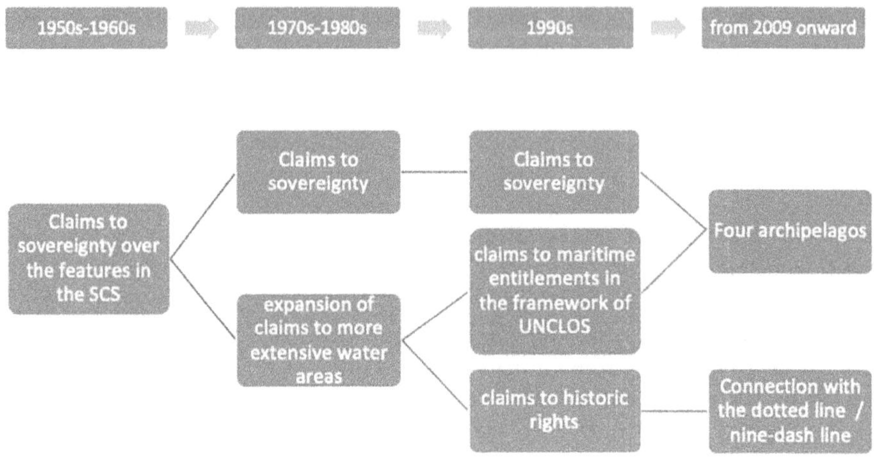

Figure 9.1 Evolution of PRC's SCS Claims in a Nutshell.
Source: Prepared by the authors.

Altogether, those elaborations by the Chinese government analyzed above have moulded the PRC's SCS claims into the following formula: sovereignty + UNCLOS-based maritime entitlements + historic rights (Figure 9.1).

China's policy towards dispute management and resolution

This part reviews the approaches that the PRC has adopted to try to manage and settle the SCS dispute. In general, China has demonstrated its preference for peaceful means such as bilateral negotiation, multilateral cooperation and joint development. In the meantime, the past seven decades also witnessed China's use of force and other kinds of unilateral actions to deal with the SCS issues.

Bilateral negotiation

Bilateral negotiation is China's most preferred method in solving the SCS dispute. Such preference has been well recorded in China's management of territorial disputes over its land borders.[22] China has long maintained the view that the SCS dispute should be peacefully resolved through friendly consultations and negotiations between countries directly concerned, a position supported by China's actual practices with other major claimants in the SCS. For example, it was through bilateral negotiation between China and Vietnam that the dispute over the Gulf of Tonkin was permanently settled in the 1990s. In the case of China and Malaysia, both sides have kept their disagreement low-profile, and so far discussion and negotiations of the dispute between the two countries have been conducted in a bilateral manner. Similar discussions are also conducted between Brunei and China.

In the case of China and the Philippines, it is worth noting that when China came to embrace the concept of joint development as an alternative approach to solving maritime dispute, it first proposed to the Philippines on a bilateral level. As mentioned in Part I of this chapter, the late Chinese leader Deng Xiaoping first tossed out the idea of joint development during his meeting with the visiting Filipino president Aquino in 1988. As part of the effort to refute the Philippines' claim that "all possibility of bilateral negotiation had been exhausted,"[23] the Chinese government listed in its 2014 Position Paper past efforts of bilateral engagements between China and the Philippines concerning the SCS dispute, demonstrating China's continuous practice of the bilateral approach. For example:

1 On 10 August 1995, China and the Philippines issued the *Joint Statement between the PRC and the Republic of the Philippines concerning Consultations on the South China Sea and on Other Areas of Cooperation*, in which both sides agreed to abide by the principles that "[d]isputes shall be settled in a peaceful and friendly manner through consultations on the basis of equality and mutual respect" and that "a gradual and progressive process of cooperation shall be adopted with a view to eventually negotiating a settlement of the bilateral disputes."
2 On 16 May 2000, China and the Philippines issued the *Joint Statement between the PRC and the Republic of the Philippines on the Framework of Bilateral Cooperation in the Twenty-First Century*, in which the two countries agreed to promote a peaceful settlement of disputes through bilateral friendly consultations and negotiations in accordance with universally-recognized principles of international law, including the 1982 UNCLOS.
3 On 1 September 2011, during the Filipino President Benigno Aquino's state visit to Beijing, the two sides issued a joint statement reaffirming that disputes will be settled through peaceful dialogue.[24]

The most recent bilateral negotiation effort undertaken by China and the Philippines is the establishment of a bilateral consultative mechanism. On 19 May 2017, the first meeting of the China-Philippines Bilateral Consultation Mechanism (BCM) on the SCS was convened, co-chaired by Chinese Vice Foreign Minister Liu Zhenmin and Philippine Ambassador to China Jose Sta. The fifth meeting of BCM was held on 28 October 2019. Bilateral consultation through the BCM has proven to be quite fruitful. Four joint working groups have been set up under the BCM, covering issues of political security, fisheries, marine scientific research and marine environment protection. China and the Philippines also agreed to engage in the cooperation of joint oil exploration and exploitation in disputed areas in the SCS. During the Philippines' President Duterte's state visit to China in Fall 2019, the two countries officially established an inter-governmental steering committee and a working group on the joint oil and gas development in the SCS.

Multilateral cooperation

Besides bilateral negotiation, multilateral engagement and cooperation is another major approach in China's toolbox for handling the SCS issues. The preference for bilateral and multilateral approaches is crystalized in China's proposal of the dual-track approach. In 2014, Chinese Foreign Minister Wang Yi, said at a press conference after the annual Association of Southeast Asian Nations (ASEAN)-China Foreign Ministers' Meeting that China supported and advocated the dual-track approach in solving the SCS issues. The "dual-track" approach includes relevant disputes being addressed by countries directly concerned through friendly consultations and negotiations and in a peaceful way, and peace and stability in the SCS being jointly maintained by China and ASEAN countries.[25]

The multilateral approach started to enter the SCS stage in the 1990s, when diplomatic discussions on the SCS issues began to appear in various multilateral venues involving China, Southeast Asian countries (including both claimant and non-claimant countries) and extra-regional countries. Gradually, multilateral engagement evolved to become a regular and effective approach for China and other claimants to managing the SCS issues. There are two reasons for such a multilateral turn in the SCS dispute management. First, as discussed in Part I of this chapter, universal application of the UNCLOS offered the SCS-bordering countries a different legal ground to assert sovereign rights and jurisdiction over many extensive areas in the SCS, thus creating overlapping claims and turning the SCS dispute into a multi-parties and multi-issue dispute. As a result, traditional bilateral state-to-state engagement was no longer sufficient in dealing with the SCS issues. It became difficult to manage the dispute and negotiate solutions in a bilateral manner because any such move would inevitably have a potential impact on the whole SCS region, as well as other parties involved. Thus, it soon became clear to the SCS countries that multilateral engagement was necessary and preferable.

The second factor motivating the multilateral turn in the SCS dispute management is related to the speedy development of China-ASEAN relationship. China and ASEAN started official engagement in 1991, in the wake of the end of the Cold War. In July 1991, Qian Qichen, then Chinese Foreign Minister, attended for the first time the opening session of the 24th ASEAN Ministerial Meeting (AMM) in Kuala Lumpur as a guest of the Malaysian Government. Subsequently, China was accorded a full Dialogue Partner status at the 29th AMM in July 1996 in Indonesia. Throughout the 1990s, the establishment and warm-up of China-ASEAN relations encouraged China and other SCS claimants to try to deal with the South China Sea dispute inside ASEAN-centred multilateral settings, such as the Workshop on Managing Potential Conflicts in the South China Sea, the ASEAN Regional Forum (ARF), ASEAN-China Forum, etc.

In these ASEAN-led multilateral networks, ASEAN's unity and concerted action persuaded and pressured China to take on a multilateral approach to the management of the SCS issues and place the SCS dispute in the context of the development of China-ASEAN relations. For example, during the second ASEAN Regional Forum in 1995, China conceded to including the SCS issues in the ARF agenda and reached consensus together with other participants on the adoption of the ARF Concept Paper. In this Concept Paper, a three-stage evolutionary process for the forum was outlined: (1) promotion of confidence-building measures (CBMs), (2) development of preventive diplomacy mechanisms (PD), and (3) development of conflict-resolution mechanisms.[26]

Following the adoption of the Concept Paper, China and ASEAN worked together towards establishing confidence-building measures as part of the efforts to implement stage 1. Their efforts were paid off in 2001, when the ARF was concluded with a consensus by all participants to move from CBMs to stage 2, PD. The encouraging progress of multilateral engagement prompted China and other SCS claimants to think about the possibility of applying PD to the SCS issues and developing a more formal multilateral arrangement in this regard. It was against this backdrop that China and ASEAN went hand in hand to explore the idea of a multilateral code of conduct.

In 1998, China and ASEAN countries started to engage in the negotiation of a regional code of conduct to prevent further escalation of conflict in the SCS. During the annual ASEAN-China Senior Officials Meeting in 1999, the two sides sped up the drafting process, although disagreement remained as to the legal nature of such a code. In 2000, a working group was established to work on the details of the code in the disputed area. Finally, in 2002, China and the ASEAN members signed the Declaration on the Conduct of Parties in the SCS (2002 DOC).[27]

From China's standpoint, the 2002 DOC is a political document and embodies the political goodwill of all parties in exercising constraint and maintaining peace and stability in the SCS. During the negotiation stage, ASEAN members, in particular, the claimant states, preferred a legally binding pact, while China insisted on a non-binding nature of such an agreement. Later, China and ASEAN reached a compromise during the 2000 SOM that the DOC would not be legally binding, but the two sides would continue to work together towards a binding code of conduct.

The 2002 DOC signified China's whole-hearted adoption of the multilateral approach to the management of the SCS, which was reaffirmed in China's proposal of the dual-track approach in 2014. In the years following the conclusion of the DOC, multilateral cooperation continued on a regular basis concerning the implementation of the DOC. For example, in 2005, energy companies from China, the Philippines and Vietnam—CNOOC, PNOC and PetroVietnam—conducted a tripartite joint exploration project in the SCS. The project, known as the Joint Marine Seismic Undertaking (JMSU), researched an area of over 14,300 km^2 in the SCS, part of which was disputed areas. In 2011, China and ASEAN agreed on the *Guidelines for the Implementation of the DOC*. Under the DOC implementation framework, multilateral talks have been held regularly. As of December 2019, China and ASEAN held 18 rounds of senior officials meetings on the implementation of DOC and 30 rounds of joint working group meetings on the implementation of DOC. These meetings have produced a number of marine cooperation and conflict projects with the aim to have "early harvest," including China-ASEAN hotline platform for maritime search and rescue, China-ASEAN senior foreign officials' hotline platform on emergencies, China-ASEAN joint exercise on search and rescue (SAR), projects on marine disaster prevention and mitigation, humanitarian relief and marine scientific research, and seminars on freedom and safety of navigation, marine ecology and biodiversity, etc. In addition to multilateral cooperation, in recent years China and ASEAN also accelerated the negotiation process of the Code of Conduct (COC). In November 2018, Chinese Premier Li Keqiang announced in Singapore that China intended to work with ASEAN to conclude the COC in three years. Once concluded, the COC would become another milestone in China's practice of multilateralism in dealing with the SCS issues.

Use of force and unilateral actions

While bilateral and multilateral negotiation and cooperation remain dominant approaches, records show that China also resorted to the use of force in dealing with the SCS dispute. There are two incidents of military confrontation in this regard. The first skirmish took place in 1974 around the Paracel Islands, and the second incident happened in 1988 in the Spratlys.

As mentioned earlier, in 1969, the Committee for Coordination of Joint Prospecting for Mineral Resources in Asian Offshore Areas conducted a scientific survey regarding the hydrocarbon potentials in the SCS. In 1971, motivated by the positive estimate of the survey, the South Vietnamese regime (RVN) initiated a programme offering oil concessions to foreign companies for exploration. At that time, the Chinese Navy (PLAN) was in control of the Amphitrite Group (Xuande) in the northeast Paracels, and South Vietnam occupied the Crescent (Yongle) Group on the southwest. In 1973, China was alerted by seismic surveys conducted by South Vietnam around Triton and Duncan islands of the Paracels and decided to adopt a more assertive posture against South Vietnam's oil exploration activities. In mid-December, the Chinese marched southwestward to establish a camp on Duncan Island. Later the crews moved to Robert island and planted flags on Money island, getting closer and closer to South Vietnam's position. South Vietnam responded quickly. On 15 January

1974, RVN announced the incorporation of the whole Paracels into Danang province and dispatched destroyers and escort ships to the islands. On 19 January, RVN ships acted first by approaching China's position and squaring off against the four PLAN boats. Chinese Navy responded and the two sides escalated into a small-scale military confrontation. When the fighting was over, RVN ships were ordered to retreat and the PLAN took control over all the Paracels.

The second armed clash took place against the backdrop of the scramble in the SCS by littoral countries. Starting in late 1970s, littoral countries in the SCS, envisioning the possibility of acquiring more extensive maritime jurisdiction, engaged in a hot race of seizing control of the features in the SCS, in particular in the Spratly area. As of the mid-1980s, the Philippines was already in control of nine islands, Malaysia three islands and Vietnam around 18 islands, while PRC had zero presence in the Spratlys. China kept a keen eye on these unilateral actions by its maritime neighbours. It gradually built up its naval capacity and sought for a good timing to catch up. In 1987, upon UNESCO's request, China was responsible for establishing an oceanic observation station in the Spratlys. Based on a scientific survey, China chose Fiery Cross Shoal as the best site for setting up observatory and construction started in January 1988. Vietnam was very anxious about China's increased activities in the vicinity of Fiery Cross Shoal including Johnson Reef (Chigua Jiao) and dispatched airplanes and navy warships to patrol in the area, monitoring China's survey and construction activities.

On 14 March, the Chinese and Vietnamese navy clashed on Johnson Reef. According to the Chinese account, the Vietnamese navy took the initiative by embarking 43 armed men on Johnson Reef, attempting to dispel the Chinese personnel on the reef. When the Chinese warned against the Vietnamese to withdraw, the Vietnamese opened fire and the two sides then exchanged fire. After the skirmish, China took control over six features, and Vietnam went on to occupy three vacant rocks in the vicinity of the Chinese-controlled islands.

The aforementioned two military clashes were both between China and Vietnam, fighting for the control of some of the SCS features. Part of the reason is that China and Vietnam had very similar sovereignty claims to the Paracels and Spratlys features and hence found themselves in a zero-sum game. Each side was eager to seize as many features as possible, as one party's gain is the other party's loss. Another important cause is that in the 1970s and 1980s, the political relationship between China and Vietnam was very tense. In fact, the two countries were involved in a military confrontation along their land borders throughout the whole 1980s.

The most recent case in which China deployed unilateral approaches is related to its land reclamation and construction activities in the SCS. In late 2013, China started land reclamation activities on its controlled features in the Spratlys, including Subi Reef (Zhubi Jiao), Mischief Reef (Meiji Jiao), Fiery Cross Reef (Yongshu Jiao), Gaven Reef (Nanxun Jiao), Johnson Reef (Chigua Jiao), Mckennan Reef (Ximen Jiao) and Cuarteron Reef (Huayang Jiao). In mid-2015, land reclamation works on those features were largely completed, followed by the second phase of facility construction. As of late 2018, all major construction works on those features were completed.

Given its impressive infrastructure capacity, China's land reclamation and facility construction works in the Spratlys pale in comparison to similar works undertaken by other claimants, raising concerns across the region. China maintained that it had indisputable sovereignty over those features and it was China's legitimate exercise of sovereignty to conduct construction works on those features. As to the purpose of its activities, China emphasized that on the one hand, China was playing "catch up" to other SCS claimants which, over the past 40 years, had continuously reclaimed land and fortified the features that they occupied; on the other hand, the facilities such as lighthouses, harbours and airfields, communication systems, meteorological equipment, maritime research and humanitarian relief facilities, were established mainly for civilian purposes and would lay a good foundation to offer much needed-public goods and services to the region in the near future.

Attitude towards compulsory dispute settlement mechanisms

China's attitude towards compulsory dispute settlement mechanisms as an option for resolving the SCS dispute is also worth noting here. Over the past several decades, China has continuously ruled out the option of a third-party dispute settlement mechanism for managing and resolving the SCS dispute.

China has long-held reservations against the settlement of disputes regime established under Part XV of UNCLOS. As early as in 1976, the Chinese delegation made a speech during the fifth session of the UNCLOS III, expressing the view that (1) disputes shall be settled by the parties directly concerned through peaceful negotiation on the basis of equality and mutual respect, and compulsory dispute settlement can only be applied on a voluntary basis, and (2) disputes concerning areas under national jurisdiction shall be settled according to the laws and regulations of the parties directly concerned, and shall not be subject to the dispute settlement mechanisms provided for in the UNCLOS.[28]

China's concern was raised again in 1996, when Chinese Vice Foreign Minister Li Zhaoxing expounded in front of the Standing Committee of the Eighth National People's Congress on four issues of concern regarding the ratification of the Convention, the fourth one of which was related to the dispute settlement regime.[29] Li acknowledged that the Chinese government had serious concerns about this regime and suggested that countermeasures should be taken in the near future to cope with the potential challenges in this regard. Consequently, in 2006 the Chinese government made, pursuant to Article 298 of UNCLOS, an optional exceptions declaration, excluding disputes concerning maritime delimitation, historic bays or titles, as well as military and law enforcement activities from the UNCLOS third-party dispute settlement procedures.[30]

China's negative attitude towards third-party dispute settlement mechanism as an option for managing and resolving the SCS dispute was highlighted in 2013 when the Philippines invoked the compulsory dispute settlement mechanism to adjudicate on the matter of the SCS dispute. Throughout the whole process of this arbitral case, the Chinese government insisted on the position of non-acceptance and non-participation, reaffirming its long-held preference for settling territorial and maritime delimitation disputes through peaceful negotiations with states directly concerned.[31]

Attitude towards the U.S.'s involvement in the SCS

The U.S. involvement in the SCS is another important factor influencing China's policy towards the SCS. Although the United States is an extra-regional country, throughout the years it has actively participated in the multilateral diplomatic settings of Asia, in particular the ASEAN-led multilateral dialogues, where the SCS issue is frequently discussed. While it has all along maintained that it does not take sides in the sovereign dispute in the SCS, in recent years the United States has increasingly involved itself in the management of the SCS issue and instigated freedom of navigation operations (FONOPs) to challenge China's maritime claims.

The United States started to show particular interests in the SCS in 2009, as part of the effort to recalibrate its foreign policy. In 2009, the newly elected U.S. president Barack Obama initiated a rebalancing of the U.S. global strategy towards Asia, also called the "Asia Pivot" or the "Rebalance to Asia." The Obama administration was determined to end decades of "benign neglect" of Southeast Asia,[32] placing the Asia-Pacific region at the top of the U.S. foreign policy agenda. In his speech delivered on 13 November 2009 in Tokyo, Obama promised at the Suntory Hall to be America's first "Pacific President."[33] On 21 July 2009, U.S. Secretary of State Hillary Clinton declared "the United States is back" upon arriving in Bangkok, Thailand, a Southeast Asian country and also a state bordering the SCS.[34] Clinton further elaborated the idea of rebalancing to Asia in her article in the November 2011 edition of Foreign Policy magazine.

Under the Asia rebalancing strategy, the United States assumed a more active role in the management of the SCS issue. Its upgraded involvement in the SCS was demonstrated on two fronts. On the diplomatic front, the United States expanded its participation in the regional maritime multilateral architecture. Through its participation, the United States played an active role in coordinating the position of other participant countries to confront China on the SCS issue and made clear to countries in the SCS region its interest in the freedom of navigation and dispute resolution in the SCS. For example, during the sixthEast Asia Summit in Bali in November 2011, the U.S. President Obama brought up the SCS issue and stated:

> While we are not a claimant in the South China Sea dispute, and while we do not take sides, we have a powerful stake in maritime security in general, and in the resolution of the South China Sea issue specifically—as a resident Pacific power, as a maritime nation, as a trading nation and as a guarantor of security in the Asia Pacific region.[35]

On the military front, theUnited States stepped up its military presence in the SCS region and directly challenged China's maritime claims by its FONOPs. The U.S. FONOPs were implemented in the SCS since 2015. As of December 2019, a total of 21 FONOPs have been conducted by the U.S. defence department. Over the years, the United States gradually increased the frequency of the FONOPs in the SCS—from a single vessel conducting a single operation to two vessels conducting two consecutive operations. For example, on 20 and 21 November 2019, a pair of U.S. FONOPs were undertaken on two consecutive days in the SCS: on Wednesday, Littoral Combat Ship USS Gabrielle Giffords conducted another FONOP near the Spratly Islands; on Thursday, Arleigh Burke-class guided-missile destroyer USS Wayne E. Meyer conducted a FONOP near the Paracel Islands. The United States also became more and more specific on the type of legal claims against which the FONOPs targeted. For instance, speaking on the FONOP on 13 September 2019, Commander Reann Mommsen, spokesperson for the U.S. 7th Fleet based in Japan said: "the USS Wayne E. Meyer challenged the restrictions on innocent passage imposed by China, Taiwan and Vietnam and also contested China's claim to straight baselines enclosing the Paracel Islands."[36]

From China's standpoint, the United States upgraded involvement in the SCS in recent years is aimed at containing China and has introduced unnecessary complications into the SCS dispute. The diplomatic confrontations between the United States and China in recent years have greatly impeded the work of various ASEAN-led multilateral dialogues and put the unity of ASEAN to test. When Chinese Foreign Minister Wang Yi proposed the dual-track approach in 2014, the message clearly conveyed was that China did not view the involvement of the United States or other extra-regional countries as an essential element in the effective management of the SCS dispute. In the meantime, China stepped up its efforts to work with other claimants as well as the ASEAN, to implement the 2002 DOC and work on a final conclusion of the COC.

As regards the U.S. security challenges in the form of FONOPs, China expressed objection from the very beginning, criticizing that the U.S. military activities were a demonstration of navigation hegemony and made no positive contribution to the peace and stability in the SCS. The Chinese government maintains that the right and freedom of navigation and overflight in the Sea Lines of Communication in the SCS has always been well respected and practiced by China and there has been no record of freedom of navigation being impeded in the SCS. To de-escalate tensions and avoid unintended incidents, China and the United States worked together on drafting the code of operation on the sea. In April 2014, during the 14th Western Pacific Naval Symposium in Qingdao, 21 Pacific nations signed the multi-national Code for Unplanned Encounters at Sea (CUES), which provided operational guidance to the Chinese and American military vessels when encountering each other in the SCS. On the other hand, the Chinese armed forces have taken countermeasures in response to the U.S. FONOPs, such as sending naval ships to closely monitor, identify and verify the U.S. warship and issued warnings requesting it to leave.

Conclusion

Over the past seven decades, China's SCS policy has gone through a series of changes. Influenced by the legal developments in the realm of the international law of the sea, today China's legal position on the SCS has been transformed into a three-layered formula that includes claims to sovereignty, UNCLOS-based maritime entitlements and historic rights. As regards China's management of the SCS dispute, by and large China's record has demonstrated a clear preference for bilateral and multilateral negotiation and consultations. However, given the strategic importance of the SCS, China's management of the dispute has increasingly attracted attention from countries outside the region. The involvement of the United States and other extra-regional countries in recent years introduces additional uncertainty to the SCS situation and it remains to see whether and to what extent China would adjust accordingly.

Notes

1 The dotted line has several names, such as the nine-dash line, the U-shaped line, nine-interrupted line, etc. In this chapter, we use the dotted line and the nine-dash line interchangeably, as these two names are most commonly used.

2 "Supplement to People's China," 1 September 1951, 1–6, cited in Lo Chi-Kin, *China's Policy towards Territorial Disputes: the Case of the SCS Islands* (New York: Routledge, 1998), 50.

3 "San Francisco Conference for the Conclusion and Signature of Treaty of Peace with Japan (1951)," Records 94305-6010, *Hoover Institution Archives* (Stanford, California), 119.

4 *Declaration of the Government of the People's Republic of China on China's Territorial Sea (English version)*, in Department of Policy, Legislation and Planning State Oceanic Administration (ed.), *Collection of the Sea Laws and Regulations of the People's Republic of China*, Fourth Edition (Beijing: Ocean Press, 2012), 295–296.

5 Preparatory meetings of the UNCLOS III started in 1971, and formal negotiations started in 1973.

6 *Beijing Review*, 18 January 1974, 3.

7 Zhenhua Han (ed.), *Collection of Historical Materials on Our Country's South China Sea Islands* (Beijing: Dongfang Publishing House, 1988), 451–452.

8 See "Shelving Disputes, Joint Developing," *Review of the History of New China's Diplomacy*, compiled by the Chinese Foreign Ministry, accessed 30 December 2019, https://www.fmprc.gov.cn/web/ziliao_674904/wjs_674919/2159_674923/t8958.shtml.

9 *Law of the People's Republic of China on the Territorial Sea and the Contiguous Zone (English version)*, in Department of Policy, Legislation and Planning State Oceanic Administration (ed.), *Collection of the Sea Laws and Regulations of the People's Republic of China*, Fourth Edition (Beijing: Ocean Press, 2012), 301–304.

10 *Law on the Exclusive Economic Zone and the Continental Shelf of the People's Republic of China (English version)*, in Department of Policy, Legislation and Planning State Oceanic Administration, (ed.), *Collection of the Sea Laws and Regulations of the People's Republic of China*, Fourth Edition (Beijing: Ocean Press, 2012), 305–308.

11 Nong Hong, "Hai Yang Fa De Guo Jia Shi Jian: Dui Nan Hai Di Qu Fa Lv Wen Hua Gong Tong Ti De Si Kao (State Practices of the Law of the Sea: Reflections on the Legal Cultural Community in the SCS Region)," *Foreign Affairs Review*, No. 5 (2017): 87.

12 *Declaration of the Government of the People's Republic of China on the Baselines of the Territorial Sea of the People's Republic of China (English version)*, in Department of Policy, Legislation and Planning State Oceanic Administration (ed.), *Collection of the Sea Laws and Regulations of the People's Republic of China*, Fourth Edition (Beijing: Ocean Press, 2012), 297–300.

13 Commission on the Limits of the Continental Shelf, "Joint Submission by Malaysia and the Socialist Republic of Viet Nam," 6 May 2009, accessed 30 December 2019, https://www.un.org/Depts/los/clcs_new/submissions_files/submission_mysvnm_33_2009.htm.

14 Commission on the Limits of the Continental Shelf, "Submission by the Socialist Republic of Viet Nam," 7 May 2009, accessed 30 December 2019, https://www.un.org/Depts/los/clcs_new/submissions_files/submission_vnm_37_2009.htm.

15 Commission on the Limits of the Continental Shelf, "Communications Received with Regard to the Joint Submission Made by Malaysia and Viet Nam to the Commission on the Limits of the Continental Shelf by China," 7 May 2009, accessed 30 December 2019, https://www.un.org/Depts/los/clcs_new/submissions_files/mysvnm33_09/chn_2009re_mys_vnm_e.pdf, and Commission on the Limits of the Continental Shelf, "Communications Received with Regard to the Submission Made by Viet Nam to the Commission on the Limits of the Continental Shelf by China," 7 May 2009, accessed 30 December 2019, https://www.un.org/Depts/los/clcs_new/submissions_files/vnm37_09/chn_2009re_vnm.pdf.

16 Commission on the Limits of the Continental Shelf, "The Philippines' 2011 Note Verbale to the UN (series no. 000228)," 5 April 2011, accessed 30 December 2019, https://www.un.org/depts/los/clcs_new/submissions_files/vnm37_09/phl_re_chn_2011.pdf.

17 See *The Philippines' Memorial - Volume I*, para. 1.7, accessed 30 December 2019, https://files.pca-cpa.org/pcadocs/Memorial%20of%20the%20Philippines%20Volume%20I.pdf.

18 The State Council of the People's Republic of China, "Position Paper of the Government of the People's Republic of China on the Matter of Jurisdiction in the South China Sea Arbitration Initiated by the Republic of the Philippines," 7 December 2014, accessed 30 December 2019, http://english.www.gov.cn/archive/press_briefing/2014/12/07/content_281475020441708.htm.

19 The nine features are: Scarborough Shoal, Mischief Reef, Second Thomas Shoal and Subi Reef, Gaven Reef, McKennan Reef (including Hughes Reef), Johnson Reef, Cuarteron Reef and Fiery Cross Reef.

20 See supra note 18.

21 Ministry of Foreign Affairs of the PRC, "Briefing by XU Hong, Director-General of the Department of Treaty and Law on the South China Sea Arbitration Initiated by the Philippines," 12 May 2016, accessed 30 December 2019, https://www.fmprc.gov.cn/mfa_eng/wjdt_665385/zyjh_665391/t1364804.shtml.

22 A majority of China's land border disputes have been settled through bilateral negotiation, see M. Taylor Fravel, "Regime Insecurity and International Cooperation: Explaining China's Compromises in Territorial Disputes," *International Security* 32, no. 2 (2005): 46–83.

23 See supra note 17, para. 1.33.

24 See supra note 18.

25 China Daily, "China Supports 'Dual-Track' Approach to Resolve Dispute," 10 August 2014, accessed 31 December 2019, http://www.chinadaily.com.cn/china/2014-08/10/content_18280181.htm.

26 See ASEAN, "The ARF Concept and Principles of Preventive Diplomacy," accessed 31 December 2019, http://aseanregionalforum.asean.org/wp-content/uploads/2019/01/ARF-Concept-Paper-of-Preventive-Diplomacy.pdf.

27 For full text of DOC, see ASEAN, *Declaration on the Conduct of Parties in the South China Sea*, accessed 31 December 2019, https://asean.org/?static_post=declaration-on-the-conduct-of-parties-in-the-south-china-sea-2.
28 See *The File Set of Chinese Delegation to the UN Conferences (1976.7-12)* (Beijing: People's Publishing House, 1977), 171.
29 Hong, supra note 11, 87.
30 Full text of China's declaration dated on 25 August 2006 is available on https://treaties.un.org/Pages/ViewDetailsIII.aspx?src=TREATY&mtdsg_no=XXI-6&chapter=21&Temp=mtdsg3&clang=_en#15.
31 China's view towards the disputes settlement mechanisms as an option for settling the dispute between China and the Philippines is well elaborated in *Statement of the Ministry of Foreign Affairs of the People's Republic of China on Settling Disputes Between China and the Philippines in the South China Sea Through Bilateral Negotiation*, and *China Adheres to the Position of Settling Through Negotiation the Relevant Disputes Between China and the Philippines in the South China Sea*, accessed 31 December 2019, https://www.fmprc.gov.cn/nanhai/eng.
32 See Diane K. Mauzy and Brian L. Job, "U.S. Policy in Southeast Asia: Limited Re-engagement after Years of Benign Neglect," *Asian Survey* 47, no. 4 (2007): 622–641.
33 The White House, "Remarks by President Barack Obama at Suntory Hall," 14 November 2009, accessed 31 December 2019, https://obamawhitehouse.archives.gov/the-press-office/remarks-president-barack-obama-suntory-hall.
34 Daily News, "U.S. 'is back' is Asia, Secretary of State Hillary Clinton Declares," 21 July 2009, accessed 31 December 2019, https://www.nydailynews.com/news/world/u-s-back-asia-secretary-state-hillary-clinton-declares-article-1.429381.
35 Jackie Calmes, "Obama and Asian Leaders Confront China's Premier," *New York Times*, 19 November 2011.
36 AFP, "US Navy Sails Ship Close to Islands Claimed by China," 14 September 2019, accessed 31 December 2019, https://news.yahoo.com/us-navy-sails-ship-close-islands-claimed-china-182438955.html.

10
MALAYSIA AND SOUTH CHINA SEA DISPUTES
Applicability of international law

BA Hamzah

Introduction

Apart from geopolitics, security, trade facilitation and resource development, Malaysia's major concern in the South China Sea is managing its maritime boundary disputes with Brunei, China, Indonesia, the Philippines, Thailand and Vietnam. Malaysia is one of the claimant states of the territories, including the continental shelf, in the disputed Spratly group of islets in the South China Sea.

Malaysia's acquisition of the continental shelf began in 1969, following a series of successful negotiations with Indonesia to delimit the continental shelf of both countries. By 1978, Malaysia decided to claim the continental shelf off Sabah and Sarawak as its maritime territories. A survey team was dispatched to the South China Sea, off Sabah waters, to claim unoccupied territories embedded on its continental shelf, not exceeding 200 nautical miles from its coast.

The Malaysian survey team comprised mainly of surveyors from the National Survey Department and officers from the Royal Malaysian Engineers. They were given instructions in 1978 to claim unoccupied territories to be included in a new Malaysian map. During the survey off Sabah waters, the team did not encounter any foreign military presence on any of the features they landed on, except the Amboyna Cay where a permanent stone marker bearing Vietnamese markings was observed. However, at the time of landing, no Vietnamese soldiers were on site. Soon after the Malaysian survey team left the area, the Vietnamese military re-occupied Amboyna Cay.

Using the data from the topographical survey, Malaysia produced a map of its continental shelf. The map included the earlier agreed continental shelf boundaries with Indonesia on the eastern side of the Malay peninsula, in the Strait of Malacca and off Tg Datu, Sarawak as well as the unilaterally claimed continental shelf off the West Coast of Sabah. Vietnam contested the inclusion of Amboyna Cay in the 1979 Malaysian map. The Philippines contested the inclusion of Commodore Reef, also in the Spratlys, which it claimed its territory. For record purposes, there were no Philippines' soldiers on the marine feature when the Malaysian survey team landed on the reef in 1978. Currently, the Philippines maintains a small military facility on Commodore Reef.

Indonesia contested the inclusion of Pulau Ligitan and Pulau Sipadan in the Celebes Sea within Malaysia's boundary. Unresolved, after years of negotiation, the two parties brought the dispute before the International Court of Justice (ICJ) at The Hague, which ruled in 2002 that the sovereignty of the two disputed islands belonged to Malaysia.[1]

The first state that Malaysia signed a boundary treaty with (apart from those left behind by the colonial powers) was Indonesia, which has been advocating for an archipelagic state status since 1927. There were three separate agreements in 1969 on the continental shelf between Indonesia and Malaysia: on the eastern side of the Malay Peninsula, in the Straits of Malacca, and off Tg Datu, Sarawak. Indonesia and Malaysia also entered into an agreement to delimit their territorial sea boundary in one small part in the Strait of Malacca in 1971. Malaysia's unilateral boundary in the Celebes Sea, as explained earlier, was contested by Indonesia and subsequently became the subject of a judicial case at the ICJ in 2002.[2]

Indonesia and Malaysia also entered into an agreement for the unsuspended passage of Malaysian vessels and aircraft through part of the Indonesian archipelagic waters and in the air space above it. This agreement is seen as part of a compromised package to facilitate the passage of the Malaysian-flagged ships within Indonesian waters of the Indonesian archipelagic regime under United Nations Convention on the Law of the Sea (UNCLOS).[3] The law requires the archipelagic state (i.e., Indonesia) "that lies between two parts of an immediately neighbouring state" to enter "an agreement with the latter (i.e., Malaysia) that has traditionally exercised rights in such waters." This agreement gives Malaysia uninterrupted access to Sabah and Sarawak through the Indonesian archipelagic waters. The 1982 Agreement[4] reaffirmed Malaysia's "legitimate rights" that its people have traditionally exercised in the Indonesian waters before the area became an archipelagic territory.

Joint development schemes

Apart from Indonesia, other neighbours including Thailand, Vietnam, Brunei and Singapore protested the inclusion of their respective territories in Malaysia's 1979 map. As an interim measure, Malaysia, Thailand and Vietnam[5] agreed to establish separate joint development areas in the disputed areas. The three parties separately agreed to shelf their boundary disputes for "a specified period of time" in favour of joint development.

Malaysia and Vietnam signed the Memorandum of Understanding for the Exploration and Exploitation of Petroleum in a Defined Area, which is better known as Block PM3 Commercial Arrangement Area (CAA) in 1992.[6] This Memorandum of Understanding has enabled the respective national oil companies from Malaysia (Petronas) and Vietnam (PetroVietnam) to undertake exploration activities in a defined area of about 2,008 km^2 for a period of 40 years. Both parties struck oil in 1997 from the unitised *Bunga Kekwa* field.

In 2009, 17 years after a successful experiment in joint development, Malaysia and Vietnam submitted a joint memorandum to the United Nations Commission on the Limits of the Continental Shelf (CLCS) in New York. Ten years later, in December 2019, Malaysia made a partial submission for the remaining portion of its continental shelf beyond 200 nautical miles in the northern part of the South China Sea.

Malaysia and Thailand agreed, as early as 1979, to establish a Joint Development Authority (JDA) as a temporary solution to explore and exploit non-living resources (mainly hydrocarbon resources) in the overlapping area of 7.25 square kilometres. After 40 years, the two countries agreed to continue with the project as both have benefitted financially. At the latest meeting celebrating the 40th anniversary of the Malaysia-Thailand Joint Area (MTJA) in November 2019, it was revealed that since the first production of gas in 2005 the MTJA has remitted a combined cumulative income of US$10 billion, with US$5 billion going to each government.[7] Though the MTJA contract would expire in 2029, it is expected to continue for another timeframe yet to be decided by both parties.

Similarly, with Singapore, after both parties failed to come to any negotiated agreement, Malaysia and Singapore finally took their boundary dispute to the ICJ.[8] The Court ruled in 2008 that the sovereignty over Pedra Branca (the disputed feature) belonged to Singapore by virtue of a *titre de souvereign*. In coming to its decision, the Court essentially examined the conduct of both states since 1953 and concluded that Malaysia's failure to protest effectively Singapore's occupation and administration of the rock was critical to its judgement.

Letter of exchange (LOE) with Brunei

Malaysia's dispute with Brunei over the ownership of the offshore territory in the South China Sea was "settled" via an LOE in 2009.[9] The disputed maritime territory is outside the Spratly proper but within the nine-dash line boundary claimed by China. When Dr Mahathir was Prime Minister, Malaysia and Brunei negotiated for more than 17 years, in search of an amicable solution. The decision to end negotiations with Brunei was, however, made during the tenure of Abdullah Badawi as Prime Minister of Malaysia. Both parties agreed to end their dispute by "exchanging" territories. The leaders of both countries held a joint press conference in May 2009 to clarify the key elements in the LOE. Essentially, both parties agreed to formally acknowledge their respective titles and ownership over the disputed land and maritime areas between them.

The joint statement also confirmed that Malaysia has "unsuspendable rights of maritime access for nationals and residents of Malaysia across Brunei's maritime zones" if Brunei's laws and regulations are observed. More importantly, for Malaysia, the LOE confirms Brunei has officially dropped its long-standing territorial claim over Limbang, a thorn in their bilateral relations.

Malaysia prefers cooperation over conflict

Malaysia's approach to overlapping claims with the neighbours in the South China Sea has always been to emphasise cooperation over conflict. However, attempts by other claimants to negotiate the overlapping territorial claims in the South China Sea, especially with China, have not been very successful. Failure to resolve their overlapping claims has led China, Taiwan, Vietnam, the Philippines and Malaysia, for example, to deploy military troops on features they have occupied in the South China Sea, including those in the Spratlys.

Although Indonesia is not a claimant state, a portion of its maritime territory off Natuna Island is included in China's nine-dash- line map. Jakarta has contested the legality of nine-dash boundary line even before the Permanent Court of Arbitration, serving as the registry to the International Tribunal. This Tribunal was established under Annex V11 to the UNCLOS (hereafter International Tribunal on the South China Sea) passed its landmark award in 2016.

In July 2017, Indonesia renamed the overlapping sea space with China's nine-dash line, which it does not recognise, as the North Natuna Sea. In early January 2020, Indonesia sent naval vessels and fighter jets to challenge the presence of China's Coast Guard vessels. Jakarta accused the Coast Guard vessels of giving protection to some 30 Chinese boats fishing illegally in the Natuna waters. Beijing contended that the disputed waters with Indonesia were part of its traditional fishing grounds.

Dr. Mahathir Mohamed, the architect of Malaysia's occupation of the Malaysian-extended maritime territories in the South China Sea, was the Deputy Prime Minister when the survey was completed, and the 1979 map was enacted later. Although Dr. Mahathir saw the initiative to extend Malaysia's maritime zone as a strategic move, as Deputy, his hands were tied. The incumbent Prime Minister was Hussein Onn, who was viewed by many as more "friendly" in his approach in dealing with Malaysia's neighbours in the South China Sea. Hussein Onn refrained from a more adventurist policy in the Spratly part of the South China Sea to avoid diplomatic spats with Vietnam and the Philippines.

When Dr. Mahathir became Prime Minister in July 1981, replacing Hussein Onn, he had a free hand in asserting Malaysia's claim of unoccupied territories in the Spratly. Hence, it was Dr. Mahathir who pushed for the occupation of the distant territories (not more than 200 nautical miles from its coast in Sabah) for strategic and economic reasons: oil, gas, fisheries and tourism. Dr. Mahathir noted in his memoir[10] that by occupying the features, he could deter Vietnam and the Philippines from encroaching into the Malaysian waters. At that time (1981–1987), the question of China occupying features in the Spratly did not arise; Beijing was nowhere to be seen in the Spratlys, although by late 1974, China had occupied the Paracels in the northern part of the South China Sea.

By 1990, after years of personal commitment to the project, Dr. Mahathir made the occupation of Layang- Layang (Swallow Reef) as his pet project. He visited the facility on numerous occasions, sometimes staying overnight, to lend moral support to the naval commandos on the ground. Once, he took the entire Cabinet to Layang-Layang for a meeting, arguably to strengthen Malaysia's claim to the feature.

To make the place liveable, he ordered the construction of accommodation amenities for soldiers guarding the artificial island. Soon after a barrack was built for the soldiers, Dr. Mahathir invited a private investor to build a resort for tourists, which stands to this day. Besides the Naval Station (Station Lima) at Layang-Layang, the Royal Malaysian Navy occupied four more strategic features. They are:

- Mariveles Reef/Terumbu Mantanani. The Royal Malaysian Navy calls this place: Station Mike (occupied since 1986).
- Ardasier Reef/Terumbu Ubi or Station Uniform (occupied since 1986).
- Erica Reef/Terumbu Siput or Station Sierra (occupied since 1999).
- Investigator Shoal/Beting Peninjau or Station Papa (occupied since 1999.[11]

The area that Malaysia has laid territorial claims in the Spratlys is now called Gugusan Semarang Peninjau. The name appears on one of the naval charts[12] published in 1988 by the National Hydrography Centre of the Royal Malaysian Navy.

Although China's expanding economic engagement with Malaysia and the other Southeast Asian States has been vital for regional peace and stability, this can hardly conceal the fact that political and security cooperation between China and some states in Southeast Asia, especially some Association of Southeast Asian Nations (ASEAN) member states, is facing formidable challenges.

Although Malaysia as well as other maritime Southeast Asian countries find China's historical claim to the entire South China Sea rather unsettling, they are prepared to continuously engage a strong China for regional peace and security. While they would not allow the unsettled territorial dispute to impede greater political and economic cooperation, they are nevertheless concerned with the activities of the People's Liberation Army (PLA), especially its naval component, the well-armed Coast Guard and other enforcement agencies in the South China Sea.

Malaysia's policy in the South China Sea is based on history, international law, economy and strategic calculations. Contrary to some observations,[13] Malaysia maintains an active, cooperative engagement and friendly policy in its waters. Recent publications[14] project Malaysia as being passive for its failure to shoo away China's Coast Guard vessels in the Laconia Shoal area where Malaysia produces oil and gas. To these commentators, an effective Malaysian policy is one that takes China to task, even if its policy is within the law. This broad anti-China approach would preclude assessing correctly Malaysia's policy in the South China Sea. Malaysia is not anti-China although it may disagree with what the latter is doing in the South China Sea.

For Malaysia, the overlapping territorial dispute in the Spratlys, important as it is, is not the most important consideration in determining Malaysia's overall relations with China. Malaysia places a premium on economic interests, cultural ties between the peoples, history and diplomatic considerations above the relatively more recent conflicting territorial claims between the two countries. This policy of active constructive engagement[15] is not only directed at China but other stakeholders too.

Like many other states in the region, Malaysia too is concerned that China's occupation and militarisation of the features in the Spratlys would put the entire semi-enclosed sea under its control. The thought that China would dominate the region politically, militarily and economically bothers many in the region, including policy makers in Malaysia.

Military control of the South China Sea would strengthen China's forward defence. It would also embolden its comprehensive maritime deterrent strategy and would give a boost to its Belt and Road policy. The maritime portion of the Belt and Road Initiative (BRI) route in South East Asia overlaps with the current sea lines of communication (SLOC) or trade route passing through the South China Sea from Europe, the Americas and Africa. Denying the use of this SLOC in crisis time to its adversaries remains China's priority military strategy in the South China Sea.

Meanwhile, it must be pointed out that China's policy in the South China Sea does not cast in stone as what extra-regional powers have made it appear to be. China is prepared to negotiate its position in the South China Sea with friendly powers but on its terms. Hence, it approaches the ASEAN proposed Code of Conduct (COC)[16] of parties in the South China Sea with some trepidation because it views it as a mechanism to restrict its movements in the South China Sea and a ploy contain its rise. But the other stakeholders in the region view the COC as necessary means that will promote a more predictable rule of engagement for all parties to minimise political fallouts. In the meantime, as a hedge against political uncertainties, almost all countries in the region have embarked on an extensive arms expansion programme.

The South China Sea has been the scenes of many showdowns between the US Navy and China's PLA-Navy and its other enforcement agencies including the well-armed China's Coast Guard over the last ten years. The US Navy has a policy of regularly challenging what it considers to be China's "excessive maritime claims" in the South China Sea via its Freedom of Navigation Operation (FONOP) programmes. Two such FONOP challenges off Mischief Reef and Fiery Cross Reef took place in August[17] and September 2019.[18] The US warships reportedly passed within 12 nautical miles of both features controlled by China. According to one source,[19] Beijing has installed anti-ship cruise missiles and surface-to-air missile systems on both features, in the case of the former since 1995. Since 2012, China has fortified military garrisons on five other features in the Spratly, which the United States claimed is a violation of international law. The US FONOPs are aimed at challenging the legality under international law of China's occupation of these features. China views FONOPs as a variant of gunboat diplomacy commonly practiced by predatory maritime powers in the early part of the 20th century.

The most recent legal attempt to undermine China's claims of the ocean space was in 2013 when the United States forced the Philippines to challenge China's excessive claims. The International Tribunal on South China Sea Arbitration, referred to earlier, delivered its award in 2016 in favour of the Philippines. According to the Tribunal, "there was no legal basis for China to claim historic rights to resources... within the sea areas falling within the nine-dash line."[20]

Mira Rapp-Hooper, an American scholar, wrote about the Tribunal's decision in *Foreign Affairs*[21] Journal, ten days after the ruling. In her opinion, the Tribunal's decision has created an immediate problem for China. The defeat was so crushing, in her view, that it left "Beijing few ways to save face." It was, as if, the entire "legal" exercise was intended to condemn China for all its activities in the Spratlys and the South China Sea (SCS). Although the author did not admit it openly, the entire proceeding had the effect of teaching China, a major power that the United States is at odds with, a lesson. Unfortunately, this lesson has backfired with China ignoring the decision. By staying on course in the South China Sea, doing much the same thing it has done before the Tribunal's condemnation, Beijing has ruffled feathers among the neo-conservative policy makers at Washington DC.

The issues in the South China Sea are not only about international law; they are also historical rights, other rights as well as responsibilities of states to maintain law and order at sea. Rights are usually supported by law. But they are not always so. But more importantly, the issues in the South China Sea are also about how states can get together to establish a regional security architecture that acknowledges each other's rights at sea. This security architecture is to prevent conflicting parties from resorting to the use of force, intimidation and bullying. This mechanism is critical to maintain a semblance of order in the enclosed sea and should uphold, among others, the Asian value of face-saving.

What ails the geostrategic environment in the South China Sea is the unsettling geopolitics arising mainly from US-Sino competition for influence and its consequent uncertainties. If we can overcome this, the current crisis can be mitigated.

Military spats will continue

While naval skirmishes and near misses are likely as some claimants and other stakeholders jockey for more influence in the South China Sea, the current US-China military spats in the South China Sea are not likely to denigrate into an open armed conflict between the contesting parties.

The involvement of extra-regional powers in the South China Sea asserting the freedom of navigation as a pretext has complicated further the fragile security situation and made it more difficult for China to make any concessions since it has already established a strong military foothold there. In the light of its competition with the United States for influence in the region, China views Washington policies in the South China Sea, Taiwan and Hong Kong as an intervention in domestic politics and as a sinister design to contain its rise.

China in fact rubbishes the Tribunal's verdict as unfair and thus is unlikely to be troubled by its decision. What China can do is to quickly move to restore confidence in the area by emphasising its positive role in preserving the freedom of navigation in the South China Sea and by taking steps to restrain from using force in its relations with other claimant states, especially in the Spratlys that is rich in oil and gas, fish and other resources. China should reassure the international community it would not undermine the safety and security of international trade (worth more than US$ 5.3 trillion) transiting the South China Sea.

China's reluctance to accept the Declaration of Conduct, which the Association of Southeast Asian Nations (ASEAN) has proposed since 2002 is viewed by many as an unfriendly act. By dragging its feet, China hopes to bide time. In July 2018, at the ASEAN Summit in Singapore, China and ASEAN agreed on a single draft negotiating text.[22] Although Premier Li Keqiang has reasserted China's willingness to finalise the COC by 2021,[23] diplomats have also yet to agree on the salient features of the non-aggression COC, such as whether it would be legally binding and the geographical scope. Vietnam has insisted the COC includes the entire South China Sea, as defined by the International Hydrographic Organisation.

China wants the COC instrument to cover only the Spratly region. In the meantime, India, Japan and the United States believe that China intends to shut them out from the South China Sea[24] by allegedly introducing a proviso that, according to them, would require prior permission or authorisation of coastal states before they could conduct military manoeuvres or exercises[25] in the South China Sea.[26] If introduced, the proviso would illegally bar access to vessels and aircraft in the South China Sea and the airspace above it. Such a policy would not go unchallenged as it is tantamount to China establishing the much-contested air defence identification zone there.

China's reluctance to adhere to a COC that covers the entire South China Sea is understandable because the disputed features are mainly in the Spratlys. Beijing's preference for a bilateral approach in the Spratlys is also quite sound; although, many see this as cherry-picking. China should not be faulted for preferring to negotiate only with the claimant ASEAN member states and not with other states with whom it has no territorial disputes.

From the claimants' vantage, however, they need friends in the region to strengthen their negotiating position with China vis-à-vis their occupied territories in the Spratlys. Like China, the claimant states too, need face-saving solutions. They too are under pressure from their people to stand up or be seen to stand up to any form of bullying and intimidation by China and other stronger powers. This is the reality of domestic politics in the claimant states that China must appreciate.

China faces a challenge in the South China Sea: how it could prevent military conflicts in the disputed Spratly area without undermining the interests of other external stakeholders? With this in mind, an interim confidence-building measure mechanism to prevent strategic miscalculations and unwanted military conflicts in the Spratly was floated in 2015. The proposal for "The Spratly Forum for Peace" was outlined in an article published in 2015.[27]

The proposal calls for the establishment of an informal information exchange centre where Commanders of enforcement units on the ground (i.e. at sea and air above it) can meet and talk, advising each other on the movements of their ships and aircraft in the area, to avoid unnecessary suspicions. The Commanders could use the existing set of rules of engagement and international regulations to facilitate the freedom of navigation and overflight, to prevent collisions and ensure safety at sea, among others.

The navies of the claimant states and other stakeholders plying the South China Sea have already adopted the COC on Unplanned Encounters at Sea (CUES) as operational guidelines since 2014.[28] But CUES are navy specific. They do not cover the grey hulls which operate in the South China Sea. Extending CUES to cover the grey hulls would not be realised without a commitment from Beijing. The claimant states and other stakeholders have also signed the 1974 International Convention for the Safety of Life at Sea (SOLAS) and the 1972 International Regulations for Preventing Collisions at Sea. Most significantly, except for the US, all the claimant states and the major stakeholders in the Spratlys have ratified UNCLOS.

In 2013, the author observed in an article[29] on how Western media treated China as a rogue state. While China's conduct in the South China Sea is not without blemish, distorted media reporting has portrayed China as an irresponsible power. By maligning China's behaviour, the Western media has downplayed China's contribution to regional security, trade, and investment, for example.

The media could be more objective in its coverage of events in the South China Sea. For example, it could point out that external powers like Great Britain, France and Japan had separately occupied the major features in the South China Sea in 1800 before China seized the Paracels in 1974. During the Vietnam War (1964–1975) the Soviet Union had maintained a large naval facility at Cam Ranh Bay, a deep-water port in Vietnam.

News of the Scarborough Shoal (Panatag/Huangyan) incident went viral in April 2010 after China barricaded the shoal. Yet, the contest for the control of the shoal had been going on for some time, almost unnoticed by the media. For example, no premier media outside the Philippines ever carried the news when a judge threw out a case against 21 Chinese fishermen caught for illegal fishing in the Scarborough Shoal in 1978.

The learned judge ruled, "there can be no legal basis as yet for the conclusion that the accused ... entered Philippine territory illegally." Since this incident, several Chinese fishermen have been arrested and fined in the Philippines for illegal fishing. In 2014, for example, the Court sentenced 12 fishermen from China to prison for illegal fishing in Tubbataha Reef off Palawan.[30] Following the 2016 arbitration which China rejected as a farce, Manila continued to arrest Chinese fishermen for illegal fishing. At the same time, there have been several reports of Chinese Coast Guard vessels seizing the catches of Filipino fishermen[31] off the Scarborough shoals where China maintains a 24/7 naval presence; that the locals have accused China's enforcement vessels of deliberately preventing them from fishing in the area.[32]

Malaysia-China relations

Malaysia's current policy of active engagement in the South China Sea is a continuation of a long-standing strategy of peaceful coexistence with China. Relations between Imperial China and the Malay states commenced in the early 7th Century, or possibly earlier. In the 15th century when China's maritime power was at its height, the Malay states had come under the limited political influence of China. Under this tributary system, China exacted tributes from maritime countries in Southeast Asia. However, unlike the Western powers, China neither colonised them nor turned them into its vassals.

Historically, long before the sovereign Malay states won independence as the Federation of Malaya in 1957, their seafaring people used to roam the nearby maritime areas, including the Spratlys for economic and military activities. The presence of Malay seafarers in the Spratlys preceded the colonial era and long before the establishment of the 1947 nine-dash line through which China stakes formal claim to the entire South China Sea. Like many seafarers from the coastal states in the region that today make up the current states of Indonesia, Cambodia and Vietnam, the seafarers from China had also sailed through the South China Sea since ancient times. The seafarers from Ming China (1368–1644), for example, were noted for their expeditions.

The seafaring peoples from the Malay Archipelago, Indochina and China who roamed the area had never laid formal claim to the features in the South China Sea of which the Spratlys is an integral part. This is unlike the Western colonial powers who resorted to various tactics, notably gunboat diplomacy, to occupy distant lands and features, away from their shores. Occupied and unoccupied features or territories belonging to weaker states were acquired through various means including the use of force. In some cases, treaties were imposed on reluctant sovereigns to "formalise" territorial acquisitions in accordance with Western norms.

It was the Western colonial powers who introduced the concept of territorial acquisition to legalise ownership of territories in distant regions. After years of perfecting their version of international law and customary rights, a code of legal norms on territorial acquisitions was introduced to legitimise acquisitions.

Since the 15th century, the Anglo-Saxon version of international law on territorial acquisition of foreign territories has rejected mere presence as evidence of ownership. Occupation, annexation, conquest, outright purchase (e.g., Alaska), prescription (long usage without contest) and cession (voluntary or by force)[33] were considered legitimate.

During the late 1940s, colonial Malaya faced insurgency problems from the Communist Party of Malaya (CPM) that maintained a close ideological relationship with the People's Republic of China. There was no denying that the military arm of the CPM received military and moral support from China and the Soviet Union. The CPM's primary objective was to free Malaya from the British colonial rule and the guerrilla tactics it waged posed a threat to the security of British Malaya. The CPM terrorised the country by killing innocent civilians and raided plantations and military camps.

The clandestine activities had alarmed the colonial government which declared a state of emergency in Malaya in 1948 for 12 years to give the government extra powers to deal with the terrorists. The counter-insurgency operations against the CPM were a protracted struggle that receded only after Great Britain granted independence to Malaya in 1957. Soon after Malaysia was formed in 1963, the second state of emergency in Malaysia was declared in 1979 lasting until 1989. By the dawn of the 1980s, without local support, the CPM attacks had lost most of its ferocity. The CPM became dysfunctional soon after Beijing cut off financial and moral support.

Malaysia supports China's infrastructure projects

Malaysia became the first original ASEAN state to establish diplomatic relations with China in May 1974. What began as a calculated diplomatic strategy has since 1990 spilled over into economic, cultural, educational and military ties.[34] Despite disagreement over China's extensive territorial claims in the Spratlys, Malaysia does not consider China a hostile power. On the contrary, following the decision to establish diplomatic ties, despite the memory of a brutal communist-China-inspired insurgency, Malaysia has adopted a friendly approach towards China.

Since the launching of the BRI in 2013, the economic ties between China and Malaysia showed tremendous improvement. China was Malaysia's largest trading partner for the last one decade with bilateral trade increased from US$63.6 billion in 2017 to US$77.7 billion in 2018.[35] China has invested over US$ 43.8 billion over the last ten years in Malaysia including taking up 49 percent equity in Proton, once the ailing National Car (Proton) project that Dr. Mahathir pioneered way back in the early 1980s.

China's multi-billion-dollar BRI projects have come under intense scrutiny by Western media describing those projects as "debt-traps" for developing countries and a plan for China to expand its geopolitical influence. For example, when the Government of Sri Lanka failed to service the loans borrowed by the previous government to develop the port at Hambantota, the new government handed over the port and 15,000 acres of land around it to China for 99 years in 2015. Some critics[36] saw this as a debt-trap rather than a normal commercial practice of recovering loans.

The story of Sri Lanka is always repeated as a warning although such seizure of assets is quite rare apart from another case in Tajikistan in 2011. While no one disputes that loans from foreign countries and multilateral financial institutions all entail risk, chastising China for its "opaque" loans for infrastructure projects as predatory does not always do justice to Beijing.

Malaysia is among the 65 countries that have participated in the BRI projects and a recipient of large foreign direct investment (FDI) from China. However, Malaysia does not share the harsh criticisms, for example, by US Vice President Mike Pence of China's BRI projects as a form of debt diplomacy to increase its political clout in the developing world.

Many of the multi-billion-dollar projects that were inked by the previous government were renegotiated after Dr. Mahathir overthrew the previous administration in the May 2018 general election.[37] Many predicted that the relationship with China would suffer because, during the 2018 general election campaigns, Dr. Mahathir criticised China for bribing Malaysian leaders to get mega projects which were largely overpriced. In fact, Dr. Mahathir promised that if elected he would cancel some of the mega projects.

Elected as Prime Minister for the second time, but under a different political party, he surprised even the Chinese when he embraced the BRI projects, thus making a 180-degree turn. Instead of cancelling the projects, he renegotiated them for a better price and insisted that Chinese companies employ more locals and source their construction materials from local companies. Interestingly, the Chinese companies agreed to cut costs and to abide by the conditions. This goes to show, contrary to some suggestions, the BRI projects can be renegotiated; they are not debt-traps, after all.

Some of the mega projects that have been renegotiated include the Bandar Malaysia and the East Coast Rail Link (ECRL). The warming up of a relationship with China under the new government in Malaysia led by Dr. Mahathir Mohamad has seen a spike in Chinese imports of, for example, palm oil, offsetting the decision of the European Union to ban the import of palm oil. This policy shift with China has earned Mahathir many critics in the country, but it has earned him the respect of Chinese leaders, eager to portray to the world their readiness to debunk any allegation of unfair agreements with the developing countries.

The criticism of China's BRI as a form of predatory politics is a misrepresentation of its real intentions. Critics of China tend to downplay China's willingness to discuss unpaid loans or projects. The Malaysian case proved otherwise: the Chinese companies were more than willing to cut cost and accept the local conditions, without much fuss.

China is seldom credited for its efforts to renegotiate the terms of its mega projects. The Malaysian case proves otherwise. President Xi must have been delighted with Dr. Mahathir's championship of BRI projects when some countries have put cold water on them. At the Second Beijing Forum on BRI (26–27 April 2019), Dr. Mahathir rubbished the claim that Beijing was using the BRI "to gain control of participating countries." Dr. Mahathir also refuted allegations that the BRI projects were debt-traps to dominate the developing world.

China must have been delighted by Dr. Mahathir's decision to embrace Huawei's 5G project which is gaining popularity in Southeast Asia. The attempts by the United States, in 2018 and 2019, to prevent the federal government and its agencies from doing business with the Chinese technology giant had not reverberated well in Southeast Asia. Washington's accusation that China is using Huawei 5G technology for spying purposes has fallen flat following Edward Snowden's exposure in 2014 of the US mass surveillance activities around the globe.

Concluding remarks

Strategically located between the Strait of Malacca and the Sulu Sea, Malaysia considers itself to be a very important geopolitical and economic force in Southeast Asia. It is a pioneer in regional cooperation and has played a leading role in creating a durable security architecture for such cooperation. But a more important contribution Malaysia has made to regional peace and security has been the leading role it has played in effecting some form of political and strategic reconciliation between Southeast Asia and China.

Despite the usual ups and downs in Malaysia's diplomatic relations with China, Kuala Lumpur does not consider Beijing as a military threat to its territorial integrity and political independence. On the contrary, some quarters in Malaysia believe that China is the victim of unfair coverage by the Western controlled international media. A more balanced reporting of events in the South China Sea could help ease tensions.

The way forward in the South China Sea is not to use force to contest China's claims in the South China Sea but to engage it more constructively. Profiling China as a rogue state will harden its negotiating position, especially in the South China Sea, where concessions are expected. However, a hostile China is not in the region's interest either. Since China walks on a tight rope in the South China Sea, it needs to act responsibly.

Malaysia's policy of active cooperative engagement in the South China Sea (i.e., the Spratlys) is not directed at China alone as it has astutely chosen a policy of accommodation over confrontation in dealing with territorial disputes with its neighbours in the South China Sea.

Malaysia's strong economic ties with China are likely to defuse political tensions arising from maritime boundary disputes in the Spratlys. For Malaysia, while the ownership of its territories in the Spratlys is important, it is not the primary concern in determining Malaysia's overall relations with China.

The focus of Malaysia's policy in the South China Sea revolves largely around maintaining friendly relations with China, claimant states and other stakeholders. However, this does not mean Malaysia has chosen the path of appeasement in its relations with China. For example, Malaysia continues to support the ASEAN- initiated COC mechanism against China in the South China Sea. Similarly, Malaysia's support for the freedom of navigation in the South China Sea reflects its responsibility to the international community and respect for rules-based international order; these two are currently at odds with China's position.

Malaysia relies on international law and diplomacy to resolve territorial disputes in its waters. Though Malaysia's 1979 map of the continental shelf has been the bone of contention with many in the region, its appeal for international law and diplomacy has produced a positive impact on its neighbours. The boundary disputes with Thailand and Vietnam, for example, have been temporarily shelved through Joint Development Schemes. The disputes with Singapore and Indonesia were resolved through the ICJ. Malaysia's reliance on international law and diplomacy to manage boundary disputes is a testimony to its active engagement policy with all the contending stakeholders in the South China Sea. In the same vein, Malaysia's reliance on the ASEAN member states to seek peaceful solutions in the South China Sea helps to reinforce its active engagement in the region.

Notes

1 For an analysis of Malaysia-Indonesia maritime boundaries, see B.A. Hamzah, VL Forbes, Jalila A. Jalil and M.N. Basiron, "The Maritime Boundaries of Malaysia and Indonesia in the Malacca Strait: An Appraisal," *Australian Journal of Maritime & Ocean Affairs* 6:4 (2014): 207–226.

2 International Court of Justice, Case Concerning Sovereignty over Pulau Ligitan and Pulau Sipadan (Indonesia/Malaysia), Order, General List No. 102, 10 November 1998. Available at www.lcj-cij.org/IDOCKtT/IINMA/iinmaorders/linmaorer981 I IO.htm.

3 See Article 47.6 of UNCLOS which states that

> if a part of the archipelagic waters of an archipelagic State lies between two parts of an immediately adjacent neigbouring State, existing rights and all other legitimate interests which the latter State has traditionally exercised in such waters and all rights stipulated by agreement between those states shall continue and be respected.

4 Treaty between Malaysia and the Republic of Indonesia relating to the legal regime of archipelagic state and the rights of Malaysia in the territorial sea and archipelagic waters as well as in the airspace above the territorial sea, archipelagic waters and the territory of the Republic of Indonesia lying between East and West Malaysia, 25 February 1982.

5 To underline their cooperative approach, on 6 May 2009, Malaysia and Viet Nam submitted jointly to the Commission on the Limits of the Continental Shelf, in accordance with Article 76, paragraph 8, of the United Nations Convention on the Law of the Sea, information on the limits of the continental shelf beyond 200 nautical miles from the baselines from which the breadth of the territorial sea is measured in respect of the southern part of the South China Sea.

6 1992 Memorandum of Understanding between Malaysia and the Socialist Republic of Vietnam for the exploration of and exploitation of petroleum in a defined area of the continental shelf involving the two countries. Adopted in Kuala Lumpur, Malaysia on 5 June 1992. A copy of this MOU is available for inspection at https://cil.nus.edu.sg/wp-content/uploads/formidable/14/1992-MOU-between-Malaysia-and-Vietnam-for-the-Exploration-and-Exploitation-of-Petroleum.pdf.

7 See "Malaysia, Thailand Look to Extend Cooperation in Joint Development Area," *New Straits Times* (11 September 2019). See also MTJDA Website https://www.mtja.org/ourwork.php Accessed on 11 September 2019.

8 Case Concerning Sovereignty over Pedra Branca /Pulau Batu Puteh, Middle Rocks and South Ledge (Malaysia/Singapore Judgement, 23 May 2008).

9 According to a press release from the Prime Minister's Office,

> the Exchange of Letters marked a historic and momentous occasion for Brunei Darussalam and Malaysia. It included the final delimitation of maritime boundaries between the two countries; the establishment of Commercial Agreement Areas (CAA) in oil and gas; and the modalities for the final demarcation of land boundaries between Brunei Darussalam and Malaysia.

https://www.kln.gov.my/web/brn_begawan/news-from-mission/-/blogs/1028210. See also report on New Era in Brunei-Malaysia Bilateral Ties, 17 March 2009, and "The Joint Statement after Brunei-Malaysia Exchange of Letters," *Borneo Bulletin* (17 March 2009). See also https://halalfocus.net/new-era-in-brunei-malaysia-bilateral-ties/.

10 Mahathir Mohamad, *A Doctor in the House: The Memoirs of Tun Dr Mahathir Mohammad* (Kuala Lumpur: MPH Publishing, 2011).

11 See Adrian David, "How Malaysia's Five Naval Stations at Spratlys were Built," *New Straits Times* (4 March 2019). https://www.nst.com.my/news/nation/2019/03/465854/how-malaysias-five-naval-stations-spratlys-were-built.

12 Private communication. See also Malaysian Chart 781, Terumbu Semarang Barat Kecil-Terumbu Peninjau, First published in 1988, Revised 2014.

13 See Parameswaran, "Malaysia's South China Sea Policy: Playing It Safe?" The *Diplomat* (6 March 2015).

14 CSIS Report, "Signalling Sovereignty: Chinese Patrols at Contested Reefs," *Asia Maritime Transparency Initiative*, Washington, DC (29 September 2019); see also Ralph Jenning, "Why China's Coast Guard Spent 258 Days in Waters Claimed by Malaysia," *Voice of America* (20 October 2019).

15 For an excellent discussion on the role of domestic politics in driving the Malaysian-China policy see Ngeow Chow Bing, "Malaysia's China Policy and the South China Sea Dispute under the

Najib Administration (2009–2018): A Domestic Policy Process Approach," *Asian Politics & Policy* 11:4 (2019): 586–605.

16 The COC is based on a 2002 Declaration on the Conduct of Parties in the South China Sea signed by China and 10 ASEAN member states.

17 See Andit Panda, "South China Sea: US Navy Warship Conducts Freedom of Navigation Operation Near Paracel Islands," *The Diplomat* (15 September 2019).

18 According to Andit Panda, The *Arleigh Burke*-class destroyer *USS Wayne E. Meyer* sailed near unspecified Chinese-held islands in the Paracel Islands in the South China Sea in September 2019. https://thediplomat.com/2019/09/south-china-sea-us-navy-warship-conducts-freedom-of-navigation-operation-near-paracel-islands/.

19 Private communication with Chew Beng Hian (29 September 2019).

20 See Press Release from the Permanent Court of Arbitration on the South China Arbitration (The Republic of the Philippines V. The Peoples' Republic of China), The Hague (12 July 2016).

21 Mira Rapp Hooper, "Parting the South China Sea: How to Uphold the Rule of Law," *Foreign Affairs* (September/October 2016).

22 See Carl Thayer, "Asean and China Set to Agree on Single Draft South China Sea Code of Conduct," *The Diplomat* (27 July 2018). https://thediplomat.com/2018/07/asean-and-china-set-to-agree-on-single-draft-south-china-sea-code-of-conduct/.

23 "We stand ready to work with ASEAN countries within the existing foundation and basis to strive for new progress in the COC, according to the three-year time frame, so as to maintain long-term peace and stability in the South China Sea," quoted in "Beijing Presses ASEAN Anew for South China Sea Code by 2021," *Nikei Asian Review* (3 November 2019).

24 Amirbhan Bhaumik, "India, Japan Oppose China's Bid on South China Sea Code," *DHNS*, New Delhi. (1 December 2019). https://www.deccanherald.com/national/india-japan-oppose-china-s-bid-on-south-china-sea-code-781449.html.

25 India, China, Malaysia, Vietnam are among the states that have made declarations at the United Nations upon ratification of UNCLOS requiring prior notification and permission before foreign military activities could conduct military manouvres in their waters.

26 See Wu Shicun, "US-China Competition Will Heat up South China Sea," *The Diplomat* (8 November 2019). https://thediplomat.com/2019/11/us-china-competition-will-heat-up-the-south-china-sea/.

27 B.A. Hamzah, "Averting Crisis in the Spratlys: Towards a Regional Naval Forum," *Institute for Policy and Security Studies*, Issue and Policy Brief (July 2015). No. 183.

28 "The Code for Unplanned Encounters at Sea (CUES) is an agreement reached at the 2014 Western Pacific Naval Symposium to reduce the chance of an incident at sea between the countries in the agreement, and - in the event that one occurred - to prevent it from escalating. Twenty-one countries have joined the agreement, including Australia, Brunei, Cambodia, Canada, Chile, China, France, Indonesia, Japan, Malaysia, New Zealand, Papua New Guinea, Peru, the Philippines, Russia, Singapore, South Korea, Thailand, Tonga, the United States and Vietnam. Taiwan, a non-signatory state also reportedly implements the Agreement." See "Code of Unplanned Encounters at Sea" in Wikipedia. https://en.wikipedia.org/wiki/Code_for_Unplanned_Encounters_at_Sea. Accessed on 10 November 2019.

29 See BA Hamzah, "A Balanced Reporting on South China Sea Required," *Din Merican: DJ Malaysian Blogger* (6 August 2013). https://dinmerican.wordpress.com/2013/08/06/a-hostile-china-is-not-good-for-our-region-asean/.

30 See Shannon Tiezzi, "Philippine Court Sentences 12 Fishermen to Prison," *The Diplomat* (6 August 2014).

31 https://www.japantimes.co.jp/news/2018/06/08/asia-pacific/philippines-protests-china-seizure-filipinos-fish-catch/#.XcePrlczaUk. Accessed on 10 November 2019.

32 The Foreign Secretary Alan Peter Cayetano has defended President Duterte's closer engagement with China has eased tensions in the disputed waters and produced positive results. He is reported to have said under Duterte Manila has "quietly protested certain Chinese actions in disputed areas and avoided noisy public protests to foster diplomatic talks." Quoted from AP report published in *Japan Times*. https://www.japantimes.co.jp/news/2018/06/08/asia-pacific/philippines-protests-china-seizure-filipinos-fish-catch/#. Accessed on 10 November 2019.

33 Robert Jennings, *The Acquisition of Territory in International Law* (Manchester University Press, 1963).

34 See for example, Ngeow Chow Bing, "Comprehensive Strategic Partners But Prosaic Military Ties: The Development of Malaysia-China Relations 1991–2015," *Contemporary Southeast Asia: A Journal of International and Strategic Affairs* 2 (August 2015): 269–304.

35 Tham Siew Yean, "Chinese Investments in Malaysia: Five Years into BRI," *ISEAS-Yusof Ishak Institute,* Singapore, 2018. No.11. *See* also China's Investment in *Malaysia: Perceptions, Issues and Prescriptions* (Kuala Lumpur: Socio-Economic Research Centre, 2018).

36 See for example Maria Abi -Habib, "How China Got Sri Lanka to Cough up a Port," *The New York Times* (25 June 2015).

37 See Ho Wah Foon, "Malaysia Set to See New Wave of China FDI," *The Star Online* (5 May 2019).

References

Maria Abi-Habib, "How China Got Sri Lanka to Cough Up a Port", *The New York Times* (25 June 2018).

China's Investment in Malaysia: Perceptions, Issues and Prescriptions (Kuala Lumpur: Socio-Economic Research Centre, 2018).

Ngeow Chow-Bing, "The Comprehensive Strategic Partners But Prosaic Military Ties: The Development of Malaysia-China Relations 1991–2015", *Contemporary Southeast Asia: A Journal of International and Strategic Affairs* (Singapore: ISEAS, No 2, August 2015): 269–304.

Ngeow Chow- Bing, "A "Model" for ASEAN Countries? Sino-Malaysian Relations: Sino-Malaysian Relations during the Xi-Jinping Era", in Alvin Cheng-Hin Lim and Frank Cibulka (eds.), *China and Southeast Asia in the Xi Jinping Era* (Lanham, MD: Lexington Books, 2018): 103–122.

Ngeow Chow-Bing, "Economic Cooperation and Infrastructure Linkage between Malaysia and China under the BRI", in Fanny M. Cheung and Ying-yi Hong (eds.), *Regional Connection under the BRI: The Prospects for Economic and Financial Cooperation* (New York: Routledge, 2019):164–191.

Ngeow Chow-Bing, "The Five Areas of Connectivity between Malaysia and China: Challenges and Opportunities", in Yang Yue and Li Fujian (eds.), *The BRI: ASEAN Countries' Perspectives* (Singapore: World Scientific, 2019): 117–139.

Ngeow Chow Bing, "Malaysia's China Policy and the South China Sea Dispute under the Najib Administration (2009–2018): A Domestic Policy Process Approach", *Asian Politics & Policy,* 11:4 (2019): 586–605.

CSIS Report, Signalling Sovereignty: Chinese Patrols at Contested Reefs in *Asia Maritime Transparency Initiative, Washington DC* (29 September 2019).

Adrian David, "How Malaysia's Five Naval Stations at Spratlys Were Built", *New Straits Times* (4 March 2019).

Ralph Emmers, *The De-escalation of the Spratly Dispute in Sino-Southeast Relations* (Singapore: RSIS, 2007).

Lye Liang Fook, "China -Malaysia Relations Back on Track?" *Yusof Ishak Institute,* Perspective, Issue 2019, No 38. (15 May 2019).

Sourabh Gupta, "Why US Analysis of Nine-Dash Line Is Flawed", *East Asia Forum* (11 January 2015).

B.A. Hamzah, "A Balanced Reporting on South China Sea Required", *Din Merican: DJ Malaysian Blogger* (6 August 2013).

B.A. Hamzah, "Averting Crisis in the Spratlys: Towards a Regional Naval Forum", *Institute for Policy and Security Studies, Issue and Policy Brief,* No. 183 (July 2015).

B.A. Hamzah, Vivian L. Forbes, Jalil A. Jalila & M.N. Basiron, "The Maritime Boundaries of Malaysia and Indonesia in the Malacca Strait: An Appraisal", *Australian Journal of Maritime & Ocean Affairs,* 6:4 (2014): 207–226.

How Wah Foon, "Malaysia Set to See New Wave of China FDI", *The Star Online* (5 May 2019).

International Court of Justice, Case Concerning Sovereignty over Pulau Ligitan and Pulau Sipadan, (Indonesia/Malaysia), Order, General List No. 102 (10 November 1998).

Ralph Jennings, "Why China's Coast Guard Spent 258 Days in Waters Claimed by Malaysia", *Voice of America* (20 October 2019).

Robert Jennings, *The Acquisition of Territory in International Law* (Manchester: Manchester University Press, 1963).

Kwame Sundaran Jomo, "Improving Malaysia-China Economic Relations", *The Star Online* (27 July 2018).

Mahathir Mohamad, *A Doctor in the House: The memoirs of Tun Dr Mahathir Mohamad* (Petaling Jaya: MPH Group Publishing, 2011).

Andit Panda, "South China Sea: US Navy Warship Conducts Freedom of Navigation Operation Near Paracel Islands", *The Diplomat* (15 September 2019).

Prashant Parameswaran, "Malaysia's Approach to the South China Sea Dispute after the Arbitral Tribunal's Ruling", *Contemporary Southeast Asia: Journal of International strategic Affairs, Singapore*, 38:3 (December 2016): 375–381.

Mira Rapp-Hooper, "Parting the South China Sea How to Uphold the Rule of Law", *Foreign Affairs* (September/October 2016).

Wu Shicun, "US-China Competition Will Heat Up the South China Sea", *The Diplomat* (8 November 2019).

Ian Storey, *Contending US and Chinese Visions for Regional Order at the Shangri-La Dialogue* (Singapore: Yusof Ishak Institute, 7 August 2019).

Siew Yean Tham, *Chinese Investment in Malaysia: Five Years into the BRI* (Singapore: Yusof Ishak Institute, Issue 2018, No 11, 27 February 2018).

Carl Thayer, "Asean and China Set to Agree on Single Draft South China Sea Code of Conduct", *The Diplomat* (27 July 2018).

Shicun Wu and Keyuan Zou (eds.), *Maritime Security in the South China Sea: Regional Implications and International Cooperation* (Farnham: Ashgate Publishing House, 2013).

Shicun Wu and Keyuan Zou (eds.), *Arbitration Concerning the South China Sea: Philippines versus China* (Abingdon: Routledge, 2016).

Mat Taib Yasin, Azhar Abdul Rahman & Johari Ramzan Ahmad (eds.), *Malaysian Pioneers in the Spratly Islands; The Untold Stories* (unpublished, 2019).

Zou Keyuan, "China's U-Shaped Line in the South China Sea Revisited", Ocean Development & International Law, 43:1 (2012): 18–34.

Zou Keyuan (ed.), Maritime Cooperation in Semi-enclosed Seas: Asian and European Experiences (Leiden/Boston: Brill/Nijhoff, 2019).

11

DECIPHERING DUTERTE'S FOREIGN POLICY ON THE SOUTH CHINA SEA

Jay L. Batongbacal

Introduction

The South China Sea disputes remain the most contentious and difficult of all territorial and jurisdictional disputes in the world. Although the South China Sea Arbitration formally laid down the first, and thus far the only, interpretation and application of United Nations Convention on the Law of the Sea (UNCLOS) to the maritime aspects of the disputes, China's continued refusal to recognize the validity of the Award in 2016, and very sharp changes in Philippine policy on the handling of the disputes since then, have only added to the uncertainty in the region's trajectory as a whole. Between President Benigno Aquino III and President Rodrigo Roa Duterte, the two administrations have induced the most dramatic changes in what used to be a mundane and dormant legal discourse, but the changes in tone and substance have been diametrically opposed. Four years into the latter's six-year term, the fate of the Philippines' maritime jurisdictions still seem to be in veritable limbo both legally and politically, due in no small part to the often-times completely opposite tracks taken by the two leaders' foreign policy on the South China Sea.

Historical background

An abridged history

The history and nuances of the Philippines-China territorial and maritime disputes are better dealt with in a separate work,[1] but suffice it to state that the disputes were dormant from the late 1960s until 1995–1999 when China's forays and activation of presence in Mischief Reef and Scarborough Shoal brought the issue closer from the periphery of Philippine foreign policy. Diplomatic tussles over the two atolls eventually led to the negotiation, in concert with Vietnam, of what became the 2002 Declaration on the Conduct of Parties in the South China Sea (DOC),[2] which was hoped to provide the basis for a lasting commitment to maintain the status quo of occupation and control in the contested region pending future dispute resolution.

With the 2002 DOC, the Philippines under the administrations of Fidel V. Ramos, Joseph E. Estrada, and Gloria Macapagal-Arroyo attempted to cultivate friendly and close economic relations with China, the latter one to the extent of being seen as "the Golden Years" of Philippines-China relations,[3] on the assumption that economic development and prosperity would bring China equally closer to accepting the prevailing system of international law that would eventually allow for a fair and equitable settlement of the maritime disputes. Agreeing with China that the South China Sea issues did not constitute the sum-total of their relations, the Philippines compartmentalized the maritime and territorial disputes and side-stepped them in favor of developing political, economic, and cultural ties. This was successful for only a brief period of time.

During the Arroyo administration, the Philippines signed a Joint Marine Seismic Undertaking (JMSU) with China in 2004, joined by Vietnam in 2005, which was celebrated as a historic landmark heralding better relations and closer cooperation in the South China Sea.[4] Three years later, however, it was perceived as a deal born of corruption and a sell-out of Philippine interests to China in exchange for kickbacks on Chinese development aid.[5] Arroyo's controversial actions precipitated Congressional action, which dusted off moribund bills amending the old Philippine baselines law resulting in the enactment of new baselines legislation that re-asserted Philippine sovereignty and jurisdiction over the Kalayaan Island Group and Scarborough Shoal.[6] But frustration and distrust over the "loss" of Mischief Reef, combined with the furor of the JMSU, found an outlet during the administration of Benigno S. Aquino, Jr. from 2012 to 2016.

The Aquino years

Only a few months into its term, the Aquino Administration's relations with China started off on the wrong foot with a hostage crisis that left eight tourists from Hong Kong dead on account of a botched police rescue operation in 2010.[7] Despite attempts to promote friendship by invoking Aquino's Chinese ancestry,[8] suspicion of Chinese intentions grew with incidents in 2011 when China Maritime Surveillance ships interfered with operations of the seismic exploration vessel *M/V Veritas Voyager* contracted by the Philippine government to conduct exploration in Reed Bank[9] and diplomatically protested the auction of petroleum blocks between Reed Bank and the Philippine island of Palawan.[10] Exploration of offshore petroleum resources had acquired a sense of urgency with projections that the Philippines' only petroleum production platform, the Malampaya Natural Gas-to-Power Project, would end its service life in the mid-2020s and would soon need a new source of natural gas, anticipated to be Reed Bank.[11] In response to the growing pressure from China to slow down or stop Philippine fishing and petroleum activities in the South China Sea and newfound confidence in the country's economic trajectory, Aquino chose to stand on the moral high ground and assert Philippine rights under national and international law. In his State of the Nation Address in July 2011, he announced his decision to upgrade the Armed Forces of the Philippines' (AFP) external defense capabilities and send a clear message that "[w]hat is ours is ours; setting foot on Recto Bank is no different from setting foot on Recto Avenue."[12]

The Scarborough Shoal incident between April and July 2012 resulted in China taking control of Scarborough Shoal and preventing Philippine private and government ships from approaching within several nautical miles from the shoal.[13] Philippines-China diplomatic relations went into free-fall as both sides traded barbs and neither side gave quarter for resuming negotiations, with the Philippines seeking a return to the *status quo ante* and China refusing to withdraw from the shoal. China pressed further in its assertive activities against the Philippines, deploying its fishing fleet into the Philippines' exclusive economic zone (EEZ) and law enforcement ships increasing pressure on Philippine outposts in the Kalayaan Islands.

The scope of the Aquino Administration's foreign policy on the South China Sea was originally announced by Foreign Secretary Albert del Rosario at a conference in Washington DC in September 2012 and described as a "rules-based approach respecting international law" meant to "help build an international system that will be just and fair to all states, regardless of economic size or power." It was comprised of three tracks: political, diplomatic, and legal.[14] Within the following months, however, each of the three tracks had taken distinct turns as relations with China further deteriorated and the diplomatic track with China closed shut.

On the political track, the Philippines had attempted to rally Association of Southeast Asian Nations (ASEAN) support behind a statement to express concern over the South China Sea disputes in the semi-annual summit at Cambodia in July that year; talks ended in deadlock and diplomatically damaged ASEAN as it was not able to issue a joint statement for the first time in its 45-year history.[15] It was hoped that the second summit in November would produce better results, but instead, the meeting ended with the Philippines denouncing the chair Cambodia for inserting into the joint statement language not agreed upon.[16] This signaled to the Philippines the difficulty of forging ASEAN unity and that regional multi-lateral engagement (and implicitly, settlement) would take more than a few years.

Frustration with interactions with ASEAN also contributed to decision-making on the legal track. The government engaged several persons to conduct studies on the feasibility of UNCLOS dispute settlement mechanisms, and in November 2012, the promulgation of judgment in the *Nicaragua v. Columbia* case[17] encouraged the pursuit of third-party dispute settlement. On 22 January 2013, the government officially announced the initiation of arbitration proceedings under UNCLOS Annex VII against China by sending a Notification and Statement of Claim.[18] The case challenged not only China's occupation of Scarborough Shoal, but the full breadth of its maritime (not territorial) claims in the South China Sea.[19]

By late 2014 and early 2015, Philippine foreign relations with China over the South China Sea could be summarized along the objectives defined by the Aquino Administration. On the legal track, the government was resolved to pursue the UNCLOS Annex VII arbitration, which led the diplomatic track to foreclose further discussions with China until after the conclusion of the proceedings. The Philippines then tried to build a unified and coordinated ASEAN position on the South China Sea disputes based on the initial consensus on the pursuit of a Code of Conduct, for which the Philippines advocated a legally binding instrument with dispute-settlement provisions. To support this effort, the Philippines also sought to mobilize international public opinion and garner moral and diplomatic support for its positions on the South China Sea disputes and the arbitration proceedings. Meanwhile, its political track was preoccupied with re-energizing its defense alliance with the United States and diversifying security partnerships. All in all, these features represented a foreign policy that sought multi-lateral support as a means of strengthening itself for future engagements with China. The Aquino Administration was able to sustain the momentum of its strategy until the end of its term in June 2016.

Turnabout under the Duterte Administration

The Aquino Administration's foreign policy largely did not survive its successor, the Duterte Administration. One unfortunate quirk in the Philippine system of government is that foreign policy is entirely the domain of the Chief Executive,[20] and thus prone to the personal preferences and inclinations of the elected President. The assumption into office of President Rodrigo Roa Duterte demolished much of what his predecessor had built and attempted to bring Philippine foreign policy with respect to China in the opposite direction.

Deciphering Duterte's mindset

The initial sign that the Duterte Administration would take a different track was broadcast nation-wide along with its first Cabinet meeting after Duterte took his oath of office on 30 June 2016.[21] During the televised meeting, Duterte openly directed his Cabinet to try to find a "soft landing" solution for China when the arbitration award was finally announced.[22] The ramifications of this statement unfolded two weeks later when the arbitral tribunal released the award on 12 July 2016.[23] Despite a sweeping victory on nearly all submissions, Foreign Secretary Perfecto Yasay officially announced the results in a very somber, almost remorseful, manner.[24] China's outright and heavy-handed rejection of the Award[25] indicated no viable way out of the long-standing deadlock.

The Duterte Administration extended the olive branch to China first by not strongly pushing for inclusion of its victory in the Joint Communique of the ASEAN Summit in Laos two weeks later,[26] and refraining from having it mentioned in the ASEAN Chairman's Statement in September.[27] It also initiated an informal "ice-breaker" meeting in Hong Kong the following August, with former President Fidel V. Ramos acting as a special envoy.[28] Informal, non-binding but free-wheeling discussions during this meeting paved the way for identifying points of *rapprochement* between the two countries,[29] and the lowering of tensions was punctuated by Duterte's first official visit to China in October 2016.

Near the conclusion of his visit, Duterte surprised everyone alike with colorful and enthusiastic comments before 200 Chinese business delegates and China's Vice Premier Zhang Gaoli, before whom he announced his "separation from the United States" in military and economic terms, and declared that "America has lost." He further stated that he "re-aligned [himself] with [China's] ideological flow," and called for an alliance between China, Russia, and the Philippines.[30] The two sides had also announced a decision for the Philippines and China to go back to direct bilateral dialogue and consultations concerning the South China Sea disputes, departing from the multi-lateral and multi-platform engagements pursued up until then.[31] This event serves as the turning point for Philippine policy and Duterte's clear departure from the course laid by the Aquino Administration before him.

Deciphering the new policy is not easy. The populist strong-man style that Duterte exudes is conveyed partly by his penchant for spontaneous and rambling soliloquy in press conferences and public events. Within his first year in office, various disjointed commentaries and candid remarks have described the parameters of a very traditional, if somewhat simple, mindset that drives his foreign policy preferences for the South China Sea. A few key points must be kept in mind to work out the method behind the madness and confusion seemingly evoked by Duterte's public performances.

China at the end of Duterte's rainbow

First and foremost, it is clear that Duterte believes in China's rise to become the pre-eminent power in the region on account of its military might and economic status. He expects transactional relations to bear fruit in terms of financial and infrastructure assistance and investments. After returning from his first visit to Beijing in October 2016, the Duterte Administration reveled in returning with 24 Billion USD worth of investment and infrastructure pledges,[32] which his officials said displayed "greater confidence" in closer economic ties for the two countries in the future.[33] Duterte often spoke very openly and of his utter need of China's financial and development assistance for his government's projects, especially his signature Build-Build-Build infrastructure program. At his press conference before departing for the Bo'ao Forum on April 9, 2018, he stated that he needed China "more than anyone else in our national life," and quite frankly, Chinese money:

> If you do not have money, you are not my friend. I go to China, plenty of money. That's the truth. I need money. Anyway, I just simply love Xi Jinping. He understood, he understands my problem and he's willing to help. And I'd like to say: Thank you, China.

Duterte never hid the fact that his personal attitude and foreign policy approach toward China is meant to secure financial favor, and this is reflected in his Administration's push for Chinese investments and assistance. China's investments rocketed from a paltry 400,000 USD in 2016 under Aquino to 930 million USD in 2018, and its official development assistance (ODA) surged from 1.5 million USD in 2016 to 364.9 million USD in 2018. The Philippines signed infrastructure loan agreements amounting to 376 million USD in 2018, and an additional 1.01 billion USD in 2019, in addition to various grants and donations. At the Belt and Road Forum for International Cooperation in April 2019, it further secured pledges from Chinese companies worth 12.1 billion USD and a separate 148 million USD pledge from President Xi Jinping. These amounts are far from enough, as the government is still seeking 14.3 billion USD in ODA to fund much of his signature Build-Build-Build infrastructure program.[34]

Duterte bet all his hopes on China's goodwill to usher in a "golden age of infrastructure" as his legacy. But four years on, the administration had to revise its ambitions to be achievable,[35] and critics have pointed out the reality that the projects underway are but a mere fraction of the scintillating pledges. Of the 24 billion USD originally announced in 2016, 9 billion USD of which were for infrastructure, only two projects worth about 924 million USD had actually materialized.[36] None of the big-ticket projects such as railways and subways had actually broken ground by the end of 2019, and the government shifted its funding strategy for Build-Build-Build away from Chinese ODA to more loans and partnerships with the Philippine private sector.[37]

Even Duterte's economic managers have expressed disappointment with the snail's pace of progress on China's promises. Socioeconomic Planning Secretary Ernesto Pernia noted that Chinese financing was not moving as fast as it should and Chinese counterparts should hold regular visits and meetings to fast-track the partnership[38] Budget Secretary Benjamin Diokno lamented that President Xi Jinping should personally "put pressure on the speed of implementation of all these projects."[39] It has been pointed that the modest assistance of the Philippines' traditional economic partner Japan has consistently and totally outpaced China despite Duterte's constant good press.[40]

In 2019, criticism of Duterte's policy has spread further into the domestic realm due to the very noticeable presence and operations of online gambling operations catering to the Chinese market from offices in the Philippines; this industry has impacted negatively upon local law and order, labor, internet access, and security, thus perceived as representing further social damages for which the country does not derive any substantial benefit.[41] These only tend to reinforce the public's perception that Duterte's policy does not result in commensurate or promised benefits, but instead bring in even more disadvantages to the country. With two years to go on his term as President, the Duterte Administration may end with precious little to show from China in exchange for the breathtaking concessions made in the West Philippine Sea.

Duterte on the West Philippine Sea

The reappearance of the South China Sea Arbitration Award in the Duterte Administration's diplomacy after nearly four years demonstrates Duterte's conflicting attitudes toward law and power. To begin with, Duterte believes that the Philippines has rights to its territories and natural resources in the West Philippine Sea. This includes the basic assumption that the Kalayaan Islands and areas under Philippine jurisdiction like Benham Rise and the EEZ indisputably pertain to the Philippines.[42] He narrates that in his first conversation with President Xi Jinping, he expressly asserted Philippine ownership of petroleum resources in the West Philippine Sea:

> We intend to drill oil there, if it's yours, well, that's your view, but my view is, I can drill the oil, if there is some inside the bowels of the earth because it is ours.[43]

This also includes persistently holding on to the validity of the award in the South China Sea Arbitration,[44] despite perceptions that early on, he had abandoned it. Although he is widely quoted to have "set aside" the ruling,[45] he frames it as a temporary concession in order to entice China back to the negotiating table. Duterte has repeatedly described the holding of discussions with China on the South China Sea Arbitration Award as a matter of "due time," such as when talks on petroleum exploration begin.[46]

In addition to time, Duterte also considers the *realpolitik* of the situation. Responding to mounting criticism over his soft stance toward China since 2016, Duterte reiterated this basic position in his 2019 State of the Nation Address:

> The West Philippine (Sea) is ours. There is no ifs and buts. (sic) It is ours but we have been acting along that legal truth and line. But we have to temper it with the times and the realities that we face today.[47]

It is with respect to "the times and the realities" that Duterte displays a jaded view of the ideal, moral, or legal high grounds of statecraft, and instead frequently falls back to conventional ideas of *realpolitik*. This creates a basic contradiction of a belief in one's rights and entitlements but acceptance of their instability under the pressure of another's greater power. For Duterte, it was not yet the "due time" to invoke the arbitration award because he was basically a newcomer in office that was only starting to create and develop different relations with China.

Four years on, it appears that the "due time" finally arrived, in the aftermath of his administration's most serious crisis with China so far: the sinking of the Filipino fishing vessel *F/B Gem-Ver* in the vicinity of Reed Bank one night in June 2019. A Chinese trawler, the *Yuemaobinyu 42212*, struck the wooden boat while it was anchored, causing it to sink. Despite seeing all 22 Filipino hands in the water, the Chinese vessel quickly departed the scene; they would have all perished had they not been able to get the assistance of a Vietnamese fishing vessel two hours away.[48] The crisis raised a public furor that lasted weeks, causing Duterte to declare that he will finally raise the issue directly in scheduled discussions with President Xi Jinping the following August.[49] As anticipated, the discussion was formally rejected by the latter,[50] and Duterte then turned to other matters without pressing further. It appears that the principal purpose of putting the arbitration award on the table was primarily to release mounting public pressure back home, rather than to leverage specific concessions. Duterte returned from the meeting with a modest set of infrastructure agreements.[51]

But having been finally raised by Duterte in talks with President Xi, subsequently, the Philippines had the opportunity to formally invoke the arbitration award at an appropriate time and venue after Malaysia unexpectedly made a submission for a continental shelf beyond 200 nautical miles in the South China Sea.[52] The Malaysian submission covered an area roughly in the center of the contested area,[53] to which China immediately submitted a protest asserting sovereignty over *Nanhai Zhudao* comprised of four islands groups including the Spratly Islands, and implying that the entire mass of islands generates all maritime zones under UNCLOS.[54] Aside from protesting the Malaysian submission,[55] the Philippines responded to China with a Note Verbale of its own, reiterating its position that it considers China's positions to be inconsistent with international law, and invoking the South China Sea Arbitration. It cited specific rulings of the award as applicable, particularly that none of the high-tide features in the Spratly Islands could generate entitlements to an EEZ or continental shelf, nor could any of the island groups be enclosed within a system of archipelagic or straight baselines so as to accord them maritime zones as a single unit.[56] China likewise responded, reiterating its rejection of the award, but also had to contend with similar positions expressed by Vietnam and Indonesia.[57] This new episode in Philippines-China relations seems to indicate a slight swing back to the situation prior to Duterte's enthusiastic embrace of China, and the official silence over the arbitration award that it entailed.

Power politics in Duterte's foreign policy

Factoring "the times and the realities" in deciding over what steps to take in the South China Sea marks how Duterte perceives the foreign policy challenges in the West Philippine Sea as simply a question of relative power. He equates the effective recognition of the country's rights and jurisdictions with the ability to enforce them without retaliation and believes that the assertion of legal rights must necessarily bow to the threat of war. He explained this thinking in a speech back in February 2017, at which he angrily answered criticism of his administration's developing silence about the arbitral award:

> I went to China. Now, you keep on pushing us, assert, assert, assert. The question — you create a friction. So I go to China. Get out, dismantle your — or else I'll come here with my Coast Guard and Navy. So if I go out and picking fights. What do you think will happen to this country? It's a massacre. Can you contend with 3,000 planes? The missiles are there in Spratly. It can hit Cagayan de Oro, it can hit Pampanga, it can hit Palawan. So you want to go to war? By what proxy? Where is the battleground? The Republic of the Philippines.[58]

Duterte is further convinced, and oftentimes tries to convince the Filipino public, that China threatens the Philippines with war if it should assert its rights strongly in the South China Sea. He claimed that when he officially stated the Philippines intended to unilaterally drill for oil, Xi Jinping responded with a threat of force:

> His response to me, 'we're friends, we don't want to quarrel with you, we want to maintain the presence of warm relationship, but if you force the issue, we'll go to war.'[59]

The threat of war is a recurring and consistent theme in Duterte's responses to criticism over his decisions on Philippine rights in the West Philippine Sea. From the very beginning of his term in 2016, he has presented relations with China as a simple dichotomy:

> So you better just say when, maybe a goodwill visit to their country to express our willingness to talk and be friendly and avoid war. It's not an option. So there is only one option left. And it is just to talk. There are two things: You talk or go to war or create trouble. If you cannot afford to go to war or do some trouble, there's only one left for you to do. And that is to talk. What is there to worry about?[60]

It was most recently reiterated in his administration's electoral campaign in 2019, in which Duterte insisted that his policy of maintaining a friendly tone with China was to avoid war over competing claims.[61] After the *F/B GemVer* incident on Reed Bank, he used the same rationale to justify his refusal to conduct fisheries law enforcement against Chinese fishing in the EEZ, arguing that war would erupt if he did not allow it.[62]

This simplistic approach highlights a fundamental and inherent contradiction in Duterte's foreign policy: friendship born out of the threat of force. Duterte's outspoken preference for China is thus double-edged because each time he has tried to convince the Filipino public of the correctness of his approach, he also subconsciously reinforces the image of China as a potential aggressor to be feared.

Duterte and the AFP

The implicit threat of war from a greater power actually ties in with Duterte's relationship with the security sector in the Philippines. Duterte's inclinations toward China for economic reasons are subtly counterbalanced by the influence of the defense and military establishment. Despite his vast Presidential prerogatives as the exclusive architect of Philippine foreign policy, the AFP plays a passive but important role in dealing with China. Duterte understands that more than anything, the AFP, together with the Philippine National Police (PNP), holds the key to ensuring his seat despite the adoption of unpopular and draconian policies such as the War on Drugs and the incarceration of an opposition Senator on the basis of dubious charges. His local political strategy is classical Machiavelli in style and content, with the cultivation of political allies and intimidation of political enemies among the basic tools of statecraft.

Since the State's means of coercion lie primarily with the military and police, Duterte needs to ensure that neither turns against him as they did in two previous Peoples' Power Revolutions to oust the sitting President in 1986 and 2011. Of the two institutions, however, the civilian police is more easily prone to co-optation because it is historically and institutionally less developed than the military establishment. The military, with much longer and professional traditions and more than 30 years of post-authoritarian institutional development intended to insulate against the vagaries of civilian politics, is a more difficult proposition since it has a clearer and more distinct institutional mission.[63] Duterte must keep the military contented and not push too radically or abruptly to ensure that it does not turn against him before he is able, through his powers as Commander-in-Chief, to appoint a pliant and allied military leadership.

This establishes the context for Duterte's sometimes rocky directions in the South China Sea. When he took over from his predecessor, the AFP was already in the early stage of its second Modernization Program; pay raises were accompanied by equipment acquisitions that used to be mere dreams. In the second half of the Aquino Administration, the Philippine Air Force had just taken delivery of F/A-50 Lead-In Fighter Trainers from South Korea;

the Philippine Navy received refurbished Hamilton-class cutters from the United States and its first brand-new multi-mission vessel, the BRP Tarlac from Indonesia; and contracts were signed or in the process of negotiations for other acquisitions of external defense assets. The Philippines had also revitalized its alliance with the United States with the conclusion of the Enhanced Defense Cooperation Agreement (EDCA) which promised capacity- and capability-building for external defense and maritime domain awareness. These were integral parts of longer-term plans to enhance the AFP's abilities to exercise and extend their defensive missions in the Kalayaan Island Group, Scarborough Shoal, and the West Philippine Sea against the only perceived external security threat posed by China.[64] The historical and institutional relationship between the Philippine and US military cannot be so easily dismantled.[65]

Although Duterte early on warned that he would take action to diminish the Philippine-US alliance,[66] the value of renewed ties between the Philippine and US military cannot be under-estimated. The "love-hate relationship" of these institutions has had many twists and turns since 1946, but the revitalization under the Aquino Administration produced markedly different levels of interoperability and cooperation. When a local armed group allied with the extremist Islamic State militants decided to take over Marawi City in an attempt to establish a Southeast Asian caliphate, the United States, as well as its ally Australia, was immediately on the scene to provide technical and intelligence surveillance, and reconnaissance support that were pivotal in crushing the extremists in a relatively short five months.[67] US training was also credited with having prepared the AFP for the battle, which was the first time the latter engaged in all-out urban warfare.[68] Cooperation between the two armed forces was immediate and Duterte did not even have a role in calling for US assistance.[69] Although Duterte frequently thanked China for their assistance (two deliveries of sniper rifles and construction equipment), he had to begrudgingly acknowledge the substantial assistance provided by the United States.[70] His verbal attacks on the alliance relationship stopped for the next two years until 2019.

Duterte's *rapprochement* with China was inconsistent with the military's interests in the alliance, and the newly-sworn President could not shift too radically and too quickly to remove the military's *raison d'etre* for its long-sought modernization and thereby lose an important institutional ally. The military adheres strongly to the principle of civilian authority over the military, and bitter experience during the Marcos Era taught it hard lessons about the need for professionalism and strong institutions, and to avoid entanglement in national politics. So while it could balance against political arbitrariness, it keeps as much as possible to its constitutional and legal duties to the Commander-in-Chief. These create a divisive security dilemma, as year after year, the AFP constantly but silently weighs the impact of Duterte's policy of accommodating China against its national security plans and goals.

Pressures from this dilemma have had numerous manifestations, such as the leak in 2017 of information about a near-confrontation between Philippine and Chinese units over Sandy Cay, a sandbar some 4–5 nautical miles from the Philippines' Pag-asa Island.[71] In 2018 another leak saw the release to a major newspaper of secret high-resolution aerial surveillance photographs of China's artificial islands.[72] After being confronted in Congress with then-unknown information that China interfered with a resupply mission to the *BRP Sierra Madre*, a grounded ship that serves as the Philippines' outpost on Second Thomas Shoal, Foreign Secretary Cayetano was forced to admit that the incident took place and laid out the Duterte Administration's "red lines," i.e., the limits to government's quietude on the South China Sea. He pointed to four: construction on Scarborough Shoal, removal of the BRP Sierra Madre from Ayungin Shoal, harassment of soldiers resupplying Philippine outposts in the Kalayaan Islands, and unilateral exploitation of the resources of the West Philippine Sea. Cayetano said that any of these conditions were breached, Duterte would be "willing to wage war on Beijing."[73] Three of the four red lines involve the main external defense missions of the AFP in the West Philippine Sea.

Persistent doubts about Duterte's policy necessitated the assurances he gave at his State of the National Address in July 2018, that improved relations with China "does not mean that we will waver in our commitment to defend our interests in the West Philippine Sea."[74] This was followed the next month by his first rare critical comment about Chinese activities in the West Philippine Sea, particularly the frequent warnings against Philippine ships and aircraft, before an audience of diplomats:

> You cannot create an island and you say that the air above the artificial island is your own. That is wrong. The right to innocent passage is guaranteed. I hope that China would temper its – at least its behavior. I do not want to quarrel with China. But at this time, because you will create – America instead of avoiding – 'get out, get out,' China would say 'we go in, we go in.' And 'get out and get out,' and one of these days, a hot head commander there would just press a trigger.[75]

After this was rebuffed by China,[76] the Duterte Administration no longer pursued the matter as it had to turn its attention to the initial negotiations for joint exploration and development of petroleum resources.[77]

In May 2018, the AFP began repair and renovation works on its largest outpost, Pag-asa Island.[78] In the months that passed, increasing numbers of Chinese fishing vessels made their presence felt around the island, sometimes anchoring as close as only one nautical mile away. Although not hostile, the fishing vessels simply kept stationary for hours on end, not conducting any fishing activity, which led to the military suspecting that they were actually part of the maritime militia monitoring the infrastructure works on the island. The Philippine military kept quiet for months until the months-long presence around Pag-asa and other Philippine-held islands was reported in March 2019.[79]

News of the incident coincided with news and visual evidence of the Chinese clam-digging activities in Scarborough Shoal, stoking public dissatisfaction even more. Unlike before, Duterte was silent, but the Department of Foreign Affairs for the first time issued a rather strongly worded statement in April 2019, calling the presence of the suspected maritime militia vessels near and around the Kalayaan Islands "illegal" for violating Philippine sovereignty, sovereign rights, and jurisdiction under international law, and

> observed that the Chinese vessels have been present in large numbers and for sustained and recurring periods – what is commonly referred to as 'swarming' tactics- raising questions about their intent as well as concerns over their role in support of coercive objectives.[80]

It went further by stating that such actions "when not repudiated by the Chinese government are deemed to have been adopted by it."[81]

The "swarming" did not cease and was the subject of another diplomatic protest the following July.[82] The marked change in tone may be associated with the personal style of Foreign Secretary Locsin, who exhibits a more forthright, forward-leaning, and assertive attitude on China policy than his predecessor. His statements and positions are more closely associated with those of Defense Secretary Lorenzana, and since taking office in November 2018, Locsin has most often described foreign policy under his watch to be "the hand, or if you will, the fist in the iron glove of the AFP,"[83] signaling alignment with the more skeptical security sector on the South China Sea.

Another factor that could account for the change in tone was the brief visit of US Secretary of State Mike Pompeo in March. During his visit, Pompeo gave assurances to Duterte and the defense establishment that "we have your back," and a pointed message expressly about the South China Sea:

> As the South China Sea is part of the Pacific, any armed attack on any Philippine forces, aircraft, or public vessels in the South China Sea will trigger mutual defense obligations under Article 4 of our Mutual defense treaty.[84]

This was a significant policy statement since it was the first time that the US expressly acknowledged the South China Sea specifically as an area of application of obligations under the 1952 Mutual Defense Treaty. It strengthened the security sector's resolve in calling out discomfort with Chinese maritime activities.

Recently, however, Duterte's mercurial personality brought about another internal crisis through his sudden announcement in February 2020 that he was terminating the Philippine-US Visiting Forces Agreement,[85] which actually gave flesh to the alliance by regulating the presence of US forces in Philippine territory and facilitating the cooperation between the two militaries. Although he had long been inclined to terminate it, Duterte could not do so due to the great value and capacity-building that the AFP was getting out of its cooperation with the United States. Even the long-delayed EDCA had just resumed implementation in 2018.[86]

The termination was precipitated by his personal fury at the reported cancellation of the US visa of his former police chief, close friend and political ally Senator Ronaldo dela Rosa on account of his role in the war against drugs.[87] It was difficult to understand Duterte's decision as nothing more than an impulse that found an opportunity during a moment of anger; both Philippine and US government officials were caught completely off-guard. Administration allies and critics alike raised the negative impact of the hasty decision,[88] but Duterte stood pat even after receiving US President Donald Trump's nonchalant and dismissive reaction.[89]

Four months later, in the midst of the coronavirus pandemic, Duterte suspended the termination process, citing unspecified "political and other developments in the region."[90] Foreign Secretary Locsin pointed to "the pandemic, and heightened superpower tensions,"[91] but if anything, the suspension offered proof of the inherent difficulties that Duterte faces in dealing with the AFP and its long-standing alliance partner. It also reflected badly on his fickle decision-making: if he were capable of sundering a long-standing international security agreement on a whim, then nothing could guarantee the stability of any other agreements with his administration.

Great powers in the South China Sea

The reality of an enduring the Philippines-US alliance is something that also complicates Duterte's foreign policy on the South China Sea. Regardless of whether right or wrong, Duterte completely blames the United States, and implicitly its allies, for the country's current practical disadvantage in the South China Sea disputes. Thus, he has no faith in the Philippines' historically rooted alliances and friendships with the West. In many speeches during his first year in office, he has repeatedly prefaced his justification for treading lightly in the South China Sea with undisguised blame for US inaction in the recent evolution of the disputes. He rationalizes that if even the US could not stop China's development of its facilities, then much less could the Philippines.[92] He further dismisses the United States for not having a word of honor and being *doble-cara* [double faced],[93] and questions why the United States did not act sooner to nip the problem in the bud by sending its military against China before the South China Sea ripened into such a complicated international issue.[94] He thinks that instead of pursuing an arbitration case, the Philippines should have called upon the United States and the ASEAN to unite and together militarily stopped China from creating its artificial islands in the South China Sea.[95] In his mind, failure to do so is what rendered the Philippines helpless before the threat of war from China in the maritime and territorial disputes.

In this light, Duterte personally resents being advised to assert the Philippines' rights at a time when, in his words, "*wala na akong magawa*" [there is nothing I can do] about China's expansion and militarization of the disputed region. To discourage critics, he frequently emphasizes the country's powerlessness by pointing to Chinese "guided missiles" in the South China Sea that can reach Manila "in seven minutes,"[96] again implicitly reinforcing the image of China as an ever-present threat whom Filipinos have no choice but be friends with. He also frequently insists that the Philippines cannot win and will be annihilated in any conflict with China, and justifies his position as being in favor of saving Filipino lives.[97] Without any other country to trust, Duterte is convinced that the Philippines-China relationship should be mediated and negotiated exclusively by the Philippines, even though by the same logic of *realpolitik* to which he subscribes, the disparity in power between the two countries logically cannot be expected to produce equitable agreements.

For Duterte, the solution lies with the party with greater power. In place of negotiated equity, Duterte expects voluntary boons; for example, when he explained his approach to President Xi and China in discussions for joint exploration and development of petroleum, he stated

> *Ang tao naman basta ganoon ang paano mo, you remain meek and humble, eh 'yung ego niya, mag-start to, and then it turns to something basic like maaawa rin.* [Any person like that, as long as your approach is you remain meek and humble, his ego will start to turn to something basic like he will pity you.][98]

This kind of attitude raises many questions since there is absolutely no guarantee of such generosity. However, it also the attitude that marks a politician steeped in local patronage politics and clientelism in the Philippines.[99] Philippine patronage politics hold that political leaders should be approachable and compassionate, demonstrating sympathy and goodwill through donations and monetary contributions,[100] which establish mutually useful relationships between the patron and the client. The better-off patron provides protection and benefits to the less-fortunate client, who in return provides assistance and support.[101] This is roughly the kind of political relationship that Duterte has cultivated and practiced all his life as mayor of Davao City, and it is clearly the kind of relationship that he has been trying to establish between the Philippines and China.

Unfortunately, local patronage politics offer no reliable guide for dealing with the party-centric politics of China. It also contributes to an inability to appreciate the complexity of decision-making in China, and therefore the identification of what could be feasible in negotiation, as the Philippines attempts to forge a mutually-acceptable compromise over the maritime disputes.

Duterte and joint development

The enormous challenge that Duterte's diplomacy faces is aptly demonstrated in his attempt to engage China in joint exploration and development of petroleum resources. After his State of the Nation Address to Congress, Duterte has indicated that China bears the burden of any cooperation initiative like joint petroleum exploration and development. He explained that

> *Naghihintay ako* [I'm waiting] when they [will] start to dig the oil. *Mahirap 'yan eh* [That's difficult, eh], we are [a] claimant, they are a claimant, so we'll have to say 'look do not forget me' and I would insist that as an owner, though conflicting with your plan, we also must have a share of the resources.[102]

The challenge, however, is that Duterte also clearly envisages China's generosity to be based on recognition of the Philippines' sovereignty and sovereign rights. This inherently clashes with China's own position for joint exploration and development, which holds primarily that sovereignty of the subject resources belongs to China.[103]

This accounts for the delay in the two countries' efforts to formulate a mutually acceptable joint exploration and development agreement for petroleum resources. After the Duterte-Xi bilateral meeting in April 2018 where the two leaders approved the start of negotiations, Foreign Secretary Cayetano promised a deal that complied with the Philippine Constitution but acceptable to China and the Chinese leadership.[104] Anything short of compliance with UNCLOS and the Constitution would be unacceptable for the Philippines, likewise for China and its own constitution and laws.[105] Cayetano also raised expectations that the deal would be "equal to or better than Malampaya,"[106] referring to the country's only offshore natural gas production platform that has been operating since 2001, and that it would be the means to implement the country's rights under UNCLOS.[107]

In reality, this sets a very high bar that could prove insurmountable for China. The Malampaya contract is based on the standard service contract issued by the Philippines that requires the service contractor to bear all of the risks and costs of exploration and development, divides the profit oil or proceeds 60 percent in favor of the Philippines and 40 percent for the contractor, and subjects the contractor to the full control and supervision of the State.[108] These conditions are based on the most substantial minimum requirements of the 1987 Constitution, particularly the cost-benefit sharing formula.[109] It is quite difficult to imagine Cayetano's "better deal" which means an arrangement wherein China bears all the risks and costs, parts with an even smaller share in profits, and subsumes itself to Philippine control and supervision. This seems to imply an over-optimistic exaggeration of the prospects of a deal.

According to Duterte, however, it was President Xi Jinping who offered the sharing formula, in exchange for setting aside the award in the South China Sea Arbitration:

> Set aside the arbitral ruling. Set aside your claim. Then allow everybody connected with the Chinese companies. They want to explore and if there is something, they said, we would be gracious enough to give you 60%, they will only get 40%. That is the promise of Xi Jinping.[110]

Duterte thus finds a joint exploration and development deal acceptable for as long as the Philippines gets a bigger share of the benefits.[111] But there is no record of any such offer having been made, whether formally or informally, and it is unlikely that China would propose such conditions that expressly acknowledges one of the most important requirements of the Constitution and petroleum laws of the Philippines, without regard to China's own laws.

In November 2018, it was thought that significant progress was achieved through the signing of a Memorandum of Understanding on Cooperation in Oil and Gas Development (MOU) in Manila.[112] But as described by Foreign Secretary Locsin, the MOU is actually only "an agreement to agree" on specific joint exploration or development projects.[113] Indeed, the principal obligation of the parties is actually "to negotiate on an accelerated basis arrangements to facilitate oil and gas exploration and exploitation in relevant maritime areas."[114] The MOU did not itself provide for any substantive legal framework as previously intended and announced, and did not even lay the needed basis for prospective joint ventures between the Philippines and China. At best, it formalized an intention to engage in more negotiations within a soft deadline of 12 months.[115] The absence of any legally binding commitment is particularly stressed, by stating that the MOU "does not create rights or obligations under international or domestic law"[116] and that all agreements made and activities undertaken in accordance with the MOU are "without prejudice to the respective legal positions of both governments."[117]

As of this writing, more than 12 months have passed but the parties have only been able to formally organize the ministerial-level Joint Committee.[118] In October 2019, the Committee met for the first time in Beijing, and issued a statement that it held "a candid, in-depth and friendly exchange on cooperation arrangements" and "agreed to further push forward communication and coordination on oil and gas development."[119] In short, it was unable to reach an agreement on anything more than its own membership. Two months later, it was confirmed that the committee was at an impasse on how to move forward from the MOU, likely due to the still-unresolved question of what legal framework will govern.[120] The Philippine Senate is also closely observing the progress and substance of the talks because as an international agreement, any deal must necessarily pass through the Senate for concurrence. This could be avoided if China simply came in as a service contractor through the China National Offshore Oil Corporation (CNOOC),[121] which most are open to and find more acceptable; but this is precisely unacceptable to China because it would be tantamount to an abandonment of its own claims and positions.

The reported deadlock comes as no surprise, given the position that the Duterte Administration has publicly started with. Philippine Ambassador to China Santiago Sta. Romana fully expected "protracted or at least intense negotiations,"[122] and it is indeed unlikely to be resolved sooner rather than later. In the meantime, however, the Philippines is foregoing offshore petroleum exploration in the West Philippine Sea despite mounting calls to lift the moratorium on all offshore service contracts in that region.[123] It is clearly more to China's advantage to prolong negotiations because it achieves its objective of not having to confront Philippine petroleum exploration in the South China Sea, a potentially crisis-inducing event it would rather avoid. If China were to act against the Philippines in the same way as it has done with Vietnam and Malaysia recently, China risks forcing the Duterte Administration, which indeed has been extremely accommodating to its demands and positions in these disputes, into an increasingly indefensible, unpopular, and potentially destabilizing political position at home. However, for as long as the Philippines is unable to move ahead with petroleum exploration on its own, it also adds to the Filipino public's resentment that good relations with China have not resulted in any benefits.

Duterte and the ASEAN-China Code of Conduct

As part of its diplomacy to entice China to the negotiating table, the Duterte Administration dropped all discussion and advocacy of the South China Sea Arbitration Award from its agenda with ASEAN. Duterte had decided that silence about the arbitration in international forums was the only means by which he could initiate talks with China. Prior to his first ASEAN Summit in September 2017, he said that he deliberately did not want to make "noise" that could endanger future bilateral talks with China.[124] Besides, as far as he was concerned, the Philippines' victory did not concern the other ASEAN members.[125] For the duration of the Philippines' tenure as ASEAN Chair, the government never raised the Award for discussion as it re-cultivated ties, and instead redirected attention to the moribund Code of Conduct negotiations.

The process was jump-started by first softening the Philippines' official stance, shifting advocacy from a binding instrument to a non-binding one, and stopping the push for binding dispute settlement provisions.[126] Upon taking over as Coordinator of the ASEAN-China Dialogue after stepping down as ASEAN Chair,[127] the Philippines then took on the responsibility of shepherding the negotiations for the Code of Conduct after Singapore produced a "Single Draft Negotiating Text" (SDNT) composed of many unfiltered proposed provisions which represented the different dialogue members' ideas of what could be included in the Code. Despite an initial expression of optimism that the Code could be finished by 2021 during the Philippines' chairmanship,[128] progress has been rather slow. One reason is that the 11 parties are able to meet only twice a year; another is the very diverse views, interests, and negotiating strategies of the parties. These were difficult enough without the consensus-based decision-making that is the hallmark of ASEAN.

A copy of the SDNT leaked just prior to the transfer of chairmanship, and it immediately appeared that there was a very wide variance in interests that make negotiations difficult.[129] The Philippines has been extremely careful to afterward not allow the evolving document to be leaked again, and as of this writing, neither the form nor any part of the content of the evolving draft have been released to any outsider to the process. What is known, however, is that Vietnam has presented a number of surely controversial proposals touching on geographic scope, the legal nature of the document, the role of external or non-regional parties, and binding dispute settlement mechanisms.[130] The tough negotiation stance was brought about another maritime confrontation between Vietnam and China over the former's petroleum exploration on Vanguard Bank.[131] By the end of 2019, Vietnam proposed additional texts, and suggested that the four difficult issues above be settled first before talks could proceed on the numerous draft provisions yet to be agreed upon. Settlement of these contentious issues would surely be difficult, and it is unlikely that consensus could be reached on the document in the few remaining meetings until 2021.

Duterte and public opinion

Amidst all these considerations it should not be forgotten that Duterte's preference for China is decidedly a minority view in the Philippines. Despite initial upticks in Duterte's first year in office, public trust in China dropped steeply and overall trended downward ever since; it remains the lowest overall among the Philippines' best-known external partners.[132] By the last quarter of 2019, China had an extremely negative trust rating of −33, compared with the high positive +72 for the US, +37 for Australia, and +35 for Japan.[133]

In his four years in office, public discourse and criticism have steadily increased over the effects of Duterte's policy; whereas 2016–2017 the attention was focused on the West Philippine Sea, by 2018–2019 there was a subtle shift toward domestic impacts such as China's unfulfilled infrastructure promises, sufferings of poor fishermen, and online gambling operations. Interest in the maritime disputes is also quite high; in 2018, polls showed that 73 percent of Filipinos wanted the government to assert the award,[134] but by 2019, the number in favor of this increased to 87 percent.[135]

Duterte's favor for China thus runs against the grain of the broader public opinion, and his foreign policy decisions are constant sources of debate among members of the Cabinet and the government at large. These debates were originally dominated by his economic managers, who held to the idea of China as the economic powerhouse of the future; but the years since have eroded some of the luster and caused even some of those members to doubt China's ability to deliver on its promises.

Due to the absence of very tangible and concrete returns from his avowed preference for China, Duterte's policy is constantly subject to and vulnerable to public criticism. In this light, Duterte's continued accommodation of China and major political concessions on the South China Sea remain a source of growing skepticism and resistance. Unless something changes drastically, Duterte will find it harder and harder to placate the electorate on this issue until the end of his term, and his successor will certainly face even bigger challenges to maintain the same level of trust and confidence similar to what he has demonstrated.

Prospects for the post-Duterte Administration

There is much more information that can be unpacked in the Duterte Administration's foreign policy, but which would take twice as long to just begin writing about. But the above provides sufficient materials for establishing a basic framework of understanding the past four years and what accounts for the great differences between Aquino and Duterte's foreign policy on the South China Sea. Comparing the outlines of Duterte's record with the three-tracked approach of the Aquino Administration at the end of its term reveals opposite directions. On the political track, Duterte moved away from advocating greater and stronger ASEAN involvement in the South China Sea disputes and limiting the Philippine focus to the negotiations of the Code of Conduct, but with a decidedly lower bar by no longer requiring a legally binding effect and dispute settlement provisions. Although the same regard is held for UNCLOS and international law in general, the South China Sea Arbitration Award does not form part of the Philippine agenda in ASEAN and instead is shunted for later bilateral discussions with China. The diplomatic track which was frozen solid by the arbitration proceedings was defrosted and fast-tracked by foregoing and compartmentalizing public discussion of the arbitration award, and instead concentrating on re-developing economic ties and inviting financial and infrastructure investments. The legal track was all but ignored and held in limbo, as the Duterte Administration saw no point in even attempting to get China to legally comply with the arbitration award in the absence of superior force on its side.

The conceptual elements that underpin Duterte's decisions and actions create a foreign policy with China that may be characterized as principally transactional, high-risk, locally centered, and unsustainable over a long term. Simply stated, Duterte's foreign policy seeks to establish a patron-client relationship between China and the Philippines, but without broader support and coordinated action from the public at large, this effort is likely to fail in the short time that he is in power.

The overall transactional nature is demonstrated by how he frames his need to get China to underwrite his over-ambitious infrastructure program in exchange for not pressing the maritime and territorial disputes in the South China Sea as publicly and provocatively as his predecessor. He has accommodated China's every wish on the maritime disputes, from not discussing it in multi-lateral forums to negotiating joint exploration and development of petroleum resources. Duterte publicly gives China his ear and utmost priority in the hopes that China will reciprocate with much-needed finances and development assistance. However, these have yet to materialize, and the government has been forced to shift from large-scale to smaller-scale infrastructure targets and diversify its funding sources.

Thus, Duterte's approach is fraught with very high risks, with the potential of too little returns in exchange for very big significant concessions. As it is, Filipinos have been informed that Duterte has allowed China to fish, jointly explore and develop petroleum resources, and militarily use the West Philippine Sea without hindrance, but there is still no satisfactory answer to the question of what the Philippines has gotten out of the relationship in exchange. Instead, what Filipinos have witnessed are the destruction of coral resources, the influx of gambling operations and associated crimes, and frequent reminders of the imaginary threat of war from China.

Meanwhile, time is running out for Duterte and China to demonstrate tangible fruits of renewed friendship and cooperation. Certain flagship projects such as the Code of Conduct and joint exploration and development of petroleum resources seem destined to extend well beyond Duterte's term in office. Despite the public displays of amity to exhibit stable and positive relations, the maritime and territorial disputes between the Philippines and China remain awash in frictions and perturbations just simmering beneath the surface.

Despite being "foreign policy," Duterte's actions with respect to the South China Sea, as well as other international issues, in truth are primarily motivated by domestic and personal concerns. "Raising the arbitration" with President Xi in 2019 is one good example, where he formally brought it up on the agenda but quickly moved on after being rebuffed. The renewal and cultivation of ties have only incidental geopolitical repercussions; what matters to Duterte is whether he can secure the financial and investments he needs to support his signature projects. Even the approach to joint exploration and development is premised on being able to essentially pass on the costs and yet still receive the lion's share of benefits. There is actually a very little large-scale geopolitical strategy in Duterte's actions and decisions; the geopolitical ramifications are actually side effects of his local political and economic objectives.

Thus, it cannot be said that Duterte's foreign policy on the South China Sea, and the changes he has introduced during his term, is permanent and enduring. Duterte himself lays the seeds for dissatisfaction by ironically painting China in an unflattering light, as a country that threatens a war that the Philippines cannot win or a wellspring of unlimited infrastructure and financing assistance, neither of which is particularly true nor endearing. This is a problem with his populist style of leadership, which unfortunately often resorts to intimidation and fear, together with a healthy dose of an exaggeration, as principal means of persuasion. Having spent decades as a tough no-nonsense mayor adept in local politics, he sees his local milieu reflected in the international arena and therefore resorts to the same practices and techniques to achieve his objectives. Duterte's foreign policy basically mirrors his personality-oriented patronage politics and the clientelism embedded in his political culture, writ large on the international stage.

Notes

1 Aileen SP Baviera and Jay L Batongbacal, *The West Philippine Sea: The Territorial and Maritime Jurisdiction Disputes from a FIlipino Perspective, A Primer* (Asian Center and Institute for Maritime Affairs & Law of the Sea 2015) 19 <https://ac.upd.edu.ph/index.php/resources/books-and-monographs/106-philippine-foreign-policy-books/1352-the-west-philippine-sea-the-territorial-and-maritime-jurisdiction-disputes-from-a-filipino-perspective>.

2 'Declaration of the Conduct of the Parties in the South China Sea' (*ASEAN*, 4 November 2002) <https://asean.org/?static_post=declaration-on-the-conduct-of-parties-in-the-south-china-sea-2> accessed 5 June 2020.

3 'Joint Statement of the People's Republic of China and the Republic of the Philippines' (*Embassy of the People's Republic of China in the Philippines*, 28 April 2005) <http://ph.china-embassy.org/eng/zfgx/zzgx/t199778.htm> accessed 5 June 2020.

4 'Oil Companies of China, the Philippines and Vietnam Signed Agreement on South China Sea Cooperation' (*Embassy of the People's Republic of China in the Philippines*, 15 March 2005) <http://ph.china-embassy.org/eng/zt/nhwt/t187333.htm> accessed 29 May 2020.

5 Dante Pastrana, 'Philippine President Accused of "Treason" over Spratlys Deal with China – World Socialist Web Site' (*World Socialist Web Site*, 29 March 2008) <https://www.wsws.org/en/articles/2008/03/phil-m29.html> accessed 29 May 2020; Miriam Grace Go, 'A Policy of Betrayal (First of Three Parts)' (*ABS-CBN News*, 14 March 2008) <https://news.abs-cbn.com/special-report/03/14/08/policy-betrayal-first-three-parts> accessed 29 May 2020.

6 'Republic Act No. 9522 (2009). An Act to Amend Certain Provisions of Republic Act No. 3046, as Amended by Republic Act No. 5446, to Define the Archipelagic Baselines of the Philippines, and for Other Purposes' (*Official Gazette of the Republic of the Philippines*, 10 March 2009) <https://www.officialgazette.gov.ph/2009/03/10/republic-act-no-9522/> accessed 29 May 2020.

7 BBC News, 'Hong Kong Hostages Die in Manila Bus Siege' (*BBC News*, 23 August 2010) <https://www.bbc.com/news/world-asia-pacific-11055015> accessed 29 May 2020.

8 'Aquino Honors Mother's Ancestors in East China' (*China Daily*, 4 September 2011) <https://www.chinadaily.com.cn/china/2011-09/04/content_13613749.htm> accessed 5 June 2020; Norman Bordadora, 'Aquino Visits Roots in Chinese Village | Global News' (3 September 2011) <https://globalnation.inquirer.net/11499/aquino-visits-roots-in-chinese-village> accessed 5 June 2020.

9 *Award, PCA Case No 2013–19 In the Matter of the South China Sea Arbitration before an Arbitral Tribunal Constituted Under Annex VII to the 1982 United Nations Convention on the Law of the Sea between The Republic of the Philippines and The People's Republic of China* [2016] Arbitral Tribunal under UNCLOS Annex VII PCA Case No. 2013–19, 2016 Perm Court Arbitr., para. 656–657 at 262–263. See also Ian Storey, 'China and the Philippines: Implications of the Reed Bank Incident' (*The Jamestown Foundation: China Brief*, 6 May 2011) <https://jamestown.org/program/china-and-the-philippines-implications-of-the-reed-bank-incident/> accessed 29 May 2020.

10 *Award, South China Sea Arbitration* (n 9)., para. 661–667 at 266–268.

11 Kristine De Guzman, 'Malampaya: When the Gas Runs Out Will Luzon Have Power?' (*CNN Philippines*, 26 June 2015) <https://cnnphilippines.com/news/2015/06/26/Malampaya-When-the-gas-runs-out-will-Luzon-have-power.html> accessed 5 June 2020; Felix Chang, 'Running Out of Gas: Philippine Energy Security and the South China Sea - Foreign Policy Research Institute' (*https://www.fpri.org/*, 6 September 2019) <https://www.fpri.org/article/2019/09/running-out-of-gas-philippine-energy-security-and-the-south-china-sea/> accessed 5 June 2020.

12 Christine O Avendaño, 'President Aquino: Philippines to Protect "What's Ours" | Inquirer News' (*Philippine Daily Inquirer*, 26 July 2011) <https://newsinfo.inquirer.net/30063/president-aquino-philippines-to-protect-%E2%80%98what%E2%80%99s-ours%E2%80%99> accessed 2 June 2020. Recto Avenue is an old and well-known street in Manila that used to be its commercial center.

13 Michael Green and others, 'Case 3: Scarborough Shoal Standoff (2012)', *Countering Coercion in Maritime Asia* (Rowman and Littlefeld 2017) <https://csis-prod.s3.amazonaws.com/s3fs-public/170530_Countering_Coercion_Study_Scarborough.pdf?vVGpl95cxLnH.c5yArfuN-PLHnu5rI4xT> accessed 29 May 2020.

14 Rappler.com, '"Rules-Based" Approach to Resolve Dispute with China: Del Rosario' (*Rappler.com*, 27 September 2012) <http://www.rappler.com/nation/13179-rules-based-to-resolve-dispute-with-china-del-rosario> accessed 29 May 2020.

15 BBC News, 'Asean Nations Fail to Reach Agreement on South China Sea' (*BBC News*, 13 July 2012) <https://www.bbc.com/news/world-asia-18825148> accessed 29 May 2020.

16 Irwin Loy, 'South China Sea Dispute Flares at ASEAN Summit' (*Voice of America*, 19 November 2012) <https://www.voanews.com/east-asia-pacific/south-china-sea-dispute-flares-asean-summit> accessed 29 May 2020; Carlyle Thayer, 'New Commitment to a Code of Conduct in the South China Sea?' (*The National Bureau of Asian Research*, 9 October 2013) <https://www.nbr.org/publication/new-commitment-to-a-code-of-conduct-in-the-south-china-sea/> accessed 29 May 2020.

17 *Judgment Territorial and Maritime Dispute (Nicaragua v Colombia)* (2012) 2012 ICJ Rep 624 (International Court of Justice).

18 Department of Foreign Affairs, 'Statement: The Secretary of Foreign Affairs on the UNCLOS Arbitral Proceedings against China, January 22, 2013 | GOVPH' (*Official Gazette of the Republic of the Philippines*, 22 January 2013) <https://www.officialgazette.gov.ph/2013/01/22/statement-the-secretary-of-foreign-affairs-on-the-unclos-arbitral-proceedings-against-china-january-22-2013/> accessed 5 June 2020.

19 *Award, South China Sea Arbitration* (n 9).

20 *Bayan v Executive Secretary* [2000] Supreme Court of the Philippines G.R No. 138570.

21 Rappler.com, 'The 1st Duterte Cabinet Meeting' (*Rappler*, 30 June 2016) <http://www.rappler.com/nation/138194-1st-duterte-cabinet-meeting> accessed 6 June 2020.

22 ABS-CBN News, 'Duterte to Seek "Soft Landing" with China after Dispute Ruling | ABS-CBN News' (*ABS-CBN News*, 30 June 2016) <https://news.abs-cbn.com/focus/06/30/16/duterte-to-seek-soft-landing-with-china-after-dispute-ruling> accessed 5 June 2020.

23 *Award, South China Sea Arbitration* (n 9).

24 Paterno Esmaquel, 'PH-China Ruling: Why Yasay Wasn't Smiling' (*Rappler.com*, 13 July 2016) <http://www.rappler.com/newsbreak/inside-track/139620-yasay-somber-statement-philippines-china-ruling> accessed 5 June 2020.

25 'Statement of the Ministry of Foreign Affairs of the People's Republic of China on the Award of 12 July 2016 of the Arbitral Tribunal in the South China Sea Arbitration Established at the Request of the Republic of the Philippines' <https://www.fmprc.gov.cn/nanhai/eng/snhwtlcwj_1/t1379492.htm> accessed 5 June 2020.

26 Paterno Esmaquel, 'Yasay Flip-Flops on Seeking ASEAN Support for Hague Ruling' (*Rappler.com*, 27 July 2016) <http://www.rappler.com/nation/141109-philippines-yasay-asean-support-hague-ruling-china> accessed 5 June 2020; Rappler.com, 'Cambodia: Yasay Dropped Bid for ASEAN to Cite Hague Ruling' (*Rappler.com*, 27 July 2016) <http://www.rappler.com/nation/141131-cambodia-philippines-yasay-asean-hague-ruling> accessed 5 June 2020.

27 Paterno Esmaquel, 'No Mention of Hague Ruling in ASEAN Chairman's Statement' (*Rappler.com*, 7 September 2016) <http://www.rappler.com/world/regions/asia-pacific/145523-asean-statement-hague-ruling-south-china-sea> accessed 29 May 2020.

28 Kristin Huang and Liu Zhen, 'Ramos the Icebreaker: Former Philippine President Heads to Hong Kong to Test China Waters' (*South China Morning Post*, 8 August 2016) <https://www.scmp.com/news/china/diplomacy-defence/article/2000842/former-philippines-president-fidel-ramos-heads-beijing> accessed 29 May 2020; Bong Miquibas, 'Fidel Ramos: Duterte's Icebreaker in South China Sea Row' (*South China Morning Post*, 12 August 2016) <https://www.scmp.com/week-asia/politics/article/2002984/fidel-ramos-dutertes-ice-breaker-south-china-sea-row> accessed 29 May 2020.

29 Kristin Huang and Catherine Wong, 'China-Philippines Fishing Deal "May Help Calm Troubled South China Sea Waters"' (*South China Morning Post*, 12 August 2016) <https://www.scmp.com/news/china/diplomacy-defence/article/2003044/china-philippines-fishing-deal-may-help-calm-troubled> accessed 29 May 2020; Miquibas (n 28).

30 Ben Blanchard, 'Duterte Aligns Philippines with China, Says U.S. Has Lost' (*Reuters*, 20 October 2016) <https://www.reuters.com/article/us-china-philippines-idUSKCN12K0AS> accessed 29 May 2020.

31 Ibid.

32 Andreo Calonzo and Cecilia Yap, 'China Visit Helps Duterte Reap Funding Deals Worth $24 Billion - Bloomberg' (*Bloomberg*, 21 October 2018) <https://www.bloomberg.com/news/articles/2016-10-21/china-visit-helps-duterte-reap-funding-deals-worth-24-billion> accessed 2 June 2020.

33 Amy R Remo, 'Itemized List of PH Projects Covered by China's $15-B Investment Pledges to Duterte' (*Philippine Daily Inquirer*, 22 October 2016) <https://business.inquirer.net/217269/itemized-list-ph-projects-covered-chinas-15-b-investment-pledges-duterte> accessed 2 June 2020.

34 ASEAN Briefing, 'Philippines and China Sign Six Agreements' (*ASEAN Business News*, 9 December 2019) <https://www.aseanbriefing.com/news/philippines-and-china-sign-six-agreements/> accessed 2 June 2020.; ibid.; Out-Law News, 'China and Philippines Sign Infrastructure Loan Agreements' (*Pinsent Masons*, 12 September 2019) <https://www.pinsentmasons.com/out-law/news/china-and-philippines-sign-infrastructure-loan-agreements> accessed 2 June 2020.; IBON Media & Communications, 'Duterte Selling Out Sovereignty for Chinese Funding - IBON' (*IBON Foundation*, 20 June 2019) <https://www.ibon.org/duterte-selling-out-sovereignty-for-chinese-funding-ibon/> accessed 2 June 2020.

35 Ralf Rivas, 'Expensive, Too Much Work: Duterte's Team Rethinks Infra Projects' (*Rappler.com*, 23 October 2019) <http://www.rappler.com/business/243206-duterte-team-rethink-infrastructure-projects> accessed 6 June 2020.

36 Raissa Robles, 'China Promised Duterte US$9 Billion. He's Had Less than US$1 Billion. Why?' (*South China Morning Post*, 26 October 2019) <https://www.scmp.com/week-asia/politics/article/3034666/china-promised-duterte-us9-billion-infrastructure-hes-had-only> accessed 2 June 2020.; Karen Lema and Martin Petty, 'Two Years after Philippines' Pivot, Duterte Still Waiting on China Dividend' (*Reuters*, 19 November 2018) <https://www.reuters.com/article/us-philippines-china-analysis-idUSKCN1NN0UO> accessed 2 June 2020.; Richard Javad Heydarian, 'Duterte Still Waiting for China's Ballyhooed Bonanza' (*Asia Times*, 30 September 2019) <https://asiatimes.com/2019/09/duterte-still-waiting-for-chinas-ballyhooed-bonanza/> accessed 2 June 2020.

37 JC Punongbayan, 'The Pipe Dream That Is Build, Build, Build' (*Rappler.com*, 16 August 2018) <http://www.rappler.com/thought-leaders/236177-analysis-pipe-dream-build-build-build-program> accessed 2 June 2020.

38 Ben De Vera, 'China "Slow" to Provide Loans for Duterte's "Build, Build, Build" — Pernia' (*Philippine Daily Inquirer*, 3 February 2020) <https://business.inquirer.net/289590/china-slow-to-provide-loans-for-dutertes-build-build-build-pernia> accessed 2 June 2020.

39 East Asia Forum, 'Skepticism of Duterte's Flirting with Beijing Mounts' (*AEC News Today*, 9 March 2019) <https://aecnewstoday.com/2019/scepticism-of-dutertes-flirting-with-beijing-mounts/> accessed 2 June 2020.

40 Panos Mourdoukoukas, 'Japan, Not China, Is The Biggest Investor In Southeast Asia's Infrastructure' (*Forbes*, 28 June 2019) <https://www.forbes.com/sites/panosmourdoukoutas/2019/06/26/japan-beats-china-in-the-philippines-singapore-and-vietnam/#741364f739d8> accessed 2 June 2020; Michelle Jamrisko, 'China No Match for Japan in Southeast Asia Infrastructure Race - Bloomberg' (*Bloomberg*, 23 June 2019) <https://www.bloomberg.com/news/articles/2019-06-23/china-no-match-for-japan-in-southeast-asia-infrastructure-race> accessed 2 June 2020.; De Vera (n 38).

41 Ben Krtiz, 'PH's POGO Problem – The Manila Times' (*Manila Times*, 13 August 2019) <https://www.manilatimes.net/2019/08/13/business/columnists-business/phs-pogo-problem/599500/> accessed 6 June 2020; Iris Gonzales, 'Special Report: POGOs: The Good and the Bad' (*Philippine Star*, 18 June 2019) <https://www.philstar.com/business/2019/06/18/1927276/special-report-pogos-good-and-bad> accessed 6 June 2020; Aika Rey, 'POGOs Linked to Crimes: Forged PH Passports, Money-Laundering, Sex Trafficking' (*Rappler.com*, 4 March 2020) <http://www.rappler.com/nation/253332-senators-link-pogos-to-crimes> accessed 6 June 2020; Geronimo Sy, 'The Non-Economic Consequences of POGO | BusinessWorld' (*BusinessWorld*, 4 October 2019) <https://www.bworldonline.com/the-non-economic-consequences-of-pogo/> accessed 6 June 2020; Dahrel Placido, 'Offshore Gaming Has "Negative" Impact on PH, Says Sen. Villanueva' (*ABS-CBN News*, 21 July 2019) <https://news.abs-cbn.com/news/07/31/19/offshore-gaming-has-negative-impact-on-ph-says-sen-villanueva> accessed 6 June 2020.

42 'Transcript of the Speech of President Rodrigo Roa Duterte at the 64th Araw Ng Hagonoy Celebration. Municipal Gymnaisum, Hagonoy, Davao Del Sur. 05 July 2017.' (2017).

43 Manuel Mogato, 'Duterte Says China's Xi Threatened War If Philippines Drills for Oil' (*Reuters*, 19 May 2017) <https://www.reuters.com/article/us-southchinasea-philippines-china-idUSKCN18F1DJ> accessed 31 May 2020.

44 *Award, South China Sea Arbitration* (n 9).

45 Nestor Corrales, 'Duterte Says He'll "Set aside" Arbitral Ruling on South China Sea' (17 December 2016) <https://globalnation.inquirer.net/150814/duterte-says-hell-set-aside-arbitral-ruling-on-south-china-sea> accessed 2 June 2020.

46 Arianne Merez, 'In Due Time? Duterte Says to Insist Rights in West PH Sea When China Drills for Oil' (*ABS-CBN News*, 22 July 2019) <https://news.abs-cbn.com/news/07/22/19/in-due-time-duterte-says-to-insist-rights-in-west-ph-sea-when-china-drills-for-oil> accessed 1 June 2020.

47 Luis Liwanag and Jojo Rinoza, 'In Speech to Congress, Philippine Leader Defends Actions Toward China' (*BenarNews*, 22 July 2019) <https://www.benarnews.org/english/news/philippine/nation-speech-07222019135406.html> accessed 1 June 2020.

48 Rambo Talabong, Sofia Tomacruz and Leanne Jazul, 'In Their Own Words: The Fishermen of Gem-Ver' (*Rappler.com*, 10 July 2019) <https://www.rappler.com/newsbreak/profiles/234971-gem-ver-fishermen> accessed 4 June 2020.

49 Bernadette D Nicolas, 'Duterte Raises Arbitral Ruling on WPS, but Xi Says China Still Won't Heed It' (*BusinessMirror*, 30 August 2019) <https://businessmirror.com.ph/2019/08/30/duterte-raises-arbitral-ruling-on-wps-but-xi-says-china-still-wont-heed-it/> accessed 6 June 2020.

50 Pia Ranada, 'Xi Refuses to Recognize Hague Ruling after Duterte Brings It Up' (*Rappler.com*, 30 August 2019) <http://www.rappler.com/nation/238890-xi-refuses-recognize-hague-ruling-after-duterte-brings-it-up> accessed 6 June 2020.

51 Pia Ranada, '6 Agreements Signed during Duterte-Xi August 29 Meeting' (*Rappler.com*, 30 August 2019) <http://www.rappler.com/nation/238881-list-agreements-signed-duterte-xi-meeting-august-29-2019> accessed 6 June 2020.

52 Commission on the Limits of the Continental Shelf, 'Continental Shelf - Submission by Malaysia' (*Commission on the Limits of the Continental Shelf*, 5 March 2020) <https://www.un.org/Depts/los/clcs_new/submissions_files/submission_mys_12_12_2019.html> accessed 7 June 2020.

53 Malaysia, 'Malaysia Partial Submission to the Commission on the Limits of the Continental Shelf Pursuant to Article 76, Paragraph 8 of the United Nations Convention on the Law of the Sea 1982 in the South China Sea. Part I: Executive Summary' <https://www.un.org/Depts/los/clcs_new/submissions_files/mys85_2019/20171128_MYS_ES_DOC_001_secured.pdf> accessed 7 June 2020.

54 Permanent Mission of the People's Republic of China to the United Nations, 'Note Verbale CML 14/2019, Dated 12 December 2019.' <https://www.un.org/Depts/los/clcs_new/submissions_files/mys85_2019/CML_14_2019_E.pdf> accessed 7 June 2020.

55 Permanent Mission of the Republic of the Philippines to the United Nations, 'Note Verbale No. 000192-2020' <https://www.un.org/Depts/los/clcs_new/submissions_files/mys_12_12_2019/2020_03_06_PHL_NV_UN_002.pdf> accessed 7 June 2020.

56 Permanent Mission of the Republic of the Philippines to the United Nations, 'Note Verbale No. 000191-2020.' <https://www.un.org/Depts/los/clcs_new/submissions_files/mys_12_12_2019/2020_03_06_PHL_NV_UN_001.pdf> accessed 7 June 2020.

57 See documents at Commission on the Limits of the Continental Shelf (n 52).

58 'Transcript of the Speech of President Rodrigo Roa Duterte at the 38th Convention of the Philippine Association of Water Districts. SMX Convention Center, SM Lanang Premier, Davao City' (2017) Speech <https://www.youtube.com/watch?v=CdScWhrOO-0>.

59 Mogato (n 43).; Julie M Aurelio, 'Duterte Recalls China Warning If PH Explores Sea for Oil' <https://globalnation.inquirer.net/177172/duterte-recalls-china-warning-if-ph-explores-sea-for-oil> accessed 1 June 2020.

60 'Transcript of the Press Conference of President Rodrigo Roa Duterte. Ahfat Seafood Plaza 1, Victoria Plaza Compound, Bajada, Davao City. 24 August 2016.' (2016).

61 Bloomberg, '"China Is Our Friend," Duterte Says amid South China Sea Tensions' (*South China Morning Post*, 3 April 2019) <https://www.scmp.com/news/asia/southeast-asia/article/3004556/philippine-president-rodrigo-duterte-calls-china-friend> accessed 31 May 2020.

62 Nestor Corrales, 'Duterte: China Can Fish in Philippines' EEZ' (*Philippine Daily Inquirer*, 26 June 2019) <https://globalnation.inquirer.net/177040/duterte-china-can-fish-in-philippines-eez> accessed 7 June 2020.

63 The Armed Forces' traditional adversaries have mostly been internal, comprised of the Communist rebellion, Islamic secessionism, and military adventurism. With all three having been defeated or neutralized, it has just turned toward enhancing its expected role of external defense, which currently faces two major threats: violent extremism in the South and potential loss of territory or jurisdiction in the West Philippine Sea.

64 Historically, the Armed Forces of the Philippines.

65 Leslie Advincula-Lopez, 'What Now? AFP Modernization in the Time of Digong Duterte' (*Rappler*, 6 August 2016) <http://www.rappler.com/thought-leaders/142032-afp-modernization-duterte-administration> accessed 5 June 2020.; Carmela Fonbuena, 'Duterte's Pivot to China Won't Be Easy for Americanized AFP' (*Rappler.com*, 30 September 2016) <https://www.rappler.com/newsbreak/in-depth/147783-duterte-pivot-china-military-war-games> accessed 5 June 2020.

66 Ted Regencia, 'Duterte to US Forces: Get out of Southern Philippines | News | Al Jazeera' (*Al Jazeera*, 13 September 2016) <https://www.aljazeera.com/news/2016/09/duterte-forces-southern-philippines-160913003704576.html> accessed 5 June 2020; Pia Ranada, 'Duterte Wants VFA Scrapped, But Will "Wait" for Trump' (*Rappler.com*, 17 December 2016) <http://www.rappler.com/nation/155785-duterte-visiting-forces-agreement-trump> accessed 5 June 2020.

67 IPD Forum, 'Lessons From Marawi' (*Indo-Pacific Defense Forum*, 23 March 2020) <https://ipdefenseforum.com/lessons-from-marawi/> accessed 4 June 2020; Neil Jerome Morales and Simon Lewis, 'U.S. Joins Battle as Philippines Takes Losses in Besieged City' (*Reuters*, 10 June 2017) <https://www.reuters.com/article/us-philippines-militants/u-s-joins-battle-as-philippines-takes-losses-in-besieged-city-idUSKBN19107I> accessed 4 June 2020.

68 Seth Robson, 'Philippine Troops Credit US Intel, Training for Helping Them Beat ISIS in Marawi' (*Stars and Stripes*, 9 November 2017) <https://www.stripes.com/news/pacific/philippine-troops-credit-us-intel-training-for-helping-them-beat-isis-in-marawi-1.496965> accessed 4 June 2020.

69 Allan Nawal, 'Duterte: I Did Not Know of US Help in Marawi Conflict Beforehand' <https://globalnation.inquirer.net/157871/duterte-not-know-us-help-marawi-conflict-beforehand> accessed 4 June 2020.

70 Carmela Fonbuena, 'Duterte on U.S. Aid in Marawi: "Nagpapasalamat Na Rin Ako"' (*Rappler*) <http://www.rappler.com/nation/172633-philippines-duterte-united-states-aid-marawi-city> accessed 4 June 2020.

71 Carmela Fonbuena, 'PH Aborts Construction on Pag-Asa Sandbar after China Protest' (*Rappler.com*, 8 November 2017) <http://www.rappler.com/nation/187690-ph-china-pagasa-standoff-lorenzana> accessed 5 June 2020.

72 Frances Mangosing, 'Exclusive: New Photos Show China Is Nearly Done with Its Militarization of South China Sea' (*Philippine Daily Inquirer*, 5 February 2018) <https://www.inquirer.net/specials/exclusive-china-militarization-south-china-sea> accessed 3 June 2020.

73 Patricia Lourdes Viray, 'Philippines, China Draw "Red Lines" in South China Sea Dispute' (*Philippine Star*, 29 May 2018) <https://www.philstar.com/headlines/2018/05/29/1819745/philippines-china-draw-red-lines-south-china-sea-dispute> accessed 2 June 2020.

74 Paterno Esmaquel, 'Duterte Vows to Defend West Philippine Sea in SONA 2018' (*Rappler.com*, 23 July 2018) <http://www.rappler.com/nation/208019-duterte-vows-defend-west-philippine-sea-sona-2018> accessed 4 June 2020.

75 Pia Ranada, 'Duterte Hopes Beijing Can "Temper" Warnings in South China Sea' (*Rappler*) <http://www.rappler.com/nation/209572-duterte-hopes-beijing-temper-south-china-sea-warnings> accessed 4 June 2020.

76 Paterno Esmaquel, 'After Duterte Tirade, China Asserts Right to Warn Planes' (*Rappler.com*, 16 August 2018) <http://www.rappler.com/nation/209726-china-rejects-duterte-criticisms-plane-warnings-west-philippine-sea> accessed 4 June 2020.

77 Paterno Esmaquel, 'China Top Diplomat to Visit PH for Joint Exploration Talks' (*Rappler.com*, 12 September 2018) <http://www.rappler.com/nation/211816-chinese-foreign-minister-wang-yi-philippine-visit-september-2018> accessed 4 June 2020.

78 Asia Maritime Transparency Initiative, 'Philippines Launches Spratly Runway Repairs' (*Asia Maritime Transparency Initiative*, 25 May 2018) <https://amti.csis.org/philippines-launches-spratly-repairs/> accessed 4 June 2020.

79 Frances Mangosing, 'Chinese Sea Militia Swarms around Pag-Asa – AFP | Global News' (*Philippine Daily Inquirer*, 30 March 2019) <https://globalnation.inquirer.net/173963/afp-notes-surge-of-chinese-fishing-vessels-around-pag-asa> accessed 4 June 2020.

80 Department of Foreign Affairs, 'Statement: On the Presence of Chinese Vessels Near and Around Pag-Asa' (*Department of Foreign Affairs*, 4 April 2019) <https://dfa.gov.ph/dfa-news/statements-and-advisoriesupdate/21089-statement-on-the-presence-of-chinese-vessels-near-and-around-pag-asa> accessed 4 June 2020.

81 Ibid.
82 Christia Marie Ramos, 'Philippines "Fires Off" Diplomatic Protest Over Chinese Vessels Circling Pag-Asa Island' (*Philippine Daily Inquirer*, 31 July 2019) <https://globalnation.inquirer.net/178458/breaking-philippines-fires-off-diplomatic-protest-over-chinese-vessels-roaming-near-pag-asa-island> accessed 4 June 2020.
83 Department of Foreign Affairs, 'Remarks of Foreign Affairs Secretary Teodoro L. Locsin, Jr. on the Presentation of the 2020 DFA Budget Proposal' (*Depaertment of Foreing Affairs*, 4 September 2019) <https://dfa.gov.ph/statement-remarks-apc/24258-remarks-of-foreign-affairs-secretary-teodoro-l-locsin-jr-on-the-presentation-of-the-2020-dfa-budget-proposal> accessed 4 June 2020.
84 Pia Ranada, 'South China Sea Covered by PH-U.S. Mutual Defense Treaty – Pompeo' (*Rappler.com*, 23 March 2019) <http://www.rappler.com/nation/224668-pompeo-says-south-china-sea-covered-philippines-us-mutual-defense-treaty> accessed 4 June 2020.
85 Daryl John Esguerra, 'Duterte Officially Orders Termination of VFA | Global News' (*Philippine Daily Inquirer*, 7 February 2020) <https://globalnation.inquirer.net/185007/breaking-duterte-officially-orders-termination-of-vfa> accessed 6 June 2020.
86 Patricia Lourdes Viray, 'First EDCA Facility Breaks Ground in Pampanga' (*Philippine Star*, 18 April 2018) <https://www.philstar.com/headlines/2018/04/18/1807117/first-edca-facility-breaks-ground-pampanga> accessed 6 June 2020.
87 Argyl Cyrus Geducos, 'Duterte Tells US: Take Back Bato's Visa Cancellation, or Say Goodbye to VFA' (*Manila Bulletin*, 27 January 2020) <https://news.mb.com.ph/2020/01/23/duterte-tells-us-take-back-batos-visa-cancellation-or-say-goodbye-to-vfa/> accessed 6 June 2020.
88 Jim Gomez, 'Philippine Official Defends US Pact after Duterte Threat' (*Associated Press*, 6 February 2020) <https://apnews.com/4404cae9d2eb241ec1f6b141c91f60fb> accessed 6 June 2020; Newsline Philippines, 'DOJ to Submit Study on VFA Termination to PRRD Jan. 27 – NewsLine. Ph' (*Newsline.ph*, 26 January 2020) <https://newsline.ph/top-stories/2020/01/26/doj-to-submit-study-on-vfa-termination-to-prrd-jan-27/> accessed 6 June 2020.; ABS-CBN News, 'PH to Lose "a Lot" of Military Training If VFA Terminated: Gordon | ABS-CBN News' (*ABS-CBN News*, 10 February 2020) <https://news.abs-cbn.com/news/02/10/20/ph-to-lose-a-lot-of-military-training-if-vfa-terminated-gordon> accessed 6 June 2020; Patricia Lourdes Viray, 'Ex-DFA Chief Warns of "national Tragedy" amid VFA Termination' (*Philippine Star*, 28 February 2020) <https://www.philstar.com/headlines/2020/02/28/1996812/ex-dfa-chief-warns-national-tragedy-amid-vfa-termination> accessed 6 June 2020; Katrina Domingo, 'Dela Rosa "Bothered" Over VFA Cancellation Notice' (*ABS-CBN News*, 11 February 2020) <https://news.abs-cbn.com/news/02/11/20/dela-rosa-bothered-over-vfa-cancellation-notice> accessed 6 June 2020.
89 Patricia Lourdes Viray, '"Thank You, next": Trump Fine with Ending Defense Pact with Philippines' (*philstar.com*, 13 February 2020) <https://www.philstar.com/headlines/2020/02/13/1992796/thank-you-next-trump-fine-ending-defense-pact-philippines> accessed 6 June 2020.
90 Frances Mangosing, 'Duterte Finds Ending VFA Untimely in Time of COVID-19, Says Lorenzana' (*Philippine Daily Inquirer*, 3 June 2020) <https://globalnation.inquirer.net/188137/duterte-finds-ending-vfa-untimely-in-time-of-covid-19-says-lorenzana> accessed 6 June 2020.
91 Willard Cheng, '"Superpower Tensions," Pandemic Led Duterte to Suspend Ending VFA: Locsin | ABS-CBN News' (*ABS-CBN News*, 3 June 2020) <https://news.abs-cbn.com/news/06/03/20/superpower-tensions-pandemic-led-duterte-to-suspend-ending-vfa-locsin> accessed 6 June 2020.
92 'Transcript of the Media Interview with President Rodrigo Roa Duterte Following His Meeting with the Filipino Community in The Republic Union of Myanmar. Grand Ballroom 1, Tharaphi Villa 2, Horizon Lake View Hotel, Nay Pyi Taw, Myanmar.' (2017).
93 'Transcript of the Media Interview of President Rodrigo Roa Duterte upon His Arrival Following His Official Visits to The Republic of the Union of Myanmar and The Kingdom of Thailand. Terminal 2, Ninoy Aquino International Airport, Pasay City, 23 March 2017.' (2017).
94 'Transcript of the Speech of President Rodrigo Roa Duterte during the Integrated Bar of the Philippines' 16th National Convention of Lawyers. Grand Ballroom, Marriott Hotel, Pasay City, 23 March 2017.' (2017).
95 'Transcript of the Speech of President Rodrigo Roa Duterte during His Attendance at the 33rd Philippine Coastguard Auxiliary National Convention. Function Room 1, SMX Convention Center, Lanang, Davao City. 19 May 2017.' (2017).; 'Transcript of the Speech of President Rodrigo Roa Duterte at the People's Day Celebration. Capitol Grounds, Malaybalay City, Bukidnon. 29 March 2017.' (2017).

96 Liwanag and Rinoza (n 47).; 'Transcript of the Speech of President Rodrigo Roa Duterte at the 38th Convention of the Philippine Association of Water Districts. SMX Convention Center, SM Lanang Premier, Davao City' (n 58).; 'Transcript of Press Conference by President Rodrigo Roa Duterte with Senate President Aquilino Pimentel III and House Speaker Pantaleon Alvarez. Malacanang Palace, 13 March 2017.' (2017); 'Transcript of Media Interview with President Rodrigo Roa Duterte Following His Second State of the Nation Address. Session Hall, House of Representatives, 24 July 2017.' (2017); 'Transcript of the Speech of President Rodrigo Roa Duterte during the 26th Anniversary of the Bureau of Fire Protection. AFP Theater, Camp Aguinaldo, Quezon City. 02 August 2017.' (2017).

97 'Transcript of Press Conference by President Rodrigo Roa Duterte with Senate President Aquilino Pimentel III and House Speaker Pantaleon Alvarez. Malacanang Palace, 13 March 2017.' (n 96); 'Transcript of the Speech of President Rodrigo Roa Duterte Upon His Departure for Official Visits to the Republic of the Union of Myanmar and the Kingdom of Thailand. Davao International AIrport, Davao City. 19 March 2017.' (2017); 'Transcript of the Media Interview with President Rodrigo Roa Duterte Following His Meeting with the Filipino Community in The Republic Union of Myanmar. Grand Ballroom 1, Tharaphi Villa 2, Horizon Lake View Hotel, Nay Pyi Taw, Myanmar.' (n 92); 'Transcript of the Speech of President Rodrigo Roa Duterte at the People's Day Celebration. Capitol Grounds, Malaybalay City, Bukidnon. 29 March 2017.' (n 95).

98 Paterno Esmaquel, 'Duterte: "Remain Meek, Humble" to Get "Mercy" of China's Xi' (*Rappler.com*, 16 May 2018) <http://www.rappler.com/nation/202674-duterte-china-xi-jinping-meek-humble-west-philippine-sea> accessed 6 June 2020.

99 Benedict J Tria Kerkvliet, 'Toward a More Comprehensive Analysis of Philippine Politics: Beyond the Patron-Client, Factional Framework' (1995) 26 *Journal of Southeast Asian Studies* 401; Julio Cabral Teehankee, 'Factional Dynamics in Philippine Party Politics, 1900–2019' [2020] *Journal of Current Southeast Asian Affairs* doi: 10.1177/1868103420913404; Meredith L Weiss, 'Patronage Politics and Parties in the Philippines: Insights from the 2016 Elections', *Strong Patronage, Weak Parties* (World Scientific 2019). <https://www.worldscientific.com/doi/abs/10.1142/9789811212604_0008> accessed 7 June 2020.; Julio Teehankee, 'Electoral Politics in the Philippines', in Gabrielle Bruns, Aurel Croissant and Marei John (eds.), *Electoral Politics in East and Southeast Asia* (Friedrich Ebert Stiftung 2002); Julio Teehankee, 'Clientelism and Party Politics in the Philippines', in Dirk Thomas and Andress Ufen (eds.), *Clientelism and Electoral Competition in Indonesia, Thailand and the Philippines* (Routledge 2012).

100 Lito Monico Lorenzana, 'Presidential System, Patronage Politics and Political Dynasties' (*Manila Times*, 28 March 2018) <https://www.manilatimes.net/2018/03/28/opinion/analysis/presidential-system-patronage-politics-and-political-dynasties/389068/> accessed 7 June 2020.

101 Teehankee, 'Clientelism and Party Politics in the Philippines' (n 99) 187.

102 Merez (n 46).

103 Ministry of Foreign Affairs of the People's Republic of China, 'Set aside Dispute and Pursue Joint Development' (*Foreign Ministry of the People's Republic of China*) <https://www.fmprc.gov.cn/mfa_eng/ziliao_665539/3602_665543/3604_665547/t18023.shtml> accessed 6 June 2020.

104 Paterno Esmaquel, 'Cayetano Off to China for Talks on Joint Exploration' (*Rappler.com*, 20 March 2018) <http://www.rappler.com/nation/198600-alan-peter-cayetano-beijing-joint-exploration-west-philippine-sea> accessed 1 June 2020.

105 Pia Ranada, 'Joint Oil, Gas Exploration Deals to Abide by Both PH, Chinese Laws – Sta Romana' (*Rappler.com*, 29 August 2019) <https://www.rappler.com/nation/238831-sta-romana-says-joint-oil-gas-exploration-contracts-to-abide-by-philippine-chinese-laws> accessed 2 June 2020.

106 Joyce Ann Rocamora, 'PH-China Oil Exploration Deal on SCS "Equal or Better" Than Malampaya' (*Philippine News Agency*, 26 July 2018) <https://www.pna.gov.ph/articles/1042729> accessed 1 June 2020.

107 Marje Pelayo, 'Cayetano Reveals PH-China Joint Exploration Plan in West Philippine Sea' (*UNTV News*, 28 August 2018) <https://www.untvweb.com/news/cayetano-reveals-ph-china-joint-exploration-plan-in-west-philippine-sea/> accessed 1 June 2020.

108 Department of Energy, 'Model Contracts: Model Petroleum Service Contract' (*Department of Energy*) <https://www.doe.gov.ph/model-contracts-petroleum> accessed 5 June 2020.

109 Art. XII, Sec. 2 of the 1987 Constitution specifically provides that all natural resource exploitation activities

> shall be under the full control and supervision of the State," and can only be undertaken by the State directly, or "it may enter into co-production, joint venture, or production-sharing agreements with Filipino citizens, or corporations or associations at least sixty per centum of whose capital is owned by such citizens.

110 Helen Regan CNN, 'Duterte Says Xi Jinping Offered Him an Oil and Gas Deal to Ignore South China Sea Ruling' (*CNN*) <https://www.cnn.com/2019/09/12/asia/duterte-xi-south-china-sea-deal-intl-hnk/index.html> accessed 31 May 2020. However, at other times, Duterte has also said that China may not be willing to accept a 60%/40% arrangement. See Aurelio (n 59).

111 Arianne Merez News ABS-CBN, 'Duterte OK with 60-40 Sharing in Joint Oil Exploration with China' (*ABS-CBN News*) <https://news.abs-cbn.com/news/08/08/19/china-plan-to-split-oil-exploration-60-40-ok-with-duterte-if-ph-gets-bigger-share> accessed 2 June 2020.

112 'Memorandum of Understanding on Cooperation on Oil and Gas Development between the Government of the People's Republic of China and the Government of the Republic of the Philippines' (*Foreign Ministry of the People's Republic of China*, 20 November 2018) <https://www.fmprc.gov.cn/mfa_eng/wjdt_665385/2649_665393/t1616644.shtml> accessed 1 June 2020.

113 ABS-CBN News, 'Manila-Beijing Oil and Gas Deal an "Agreement to Agree," Says Locsin | ABS-CBN News' (*ABS-CBN News*, 22 November 2019) <https://news.abs-cbn.com/business/11/22/18/manila-beijing-oil-and-gas-deal-an-agreement-to-agree-says-locsin> accessed 1 June 2020.

114 'Memorandum of Understanding on Cooperation on Oil and Gas Development between the Government of the People's Republic of China and the Government of the Republic of the Philippines' (n 112) s II.

115 Ibid. III.D.

116 Ibid. IV.

117 Ibid.

118 Pia Department of Foreign Affairs, 'Joint Press Release: PH-CN Joint Committee on Oil & Gas Dev't Hold 1st Meeting in Beijing' (*Rappler.com*, 29 August 2019) <https://dfa.gov.ph/dfa-news/dfa-releasesupdate/24875-joint-press-release-first-meeting-of-philippines-china-inter-governmental-joint-steering-committee-on-cooperation-on-oil-and-gas-development-was-held-in-beijing> accessed 2 June 2020. A second meeting was scheduled for "early 2020", but has been postponed due to the coronavirus pandemic that began spreading throughout the region.

119 Pia Lee-Brago, 'Philippines, China Convene Steering Committee on Joint Exploration' (*Philippine Star*, 31 October 2019) <https://www.philstar.com/headlines/2019/10/31/1964844/philippines-china-convene-steering-committee-joint-exploration> accessed 2 June 2020.

120 Jet Encila, 'China, PH Officials to Meet on South China Sea Oil Venture Impasse' (*Business Times*, 8 January 2020) <https://www.btimesonline.com/articles/124568/20200108/china-philippines-oil-project-china-philippines-gas-project-china-gas-venture.htm> accessed 2 June 2020.

121 Ibid.

122 Ranada, 'Joint Oil, Gas Exploration Deals to Abide by Both PH, Chinese Laws – Sta Romana' (n 105).

123 Lenie Lectura, 'Cusi Bares Details on PHL-China MOU on Joint Oil, Gas Exploration' (*Business Mirror*, 23 November 2018) <https://businessmirror.com.ph/2018/11/23/cusi-bares-details-on-phl-china-mou-on-joint-oil-gas-exploration/> accessed 2 June 2020.

124 Pia Ranada, 'Duterte Won't Bring Up West PH Sea in ASEAN Summit' (*Rappler.com*, 17 August 2016) <http://www.rappler.com/nation/143382-duterte-west-philippine-sea-asean-summit> accessed 5 June 2020; Associated Press, 'Duterte Won't Bring Up South China Sea Arbitration Victory at Southeast Asia Summit' *Wall Street Journal* (27 April 2017) <https://www.wsj.com/articles/duterte-wont-raise-south-china-sea-arbitration-win-at-southeast-asia-summit-1493298290> accessed 2 June 2020; Reuters, 'Duterte Won't Raise Arbitral Ruling at ASEAN Summit' (*Manila Bulletin*, 28 April 2017) <https://news.mb.com.ph/2017/04/28/duterte-wont-raise-arbitral-ruling-at-asean-summit> accessed 2 June 2020.

125 Associated Press (n 124).

126 Paterno Esmaquel, 'Cayetano Wary of "legally Binding" Rules in South China Sea' (*Rappler.com*, 19 May 2017) <http://www.rappler.com/nation/170373-dfa-cayetano-code-conduct-south-china-sea> accessed 5 June 2020.

127 Joyce Ann Rocamora, 'PH Assumes Coordinatorship for ASEAN-China Dialogue' (*Philippine News Agency*, 5 August 2018) <https://www.pna.gov.ph/articles/1043786> accessed 5 June 2020.

128 Luchi De Guzman, 'ASEAN Targets Completion of Code of Conduct within Three Years' (*CNN Philippines*, 4 November 2019) <https://www.cnnphilippines.com/news/2019/11/4/asean-china-code-of-conduct-south-china-sea.html> accessed 5 June 2020.; Jitairee Thongnoi, Kyodo and Reuters, '"Major Progress" on South China Sea Code of Conduct Talks: Wang' (*South China Morning Post*, 31 July 2019) <https://www.scmp.com/news/asia/southeast-asia/article/3020838/major-progress-south-china-sea-code-conduct-chinese> accessed 5 June 2020.

129 Carl Thayer, 'A Closer Look at the ASEAN-China Single Draft South China Sea Code of Conduct' <https://thediplomat.com/2018/08/a-closer-look-at-the-asean-china-single-draft-south-china-sea-code-of-conduct/> accessed 5 June 2020.

130 Wenwen Wang, 'China, ASEAN Read South China Sea Code of Conduct - Global Times' (*Global Times*, 30 July 2017) <http://www.globaltimes.cn/content/1159604.shtml> accessed 5 June 2020; Greg Torode, 'Tough South China Sea Talks Ahead as Vietnam Seeks to Curb China's Actions' (*Reuters*, 31 December 2018) <https://www.reuters.com/article/us-china-southchinasea-asean-idUSKCN1OT0ML> accessed 5 June 2020.

131 Pia Ranada, 'Duterte to Vietnam's Quang: Bilateral Talks with China "Necessary"' (*Rappler.com*, 29 September 2016) <http://www.rappler.com/world/regions/asia-pacific/147721-duterte-vietnam-president-bilateral-talks-china> accessed 5 June 2020.

132 Social Weather Stations, 'Third Quarter 2019 Social Weather Survey: Net Trust for China Falls to "Bad" -33; Net Trust Stays "Excellent" for the United States, "Good" for Australia and Japan, and "Moderate" for Singapore' (*Social Weather Stations*, 7 December 2019) <https://www.sws.org.ph/swsmain/artcldisppage/?artcsyscode=ART-20191120154738> accessed 5 June 2020.

133 Ibid.

134 Frances Mangosing, '73% of Filipinos Want Duterte Admin to Assert Rights in West Philippine Sea' (*Philippine Daily Inquirer*, 12 July 2018) <https://globalnation.inquirer.net/168371/73-filipinos-want-duterte-admin-assert-rights-west-philippine-sea> accessed 6 June 2020.

135 Sofia Tomacruz, '3 Years Later, 87% of Filipinos Want Gov't to Assert Hague Ruling' (*Rappler.com*, 12 July 2019) <http://www.rappler.com/nation/235259-filipinos-want-government-assert-hague-ruling-sws-survey-2019> accessed 6 June 2020.

12
VIETNAM'S SOUTH CHINA SEA POLICY

Nguyen Hong Thao

Introduction

Vietnam is one of the key countries in the South China Sea competition. The Nation has a long history to consolidate sovereignty over the offshore islands in the South China Sea, the earliest record of which dated back to the 17th century. It is the only country in the region that had armed confrontations with China's Navy in the islands in 1974 and 1988. Vietnam declared its 200-nautical-mile exclusive economic zone and continental shelf in 1977. It insists on maintaining the South China Sea as a sea of peace, stability, cooperation, and prosperity. Therefore, it consistently holds against attempts to impose unlawful maritime claims, such as the expansive maritime claims based on the "nine-dotted line." It has contributed great effort to achieving a legal document to manage the potential conflicts in the South China Sea, from the adoption of the Declaration on the Conduct of Parties (DOC) to the ongoing negotiation of the Code of Conduct (COC) of Parties. An overview of the South China Sea situation and available solutions will be insufficient without a study on Vietnam's policy. In the framework of this Handbook with limited pages, the author will not go into details of the legal arguments on sovereignty claims or actions in the field. The analysis focuses on the comprehensive strategy of Vietnam to realize its own targets in safeguarding the sovereignty claims over Hoang Sa (Paracels) and Truong Sa (Spratlys) islands, peacefully settling maritime disputes, maintaining a rules-based international order at sea, and developing a sustainable maritime economy. Therefore, the chapter will consist of four parts: (1) importance of the South China Sea to Vietnam, (2) exploring history in the South China Sea (or the East Sea as called by the Vietnamese people), (3) Vietnam's policy on the South China Sea, and (4) the United Nations Convention on the Law of the Sea (UNCLOS) – the tool to implement this policy.

Importance of the South China Sea to Vietnam

A well-known Vietnamese legend illustrated the importance of the East Sea (Bien Dong in Vietnamese) and the tradition of moving seaward since the earlier days of nation-building. The first King Lac Long Quan and his wife Au Co in 4000 years BC had one hundred children. Half of them went with their mother to settle in the mainland and the forests.

Fifty others went with their father to the sea. The coastal and marine zones of Vietnam have important roles, at least in the four points below. *First*, with the long coastlines of 3,260 kilometers and more than 3,000 islands scattered around (not including the Paracels and Spratlys), Vietnam has the favorable condition to extend maritime zones under the international law of the sea. The ratio of coastal front to land area (330,000 km^2) of Vietnam is 0.01, while Thailand's is 0.007. It allows the State to have a capacity to gain maritime zones more than two times of its land area, only behind Brunei, Indonesia, and the Philippines in the South China Sea. *Second*, the long coastline allows Vietnam to develop the navigation, port infrastructure, research, search, and rescue services. Vietnam has more than 90 maritime ports. Most of the sea lanes across the South China Sea pass through the maritime zones under the jurisdiction of Vietnam. *Third*, the coastal and marine zones of Vietnam are rich in flora and fauna, including over 2000 marine fish species, 300 species of coral, an unknown number of plant species that is moreover characterized by 13 major ecosystems.[1] The fisheries industry is extremely important to Vietnam. The other national resource is petroleum with an estimated oil reservoir of 700 million tons. *Fourth*, Vietnam serves as a gate to the sea for land-locked States (Laos), or geographically disadvantaged States or areas (Cambodia, Yunnan province of China). However, the sea also creates negative impacts to the national security of Vietnam. The State is threatened by foreign attacks from the sea. In addition, Vietnam engages in 8 over 20 maritime disputes in the region.[2] Maritime disputes are concerned with not only two but three (Vietnam, China, and Taiwan on Paracels islands) or six parties (Vietnam, the Philippines, Malaysia, Brunei, China, and Taiwan) on Spratly islands.

Exploring history in the South China Sea (East Sea)

International ports for maritime trade were opened in the early period, Van Don in the 11th and Hoi An town in the 16th centuries.[3] Vietnamese official historical accounts and later, the Western and Chinese record books had noted the activities of maritime brigades under the Vietnamese Nguyen Dynasty in the Paracels and Spratlys since the beginning of the 17th century. Among them, the most important were made by the National Institute of History under the Nguyen Dynasty (Quoc Su Quan), including *Dai Nam Thuc Luc Tien Bien* (Accounts of Dai Nam's Former Dynasties, 1600–1775) and *Dai Nam Thuc Luc Chinh Bien* (Accounts of Dai Nam's Present Dynasty, 1865–1882), *Dai Nam Nhat Thong Chi* (Geography of Reunified Dai Nam, 1865–1882), *Kham Dinh Dai Nam Hoi Dien Su Le* (The Dai Nam Administrative Repertory 1843–1851), Phan Huy Chu, *Lich Trieu Hien Chuong Loai Chi* (Regulations of Successive Dynasties by Subject-Matter, 1821), *Hoang Viet Dia Du Chi* (Geographical Treatise of Imperial Vietnam, 1833), *Viet Su Cuong Giam Khao Luoc* (Brief History of Vietnam 1876), etc.

Dai Nam Thuc Luc Tien Bien 1844 (Accounts of Dai Nam's Former Dynasties 1600–1775) described the process of establishment and functions of Hoang Sa company sent by Dynasty of Nguyen to the Paracels and Spratlys as follows:

> Far out in the middle of the sea beyond the coast of An Vinh village, Binh Son subdistrict, Quang Ngai district there are over 130 sandbanks separated by sea distances of a full day's voyage or just a few watches' and scattered on a length of several thousand dam, hence the popular designation of Van Ly Hoang Sa. Fresh water springs are found on many sandbanks. Sea products there include seacucumbers, conches, tortoises, turtles, etc.
>
> During the early days of the dynasty, the Hoang Sa detachment was created and it was made up of 70 men recruited from among An Vinh villagers. It set out every year in the third month and used to reach the islands after a three days and nights voyage. There the

> men collected articles from wrecked ships. Its home trip would normally begin in the eighth month of the year. In addition, there was a Bac Hai team whose members were recruited from Tu Chinh commune in Binh Thuan province or from Canh Duong village. The team was sent to Bac Hai areas and the island of Con Lon to gather articles from wrecked ships. The Bac Hai team was placed under the Hoang Sa detachment commander.'[4]

Foreign articles, documents, and maps at that time recorded the activities of the Hoang Sa Company and recognized that in 1816 the Vietnamese Emperor took possession of the Paracels.[5] Some Chinese history books and documents depicted the Paracels as "*Van Ly Truong Sa is a sandbank rising above the sea. Several thousand leagues in length, it forms a rampart on the periphery of the Kingdom of Annam (Vietnam).*"[6] In the earlier period, the Vietnamese believed that the two archipelagos were unique. The popular Vietnamese names of Hoang Sa (Cat Vang - Yellow Sand) or Van Ly Truong Sa (Ten-Thousand-Ly Long Sand) were used to indicate the offshore group of dangerous islets stretched a hundred miles in the open sea. Later, each archipelago had its own name: Hoang Sa for the Paracels and Van Ly Truong Sa for the Spratlys. However, they were still presented on the *Dai Nam Nhat Thong Toan Do* (The Complete Map of the Unified Dai Nam) published in 1838 as two groups of islands in one unit encircled by dotted lines.[7]

Vietnamese stand to the sovereignty over the Paracels and Spratlys is based on the effective occupation theory. Operations of Hoang Sa and Bac Hai companies were considered as State activities because those detachments were established by the orders of the King and put under the commandment of navy officers and military discipline. The members of companies enjoyed immunities and privileges such as tax exemption. Those military units had public functions. Every year, from March to August, they were sent to Paracels and Spratlys to collect remains from shipwrecks. They went to "*the Hoang Sa to study and to chart the maritime routes*"[8] as well as for the building of shrines and temples, and the planting of trees as a symbol of sovereignty over the islands.[9] J. Gutzlaff, in 1849, wrote about a "*small garrison on the spot to collect the duty on all visitors, and to ensure protection to its own fishermen.*"[10] Western documents revealed also the cases when the Kingdoms of Nguyen provided assistance to foreign vessels in distress in the Paracels and Spratlys. The Vietnamese activities on the archipelagoes hadn't met any competition from neighboring countries. Historic records gave evidence to the Chinese indifference to the Paracels. Chinese authority denied any liability to the German ship 'Bellona' and the Japanese ship 'Imegi Maru' shipwrecked in 1895–1896.[11] In other cases, Chinese authorities even gave assistance to Vietnamese sailors operating in the Paracels.[12] The official position of Vietnam is that "*Vietnam has sufficient legal foundations and historical evidence proving its sovereignty over Hoang Sa and Truong Sa archipelagos.*"[13] The activities of the Hoang Sa and Bac Hai companies during the Kingdom of Nguyen were comprehensive, continuous, peaceful, and uncontested. They went in line with requirements of effective occupation theory of international law that are reconfirmed by State practice and through judicial judgments.[14] Vietnam was the owner of those archipelagos before the arrival of the French.

The French colonial authority in Indochina, which was responsible for the external relations of the Vietnamese Kingdom, recognized its State succession status over the Hoang Sa islands from the Vietnamese Kingdom. However, France occupied the Spratlys and incorporated to Cochinchina (Nam Ky of Vietnam but under the French colony) in 1930 and 1933 with the argument that the archipelago was *terre nullius.*[15] The Treaty of Ha Long Bay in 1949 rectified this mistake by the fact that the French officially transferred the sovereignty over Cochinchina, including the Spratlys, to the Bao Dai Administration.[16] At the San Francisco Peace Conference in 1951, Prime Minister and Minister of Foreign Affairs Tran Van Huu from the Associated State of Vietnam solemnly declared that the two islands should belong to Vietnam.[17] This declaration did not elicit any protest from the other delegates of the Conference. The Paracels and Spratlys were put under the administration of the Republic of Vietnam in accordance with the Geneva Accords of 1954.[18] The Paracels were totally occupied by the Chinese Navy force in 1974 before Vietnam's reunification in 1975. Later, again in 1988, China used the force to land on some low-tide elevations in the Spratlys. Vietnam continues to affirm its indisputable sovereignty over both archipelagos.

Vietnam's policy on the South China Sea

After its reunification in 1975, the Vietnam government pursues a consistent policy with two main objectives: defense of national security and development of the national economy. The realization of both objectives relies mainly on the policy of moving seaward. This policy is realized through main directions: improvement of national legislation in conformity with international law; the advancement of peaceful settlement of maritime disputes; policy of befriending all nations; and maritime sustainable development.

During the Third United Nations Conference on the Law of the Sea, Hanoi established the 200 nm exclusive economic zone (EEZ) and continental shelf by the Declaration on Vietnam's maritime zones on 12 May 1977.[19] Before signing the UNCLOS, Vietnam published the Government Declaration on the baselines used for determination of Vietnam's territorial sea on 12 November 1982.[20] Both documents created a basic legal foundation for the building of Vietnam's system of marine legislation. On 23 June 1994, Vietnam became the 63rd State having ratified the UNCLOS. The Resolution on the Ratification of the UNCLOS reflected the determination of Vietnam to build a just and equitable legal order for the seas, encouraging marine development and cooperation. It also confirmed the sovereignty of Vietnam over its internal waters and territorial sea, sovereign rights, and jurisdiction over the contiguous zone, the EEZ, and the continental shelf on the basis of the provisions of the UNCLOS and principles of international law.[21] The 2012 Law of the Sea of Vietnam, of which Article 8 stipulates that the Government defines baselines in areas where the baselines have not been defined and publishes them after getting approved by the Standing Committee of the National Assembly. Regarding the legal regime of the contiguous zone, the 2012 Law of the Sea of Vietnam wrote off the jurisdiction on security in the contiguous zone that stipulated in the Government Declaration of 1977. It confirmed the right of Vietnam to extend its continental shelf beyond 200 nm.[22] This right was realized through the joint submission by Malaysia and Vietnam to the Commission on the Limits of the Continental Shelf (CLCS) made on 6 May 2009 and Vietnam's individual submission to the CLCS made on 7 May 2019.[23] The Law corrected limitations in the Government Declaration of 1977 and fully respects the UNCLOS. The Law of 2012 reconfirmed the sovereignty over the Paracels and Spratlys and underlined the policy to settle maritime disputes through peaceful means.

Hanoi believes that a peaceful and favorable international environment is indispensable for economic development. Since the implementation of *Doi Moi* (Renovation), Vietnam's foreign policy is "*to be friend with all countries in the world.*"[24] Hanoi persistently advocates for the peaceful settlement of maritime disputes in accordance with the UNCLOS. The Resolution on the Ratification of the UNCLOS in 1994 affirmed Vietnam's position:

> to settle disputes over territorial sovereignty and other differences related to the East Sea through peaceful negotiation in the spirit of equality and mutual understanding and respect, respect for international law, especially the United Nations Convention on the

> Law of the Sea, respect for sovereign rights and jurisdiction of coastal countries over their exclusive economic zones and continental shelves...[25]

The 2012 Law of the Sea of Vietnam states: "*The State shall settle disputes related to the sea and islands with other countries through peaceful measures, in conformity with the United Nations Convention on the Law of the Sea, international law and practices.*"[26] Vietnam's standing fully accords with Article 33 of the United Nations Charter, Articles 15, 74, 83, 279, and 280 of the 1982 Convention, the general trend of the regional countries, as well as international law and State practices. In practice, Vietnam is among the regional countries taking the lead in applying the provisions of the UNCLOS in the settlement of marine disputes by peaceful means. It concluded maritime delimitation with Thailand in 1997,[27] with China in the Tonkin Gulf in 2000,[28] signed an agreement on the delineation of the continental shelf with Indonesia in 2003.[29] Vietnam also signed two joint marine exploitation agreements, one with Cambodia in the common historical waters in 1982 and another with Malaysia in the overlapping continental shelves in the Thailand Gulf in 1992. A joint fishery zone in the Tonkin Gulf was set up by the agreement between Vietnam and China in 2004. Hanoi, together with Manila, was the co-drafter of the Association of Southeast Asian Nations (ASEAN) Declaration on the COC of Parties in the South China Sea, played an active role in achieving the ASEAN-China Declaration on the Code of Conduct of Parties in the South China Sea (DOC), and is striving together with concerned countries to reach a COC of Parties in the South China Sea.[30] In October 2011, China and Vietnam reached an "Agreement on Basic Principles guiding the Settlement of Sea-related Issues."[31] To implement the Agreement, the two countries have carried out expert-level talks, one on "demarcation of areas outside the mouth of the Gulf of Tonkin," and another on "co-operation in less sensitive fields at sea." Vietnam holds that bilateral disputes will be settled bilaterally, multilateral disputes will be settled by all parties concerned. Vietnam persistently proposes for talks with China on the sovereignty of the Paracels, while it continues to cooperate with other claimants to solve the disputes over the Spratlys.

In realizing the policy to befriending all States, Vietnam flexibly implements the three-Nos defense policy, that is no military alliances, no aligning with one country against another, and no foreign military bases on Vietnamese soil. The three Nos policy was published in Vietnam's 1998 Defense White Paper and then repeated in subsequent Defense White Papers of 2004 and 2009. The new Defense White Paper, released in 2019, underlined the fourth "No" – principle of "no using force or threatening to use force in international relations."[32] The four-Nos policy permits Vietnam to balance the influence of the two strategic competitors in the region for its own interest. The four-Nos policy is aimed at creating a favorable international environment and conducive conditions to serve the cause of national construction and defense. It maintains a peaceful environment to solve territorial and maritime disputes with other countries exclusively by peaceful means. A provision for "acting together," is also added with the meaning that if Vietnam is attacked it will review its "four-Nos policy" and be ready to engage with other countries to counter a common enemy based on the implementation of a legitimate right to self-defense. Vietnam's 2019 Defense White Paper reaffirms:

> Viet Nam's national defense policy is peaceful and self-defensive in nature. Viet Nam resolutely and consistently settles all disputes and divergences through peaceful means on the basis of international law, actively and proactively prevents and repulses the risks of war, realizes the motto of defending the Homeland from afar, and is prepared to fight against wars of aggression.[33]

Vietnam does not allow the South China Sea issues to negatively affect the cooperation aspect or overall bilateral relationships in the region.

The success in resolving maritime disputes by peaceful means creates favorable conditions to realize the policy of moving seaward. The Resolution of the Central Committee of Vietnam's Communist Party on the strategy for sustainable development of the Vietnamese marine economy up to 2030, with a vision toward 2045[34] laid an objective to make Vietnam a strong and rich country based on the sea. This Resolution continues the path drawn by the Resolution, adopted in 2007, on Vietnam Marine Strategy to 2020 with the goal of turning Vietnam into a prosperous country from the sea. The new Resolution affirms that the sea is a component of the national sovereignty, a living space, an international gateway closely associated with the national construction and defense. It says that Vietnam will sustainably develop its maritime economy while ensuring national defense and security, firmly maintaining independence, sovereignty, and territorial integrity, enhancing external relations and international cooperation on the sea, contributing to maintaining a peaceful and stable environment conducive to development. The Resolution sets forth various objectives for 2030. Sea-based industries will contribute about 10 percent and the economy of the 28 coastal provinces and cities will make up 65–70 percent of the country's GDP. At least half of Vietnam's maritime zones will be surveyed in terms of marine resources and environment and presented on maps of the 1:500.000 scales. By 2045, according to the Resolution, Vietnam will become a powerful marine country, with the marine economy making remarkable contributions to the national economy. It will proactively and responsibly participate in addressing international and regional issues of the sea and the ocean. By 2030, Vietnam's priority would concentrate on some main sectors: (1) Tourism and marine services, (2) Maritime economy, (3) Exploitation of oil and gas and other marine mineral resources, (4) Aquaculture and fishing, (5) Coastal industry and (6) Renewable energy and new marine economic sectors.[35]

To achieve the sustainable marine development target, Vietnam has introduced a raft of specialized laws, particularly the 1980 Maritime Code, amended in 2005 and 2015; the 1993 Petroleum Law, revised in 2000, 2008, and 2014; the 1993 Law on Environmental Protection, amended in 2014; the 2015 Criminal Code, the 2015 Law on Marine and Island Resources and Environment; the 2003 Fisheries Law, amended in 2017; and the 2018 Law on the Vietnam Coast Guard. The country has also signed a total of 11 conventions of the International Maritime Organization, including the Convention for the Safety of Life at Sea (SOLAS), Convention for the Prevention of Pollution from Ships (MARPOL), Convention on Civil Liability for Oil Pollution Damage (CLC), Convention on Facilitation of Maritime Traffic (FAL), and Convention on Maritime Search and Rescue (SAR).

Vietnam realizes the need to reform the marine management apparatus. In 1998, the task of developing a national plan for oil spill incident prevention and response was transferred from the Ministry of Science, Technology, and Environment to the National Committee for Air and Sea Search and Rescue, helping the latter strengthen and expand its activities in Vietnam's waters, meeting the requirements of new tasks. The regional oil spill response centers have been established for the Northern, Central, and Southern regions.[36] In 2007, the Ministry of Fisheries was merged into the Ministry of Agriculture and Rural Development, and the Vietnam Administration of Seas and Islands was established within the Ministry of Natural Resources and Environment to enhance the approach of unified, multi-disciplinary, and multi-functional management to the marine environment.[37] In 1998, the Vietnam Marine Police was established. It was in charge of ensuring order and security at sea, as well as handling administrative violations beyond the baseline from which the territorial sea is measured to the outer limit of the exclusive economic zone and continental shelf. In 2008 this force changed the name to the Vietnam Coast Guard (VCG). The Law on Vietnamese Coast Guard in 2018 extends the competence of the VCG to adapt the development in the South China Sea. The Vietnam Coast Guard has the competence to operate in all maritime zones of Vietnam, including internal waters, territorial sea, the exclusive economic zone, and the continental shelf of Vietnam, aimed at ensuring security, order, and safety as well as maintaining law enforcement at sea and defending national sovereignty, sovereign rights and jurisdiction. It can conduct checks and controls to protect sovereignty and national resources; prevent and control environmental pollution; preserve security, order, and safety; and detect, prevent and combat human trafficking, illegal transportation and trading of narcotics, piracy, and other violations.[38] The VCG is responsible for carrying out international cooperation concerning security, order, peace and stability in international and regional maritime zones on the basis of observance of Vietnam's laws, treaties that Vietnam is a party, in respect of basic principles of international law. To aid the VCG, another force, namely the Vietnam Fisheries Resources Surveillance Force (VFRSF) has been reestablished since 2014. The VFRSF is tasked with patrolling, checking, controlling, inspecting fisheries, and handling violations of fishery law in Vietnam's seas; participating in search and rescue and relief; protecting fishing grounds and fishermen; developing marine economy; and protecting the country's sacred sovereignty over seas and islands. This force, coordinating with the VCG, was at the frontline in opposing the encroachments on Vietnam's EEZ and continental shelf by the Chinese oil rig HYSY 981 in 2014 and the survey vessel Haiyang Dizhi 8 in 2019.

The implementation of the moving seaward policy has also brought about new problems. Since 2007, the Vietnamese Government has encouraged Vietnamese fishing vessels to operate farther in its EEZ. Nevertheless, in the situation where maritime boundaries have not been delimited clearly, fishermen having insufficient legal knowledge can sail into the waters under the sovereign rights and jurisdiction of other countries, leading to the risk of violating Illegal, Unregulated and Unreported (IUU) fishing regulations. To combat IUU fishing, Vietnam replaced the Law on Fisheries in 2003 by the Law on Fisheries in 2017 that is effective from 2019. This Law is expected to intensify the management of fisheries resources toward sustainable development, management of fishermen and fishing vessels as well as capture activities.[39] Vietnam also promotes education, awareness-raising, and knowledge development on the sea and the ocean, survival skills, adaptation to climate change, sea-level rise, and disaster prevention for pupils and students in all levels of education. The successful implementation of Vietnam's marine policy is linked closely with the promotion of regional and international cooperation on sustainable management, use, and conservation of seas and oceans. Vietnam's marine strategy is in line with the world's seaward advancing trend for which the 1982 UNCLOS has laid the foundation.

UNCLOS – the tool for the implementation of Vietnam's marine policy

The UNCLOS is highly respected and implemented by Vietnam. As a developing country, Vietnam has high hopes in upholding the international legal order at seas and oceans, created by the UNCLOS. It is seen as an effective tool to resolve maritime disputes and create favorable conditions for maritime cooperation and sustainable development. Vietnam actively participated in the negotiation, signature, and ratification of the UNCLOS. Vietnam is also a party to the agreement relating to the implementation of Part XI of the UNCLOS (27 April 2006) and the 1995 Convention on Straddling Fish Stocks and Highly Migratory Fish Stocks (18 December 2018).[40]

The UNCLOS plays an important role in resolving maritime issues that Vietnam has to cope with. Vietnam's interpretation and application of the UNCLOS contribute to clarifying and reinforcing the role of the UNCLOS in maintaining international order at sea as well as peace, stability, and sustainable cooperation and development in the South China Sea.

Maritime delimitation

Since 1997, Vietnam has concluded three maritime boundary agreements with neighboring states. Those agreements have some similar points. They are primarily bilateral ones that resulted from direct negotiations. They are based on equitable principle. All cases have the presence of Vietnamese islands that enjoyed only a partial effect on delimitation. They are maritime delimitation between States with opposite coasts, except the case of the Gulf of Tonkin where maritime delimitation is carried out between the two States with opposite and adjacent coasts. This practice demonstrates that direct negotiation is preferable among peaceful means for Vietnam. The Government's Declaration of 1977 and Resolution of 1994 mentioned only "*peaceful negotiation*" to settle disputes over territorial sovereignty and other differences related to the East Sea. The 2012 Law of the Sea of Vietnam marked the turning point in Vietnam's approach to use "*peaceful measures*" in resolving maritime disputes, in conformity with the UNCLOS and international law and realities. Vietnam has not stated its choice of the procedures provided for in Article 287 of the UNCLOS. Before the South China Sea Tribunal Award, on 7 December 2014, the Vietnamese Foreign Ministry sent to the Tribunal a statement on its position to the case. Vietnam expressed its strong support for "*contracting states to the Convention in seeking solutions to their disputes concerning the interpretation and application of the Convention, based on the procedures set out in Part XV of the Convention.*" The Statement says "*Vietnam has no doubt that the Tribunal has jurisdiction in this case*" and wishes the Tribunal "*could clarify the legal position of the parties to the case and the third parties that are interested in the case.*"[41] Obviously, Hanoi tries to have a more open view in the selection of peaceful means to settle disputes, from "direct negotiation" to readiness to use other peaceful means, including the compulsory procedures of settlement of disputes provided in Annexes V or VII to the 1982 Convention.

Vietnam's approach to maritime delimitation is consistently based on the equitable principle. In the course of the Third UN Conference on the law of the Sea, Vietnam joined the group of 29 coastal States supporting the equitable principle. According to Vietnamese practice, the equitable principle often presents in an equidistant line adjusted by special circumstances to achieve a mutually acceptable solution to the parties. In the Thailand – Vietnam case of 1997, the overlapping area was created by the different views of the parties on the location of offshore formations. South Vietnam in 1971 claimed a median line between the offshore islands of Tho Chu and Poulo Wai and the opposite coast of Thailand without taking into account Ko Kra and Ko Losin rocks of Thailand. In its turn, Thailand's median line of 1973 intentionally ignored the Vietnamese Tho Chu archipelago and Poulo Wai Island of Cambodia. Tho Chu is 55 nm away from Phu Quoc Island, while Ko Kra and Ko Losin are located 26 and 37 nm from Thailand's coast, respectively. During the negotiation on the delimitation of the continental shelf in the Gulf of Thailand from 1992 to 1997, the fact that Tho Chu is far from Phu Quoc is taken to adjust the median line giving two-thirds of the area of the overlapping continental shelf claims to Thailand and one-third of the said area to Vietnam. This goodwill was well received in settling definitively and simultaneously the pending issues of the continental shelf and EEZ overlapping claims by a single boundary.[42]

In the Gulf of Tonkin, China and Vietnam agreed to "*apply the international law and consult international practices, following the principle of equitable and accounting all relevant circumstances in the Gulf, in order to achieve an equitable solution*". For Vietnam, an equitable solution was an equidistance line adjusted by relevant circumstances. For China, an equitable solution was equal division of the Gulf without giving any effect to islands. The main difficulty is the effect of Bach Long Vy Island on the maritime delimitation. This island locates in the middle of the Gulf (110 km from the nearest Vietnamese coast and 130 km from the Hainan Island). The Vietnamese approach to consider Bach Long Vy a special circumstance that deserved a partial effect on maritime delimitation was supported by the international practices and judgments of the ICJ. In most cases, such as the Malta/Libya,[43] Greenland/Jan Mayen,[44] or maritime delimitation in the Black Sea (Romania v. Ukraine),[45] an equidistance line was taken as a starting line, which would be adjusted by relevant circumstances to achieve an equitable solution. Finally, both sides agreed to give the Bach Long Vy island an effect of 15 nautical miles and to the Con Co island a half effect in maritime delimitation. Considering the proportionality test of the ratio between the length of coastlines and the received area, the relation of the relevant coastlines of Vietnam and China is found to be 1,1/1 and the sea areas of Vietnam and China stand in a proportion of 1,135/1.[46]

In the case of continental shelf boundary delimitation between Vietnam and Indonesia, the equitable principle applied by Vietnam is based on the mutual agreement to narrow down the overlapping area constituted by the initial claims of both sides, before dividing it. In 1972, Indonesia proposed to divide the continental shelf by the median line between North Natura Island (Indonesia) and Con Lon Island (Vietnam). The Republic of Vietnam applied the same method but with different reference points, resulting in a median line between the mainland of the two countries (the Vietnamese coast and the coast of the biggest island of Indonesia – Borneo). Saigon rejected the North Natura island because of its small dimension and its distance from Borneo (178 nm) is three times bigger than the distance between Con Dao Island and the Vietnamese mainland (48 nm). In 1978, Indonesia and the Socialist Republic of Vietnam(SRV) renewed the negotiation on the equitable principle. On 26 June 2003, the agreement between the Government of the SRV and the Government of the Republic of Indonesia concerning the delimitation of the continental shelf boundary was concluded.[47] However, Indonesia has not accepted the proposal of Vietnam to take this continental shelf delimitation line as the single boundary for both EEZ and continental shelf. The two sides agreed to continue the negotiation on the delimitation of the EEZ.

Joint development (JD) orcooperation for mutual development (CFMD)

Articles 74 and 83 of the UNCLOS set forth "joint development" (JD) as a type of "provisional arrangements of a practical nature", applied during a "transitional period", awaiting "the final delimitation". Several inferences can be drawn from these provisions: (1) JD is an agreement between states; (2) JD is a provisional solution of a practical nature; (3) JD only applies in maritime areas awaiting delimitation, not in areas that have been delimited; (4) JD can be applied to both living resources (Article 83) and non-living resources (Article 74); (5) JD only occurs in the EEZ and continental shelves; (6) JD is for mutual benefits; (7) JD is without prejudice to states' position in delimitation; (8) JD, as a provisional measure, is designated to be applied for maritime areas having overlapped legal titles accorded in conformity with the UNCLOS; and (9) JD is not applied for territorial sovereign disputes settlement.

However, the term "joint development" is interpreted by China and Vietnam differently. On 24 September 1975, Chinese Vice Premier Deng Xiaoping put forward the initial idea of "setting aside disputes" in his meeting with General Secretary of the Communist Party of Vietnam, Le Duan. On this occasion, he argued, "*between us there is still dispute on Xisha Islands and Nansha Islands…, of course this problem can be discussed later.*"[48] In August 1990, Premier Li Peng announced that the People's Republic of China "*is willing to support the joint efforts of South East Asian countries in setting aside disputes to pursue joint development of the Nansha Islands.*"[49] In fact, China wants to legitimize its nine-dash lines claim in its proposed concept of JD. It includes four elements: (1) the islands and maritime zones inside the nine-dash line claim belong to China, (2) the Four Sha (four groups of geographical features in the middle of the South China Sea) have 200 nm EEZ and continental shelf, (3) the dispute is set aside, and (4) the parties pursue joint development.[50] This concept is inconsistent with international law and the UNCLOS in at least 4 respects. Firstly, the concept stresses that sovereignty belongs to one country and no overlapping claims exist, which is contrary to the very rationale of "setting aside dispute." Secondly, the concept extends disputes to irrelevant territories rather than setting aside disputes. Thirdly, it intends to apply archipelagic baselines for the Four Sha. Finally, the concept promotes joint development in maritime areas where under the UNCLOS, China's sovereign rights and jurisdictions are not founded. In relation to Vietnam, China has insisted on applying this JD model to the Tu Chinh bank (Vanguard Bank) since 1992. Three-fourths of this area fall within the 200 nautical-mile radius measured from Vietnam's coastline, while the rest wholly lies in Vietnam's extended continental shelf established by the Malaysia-Vietnam Joint Submission to the CLCS in 2009. On 8 May 1992, China National Offshore Oil Corporation (CNOOC) entered into an oil development contract with a US company, Crestone Energy Corporation, that covered an area of 25,155 square kilometers, named Wan An Bei-21. China claimed that this area was within its nine-dash line claim and within the 200 nautical-mile radius measured from the Spratly Islands. The 2016 South China Sea Arbitration has made a historic conclusion that all high-tide features in the Spratly Islands had only a 12-nautical mile territorial sea[51] while denying the low-tide elevations the legal status of rocks. The Tribunal found that China's claim of historic rights in the nine-dash line was "*contrary to the Convention and without lawful effect to the extent that they exceed the geographic and substantive limits of China's maritime entitlements under the Convention.*"[52] The pinnacle of clash is the deep encroachment of the Chinese geological survey vessel group Haiyang Dizhi 8 in 2019 in Vietnam's EEZ and continental shelf. Vietnam's Ministry of Foreign Affairs issued consistent statements, condemning any Chinese attempt to insert Chinese jurisdiction over those maritime areas that legally are under the sovereign rights of Vietnam in accordance with the UNCLOS.[53] Vietnam confirmed that all of its maritime economic activities, including oil and gas exploitation, have been carried out within Vietnam's EEZ and continental shelf as defined from the land territory in line with the UNCLOS, to which both Vietnam and China are parties. According to the UNCLOS, no State party is entitled to lay claims on waters in the East Sea that exceed the geographical and substantive limits set out in the Convention. Illegal and unsubstantiated claims which are not in conformity with the UNCLOS cannot be used as the foundation to create the so-called disputed or overlapped waters. Vietnam clearly supports the 2016 Award of the Arbitral Tribunal on the South China Sea, which ruled that claims of historic rights to natural resources cannot replace the legal status of maritime institutions, such as EEZ or continental shelf, provided for by the UNCLOS, and all high-tide features of the Spratlys have only 12 nm territorial seas.[54]

The note dated 30 March 2020 affirmed that UNCLOS provides the sole legal basis for defining, in a comprehensive and exhaustive manner, the scope of their respective maritime entitlements in the East Sea. It rejects also the new concept of Nanhai Zhudao that China stated.[55]

Vietnam shows its flexibility in applying the joint development model in accordance with the UNCLOS. It leads the region with 5 agreements on joint development, namely the Kampuchea -Vietnam Agreement on Historic Water in 1982,[56] the Malaysia-Vietnam Joint Development Memorandum in the Gulf of Thailand in 1992,[57] the Sino-Vietnamese Agreements on Fishery Cooperation in the Gulf of Tonkin in 2000-2004,[58] the PetroVietnam- CNOOC agreements on the common exploration zone in the Gulf of Tonkin in 2004–2013[59] and the Tripartite Agreement for Joint Marine Seismic Undertaking in the Agreement Area in the South China Sea concluded by CNOOC, PNOC (Philippine National Oil Company), and PetroVietnam in 2005.[60] They include JD on oil and gas and JD on fishery resources, in overlapping or delimited areas.

To counter the Chinese JD concept, Vietnam, based on its practical experience, advanced the policy of ""CFMD". It has five principal characteristics. First, CFMD is a comprehensive solution, based on the principle of cooperation recognized in the Preamble, Articles 74 and 83 on maritime delimitation or 123 on the cooperation in enclosed or semi-enclosed waters of the UNCLOS. Second, while JD is agreed upon and implemented by States, CFMD may involve the participation of private actors, such as companies. One of the examples is the participation of the three national oil and gas companies of China, Vietnam, and the Philippines in the tripartite agreement in 2005. Third, CFMD can be implemented in all sea areas, including not only areas subjected to the sovereignty or jurisdiction of one or more states (internal waters, territorial sea, EEZ, continental shelf) but also areas beyond 200 nautical miles (the high sea and the area). As mentioned above, CFMD may take the form of joint development in areas of overlapping claims, disputed waters, or in oil fields crossing the borders of different states. It can also take place within an area subject to the sovereignty of one State only. Fourth, CFMD has a large scope of implementation, ranging from exploration and exploitation of resources, protection, and preservation of the marine environment, maritime search, and rescue, disaster prevention, and control, to repression of piracy, etc. These are consistent with the 1982 UNCLOS, as well as the DOC and the forthcoming South China Sea COC. Fifth, CFMD is a permanent and long-term measure, while JD is a "provisional arrangement." It needs a clear, defined area with a sound legal basis for long-term cooperation. Thus, CFMD prevents the abusive behavior of States while aiming at sustainable development and mutual understanding rather than merely preventing the dispute from escalating or expanding to other fields.

Based on the new theory of CFMD, Vietnam is confident in managing the negotiations with China in the mouth of the Gulf of Tonkin and hopes to pave the way for further cooperation in the South China Sea.

COC of the Parties in the South China Sea

In the South China Sea, the COC is expected to be a sustainable and effective tool to reduce the tension and create an atmosphere of confidence and cooperation for the management of conflicts in the region. Vietnam has been active in the process of developing the COC. It signed with the Philippines a bilateral COCs in the Joint Statement on the Fourth Annual Bilateral Consultations between the two countries in November 1995.[61] The two States were co-authors of the first ASEAN draft of the COC in 1999 and played a crucial role in persuading China to accept the negotiation and conclusion of the DOC in the South China Sea in 2002, the first step to the COC.[62] The DOC is designed to encourage the exercise of self-restraint; reduce tensions, promote cooperation in less sensitive areas; build confidence between ASEAN and China; respect for the freedoms of maritime navigation and flight, and create favorable conditions for settlement of disputes in the South China Sea through peaceful negotiations, consultations, cooperation, and other confidence-building measures. Vietnam actively involves in the implementation of the DOC. It was designated as the host country for the Workshop on Regional Oceanographic and Climate Exchanges in the South China Sea, one of the six projects to be implemented in the scope of the DOC since 2006. The Joint Oceanographic Marine Scientific Expedition in the South China Sea (JOMSRE)-South China Sea, a joint initiative of the Philippines and Vietnam to promote marine scientific research, opened for outside participants, including American and Canadian observers. In April 2007, for the JOMSRE-South China Sea IV, China expressed willingness to join the research as a signatory of the DOC. However, the DOC did not fully meet the expectations to manage the conflict in the South China Sea. It has some limitations to prevent effective implementation. The scope of application and legal status of adjacent maritime areas are not clear. The DOC is not a legally binding document; implementation bases on the goodwill of the parties. It does not clarify what kind of activities might complicate or escalate the disputes and must be prohibited. It has no enforcement mechanisms for controlling the CBM's implementation. There are different views on the status of the DOC when China interpreted that it signed the DOC with each member of the ASEAN but not with the Association on the whole. The Chinese land reclamation in 2014–2018 in the South China Sea pushed other countries into realizing the need for a new COC. However, the process of negotiation on the new COC has been very slow. The limitations that weaken the DOC were major questions to be addressed in the talk on the COC. In August 2017, the framework for a COC was endorsed by the foreign ministers of the ASEAN and China. Negotiation on ASEAN-China COC began in March 2018 in Hanoi with the objective to finalize it within three years. Vietnam proposed a long list of 27 points to accelerate the COC negotiations.[63] It requires that the COC will be applicable to all disputed features and overlapping maritime areas claimed under the UNCLOS in the South China Sea; disputes are settled through friendly negotiation, inquiry, mediation, conciliation, and other means and nothing in the COC prevents the peaceful settlement of disputes through arbitration, judicial settlement, resort to regional agencies or arrangements, or other peaceful means decided by the parties concerned; respect for maritime zones as provided for and established in accordance with the 1982 UNCLOS; 60 days notification of impending joint/combined military exercise/drill; no construction on any artificial island; no militarization of the features; no blockade of vessels carrying provisions or personnel for rotation; no declaration of an Air Defense Identification Zone (ADIZ) in the South China Sea; and no simulated attacks at the vessels and aircraft of other countries. Vietnam strongly emphasized the COC as being legally binding. Pending a final COC, Vietnam continues to underline the importance of fully respecting and implementing the DOC, treating it as an essential tool to protect the interests of parties in the South China Sea.

Conclusion

Being a coastal country of the South China Sea and with a long history of using and exploiting the Sea, as well as consolidating its sovereignty over the Paracel and the Spratly Islands, Vietnam plays an important role in the process of reaching any solution for the South China Sea disputes. The Vietnamese Government actively participated in the process of concluding and implementing the UNCLOS. The Convention has become a legal framework and an effective tool for Vietnam and other regional countries to protect their legitimate marine interests against attempts based on force and raw power with the aim to abolish the order established by the UNCLOS. Vietnam has adjusted its national legislation in accordance with provisions of the UNCLOS. A substantive and legally binding COC is what Vietnam wants to work for, in cooperation with its ASEAN counterparts and China, to maintain peace, security, legal order, and prosperity in the South China Sea.

Notes

1 Konstantin A. Lutaenko, Kwang-Sik Choi, Thái Ngọc Chiến, "Coastal Marine Biodiversity of Vietnam: Regional and Local Challenges and Coastal Zone Management for Sustainable Development," *Asia-Pacific Network for Global Change Research Project ARCP2011-10CMY-Lutaenko* (2011) available at <https://www.apn-gcr.org/resources/files/original/1a4cea0e652bba8aeb03603f48d6b3a7.pdf>.

2 Sam Bateman, Joshua Ho, Jane Chan, *Good Order at Sea in Southeast Asia*, RSIS Policy Paper April (2009): 16.

3 Pierre-Yves Manguin, *Les Portugais sur les cotes du Vietnam et du Campa, Etude sur les routes maritimes et les relations commerciales, d'apres les sources portugates* (16e, 17e, 18e siècle), L'Institut d'Extrême Orient, Paris (1972). See also Pierre-Yves Manguin, "La traversee de la mer de chine meridionale, des detroits a Canton, jusqu'au XVIIe siecle (La question des iles Paracels)," *Asie de Sud-Est continentale-actes du XXIXE Congres International des Orientalistes* (1976): 110–115.

4 Ministry of Foreign Affairs of the Socialist Republic of Vietnam, *The Hoang Sa And Truong Sa Archipelagos Vietnamese Territories* 9–11 (1981) [Vietnam White Paper 1981].

5 Le Memoire sur la Cochichine de Jean Baptiste Chaigneau par Salles A, in *Bulletin des Amis du vieux Hue* No. 3 Avril-Juin (1923): 25–83.

6 Hai Lu, Volume 13, folio 4, at 2 of *Hai Quoc Do Chi*, written in the 22nd year of the reign of Dasquang of the Qing (1730), Archives of the French Foreign Ministry (AS 1840 China 797).

7 Institute of National History, *Dai Nam Nhat Thong Toan Do* (The Complete Map of the Unified Dai Nam, 1838); Ministry of Foreign Affairs of the Socialist Republic of Vietnam, *The Hoang Sa And Truong Sa Archipelagos Vietnamese Territories* (1981): 19. *See also* http://biengioilanhtho.gov.vn/eng/Album.aspx (last visited on Apr. 1, 2012).

8 Institute of National History, 165:2 *Dai Nam Thuc Luc Chinh Bien* (Accounts of Dai Nam's Present Dynasty, 1865–1882), vol. 165, (1848): 2.

9 Ministry of Foreign Affairs of the Socialist Republic of Vietnam, *Vietnam's Sovereignty over the Hoang Sa And Truong Sa Archipelagos*, [Vietnam White Paper 1979]. Hanoi (1979): 7, available at <https://www.cia.gov/library/readingroom/docs/CIA-RDP08C01297R000300180007-5.pdf>; *The Hoang Sa And Truong Sa Archipelagos Vietnamese Territories* 9–11 (1981), available at <nghiencuubiendong.vn › trung-tam-du-lieu-bien-dong › doc_download › 1...>; *The Hoang Sa (Paracel) and Truong Sa (Spratly) Archipelagos and International Law* [Vietnam White Paper 1988]: 32 (1988), available at <nghiencuubiendong.vn › download › doc_download › 132-white-paper-o...> last accessed 23 September 2019.

10 J. Gutzlaff, "Geography of the Cochin-Chinese Empire," *Journal of Georaphical Society*, 19 (1849): 93–94, London.

11 Letter No. 704 — A — Ex, dated 20 March 1930, from the Governor General of Indochina, Hanoi to the Minister for the Colonies, Paris. See Annex 5, Monique Chemillier-Gendreau, *Sovereignty over the Paracel and Spratly Islands*, La Haye, Kluwer Law International, 265 (2000): 166–167.

12 Le Quy Don, *Phu Bien tap luc* (Miscellany on the Government of the Marches), Book II (1994).

13 *Foreign Ministry's Spokeswoman Le Thi Thu Hang, such as the Speech on April 24, 2018 in Response to Reporters' Queries about China's Recent Activities in the Areas of Vietnam's Hoang Sa and Truong Sa Archipelagos*, available at <https://en.nhandan.com.vn/politics/item/6079702-vietnam-has-sufficient-legal-foundations-and-historical-evidence-proving-its-sovereignty-over-hoang-sa-and-truong-sa-archipelagos.html>.

14 See Island of Palmas case (Netherland/US) (1925), available at <https://pca-cpa.org/en/cases/94>/, Clipperton Island case (France/Mexico) (1932), <https://heinonline.org/HOL/LandingPage?handle=hein.journals/ilanrelat2&div=28&id=&page=>, Sovereignty over Pulau Ligitan and Pulau Sipadan (Indonesia/Malaysia) (2001), <https://www.icj-cij.org/files/

case-related/102/102-20011023-JUD-01-00-EN.pdf> or Case concerning sovereignty over Pedra Blanca/Pulau Batu Puteh, Middle Rocks and South Ledge (Malaysia/Singapore) (2008), <https://www.icj-cij.org/files/case-related/130/130-20080523-JUD-01-00-EN.pdf>.

15 Journal Officiel de la Republique Francaise N. 26, 7837 (1933).

16 Supra note 11, p. 242.

17 Le Monde (Sept. 9–10, 1951).

18 Geneva Agreement on the Cessation of Hostilities in Viet - Nam 20 July 1954, available at <https://peacemaker.un.org/sites/peacemaker.un.org/files/KH-LA-VN_540720_GenevaAgreements.pdf>.

19 Statement on the Territorial Sea, the Contiguous Zone, the Exclusive Economic Zone and the Continental Shelf of 12 May 1977, available at <https://www.un.org/Depts/los/LEGISLATIONANDTREATIES/PDFFILES/VNM_1977_Statement.pdf>.

20 Statement of 12 November 1982 by the Government of the Socialist Republic of Viet Nam on the Territorial Sea Baseline of Viet Nam, available at <https://www.un.org/Depts/los/LEGISLATIONANDTREATIES/PDFFILES/VNM_1982_Statement.pdf>.

21 Hong Thao Nguyen & Hai Oanh Hoang, "The Implementation of the 1982 Convention in Vietnam," 2 *PetroVietnam* 2 (2005): 36–44.

22 Law of the Sea of Vietnam 2012, *Vietnam Law and Legal Forum*, available at <http://vietnamlawmagazine.vn/law-of-the-sea-of-vietnam-4895.html>.

23 See <https://www.un.org/depts/los/clcs_new/submissions_files/submission_mysvnm_33_2009.htm> and <https://www.un.org/depts/los/clcs_new/submissions_files/submission_vnm_37_2009.htm>. See also Nguyen Hong Thao & Ramses Amer, "Coastal States in the South China Sea and Submissions on the Outer Limits of the Continental Shelf," *Ocean Development & International Law*, 42:3 (2011): 245–263, available at <https://www.tandfonline.com/doi/abs/10.1080/00908320.2011.592473>.

24 Douglas Pike, "Vietnam in 1991: The Turning Point," *Asian Survey*, 32:1, A Survey of Asia in 1991: Part I (January 1992): 74–81, Documents of the 7th National Party Congress in June 1991; see also Article 12 of the 2013 Constitution of Vietnam, available at <http://constitutionnet.org/sites/default/files/tranlation_of_vietnams_new_constitution_enuk_2.pdf>.

25 Vietnam's Declaration dated 25 July 1994 on its Ratification of UNCLOS, available at <http://treaties.un.org/pages/ViewDetailsIII.aspx?&src=TREATY&mtdsg_no=XXI~6&chapter=21&Temp=mtdsg3&lang=en#13>.

26 Supra note 22.

27 Nguyen Hong Thao, "Vietnam's First Maritime Boundary Agreement," *IBRU Boundary and Security Bulletin*, 5:3 (Autumn 1997): 74–78.

28 Nguyen Hong Thao, "Maritime Delimitation and Fishery Cooperation in the Tonkin Gulf," *Ocean Development & International Law*, 36:1 (2005): 25–45.

29 See <https://www.un.org/Depts/los/LEGISLATIONANDTREATIES/STATEFILES/VNM.htm>.

30 Nguyen Hong Thao, "Vietnam and the Code of Conduct for the South China Sea," *Ocean Development & International Law*, 32:2 (2001): 105–130.

31 China and Vietnam Agree Principles for Resolving Maritime Disputes," *IBRU Boundary and Security Bulletin*, Durham University 2011, available at <https://www.dur.ac.uk/ibru/news/boundary_news/?itemno=12969>.

32 *Vietnam National Defense* (2019): 23, available at <https://daisukybiendong.files.wordpress.com/2019/12/vietnams-defense-white-paper-2019.pdf>.

33 Ibid.

34 "Vietnam Set to Become a Powerful Marine Nation by 2030," *Vietnam Law and Legal Forum*, 31 December 2018, available at <http://vietnamlawmagazine.vn/vietnam-set-to-become-a-powerful-marine-nation-by-2030-6513.html>.

35 *Party's Resolution on Strategy for Sustainable Development of Marine Economy*, available at <http://news.chinhphu.vn/Home/Partys-Resolution-on-strategy-for-sustainable-development-of-marine-economy/20191/35784.vgp>.

36 Nguyen Huy Trong, *Oil Spill Preparedness and Response in Vietnam: Current Status and Recommendations*, The National Southern Oil Spill Response Center (NASOS), Vietnam, available at <http://www.pcs.gr.jp/doc/esymposium/2014/5_Mr_Nguyen_Huy_Trong_word_E.pdf>.

37 UNEP, *Fisheries Subsidies, Supply Chain and Certification in Vietnam*, Summary Report, (2009): 15, available at <https://unep.ch/etb/areas/fisheries%20country%20projects/vietnam/Final%20Summary%20Report%20Vietnam.pdf>.

38 Nguyen Hong Thao, "Law on the Coast Guard: New Development of Maritime Law Enforcement Agencies in Vietnam," *Vietnam Law & Legal Forum*, 25:298 (June 2019): 9–13.

39 Nguyen Hong Thao, "The 2017 Fisheries Law and the Fight against Illegal Fishing," *Vietnam Law and Legal Forum*, 24:2–3 (2018): 8–12.
40 *UN Oceans & Law of the Sea*, available at <https://www.un.org/depts/los/reference_files/chronological_lists_of_ratifications.htm#Agreement%20for%20the%20implementation%20of%20the%20provisions%20of%20the%20Convention%20of%2010%20December%201982%20relating%20to%20the%20conservation%20and%20management%20of%20straddling%20fish%20stocks%20and%20highly%20migratory%20fish%20stocks>.
41 Arbitration Tribunal Rules to Have Jurisdiction over East Sea-Related Case Filed by the Philippines against China, Vietnam Law and Legal Forum 1/2016, available at <http://vietnamlawmagazine.vn/arbitration-tribunal-rules-to-have-jurisdiction-over-east-sea-related-case-filed-by-the-philippines-against-china-5140.html>.
42 *Supra* note 22.
43 Continental Shelf (Libyan Arab Jarnahiriya/Malta), Judgment, *I. C.J. Reports* (1985): 13–49, available at <https://www.icj-cij.org/files/case-related/68/068-19850603-JUD-01-00-EN.pdf>.
44 Maritime Delimitation in the Area between Greenland and Jan Mayen, Judgment, *I.C.J. Reports* (1993): 38–80, available at <https://www.icj-cij.org/files/case-related/78/078-19930614-JUD-01-00-EN.pdf>.
45 Maritime Delimitation in the Black Sea (Romania v. Ukraine), Judgment, *I.C.J. Reports* (2009): 61–132, available at <https://www.icj-cij.org/files/case-related/132/132-20090203-JUD-01-00-EN.pdf>.
46 Nguyen Hong Thao, "Maritime Delimitation and Fishery Cooperation in the Tonkin Gulf," *Ocean Development & International Law*, 36:1 (2005): 25–45; Zou Keyuan, "Maritime Boundary Delimitation in the Gulf of Tonkin," *Ocean Development & International Law*, 30:3 (1999): 235–254.
47 *The Law of the Sea Bulletins* No.67 (2008): 39, available at <https://www.un.org/Depts/los/doalos_publications/LOSBulletins/bulletinpdf/bulletin67e.pdf>.
48 *The Hoang Sa (Paracel) and Truong Sa (Spratly) Archipelagos and International Law* [Vietnam White Paper 1988) 32 (1988): 28.
49 Ji Guoxing, "China vs. South China Sea security," *Security Dialogue*, 29:1 (1988): 101.
50 China's Ministry of Foreign Affairs, *Set Aside Dispute and Pursue Joint Development*, available at <http://www.fmprc.gov.cn/mfa_eng/ziliao_665539/3602_665543/3604_665547/t18023.shtml>, accessed 16 September 2019.
51 PCA Case No. 2013–19: The South China Sea Arbitration Award of 12 July 2016 (The Republic of the Philippines v. The People's Republic of China), paragraph 646, p. 260 available at <https://pcacases.com/web/sendAttach/2086>.
52 Ibid., para 278.
53 "China Asked to Withdraw Ships from Việt Nam's Territorial Waters," *Vietnamnews*, 16 August 2019, available at <http://vietnamnews.vn/politics-laws/524144/china-asked-to-withdraw-ships-from-viet-nams-territorial-waters.html#f8BJ5ovFfTAX5Fh1.99> and "Vietnam Demands China to Withdraw Ships from Its Territorial Waters," *Nhan Dan*, 12 September 2019, available at <https://en.nhandan.org.vn/politics/item/7910702-vietnam-demands-china-to-withdraw-ships-from-its-territorial-waters.html>.
54 Ministry of Foreign Affairs of SRV, Note on 7 December 2014 to the Tribunal on the South China Sea case. See PCA Award on Jurisdiction and Admissibility 29 October 2015, paragraph 54, p. 20, available at <https://pcacases.com/web/sendAttach/2579>.
55 Note No. 22/HC-2020 of the Permanent Mission of the Socialist Republic of Viet Nam to the United Nations on 30 March 2020, available at https://www.un.org/Depts/los/clcs_new/submissions_files/mys_12_12_2019/VN20200330_ENG.pdf).
56 Ramses Amer, "Border Conflicts between Cambodia and Vietnam," IBRU *Boundary and Security Bulletin*, 5:2 (Summer 1997): 80–92.
57 Nguyen Hong Thao, "Joint Development in the Gulf of Thailand," *Boundary and Security Bulletin*, 7:3 (Autumn 1999). 79–88, available at <http://www.dur.ac.uk/resources/ibru/publications/full/bsb7-3_thao.pdf>.
58 Yao Huang and Mingming Huang, "Implementation of the Sino-Vietnamese Fishery Agreement: Mainly Chinese Perspective," *Beijing Law Review*, 4:3 (2013): 103–119.
59 "Vietnam, China Renew Joint Exploration Agreement," *Nhan Dan*, 20 August 2013, available at <https://en.nhandan.org.vn/politics/external-relations/item/1808402-vietnam-china-renew-joint-exploration-agreement.html>.

60 CNOOC/ PETROVIETNAM/ PNOC, *Joint Statement on the Signing of a Tripartite Agreement for Joint Marine Seismic Undertaking in The Agreement Area in the South China Sea*, 14 March 2005, available at <http://ph.china-embassy.org/eng/zt/nhwt/t187333.htm> last accessed 25 September 2019.
61 Liselotte Odgaard, *Deterrence and Cooperation in the South China Sea. An Analysis of the Spratly Dispute and Its Implications for Regional Order between the PRC and Southeast Asia after the Cold War*, University of Aarhus, Denmark (1997): 329.
62 Nguyen Hong Thao, "Vietnam and the Code of Conduct for the South China Sea," *Ocean Development and International Law*, 32 (2000): 105–130; Nguyen Hong Thao, "Declaration on Parties' Conduct in South China Sea (the East Sea) – a Step towards the Establishment of the Code of Conduct for the Region," *Vietnam Law & Legal Forum*, 9:99 (2002): 19–21.
63 Le Hong Hiep, "Vietnam's Position on the South China Sea Code of Conduct," *ISEAS Perspective*, 22 Singapore (2019): 1–8.

PART IV

Natural resources and environment

13

FISHERIES MANAGEMENT IN THE SOUTH CHINA SEA

Dustin Kuan-Hsiung Wang

Introduction

This chapter focuses on the issues concerning fisheries management in the South China Sea region. First of all, it will explore the situation of abundant fishery resources in the South China Sea and the dependence on fishery resources for nationals of the countries surrounding the South China Sea. Obviously, fishery resources are not only an important source for animal protein but also national income and employment opportunities. The second part is to analyze the situation and causes of the destruction of fishery resources in the South China Sea, mainly from two aspects; one is the result of excessive economic development, and the other is the over-exploitation from fishing activities, especially the illegal, unregulated and unreported (IUU) fishing. The third part is to touch upon the existing multilateral mechanisms and bilateral arrangements related to fishery management in the region. The author suggests that the tension between the claimants of the South China Sea dispute could be reduced through fishery management cooperation. Hence, engagement in a well-designed fishery management arrangement can not only fulfill the responsibility of managing fishery resources and protecting the marine environment but also lay the groundwork for peace and security of the region.

Fishery resources of the South China Sea

Bordering by China, Taiwan, the Philippines, Malaysia, Brunei, Indonesia, Singapore, Thailand, Cambodia and Vietnam, also including Taiwan Strait, Bashi Channel, Karimata Strait and Malacca Strait, the South China Sea is one of the most important and abundant commercial fishing grounds in the world. It is also categorized as a Large Marine Ecosystem (LME). Although it covers only 3.1 million km^2 and represents 8.6 percent of the ocean's surface, it harbors 3,790 fish species, i.e., 22 percent of the 17,200 reported from the world's oceans,[1] and contains 7.04 percent and 0.93 percent of the world's coral reefs and seamounts, respectively.[2] Shared stocks, such as scads and mackerels, and highly migratory species, such as tuna and tuna-like stocks, are the most common commercial stocks in this region.

It is a general situation that organic production and nutrient levels are higher in coastal areas, especially around the mouths of rivers. For example, the discharge from the Mekong River makes the southern portion of the South China Sea, stretching from the Gulf of Siam to Singapore, a particularly rich fishing ground. Similarly, the rivers flowing through the volcanic areas of Sumatra and discharging into the Malacca Strait also encourage the growth of fish nutrients and fish stocks.[3]

Various marine species are distributed throughout the South China Sea. The main species include the coastal tunas (*Euthynnus*, *Thunnus* and *Auxis* spp.), mackerels (*Rastrelliger* spp.), scads (*Decapterus* spp.), king mackerels (*Scomberomorus* spp.), anchovies (*Stolephorus* spp.), sardines (*Sardinella* spp.) and carangids. Larger tuna species, such as skipjack, are taken in the deep-water areas, such as the Celebes Sea; and smaller species are taken in the shallow-water areas close to the exclusive economic zones (EEZs) of the littoral states.[4]

Pelagic fisheries are the most popular and important fishing practices for the littoral states in the region. The fisheries in this region can be divided into two distinct subsectors, namely coastal and deep-sea fisheries. Fisheries in the deep-sea area are generally less diverse than the ones in the coastal waters. The high diversity of resources and low dominance of any species or species groups result in non-targeted, multi-species type fisheries. Coastal pelagic fish are caught in the coastal areas of the central Philippines, the Gulf of Thailand, the Gulf of Tonkin, Sarawak, Brunei, Taiwan, along the coasts of Vietnam, Hainan Island, Mindoro Island, Palawan Island and Natuna Island.[5]

Inevitably, such abundant fishery resources have a huge impact on the lifestyle and livelihood of Southeast Asian peoples, as it provides a source of food, is a major component of the economy, and is a source of employment. Table 13.1 shows the consumption and contribution of fish to the littoral states in 2016. The per capita consumption of fish per year for every state in this region is above the world average. For some of them, such as Malaysia, Singapore, Brunei, Cambodia and China,[6] the consumption is much higher than the one for the world. In addition, fish is the single most important source of animal protein for the people in this region. More than one-third of the total intake of animal protein by the average Southeast Asian person comes from fish.

As an animal-based protein, fish plays a critical role in maintaining food security in this region because it is more accessible and often cheaper. Table 13.1 also illustrates the result of fish consumed into levels of protein consumption. It is clear that fish provided the highest

Table 13.1 Fish and Fishery Products Consumption and Contribution for States Surrounding South China Sea, 2016

	Fish and Fishery Products Per Capita Supply (kg/year)	*Fish Contribution to Protein Supply (Fish/Animal Proteins, %)*
Brunei	46.4	22.8
Cambodia	42.2	69.8
China	38.9	23.6
Indonesia	30.5	55.2
Malaysia	57.3	38.9
Philippines	28.6	36.8
Singapore	49.1	21.8
Taiwan	30.2	18.6
Thailand	27.2	37.5
Vietnam	35.6	31.3
World	**19.7**	**17.4**

Sources: FAO, *Food Balance Sheets and Fish Contribution to Protein Supply*, by world continent and economic groups, 2016 and 1961–2016, available at http://www.fao.org/fishery/static/Yearbook/YB2017_USBcard/root/food_balance/section1.pdf (accessed 19 November 2020).

levels of protein in the diet in Cambodia, accounting for 69.8 percent of total protein consumed followed by Indonesia at 55.2 percent. The lowest level was recorded in Taiwan where fish represented 18.6 percent of protein intake. Nonetheless, it is also understandable that even the lowest is still higher than the world average at 17.4 percent.

Fisheries create jobs for a large number of the coastal populations in the region, which play an important role in providing employment opportunities. For instance, engagement in fisheries and aquaculture in China remained between 14.2 million and 14.6 million in the period of 2012–2016 (about 25 percent of the world total).[7] Almost in the same period, in 2014, 76 percent of the global population engaged in the fisheries and aquaculture sector came from Asia (excluding Southeast Asia) followed by Southeast Asia (11 percent) and this represents 8.17 million fishers and fish farmers.[8] In terms of fishing capacity, there are 1,770,000 fishing vessels operating in the South China Sea.[9] These figures illustrate the importance of the social-economic development of this region.

In addition, fishery is one of the foundations for many other economic sectors in the coastal regions as well as an important source of foreign currency for the states in the region. For instance, with nearly 10,000 processing companies which heavily rely upon the marine catch sector for raw materials, China is not only the biggest fishery producer, but also is the largest fishery processing sector in the world. Similarly, marine fishery is important for the development of marine tourism, shipbuilding, and onshore catering sectors of China and ASEAN countries.[10]

In 2014, Asia contributed to a third of global seafood exports. China, Vietnam and Thailand rank among the top five fishery exporters in the world. China is by far the largest fishery exporter in the world. China's exports totaled nearly USD 21 billion, accounting for 12.5 percent of total global exports in 2014. As for Thailand and Vietnam, fishery exports are one of the key sources of foreign exchange. Indonesia, as the second-largest fishery producer in the world, has boosted the country's fishery exports in recent years as well. Indonesia's global exports of fishery products reached USD 3.6 billion in 2015.[11]

From the aforementioned facts, it is understandable that fisheries have been the leading industry of the major source of animal protein, employment, livelihood and foreign exchange, which have a great impact on the livelihoods of those littoral nationals of the South China Sea.

Factors that harm fishery resources

Environmental pollution

The issues of environmental pollution in the South China Sea are generally originated from population growth and urbanization in coastal cities, economic growth and increased consumption, as well as highly polluting technologies for energy production and primary resource extraction. In addition, there has been an increase in oil spills and waste dumping by transit vessels as a result of increasing trade and transport of raw materials, fossil fuels and commodities across the region's shipping lanes.[12]

The South China Sea has been undergoing serious environmental degradation caused by land-based pollution, sea-based pollution, habitat loss, etc.[13] In terms of land-based pollution, the South China Sea is surrounded by quite a few large and rapidly growing cities, e.g. Guangzhou, Hong Kong, Ho Chi Minh City, Bangkok, Manila, Jakarta and Singapore. Wastewater from those cities has been flowing into the sea without being appropriately treated due to insufficient sewage treatment facilities. Additionally, pesticides are used epidemically so that they become one of the major contributors to environmental degradation in the South China Sea region.[14]

As to sea-based pollution, the major causes of oil pollution are ships, oil and gas exploration, and production platforms. Because of its rich oil and natural gas reserves, the activities of exploiting these resources in the South China Sea have become frequent, and it is particularly important to avoid accidents. The U.S. Energy Information Administration (EIA) estimates in 2013 that the South China Sea holds approximately 190 trillion cubic feet of natural gas and 11 billion barrels of oil in proved and probable reserves, most of which lie along the margins of the South China Sea rather than under disputed islets and reefs. According to the U.S. Geological Survey (USGS) 2010 study, it is estimated that there could be between 5 and 22 billion barrels of oil and between 70 and 290 trillion cubic feet of gas in the South China Sea region. Moreover, in November 2012, the Chinese National Offshore Oil Company (CNOOC) estimated that the area holds around 125 billion barrels of oil and 500 trillion cubic feet of natural gas in undiscovered resources.[15] These figures express the fact that the South China Sea is rich in resources as well as holds significant influence in political and economic power.

However, under the situation of the rapid growth of Asian economies, such as Taiwan, Japan, Korea or China, the increase of oil demand will bring on the growth of oil transportation via the sea,[16] which will eventually increase the risk of oil spills. This issue had been discussed in 2006 at the second East Asian Seas Congress held in Haikou, Hainan, China. It was recognized that the large volumes of oil being transported and this increased oil tanker traffic and associated spill risks. Furthermore, it will contribute to the incidents in the region. Therefore, it emphasized the need to strengthen the region's preparedness through effective legal frameworks and contingency plans.[17]

Nevertheless, as the littoral states around the South China Sea keep expanding their economies and consuming more fossil fuel resources, in the same manner, they also produce a large amount of pollution. Many of these states are now making important decisions about technology and infrastructure with critical implications for long-term environmental change. Many of them face competitive market pressures to produce at the lowest, short-term cost as possible. As long as governments compete with each other for investment in an increasingly integrated world economy, they are reluctant to impose costly regulations to maintain environmental standards, which might discourage investment and output. From the individual national, short-term view, pollution control programs may hinder economic performance and increase consumer prices. States that do impose charges on polluters are thought to give business enterprises an incentive to relocate to countries with more lenient standards. As a result, many environmental pollution problems are often overshadowed by concerns over economic growth.[18]

Overfishing and IUU fishing

Because of the extensive continental shelves, relatively shallow depths, and the influx of numerous large continental rivers, the South China Sea has become a highly productive body of water in terms of fisheries and other marine living resources. In addition to this, habitats in the South China Sea include mangrove forests, seagrass beds, coral reefs and soft-bottom communities, all of which may post highly productive ecosystems. The South China Sea has also the world's highest level of biodiversity. According to a study, species abundance in the South China Sea region includes 1,027 fish, 91 shrimp and 73 cephalopod species in the northern continental shelf; approximately 205 fish and 96 shrimp species in the continental slope; and more than 520 fish species around the islands and reefs of the southern waters. The fisheries resources of the South China Sea are of great local, national and international importance as well as being a major contributor to both food and income of the nationals in the region. In total, the South China Sea produces around 5 million tonnes of catch each year, some 10 percent of the total global catch.[19]

In its development history, trawlers were introduced to the Southeast Asian countries in the 1960s. With their efficiency and higher production rate, trawlers became a popular fishing method. At the outset, there is neither a fishing policy nor the concept of fishery resources management for those littoral states to limit the increase of fishing efforts. More specifically, in order to meet the demand for fishery resources, states tend to improve their fishing yields.

Cambodia

Cambodia's capture fisheries produced 649,500 tonnes in 2017. Its freshwater fisheries are among the most productive in the world due to the presence of large floodplains around the Great Lake and along the Tonle Sap and the Mekong Rivers. These inland fisheries have produced 528,500 tonnes in 2017. By comparison, the total marine fishery production was 121,000 tonnes.[20]

China[21]

China has been the world's largest exporter of fish and fishery products since 2002, with exports reaching USD 19.7 billion in 2015. Also in 2015, China produced 65.2 million tonnes of food fish, with 47.6 million tonnes (73 percent) from aquaculture and 17.6 million tonnes (27 percent) from capture. Catches reported for Chinese vessels operating in distant waters (areas outside fishing area "61-Northwest Pacific") grew significantly reaching almost 1 million tonnes in 2015, but it is thought that catch data by distant fleets may still be underreported. The fishery sector provided jobs for over 14 million people in 2015 in all sectors.

Indonesia[22]

In 2012, Indonesia's fishery production reached approximately 8.9 million tonnes, of which inland and marine catch accounted for about 5.8 million tonnes and aquaculture 3.1 million tonnes in addition to 6.5 million tonnes of seaweeds. About 95 percent of fishery production comes from artisanal fishermen. The marine fishing fleet comprised 620,830 vessels in 2012, with 28 percent of non-powered boats and 39 percent of the out-board engine. An additional 184,900 vessels (of which 23 percent had an engine) composed the fleet operating in inland waters. In 2012, about 6.4 million people were engaged in inland and marine fishing and fish farming.

Malaysia[23]

In 2017, total fishery production amounted to 1.7 million tonnes, including 1.5 million tonnes from capture and 0.2 million tonnes from aquaculture (excluding seaweeds). Malaysia produced 0.2 million tonnes of farmed seaweeds as the world's seventh-largest producer, as well as ranked third for tropical carrageenan seaweed farming. Marine capture fisheries are subdivided into coastal fisheries and offshore subsector. The total number of fishermen in 2017 was estimated to be about 132,305 with an additional 21,156 people who were engaged in aquaculture.

Philippines[24]

In 2012, the Philippines ranked among the major fish producing countries in the world with a total production of 3.1 million tonnes of fish and other aquatic products. Aquaculture contributed 790,900 tonnes (25.4 percent) to the total fish production. Much of its production is consumed locally. In addition, the Philippines is the world's third-largest producer of farmed seaweeds with a production of 1.8 million tonnes in 2012. The fisheries and aquaculture industry employed an estimated 1.5 million people in 2010 nationwide, with fisheries accounting for more than 1 million.

Taiwan[25]

Taiwan's total fishery production was about 1 million tonnes in 2016, with 0.73 million tonnes (73 percent) from distant water fisheries,[26] 0.17 million tonnes from coastal and offshore fisheries, and 0.03 from aquaculture. There were about 330,000 people engaged in the work of fisheries.

Thailand[27]

Thailand's total fishery production was 2.4 million tonnes in 2017, with marine and inland capture fisheries contributing 1.5 million tonnes and aquaculture contributing 0.9 million tonnes. An estimated total of 445,000 people was engaged in the aquaculture and marine fishing sector in 2017. The fishing fleet, equipped with engines was 25,002 marine fishing vessels. In 2017, the farming production of marine shrimp represented almost 40 percent of the total inland and marine culture production. Thailand is the world's sixth-largest producer of cultured marine shrimps in 2017.

Vietnam[28]

Vietnam was the fourth major producer of fishery and aquaculture with a total production of 6.4 million tonnes in 2016 and the third major exporter of fish and fishery products with a value at USD 8.5 billion in 2017 in the world. Aquaculture was the major contributor to total fisheries production and reached 3.6 million tonnes in 2016. Marine capture fishery produced 2.7 million tonnes in 2016. In 2015, a total of 28,719 vessels were reported. Approximately 4.4 million people are employed in the marine and aquaculture fisheries.

In order to have a better understanding of the fisheries condition as well as have a better management of fishery resources, and specifically have a better understanding on fisheries catch statistical data, the world oceans are divided into several fishing areas and the catch data is maintained by the FAO. The South China Sea region is within the Area 71, which is under the title of Western Central Pacific.[29]

In terms of global production of marine capture fisheries, it reached 79.3 million tonnes in 2016. Taking a more detailed observation, the top five marine capture Areas are Northwest Pacific with 22.4 million tonnes (28.2 percent of the global marine catch), Western Central Pacific with 12.7 million tonnes (16.0 percent), Northeast Atlantic with 8.3 million tonnes (10.5 percent), Eastern Indian Ocean with 6.4 million tonnes (8 percent) and Southeast Pacific with 6.3 million tonnes (7.9 percent).[30] In other words, the area of the Western Central Pacific, where the South China Sea locates, contributes about 16 percent of global marine production. Despite this apparently positive situation, there are reasons for concern regarding the state of the resources, with most stocks being either fully exploited or overexploited (many also depleted), particularly in the western part of the South China Sea. The high catches have probably been maintained through the expansion of the fisheries to new areas, and possible double-counting in the transshipment of catches between fishing areas, which leads to bias in estimates of production, potentially masking negative trends in stock status.[31] Another research shows that 80 percent of coral reefs in the South China Sea were at risk, two-thirds of the major fish species[32] and several of the region's most important fishing areas are fully or over-exploited by the destructive measures employed.[33]

IUU fishing is one of the most dangerous practices which contributes to the depletion of fish stocks in the South China Sea.[34] The impact of illegal fishing emerges in an endless stream. As IUU fishing practices may result in the decline or depletion of a fish stocks, or the adverse impact on efforts to recover depleted stocks, and it will cause damage to the conservation of marine living resources. More seriously, it will also have an impact on maintaining the diversity of marine living resources. Among all the law and order challenges at sea in this region, IUU has the most immediate and serious impact on economic development and environmental sustainability.

According to the study of a South China Sea Expert Working Group which is supported by the Asia Maritime Transparency Initiative (AMTI), total fish stocks in the South China Sea have been depleted by 70–95 percent since the 1950s, and catch rates have declined by 66–75 percent over the last 20 years.[35] Furthermore, common methods such as dynamite fishing, cyanide poisoning, and bottom trawling have wreaked havoc in regional ecosystems and threaten the future of the regional fishing market. It is estimated that 40 percent of the South China Sea's fish stocks have already disappeared and 70 percent of the South China Sea's coral reefs are rated to be in fair or poor condition.[36] The entire South China Sea fishery, which employs millions of people and helps feed hundreds of millions, is now in danger of collapse unless claimants act urgently to arrest the decline.

The resources of the South China Sea, either living or non-living, are rapidly being exploited by the people of the region, who are concentrated along with the heavily developed coastline areas. Overfishing and IUU fishing are compounded by sovereignty claims in the South China Sea. Fishing boats are traveling farther from their territorial waters because there are fewer fish to be found in traditional fishing grounds. Part of the reason the claimants are asserting sovereignty over islands, rocks, shoals, and reefs is because of the fish in the surrounding waters. Ambiguous territorial claims, unilateral fishing restrictions, illegal fishing activities and uncertain law enforcement among the claimants would surely worsen this situation.

Multilateral and bilateral practices of fishery management

Legal framework for fishery cooperation

The South China Sea meets the criteria set out in Article 122 of the 1982 United Nations Convention on the Law of the Sea (UNCLOS) defining the term "semi-enclosed sea":

> [E]nclosed or semi-enclosed sea' means a gulf, basin or sea surrounded by two or more States and connected to another sea or the ocean by a narrow outlet or consisting entirely or primarily of the territorial seas and exclusive economic zones of two or more coastal States.

On this ground, any change in the eco-system of the semi-enclosed sea will have a significant impact on the whole area. It is generally recognized that the living resources in the South China Sea area migrate from one EEZ to another, particularly those highly migratory species, such as tuna and other shared stocks. Each country may already have its own assessment of its living resources in its EEZ, assuming that the definition and delineation of each EEZ are clear. The problem is that many of those EEZ boundaries are not well defined or mutually agreed upon by the relevant parties. Likewise, there are various conflicting claims to islands that complicate and defer the determination of the EEZ boundaries. For this reason, there is a need to cooperate on the assessment of the living resources in the South China Sea area without regard to jurisdictional boundaries. The basis for this endeavour would be Article 123 of the UNCLOS regarding the responsibilities of the coastal states surrounding enclosed or semi-enclosed seas. Article 123 provides:

> States bordering an enclosed or semi-enclosed sea should co-operate with each other in the exercise of their rights and in the performance of their duties under this Convention. To this end they shall endeavour, directly or through an appropriate regional organisation:
>
> a to co-ordinate the management, conservation, exploration and exploitation of the living resources of the sea;
> b to co-ordinate the implementation of their rights and duties with respect to the protection and preservation of the marine environment;
> c to co-ordinate their scientific research policies and undertake where appropriate joint programmes of scientific research in the area;
> d to invite, as appropriate, other interested states or international organisations to co-operate with them in furtherance of the provisions of this article.

Therefore, all parties concerned should be aware that fish are migratory and fishery resources are exhaustible, so that rational use of the South China Sea and the preservation of its marine environment are important to all parties. Thus, cooperation among littoral states in the region is essential. In order to avoid overfishing or depletion of resources, the related states should take conservation measures as the cooperation measures. Such measures are not possible without regional cooperation and require close coordination among the parties concerned especially in a semi-enclosed sea like the South China Sea.

A semi-enclosed sea concept could provide a legal basis for promoting cooperation and coordination in fishery resources management in countries surrounding the South China Sea. Under such circumstances, for all the littoral states to make the boundary delimitation issue as the first priority would be unwise. Instead, concentrating upon their common interests can be an essential motivation to resolve conflicts rationally. Under this situation, fishery cooperation could be the most feasible course of action for the littoral states since through cooperation, fishery resources could be properly conserved and managed such that economic waste and overexploitation may be avoided.

In the same fashion, there are several other documents that express the willingness to cooperate among the related states in the region. The first one is the Declaration on the Conduct (DOC) of the Parties in the South China Sea signed in 2002 between ASEAN member states and China.[37] DOC notes the Parties desire to peacefully resolve all territorial and jurisdiction disputes between them. Although the term 'fishery cooperation' is not provided in the DOC, it is understandable that some of the cooperative activities, such as 'marine environmental protection' or 'marine scientific research' could be interpreted as fishery cooperation related matters. A similar expression is also included in the 1992 ASEAN Declaration on the South China Sea[38] and the 1976 Treaty of Amity and Cooperation in Southeast Asia.[39]

Multilateral fishery management cooperation

As a persistent inter-relation, fisheries impact not only on the stocks exploited, but also on the ecosystems in which the stocks are embedded. This is particularly true for demersal trawl fisheries, which are non-selective and also have an impact on the habitat on which the fish depend. Indeed, contrary to a still widely spread perception, fisheries are causing a major impact on marine ecosystems, far outweighing effects such as pollution and environmental changes.[40] It is also true that the South China Sea is regarded as the semi-enclosed sea. Therefore, cooperation among the littoral states is important. The following is a list of several regional organizations or arrangements that existed among littoral states of the South China Sea which reflects the general willingness to resolve mutual problems through cooperation.

Western and Central Pacific Fisheries Commission (WCPFC)

WCPFC is one of the regional fishery management organizations (RFMOs)[41] and probably the only one RFMO's convention area covers the South China Sea. It was established by the Convention for the Conservation and Management of Highly Migratory Fish Stocks in the Western and Central Pacific Ocean, which entered into force in 2004.[42] The objective of the Convention is to ensure, through effective management, the long-term conservation and sustainable use of highly migratory fish stocks in this area. The WCPF Convention draws on many of the provisions of the UN Fish Stocks Agreement (UNFSA) while, at the same time, reflecting the special political, socio-economic, geographical and environmental characteristics of the Western and Central Pacific Ocean (WCPO) region. The WCPFC Convention seeks to address problems in the management of high seas fisheries resulting from unregulated fishing, over-capitalization, excessive fleet capacity, vessel re-flagging to escape controls, insufficiently selective gear, unreliable databases and insufficient multilateral cooperation in respect to conservation and management of highly migratory fish stocks.[43] Its headquarters is in Pohnpei, Federated States of Micronesia and has 26 members.[44]

Article 3 of the WCPFC Convention stipulates that the area of competence of the Commission (hereinafter referred to as "the Convention Area") comprises all waters of the Pacific Ocean bounded to the south and the east by the following line:

> From the south coast of Australia due south along the 141° meridian of east longitude to its intersection with the 55° parallel of south latitude; thence due east along the 55° parallel of south latitude to its intersection with the 150° meridian of east longitude; thence due south along the 150° meridian of east longitude to its intersection with the 60° parallel of south latitude; thence due east along the 60° parallel of south latitude to its intersection with the 130° meridian of west longitude; thence due north along the 130° meridian of west longitude to its intersection with the 4° parallel of south latitude; thence due west along the 4° parallel of south latitude to its intersection with the 150° meridian of west longitude; thence due north along the 150° meridian of west longitude.

It is clear that the area covered by the WCPFC Convention covers almost 20 percent of the Earth's surface. Although the western boundary notionally extends to the East Asian seaboard, it is understood that the Convention Area does not include the South China Sea. In the east, the Convention Area adjoins, or overlaps, the area of competence of the Inter-American Tropical Tuna Commission. The southern boundary extends to 60 degrees south and the northern boundary extends to Alaska and the Bering Sea. Obviously, the Convention Area does not cover those fishery issues that happened in the South China Sea.

WCPFC is the first RFMO to adopt "Boarding and Inspection Procedures" on the high seas within its convention area.[45] "Boarding and Inspection Procedures" is one of WCPFC's principal enforcement tools, which authorizes member states to board and inspect fishing vessels on the high seas but within its convention area engaged in a regulated fishery to verify compliance with the Commission's conservation and management measures. The Procedures is critical of being a deterrence and enforcement mechanism. It is because, on the high seas, no single state may assert sovereignty nor enact unilateral conservation and management measures regarding the living marine resources, making these resources particularly susceptible to IUU fishing. The enforcement and deterrence benefits of boarding and inspection also extend to the EEZs of neighboring states, whose conservation and management measures can easily be subverted by illegal fishing in adjacent high seas areas, or by the use of such areas to support illegal activities within adjacent EEZs.[46]

Asia-Pacific Fishery Commission (APFIC)

The APFIC was founded in 1948, with the original name of the Indo-Pacific Fisheries Council (IPFC),[47] to promote the full and proper use of living aquatic resources in the region from the Indian Ocean to the Pacific Ocean. The Commission assists member countries to achieve their objectives by helping with the development and management of fishing and culture operations, processing and marketing. APFIC works to improve understanding, awareness and cooperation concerning fisheries issues in the Asia-Pacific region. Twenty-one countries are now members of the Commission,[48] which maintains its Secretariat at the FAO Regional Office for Asia and the Pacific in Bangkok, Thailand.

As a regional fishery body established by FAO, the main function of the APFIC is "to promote the full and proper utilization of living aquatic resources by the development and management of fishing and culture operations and by the development of related processing and marketing activities in conformity with the objectives of its members."[49] The APFIC is committed to acting as a regional consultative forum, providing member countries, regional organizations and fisheries professionals in the region with the opportunity to review and discuss the challenges facing the region's fisheries sector and helping them decide on the most appropriate actions to take.[50]

To meet its objectives, the APFIC has a broad mandate in formulating and recommending measures for conservation and management of the resources. There is no specific system in place to collect data on catches in the agreement area,[51] but APFIC provides a regional overview of fisheries and aquaculture on its website, with biannual reports. APFIC has supported measures for the adoption of VMS in the agreement area since 2014. APFIC has developed regional guidelines for the management of tropical trawl fisheries, including a recommendation to implement VMS on all large vessels.[52] APFIC has carried out a number of workshops focusing specifically on combating IUU fishing and APFIC has also supported actions to implement port State measures since 2014 by providing training courses and producing material on the subject.[53]

The Southeast Asia Fisheries Development Center (SEAFDEC)

SEAFDEC is an autonomous intergovernmental body established in 1967 by the Agreement Establishing the Southeast Asian Fisheries Development Center to promote fisheries development in Southeast Asia.[54] The purpose of SEAFDEC is to contribute to the promotion of fisheries development in Southeast Asia by mutual cooperation among the member governments of it and through collaboration with international organizations and governments external to it.[55]

Wording of Paragraph 2 of the SEAFDEC Agreement express that

> [The Contracting Governments] realizing that, in order to promote the fisheries development in this region, further efforts should be made in the fields of training of fisheries technicians, research on fisheries techniques and investigation of fisheries resources and in other relevant fields.

Obviously, SEAFDEC aims specifically to develop the fishery potentials in the region through training, research and information services to improve the food supply by rational utilization and development of the fisheries resources. Its services cover the broad areas of fishing gear technology, marine engineering, fishing ground surveys and stock assessment, post-harvest technology as well as development and improvement of aquaculture techniques. Moreover, the mission of SEAFDEC considered and adopted by the Special Meeting of the SEAFDEC Council 2017 is "To promote and facilitate concerted actions among the Member Countries to ensure the sustainability of fisheries and aquaculture in Southeast Asia."[56] There are eleven members so far[57] and its secretariat is in Thailand.

SEAFDEC supports its members in combating IUU fishing in various ways, including projects on applying catch certification for international trade in fish and fishery products, developing a regional fishing vessel record for vessels longer than 24 metres, and supporting the implementation of port State measures through regional cooperation. SEAFDEC has endorsed and is working to implement the ASEAN guidelines for preventing the entry of fish and fishery products from IUU fishing activities into the supply Chain.[58]

Regional Plan of Action to promote responsible fishing practices including combating Illegal, Unreported and Unregulated fishing in the region (RPOA-IUU)

The RPOA-IUU was endorsed by Ministers responsible for fisheries in Bali, Indonesia, in May 2007. Eleven countries, including Australia, Brunei Darussalam, Cambodia, Indonesia, Malaysia, Papua New Guinea, Philippines, Singapore, Thailand, Timor-Leste and Vietnam and four regional fisheries organisations provide technical advice and assistance, which are FAO/Asia-Pacific Fishery Commission (APFIC), Southeast Asian Fisheries Development Centre (SEAFDEC), InfoFish and WorldFish Center. The objectives of RPOA are to enhance and strengthen the overall level of fisheries management in the region, in order to sustain fisheries resources and the marine environment, also to optimize the benefit of adopting responsible fishing practices. The actions cover conservation of fisheries resources and their environment, managing fishing capacity, and combating IUU fishing in the areas of Sub-Regional Southern and Eastern of South China Sea and Sulu-Sulawesi Seas (SESCS SSS), Sub-Regional Gulf of Thailand, and Sub-Regional Arafura-Timor Seas.[59]

Network of Aquaculture Centres in Asia-Pacific (NACA)

NACA was formed by an international treaty, Agreement on the Network of Aquaculture Centres in Asia and the Pacific, which was signed in Bangkok on 8 January 1988.[60] The purpose of the NACA is the recognition of the importance of fisheries in the Asia Pacific region, where aquaculture plays a vital role in the promotion and better use of fishery resources and that the maintenance of a network of aquaculture centres in the region can make a significant contribution to the development of aquaculture. NACA has 18 members[61] and its headquarters is based in Kasetsart University, Bangkok.

Bilateral fishery management cooperation

1974 Agreement on fisheries between the Philippines and Indonesia[62]

Both Governments shall promote mutual cooperation in the development of the fishing industries of both countries pursuant to their respective investment and other laws; both Governments shall promote mutual consultation and exchange of technical assistance and research findings on all phases of fisheries, including utilization of by-products; both Governments shall continue discussions through the agencies designated in the Basic Agreement to explore other means of promoting further cooperation in the field of fishing industry in both countries.

1996 Memorandum of agreement between the government of the republic of the Philippines and the government of Malaysia on the establishment of the Turtle Island heritage protected area

Both Parties agree to establish the Turtle Island Heritage Protected Area (TIHPA) composed of six islands designated by the Philippines and three islands designated by Malaysia. These nine islands are located in the Sulu-Sulawesi region in the border areas between the province of Tawi-Tawi, the Philippines and Sabah, Malaysia. Both Parties shall jointly manage and protect the Turtle Islands Heritage Protected Area as a green and hawksbill turtle sanctuary. The area is the largest remaining nesting site for green turtles in Southeast Asia.[63]

2000 Agreement on fishery cooperation in the Beibu Gulf between China and Vietnam[64]

Overexploitation of fishery resources in the Gulf of Tonkin is evident. According to one scientific estimation, the sustainable catch in the Gulf is 600,000 tonnes per year. In recent years, however, the catch by the two sides has exceeded 1 million tonnes. If this situation were allowed to continue, the fishery resources in the Gulf would be depleted within a short period. In order to conserve fishery resources, protection measures are necessary.

The Agreement on Fishery Cooperation in the Beibu Gulf establishes a Common Fishery Zone, a buffer zone for small fishing boats, and a zone for transitional arrangements. The Common Fishery Zone, about 30,000 square kilometres, covers most of the fishing grounds of high productivity in the Gulf. The Fishery Agreement also indicates that there is to be a Transitional Zone that is to last for four years. The Transitional Zone is to be defined by a separate protocol to the Fishery Agreement. This special arrangement is to allow Chinese fishermen to have time to adjust their fishing patterns to the new and changed conditions. Another two additional agreements followed up, one is the Supplementary Protocol, and the other is the Management Measures for the Conservation of the Resources in the Common Fishery Zone in the Gulf of Tonkin.[65]

2003 Protocol amending the arrangement between Indonesia and Thailand on the utilization of part of the total allowable catch in the Indonesian exclusive economic zone[66]

Both Parties agree that Thai fishing vessels are granted the right to access to part of the TAC of demersal and large-pelagic fish stocks in the Indonesian EEZ in the South China Sea, measured from the Indonesian straight archipelagic baselines as indicated in the relevant Indonesian laws and regulations, and the Indonesian EEZ in the Arafura Sea between 132°E and 140°E.

2005 Memorandum of understand between Taiwan and the Philippines on agricultural and fishery cooperation[67]

Both Parties, in conformity with their respective laws and regulations, including those on conservation and management of natural resources, shall promote scientific, technical and economic cooperation in the fields of agriculture and fisheries. They agree to establish a mechanism to help prevent poaching activities including expeditious resolution of alleged poaching cases on the waters of both sides.

2011 Letter of intent between Indonesia and Brunei Darussalam on Marine and fisheries cooperation[68]

Two countries intend to establish marine and fisheries cooperation, in accordance with their prevailing laws and regulation, in the following areas of cooperation: (1) Sustainable aquaculture development; (2) Marine capture fisheries cooperation through joint venture investment; (3) Fishery product processing and marketing; (4) Fish quarantine and inspection; (5) Preventing, combating and eliminating IUU Fishing; (6) Marine conservation, integrated coastal zone management and marine eco-tourism; (7) Research, development and capacity building; and (8) Exchange of data and information on marine and fisheries.

2012 Memorandum of Understanding (MoU) in respect to the Common Guidelines concerning Treatment of Fishermen by Malaysia and Indonesia[69]

The objective of the Common Guidelines is to establish guidance for agreed activities in dealing with fisheries issues between the Parties with particular emphasis on ensuring the wellbeing of the fishermen of the Parties. The Common Guidelines includes the following points:

1 The highest priority is given to maintaining good relations, close cooperation and mutual understanding between the Parties;
2 Every action and maneuver undertaken by maritime law enforcement agencies should avoid any violence and be carried out without use of force.
3 Impartial treatment should be extended to the fishermen in accordance with their fundamental human rights.
4 Actions to be taken upon encroachment incidents/cases:
    A Inspection and request to leave the area shall be conducted promptly towards all fishing boats, except for those using illegal fishing gears, such as explosives, electrical and chemical fishing gears;
    B Notification on the inspection and request to leave the area shall be reported promptly to Focal Points; and
    C Conducting an open and direct communication among the maritime law enforcement agencies of the Parties promptly and expeditiously.

2015 Agreement Concerning the Facilitation of Cooperation on Law Enforcement in Fisheries Matters between Taiwan and the Philippines[70]

Both Parties agree:

1. Avoiding the use of violence or unnecessary force: The relevant authorities of the Parties shall avoid using violence or unnecessary force in the implementation of their fisheries laws and other relevant regulations consistent with international law and practice.
2. Notifying, without delay, to the other Party when a fishing boat of the other Party is in breach of the provisions of the Agreement and the action taken by its law enforcement agencies against fishing vessels from the other Party. The other Party shall respect the notifying Party's notification.
3. Providing the other Party with a result report of the law enforcement action taken against said Party's fishing vessel.
4. Formulating other concrete measures of cooperation, including sharing of law enforcement methods and procedures and relevant laws and regulations.

2017 Joint Statement between China and the Philippines[71]

Both sides agree to strengthen cooperation on agriculture and fisheries. China is willing to support the Philippines to develop science and technology-driven agriculture, improve rice production capacity, and offer funding and technical support to the agriculture and fisheries industry of the Philippines.

2018 Joint Communique on Voluntary International Cooperation to Combat Illegal, Unreported and Unregulated (IUU) Fishing and to Promote Sustainable Fisheries Governance between Indonesia and Vietnam[72]

Both Parties strengthen cooperation in the followings:

1. Supporting efforts to prevent, deter and eliminate IUU Fishing based on the existing national, regional and international effective tools and measures.
2. Enhancing effort and measures to promote responsible fishing practices and to combat IUU fishing through information sharing and capacity building activities.
3. Exercising the precautionary principles in sustainable fisheries governance, including taking necessary action in reducing fishing efforts.

2018 Joint Statement between China and the Philippines[73]

Both sides reaffirm the importance of existing China-Philippines bilateral dialogue mechanisms, such as the Joint Committee on Fisheries, in enhancing understanding, broadening cooperation, and striving for a stronger partnership. They will step up cooperation in the fishery and other fields.

Conclusion

It is a fact that the South China Sea has abundant fishery resources, and the people of the littoral states rely upon such resources on the animal protein supply as well as the employment.

However, fishery resources are fragile and dependent upon sound governance. Environmental degradation, overfishing for short-term gain, and illegal fishing activities will cause damage to the stability of stocks' existence.

Fish are by nature migratory and do not abide by territorial boundaries. It has been suggested that the best approach for managing potential conflicts in the South China Sea is for the relevant parties to set aside their competing sovereignty claims and focus on joint development and management of the natural resources in the region, fishery management is one of the solutions.

The absence of a regional governing body or a multilateral agreement to govern fisheries is one of the key contributors to the increasing levels of overfishing, IUU fishing and fishing-related conflicts in the South China Sea. Nonetheless, there is no RFMO to deal with fishery issues in the South China Sea. As far as multilateral fishery management cooperation in the previous section is concerned, none is actually in a position to serve as a basis for effective fishery management in the South China Sea region because of their limited jurisdiction on fishing activities and their limited functions on management.

The establishment of an RFMO in the South China Sea is considered imperative to manage the region's fishery issues. Cooperation through an RFMO not only could reduce fishery disputes in the area, but also help to alleviate other possible disputes in the South China Sea, particularly territorial disputes. Nonetheless, we witness the positive development of bilateral cooperation on fishery management. We also find that the littoral states of the South China Sea are willing to cooperate in the fishery resources management matters, especially coordination in combating IUU fishing activities. Perhaps they realize that most fish species in the South China Sea are considered to be fully utilized or over-utilized, and it is impossible for fishing output to increase further, or to continue to focus on increasing production will lead to the complete destruction of fishery resources. Under such circumstances, it might be a better solution to refine the fishery management and to build up an RFMO through the meshwork of cooperation between littoral states.

Notes

1 Daniel Pauly and Cui Liang, "The Fisheries of the South China Sea: Major Trends since 1950," (2019) *Marine Policy*, doi: 10.1016/j.marpol.2019.103584. (accessed 22 April 2020)
2 S. Heileman, "South China Sea: LME #36," in Kenneth Sherman and Gotthilf Hempel eds., *The UNEP Large Marine Ecosystem Report: A Perspective on Changing Conditions in LMEs of the World's Regional Seas*, UNEP Regional Seas, Report and Studies No. 182 (UNEP, 2008).
3 Lee Yong Leng, *Southeast Asia and the Law of the Sea: Some Preliminary Observations on the Political Geography of Southeast Asian Seas* (Singapore University Press, 1978) 31–32.
4 Hiroyuki Yanagawa, "Small Pelagic Fisheries in the South China Sea," in Asia-Pacific Fishery Commission, Small Pelagic Resources and Their Fisheries in the Asia-Pacific Region, Proceedings of the First Session of the APFIC Working Party on Marine Fisheries (Bangkok, Thailand, 13–16 May 1997) 365–380. Also, Shui-Kai Chang et al., "A Step Forward to the Joint Management of the South China Sea Fisheries Resources: Joint Works on Catches, Management Measures and Conservation Issues," (2019) *Marine Policy*, doi: 10.1016/j.marpol.2019.103716. (accessed 22 March 2020)
5 Joseph Morgan and Mark Valencia eds., *Atlas for Marine Policy in Southeast Asian Seas* (University of California Press, 1983) 36.
6 Take China for instance, there are very distinct patterns in the consumption of aquatic products between the different regions in China. Major consumers are in China's coastal south and southeast provinces. Aquatic products are consumed less in China's western provinces, especially in the northwest. This trend is generally reflected in both urban and rural consumption patterns. Meanwhile, fish is the second most important source of animal protein in Chinese diet after pork for both rural and urban dwellers. Steve Needham & Simon Funge-Smith, The consumption of

fish and fish products in the Asia-Pacific region based on household surveys, RAP PUBLICATION 2015/12 (Bangkok, FAO Regional Office for Asia and the Pacific, 2015) 19–22, available at http://www.fao.org/3/a-i5151e.pdf. (accessed 22 March 2020)

7 FAO, *The State of World Fisheries and Aquaculture 2018: Meeting the sustainable development goals* (FAO, 2018) 30, available at http://www.fao.org/3/i9540en/I9540EN.pdf. (accessed 22 January 2020)

8 Southeast Asian Fisheries Development Center, Southeast Asian State of Fisheries and Aquaculture 2017 (Southeast Asian Fisheries Development Center, 2017) 15; K. Kuperan Viswanathan, "Enhancing Governance in Fisheries Management in Southeast Asia Towards 2020: Issues and Perspectives," The ASEAN-SEAFDEC Conference on Sustainable Fisheries for Food Security towards 2020 "Fish for the People 2020: Adaptation to a Changing Environment," January 2011, available at https://www.researchgate.net/profile/KKuperan_Viswanathan/publication/216306639_Enhancing_governance_in_Fisheries_Management_in_Southeast_Asia_Towards_2020_Issues_and_Perspectives/links/0bf7c66629116d03cb088867/Enhancing-governance-in-Fisheries-Management-in-Southeast-Asia-Towards-2020-Issues-and-Perspectives.pdf. (accessed 22 January 2020)

9 Louise Teh et al., "Status, Trends, and the Future of Fisheries in the East and South China Seas," (2019) 27-1 *Fisheries Centre Research Reports* 13-14.

10 Hongzhou Zhang, "Fisheries Cooperation in the South China Sea: Evaluating the Options," (2018) 89 *Marine Policy* 69.

11 *Ibid.*

12 David Rosenberg, "Environmental Pollution around the South China Sea: Developing a Regional Response," (1999) 21-1 *Contemporary Southeast Asia*, available at https://www.researchgate.net/publication/228689561_Environmental_Pollution_around_the_South_China_SeaDeveloping_a_Regional_Response. (accessed 21 January 2020)

13 Shicun Wu and Keyuan Zou, *Maritime Security in the South China Sea: Regional Implications and International Cooperation* (Ashgate Publishing, 2009) 232.

14 *Ibid.*

15 US Energy Information Agency (EIA), South China Sea Region Report, 7 February 2013, available at https://www.eia.gov/international/analysis/regions-of-interest/South_China_Sea; Asia Maritime Transparency Initiative (AMTI), South China Sea Energy Exploration and Development, available at https://amti.csis.org/south-china-sea-energy-exploration-and-development/. (accessed 22 January 2020)

16 For example, China is the world's second-largest consumer of oil behind the United States, and the second-largest net importer of oil as of 2009. And, Korea is the second-largest importer of liquefied natural gas in the world behind Japan. See US Energy Information Administration, available at www.eia.gov/countries/. (accessed 22 January 2020)

17 The East Asian Seas (EAS) Congress, "Summary of the East Asian Seas Congress 2006, 12–16 December 2006," (2006) 131-5 *EAS Congress 2006 Bulletin*, available at https://enb.iisd.org/download/pdf/sd/ymbvol131num5e.pdf. (accessed 22 January 2020)

18 David Rosenberg, An Introduction to the Website of The South China Sea, available at http://www.southchinasea.org/why-a-south-china-sea-website-an-introductory-essay/. (accessed 22 January 2020)

19 Pakjuta Khemakorn, *Sustainable Management of Pelagic Fisheries in the South China Sea Region* (United Nations–The Nippon Foundation Fellow, 2006) 18–20.

20 FAO, Fishery and Aquaculture Country Profiles: The Kingdom of Cambodia, available at http://www.fao.org/fishery/facp/KHM/en. (accessed 31 March 2020)

21 FAO, Fishery and Aquaculture Country Profiles: The People's Republic of China, available at http://www.fao.org/fishery/facp/CHN/en. (accessed 31 March 2020)

22 FAO, Fishery and Aquaculture Country Profiles: The Republic of Indonesia, available at http://www.fao.org/fishery/facp/IDN/en. (accessed 31 March 2020)

23 FAO, Fishery and Aquaculture Country Profiles: Malaysia, available at http://www.fao.org/fishery/facp/MYS/en. (accessed 31 March 2020)

24 FAO, Fishery and Aquaculture Country Profiles: The Republic of the Philippines, available at http://www.fao.org/fishery/facp/PHL/en. (accessed 31 March 2020)

25 Fisheries Agency, Taiwan, *Fisheries of Taiwan*, available at https://www.fa.gov.tw/upload/174/%e4%b8%ad%e8%8f%af%e6%b0%91%e5%9c%8b%e6%bc%81%e6%a5%ad%e7%b0%a1%e4%bb%8b.pdf. (accessed 2 April 2020)

26 Fishing activities conducted in areas outside the EEZ of Taiwan.
27 FAO, "Fishery and Aquaculture Country Profiles: The Kingdom of Thailand," available at http://www.fao.org/fishery/facp/THA/en. (accessed 31 March 2020)
28 FAO, Fishery and Aquaculture Country Profiles: The Socialist Republic of Vietnam, available at http://www.fao.org/fishery/facp/VNM/en. (accessed 31 March 2020)
29 Http://www.fao.org/fishery/area/Area71/en. However, due to the reasons of the South China Sea occupies only the west part of Area 71 and the statistical date are from different methodology, there are other research methods have been utilized. For example, Daniel Pauly and Cui Liang, *supra* note 1.
30 FAO, *The State of World Fisheries and Aquaculture 2018: Meeting the Sustainable Development Goals* (FAO, 2018) 4, 13.
31 FAO, *World Review of Fisheries and Aquaculture* (FAO, 2010) 39.
32 The steady increase of the reported landings, from 490,000 t in 1950 to a peak of over 6 million tonnes in 2001 is primarily due to a significant increase in the landings of unidentified fishes (included in 'mix group'), which account for two-thirds of the landings in recent years. In general, a high proportion of unidentified fishes in landings statistics is a symptom of deficiencies in a reporting system. The marine fisheries target groups that include tuna, billfishes, mackerels and sharks for the pelagic species, and a huge array of demersal fish and invertebrates, especially penaeid shrimps. See "LME 36 – South China Sea," Transboundary Water Assessment Programme, 2015, available at http://onesharedocean.org/public_store/lmes_factsheets/factsheet_36_South_China_Sea.pdf. (accessed 31 March 2020)
33 Scott Snyder, Brad Glosserman, and Ralph A. Cossa, "Confidence Building Measures in the South China Sea," (2001) 2-01 *Issues and Insights*, Pacific Forum CSIS, Honolulu, Hawaii.
34 The term IUU was first used in the meeting of the Commission for the Conservation of Antarctic Marine Living Resources (CCAMLR) in 1997. It is important to understand that IUU fishing activities do not occur only in specific geographic sea areas, their scope also appear in global fish commodities trade. A clear definition on IUU could be found in Article 3 of International Plan of Action on IUU, http://www.fao.org/3/a-y1224e.pdf. (accessed 12 March 2020)
35 Asia Maritime Transparency Initiative (AMTI), A Blueprint for Fisheries Management and Environmental Cooperation in the South China Sea, 13 September 2017, available at https://amti.csis.org/coc-blueprint-fisheries-environment/. (accessed 15 March 2020)
36 Nina Hachigian, "The Other Problem in the South China Sea: Territorial Disputes Are Not the Only Issue to Trouble This Vital Maritime Region," (2015) *The Diplomat*, available at http://thediplomat.com/2015/04/the-other-problem-in-the-south-china-sea/. (accessed 2 March 2020)
37 2002 Declaration on the Conduct of the Parties in the South China Sea, available at https://asean.org/?static_post=declaration-on-the-conduct-of-parties-in-the-south-china-sea-2. (accessed 31 March 2020)
38 The Declaration urges a positive environment for the resolution of all disputes over the water body. The Parties agree, without prejudicing the sovereignty and jurisdiction of countries having direct interests in the area, to explore the possibility of cooperation in the South China Sea relating to the safety of maritime navigation and communication, protection against pollution of the marine environment, coordination of search and rescue operations, efforts towards combatting piracy and armed robbery as well as collaboration in the campaign against illicit trafficking in drugs. 1992 ASEAN Declaration on the South China Sea, available at https://cil.nus.edu.sg/wp-content/uploads/2017/07/1992-ASEAN-Declaration-on-the-South-China-Sea.pdf. (accessed 20 February 2020)
39 Article 1 of the Amity Treaty stipulates that "The Purpose of This Treaty Is to Promote Perpetual Peace, Everlasting Amity and Cooperation among Their Peoples Which Would Contribute to Their Strength, Solidarity and Closer Relationship." *1976 Treaty of Amity and Cooperation in Southeast Asia*, available at https://asean.org/treaty-amity-cooperation-southeast-asia-indonesia-24-february-1976/.(accessed 3 February 2020)
40 Villy Christensen *et al.*, "Fisheries Impact on the South China Sea Large Marine Ecosystem," in V. T. Christensen et al., eds., Assessment, Management and Future Directions for Coastal Fisheries in Asian Countries, WorldFish Conference Proceedings 67(WorldFish Center, 2003) 51–52.
41 RFMOs have mandates to adopt international legally binding conservation and management measures concerning fishing operations and associated activities based on the best scientific

evidence. Terje Løbach, Matilda Petersson, Eliana Haberkon, and Piero Mannini, Regional Fisheries Management Organisations and Advisory Bodies: Activities and Developments, 2000–2017, FAO Fisheries and Aquaculture Technical Paper No. 651 (FAO, 2020), available at https://doi.org/10.4060/ca7843en. (accessed 20 January 2020)

42 Convention for the Conservation and Management of Highly Migratory Fish Stocks in the Western and Central Pacific Ocean, available at https://www.wcpfc.int/doc/convention-conservation-and-management-highly-migratory-fish-stocks-western-and-central-pacific. (accessed 15 February 2020)

43 Løbach et al., *supra* note 41; and WCPFC website, About WCPFC, available at https://www.wcpfc.int/about-wcpfc. (accessed 15 February 2020)

44 WCPFC members: Australia, China, Canada, Cook Islands, European Union, Federated States of Micronesia, Fiji, France, Indonesia, Japan, Kiribati, Republic of Korea, Republic of Marshall Islands, Nauru, New Zealand, Niue, Palau, Papua New Guinea, Philippines, Samoa, Solomon Islands, Chinese Taipei, Tonga, Tuvalu, United States of America, Vanuatu.

45 WCPFC, "Boarding and Inspection Procedures: Conservation and Management Measure 2006–08," available at https://www.wcpfc.int/file/284/download?token=9EXQmfhU. (accessed 15 February 2020)

46 Andrew Norris, "Fishy Business: The High Seas Boarding and Inspection Regime in the Western and Central Pacific Ocean," (2015) 46-4 *Ocean Development & International Law* 331–344.

47 FAO, Agreement for the Establishment of the Indo-Pacific Fisheries Council, 1948, available at https://www.loc.gov/law/help/us-treaties/bevans/m-ust000004-0694.pdf. (accessed 15 January 2020) In 1976, the title of "Indo-Pacific Fisheries Council" was changed to "Indo-Pacific Fishery Commission" and the Agreement was also amended to enable the Commission to act directly related to fisheries management and development in its area of competence. Further amendments to the Agreement were made in 1993 and the title was changed to Asia-Pacific Fishery Commission (APFIC). FAO, Asia-Pacific Fishery Commission, "About the Asia-Pacific Fishery Commission," available at http://www.fao.org/apfic/background/about-asia-pacific-fishery-commission/en/. (accessed 15 January 2020)

48 Member countries of the APFIC are: Australia, Bangladesh, Cambodia, China, France, India, Indonesia, Japan, Malaysia, Myanmar, Nepal, New Zealand, Pakistan, Philippines, Republic of Korea, Sri Lanka, Timor-Leste, Thailand, United Kingdom, United States of America, and Vietnam.

49 APFIC Agreement, Article IV, available at http://www.fao.org/apfic/background/apfic-agreement/en/.(accessed 15 January 2020)

50 FAO, Asia-Pacific Fishery Commission (APFIC), available at http://www.fao.org/asiapacific/apfic/en/.(accessed 15 January 2020)

51 APFIC Agreement, Article VI (Area) provides: The Commission shall carry out the functions and responsibilities set forth in Article IV in the Asia-Pacific Area.

52 FAO, APFIC/FAO Regional Expert Workshop on "Regional Guidelines for the Management of Tropical Trawl Fisheries in Asia." Phuket, Thailand, 30 September–4 October 2013. FAO Regional Office for Asia and the Pacific, Bangkok, Thailand. RAP Publication 2014/01. Available at http://www.fao.org/3/a-i3575e.pdf. (accessed 15 January 2020)

53 For example, FAO/APFIC Workshop on "Implementing the 2009 FAO Agreement on Port State Measures to Combat Illegal, Unreported and Unregulated Fishing," Bangkok, Thailand, from 23 to 27 April 2012, available at http://www.fao.org/apfic/publications/detail/en/c/421244/; APFIC Regional Consultative Workshop on Fishing Capacity Management and IUU Fishing, Phuket, Thailand, 13–15 June 2007, available at http://www.fao.org/apfic/publications/detail/en/c/421246/.(accessed 15 January 2020)

54 Agreement Establishing the Southeast Asian Fisheries Development Center (SEAFDEC Agreement), available at http://www.fao.org/fishery/docs/DOCUMENT/seafdec/Agreement-EstablishingSEAFDEC.pdf. (accessed 15 January 2020)

55 SEAFDEC Agreement, Article 1.

56 SEAFDEC website, About SEAFDEC, available at http://www.seafdec.org/about/.(accessed 12 January 2020)

57 They are Brunei, Cambodia, Indonesia, Japan, Lao PDR, Malaysia, Myanmar, Philippines, Singapore, Thailand, and Vietnam. SEAFDEC Council Member List, available at http://www.seafdec.org/council-members/. (accessed 15 January 2020)

58 Løbach, supra note 41, p. 103. For ASEAN-SEAFDEC Guidelines for Preventing the Entry of Fish and Fishery Products from IUU Fishing Activities into the Supply Chain, available at https://www.asean.org/wp-content/uploads/images/2015/November/AMAF/App%20 9%20-%20ASEAN%20Guidelines%20IUU%20SSOM36th%20AMAF%20final.pdf. (accessed 20 December 2019)

59 RPOA-IUU, http://www.rpoaiuu.org/; Australian Government, Department of Agriculture, Water and the Environment, "Compliance: Illegal, Unreported and Unregulated Fishing," available at https://www.agriculture.gov.au/fisheries/iuu/compliance. (accessed 20 December 2019)

60 Agreement on the Network of Aquaculture Centres in Asia and the Pacific, available at https://enaca.org/enclosure.php?id=853. (accessed 20 December 2019)

61 Members of the NACA: Australia, Bangladesh, Cambodia, China, Hong Kong, India, Indonesia, Iran, Lao PDR, Malaysia, Maldives, Myanmar, Nepal, Pakistan, Philippines, Sri Lanka, Thailand, Vietnam.

62 Agreement on Fisheries between the Government of the Republic of the Philippines and the Government of the Republic of Indonesia, 1974, Article 1, available at https://treaties.un.org/doc/publication/unts/volume%20987/volume-987-i-14436-english.pdf. (accessed 20 December 2019)

63 WWF-Philippines, Turtle Islands: Resources and Livelihoods under Threats (WWF-Philippines, 2005) 5.

64 Agreement on Fishery Cooperation in the Beibu Gulf between the Government of the People's Republic of China and the Government of the Socialist Republic of Vietnam, available at http://extwprlegs1.fao.org/docs/pdf/bi-51872.pdf. (accessed 20 December 2019)

65 Zou Keyuan, "The Sino-Vietnamese Agreement on Maritime Boundary Delimitation in the Gulf of Tonkin," (2005) 36-1 *Ocean Development and International Law* 13–24; Yunjun Yu and Yongtong Mu, "The New Institutional Arrangements for Fisheries Management in Beibu Gulf," (2006) 30 *Marine Policy* 249–260.

66 Protocol Amending the Arrangement between the Ministry of Marine Affairs and Fisheries of the Republic of Indonesia and the Ministry of Agriculture and Cooperatives of the Kingdom of Thailand on the Utilization of Part of the Total Allowable Catch in the Indonesian Exclusive Economic Zone, 2003, available at https://treaty.kemlu.go.id/apisearch/pdf?filename=-THA-2003-0029.pdf. (accessed 22 April 2020)

67 Memorandum of Understanding between the Taipei Economic and Cultural Office in the Philippines and the Manila Economic and Cultural Office in Taiwan on Agricultural and Fishery Cooperation, 2005, available at https://law.moj.gov.tw/ENG/LawClass/LawAll.aspx?p-code=Y0110488. (accessed 22 April 2020)

68 Letter of Intent between the Ministry of Marine Affairs and Fisheries of the Republic of Indonesia and the Ministry of Industry and Primary Resources of Brunei Darussalam on Marine and Fisheries Cooperation, 2011, available at https://treaty.kemlu.go.id/apisearch/pdf?file-name=BRN-2011-0009.pdf. (accessed 22 April 2020)

69 Memorandum of Understanding (MoU) in Respect to the Common Guidelines Concerning Treatment of Fishermen by Maritime Law Enforcement Agencies of Malaysia and the Republic of Indonesia, 2012, Articles 1–3, available at http://treaty.kemlu.go.id/apisearch/pdf?file-name=MYS-2011-0127.pdf. (accessed 22 April 2020)

70 Agreement Concerning the Facilitation of Cooperation on Law Enforcement in Fisheries Matters between the Taipei Economic and Cultural Office in the Philippines and the Manila Economic and Cultural Office in Taiwan, 2015, available at https://law.moj.gov.tw/ENG/LawClass/LawAll.aspx?pcode=Y0110542. (accessed 22 April 2020)

71 Joint Statement between the Government of the People's Republic of China and the Government of the Republic of the Philippines, 2017, available at https://www.fmprc.gov.cn/mfa_eng/wjdt_665385/2649_665393/t1511299.shtml. (accessed 20 April 2020)

72 Joint Communique on Voluntary International Cooperation to Combat Illegal, Unreported and Unregulated (IUU) Fishing and to Promote Sustainable Fisheries Governance between Indonesia and Vietnam, 2018, available at https://treaty.kemlu.go.id/apisearch/pdf?file-name=VNM-2018-0095.pdf. (accessed 22 April 2020)

73 Joint Statement between the People's Republic of China and the Republic of the Philippines, 2018, available at http://www.xinhuanet.com/english/2018-11/21/c_137622271.htm. (accessed 22 April 2020)

14

GOVERNANCE OF NON-LIVING RESOURCES IN THE SOUTH CHINA SEA

Yen-Chiang Chang

Introduction

Non-living resources can be defined as resources that exist naturally in the environment and are relatively untouched by humankind, in their natural form. They exist in various ecosystems of the earth and have played an essential role in not only maintaining the balance of the natural ecological system but also in helping to transform human life into the modern world. By using non-living resources, living standards can be improved via developed healthcare and education systems, increased productivity, infrastructure development, digital connectivity and much more.[1] Non-living resources can be further divided into non-renewable and renewable resources.

Non-renewable resources are those natural resources that are presented in limited amounts and are, sometimes referred to as exhaustible resources, which are derived from fossil fuels. Due to the limitations of technology, the total quantity in existence may not yet be fully acknowledged. As they are fixed in quantity and cannot be replenished or reproduced, the more the resources are extracted and used today, the less will remain for future generations.[2] Thus, the consumption of quantities of a non-renewable resource at any time carries an opportunity cost, i.e. the value of consuming that resource in the future. This opportunity cost of consumption is usually given the name 'user cost'.[3] The nature of non-renewable resources means that the critical economic question is when to use them. Leaving aside issues of recycling, the use of coal, oil, metal ores, limestone and so on, reduces the quantity that can be consumed by future generations.[4] Also, non-renewable resources are not necessarily reserved for maritime zones, but the majority of them lie in ocean areas.

Human civilisation is, however, currently reliant on non-renewable resources as its primary source of energy. As they are rich in energy and relatively cheap to process, human dependence on fossil fuels has continuously increased since early times. Every year, approximately 80 percent of the overall volume of energy consumed globally, is derived from non-renewable resources.[5] The major problem with non-renewable resources, apart from being in limited quantity, is that their usage emits carbon dioxide into the atmosphere. Rising levels of heat-trapping carbon dioxide in the atmosphere is perceived to be the leading cause of global warming. Hence, with the challenge of the global energy crisis and the requirement for environmental protection and sustainable economic development, it has become essential for developed countries and some developing countries, to develop and utilise renewable sources of energy.

Marine non-living renewable energy is a form of zero-emission clean energy, such as offshore wind, waves, tides and currents, which could (with scale) replace fossil fuels and effectively reduce the emission of greenhouse gases and pollutants such as carbon dioxide and sulphur dioxide.[6] The comprehensive utilisation of marine renewable energy could bring significant benefits, both economically and socially.[7] The United Nations Secretary-General, in the 67th annual report, *Oceans and the Law of the Sea*, made a preliminary statement indicating a governance policy and legal framework for marine renewable energy. The report also recommended establishing a relevant legal regime but did not specify any details.[8] Legislative and research work have positive effects in facilitating marine renewable energy programmes, which is also a necessary precondition for creating a relevant legal governance regime if it is to establish a concrete marine renewable energy programme.[9]

The 1982 United Nations Convention on the Law of the Sea (UNCLOS) can be seen as the basic legal framework for marine renewable energy, with other international, regional and national legal instruments and measures being necessary supplements,[10] all of which should be referred to in the construction of a new legal system for marine renewable energy. Such a system would need to address the following issues: legal rights and obligations of coastal States in different maritime zones; rights and obligations concerning the utilisation of resources discovered in different maritime zones; the installation and use of facilities and structures for energy development in maritime zones; transportation of produced energy; protection and conservation of the marine environment; and the prevention of potential adverse effects from activities relating to energy exploration, deployment, development and transportation.[11] The development of marine renewable energy requires a balance of benefits between maritime space, owners and users of resources,[12] a balance of rights and obligations regarding marine renewable energy, and other relevant issues regulated by other international instruments.[13]

In this chapter, the governance of marine non-living resources in the South China Sea is discussed. Presently the littoral States in the South China Sea are at crossroads as regards the control and exploration of the non-living resources. Every disputing State has occupied some islands in the South China Sea and is exploring the resources from offshore, with many overlapping claims of maritime jurisdiction. In order to resolve territorial disputes in the South China Sea, it is essential to resolve the issue of control of non-living resources. Furthermore, to resolve the dispute over the control of non-living resources, it is essential to have a communique on the governance of the non-living resources among the disputing parties. This chapter is an attempt to understand the stumbling blocks in the governance of non-living resources and also tries to provide a workable solution.

Non-living resources in the South China Sea

Non-living marine resources provide valuable economic, social and cultural means, to the major littoral States and small island States. In the 21st century, with the help of modern technology and a greater understanding of environmental protection norms, new opportunities have emerged that are gradually being realised in the form of a 'Blue Economy'. It acknowledges the necessity to capitalise on the massive economic potential offered by the ocean while protecting its eco-systems.[14] The significance of oceans and seas for sustainable development is widely understood by the international community and exemplified in Chapter 17 of Agenda 21,[15] the Johannesburg Plan of Implementation and various decisions taken by the Commission on Sustainable Development.[16] Therefore, the significance of marine non-living resources matters much ventures for the world economies. To comprehend such avenues in the South China Sea, it is pertinent to mention here that regional distribution of non-renewable energy resources (Hydrocarbons) in the South China Sea includes: (1) South of Hainan Island – 210 million barrels, (2) Southern China – 1500 million barrels, (3) Gulf of Tonkin – 95 million barrels, (4) South Vietnam – 2847 million barrels, (5) Sunda Shelf – 180 million barrels, (6) Borneo/Sarawak – 9260 million barrels, and (7) The Philippines – 409 million barrels.[17]

Non-renewable resources

Oil

Although total assessments differ, the U.S. Energy Information Agency estimates that the South China Sea region contains around 11 billion barrels of proven oil reserves.[18] An earlier Chinese estimate, however, indicates that the actual potential reserves might be as great as 213 billion barrels.[19] If the latter is accurate, this would be equal to around 80 percent of the oil reserves of Saudi Arabia. In addition, China National Offshore Oil Corporation (CNOOC), a major state-owned oil company, which holds rights to most of China's offshore hydrocarbon development, estimates that the region holds around 125 billion barrels of oil.[20] These diverging estimates show that there is no unanimity concerning the quantity of reserves. New Chinese studies suggest that the Spratly and Paracel Islands may also contain oil reserves.[21]

Natural gas

Natural gas is the largest hydrocarbon resource in the South China Sea, with most of the hydrocarbon fields surveyed in the region containing natural gas. According to a U.S. Geological Survey, about 60–70 percent of the hydrocarbon in this region is in the form of natural gas. A study in China estimates a total of 30–72 trillion cubic metres (TCM) of natural gas, is reserved in this region.[22] Since the mid-1970s, the U.S. estimates suggest the value of hydrocarbon in the South China Sea as being between US$3 and US$8 trillion, whereas, Chinese estimates suggest a value between US$25 and US$60 trillion.[23] Similar to oil estimations, the figures relating to the region's natural gas resources also vary widely. The U.S. Energy Information Administration estimates that the natural gas reservation in the South China Sea is approximately 190 trillion cubic feet.[24] A Chinese study estimates natural gas reserves to be around two quadrillion cubic feet.[25] Another Chinese report estimates that total gas reserves represent 225 billion barrels in the Spratly Island alone.[26] If the latter is true, then, the total gas resources against the proved gas reserves would be almost 900 trillion cubic feet in the South China Sea.[27] This would be equal to the total amount of natural gas in Qatar, which has the third-largest natural gas reserves in the world.

Rare-earth metals

Other than oil and gas, the most intensively explored mineral deposits in the South China Sea are near-shore placer minerals such as titaniferous magnetite, zircon, monazite, tin, gold and chromite.[28] According to the International Union of Pure and Applied Chemistry, rare earth metals are a set of 17 chemical elements in the periodic table, these also being referred to as Rare Earth Elements (REE) and Rare Earth Yttrium (REY).[29] Total REY contents in the South China Sea scale from 69.1×10^{-6} to $2\,919.4 \times 10^{-6}$, with a median value of $1\,459.5 \times 10^{-6}$.[30] The South China Sea's two major sources of dissolved REEs are in fluvial and coastal input to the surface ocean and a bottom release into the deep water, in the Luzon Strait.[31] These metals have become very important in the modern world, as they provide critical components in next-generation technology, and today, everything from high-end smartphones to flat-screen TVs, and hybrid cars to rockets, has rare earth metal elements. In 2018, Chinese deep-sea exploration in the South China Sea discovered polymetallic nodules and ancient hydrotherms, which will help in exploiting metal resources and will provide the materials needed to manufacture military and aerospace equipment.[32]

Oceanic methane hydrate

Methane hydrate is a solid clathrate compound, formed from methane and water, under appropriate conditions (e.g., temperature, pressure and pH levels). The compound may break down to release methane (>90 percent) and is colloquially referred to as, 'flammable ice'.[33] Methane hydrate deposits are mainly found in two types of environment, namely, permafrost regions and on ocean floors,[34] hence, their categorisation as continental methane hydrate and oceanic methane hydrate, respectively. The estimated reserves in the South China Sea could be as large as 70 billion tonnes of oil equivalent (toe).[35] Methane hydrate is widely distributed underground; therefore, if sovereignty over the land or sea is unclear, ownership of the methane hydrate may also be disputed. The fact that methane hydrate is an important alternative energy source, and consists of the potential to trigger more or to intensify existing disputes since there are large methane hydrate reserves in the South China Sea. Given the ongoing sovereignty disputes in the region, ownership of the methane hydrate could well further exacerbate the tension.[36]

Renewable resources

Tidal energy

Tidal energy is one of the more abundant marine renewable energy sources and is created with the help of the gravitational forces of the sun and moon, along with the rotation of the earth.[37] Most of the tides arise twice each lunar day, due to the centrifugal force of the rotational cycle of the moon-earth system and the gravitational pull applied by the moon upon the earth.[38] With the steep continental slope and numerous seamounts, the extremely complicated topographies make the South China Sea a preferred region for dissipation of internal tides, generated both locally and remotely.[39] A study to check the tidal energy fluxes was conducted in the South China Sea from June 2011 to August 2011.[40] It was found that, the Westward, mode-1 diurnal and semidiurnal fluxes exceeded 40 and 30 kW m^{-1}. Other studies have shown that two parallel ridges in the Luzon Strait generate around >60 kW m^{-1} depth-integrated energy fluxes, which are considered as among the larger internal tides in the ocean.[41]

Wind energy

Offshore wind power is one of the more developed forms of marine, renewable energy in terms of policy frameworks, installed capacity and technology development.[42] On average, winds move faster and more consistently at sea than on land and a faster and steadier wind implies less wear on the turbine machinery, and extra electricity is produced per turbine.[43] In the South China Sea area, wind power has alternated between 96.27 watts per square meter (hereinafter W/m^2) in May and 527.03 W/m^2 in December.[44] Furthermore, strong trends in wind power exist in the Luzon Strait in the northern South China Seas, as well as Paracel, Liyue and Macclesfield Banks, in the central South China Sea, which are evaluated as being high wind potential regions and which may be rated as suitable locations for the installation of large wind turbines for electrical energy generation.[45]

Wave energy

As the wind flows over the ocean, the air-sea interface processes transfer some of the wind energy to the water, forming waves, which store this energy as potential and kinetic energy. The wave power density is greater than 24 kilowatts per meter (hereinafter kW/m) in the South China Sea high-wind-speed area and above 27 kW/m in the Luzon Strait area.[46] The maximum annual wave power is found in the northern region of the South China Sea, with amplitudes exceeding 20 kW/m.[47] The South China Sea wave energy varies from 4 to 7 percent. In the neighbouring waters of Taiwan Island, the Beibu (Tonkin) Gulf, which lies in the northern area of the South China Sea, it is about 4 percent.[48] In the western waters of Kalimantan and the western waters of Luzon, it is between 4 and 5 percent.[49] In the southeast region of the Indo-China Peninsula, it is stable at 7 percent.[50]

Ocean current energy

The constant flow of ocean water in particular directions, driven by gravity, salinity, wind flows, temperature gradients and the earth's rotation, is regarded as ocean current energy.[51] Most of the currents on the surface are driven by winds, whereas thermohaline circulation is the cause of deep-sea currents.[52] There is a huge potential of ocean current in the South China Sea,[53] there being four major currents in the upper layer (0~400 m) of the Southern part of South China Sea: the North Nansha Current (NNC), the Nansha Eastern Coastal Current (NECC), the Nansha Western Coastal Current (NWCC), and the Nansha Counter-wind Current (NCC).[54]

Ocean thermal energy

Ocean Thermal Energy Conversion (OTEC) is a process by which the natural thermal gradient in the ocean, which lies on the surface and subsurface of the ocean waters, is used to produce electricity.[55] According to 2013 World Ocean Atlas data, the greatest steady-state OTEC electrical power in the South China Sea is about 0.5 TW, in consideration of Carnot efficiency.[56] At the moment, China is constructing the world's largest OTEC station and once operational, it will have the capacity to generate 10 MW of electricity, which is sufficient to light a large city.[57] Furthermore, research suggests that, with more such stations being constructed, this will help generate 100 MW of electricity.[58]

Osmotic power

Osmotic power is generated from the salinity gradient, which is obtained from the freshwater from river flows into the sea, where it mixes with saline water.[59] According to estimation, the osmotic power capacity near the Pearl River estuary alone is around 24.555 million KW.[60]

Marine biomass energy

Marine biomass, like marine algae and seaweeds, can be used as a sustainable source of biofuel. The potential growth of algae is ten times greater than with traditional land-based crops. If coral reefs are protected, they have the potential to grow in abundance.[61] Algae, from there, can be effectively processed into biofuels, including biodiesel and bioethanol.[62] Algae cultivated for biofuels can also help in absorbing carbon dioxide, thereby helping the environment. At the moment, however, little work has been done regarding the potential marine biomass energy in this region.

Legal basis for the governance of non-living resources in the South China Sea

While a large number of policy experts, academics, government agencies and even non-governmental organisations have discussed the South China Sea issues, most attention has been given to political and territorial disputes in the region, without more consideration of what is at the core of these conflicts, which is control and exploration of energy resources. UNCLOS has set out legal guidelines for the use of the oceans, in general. UNCLOS asserts that States with overlapping maritime claims should settle disputes through negotiation in good faith. Despite this, disputes still exist and seem unlikely to resolve any time soon. This section briefly deals with the legal basis from UNCLOS, the Declaration of Conduct of Parties (DOC) for the South China Sea, the Code of Conduct (COC) for the South China Sea, in dealing with the governance of non-living resources in the South China Sea.

The legal basis from UNCLOS

UNCLOS has established a universal legal directive within which all activities on the seas must be carried out. As an all-encompassing legal basis for the law of the sea, UNCLOS has expounded the rights and responsibilities of all States, comprising coastal, land-locked as well as geographically disadvantaged States.[63] UNCLOS allocates a substantial part of its provisions to the settlement of maritime disputes.[64] Provisions regarding the governance of non-living resources are discussed in the following paragraphs.

According to Article 77, 'the coastal State exercises sovereign rights over the continental shelf to explore it and exploit its natural resources'. No State can exploit resources from the continental shelf of other State without its consent. The natural resources referred to here consist of the minerals and other living organisms belonging to sedentary species, as well as the non-living resources of the seabed and subsoil.[65] Furthermore, Article 137 states that no State shall allege or exert autonomy or sovereign rights over any part of the area or its resources, nor shall any juridical or natural person or State can appropriate any part. All rights in the resources of the area are bestowed in humankind as a whole, and the Authority shall act on their behalf.[66] In addition, Article 153, defines that, activities in the area shall be organised and conducted in a controlled environment by the Authority on behalf of humankind.[67] It further states that the activities in the area shall be conducted in accordance with a formal written plan of work, in accordance with Annex III and endorsed by the Council after review by the technical and legal commission.[68] States should collaborate on a global basis and as appropriate, on a regional basis, directly or through proficient international organisations, in formulating and elaborating international rules.[69]

In terms of dispute settlement, Article 280 states that any peaceful methods shall do the settlement of disputes opted for by the parties. Suppose the disputing States, have agreed, through a general, regional or bilateral agreement or otherwise, that such disputes, at the request of any party to the dispute, shall be submitted to a procedure that necessitates a binding verdict. In that case, that procedure shall apply in lieu of the procedures provided for in Part XV of UNCLOS, unless the parties to the dispute agree otherwise.[70] Articles 297 and 298, nonetheless, provide automatic and exceptional exceptions to the compulsory jurisdictions of UNCLOS.[71] Under Article 297, disputes, such as overflying, rights to navigation, and laying submarine cables, are automatically excluded from the compulsory jurisdiction. Under Article 298, if a State party to UNCLOS says that it does not accept any one or more of the compulsory procedures in relation to certain disputes, other parties cannot use compulsory procedures against them.

As a result of the foregoing, it becomes challenging to resolve a dispute under UNCLOS. In a way, it handicaps the entire dispute resolving procedure, as if even one State among the disputing parties refuses to accept the compulsory procedure, then the equation goes back to zero. If the governance of the non-living resources is to be successful, all the disputing States should consider accepting all of the above-mentioned provisions. It is only when the States stop favouring individual gain over the collective benefits that they will realise the potential of the joint working group, technology sharing, and governance of resources. Once the States agree on the terms in governing non-living resources, this will play a decisive role in conservation and the distribution of resources among the disputing States.

DOC for the South China Sea

The differences between the disputing parties over the control of resources are the key factor in the South China Sea dispute over sovereignty and jurisdiction. If the disputes over the sovereignty and jurisdiction in the South China Sea are to be resolved, it is essential to have a communique among the disputing parties over the exploration and utilisation of non-living resources. It is important that these disputes shall be resolved through dialogue and peaceful co-operation based on international law.

The genesis of the Code of Conduct for the South China Sea lies in the ASEAN Declaration on the South China Sea on 22 July 1992, in Manila, popularly known as the 1992 Declaration. The Declaration stressed that all the sovereignty and jurisdictional issues relating to the South China Sea shall be resolved peacefully, without the use of force. It also asks the concerned parties to practise restraint and help create a positive climate for the ultimate resolution of all disputes.[72] On 4 November 2002, DOC was signed between the ASEAN States and China.

The content of the DOC reveals two main purposes relating to non-living resources, as mentioned below:

1 Relating to building trust and confidence measures:

The disputing parties shall engage in activities, such as holding dialogues and exchanges of views among their defence and military officials, ensuring humane treatment of refugees and exchanging relevant information on a voluntary basis.[73]

2 Relating to co-operative activities:

Despite the lack of settlement of the disputes, the concerned parties shall undertake co-operative activities: a. marine scientific research; b. search and rescue operations; c. address safety of navigation and communication at sea; d. marine environmental protection; and e. combating transnational crime, comprising but not restricted to trafficking in illicit drugs, piracy and armed robbery at sea and illegal trafficking of arms.[74]

Although initially, the disputing parties tried to co-operate on the DOC, as when in 2003, they decided to regularly encourage ASEAN and China Senior Official's Meeting to oversee the smooth implementation of the DOC. Further joint working groups were established to develop guidelines for the implementation of DOC. Ultimately in July 2011, at the China-ASEAN Foreign Ministers' Meeting, ASEAN and China agreed to conclude the DOC implementation guidelines.[75] One achievement of the DOC can be attributed to the tripartite, joint seismic study by China, Vietnam and the Philippines, from 2005 to 2008.[76] Despite much publicity, however, DOC did not play a significant role in changing the ground reality, as it was not backed by legal bindings. As a result, most of the States ignored or conveniently interpreted the rules made by DOC.[77] As DOC did not clearly define the areas of co-operation in the South China Sea, many States went ahead with unilateral changes, citing the region as being their exclusive economic zone.[78]

COC for the South China Sea

The ASEAN senior officials were engaged in drafting a COC document during late 2011 and early 2012. The first document containing the major elements of COC was presented to China during the July 2012 ASEAN Foreign Ministers meeting in Phnom Penh. The first China-ASEAN Senior Official's Meeting on the COC was convened in Suzhou, China, on 15 September 2013. After a series of negotiations, the ASEAN and China agreed on the Single Draft South China Sea Code of Conduct Negotiating Text, in August 2018.[79] In November 2018, they reached an agreement to fully finalise the COC in the following three years, starting from 2019.[80]

The COC deals with five issues in the South China Sea: 1. geographic scope; 2. dispute settlement; 3. the duty to cooperate; 4. the role of third parties; and 5. the legal status of the final Code of Conduct for the South China Sea.[81]

1 Geographic scope:

The COC does not explicitly classify the regions which would come under it. Despite the fact that some general suggestions being made by States such as Vietnam, Indonesia, Malaysia and Singapore, a clear geographic scope has yet to be finalised. It is essential to define the geographic scope in COC, which will provide a clear picture of the regions included and excluded in the COC and help to reduce the current uncertainty over the governance of non-living resources.

2 Dispute settlement:

The COC takes the initiative to prevent, manage and settle any dispute among the disputing States in the South China Sea. The COC also ratifies the commencing of consultations on environmental preservation and the protection of fisheries and other non-living resources, in the areas with overlapping claims.[82]

3 Duty to cooperate:

The COC has adopted UNCLOS provision, which defines that, all the signatories to UNCLOS should co-operate to protect the marine environment in a semi-enclosed sea. It further states that, pending the settlement of disputes, the States should enter into a co-operative arrangement. It is essential that the disputing States cooperate on marine archaeology and joint research to help the local people in understanding the shared history of the South China Sea, in which the resources from the sea were peacefully shared among the littoral States.[83] This will help to identify those not inclined to cooperate in these States and may open the door to the peaceful exploration of the non-living resources. There is still, however, no unanimity on the subjects of duty to co-operate, promotion of practical maritime co-operation, prevention of incident escalating issues, self-restraint and promotion of trust and confidence.

4 Role of third parties:

The third-party States which are not signatories to the COC, have been excluded or will have limited capacity in the COC. This will limit the role played by States from outside the region.

5 Legal status:

Presently, the COC is not referred to as a treaty under international law; it is not having a legal binding force. As the COC is a working document, the concerned parties have the liberty to add or subtract terms at the drafting stage. If the terms within the COC are not brought under the ambit of legal binding, then it will be a 'toothless tiger'.

If peace and stability are to prevail in the South China Sea, the COC should achieve effectiveness in ensuring that, respective parties exercise self-restraint, engage in confidence-building measures and co-operate in the undisputed areas. If, however, the COC for the South China Sea is to be successful, it must achieve legally binding authority.

State practice in the exploration of non-living resources in the South China Sea

As a large number of non-living resources have been discovered in the 21st century, many littoral States have initiated offshore exploration, as an alternative to exploring land-based resources. On the one hand, however, due to over-exploitation, the non-living resources on land have become scarce, and on the other hand, due to technological advancement, offshore exploration is increasingly becoming more feasible. In the case of the South China Sea, the littoral States have affirmed ownership of the islands and subsequently claimed the surrounding sea and its resources. This section analyses the State practice in the exploration of non-living resources.

Table 14.1 The South China Sea Estimated Proved and Probable Reserves

Country	*Crude Oil and Liquids Reserves (Billion Barrels)*	*Natural Gas Reserves (Trillion Cubic Feet)*
China	1.3	15
Brunei	1.5	15
Indonesia	0.3	55
Malaysia	5.0	80
Philippines	0.2	4
Thailand	-	1
Vietnam	3.0	20
Total	11.2	190

Sources: US Energy Information Administration, Oil & Gas Journal, IHS, CNOOC, PFC Energy, 15 October 2019 (public domain). Modelled from data from U.S. Energy Information Administration, Oil & Gas Journal, IHS, CNOOC, PFC Energy.

China

China, with its rapid economic and military growth, has become a major player in determining the geopolitics of the world in general and Asia-Pacific in particular.[84] In the longer term, China may well wish to succeed in current America's pre-eminence. In the shorter to medium term, however, it is preoccupied with domestic problems, with trying to expand its influence in neighbouring regions and warding off perceived United States pressures or designs, which are seen as inimical in China's interests.[85] China is the largest consumer of non-living resources in the region, and it has heavily invested in onshore and offshore gas production. The three largest State oil companies, China Petroleum & Chemical Corporation (Sinopec), China National Petroleum Corporation (CNPC), and CNOOC, have been engaged in exploration in the South China Sea. CNOOC is the most experienced in offshore oil production and is the largest investor in the South China Sea. To handle maritime disputes with its neighbours, China favours direct bilateral discussion and negotiations.[86] China has always opposed any form of third-party involvement, including judicial settlement, mediation, and conciliation.

China was one of the initial advocates of 'pursuing joint development while shelving disputes'.[87] CNOOC signed its first contract with foreign companies for offshore activity in the South China Sea in 1983, allowing BP, Petro-Canada, Petrobras and BHP Billiton, to develop several blocks jointly, at the mouth of the Pearl River Basin.[88] In November 2017, China and Vietnam decided to carry out follow-up works of joint inspection of the waters outside the Beibu (Tonkin) Gulf, as addressed in the joint statement.[89] In November 2018, China and the Philippines signed a Memorandum of Understanding on Co-operation on Oil and Gas Development.[90] In September 2019, China and Malaysia agreed to set up a South China Sea dialogue mechanism, which is the first of its kind between the two States.[91] To enlarge its political and economic space and to conscribed the United States from undertaking perceived anti-China moves in this region, China has been building various co-operative multilateral institutions and bilateral partnerships, with neighbouring States.[92]

The Philippines

In the 1970s, the Philippines had started surveying the Reed Bank area of the Spratly Islands and successfully tested a gas well in 1976. Further oil was discovered in the Nido oil field, of the Palawan-Sulu seabed. Commercial production commenced in 1979 and generated 8.8 million barrels. The Philippine National Oil Company, in a joint venture with Shell, operates the Malampaya gas platform sited in the northern Palawan basin. Several administrations of the Philippines' have willingly conveyed their readiness to set aside disputes, for the sake of co-operation. China and the Philippines reached an eight-point agreement on 11 August 1995, 'code of conduct' concerning disputes in the South China Sea, in which both States highlighted the significance of confidence-building and increasing trust between the two States.[93] In October 2019, China and the Philippines established the Joint Body for Energy Exploration in the South China Sea,[94] which will help them to work out the rules and regulations and other policies relating to joint exploration.[95]

Vietnam

Vietnam wishes to increase offshore production in the South China Sea, not only as a way of meeting domestic demand but also to augment State funds. Vietnam's national oil company,

Petro Vietnam, handles all oil and gas, processing, storage and distribution. In addition to operating as a partner with foreign companies in almost all new advancements and refinery ventures, it directly controls half of the gas production and 20 percent of the country's oil production. As the Vietnamese Government encourages the awarding of foreign contracts, major foreign oil companies now have a strong presence in Vietnam's offshore production, in production-sharing contracts (PSCs) with Petro Vietnam. Vietnam, Malaysia and Indonesia entered into a joint oil exploration venture in 2002. China and Vietnam have started joint ventures in the Beibu (Tonkin) Gulf in 2004, which was for 12 years but was further extended for three years. In addition, the Vanguard Bank basin is in the westernmost reef of the Spratly and is known for its rich oil and gas reserves. The Vietnamese Government divides the Vanguard Bank area into several blocks and has dozens of oil rigs in the area. Vietnam has signed more than 50 exploitation contracts with foreign oil companies registered in Japan, Russia, United Kingdom, United States, Spain and so on. Recently, Vietnam's national oil company and Exxon Mobil Corporation reached an agreement to launch a project namely "blue whale" in Block 118, which had been announced to be put into operation in 2022.[96]

Malaysia

Malaysia is the largest producer of oil and gas in the South China Sea. Malaysia's National Oil Company, Petronas, owns the majority of the country's oil and gas assets. Exxon Mobil is Malaysia's major foreign oil and gas producer, with around 50,000 barrels per day. Malaysia is open to joint ventures, and in several instances, its leaders have voiced their readiness for joint ventures in disputed waters. The State has carried out several joint ventures with its neighbours such as the 1979/1990 Malaysia-Thailand Joint Venture and the 1992 Vietnam-Malaysia Joint Venture.

Indonesia

Most of Indonesia's larger producing oil fields, such as those at Duri and Minas, are located outwith the South China Sea. Likewise, most of its natural gas reserves are also located outwith the South China Sea. Currently, Indonesia's oil and gas industry plays a limited role in the South China Sea, however, to meet growing domestic demand, the National Oil Company of Indonesia has made attempts to gain more stakes in the Natuna's D-Alpha Block and offshore blocks near Vietnam. The company wishes to find new discoveries, through joint exploration with Vietnam and Malaysia.

Brunei

The Brunei National Petroleum Company handles all the offshore activities in Brunei, but Brunei-Shell Petroleum has a joint venture with Shell, the only foreign oil producer in Brunei. After Malaysia and Brunei resolved their offshore territorial dispute in March 2009, both successfully entered into a production sharing agreement. In 2011, they started joint drilling in several offshore oil and gas fields, off the coast of Brunei.[97] In 2013, China and Brunei signed the cooperation agreement between the China National Offshore Oil Corporation and the Brunei National Petroleum Company Sendirian Berhad. The PBS-COSL Oilfield Service Company was registered a year later to push forward the cooperation on the Hengyi Industries Sdn Bhd refinery and petrochemical plant, and to promote the 'Brunei-Guangxi Economic Corridor'.[98] It is noteworthy that, Hengyi Industries Sdn Bhd – a joint petrochemical venture between China and Brunei – went into full operation in November 2019 and planned to expand into the second phase construction of its oil refinery and petrochemical project at an industrial park on an island at the Brunei Bay.[99]

Conclusion

Competition concerning obtaining the non-living resources has led to an impasse among the disputing States in the South China Sea, especially those between China, Vietnam and the Philippines. There is a slight possibility of co-operation in renewable energy, as it is abundant in nature and can be re-produced offshore from the respective States. Currently, however, meaningful progress regarding co-operating on non-renewable energy situated in the disputed areas is proving problematical, as there is no mandatory provision in UNCLOS asking a State to co-operatively manage the resources in a marginal sea. This is despite the fact that Articles 74 and 83 indicate obligations for mutual restraint and the establishment of mutual provisional arrangements, e.g. DOC and COC in the case of the South China Sea. The lack of legal binding force and unwillingness to compromise has, however, reached an impasse, in efforts to resolve the dilemma. In order to resolve this dilemma, China being the largest and the most powerful State is encouraged to take the initiative and play a major role in establishing mutually beneficial dispute management measures. It is essential to appreciate that, not all disputes can be solved on a legal basis as, sometimes States have to compromise and cooperate on the humanitarian grounds, in order to create a mutually beneficial outcome.

Notes

1 H. Ritchie, 'Energy', Our World nData.org, 2014, 'https://ourworldinda ta.org/energy', (accessed 13 June 2020).
2 Y.C. Chang, 'Ocean Governance: A Way Forward', *Springer Science & Business Media*, 2011, p. 85.
3 Ibid.
4 J. Bowers, *Sustainability and Environmental Economics: An Alternative Text* (Addison Wesley Longman Limited, 1997), p. 181.
5 IEA Statistics, Fossil Fuel Energy Consumption (% of total), The World Bank Data, 2014, https://data.worldbank.org/indicator/EG.USE.COMM.FO.ZS, (accessed 12 June2020).
6 N. Wang and Y.C. Chang, 'Carbon Print Studies for the Energy Conservation Regulations of the UK and China', *Energy & Buildings*, vol. 42, 2010, p. 695; Y.C. Chang and N. Wang, 'Environmental Regulations and Emissions Trading in China' *Journal of Energy Policy*, vol. 38, 2010, p. 3356.
7 L. Zhuangyan, 'Construction and Perfection of Legal Systems of China's Marine Renewable Energy', Graduate Thesis of Xiamen University, 2009, pp. 9–20. (in Chinese)
8 United Nations, Oceans and the Law of the Sea, Report of the Secretary-General, 2012, A/67/79.
9 Y.C. Chang, N. Wang and S. Durak, 'Ship Recycling and Marine Pollution', *Marine Pollution Bulletin*, vol. 60, no. 9, 2010, p. 1390.
10 Y.C. Chang, 'International Legal Obligations in relation to Good Ocean Governance', *Chinese Journal of International Law*, vol. 9, 2010, p. 589.
11 Y. C. Chang, 'Good Ocean Governance', *Ocean Yearbook*, vol. 23, 2009, p. 119; Y. C.Chang, 'Maritime Clusters—What Can be Learnt from the South West of England', *Journal of Ocean and Coastal Management*, vol. 54, 2011, p. 494; Y. C. Chang, N. Wang and K. Sumser-Lupson, 'Port Social and Culture Survey in the South West of England', *Journal of Coastal Research*, vol. 27, 2011, p. 161.
12 Y. C. Chang, N. Wang and Y. Zhao, 'The Current Development of the Ocean Governance Mechanism in China' *Coastal Management*, vol. 41, 2013, p. 133.
13 Y.C. Chang, 'A Note on a Comparison of the Ocean Governance System between Mainland China and Taiwan', *Ocean Development &International Law*, vol. 43, 2012, p. 329.

14 J.A. Leggett and N.T. Carter, 'Rio+20: The United Nations Conference on Sustainable Development', *Congressional Research Service*, 18 June 2012, https://fas.org/sg p/crs/row/R42573.pdf, p. 8, (accessed 12 June 2020).
15 'Agenda 21 UNCED, Sustainable Development Goals', 1992, https://sustainabledevelopment.un.org/index.php?page=view&type=400&nr=23&menu=35, (accessed 16 June 2020).
16 Ibid.
17 'Swire Institute of Marine Science and Department of Ecology and Biodiversity', University of Hong Kong, http://http.fisheries.ubc.ca/l.teh/destructive%20fishing/South%20c hina%20sea.pdf, (accessed 12 June 2020).
18 'Asia Maritime Transparency Initiative', https://amti.csis.org/south-china-sea-energy-exploration-and-development/, (accessed 16 June 2020).
19 T. Daiss, 'Why The South China Sea Has More Oil Than You Think, Forbes', 22 May 2016, https://www.forbes.com/sites/timdaiss/2016/05/22/why-the-south-china-sea-has-more-oil-than-you-think/#19f46ff1dd8f, (accessed 16 June 2020).
20 Ibid.
21 IBP USA, 'China Investment and Business Guide' Volume 1 Strategic and Practical Information', 2013, p. 38.
22 G. Li, 'China Sea Oil and Gas Resources', *China Institute of International Relations*, 11 May 2020, https://www.globalsecurity.org/military/world/war/spratly-oil.htm, (accessed 16 June 2020).
23 A. Corr, 'China's $60 Trillion Estimate of Oil and Gas in the South China Sea: Strategic Implications', *Journal of Political Risk*, vol. 6, no.1, p. 5.
24 'US Energy Information Administration, South China Sea', 15 October 2019, https://www.eia.gov/international/analysis/regions-of interest/SouthChinaSea, (accessed 16 June 2020).
25 'Global Security.org', South China Sea Oil and Natural Gas, https://www.globalsecurity.or g/military/world/war/spratly-oil.htm, (accessed 12 June 2020).
26 Ibid.
27 X. Vagg, 'Resources in the South China Sea', 04 December 2012, https://www.ame ricansecurityproje ct.org/resources-in-the-south-china-sea/, (accessed 18 June 2020).
28 A. Clark and C. Li, 'Marine Mineral Resources of the South China Sea', *Marine Georesources & Geotechnology*, vol. 11, no.1, 1993, p. 126.
29 X. Vagg, 'Resources in the South China Sea', 04 December 2012, https://www.americansecurityproje ct.org/resources-in-the-south-china-sea/, (accessed 18 June 2020).
30 Y. Zhong et al., 'Rare Earth Elements and Yttrium in Ferromanganese Deposits from the South China Sea: Distribution, Composition and Resource Considerations', *Acta Oceanol. Sin.*, vol. 37, 2018, p. 54.
31 D.S. Alibo and Y. Nozaki, 'Dissolved Rare Earth Elements in the South China Sea: Geochemical Characterization of the Water Masses', *Journal of Geophysical Research, Oceans*, vol. 105, no. 12, 15 December 2000, p. 28783.
32 H. Zhang, 'Scientists Find Materials in SouthChina Sea Needed in Military, Aerospace Equipment', *Global Times*, 16 May 2018, http://www.globaltimes.cn/content/1102629.shtml, (accessed 21 June 2020).
33 Z. Haifeng, L. Haibin and T. Fangzheng, 'Research and Development Prospect of Natural Gashydrate', *Liaoning Chemical Industry*, vol. 4, 2016, p. 533. (in Chinese)
34 Office of Fossil Energy, 'Methane Hydrate', https://www.energy.gov/fe/science-innovation/oil-gas-research/methane-hydrate; (accessed 21 June 2020).
35 S. Zhongni, 'Resources Distribution of Gas Hydrate and Its Exploration and Development Advances', *5 Contemporary Petroleum and Petrochemical*, vol. 24, 2007, p. 26. (in Chinese).
36 X.W. Wang and Y.C. Chang, "Sea Law Phalanx" Initiative: Conference Report', *Marine Policy*, vol. 72, 2016, p. 13.
37 Y.-L. Zhang, Z. Lin and Q.L. Liu, 'Marine Renewable Energy in China: Current Status and Perspectives', *Water Science and Engineering*, vol. 7, no. 3, 2014, p. 305.
38 J. Zhenga, P. Daib and J. Zhanga, 'Tidal Stream Energy in China', *8th International Conference on Asian and PacificCoasts(APAC 2015), Procedia Engineering*, vol. 116, 2015, p. 887.
39 X. Wang et al., 'Tidal Mixing in the South China Sea: An Estimate Based on the Internal Tide Energetics', *Journal of Physical Oceanography*, vol. 46, no. 1, 2016, p. 124.
40 T.M. Shaun Johnston et al., 'Internal Tidal Energy Fluxes in the South China Sea from Density and Velocity Measurements by Gliders', *Journal of Geophysical Research*, vol. 118, no. 8, 2013, p. 3949.

41 Alford, M.H. et al., 'Energy Flux and Dissipation in Luzon Strait: Two Tales of Two Ridges', *Journal of Physical Oceanography*, vol. 41, 2011, p. 2222.
42 A, Dhanju, Golmen et al., 'Chapter 22. Other Marine-Based Energy Industries', 2016, https://www.un.org/depts/los/globalreporting/WOARPROC/Cha pter_22.pdf, (accessed 21 June 2020).
43 W. Musial, S. Butterfield and B. Ram, '*Energy from Offshore Wind*. Conference paper presented at Offshore Technology Conference, Houston, TX, May, 2006, p. 4.
44 A. Ayodotun et al., 'Wind Energy Potentials and Its Trend in the South China Sea', *Energy and Environment Research*, vol. 6, no. 2, 2016, p. 51.
45 Ibid.
46 G. Lin et al., 'Assessment of Wave Energy in the South China Sea Based on GIS Technology, Advances in Meteology', *Hindawai*, 2017, https://www.hindawi.com/journals/amete/2017/1372578/, (accessed 22 June 2020).
47 A. Mirzaei, F. Tangang and L. Juneng, 'Wave Energy Potential Assessment in the Central and Southern Regions of the South China Sea', *Renewable Energy*, vol. 80, 2015, p. 470.
48 G. Lin et al., 'Assessment of Wave Energy in the South China Sea Based on GIS Technology, Advances in Meteology', *Hindawai*, 2017, https://www.hindawi.com/journals/amete/ 2017/1372578/, (accessed 22 June 2020).
49 Ibid.
50 Ibid.
51 'U.S Department of Energy (DOE), *Assessment of Energy Production Potential from Ocean Currents Along the United States Coastline*, http://www1.eere.energy.gov/water/pdfs/energyproduction-oceancurrentsus.pdf, (accessed 23 June 2020).
52 National Oceanic and Atmospheric Administration (NOAA) *Welcome to Currents*, 2007, http://oceanservice.noaa.gov/education/tutorial_currents/lessons/currents_tutorial.pdf. (accessed 23 June 2020).
53 J. Hu, H. Hong and Y. Qi, 'A Review on the Currents in the South China Sea: Seasonal Circulation, South China Sea Warm Current and Kuroshio Intrusion', *Journal of Oceanography*, vol. 56, no. 6, 2000, p. 624.
54 W.D. Fang, Z.X. Guo and Y.T. Huang, 'Observation and Study on the Circulation in the Southern South China Sea', *Chinese Science Bulletin*, vol. 42, no. 21, 1997, p. 2271.
55 A. Dhanju et al., 'Chapter 22. Other Marine-Based Energy Industries', 2016, https://www.un.org/depts/los/global_reporting/WOARPROC/Cha pter_22.pdf, (accessed 24 June 2020).
56 S. Zhang et al., 'An Assessment of Ocean Thermal Energy Conversion Resources in the South China Sea,' *OCEANS 2016 - Shanghai*, Shanghai, 2016, p. 6.
57 Sharda, World's Largest Ocean Thermal Energy Conversion (OTEC) Power Plant To Come Up in China, Marine Insight, 11 December 2019, https://www.marineinsight.com/offshore/worlds-largest-ocean-thermal-energy-conversion-otec-power-plant-to-come-up-in china/#:~:text=April%2030%2C% 202019-\,World's%20Largest%20Ocean%20Thermal%20Energy%20Conversion%20(OT EC)%20 Power%20Plant%20To,global%20OTEC%20construction%20and%20development., (accessed 24 June 2020).
58 Ibid.
59 F. Gallucci and M.S. Annaland, *Process Intensification for Sustainable Energy Conversion*, John Wiley & Sons, 12 May 2015, p. 290.
60 C. Zheng et al., *21st Century Maritime Silk Road: A Peaceful Way Forward*, Springer, 17 Mar 2018, p. 71.
61 A. Dhanju et al., 'Chapter 22. Other Marine-Based Energy Industries', 2016, https://www.un.org/depts/los/global_reporting/WOARPROC/Cha pter_22.pdf, (accessed 24 June 2020).
62 Ibid.
63 D.M. Nguyen, 'Settlement of Disputes under the 1982 United Nations Convention on the Law of the Sea The Case of the South China Sea Dispute', UN-Nipon Foundation, December 2005, p. 3.
64 Part XV: Settlement of dispute with 21 Articles; Annex V: Conciliation with 14 Articles; Annex VI: Status of the International Tribunal for the Law of the Sea with 41 Articles; Annex VII: Arbitration with 17 Articles; Annex VIII: Special Arbitration with 5 Articles. Besides that, Articles deal with dispute settlement can be found in Articles 15, 74 and 83 relating to the delimitation of territorial sea, exclusive economic zone and continental shelf; Article 59, Article 263, Article 265 and Part XI. https://www.un.org/depts/ los/conventionagreements/texts/unclos/unclos_e.pdf, (accessed 18 June 2020).

65 Ibid., p. 51.
66 Ibid., p. 67.
67 Ibid., p. 79.
68 Ibid., p. 79.
69 Ibid., p. 99.
70 Ibid., p. 130.
71 S. Rosenne and L.B. Sohn, *The United Nations Convention on the Law of the Sea: A Commentary*, 1998, 5, p. 87.
72 R.C. Severino, 'ASEAN and the South China Sea', *Security Challenges*, vol. 6, no. 2, 2010, p. 47.
73 Ibid.
74 Ibid.
75 C. Thayer, 'ASEAN, China and the Code of Conduct in the South China Sea', *SAIS Review of International Affairs*, vol. 33, 2013, p. 84.
76 Ibid.
77 J. Kim, 'Territorial Disputes in the South China Sea: Implications for Security in Asia and Beyond', *Strategic Studies Quarterly*, vol. 9, no. 2, 2015, p. 141.
78 Ibid.
79 C. Thayer, 'A Closer Look at the ASEAN-China Single Draft South China Sea Code of Conduct', *The Diplomat*, 03 August 2018, https://thediplomat.com/2018/08/a-closer-look-at-the-asean-china-single-draft-south-china-sea-code-of-conduct/, (accessed 24 June 2020).
80 N.M. Quang, 'Saving the China-ASEAN South China Sea Code of Conduct', 29 June 2019, https://thediplomat.com/2019/06/saving-the-china-asean-south-china-sea-code-of-conduct/, (accessed 16 June 2020).
81 C. Thayer, 'A Closer Look at the ASEAN-China Single Draft South China Sea Code of Conduct', *The Diplomat*, 03 August 2018, https://thediplomat.com/2018/08/a-closer-look-at-the-asean-china-single-draft-south-china-sea-code-of-conduct/, (accessed 24 June 2020).
82 South China Sea Expert Working Group, 'A Blueprint For A South China Sea Code Of Conduct', *Asia Maritime Transparency Initiative*, 11 October 2018, https://amti.csis.org/blueprint-for-south-china-sea-code-of-conduct/, (accessed 3 July 2020).
83 Ibid.
84 S. Lokhande, 'South China Sea a Sea of Dispute', *Chaurahha The Crossroad*, 10 March 2013, https:/ /chaurahha.wordpress.com/tag/east-asia-summit/, (accessed 29 June 2020).
85 D. Singh, 'Asia-Pacific Political & Security Dynamics', *Political & Security Dynamics of South & SEA*, (ISEAS), 2007, p. 27.
86 J. Li and P. Chen, 'Joint Development in the South China Sea: Is the Time Ripe?', *Asian Yearbook of International Law: Volume 22* (2016), edited by Seokwoo Lee et al., Brill, LEIDEN; BOSTON, 2019, p. 158.
87 H. Qi, 'Joint Development in the South China Sea: China's Incentives and Policy Choices', *Journal of Contemporary East Asia Studies*, vol. 8, no. 2, 2019, p. 239.
88 US Energy Information Administration, South China Sea, 15 October 2019, https://www.eia.gov/international/analysis/regions-of interest/SouthChinaSea, (accessed 22 June 2020).
89 Xinhua, 'China, Vietnam Reach Consensus on Trade, Maritime Cooperation: Joint Statement', 13 November 2017, (accessed 16 June 2020).
90 Chinese Ministry of Foreign Affairs, 'Memorandum of Understanding on Cooperation on Oil and Gas Development between the Government of the People's Republic of China and the Government of the Republic of the Philippines', 27 November 2018, https://www.fmprc.gov.cn/mfa_eng/wjdt_665385/2649_665393/t1616644.shtml, (accessed 20 June 2020).
91 Reuters, 'China, Malaysia to Set Up South China Sea Dialogue Mechanism', 12 September 2019, https://www.reuters.com/article/us-china-malaysia/china-malaysia-to-set-up-south-china-sea-dialogue-mechanism-idUSKCN1VX0JN, (accessed 16 June 2020).
92 S. Lokhande, 'South China Sea a Sea of Dispute', Chaurahha The Crossroad, 10 March 2013, https:/ /chaurahha.wordpress.com/tag/east-asia-summit/, (accessed 23 June 2020).
93 H.T. Nguyen, 'Vietnam and the Code of Conduct for the South China Sea', *Ocean Development and International Law*, vol. 32, no. 2, 2001, p. 126.
94 J. Rinoza and L. Liwanag, 'Manila, Beijing Establish Joint Body for Energy Exploration in South China Sea', 30 October 2019, https://www.benarnews.org/english/news/philipine/South-China-Sea-10302019152758.html, (accessed 16 June 2020).

95 R. Robles, 'Officials from Philippines, China to Meet on Stalled South China Sea Joint Oil-exploration Deal: Senator', *South China Morning Post*, 7 January 2020, https://www.scmp.com/week-asia/politics/article/3045050/officials-philippines-china-meet-stalled-south-china-sea-joint, (accessed 29 June 2020).

96 T. Daiss, 'All the Reasons ExxonMobil May Leave Vietnam', *Asia Times*, 17 September 2019, https://asiatimes.com/2019/09/all-the-reasons-exxonmobil-may-leave-vietnam/, (accessed 12 October 2020).

97 US Energy Information Administration, Oil & Gas Journal, IHS, CNOOC, PFC Energy, 15 October 2019, https://www.eia.gov/international/analysis/regions-of-interest/SouthChinaSea, (accessed 22 June 2020).

98 Asia Pacific Energy Research Centre, 'APEC Energy Overview 2019', (2019), p. 26.

99 BANDAR SERI BEGAWAN, 'China-Brunei Joint Venture Delivers 1st Supply of Refined Fuel Products', *XinHua Net*, 18 May 2020, http://www.xinhuanet.com/english/2020-05/18/c_139067323.htm, (accessed 12 October 2020).

15
BIODIVERSITY AND CONSERVATION

Vu Hai Dang[1]

Introduction

The South China Sea is the body of water, part of the Pacific Ocean, located between the Strait of Malacca in the Southeast and the Strait of Taiwan in the Northeast.[2] Considered one of the largest semi-enclosed seas in the world, the South China Sea has an estimated area of about 3.500.000 km^2 and an average depth of 1212 m.[3] The regional sea is surrounded by China, the territory of Taiwan (hereafter called Taiwan), the Philippines, Brunei, Indonesia, Singapore, Malaysia, Thailand, Cambodia and Vietnam. From a socioeconomic point of view, the coastal area of the South China Sea is home to the world's most dynamic economies over the last decades, which are China and the ASEAN countries. Main exploitation of the sea includes fisheries, mariculture, oil and gas, shipping and tourism.[4]

While the South China Sea is well known in international media for its hot and complicated territorial and maritime disputes;[5] the marine region is also a recognized world hub for marine biodiversity. The problem is while countries are disputing over ownership and jurisdiction in its waters, the South China Sea marine environment is degrading at an alarming rate due to both human activities and climate change. This chapter provides an evaluation of the cooperation at the regional level between coastal States in the South China Sea towards the conservation of its marine biodiversity.

It first sets out a comprehensive picture of the current threats to the biodiversity in the South China Sea and affirms that regional cooperation to conserve marine biodiversity is an established norm of international law. It then takes stock of what has been undertaken at the regional level to help protect the South China Sea biodiversity.

Biodiversity in the South China Sea: values and threats

This section analyses the important values of the South China Sea in terms of marine biodiversity and the threats that it is currently facing.

Values

The South China Sea lies within the Indo-West Pacific region, recognized as a global center of biodiversity. In terms of the distribution of valuable natural habitat, estimates state that the South China Sea has 12 percent of the world's and about 30 percent of Asia's mangrove forests. It is also recognized that the South China Sea supports 20 percent of Southeast Asia's coral reefs which account for 34 percent of the world total. The South China Sea's coastal area also has various large seagrass beds of dozens of thousands of hectares, of which the largest is probably the connected seagrass meadows of Kampot, Cambodia and Phu Quoc, Viet Nam (37.000 hectares).[6]

In terms of species richness, it is estimated that South China Sea has about 8600 species of plan and animals.[7] According to researches undertaken by China, the South China Sea has the largest number of species per 100 km of coast in comparison with all marine regions surrounding the country, with the domination of tropical fauna and flora.[8] For flora, the greatest number of true mangroves are observed in Malaysia where 41 species have been recorded, followed by Indonesia and Viet Nam with 37 species each. Eighteen out of 50 known species of seagrass worldwide are also found in, and adjacent to the coastal waters of the South China Sea.[9]

For fauna, according to D. Huang *et al.*, the total number of corals recorded in all the areas of the South China Sea reaches 571 species, ranging from 95 in its northern part to 433 in its southern part. This richness can be equivalent to the famous neighboring Coral Triangle, which has about 566 species of coral reefs.[10] Some scholars even trace the high diversity of corals in the Coral Triangle from the transport of fish larvae from the South China Sea.[11] Lutaenko affirms that the South China Sea has the most diverse bivalve fauna in the world, with from 1200 to 1500 species.[12] Valez says that the South China Sea is "the world's most diverse shallow water area" with, among others, seven of nine known species of giant clams, three of four identified species of horseshoe crabs.[13] According to the Seas Project from the Oregon Institute of Marine Biology, the South China Sea also has over 530 species of phytoplankton, over 850 species of algae and various marine mammals such as humpback dolphins and finless porpoises.[14]

The South China Sea is an important fishing ground for countries in the region. Most of the region belongs to the Western Central Pacific,[15] which produced, in 2017, 12.5 million tons of fishes, ranking second among the world's 19 fishing zones in terms of total annual marine production.[16] The most comprehensive assessment estimates that the South China Sea has 3,365 species of marine fishes belonging to 263 families, most of which are highly migratory. Main species fished pelagic species such as flying fishes, tunas, billfishes and mackerels; demersal fishes such as snappers and soles; invertebrates such as crabs, shrimps and squids; reef fish such as groupers, parrotfish and rabbitfish; small coastal pelagic fish such as herring, sardine and anchovy; and sharks.[17]

Fisheries have an important socio-economic role in South China Sea countries. It is estimated that currently, 1.77 million fishing vessels are operating in the waters of the South China Sea (which corresponds to 55 percent of the number of fishing vessels worldwide) of which the majority (86 percent) are small-scale vessels. The employment in South China Sea's marine fishery is estimated at about 3.7 million people but it is likely an underestimation.[18] The consumption of marine fish in the food supply in East and Southeast Asia is about 2.96 kg per capita per year, much higher than the world's average of 1.09 kg per capita per year.[19]

Threats

The most updated comprehensive assessment of the status of the marine biodiversity in the South China Sea so far was undertaken under the Reversing Environmental Degradation Trends in the South China Sea and Gulf of Thailand project which was terminated in 2007.[20]

At the time, it has been generally agreed that the most serious threats to the marine biodiversity of the South China Sea are habitat loss and degradation, depletion of marine living resources and land-based pollution. More recent studies on the marine environment of the South China Sea seem to indicate that the degradation trends in the South China Sea biodiversity have been exacerbated.

Estimates from the mid- to late 2000s state that 70 percent of the region's mangroves have been lost due mainly to the conversion of coastal land to pond aquaculture (especially for shrimp), cutting of wood, urban and port development and coastal settlement. Eighty percent of the South China Sea's coral reefs have been degraded or under serious threats in places[21] from sediment, overfishing and destructive fishing practices (such as the use of poison and dynamite), pollution and climate change, which makes them become the most threatened and damaged reefs in the world. Twenty to 50 percent of the seagrass beds have been damaged in many places in the region (Indonesia, Malaysia, Philippines and Thailand) through destructive fishing, sedimentation, wastewater, effluents, nutrients, coastal construction and overfishing. The wetlands of the South China Sea have also suffered a widespread loss due to the conversion of the land for agriculture, human settlement, urbanization, industrialization and tourism, and degradation of the ecosystem from pollution, overfishing, deforestation and natural disasters.[22] Overall, the overall decadal losses of these habitats until 2006–2007 are 30 percent of seagrass, 16 percent of mangroves, and 16 percent of live coral cover.[23]

Recently, China has received a lot of critics from scientists due to the land reclamation activities in several disputed features in the South China Sea.[24] John McManus from the University of Miami said that about 16.8 kilometer square of coral reefs in the Spratlys was permanently destroyed by China, equivalent to more than 10 percent of the Spratlys' total shallow reef area.[25] Edgar Gomez from the University of Philippines estimates that coral reefs in the Spratlys provide a value of 350.000 USD per year per hectare thus China's land reclamation activities are causing a total loss of 108.9 million USD annually to coastal countries in the South China Sea.[26] Leland Smith *et al.* states that China's dredging activities led to a decrease in the biological health of the region resulting from the smothering of natural benthic habitats and reef complexes with sediment. They opine further that the potential causality between Chinese island-building operations and environmental degradation is potentially significant, as the Spratly Islands in the South China Sea form a distinct marine ecosystem, which serves as a significant source of larvae for regional coral reefs.[27]

Although no recent stock assessment for the South China Sea has been undertaken, it has been generally agreed that marine living resources in the South China Sea have been heavily over-exploited.[28] Studies have shown that the majority of the assessed stocks in the South China Sea are either overfished or fully fished, as little as reaching only about 5 percent of the 1950s level. Catch per unit effort in most fisheries has declined steadily, equivalent to a third of catch 30–40 years ago, and "fishing down the web" is widespread in all South China Sea countries.[29] The widespread use of destructive fishing practices such as bottom trawling, poisoning and blast fishing exacerbates the degradation of marine habitat and depletion of fish stocks.[30]

The most important sources of pollution in the South China Sea are land-based, consisting of contributions from domestic and industrial waste,[31] agriculture, aquaculture as well as sediments and solid waste as the most dominant.[32] Lately, an alarm has been raised about plastic waste in the region's ocean. According to studies, it is estimated that every year about 8 million tons of plastic have been leaked to the sea, of which more than half comes from South China Sea states, namely China, Indonesia, Philippines, Viet Nam, Thailand and

Malaysia. If no action is taken, the ocean is expected to contain one ton of plastic for every three tons of fish by 2025 and more plastics than fish by 2025.[33] A recent experiment also shows that the level of microplastics in the South China Sea reached 360 particles per square metre in a marine area close to the Philippines.[34]

Besides these human-induced threats, the marine biodiversity of the South China Sea is also at the risk of being adversely affected by climate change. The Intergovernmental Panel on Climate Change projected that the effects of climate change in Asia until the late 21st century would include an increase in mean annual temperature, especially in the ocean surface (an increase of 3 degree Celsius in Southeast Asia) and more extreme precipitation in East and Southeast Asia.[35] The panel also predicted the sea level of the South China Sea to rise to 64.1 cm by the end of the century and to become 0.3 to 0.35 pH more acidic.[36] These would likely cause changes in the growth, development and distribution of mangroves; decrease in distribution, abundance, and size of marine species in the tropic region; large declines in coral-dominated reefs; negative impacts on calcified marine organisms (algae, molluscs, larval echinoderms) and increasing coastal flooding, erosion, and saltwater intrusion into surface and groundwaters.[37] It is stated that 40 percent of the coral reef were bleached on Pratas Island in the northern part of the South China Sea due to a two degree Celsius sea surface temperature rise during the 2015 El Niño event.[38] Recently, the Washington-based Climate Central issued even much gloomier projections for the region. According to the organization's report on global vulnerability to sea-level rise and coastal flooding, by 2050, Asia will suffer the most serious impact from sea-level rising with about 300 million people affected.[39] In the South China Sea region, large parts of Viet Nam's Mekong and Red River Deltas, and China's Pearl River Delta are expected to be below annual flood level by then.[40]

International legal framework for the conservation of marine biodiversity in the South China Sea

The duty to conserve and sustainably use marine biodiversity, including through regional cooperation, appears in many international instruments, both treaties and soft law instruments. This section focuses on how this duty is formulated under the framework of two major conventions relating to the protection of marine biodiversity; namely the United Nations Convention on the Law of the Sea, 1982 and the Convention on Biological Diversity, 1992; and United Nations' most important soft law instruments on the marine environment. Relevant conclusions of the Arbitral Tribunal in the South China Sea Arbitral Award are also analysed to see how international law's rules relating to the protection of marine biodiversity are applied in the South China Sea.

United Nations Convention on the Law of the Sea (UNCLOS), 1982

UNCLOS[41] contains many provisions relating to the conservation of marine biodiversity. For instance, UNCLOS also imposes on States the general obligation to protect the marine environment[42] and an obligation to protect and preserve rare or fragile ecosystems as well as the habitat of depleted, threatened or endangered species and other forms of marine life.[43] The UNCLOS also imposes on States a duty to protect marine living resources in both waters under their jurisdiction as well as in the high seas.[44]

Regional cooperation or similar words implying the same thing appears in many of the UNCLOS's stipulations relating to the protection and preservation of the marine environment. Article 197 asks States to cooperate

> as appropriate, on a regional basis, directly or through competent international organizations, in formulating and elaborating international rules, standards and recommended practices and procedures consistent with this Convention, for the protection and preservation of the marine environment, taking into account characteristic regional features.[45]

Article 123 requires the relevant coastal States to have a semi-enclosed sea endeavor to coordinate, whether directly or through the appropriate regional organization, in the exploitation, management and conservation of marine living resources and the protection and preservation of the marine environment. It also encourages these States to invite other interested States or international organizations to cooperate with them in the implementation of such initiatives.[46] Relating to the conservation of the marine living resources, States are required to cooperate regionally in the exploitation, management and protection of shared stocks.[47] Article 66 relating to the conservation, exploitation and management of anadromous stocks also specifies the States of origin of these stocks and the other States fishing there to "make arrangements" for its implementation.[48]

Convention on biological diversity, 1992

The Convention on Biological Diversity (CBD) provides the most comprehensive international legal framework for the conservation of biodiversity, including marine biodiversity. Under the CBD, States are required to take actions to achieve three objectives: conservation of biological diversity, sustainable use of its components and fair and equitable sharing of the benefits arising out of the utilization of genetic resources.[49] These include to identification and monitoring of components of biological diversity important for its conservation and sustainable use, processes and activities which have or likely to have significant adverse impacts on the conservation and sustainable use of biological diversity;[50] to implement *in-situ* and *ex-situ* conservation measures;[51] and measures to ensure the sustainable use of components of biological diversity.[52]

Relating to regional cooperation, the CBD imposes on States a duty to cooperate with the other contracting States directly or through competent international organizations, in respect of areas beyond national jurisdiction and on other matters of mutual interests for the conservation and sustainable use of biological diversity.[53] This duty to cooperate includes providing financial and other support such as research and training for *in-situ* and *ex-situ* conservation, in particular for developing countries;[54] dealing with transboundary threats on biological diversity;[55] access to and transfer of technology;[56] exchange of information;[57] and promotion of technical and scientific cooperation.[58]

Measures for the conservation of marine biodiversity are adopted also under the framework of the Conference of the Parties of the CBD. For instance, a Strategic Plan for Biodiversity 2011–2020 was adopted at the 10th meeting of the Conference of the Parties (COP) of the CBD in 2010 in order to

> take effective and urgent action to halt the loss of biodiversity in order to ensure that by 2020 ecosystems are resilient and continue to provide essential services, thereby securing the planets variety of life, and contributing to human well-being, and poverty eradication.[59]

To achieve the goal of improving the status of biodiversity by safeguarding ecosystems, species and genetic diversity, Strategic Plan fixes as target to achieve by 2020,

> at least 17 percent of terrestrial and inland water areas, and 10 percent of coastal and marine areas, especially areas of particular importance for biodiversity and ecosystem services, are conserved through effectively and equitably managed, ecologically representative and well-connected systems of protected areas and other effective area-based conservation measures, and integrated into the wider landscapes and seascapes.[60]

Currently, a post-2020 global biodiversity framework is being developed under the CBD to replace the Strategic Plan for Biodiversity 2011-2020. This new framework is to be adopted by the 15th COP of the CBD which will be held tentatively in Kunming, China in November 2021.[61] According to a zero draft of this framework, it determine new action targets to be achieved by 2030 but with a longterm vision until 2050.[62]

A programme of work on marine and coastal biological diversity was adopted at the 3rd COP of the CBD meeting in 1998 in Bratislava, Slovakia to implement the "Jakarta Mandate on Marine and Coastal Biological Diversity" of 1995 which affirms the "critical need for the Conference of the Parties to address the conservation and sustainable use of marine and coastal biological diversity".[63] The programme has five elements: integrated marine and coastal area management, marine and coastal living resources, marine and coastal protected areas, mariculture and alien species and genotypes. Within each element, it defines operational objectives and priority activities with a timeline to achieve these objectives.[64]

Important soft law instruments

Conservation and sustainable use of marine biodiversity is also a critical topic in United Nations' most important declarations, plans of action and resolutions relating to environmental protection. For instance, in the Agenda 2030 for Sustainable Development adopted at the United Nations Sustainable Development Summit in 2015, the 14th goal is to conserve and sustainably use the oceans, seas and marine resources for sustainable development. Under this goal, States set as targets, *inter alia*, by 2020, to sustainably manage and protect marine and coastal ecosystems and take action for their restoration in order to achieve healthy and productive oceans and to conserve at least ten percent of coastal and marine areas, consistent with national and international law and based on the best available scientific information.[65] At the United Nations Conference to Support the Implementation of Sustainable Development Goal 14, organized in June 2017,[66] participants, including Heads of State and Government and high-level representatives, were committed to halting and reversing the decline in the health and productivity of the ocean and its ecosystems and to protecting and restoring its resilience and ecological integrity.[67] They also stress the need for enhanced cooperation, coordination and policy coherence at all levels and emphasize the critical importance of effective partnerships enabling collective action.[68] Furthermore, in the annually adopted resolutions regarding Ocean and the law of the sea by the United Nations General Assembly, the call for States to take concrete actions in order to conserve and sustainably use the biodiversity of the oceans, including the strengthening of regional cooperation, has been repeatedly affirmed.[69]

The South China Sea Arbitral Award and conservation of marine biodiversity in the South China Sea

The Award issued by the Arbitral Tribunal in the South China Sea Arbitration between the Philippines and China in 2016,[70] in addition to its conclusions relating to maritime entitlement, also has an important reference to the conservation and sustainable use of marine biodiversity in the South China Sea. Concretely, it gives examples of what could be considered as a violation of the duty to protect and preserve the marine environment under the UNCLOS. An analysis of the relevant part of the Award follows.

In the Award, the Arbitral Tribunal concludes that two types of activities from China are in violation of the obligations to protect and preserve the marine environment under UNCLOS:

- Toleration, protection and failure to prevent harmful harvesting activities of endangered species: First, the Arbitral Tribunal states that Chinese fishing vessels have been involved in the harvesting of threatened or endangered species such as corals, giant clams and marine turtles on various occasions based on the shreds of evidence submitted by the Philippines.[71] Among these, the Arbitral Tribunal considers the harvesting of sea turtles, species threatened with extinction constitute harm to the marine environment. As for the corals and giant clams, the Arbitral Tribunal states that harvesting at a large scale has an adverse impact on the fragile marine environment. Thus, the Arbitral Tribunal concludes that the failure to prevent these practices by China is a breach of articles 192 and 194(5) of UNCLOS.[72] The Arbitral Tribunal also condemns the use of cyanide and dynamite, considered by independent experts "highly destructive methods" and "the most highly destructive of all fishing method,"[73] as a violation of articles 194, 194(2) and 194(5) of UNCLOS.[74]
- Islands-building activities: The Arbitral Tribunal recognizes that despite the fact that early construction and land reclamation works on the occupied features in the South China Sea have had negative impacts on its coral reefs, the most serious destruction comes from China's recent construction.[75] According to the Arbitral Tribunal, China's artificial island-building activities violated the obligation under article 192 to protect and preserve the marine environment and the obligation under article 194(1) to ensure that activities under their control do not cause damage by pollution to the environment. China also violated the obligation under article 194(5) to take measures necessary to protect and preserve rare or fragile ecosystems as well as the habitat of depleted, threatened or endangered species and other forms of marine life.[76]

The Arbitral Tribunal further states that by undertaking the island-building activities, China failed to respect two obligations under the duty to cooperate for the protection and preservation of the marine environment. First, China did not respect the obligation to cooperate on a regional basis to formulate standards and practices for the protection and preservation of the marine environment as required by article 197. Second, China did not respect the one to endeavor to coordinate the implementation of their rights and duties with respect to the protection and preservation of the marine environment in a semi-enclosed sea as required by article 123.[77]

Regional cooperation for the conservation of marine biodiversity of the South China Sea

This section looks at how coastal States in the South China Sea cooperate to conserve the marine biodiversity of the South China Sea both in words and in deeds. Concretely, it studies the commitments and cooperative activities relating to the conservation of marine biodiversity in general and conservation of the South China Sea biodiversity in particular, under four most relevant regional mechanisms: Coordinating Body for the Seas of East Asia, Partnership in Environmental Management for the Seas of East Asia, ASEAN-China cooperation and the Workshops for managing potential conflicts in the South China Sea.

The Coordinating Body for the Seas of East Asia (COBSEA)

COBSEA, one of the world's 13 Regional Sea Programmes, was established is to oversee the implementation of the Action Plan for the Protection and Sustainable Development of the Seas of East Asia.[78] The objective of the Action Plan is to provide a comprehensive strategy for the protection of the environment and promote sustainable development in the East Asian Seas.[79] It provides for the undertaking of measures to rehabilitate damaged natural habitats and replenish depleted species population in order to restore sustainable productivity and establishment of a network of properly managed marine protected areas to conserve biodiversity and maintain productivity.[80]

Regional action in conserving marine biodiversity under COBSEA has been more focused on monitoring, management, and protection and establishment of demonstration sites for management of coral reefs.[81] With regards to the South China Sea, from 2002 to 2008, COBSEA has developed and implemented the Global Environment Facility/ UN Environment Programme (GEF/UNEP) Project "Reversing the Environmental Degradation Trend in the South China Sea and Gulf of Thailand" (South China Sea Project), which seeks to protect the region's most important habitats such as mangroves, coral reefs, seagrasses and wetlands.[82] The most important output of the project was the adoption of a South China Sea's Strategic Action Programme (SAP) for future cooperative activities to enhance the conservation of the regional seas' most valuable habitats such as mangroves, coral reefs, seagrasses and wetlands as well as prevention of land-based pollution and conservation of fish stocks.[83] Two other projects have been adopted to implement the SAP, namely the "Implement the Strategic Action Programme for the South China Sea" Project[84] for the conservation of habitat and prevention of pollution components and the "Establishment and Operation of a Regional System of Fisheries *Refugia* in the South China Sea and Gulf of Thailand" Project[85] for the conservation of fish stocks component. To date, the Fisheries Refugia project seems to make more progress than the former as it has been launched since November 2016.[86] As for the SAP Implement project, it is in the process of undertaking national consultations and developing national assistance tools.[87]

According to the COBSEA Strategic Directions 2018–2022, in the years to come, COBSEA action will focus on two areas: land-based marine pollution and marine and coastal planning and management. In marine and coastal planning and management, COBSEA's aims include strengthening biodiversity conservation in line with Aichi targets, including increasing conservation of marine and coastal area to 10 percent in the COBSEA region; facilitating the formulation of national and regional policy on ecosystem-based marine and coastal planning and management; and strengthening and mainstreaming action plans for ecosystem-based marine and coastal planning and management. The planned activities to achieve these objectives are a review of national and regional legal and policy frameworks; development of regional guidelines; building capacity, exchange of information and knowledge, establishing COBSEA network of MPAs and evaluating management effectiveness of MPAs.[88]

The Partnerships in Environmental Management for the Seas of East Asia (PEMSEA)

PEMSEA was established by the project "Building Partnership for Environmental Protection and Management in the East Asian Seas," 1999–2007 to implement the Sustainable Development Strategy for the East Asian Seas (SDS-EAS).[89] The SDS-EAS, adopted by the Putrajaya Declaration on 12 December 2003 and then updated by the

Da Nang Compact on 20 November 2015,[90] contains a package of applicable principles, objectives and implementation approaches for achieving sustainable development of the seas of East Asia.

The SDS-EAS set out various objectives for action for the conservation of marine biodiversity such as conservation and redress of biological diversity; safeguarding of the rare, threatened endangered species and genetic resources, and stopping coastal and marine degradation from land-based human activities. To achieve these objectives, PEMSEA members will undertake action programmes such as developing a national policy to integrate the management of natural/biological resources and economic development and crafting an agreed approach to determining coastal and marine areas of significant biological diversity and natural value and identifying the allowable limits of their use. They will also expand regional cooperation to conserve and manage environmental resources, including overexploited and endangered migratory species and coastal areas of transboundary importance.[91]

To achieve these above-mentioned objectives, PEMSEA focuses on enhancing integrated coastal management in its Country Partners through activities such as establishing a regional knowledge bank on integrated coastal management, capacity building, training, conducting research with Partners on specific topics (such as sustainable financing), the publication of manuals and undertaking consultation for implementation of targeted research. For the objective of conservation of marine biodiversity, PEMSEA activities on helping Country Partners in conducting baseline, risk and vulnerability assessments and preparation of management plans for local sites focusing on improving MPA management effectiveness, sustainable fisheries/ecosystem approach to fisheries management, and ecosystem friendly alternative livelihood activities.[92] According to the SDS-EAS Implementation Plan 2018–2022, PEMSEA aims towards achieving three targets in biodiversity conservation and management by 2022: (i) increasing the areal extent of healthy and resilient coastal and marine habitats; (ii) expanding and strengthening Marine Protected Areas (MPA) and MPA networks for the protection and conservation of marine biodiversity and threatened marine animals; and (iii) enhancing the use of green infrastructure and blue carbon for climate adaptation and mitigation and biodiversity conservation.[93]

To date, it is estimated that PEMSEA's ICM programmes have covered a total of more than 40.000 km of coastline of the East Asian Seas region[94] and the organization is aiming towards having ICM programmes covering at least 25 percent of the region's coastline and contiguous watershed areas by 2021.[95]

ASEAN-China cooperation in conservation of marine biodiversity in the South China Sea

The ASEAN-China cooperation in the conservation of marine biodiversity in the South China Sea is carried out under two frameworks: the cooperation between ASEAN and China in environmental protection and the implementation of the Declaration of Conduct of Parties in the South China Sea.

The "bilateral" cooperation between ASEAN and China in environmental protection started in 2004 with the organization of the China-ASEAN Dialogue on Environmental Policies organized in Sanya, China.[96] Since then, environmental protection has become a component of the Plans of Action to Implement the Joint Declaration on ASEAN-China Strategic Partnership for Peace and Prosperity.[97] In the most recent Plan of Action for the period 2016–2020 adopted in 2015, the two sides committed to exploring possible cooperative initiatives to support the ASEAN Centre for Biodiversity and on the management of priority areas for biodiversity conservation such as ASEAN Heritage Parks and the implementation of biodiversity-related environmental agreements, including the CBD.[98]

The first instrument between China and ASEAN specifically relating to environmental protection cooperation is the China-ASEAN Strategy on Environmental Protection Co-operation 2009–2015, jointly developed and adopted by ASEAN and China in 2009. The Strategy identified seven areas of cooperation in environmental protection to be developed between ASEAN and China, including the area of biodiversity conservation.[99] Under the Strategy, a number of activities were implemented to promote cooperation on biodiversity and ecological conservation, such as the development of an "ASEAN-China biodiversity and ecological protection cooperation plan" project to support China and the ASEAN Member States to develop and implement policies, plans and actions of biodiversity and ecological conservation. A number of workshops on biodiversity conservation practice in ASEAN and China were also organized such as the "Workshop on ASEAN-China implementation of biodiversity conservation strategy and Aichi target capacity building" and "Seminar on China – ASEAN biodiversity conservation practice" organized in Kunming, China in July 2013.[100] Currently, China and ASEAN have completed the implementation of the ASEAN-China Strategy on Environmental Cooperation 2016–2020[101] and are in the process of finalising the Framework of ASEAN-China Environmental Cooperation Strategy and Action Plan (2021-2025).[102]

The cooperative activities between ASEAN and China in the conservation of marine biodiversity in the South China Sea are also implemented under the framework of the Declaration on the Conduct of Parties in the South China Sea (DOC). Also with regard to conflict prevention in the South China Sea, cooperation between ASEAN and China has started with the negotiations for a Code of Conduct in the South China Sea since the 2000s.[103] The DOC was adopted by ASEAN and China in 2002 to prevent the escalation of conflicts in the South China Sea and providing an environment favorable to the peaceful settlement of the South China Sea dispute.[104] Pursuant to paragraph 6 of the Declaration, pending the resolution of the dispute, the Parties may explore and undertake cooperative activities in several areas, including marine environmental protection.[105] Under this framework, ASEAN and China have conducted a number of workshops and seminars, including on the topic of marine ecosystem and biodiversity.[106]

On the occasion of the 20th ASEAN-China Summit and the 15th anniversary of the signing of the DOC in Manila, Philippines, on 13 November 2017, Heads of States of ASEAN and China issued the Declaration for a Decade of Coastal and Marine Environmental Protection in the South China Sea (2017–2027). The Declaration affirms that coordinated and cooperative regional efforts are essential for the scientific conservation and management of marine resources and environment, biodiversity, and coastal zone of the ecosystem of the South China Sea. It also acknowledges that conservation of endangered and migratory wildlife species warrants cooperation from countries within the region where such species spend any part of their life cycle. Most importantly, it calls on the governments of ASEAN and China to action to meet these aspirations.[107]

Workshops to manage potential conflicts in the South China Sea

The workshops to manage potential conflicts in the South China Sea (or South China Sea workshops) were are a series of informal workshops organized by Indonesia since 1990 with the participation of all the claimants in the Paracels and Spratlys islands dispute, including Taiwan, and other ASEAN countries. The purpose of the workshops is to develop confidence-building measures in the South China Sea and to promote cooperation activities between the littoral States. The participants at the meetings include government and military officials, academics and scientists from the region.[108] So far, a total of 29 workshops have been organized by Indonesia with the latest one in September 2019.

Under the South China Sea Workshops, a wide range of issues have been discussed at its different meetings which covers also resource management, environment, ecology and marine scientific research.[109] A number of cooperative activities were also proposed and implemented, which include the organization in 2002 of an expedition for biodiversity studies in the Anambas and Natunas islands of Indonesia (Anambas Expedition). During this expedition, a total of 60 sites were explored, 3,000 specimens collected among which some were unknown previously.[110] Currently, Indonesia suggests organizing a second expedition, the Anambas II Expedition, to study biodiversity and pollution in the South China Sea.[111]

Conclusions

This chapter provides an account of how coastal States have fulfilled the duty under international law to cooperate at the regional level to conserve the marine biodiversity of the South China Sea. It could be observed that the conservation of marine biodiversity in general and the conservation of the South China Sea biodiversity is very high in the agenda for regional cooperation. However, cooperative initiatives undertaken have most of the time not gone further than organizing conferences, seminars, and joint studies relating to marine biodiversity. The existing territorial and maritime disputes in the regional waters could be blamed as the major obstacle for deeper cooperation to protect its environment. However, relevant States should be conscious of the level of urgency in dealing with the environmental issues, in particular the loss of biodiversity, in the South China Sea. With this current rate of degradation of the marine environment does not slow down, what they will have is a "dead sea" before any solution for the disputes could be reached. What is more, the depletion of marine resources could also be a cause for heightened tension, as it has been witnessed with the increase in fishing incidents in the South China Sea. For these reasons, it is time for South China Sea States to find a way to prevent disputes to block regional cooperation in the protection of the marine environment in general and the conservation of marine biodiversity in particular.

Notes

1 The author would like to thank his colleagues Ms. Youna Lyons and Ms. Dita Liliansa for their help in completing this chapter. Funding was provided to CIL by a Singapore Maritime Institute (SMI) grant.

2 For the delimitation of the South China Sea, see International Hydrographic Organization, *Limits of the Oceans and Seas*, Special Publication No.23, 3rd ed. (Monte-Carlo: International Hydrographic Organization, 1953) 30 and C. Wilkinson *et al.*, *South China Sea*, GIWA Regional Assessment 54, (University of Kalmar, 2005) 14. At the time, it should be noted that the Gulf of Thailand is considered part of the South China Sea in some recent definitions but not in the one provided by International Hydrographic Organization, see for example: S. T. Vo, J. C. Pernetta & C. J. Patterson, "Status and Trends in Coastal Habitats of the South China Sea," (2013) 85 *Ocean and Coastal Management* 153–163 and A. Valez, "Beyond the Arbitral Ruling: A Transboundary Environment Impact Assessment in the South China Sea," (2019) 9 *Asian Journal of International Law* 251–273.

3 J. Y. Liu, "Status of Marine Biodiversity in China Seas," (2013) 8 *PLoS* 1–24 at 4.

4 L. Talaue-McManus, *Transboundary Diagnostic Analysis for the South China Sea*, EAS/RCU Technical Report Series No.14 (UNEP, 2000) 1; S. Chen, "Instrumental and Induced Cooperation:

Environmental Politics in the South China Sea," (2005) (unpublished PhD thesis, University of Maryland) 109 and K. Sherman & G. Hempel (eds.), *The UNEP Large Marine Ecosystem Report: A Perspective on Changing Conditions in LMEs of the World of Regional Seas*, UNEP Regional Seas Report and Studies No.182 (UNEP, 2009) 255 and 297.

5 For a summary on the South China Sea disputes, see: "Explained: South China Sea Dispute," *South China Morning Post*, 16 February 2019, available at https://www.scmp.com/week-asia/article/2186449/explained-south-china-sea-dispute, (accessed 19 September 2019).

6 Vo, Pernetta & Patterson, *supra* note 2. See also Talaue-McManus, *supra* note 2 at 1 and Wilkinson *et al.*, *supra* note 2 at 18.

7 T. Arai, "Diversity and Conservation of Coral Reef Fishes in the Malaysian South China Sea," (2015) 25 *Reviews in Fish Biology and Fisheries* 85–101 at 86.

8 Liu, *supra* note 3 at 9.

9 UNEP, *Mangroves in the South China Sea*, UNEP/GEF/SCS Technical Publication No.1 (UNEP, 2004) 2; UNEP, *Coral Reefs in the South China Sea*, UNEP/GEF/SCS Technical Publications No.2 (UNEP, 2004) 2; Talaue-McManus, *supra* note 4 at 9 and UNEP, *Seagrasses in the South China Sea*, UNEP/GEF/SCS Technical Publications No. 3 (UNEP, 2004) 2.

10 D. Huang *et al.*, "Extraordinary diversity of reef corals in the South China Sea," (2015) 45 *Marine Biodiversity* 157–168 at 162.

11 Valez, *supra* note 2 at 254.

12 K. A. Lutaenko, "Biodiversity of Bivalve Mollusks in the Western South China Sea: An Overview" in A. V. Adrianov & K. A. Lutaenko (eds.), *Biodiversity in the Western Part of the South China Sea* (Dalnauka, 2016) 315.

13 Valez, *supra* note 11 at 254.

14 The South China Sea (2010), The Seas Project, available at <http://theseasproject.weebly.com/south-china-seas.html>, accessed 8 August 2019.

15 P. Martosubroto, "Western Central Pacific: FAO Statistical Area 71," in FAO, *Review of the State of the World Fisheries Resources*, FAO Fisheries Technical Paper 457 (FAO, 2005), available at http://www.fao.org/docrep/009/y5852e/y5852e00.htm, (accessed 17 June 2010).

16 FAO Fishery Statistical Collections, available at http://www.fao.org/fishery/statistics/global-capture-production/en, (accessed 10 August 2019).

17 U. R. Sumaila & W. W. L. Cheung, *Boom or Bust: The Future of Fisheries in the South China Sea*, Research Project, November 2015, Oceans Asia Project, at 4.

18 Ibid.at 9.

19 FAOSTAT, *Statistics Relating to Fish in Food Supply*, available at http://faostat.fao.org/site/610/default.aspx#ancor, (accessed 21 January 2013).

20 For more details about this project, see Reversing Environmental Degradation Trends in the South China Sea and Gulf of Thailand, available at http://www.unepscs.org/Project_Background.html, (accessed 22 August 2019). See also Vo, Pernetta & Patterson, *supra* note 2 for a scholarly analysis of the results of the Project.

21 Such as the coastal waters near China.

22 Sherman and Hempel (eds.), *supra* note 4 at 304; Wilkinson *et al.*, *supra* note 2, Chen, *supra* note 4 at 122; Talaue-McManus, *supra* note 2 at 22 and UNEP, *Strategic Action Programme for the South China Sea*, UNEP/GEF/SCS Technical Publication No.16 (2008) 3, 9 and 21 [UNEP, SAP].

23 Vo, Pernetta & Patterson, *supra* note 2 at 15.

24 From late 2013 to mid-2017, China undertook massive land reclamation activities on number of disputed features in the South China Sea, namely Subi Reef, Fiery Cross Reef, Mischief Reef, Gaven Reef, Hughes Reef, Johnson South Reef, Cuarteron Reef, North Cay and Tree Island. According to the Asia Maritime Transparency Initiative, China's land reclamation in the Spratlys alone has created almost 1300 hectares of new land in these islands, see China Island Tracker, available at https://amti.csis.org/island-tracker/china/, (accessed 15 August 2019).

25 M. Ives, "The Rising Environmental Toll of China's Offshore Island Grab," Yale Environment 360, (October 10, 2016) available at https://e360.yale.edu/features/rising_environmental_toll_china_artificial_islands_south_china_sea, (accessed 12 August 2019).

26 "DA-BFAR, National Scientist Condemn the Destruction of Marine Resources in the West Philippine Sea," Philippines' Official Gazette (April 23, 2015), available at https://www.officialgazette.gov.ph/2015/04/23/da-bfar-national-scientist-condemn-the-destruction-of-marine-resources-in-the-west-philippine-sea/, (accessed 15 August 2019).

27 L. Smith *et al.*, "Evidence of Environmental Changes Caused by Chinese Island-Building," (28 March 2019) *Nature* available at https://www.nature.com/articles/s41598-019-41659-3.pdf (accessed 8 August 2019).

28 S. Funge-Smith, M. Briggs & W. Miao, *Regional Overview of Fisheries and Aquaculture in Asia and the Pacific* (2012) RAP Publication 2012/26, Asia-Pacific Fishery Commission, FAO Regional Office for Asia and the Pacific at 10. See also Sumaila & Cheung, *supra* note 17, at 3; *The Future of Indian Ocean and South China Sea Fisheries: Implications for the United States*, National Intelligence Council Report (30 July 2013) NICR 2013-38, at 16; L. S. T. Teh *et al.*, "What Is at Stake? Status and Threats to South China Sea Marine Fisheries," (2017) 46 *Ambio* 57–72 at 61.

29 Funge-Smith, Briggs & Miao, *ibid.* at 10; Sumaila & Cheung, *supra* note 17 at 6; M. Tsirbas, "Saving the South China Sea Fishery: Time to Internationalise," No. 3, National Security College Policy Options Paper, (June 2017).

30 The Future of Indian Ocean and South China Sea Fisheries: Implications for the United States, *supra* note 27 at 16.

31 It is estimated that South China Sea States generate one million metric tonnes of sewage per year. A large proportion of this domestic waste is discharged directly into the sea without proper treatment. Besides, industries release a minimum of 430,000 tonnes of biochemical oxygen demand (an industrial waste capable of suppressing microbiological growth or activity) into the aquatic system interacting with the South China Sea, see Chen, *supra* note 4 at 124; UNEP, *Land-Based Pollution in the South China Sea*, UNEP/GEF/SCS Technical Publications No. 10 (Bangkok: UNEP, 2007) 3 and Sherman & Hempel (eds.), *supra* note 4 at 303.

32 A high level of suspended solids are found in coastal waters through most of the region due to activities such as extensive deforestation, logging, mining, land reclamation, dredging, urban development and erosion, see Sherman & Hempel (eds.), *supra*. note 4 at 303.

33 J. R. Jambeck, "Plastic Waste Inputs from Land into the Ocean," (February 13, 2015) 347:6223 *Science* World Economic Forum, *The New Plastics Economy: Rethinking the Future of Plastics* (January 2016) at 14; and Ocean Conservancy and McKinsey Center for Business and Environment, *Stemming the Tide: Land-Based Strategies for a Plastic- Free Ocean* (September 2015).

34 N. Careem, "Microplastics in South China Sea at Its Highest Levels, According to Samples Taken by Volvo Ocean Race Crew Member" (May 15, 2018) *South China Morning Post*, available at https://www.scmp.com/sport/hong-kong/article/2146072/microplastics-south-china-sea-its-highest-levels-according-samples, (accessed 21 August 2019).

35 Y. E. Lin *et al.*, "Asia" in V. R. Barros *et al.* (eds.), *Climate Change 2014: Impacts, Adaptation, and Vulnerability. Part B: Regional Aspects. Contribution of Working Group II to the Fifth Assessment Report of the Intergovernmental Panel on Climate Change* (Cambridge University Press, 2014) 1327–1370 at 1334.

36 H. Chuanjiang & Q. Fangli, "Sea Level Rise Projection in the South China Sea from CMIP5 Models" (2015) 34:3 *Acta Oceanologica Sinica* 31–41 at 39; J. C. Trajano *et al.*, *Marine Environmental Protection in the South China Sea: Challenges and Prospect*, Part 1, NTS Insight, no. IN17-04, December 2017 at 13.

37 Lin *et al.*, *supra* note 35 at 1342; W. W. L. Cheng, R. Watson & D. Pauly, "Signature of Ocean Warming in Global Fisheries Catch" (May 16, 2013) 497 *Nature* 365–367 and M. D.P. Godoy & L. D. De Lacerda, "Mangroves Response to Climate Change: A Review of Recent Findings on Mangrove Extension and Distribution" (2015) 87:2 *Annals of the Brazilian Academy of Sciences* 651–667 at 2.

38 J. C. Trajano *et al.*, *supra* note 36 at 13 and M. Sembiring, *Climate Change Adaptation: Case of South China Sea*, RSIS Commentary No. 116-12 June 2017.

39 Climate Central, Report: Flooded Future: Global vulnerability to Sea Level Rise Worse Than Previously Understood (29 October 2019), available at https://www.climatecentral.org/news/report-flooded-future-global-vulnerability-to-sea-level-rise-worse-than-previously-understood, (accessed 10 November 2019)

40 Climate Central, Land Projected to Be Below Flood Level by 2050, available at https://coastal.climatecentral.org/map/9/106.8422/20.9652/?theme=sea_level_rise&map_type=coastal_dem_comparison&elevation_model=coastal_dem&forecast_year=2050&pathway=rcp45&percentile=p50&return_level=return_level_1&slr_model=kopp_2014, (accessed 10 November 2019). See also: S. A. Kulp & B. H. Strauss, "New Elevation Data Triple Estimates of Global Vulnerability to Sea-Level Rise and Coastal Flooding," (29 October 2019) 10:4844 *Nature Communications* 1–10.

41 The UNCLOS, signed in 1982 at Montego Bay, Jamaica is considered as "a Constitution for the Oceans", see Remarks by Tommy T.B. Koh, President of the Third United Nations Conference

on the Law of the Sea, United Nations-Division for Ocean Affairs and the Law of the Sea, *United Nations Convention on the Law of the Sea of 10 December 1982: Overview and Full Text*, available at http://www.un.org/Depts/los/convention_agreements/convention_overview_convention.htm, (accessed 20 September 2019). Since its adoption in 1982, the UNCLOS has received ratifications from 168 countries in the world and entered into force in 1994, see United Nations-Division for Ocean Affairs and the Law of the Sea, *Status of the United Nations Convention on the Law of the Sea, of the Agreement Relating to the Implementation of Part XI of the Convention and of the Agreement for the Implementation of the Provisions of the Convention Relating to the Conservation and Management of Straddling Fish Stocks and Highly Migratory Fish Stocks*, available at https://www.un.org/Depts/los/reference_files/chronological_lists_of_ratifications.htm#The%20United%20Nations%20Convention%20on%20the%20Law%20of%20the%20Sea, (accessed 20 September 2019).

42 UNCLOS, 10 December 1982, 1833 U.N.T.S. 3 art. 192.
43 UNCLOS, *ibid.*, art. 194.
44 UNCLOS, *ibid.*, arts 61(6) and 117.
45 UNCLOS, *ibid.*, art. 197.
46 UNCLOS, *ibid.*, art. 123.
47 UNCLOS, *ibid.*, arts 61(2), 63 and 64. FAO distinguishes between four types of shared fish stocks, namely "transboundary stocks", "highly migratory species", "straddling stocks" and "discrete high seas fish stocks", see G. Munro, A. Van Houtte and R. Willmann, *The Conservation and Management of Shared Fish Stocks: Legal and Economic Aspects*, FAO Fisheries Technical Paper 465 (FAO Legal Office, 2002) 3.
48 UNCLOS, *supra* note 40, art. 66.
49 CBD, 5 June 1992, 760 U.N.T.S 79.
50 CBD, *ibid.*, art.7.
51 CBD, *ibid.*, arts 8 and 9.
52 CBD, *ibid.*, art.10.
53 CBD, *ibid.*, art. 45.
54 CBD, *ibid.*, arts 8, 9 and 12.
55 CBD, *ibid.*, art. 14.
56 CBD, *ibid.*, art. 16.
57 CBD, *ibid.*, art. 17.
58 CBD, *ibid.*, art. 18.
59 CBD, *Strategic Plan for Biodiversity 2011–2020*, Decision X/2, 10th Meeting of the Conference of the Parties to the Convention on Biological Diversity, Nagoya, Japan, 18–29 October 2010, Annex, line 12.
60 Ibid., line 13.
61 CBD, "Preparation for the Post-2020 Biodiversity Framework", available at https://www.cbd.int/conferences/post2020 (accessed 3 April 2021).
62 Convention on Biological Diversity, Update of the zero draft of the post-2020 global biodiversity framework, UNEP OR, Doc. No. CBD/POST 2020?PREP/2/1 (17 August 2020).
63 "The Jakarta Ministerial Statement on the implementation of the Convention on Biological Diversity" in UNEP, *Report on the 2nd Meeting of the Conference of the Parties of the Convention on Biological Diversity*, UN Doc.UNEP/CBD/COP/2/19, 30 November 1995, Appendix.
64 *Conservation and Sustainable Use of Marine and Coastal Biological Diversity, Including a Programme of Work*, Decision IV/5, Annex, 4th Meeting of the COP to the Convention on Biological Diversity, Bratislava, Slovakia, 4–15 May 1998.
65 *Transforming Our World: The 2030 Agenda for Sustainable Development*, UNGA Resolution, UNGA OR A/Res/70/1, 7th session, 21 October 2015, at 24/35.
66 See *Our Oceans, Our Future: Partnering for the Implementation of Sustainable Development Goal 14*, available at https://oceanconference.un.org/about, (accessed 11 September 2019).
67 *Our Ocean, Our Future: Call for Action*, UNGA Resolution, UNGA OR A/Res/71/312, 71st session, 14 July 2016, p. 2/6.
68 Our Ocean, Our Future: Call for Action, *ibid.*, p. 2/6.
69 See for example *Oceans and the Law of the Sea*, UNGA Resolution, UNGA OR A/Res/73/124, 73rd session, 31 December 2018.
70 For a background on the South China Sea Arbitration, see: Permanent Court of Arbitration, The South China Sea Arbitration, available at https://pca-cpa.org/en/cases/7/, accessed 11 September 2019.

71 Permanent Court of Arbitration, *Award*, 12 July 2016, PCA Case No. 2013–19 in the matter of an Arbitration before an Arbitral Tribunal Constituted under the Annex VII to the 1982 United Nations Convention on the Law of the Sea between the Republic of the Philippines and the People's Republic of China, available at https://pca-cpa.org/en/cases/7/, (accessed 4 September 2019) 379 [South China Sea Arbitration].
72 South China Sea Arbitration, *ibid.*, 382.
73 South China Sea Arbitration, *ibid.*, 386.
74 South China Sea Arbitration, *ibid.*
75 South China Sea Arbitration, *ibid.*, 389.
76 South China Sea Arbitration, *ibid.*, 394.
77 South China Sea Arbitration, *ibid.*, 394.
78 The Action Plan was adopted in 1981 by Indonesia, Malaysia, Philippines, Singapore and Thailand; see UNEP Regional Seas, *Action Plan for the Protection and Sustainable Development of the Marine and Coastal Areas of The East Asian Region*, UNEP Regional Seas Reports and Studies No.24 (Bangkok: UNEP, 1983). It was then modified in 1994 to include the participation of Australia, China, Cambodia, Republic of Korea and Vietnam, see COBSEA, *About COBSEA*, available http://www.cobsea.org/aboutcobsea/background.html, (accessed 4 June 2012). Since 2011, Australia is no longer a member, see COBSEA, COBSEA Strategic Directions 2018–2022 (Bangkok: COBSEA and UNEP, 2018) 5.
79 UNEP Regional Seas, *Action Plan for the Protection and Sustainable Development of the Marine and Coastal Areas of the East Asian Region*, Annex IV, Doc. COBSEA (OCA)/EAS IG5/6 (1994) [Action plan for the Protection and Sustainable Development of the Marine and Coastal Areas of the East Asian region].
80 Action plan for the Protection and Sustainable Development of the Marine and Coastal Areas of the East Asian region, *ibid.* at 5.
81 COBSEA, *Monitoring Coral Reefs for Better Management Schemes: UNEP EAS/RCU Small Grants Fund Programme 2002–2003* (UNEP, 2004) 1 and COBSEA, *Report of The Meeting of the Regional Group of Experts on the International Coral Reef Action Network*, Phuket, Thailand, 28–30 January 2002.
82 For details about the South China Sea Project, see Christopher J. Patterson, *UNEP/GEF South China Sea Project Document*, (29 August 2006), *The South China Sea Project*, available at http://www.unepscs.org/remository/startdown/381.html, (accessed 13 September 2019).
83 UNEP, *Strategic Action Programme for the South China Sea*, UNEP/GEF/SCS Technical Publication No.16 (UNEP, 2008).
84 *Report of 10th Meeting of the Regional Scientific and Technical Committee for the UNEP/GEF South China Sea Project*, Pattaya, Thailand, 17–19 December 2008, Doc. UNEP/GEF/SCS/RSTC.10/3, Annex 5.
85 *Report of 8th Meeting of the Regional Scientific and Technical Committee for the UNEP/GEF South China Sea Project*, Trat Province, Thailand, 11–14 December 2007, para. 12.2.
86 *Report of the 23rd Meeting of the Coordinating Body of the Seas of East Asia*, Bangkok, Thailand, 27–28 February 2017, Document no. UNEP/ COBSEA IGM 23/7, para. 76.
87 *Report of the 24th Meeting of the Coordinating Body of the Seas of East Asia*, Bali, Indonesia, 19–20 June 2019, Document no. UNEP/COBSEA IGM 24/11.
88 COBSEA, *COBSEA Strategic Directions 2018–2022* (COBSEA and UNEP, 2018) 10.
89 Currently, PEMSEA has 11 Country Members, namely: Cambodia, China, DPR Korea, Indonesia, Japan, Laos, Philippines, RO Korea, Singapore, Timor-Leste, and Viet Nam.
90 See *Putrajaya Declaration of Regional Cooperation for the Sustainable Development of the Seas of East Asia*, East Asian Seas Congress 2003, Putrajaya, Malaysia, 12 December 2003 and *Danang Compact on the Sustainable Development Strategy for the East of East Asia*, 5th Ministerial Forum, East Asian Sea Congress 2015, 20 November 2015, Da Nang, Viet Nam.
91 PEMSEA, *Sustainable Development Strategy for the Seas of East Asia* updated 2015 (PEMSEA, 2015) at 55 & 56.
92 PEMSEA, *Proceeding of 11th East Asian Seas Partnership Council Meeting*, 24–26 July 2019, Surabaya, Indonesia at 16.
93 PEMSEA, *SDS-SEA 2018–2022: Implementation Plan Sustainable Development Strategy for the Seas of East Asia* (PEMSEA, 2018) 5.
94 PEMSEA, *PEMSEA Annual Report 2018* (PEMSEA, 2019) 5.

95 *Danang Compact on the Sustainable Development Strategy for the East of East Asia*, the 5th Ministerial Forum, East Asian Sea Congress 2015, 20 November 2015, Da Nang, Viet Nam.

96 See *China-ASEAN Strategy on Environmental Protection Cooperation 2009–2015*, joint developed by Ministry of Environmental Protection of China and ASEAN Member States in 2009, China – ASEAN Environmental Cooperation Center, available at http://www.chinaaseanenv.org/english/events/271416.shtml, (accessed 5 April 2012). Before that date, there was the ASEAN plus Three (China, Japan and Republic of Korea) Environment Ministers' Meetings hosted by ASEAN since 2002.

97 See *Joint Declarations of the Heads of State/Government of the Association of Southeast Asian Nations and the People's Republic of China on Strategic Partnership for Peace and Prosperity*, 8 October 2003, adopted at 9th ASEAN Summit, Bali, Indonesia, 7–8 October 2003, available at http://www.aseansec.org/15265.htm, (accessed 5 April 2012) and *Plan of Action to Implement the Joint Declaration on ASEAN-China Strategic Partnership for Peace and Prosperity (2005–2010)* adopted at 10th ASEAN Summit, Vientiane, Laos, 29–30 November 2004, available at http://www.aseansec.org/16805.htm, (accessed 5 April 2012).

98 See *Plan of Action to Implement the Joint Declaration on ASEAN-China Strategic Partnership for Peace and Prosperity (2016–2020)*, 18th ASEAN-China Summit, 21 November 2015, Kuala Lumpur, Malaysia, available at https://www.asean.org/storage/images/2015/November/27th-summit/ASEAN-China%20POA%20%202016-2020.pdf, (accessed 16 September 2019), 3.6.9 and 3.6.11.

99 *China-ASEAN Strategy on Environmental Protection Cooperation 2009–2015* (2009), available at http://www.chinaaseanenv.org/english/events/271416.shtml>, (accessed 5 April 2012).

100 *ASEAN-China Strategy on Environmental Cooperation 2016–2020*, available at https://environment.asean.org/wp-content/uploads/2017/02/ASEAN-China-Strategy-on-Environmental-Cooperation-2016-2020.pdf, (accessed 16 September 2019), p. 7.

101 *Ibid.*

102 Chairman Statement of the 23rd ASEAN - China Summit, 12 November 2020, videoconference host by Viet Nam, para.25.

103 N. H. Thao, "The Declaration on the Conduct of Parties in the South China Sea: A Vietnamese Perspective, 2002–2007" in S. Bateman and R. Emmers (eds.), *Security and International Politics in the South China Sea: Towards a Co-operative Management Regime* (Taylor and Francis, 2009) 207 at 209.

104 *Declaration of the Conduct of Parties on the South China Sea*, Phnom Penh, 4 November 2002, available at http://www.aseansec.org/20185.htm, (accessed 17 September 2019).

105 *Ibid.*, paragraph 6.

106 Ministry of Foreign Affairs of Indonesia, "ASEAN-China Senior Officials Meeting on the Implementation of the DOC in the South China Sea, Beijing, China, 13–14 January 2012" (2012), available at https://ex.kemlu.go.id/en/berita/siaran-pers/Pages/ASEAN-China-Senior-Officials-Meeting-On-the-Implementation-of-the-DOC-in-the-South-China-Sea-Beijing.aspx, (accessed 17 September 2019) and Ministry of Foreign Affairs of Thailand, "The 10th ASEAN-China Joint Working Group on the Implementation of the Declaration on the Conduct of Parties in the South China Sea," Press Release, 19 March 2014, available at http://www.mfa.go.th/main/en/media-center/14/44171-The-10th-ASEAN-China-Joint-Working-Group-on-the-Im.html, (accessed 17 September 2019).

107 *Declaration for a Decade of Coastal and Marine Environmental Protection in the South China Sea (2017–2027)*, Manila, Philippines, 13 November 2017.

108 Yann-Huei Song, "Managing the Potential Conflicts in South China Sea: Taiwan's Perspectives," East Asian Institute Paper No.14 (World Scientific Publishing and Singapore University Press, 1999) 20 and Chen, *supra* note 4 at 218.

109 For a list of issues discussed under the South China Sea Workshops, see Hasjim Djalal, "The South China Sea: The Long Road towards Peace and Cooperation," in Bateman and Emmers (eds.), *supra* note 98 at 183.

110 N. Nivasothi, *Progress Report for EX ANAMBAS 2002, an Initiative of the Workshop on Managing Potential Conflicts in the South China Sea*, 13th Workshop on Management of Potential Conflicts in the South China Sea, 17–18 September 2003, Medan, Indonesia.

111 Ministry of Foreign Affairs of Indonesia, "Batam Hosts Workshop on Managing Potential Conflict in the South China Sea," available at https://kemlu.go.id/portal/en/read/587/berita/batam-hosts-workshop-on-managing-potential-conflict-in-the-south-china-sea, (accessed 18 September 2019).

16

THE SOUTH CHINA SEA ENVIRONMENT

The need for formalised institutional interaction between science, policy and law

David M. Ong

Introduction

This chapter is a survey of the conjunction and interaction between the scientific, policy and legal disciplines devoted to the protection of the South China Sea's environment. It will first assess the state of scientific research on this water body, and then explore the connexions between the results of this scientific research with the policy initiatives and legal instruments designed to address the specific pollution issues and general degradation of this semi-enclosed sea. Much scientific research has already been undertaken and continues to be carried out both within and across this marine region. However, the absence of an overarching legal and institutional framework for such scientific research to feed into concrete region-wide policy decisions, as well as legal measures and actions directed solely, or at least mainly, towards environmental protection, is notable.

The present study is therefore predicated on the assumption that there is a continuing need for *formalised institutional cooperation* on the marine scientific research efforts into this body of water as a necessary pre-requisite, *inter alia*, to establish the environmental baseline standards for measuring land-based sources of pollution into the South China Sea from its littoral States, as well as other pollution sources such as international shipping through this busy waterway between several of the biggest economies in the world. Such *formalised institutional co-operation* over marine scientific research can then form the basis for targeted policy decisions and specific legal measures designed to address the environmental threats uncovered by the concerted and collated marine scientific research on the South China Sea. It will be argued that increased and improved levels of *formalised institutional cooperation* over marine scientific research in the South China Sea can in turn lead to more effective global, regional, bilateral and national environmental protection instruments for this area. This is in marked contrast to both previous and current efforts to mitigate potential disputes over the South China Sea, which are characterised by their emphasis on geopolitical, legal and resource-led economic perspectives, rather than environmental concerns *per se*.[1]

When considering the current international governance efforts at addressing South China Sea environmental concerns, a structured approach based on the following (nominally) geographical tiers will be utilised. First, broader East Asian and/or wider South China Sea regional initiatives are discussed, before sub-regional, Southeast Asian-based efforts are considered, and finally, bilateral initiatives between the South China Sea (specifically, the Gulf of Thailand) littoral countries are addressed. While the following discussion will attempt to adhere to this nominally geographical approach, it should be appreciated that some of the regional efforts covered within individual sections overlap with each other in terms of their (State) membership, both from within and without this marine region.

Background

While the South China Sea continues to be a region of significant geostrategic intrigue,[2] by far the most pressing set of issues arising from this largest of semi-enclosed seas revolve around its well-being as a large marine ecosystem (LME).[3] Chief among the environmental threats to the South China Sea is the influx of pollution resulting from human activities, caused in turn by the sheer weight of population increases over the last few decades. Southeast Asia's population, especially when taking into account the southern flank of the Chinese mainland that also abuts the northern aspect of the South China Sea, easily amounts to more than half a billion people today. Rising per capita consumption due to rapidly growing regional economies have also contributed to the burgeoning material aspects of marine pollution. Indeed, reports suggest that the wider 'East Asian Seas' region may now generate as much as half the world's marine plastic litter.[4] These relatively new but growing sources of pollution are now beginning to have a real impact on biodiversity, for example, plastic waste entanglement with turtles, seabirds, and fish.

These *accumulated* marine environmental protection issues are now well known and scientifically documented as far back as the beginning of the present millennium, *i.e.* nearly 20 years ago and indeed, even before this. A 2005 Global International Waters Assessment (GIWA) report presented the results of several scaling, scoping, causal chain and policy options analyses conducted for the South China Sea (designated as GIWA region 54) in 2001–2002.[5] This assessment determined that the most severe environmental issues facing the South China Sea include:

> Suspended solids resulting from deforestation and agriculture in hundreds of watersheds; Habitat loss and modification, through massive deforestation and associated siltation, conversion to agriculture and other land uses (freshwater, coastal and estuarine habitats) and destructive fishing practices (coastal, estuarine and marine habitats); Over-exploitation and destructive fishing practices.[6]

Unfortunately, scientific recognition of these accumulated environmental problems and multiple assessments of their severity has not prevented the South China Sea environment from continuing to be subsumed within the regional and extra-regional machinations of Great Power rivalry over this geopolitically significant area. Lying as it does amongst and between some of the biggest and fastest-growing economies in the world today, this water body will always attract the attention of those who want to control, or at least influence, global shipping lanes. Moreover, as Tagliacozzo observes when beginning his *longue duree* historical account:

> The South China Sea has been one of the busiest waterways in global history; its pedigree is ancient, even as its modern geopolitical importance remains undisputed.... Yet the history of connection, both via trade and via political contacts, between China and the various polities of Southeast Asia has been more steady and influential than any more recent history of geostrategic unease.[7]

Later on in his account, however, he cautions that

> (i)t is in fact, the South China Sea of the twentieth into the twenty-first centuries that shows us how fragile this history of movement, trade and political accommodation has become. This broad maritime space is still criss-crossed by shipping as it always has been; indeed, the raw tonnage of transport is higher now than it ever has been in historical time. Yet there are worrying signs that an epoch of *mare clausum* – closed seas – could be approaching.[8]

Mutual wariness and distrust of motives among the littoral States over these contested waters, in part caused by the extraneous over-reach of regional and global hegemons such as China, and the USA, respectively, as well as middle-order powers such as the UK, Japan, Australia, and even India,[9] speak volumes to the lack of international co-ordination on the environmental front. This extends to the relative lack of *concerted* scientific research being undertaken in this region towards assessing the parlous state of the South China Sea's environment. Even an initially successful trilateral agreement between the national oil companies of China, Viet Nam and the Philippines for cooperation over seismic activities in the northern reaches of the South China Sea,[10] stalled over the underlying territorial and maritime jurisdictional issues that this arrangement was originally designed to downplay. It is no surprise then to find that international cooperation levels over this regional marine environment are still generally low, and regular, scientific assessments for the region as a whole are few and far between. Specifically, established and long-standing *institutionalised* regional initiatives remain nascent.

On the other hand, it is possible to underestimate the scale of the task at hand, given the comparatively large geographical size, as well as hydrographical and biological complexity, of the South China Sea. It should be noted however that these high levels of geographical, historical, scientific, economic, political and legal complexity have not deterred expansive academic efforts at bringing them together within a single resolutive mechanism. One radical alternative along these lines proposes that: 'Given the rapid proliferation of international peace parks around the world, it is time to take positive steps toward the establishment of a Spratly Islands Marine Peace Park. Its purpose would be to manage the area's natural resources and alleviate regional tensions via a freeze on claims and claim supportive actions,'[11] thus testifying to the unlimited ambitions of academic ingenuity in responding to such complexities. While applauding such attempts to cut the Gordian knot of South China Sea complexities, the present effort is arguably less speculative in its approach but no less ambitious in its prescriptive injunctions. It begins by highlighting the relative lack of correlation between accumulated scientific evidence of environmental degradation and then focuses on the corresponding need for a robust international (regional) policy and legal framework for addressing this environmental malaise within the South China Sea governance matrix.

Within this context, it is significant to note that in 2002, as an essential aspect of intra-regional efforts to reduce the geopolitical tension which continues to afflict this part of the world to this day, the Association of Southeast Asian Nations (ASEAN) Member States and the People's Republic of China adopted a Declaration on the Conduct of Parties in the South China Sea,[12] providing, *inter alia*, the following statements:

> '1. The Parties reaffirm their commitment to the purposes and principles of the Charter of the United Nations, the 1982 UN Convention on the Law of the Sea, the Treaty of Amity and Cooperation in Southeast Asia, the Five Principles of Peaceful Coexistence,

and other universally recognized principles of international law which shall serve as the basic norms governing state-to-state relations;

...

4. The Parties concerned undertake to resolve their territorial and jurisdictional disputes by peaceful means, without resorting to the threat or use of force, through friendly consultations and negotiations by sovereign states directly concerned, in accordance with universally recognized principles of international law, including the 1982 UN Convention on the Law of the Sea;

...

6. Pending a comprehensive and durable settlement of the disputes, the Parties concerned may explore or undertake cooperative activities. These may include the following:

a marine environmental protection;
b marine scientific research; (emphasis added)

...

The modalities, scope and locations, in respect of bilateral and multilateral cooperation should be agreed upon by the Parties concerned prior to their actual implementation.

7. The Parties concerned stand ready to continue their consultations and dialogues concerning relevant issues, through modalities to be agreed by them, including regular consultations on the observance of this Declaration, for the purpose of promoting good neighbourliness and transparency, establishing harmony, mutual understanding and co-operation, and facilitating peaceful resolution of disputes among them;

8. The Parties undertake to respect the provisions of this Declaration and take actions consistent therewith;

9. The Parties encourage other countries to respect the principles contained in this Declaration;

10. The Parties concerned reaffirm that the adoption of a code of conduct in the South China Sea would further promote peace and stability in the region and agree to work, on the basis of consensus, towards the eventual attainment of this objective.'[13]

The explicit inclusion of *marine environmental protection* and *marine scientific research* (in that order) within the above Code of Conduct serves to highlight the growing recognition of both the importance of these two themes, as well as their intimate connexion in the furtherance of a comprehensive marine environmental governance regime for the South China Sea.

International scientific research initiatives on the South China Sea environment

When it comes to regional marine environmental protection generally, attention naturally shifts to the UN Regional Seas Programme, which is now nearly 40 years in operation.[14] According to the UN Environment Programme (UNEP) which administers, coordinates, and/or otherwise supports this long-standing initiative from its Nairobi headquarters, the Regional Seas Programme 'aims to address the accelerating degradation of the world's oceans and coastal areas through a "shared seas" approach – namely, by engaging neighbouring countries in comprehensive and specific actions to protect their common marine environment. Today, more than 143 countries have joined 18 Regional Seas Conventions and Action Plans for the sustainable management and use of the marine and coastal environment. In most cases, the Action Plan is underpinned by a strong legal framework in the form of a regional Convention and associated Protocols on specific problems. All individual Conventions and Action Plans reflect a similar approach, yet each has been tailored by its own governments and institutions to suit their particular environmental challenges.'[15] These (regional) scientific evidence and policy bases, in turn, inform the legal basis for the applicable rules and standards to be included (or directly referenced within) the Framework-type Convention adopted by the participating States for the marine region in question.[16] Indeed, '(t)he UNEP Regional Seas Conventions and Actions Plans have emerged over the last 40 years as the world's *only* legal framework for protecting the oceans and seas *at the regional level.* In particular, the Regional Seas Conventions and Action Plans have worked ... to protect and restore the health, productivity and resilience of oceans and marine ecosystems, and to maintain their biodiversity. They implement protocols on land-based pollution, strengthen capacities at the national level on marine and coastal governance, and work to decouple economic growth from environmental pressures in the marine and coastal environment'[17] (emphasis added).

As mentioned above, across the globe, the Regional Seas programme now numbers at least 18 distinct marine regions in all, with 14 of these being formally established by a multilateral treaty instrument, followed in many cases by detailed Protocols around specific environmental threats or issues. For example, in the case of the first of these treaties, the 1976 Barcelona Convention on the Mediterranean Sea[18] has been followed up by no less than seven so-called 'landmark' protocols.[19] Similar efforts were made towards a Convention specifically for the South China Sea region but so far to no avail. In retrospect, the absence of any formalised, institutional co-operation underpinned by a Regional Seas-type Convention based on the template of UNEP's eponymous programme for specific marine regions is symptomatic of the continuing tensions that beset this part of the world.

Aside from the South China Sea being a notable exception to the otherwise global reach of the UNEP Regional Seas Programme's codifying efforts, what is also significant about this UNEP programme is its emphasis on the initial Action Plan as a platform to build and consolidate accumulated scientific information and hence evidence on the specific environmental issues related to the marine region concerned. As the UNEP itself notes,

> Most of the Regional Seas Programmes function through Action Plans, which are adopted by member governments in order to establish a comprehensive strategy and framework for protecting the environment and promote sustainable development. An action plan outlines the strategy and substance of the programme, based on the region's particular environmental challenges as well as its socio-economic and political situation.[20]

Within the individually designated marine regions, the Regional Seas programme's Action Plans work through Secretariats or Regional Coordinating Units (RCUs) and Regional Activity Centers (RACs). The RCU is the nerve centre and command post of the Action Plan's activities and has the overall and practical responsibility for the implementation of the decisions of member countries (or contracting parties) regarding the operation of the action plan. The RCU is responsible for the follow-up and implementation of legal documents, the programme of work and strategies and policies adopted by the member countries. The RCU also carries out the diplomatic, political and public relations functions of the action plan. Finally, the RCU cooperates with governments, other UN and non-UN agencies and NGOs, and facilitates the capacity building of its own regional activity centres and member governments. The RACs serve all member states by carrying out activities related to the action plan as agreed and guided by the Conference of the Parties or intergovernmental decisions. The Regional Activity Centres (RACs) play key roles in the implementation of various components and activities of the action plan at regional, sub-regional, national and sometimes local levels. The RACs are an integral part of the Action Plan and report directly to the RCU. They are usually financially supported by the contracting parties and by the host country through the financial mechanisms of the action plan.[21]

East Asian Seas Action Plan & Coordinating Body on the Seas of East Asia (COBSEA)

As far back as in 1977, having been primed by a number of East Asian States, the UNEP Governing Council decided that 'steps are urgently needed to formulate and establish a scientific programme involving research, prevention and control of marine pollution and monitoring' for a regional action plan in East Asia.[22] The Intergovernmental Meeting on the Protection and Development of the Marine Environment and Coastal Areas of the East Asian Region (Manila, 27–29 April 1981), attended by representatives of Indonesia, Malaysia, the Philippines, Singapore and Thailand, adopted the Action Plan for the Protection and Development of the Marine Environment and Coastal Areas of the East Asian Region, also known as the 'East Asian Seas Action Plan.'[23] This Action Plan in turn established the COBSEA as the regional inter-governmental policy forum that is the sole decision-making body for the East Asian Seas Action Plan and oversees its implementation.[24] At the request of participating countries, UN Environment also established the Regional Coordinating Unit for the East Asian Seas Action Plan in 1993, functioning as a Secretariat for COBSEA. The COBSEA Secretariat provides overall technical coordination and supervision of the implementation of the action plan.[25] The Secretariat is hosted by Thailand and administered by UN Environment. National Focal Points in each participating country act as a channel of communication, to coordinate the participation of and guide national institutions in the implementation of COBSEA-approved programmes.[26] National institutions provide the institutional basis for carrying out the projects under the action plan.[27]

A decision to revise the East Asian Seas Action Plan was taken at the 10th meeting of the Coordinating Body on the Seas of East Asia (COBSEA) held in Bangkok, Thailand on 9–10 July 1993. This step was in line with the revision of the Long-Term Strategy of COBSEA which had to take into consideration Chapter 17 of Agenda 21.[28] The two major factors guiding this revision were the expansion of COBSEA to include first, the wider East Asian Seas region,[29] and second, the need for the Long-Term Strategy to be problem-oriented, management-driven and integrated in approach, with the 'ultimate goal of an actual and real improvement in coastal and marine environmental quality.'[30] Thus, in 1994, the Action Plan was revised to involve another five countries – Australia, Cambodia, People's Republic of China, Republic of (South) Korea and Viet Nam,[31] although Australia withdrew its membership of this Plan in 2011. In a nutshell, the early organizational efforts coalesced around the 'Development of a regional database,' and the revised Action Plan was able to report that:

> '4. Since the inception of the action plan, activities arising from it, together with related programmes carried out in the region, have resulted in the following accomplishments:
>
> 4.1 Baseline information on the structure, distribution and dynamics of major marine ecosystems (e.g. coral reefs, mangroves, seagrass beds, soft bottoms) situated in the different countries;

4.2 Information on levels and trends in the distribution of important non-oil pollutants originating from land-based and offshore sources;
4.3 Information on levels and trends in the distribution of oil pollutants, from both land-based and offshore sources (including shipping);
4.4 Directories of scientific institutions, research centres, information centres and data sources in the region; and
4.5 Bibliographies of publications on relevant marine environmental issues in the region.'[32]

Moreover, the Plan had already envisaged the need for '5. A regularly updated database (that) should integrate all this information into a compatible format including risk assessment estimates readily assessable to and usable through electronic networking by policy/decision makers, managers and other scientists.'[33] In this regard, the revised Action Plan was able to report (in 1994) that

> 6. A database on the status and distribution of marine ecosystems and their associated species has been developed by the ASEAN-Australia Economic Cooperation Programme (AAECP) Marine Science Project: Living Coastal Resources. A new phase of AAECP aims at establishing national decision-support systems by integrating different databases relevant to the coastal and marine environment. An important activity of the action plan would be to build on and expand these valuable databases to incorporate all information generated pertaining to the East Asian Seas. This will provide decision makers with a sound basis for the management and protection of the marine and coastal environment on a regional basis.[34]

However, there is little evidence that these early databases have been consolidated into an accessible repository of all (or at least most) information on the evolving state of the South China Sea over several decades now.

As noted above, the overall authority for the implementation of this Action Plan is the COBSEA, which, *inter alia*, determines the content of the action plan, reviews its progress and approves its programme of implementation, including the financial implications.[35] The Regional Coordinating Unit of the East Asian Seas Action Plan (EAS/RCU) will assist COBSEA in the implementation of the action plan by serving as the Secretariat for the action plan.[36] The channel of communication between the EAS/RCU and the participating Governments in the East Asian Seas Action Plan will be through the respective National Focal Points. In matters of technical nature, the EAS/RCU may communicate with individuals and/or institutions concerned, providing copies of communications to the relevant National Focal Points.[37] Thus, COBSEA provides an inter-governmental mechanism for science-based policy-setting at the regional level.[38]

Coral Triangle Initiative – A positive model for (informal) South China Sea environmental cooperation?

The so-called 'Coral Triangle Initiative' (CTI) extends across a vast marine area of the south-western aspect of the Pacific Ocean. It is bordered by the Philippines, Indonesia (central and eastern), Malaysia (Sabah on Borneo island), Timor Leste, Papua New Guinea, and the Solomon Islands.[39] Geographically therefore it lies beyond the confines of the South China Sea, but it is introduced here as a model example of how an ostensibly (international) scientific research programme has transcended its relatively narrow beginnings to become a successful stakeholder forum for relevant and concerned actors in this region, beyond just the governments themselves.

Fidelman *et al* have recently charted this progress towards inculcating multiple stakeholder views within the nascent international governance framework of the CTI.[40] They focused on identifying influential stakeholders, their beliefs and interests, their network relations, and their capacity to leverage resources towards meeting CTI goals.[41] They then applied the 'Advocacy Coalition Framework'[42] to examine the views of main CTI stakeholders to better understand their efforts to design and implement marine management policies. Fidelman *et al* conclude *inter alia* that

> The CTI presents many characteristics of a nascent, collaborative policy subsystem, one which is newly formed or in the process of forming and involves collaborative over adversarial relations. Among the stakeholders consulted, there is largely strong support for the CTI objectives, convergence in policy beliefs (e.g., pro community-based conservation), and instances of collaboration at different levels. It is important to note that in collaborative policy subsystems, there are still disagreements among stakeholders. However, these disagreements are overcome by finding enough common ground to cooperate. In other words, despite the differences among CTI stakeholders, the goals of the Initiative may be close enough to their policy preferences and beliefs to enable collaborative action to achieve similar or related objectives.[43]

Transboundary diagnostic analysis (TDA)for the South China Sea

A relevant, South China Sea-focused scientific research exercise that has the potential to emulate the nascent success achieved by the Coral Triangle Initiative described above is the 'Transboundary Diagnostic Analysis for the South China Sea.'[44] As the narrative provides in the final report/study of this project, 'Purpose of the Transboundary Diagnostic Analysis (TDA)':

> The transboundary diagnostic analysis of the South China Sea and its associated catchment areas, is a process that focuses on identifying water-related problems and concerns, their socio-economic root causes, and the sectoral implications of actions needed to mitigate them. The analysis further seeks to determine those issues which have transboundary, i.e. involves more than one country, causes and/or impacts, appropriate mitigation of which will have to be done on a regional or bilateral basis. The analysis then becomes the basis for a strategic action program which is coordinated both at the national and regional levels.[45]

Following on from the TDA, a further scientific research project entitled 'Reversing Environmental Degradation Trends in the South China Sea and the Gulf of Thailand,' funded by the Global Environment Facility (GEF) and implemented by UNEP in partnership with seven riparian states bordering the South China Sea became fully operational in February 2002. This project addressed three priority areas of concern identified in the TDA, namely the loss and degradation of coastal habitats, over-exploitation of fisheries in the Gulf of Thailand, and land-based pollution. As the final report on this project notes, it

> was rather unusual for a GEF project in that project execution is undertaken by, national level institutions contracted directly to UNEP as the Implementing Agency of

> the GEF. In contrast, most projects are implemented through an intermediate organization such as a regional commission or regional office of an International agency or NGO that becomes responsible for the contractual arrangements, fund management and due diligence monitoring of national level actions. Not only does this increase the overall transactions costs but it removes by one further step the GEF from its client the countries.[46]

This final report then makes an interesting evaluation of the unusual nature of this particular GEF project being undertaken by national institutions, as follows: 'Since no regional commission exists with a specific mandate focused on the environment of the South China Sea, UNEP deals directly with the countries, which are now truly in charge, without filters, without false ambassadors, and money starved intermediaries.'[47] This preference for nationally-focused interactions and funding streams by relevant international organizations and agencies is supported by a more recent academic survey of marine and coastal management initiatives in East Asian seas, leading to the conclusion that

> to scale up investments and to leverage larger amounts of co-financing to future GEF projects and programs, there should be an increased emphasis on funding to single country projects, as they are on average mobilizing many times as much co-financing as regional projects.[48]

As a (preliminary) conclusion to this section and introduction to the next section of this essay, we can observe that these extra-regional and regional initiatives, programmes, action plans, and projects, were initially devoted towards developing marine scientific research database(s) on the South China Sea environment, before being increasingly followed up by regional management and governance-oriented initiatives and efforts. However, these follow-up efforts are not always undertaken in the most co-ordinated and transparent ways, as we shall see below.

International governance frameworks for environmental protection in the South China Sea

This section assesses current international *governance* (as opposed to *legal*) frameworks devoted to environmental protection within the South China Sea. It takes a broadly geographical approach, mapping these extra-regional, regional, sub-regional, and bilateral arrangements onto two separate sections of discourse, namely, (a) the wider South China Sea region, and (b) South China Sea sub-regional and bilateral initiatives, always taking into account the overlapping nature of these arrangements in its discussion. Cumulatively, these projects were supposed to be laying the ground for strong(er) international policy and legal frameworks to address the identified environmental threats therein but as already noted, there is arguably a continuing paucity of international *legal* (as opposed to *governance*) frameworks for, and within the South China Sea region itself. This is notwithstanding the continuing adoption of extra-regional, regional and sub-regional arrangements devoted to scientific and management-oriented actions for South China Sea environmental protection. These multi-varied arrangements, however, appear to have ongoing institutional coordination issues, with very little evidence of collaboration between them, despite ostensibly covering similar themes of South China Sea environmental protection.

Wider South China Sea regional initiatives

Strategic action programme for the South China Sea

Following on from the main scientific research-based regional arrangements discussed above, a (more) policy-oriented instrument that was approved on 25 June 2008 is the Strategic Action Programme (SAP) for the South China Sea.[49] Seven riparian States of the South China Sea initially signed-up to participate and implement this SAP, namely, Cambodia, People's Republic of China, Indonesia, Malaysia, Philippines, Thailand and Viet Nam. The draft SAP was based on the findings of the regional TDA, outlined above. The rationale for regional co-operation in the form of the SAP was stated as follows:

> The environment of the South China Sea continues to degrade despite actions taken at the national, sub-regional and regional levels. Part of the problem stems from the transboundary marine problems in the region and their impact on the ecosystems and resources of the South China Sea. This provides the ecological impetus for co-operation that is also based on the fact that the region is a large marine ecosystem with intrinsic integrity and inter-connections between all trophic levels.[50]

As the SAP itself observes when charting the history of its own development, '(a) key element in this process has been the development of detailed National Action Plans by each country that addresses the specific concerns and issues relevant to the components of the draft Strategic Action Programme,'[51] all of these were planned for implementation by the end of 2007. A further significant and perhaps even unique element of this SAP is 'the inclusion of detailed economic values for coastal habitat goods and services and their use in the determination of regionally applicable Total Economic Values.'[52]

From a legal perspective, the SAP was envisaged as part of an overarching proposed Framework for Management of the Marine Environment of the South China Sea, which was supposed to be underpinned by a Memorandum of Understanding (MOU) signed by the Environment Ministers of the countries involved, under which the SAP would interact with 'sub-regional and bilateral agreements' and 'national action plans.'[53] But there appears to have been no further actions in this regard. This is in line with the observation made earlier on in this analysis that ongoing tensions between the littoral States over territorial and maritime jurisdictional issues, as well as overflight and navigational issues involving extra-regional powers, continue to blight the outlook for co-operation within the South China Sea. As the SAP itself noted: 'Due to the geopolitical sensitivity of the South China Sea marine basin the countries expressed the wish that no international or regional entities, other than UNEP be involved in the management of the project.'[54]

Nevertheless, the SAP identified continuing obstacles to formal regional undertakings of scientific, and management co-operation as follows:

- Financial constraints; continued long-term financing;
- Lack of understanding of the root causes of regional marine environmental problems;
- Lack of consideration of long-term impacts;
- Inability to predict the impacts of future threats;
- Lack of a regional and global perspective;
- Lack of respect and recognition of regional expertise among some high-level decision-makers;
- Lack of a regional political consensus;

- Lack of a regional network and mechanism for action; and,
- Lack of understanding of the benefits of regional cooperation.[55]

To address these continuing obstacles and based on regional consultations, the SAP identified the following criteria and pathways to formal institutionalised cooperation for the South China Sea environment:

- A process-oriented focus to improving the effectiveness of actions and implementation is appropriate for regional cooperation;
- A strong, proactive institutional mechanism empowered to act effectively, results in the most effective regional co-operation; and lastly
- That regional co-operation may take many forms, but it must be appropriate to the regional ethos and culture.[56]

However, it was significant to note that the international consultation exercise conducted under SAP auspices also revealed that the regional consensus on the optimum way forward in this region was the preparation of a non-legally binding framework.[57] Moreover, the overall goals of this framework would be to create an environment at the regional level, in which collaboration and partnership in addressing environmental problems of the South China Sea, between all stakeholders, and at all levels are fostered and encouraged; and to enhance the capacity of the participating governments to integrate environmental considerations into national development planning.[58] According to the SAP, 'the recommended framework must also be functional and effective in resolving environmental problems and fostering strong regional cooperation and coordination of appropriate cost-effective actions. The framework must include, *inter alia*

- Sound science. The use of sound science must be incorporated into policy-making processes and underpin decisions to foster ecological and economic soundness.
- Ecologically effective actions. It is increasingly recognised that many laws, policies and actions are ineffective in terms of ecological improvements. Ecological ineffectiveness also results in waste of scarce financial resources. Ecologically effective actions must be based on sound science and not on perceptions.
- Cost effective actions.
- Economic valuation. Economic valuation of environmental goods and services as a tool for sound development planning.
- Knowledge-based decision-making. This entails gathering all relevant information for the purpose of making effective decisions. Studies indicate that working towards a consensual knowledge-base for decision-making purposes improves the effectiveness of decisions and also improves cooperation.
- Consensual knowledge base. Promoting and building a consensual knowledge base (a base of information that the parties agree is applicable) facilitates cooperation and decision-making processes. This is particularly true where progress on regional cooperation is stalled or slowed due to complexities or uncertainty surrounding the issue.
- Communication. The lack of effective vertical and horizontal communication has been identified as a serious impediment to effective cooperation.
- Periodic assessment and review and revision of instruments or actions as required. Significant amounts of money and valuable resources are wasted due to the failure to assess

or review laws, policies, mechanisms and measures to ensure they are effective or even implemented. Where assessments indicate problems, it is imperative that revisions are undertaken.
- Adaptive management. This provides a flexible approach that allows for the inclusion of new information.'[59]

According to the SAP, the main areas for cooperation to be covered by the framework include:

1 Establishment and management of regional database;
2 To identify and collect data & information in the areas of:
    - Marine and coastal legislation, regulation and institutional arrangement and coordination related to the analyse of the contents of the Draft National Action Plan from the Perspective of the Regional Strategic Action Programme.
    - Ratified international and regional conventions and agreements on marine and coastal issues to find out the similarities and differences of all countries involved for Regional Cooperation perspectives.
    - Scientific and technical data and information, including monitoring data, economic data related to marine and coastal environment.
    - Experts and institutions in the region.
    - Experience of each country, including pilot projects that can serve as models;
3 Exchange of data, information and experience;
4 Regional prioritisation of environmental issues;

    The coastal States should cooperate on a sub-regional or regional basis to identify and prioritize regional and transboundary environmental issues. States should co-operate with each other in addressing the prioritized marine environmental issues in the South China Sea. Each Party should mobilize necessary resources, capacities and services, as well as develop legal, financial and economic arrangements, including the adoption of a strategic plan for the management and conservation of coastal and marine resource to reach the targets stated in the South China Sea SAP.
5 Public Awareness and Education

    Public awareness should be raised through countries' education systems, campaigns and other activities at the regional, national, and local community levels, especially those living along the coastlines, on the following issues:
    - Ecological unity of the South China Sea and Gulf of Thailand;
    - Social, economic and environmental benefits arising from the proper exploitation, management and conservation of marine resources of the South China Sea and Gulf of Thailand;
    - Social, economic and environmental adverse impacts possibly arising from the degradation of the ecosystems of the South China Sea and Gulf of Thailand; and
    - Necessity of regional cooperation on the exploitation, management and conservation of the marine resources of the South China Sea and Gulf of Thailand.'[60]

    All of the above policies, measures and actions are to be undertaken within a management framework that:
    - Restricts the membership of the policy/decision-making body to government representatives only;
    - The policy/decision-making body may invite a limited number of observers from regional and international agencies and institutions as deemed appropriate;

- Includes a high level scientific and technical body that serves: (a) as a forum for reconciling both sectoral and national interests and priorities; and (b) as the source of independent scientific and technical advice to the policy-making body;
- Ensures and maintains a separation between discussions of scientific and technical matters from discussions dealing with policy and principles at both the national and regional levels;
- Facilitates and ensures the incorporation of sound scientific and technical advice and information into politically based decision-making;
- Emphasises the use of experts and consultants from the participating countries, having regional knowledge and perspectives;
- Fosters the establishment of epistemic communities within the region and utilises effectively their advice and experience;
- Permits and encourages networking and interactions among and between specialist epistemic communities;
- Emphasises and fosters networking at all levels and amongst all stakeholders;
- Fosters and strengthens both "horizontal" (inter-country) and "vertical" (intra-country) interactions and networking between individuals at all levels of SAP implementation and execution;
- Encourages adaptive management, which is subject to periodic review in line with the reviews of the SAP;
- Is developed through a process of detailed planning and consultation that ensures consensus regarding the final, agreed management framework; and,
- Is managed and operated by committed, experienced, independent, and full-time professionals, guided by and responsible to the policy/decision-making body.[61]

Moreover, according to the SAP, the proposed management framework should contain the following components:

'Memorandum of Understanding adopted at the ministerial levelserves as the political instrument for the implementation of the entire Strategic Action Programme'.

REGIONAL STRATEGIC ACTION PROGRAMME

The regional Strategic Action Programme will be the operational arm of the Memorandum of Understanding and outlines the actions that need to be taken to address environmental degradation in the South China Sea and Gulf of Thailand.

SUB-REGIONAL AND BI-LATERAL AGREEMENTS

Countries are encouraged to enter into sub-regional and bi-lateral agreements to address issues relating to the implementation of the SAP. The Memorandum of Understanding will form the umbrella under which these sub-regional and bilateral agreements are negotiated and implemented.

EXISTING NATIONAL ACTION PLANS

During the course of the UNEP/GEF project entitled "Reversing Environmental Degradation in the South China Sea and the Gulf of Thailand", participating countries have prepared

National Action Plans (NAPs) for habitats, fisheries and land-based pollution. The existing NAPs will form the national basis for action in implementation of the SAP.'[62]

Finally, and bringing us right up to date, a further UNEP/GEF initiative entitled 'Implementing the Strategic Action Programme for the South China Sea' was launched in 2016 and projected to run until 2021,[63] in partnership with six out of the seven environment Ministries that originally adopted the SAP (excluding Malaysia). The overall objective of this initiative is to assist these participating countries in meeting the targets of the approved SAP for the South China Sea through the provision of technical assistance as required in implementing national activities in support of the SAP; and the provision of strong regional coordination of the process of SAP implementation.[64]

COBSEA & Regional Action Plan on marine litter

Reverting to COBSEA's governance role within the wider South China Sea-East Asian Seas region, it should be noted that presently, COBSEA activities are guided by the Strategic Directions 2018–2022.[65] These Strategic Directions 2018–2022 focus on two substantive themes: 'Land-based Marine Pollution'; and 'Marine and Coastal Planning and Management'; as well as an over-arching 'Governance' theme.[66] The two substantive themes identify priority issues relevant to the region's marine and coastal environment and sustainable development, where COBSEA has a particular mandate or comparative advantage to catalyse and deliver policy development, projects and other activities. The 'Governance' theme, on the other hand, addresses COBSEA as a regional policy mechanism and identifies priorities in creating the necessary conditions for COBSEA and its Secretariat to efficiently deliver their mandates.[67] By serving as a forum for the exchange of experiences, policy and practice related to the two substantive themes, COBSEA's role as a coordinating regional body is thereby confirmed.

Moreover,

> COBSEA activities towards implementation of the East Asian Seas Action Plan under the "New Strategic Direction for COBSEA (2008–2012)" have focused on Information Management; National Capacity Building; Strategic and Emerging Issues; and Regional Cooperation, emphasizing, in particular, land-based sources of marine pollution, sustainable management of critical habitat, related spatial planning including to build climate change resilience, as well as assessment and knowledge management.[68]

As the COBSEA reports,

> (n)otable achievements include development of a State of the Marine Environment Report, adoption of a Regional Action Plan on Marine Litter, implementation of a regional project on coastal and marine spatial planning, development of two UN Environment GEF projects for implementation of the Strategic Action Programme for the South China Sea, and implementation of sub-regional projects addressing coastal erosion, environmental sustainability in the dive tourism industry, and participation in natural resource governance on small islands.[69]

Specifically, in relation to marine litter, participating countries and the COBSEA Secretariat are now also guided by the Regional Action Plan on Marine Litter (RAP MALI) adopted by the 24th Intergovernmental Meeting in 2019. According to paragraph 8 of this Action Plan, the specific objectives are to:

'Prevent and reduce to the minimum marine litter pollution in the marine and coastal environment of the East Asian Seas Region;
Foster sustainable consumption and production in a multi-stakeholder whole lifecycle approach to prevent and reduce leakage at source;
Remove to the extent possible already existent marine litter by using environmentally acceptable methods;
Improve monitoring and assessment of marine litter and its impacts for a science-based approach;
Enhance knowledge sharing and awareness about marine litter and its impacts amongst all stakeholders and all groups of society in the East Asian Seas Region;
Support national efforts towards adequate institutional, policy and implementation frameworks, cross sector coordination and regional and international cooperation.'[70]

This Marine Litter Action Plan comprises four main actions, of which the third is most pertinent to the thesis advanced by this essay, namely, 'Action 3: Monitoring and Assessment of Marine Litter and assessment programmes,' which observes that: 'One of the significant barriers to addressing marine litter is the absence of adequate *science-based monitoring and assessment programmes*'[71] (emphasis added). The Plan also notes that:

> Monitoring and assessment are indispensable in identifying marine litter status and trends and its most critical impacts, and to support development, tracking and evaluation of policy and management interventions. There is a need to improve knowledge on the main types, sources and amounts of litter that enter the marine and coastal environment, to enable assessment of marine litter status and trends, the impact of marine litter on the marine and coastal environment and human health, as well as the socio-economic aspects of marine litter. Sound marine litter monitoring and reporting is also required to track progress towards the Sustainable Development Goals (SDGs), including target 14.1, and contribution to other relevant SDGs and associated targets.[72]

Complementing this COBSEA Regional Action Plan on Marine Litter, the COBSEA Working Group on Marine Litter was established to promote the implementation of this Action Plan, provide strategic as well as technical support and advice to the COBSEA Intergovernmental Meeting and COBSEA Secretariat; exchange information that supports the implementation of the COBSEA Regional Action Plan on Marine Litter; and promote regional cooperation in the context of the COBSEA Regional Action Plan on Marine Litter. To fulfil its functions, the COBSEA Working Group on Marine Litter will, *inter alia*,

> Identify and share knowledge and scientific evidence where available, identify capacity and other gaps and needs, and provide guidance on information exchange, knowledge management, technical cooperation, education, training and technology transfer or other efforts to address such gaps and needs; ...[73]

Partnerships in Environmental Management for the Seas of East Asia (PEMSEA)

Separately, under the auspices of UNEP's sister programme, the UN Development Programme (UNDP), the 'Partnerships in Environmental Management for the Seas of East Asia (PEMSEA) was created with a similar mission – to foster and sustain healthy and resilient coasts and oceans, communities and economies across the Seas of East Asia through integrated management solutions and partnerships.'[74] Unlike COBSEA, PEMSEA draws its 14 State membership from the wider East Asian region, encompassing Japan, the Republic of (South) Korea and even the Democratic People's Republic of (North) Korea, as well as most of the South China Sea regional States, latterly even including Timor-Leste (East Timor).[75] However, there is arguably little direct evidence of much-needed coordination, collaboration and/or co-operation between this arrangement and that of COBSEA – considered above.

According to PEMSEA, which is based in Quezon City, the Philippines, it has provided solutions for effective management of coasts and oceans across the shared seas of East Asia for over two decades,[76] in the following ways:

> PEMSEA aims to proactively build effective intergovernmental and intersectoral partnerships and expand the capacities of countries and other stakeholders with innovative, cross-cutting policies, tools and services for integrated coastal and ocean management. PEMSEA applies integrated coastal management (ICM) as its primary approach for generating and sustaining healthy oceans, people and economies.[77]

Moreover, PEMSEA is the regional coordinating mechanism for the Sustainable Development Strategy for the Seas of East Asia (SDS-SEA), a shared marine strategy among 14 countries in the region. In this role, PEMSEA works with national and local governments, companies, research and science institutions, communities, international agencies, regional programmes, investors and donors towards the implementation of the SDS-SEA. The SDS-SEA was initially adopted by 12 governments in December 2003, namely: Brunei Darussalam; Cambodia; China; Democratic People's Republic (DPR) of Korea; Indonesia; Japan; Malaysia; Philippines; Republic of Korea; Singapore; Thailand; and Viet Nam, with the signing of the Putrajaya Declaration of Regional Cooperation for Sustainable Development of the Seas of East Asia. In 2006, the governments of Lao People's Democratic Republic and Timor-Leste also adopted the SDS-SEA. In 2009, PEMSEA was granted international legal personality, and together with the SDS-SEA was recognized as the regional governance mechanism and framework for the sustainable management of the seas of East Asia.[78]

As originally drafted, the SDS-SEA did not create a new set of obligations but rather complemented existing ones. Following a review of the SDS-SEA in 2015,[79] it was updated to address the changing context in ocean governance, in light of new or amended international and regional agreements, and especially the 2015 SDGs. It now provides a framework for policy and programme development and implementation at the regional, national and local levels for achieving the goals and targets set by these various global instruments. The SDS-SEA 2015 contains seven strategies, and related objectives and action programmes for sustainable development of coasts and oceans. While the SDS-SEA 2015 is considered to be non-binding, over time countries have developed confidence in the development and application of integrated coastal and ocean management as an effective tool for achieving the

SDS-SEA objectives.[80] Building on this progress, strategic targets have been identified for monitoring and assessing progress with SDS-SEA 2015 implementation across the region. The SDS-SEA 2015 and strategic targets were adopted during the Fifth Ministerial Forum on 20 November 2015 in Danang, Viet Nam. According to PEMSEA, '(t)he updated strategy is the region's concrete response to the UN SDGs, and will lay down a stronger commitment from the countries of the region to ensure a sustainable path for the Seas of East Asia.'[81] The four specific SDS-SEA 2015 Targets are as follows:

'Target 1:

By 2017, a self-sustaining PEMSEA Resource Facility (PRF) managing and coordinating a suite of products, services and financing mechanisms for advancing SDS-SEA implementation at the regional, national and local levels.

Target 2:

By 2018, a regional State of Oceans and Coasts reporting system to monitor progress, impacts and benefits, and to continually improve planning and management of SDS-SEA implementation.

Target 3:

By 2021, national coastal and ocean policies, and supporting legislation and institutional arrangements set up and functional in 100% of PEMSEA Partner Countries, consistent with international environmental and sustainable development commitments and based on best available scientific information.

Target 4:

By 2021, ICM programs for sustainable development of coastal and marine areas covering at least 25% of the region's coastline and contiguous watershed areas, supporting national priorities and commitments under the UN SDGs, UNFCCC, Aichi Biodiversity Targets, UNISDR Post-2015 Framework for Disaster Risk Reduction, and other relevant environmental and sustainable development targets subscribed to by PEMSEA Partner Countries.'[82]

Furthermore, a 2018–2022 SDS-SEA Implementation Plan (IP) has been established, composed of three Priority Management Programmes and three Governance Programmes. The Priority Management Programmes include: (a) Biodiversity Conservation and Management; (b) Climate Change and Disaster Risk Reduction and Management; and (c) Pollution Reduction and Waste Management. The cross-cutting Governance Programmes include: (a) Ocean Governance and Strategic Partnerships; (b) Knowledge Management and Capacity Development; and (c) Blue Economy Investment and Sustainable Financing.[83] In turn, each Priority Management and Governance program includes three parts: (1) an introductory section providing an overview of the priority issue area/program, the region's current situation and major efforts undertaken, and remaining gaps and challenges; (2) a summary of key international and regional commitments directly relevant to respective priority program; and (3) a matrix of the overall objective of the priority program, expected outcomes to 2022, indicators of benefit/impact, and targeted actions and schedule to which PEMSEA Country and Non-Country Partners may indicate/identify relevant activities of possible collaboration/initiatives (ongoing/planned) that would help contribute to achieving the region's targets.[84]

As a living document, the PEMSEA Partners, in coordination with the Secretariat of the PRF, will continue to collaboratively identify priorities, outputs and indicative actions that align with the SDS-SEA IP 2018–2022, and jointly implement initiatives/activities that would be identified.[85] To ensure regular monitoring of progress and gaps, progress/achievements of Partners and collaborating organizations will be highlighted during national and regional events, as well as documented via PEMSEA's Annual Report and the triennial State of Oceans and Coasts (SOC) Report.[86] As Kirk has recently observed in an overview of PEMSEA's role and activities within the context of UNDP's contribution to global ocean governance,

> (t)hese examples point to the development of regional regimes by focusing on the use of practice to develop shared understandings – the regime building approach. … the key element appears to be creation of common understandings at the regional level.[87]

At this juncture, however, it may be reiterated that neither the COBSEA nor PEMSEA arrangements described in the last two sub-sections *explicitly* refer to dovetailing efforts to ensure non-replication of their collective efforts. The lack of explicit co-ordination with each other can be partially explained by their different (State) memberships, albeit with a significant number of States being members of both organizations. On the other hand, this apparent discrepancy between UNEP-led COBSEA & UNDP-led PEMSEA efforts over largely the same area of marine space lends credence to the argument that there is now a need for a single, overarching, formalised institutional framework to bring all scientific research results, management options, and policy decision-making structures under one umbrella-type *governance* (or even *legal*) arrangement for the South China Sea's environment.

South China Sea sub-regional and bilateral initiatives on the marine environment

ASEAN initiatives on the South China Sea environment

A further significant, Southeast Asian region-wide initiative that adopts a comprehensive and holistic approach to the environment of the South China Sea is the Declaration for a Decade of Coastal and Marine Environmental Protection in the South China Sea (2017–2027) adopted by the ten ASEAN Member States and China.[88] This Declaration provides, *inter alia*, as follows:

'Affirming the commitment of Governments under the Declaration on the Conduct of Parties in the South China Sea (DOC), particularly on undertaking cooperative activities on marine environmental protection;

Recognizing that the preservation and sustainable management of the coastal and marine environment is vital to the economic well-being and enhanced quality of life of the peoples of ASEAN Member States and China;

Noting that the current environmental situation in the South China Sea requires collective attention and action to protect the marine ecosystem and biodiversity, in particular on vulnerable marine ecosystems and their physical and biogenic structure, including coral reefs, cold water habitats, hydrothermal vents and seamounts, of certain human activities;

Emphasizing the need to promote responsible fishing practices, environmentally friendly fishing methods, and combatting illegal, unreported and unregulated fishing (IUUF), to ensure sustainable fishery resources and achieve food security; …

Noting that a precautionary and ecosystem-based approach based on the best available science in marine resources management to ensure its rational and sustainable development could be applied as appropriate;

Noting that coordinated and cooperative regional efforts are essential for the scientific conservation and management of marine resources and environment, biodiversity, and coastal zone of the ecosystem of the South China Sea;

Acknowledging that conservation of endangered and migratory wildlife species warrants cooperation from countries within the region where such species spend any part of their life cycle;

Reiterating the need to continue developing and sustaining environmentally-friendly mechanisms to mitigate the effects of climate change and transboundary marine environmental pollution and degradation;

Recognizing the significance of the sustainable management and conservation of fresh water eco-systems such as lakes and rivers, wetlands, and adjacent estuaries along coastal areas in the overall health of the marine environment; Further recognizing the importance of protecting the South China Sea as a natural resource base for economic and social development for the present and future generations and recognising the benefits that would be gained from having the South China Sea as a sea of peace, stability and prosperity; ...'[89]

The ASEAN framework of action on marine debris

Recognising that marine debris is a transboundary issue which requires integrated regional cooperation in addition to robust national strategies and actions to address marine debris, the ASEAN Framework of Action on Marine Debris was developed to act on the recommendations from the ASEAN Conference on Reducing Marine Debris in ASEAN Region in Phuket in November 2017, taking into account the East Asia Summit (EAS) Conference on Combating Marine Plastic Debris in Bali in September 2017. This Framework of Action was formally welcomed by all ASEAN Member States at the Special ASEAN Ministerial Meeting on Marine Debris on 5 March 2019 in Bangkok, Thailand,[90] and then followed-up by the Bangkok Declaration on Combating Marine Debris in ASEAN Region *(sic)* adopted on 22 June 2019.[91] Of these two related initiatives, the Framework of Action is more comprehensive and pithy, initially comprising four (4) priority areas, namely: (i) Policy Support and Planning; (ii) Research, Innovation, and Capacity Building; (iii) Public Awareness, Education, and Outreach; and (iv) Private Sector Engagement. Each priority area then provides further 'Frameworks' for collaborative actions and activities, summarised as follows:

Under Framework I: Policy Support and Planning:

A Promote and organise regular regional policy dialogue, sharing information and knowledge, and strengthening regional coordination on prevention and reduction of marine debris from land- and sea-based activities.

B Mainstream multi-sectoral policy measures to address marine debris in national and ASEAN's development agenda and priorities, including having comprehensive waste management systems to prevent pollution and circular economy approaches; develop and implement extended producer responsibility (EPR) policies and schemes, including deposit refund, and take-back for reusing and recycling; encourage national authorities in collaboration with businesses to develop and promote product sustainability and circularity criteria to stimulate the market for sustainable products and secondary raw materials while concurrently, addressing the unsustainable use and disposal of single-use plastic products; develop/strengthen upstream policies for land-based leakage (including single-use plastics), and sea-based leakage (e.g. ghost nets, and waste from fishing vessels, maritime transport and marine tourism); welcome inter-sectoral initiatives and collaboration to effectively address marine debris through various relevant ASEAN-led mechanisms; encourage national and local governments to incorporate marine debris issues in their priorities.

C Encourage ASEAN Member States to implement relevant international laws and agreements related to waste management – such as MARPOL Annex V ship-generated waste, Basel Convention, and UN Environment Assembly resolutions 3/7 on Marine Litter and Microplastics, by incorporating these international laws and agreements related to waste management into regional platforms; provide support for enabling conditions to the implementation of the international laws and agreement; conduct regular dialogue through webinar and/or through Basel Convention Regional Centre for South-East Asia (BCRC-SEA).

D Develop a regional action plan on combating marine debris in the ASEAN

Region by applying integrated land-to-sea policy approaches; establish a task force on the development of ASEAN regional action plan on combating marine debris as a mean to:

1.1 exchange information on existing national policy instruments to combat marine debris.
1.2 develop elements for a regional action plan.
1.3 compile the regional action plan in accordance with the national and regional context.

2 Review and analyse best practices of Regional Seas Programmes to combat marine debris.
3 Conduct feasibility study/consultative meeting on the development of an ASEAN agreement on the management of marine debris pollution.
4 Conduct feasibility study/consultative meeting on the establishment of an ASEAN Centre on Combating Marine Debris.
5 Contribute to EAS efforts to develop the regional plan of action on combating marine plastic debris.

Framework II: Research, Innovation and Capacity Building:

A Compile regional baseline on status and impacts of marine debris in the ASEAN Region; review and analyse information and data on status and impacts of marine debris in the ASEAN region, and develop a regional baseline report; assess information and data gaps, and identify possible approaches to bridge the gaps.

B Strengthen regional, national and local capacities to develop and implement national action plans/initiatives; explore standardisation of methods for the measurement and monitoring of marine debris, based on existing/established protocols; conduct capacity assessment on addressing marine debris issue where appropriate and when requested to assess the existing capacity and capacity need of the ASEAN Member States to address marine debris issues; provide trainings on combating marine debris among ASEAN Member States as well as with support from external parties including monitoring and management of marine debris.

C Enhance scientific knowledge, transfer marine technology and promote innovative solution to combat marine debris; support research and sharing of scientific knowledge, technology and innovation development among ASEAN Member States, including by engaging research institutions, public and private sectors, international partners, and other relevant stakeholders; promote cooperation and partnership across research institutions to collect and exchange data and information and develop collaboration on combating marine debris including through national and international events/meetings, exchange visits; promote efforts to identify and replicate innovative solutions implemented by cities for combating marine debris; enhance research/study on marine debris, including plastics and microplastics; explore the possible development of a network for sharing marine debris data and information; promote efforts on research and development cooperation on the development of environmentally-friendly alternatives in combating marine debris.

D Promote integration and application of scientific knowledge to enhance science-based decisions and policies on marine debris prevention and management; promote science-policy interface in order to enhance interaction between scientist and policy maker, and accessibility to scientific information; disseminate scientific knowledge through various communication channels such as peer-review publication, conferences/meetings and mass media; encourage the participation of scientist in the policy-making process, when appropriate, in order to provide evidence-based inputs to the policy; encourage scientists to incorporate multiple points of view, especially from policy maker, into study design, delivery and communication.

Framework III: Public Awareness, Education and Outreach:

A Promote public awareness on status and impacts of marine debris and microplastics; develop communication materials on status and impacts of marine debris by incorporating science-based information; disseminate the information/materials to the general public via advance communication platforms, mass media and public events.

B Accelerate advocacy strategy/programme to promote behavior change to combat marine debris, and to incorporate marine debris issue into ASEAN's Culture of Prevention Initiative; develop a communication plan to promote public awareness and behavior change; adapt and apply best practices and campaigns which successfully change behaviour; share alternative solutions and practices to prevent and reduce land- and sea-based debris; integrate scientific finding on status and impacts of marine debris in advocacy strategy/programme; engage multi-stakeholders including youth, public and private sectors, and government agencies in advocacy programmes and outreach activities on combating marine debris.

C Promote platforms for knowledge sharing, innovative solutions and best practices to combat marine debris; organise expert exchange platforms and/or study-trip programmes; establish ASEAN information platform to exchange information and share innovative solution and best practices.

Framework IV: Private Sector Engagement:

A Promote collaborative actions with the private sector and industry associations to implement measures to address marine debris issues; support private sectors to implement measures to address marine debris issues.

B Encourage private sector investment in and contribution to combat marine debris; engage the private sector in campaigns such as programme and campaign on the circular economy, product life-cycle management, sustainable consumption and production and "3R" approaches; mainstream private sectors support to develop research and innovation such as through project funding, and prioritise Corporate Social Responsibility (CSR) activities on combating marine debris; promote private sector investment in redesigning products/packaging and alternative materials; engage value chain stakeholders to establish enabling mechanisms/infrastructure to increase waste recovery and recycling rates.[92]

The 2008 Cambodia-Vietnam (provincial) arrangement for coastal ecosystems and natural resources management

There is growing evidence that the above extra-regional, regional and sub-regional initiatives have spawned specific bilateral intra-governmental arrangements on shared marine environments. An example of this is the Memorandum of Agreement (MoA) was entered into between the People's Committee of Kien Giang Province (Viet Nam) and the Governor of Kampot Province (Cambodia) on 29 March 2008 in Kampot, Cambodia. Under this MoA the two parties agree to implement the policy and framework for cooperation in the management of coastal ecosystems and natural resources between the provinces of Kien Giang and Kampot in order to strengthen environmental protection, biodiversity conservation, and welfare of each province.[93]

Conclusions and recommendations

This essay has explored the scope of current interaction between the science, policy and law disciplines as they converge around the blighted marine environment of the South China Sea. In doing so, this essay has conducted an outline survey and assessment of the range of international scientific research initiatives, international governance efforts, policy decisions, as well as legal measures and actions attempting to address the parlous state of this particular marine environment. This survey of international initiatives and efforts has covered a number of applicable extra-regional, regional, sub-regional, and bilateral initiatives, programmes, action plans and projects devoted to assessing the sources of pollution affecting the ecosystem health and biodiversity levels of this semi-enclosed sea. Summarising the results of these assessments has revealed that the rich sources of information on the environmental threats developed by the cooperative efforts on scientific research are arguably not matched by correspondingly robust, *formalised institutional* governance frameworks, policy decisions, and legal measures environment that co-operation at the region-wide level now demands. Moreover, there appears to be a lack of provision for institutional co-ordination and collaboration between and amongst the plethora of initiatives that now converge on the South China Sea environment, even though their organizational entities are at least partially supported by the UN, albeit through different programmes, namely, the UNEP & UNDP, respectively.

Overall, therefore, this non-exhaustive exercise of collating previous and continuing *collective* regional marine scientific research efforts has identified the need for a *formalised institutional* approach to continue developing the informational database drawn from present and future scientific research endeavours in the South China Sea. Both previously and presently, marine scientific research on the South China Sea environment has proceeded on an individually conceived project-to-project basis. Although there is some evidence of continuity between these individual projects, building towards a comprehensive set of environmental data on the South China Sea, the formal establishment of a designated institutional repository of regional data on the South China Sea marine environment would serve to consolidate all (or at least most) of this data in one place. A *formalised institutional* governance framework for regional, bilateral and national marine scientific research activities (incorporating an established repository for all scientific databases) would also fulfil a vital co-ordinating role between these research activities. Following the above prescriptions could also, *inter alia*, prevent replication of similarly conceived research efforts and thus avoid wasteful endeavours.

Other international policy-oriented exercises have advocated similar actions. For example, the Center for Strategic & International Studies (CSIS) Working Group on the South China Sea has recommended that the littoral States, *inter alia*, 'Cooperate on marine scientific research, which is necessary to assess the health of the maritime environment and effectively implement conservation efforts,' in the following ways:

- 'Claimants should coordinate joint marine scientific research cruises throughout the South China Sea with experts from all claimants invited to participate.
- Each claimant should facilitate visits by experts from other claimant nations to conduct research on islands and reefs that it occupies, with due regard given to the need to restrict access to sensitive military sites. Claimants should all agree that research trips would be organized without prejudice to the outstanding claims of other parties and that participation would not imply recognition on the part of individual researchers or governments of the claims of the organizer.
- Claimants should host regular scientific workshops supported by all neighboring governments with participation of experts from across the region and beyond.
- Governments should invest, both individually and as a group, in programs to raise public awareness of the importance of and threats to fisheries as a common, renewable resource.'[94]

While it is important to note that the Strategic Action Programme for the South China Sea has already promoted similar actions to that suggested here, it is nevertheless submitted that an international governance body such as a 'South China Sea Marine Scientific Research Institute,' could become a necessary and significant stepping-stone in the pathway to a binding international legal instrument addressing the environmental threats affecting the South China Sea today. Towards this end, the establishment of such an entity could be underpinned initially by a Memorandum of Understanding or similar type of formal, albeit perhaps not legally binding, an agreement between all the regional States of the South China Sea, with possible provision for associate membership to extra-regional States that are keen to support and participate in research activities within this marine basin. Such an entity would deliver up-to-date, comprehensive, over-arching scientific studies on the state of the South China Sea environment, consolidating the accumulated but arguably disparately located scientific evidence on this vital subject. These comprehensive studies will in turn form the basis for, *inter alia*, agreeing and establishing the requisite environmental baselines to measure pollution and biodiversity levels against. These environmental quality gauges can then feed into an international (regional) policy and legal framework with a view to forming the bases for concrete legal actions by individual States, both to reduce toxic output into the South China Sea, as well as build a network of marine protected areas for fragile ecosystems across this Sea. All of this hopefully should be undertaken before it is too late for the South China Sea environment.

Notes

1 For example, since 1990, the Indonesian government has organized so-called 'Track Two' Workshops on Managing Potential Conflicts in the South China Sea, attended by government and military officials in their private capacities, as well as by academics drawn mainly from the littoral States of the South China Sea and external experts. This continuing dialogue process aims to manage potential conflicts by exploring areas of cooperation among the littoral States in the South China Sea area, but it has only recently been devoted to exploring the environmental threats to this region. For an initial account of the semiotics of these workshops, see: Ted L. McDorman, 'The South China Sea Islands Dispute in the 1990s – A New Multilateral Process and Continuing Friction', *International Journal of Marine and Coastal Law*, Vol. 8, Issue 2 (May 1993), 263–285. For a recent study of their implications on regional and bilateral relationships among littoral South China Sea States, see, for example, Yann-Huei Song (Billy), 'The South China Sea Workshop Process and Taiwan's Participation', *Ocean Development & International Law*, Vol. 41, Issue 3 (2010), 253–269.

2 Recent contributions to this genre include Sarah Raine and Christian Le Miere, *Regional Disorder: The South China Sea Disputes*, London: IISS/Routledge (2017).

3 D. A Feary, A. M. Fowler and T. J. Ward, 'Developing a Rapid Method for Undertaking the World Ocean Assessment in Data-poor Regions – A Case Study Using the South China Sea Large Marine Ecosystem', *Ocean & Coastal Management*, Vol. 95 (July 2014), 129–137.

4 See: J. R. Jambeck et al., "Plastic Waste Inputs from Land into the Ocean," *Science*, Vol. 347, Issue 6223 (2015): 768–771.

5 For the purpose of this assessment, the South China Sea region was defined as comprising of nine nations; China, Vietnam, Cambodia, Thailand, Malaysia, Singapore, Indonesia, Brunei and the Philippines. According to the report, this Large Marine Ecosystem and its catchments are bounded to the west by the Mekong River (GIWA region 55), north by East China Sea (GIWA region 36), east by the Sulu-Celebes (Sulawesi) Sea (GIWA region 56) and Small Island States (GIWA region 62), and south and southeast by Indonesian Seas (GIWA region 57). See: Executive Summary, Global International Waters Assessment South China Sea, GIWA Regional assessment 54, Published by the University of Kalmar on behalf of UNEP (2005) at 9.

6 Ibid., at 9.

7 Eric Tagliacozzo, 'The South China Sea', in David Armitage, Alison Bashford, and Sujit Sivasundaram (eds.), *Oceanic Histories*, Cambridge: Cambridge University Press (2018), 113–133, at 113.

8 Ibid., at 129.

9 For recent contributions on the Indian perspective in the South China Sea, see, for example, Nandini Jawli, 'South China Sea and India's Geopolitical Interests', *Indian Journal of Asian Affairs*, Vol 29, Issue 1/2 (June–December 2016), 85–100; and David Scott, 'India's Role in the South China Sea: Geopolitics and Geoeconomics in Play', *India Review*, Vol. 12, Issue 2 (2013), 51–69.

10 See: China National Offshore Oil Corporation (CNOOC), Vietnam Oil and Gas Corporation (PETROVIETNAM), and Philippine National Oil Company (PNOC), Joint Statement on the Signing of a Tripartite Agreement for Joint Marine Seismic Undertaking in The Agreement Area in the South China Sea, adopted on March 14, 2005, accessible at: http://ph.china-embassy.org/eng/zt/nhwt/t187333.htm.

11 John W. McManus, Kwang-Tsao Shao and Szu-Yin Lin, 'Toward Establishing a Spratly Islands International Marine Peace Park: Ecological Importance and Supportive Collaborative Activities with an Emphasis on the Role of Taiwan', *Ocean Development &International Law*, Vol. 41, Issue 3: Issues in the South China Sea (2010), 270–280.

12 Done on the Fourth Day of November in the Year Two Thousand and Two (2002) in Phnom Penh, the Kingdom of Cambodia, accessible at: https://asean.org/?static_post=declaration-on-the-conduct-of-parties-in-the-south-china-sea-2.

13 Ibid.

14 Information on this Programme can be accessed at: https://www.unenvironment.org/explore-topics/oceans-seas/what-we-do/working-regional-seas/regional-seas-programmes.

15 See UNEP, Regional Seas Programme website at: https://www.unenvironment.org/explore-topics/oceans-seas/what-we-do/working-regional-seas/why-does-working-regional-seas-matter.

16 Ibid.

17 See UNEP, Regional Seas Programme website at: https://www.unenvironment.org/explore-topics/oceans-seas/what-we-do/working-regional-seas/why-does-working-regional-seas-matter-0.

18 Full title: Convention for the Protection of the Mediterranean Sea against Pollution was initially adopted in 1976 and entered into force in 1978, before being amended in 1995, and renamed Convention for the Protection of the Marine Environment and the Coastal Region of the Mediterranean, with this amended version in force in 2004.
19 See: UNEP, Regional Seas Programme, 'Mediterranean' webpage, accessible at: https://www.unenvironment.org/explore-topics/oceans-seas/what-we-do/working-regional-seas/regional-seas-programmes/mediterranean.
20 Ibid.
21 Ibid.
22 UNEP Governing Council, Decision 88 (v), 1977.
23 UNEP/IG.26/6, Annex IV.
24 See: para.52 of the East Asian Seas Action Plan. More information on COBSEA is accessible at: https://www.unenvironment.org/cobsea/who-we-are.
25 Ibid., at para.55.
26 Ibid., at para.59.
27 Ibid., at para.60.
28 UNEP(OCA)/EAS IG.4/7, para.58.
29 Now including Cambodia, People's Republic of China, Republic of Korea, and Viet Nam, in addition to the original COBSEA member States, namely, Indonesia, Malaysia, the Philippines, Singapore and Thailand.
30 UNEP(OCA)/EAS IG.4/7, Annex V.
31 UNEP(OCA)/EAS IG5/6 (1994) Annex IV.
32 UNEP(OCA)/EAS IG.5/6 Annex IV, at 1.
33 Ibid.
34 Ibid., at 2.
35 Ibid., at para.34, p.6.
36 Ibid., at para.35, p.7.
37 Ibid., at para.36, p.7.
38 See: COBSEA Strategic Directions 2018–2022. Secretariat of the Coordinating Body on the Seas of East Asia (COBSEA) and United Nations Environment Programme, Bangkok (2018), at para.14, accessible at: https://wedocs.unep.org/bitstream/handle/20.500.11822/31820/COBSEA2022.pdf?sequence=1&isAllowed=y.
39 Full title: The Coral Triangle Initiative on Coral Reefs, Fisheries, and Food Security (CTI-CFF). The CTI is a multilateral partnership working together to sustain extraordinary marine and coastal resources by addressing crucial issues such as food security, climate change and marine biodiversity. It was established in 2009 and is now underpinned by an Agreement on the Establishment on the Regional Secretariat of the Coral Triangle Initiative on Coral Reefs, Fisheries and Food Security (CTI-CFF) scheduled to enter into force on 20th November 2014. More information on the CTI is accessible at: http://www.coraltriangleinitiative.org/.
40 Pedro Fidelman, Louisa S. Evans, Simon Foale, Christopher Weible, Franciska von Heland, and Dallas Elgin, 'Coalition Cohesion for Regional Marine Governance: A Stakeholder Analysis of the Coral Triangle Initiative', *Ocean & Coastal Management*, Vol. 95 (2014), 117–128, at 117.
41 Ibid., at 125.
42 Initially designed by Paul Sabatier and Hank Jenkins-Smith to explain political behaviour and policy change, see: Sabatier and Jenkins-Smith, *Policy Change and Learning: an Advocacy Coalition Approach*, Westview Press, Boulder, CO. (1993).
43 Fidelman *et al.* (2014) at 125.
44 L. Talaue-McManus, Transboundary Diagnostic Analysis for the South China Sea. EAS/RCU Technical Report Series No. 14. UNEP, Bangkok, Thailand (2000), accessible at: https://wedocs.unep.org/handle/20.500.11822/28960.
45 Ibid., at para.1.2.
46 Managing Multi-Lateral, Intergovernmental Projects and Programmes, the Case of the UNEP/GEF Project, entitled: Reversing Environmental Degradation Trends in the South China Sea and Gulf of Thailand', IW-Learn Knowledge document UNEP/GEF/SCS/Inf.1, UNEP (2005), accessible at: http://wedocs.unep.org/bitstream/handle/20.500.11822/28960/TDA.pdf?sequence=1&isAllowed=y.
47 Ibid.

48 Anna Tengberg and Annadel S Cabanban, 'Lessons Learned from Investing in Marine and Coastal Management Initiatives in the East Asian Seas', *Marine Policy*, Vol. 38 (2013), 355–364, at 363.
49 Strategic Action Programme for the South China Sea. UNEP/GEF/SCS Technical Publication No. 16, UNEP (2008), accessible at: https://scssap.org/documents/06-FR-Inc-SCS-Strategic-Action-Programme.pdf.
50 Strategic Action Programme (SAP) for the SCS (2008) at 61.
51 Ibid., at 2.
52 Ibid., at 2.
53 See Diagram in SAP, ibid., on front/cover page of SAP document.
54 Ibid.
55 Ibid., at 61.
56 Ibid., at 61–62.
57 Ibid., at 62.
58 Ibid., at 62.
59 Ibid., at 62–63.
60 Ibid., at 63.
61 Ibid., at 63.
62 Ibid., at 64.
63 See: Project Document, accessible at: https://view.officeapps.live.com/op/view.aspx?src=https%3A//scssap.org/documents/UNEP-SCS-SAP-ProDoc-Draft-10-cp.doc.
64 Accessible at: https://scssap.org/.
65 See: COBSEA Strategic Directions 2018–2022. Secretariat of the Coordinating Body on the Seas of East Asia (COBSEA) and United Nations Environment Programme, Bangkok (2018) *op. cit.*
66 Ibid., at para.19.
67 Ibid.
68 Ibid., at para.13.
69 Ibid.
70 See COBSEA Regional Action Plan on Marine Litter 2019. Secretariat of the COBSEA and United Nations Environment Programme, Bangkok, COBSEA (2019), at para.8.
71 Ibid., at para.11.
72 Ibid., at para.11.
73 See: Para.5 of Appendix 3: Terms of Reference of the Cobsea Working Group on Marine Litter, Cobsea Regional Action Plan on Marine Litter 2019.
74 See: 'About PEMSEA', accessible at: http://www.pemsea.org/about-PEMSEA.
75 Although there is some uncertainty here, as only 12 States are identified as PEMSEA 'Country Partners' on its website, accessible at: http://pemsea.org/about-pemsea/our-partners/country-partners.
76 See: 'About PEMSEA', ibid.
77 Ibid.
78 See: PEMSEA's 'History', accessible at: http://www.pemsea.org/about-pemsea/history.
79 Full title: Regional Review (of the) Implementation of the Sustainable Development Strategy for the Seas of East Asia (SDS-SEA) 2003–2015, PEMSEA, November 2015, accessible at: http://pemsea.org/publications/reports/regional-review-implementation-sustainable-development-strategy-seas-east-asi-0.
80 See: PEMSEA's Regional Marine Strategy', at: http://www.pemsea.org/our-work/regional-marine-strategy.
81 Ibid.
82 Ibid.
83 Ibid.
84 Ibid.
85 Ibid.
86 Ibid.
87 Elizabeth A. Kirk, 'UNDP and Ocean Governance', in Attard, Fitzmaurice and Ntovas (eds), *The IMLI Treatise on Global Ocean Governance, Vol.II: UN Specialized Agencies and Global Ocean Governance*, Oxford University Press (2018), 81–101, at 92.
88 Accessible at: https://asean.org/storage/2017/11/Declaration-for-a-Decade-of-Coastal-and-Marine-Environmental-Protection-in-the-South-China-Sea-2017-2027.pdf.

89 Ibid.
90 Accessible at: https://asean.org/asean-framework-action-marine-debris/.
91 Accessible at: https://asean.org/bangkok-declaration-combating-marine-debris-asean-region/.
92 Accessible at: https://asean.org/storage/2019/06/3.-ASEAN-Framework-of-Action-on-Marine-Debris-FINAL.pdf.
93 Accessible at: http://www.unepscs.org/Demonstration_Sites/Demonstration_Sites/Cambodia_and_Vietnam_Sign_MoA.html.
94 A Blueprint for Fisheries Management and Environmental Cooperation in the South China Sea, CSIS Expert Working Group on the South China Sea, September 13, 2017, accessible at: https://amti.csis.org/coc-blueprint-fisheries-environment/.

PART V

Cooperation and institutions

17

SEMI-ENCLOSED SEAS COOPERATION UNDER UNCLOS

Seokwoo Lee and Lowell Bautista

Introduction

It is self-evident that the South China Sea – a body of water surrounded by China, Vietnam, Philippines, Malaysia, Brunei, Singapore, and Indonesia – is an example of a semi-enclosed sea. The United Nations Convention on the Law of the Sea (UNCLOS) in Article 122 defines a semi-enclosed sea as one that is "surrounded by two or more States and connected to another sea or ocean by a narrow outlet, or consists entirely or primarily of the territorial seas or exclusive economic zones of two or more coastal States."[1] The specific geographical, environmental, and ecological vulnerabilities of semi-enclosed seas render them exposed to unique threats of pollution, navigation, depletion of marine resources, which compel a special regime. Whilst the duty to cooperate, in letter or spirit, is positively reflected or tacitly espoused in most if not all provisions of UNCLOS, Article 123 reflects the reality that States bordering a semi-enclosed sea are under an enhanced duty to cooperate.[2]

The emphasis of most literature on the South China Sea in relation to UNCLOS lies on issues of competing territorial claims and issues associated with uncertain maritime boundaries. In particular, recent scholarly work on the South China Sea has mostly focused on the decision of the South China Sea Arbitral Tribunal set up in accordance with Annex VII of UNCLOS in the case filed by the Philippines against the People's Republic of China on 12 July 2016.[3]

Semi-enclosed seas, from a marine space perspective, inherently entail an adversarial competition for resources and boundaries due to the natural geographical difficulty of bordering States to claim a full 200-nautical-mile exclusive economic zone and continental shelf, or even a full 12-nautical-mile territorial sea, which potentially overlap with the maritime zone claims of the neighbouring opposite or adjacent States.[4] The UNCLOS-related discourse regarding the South China Sea also examines interstate cooperation, due to the transnational nature of issues such as environmental degradation, human trafficking and smuggling, and maritime terrorism which are faced by its littoral States.[5]

However, for the most part, scholarly literature on cooperation in the South China Sea only broadly involves UNCLOS in two ways. First, tangentially as the overarching framework for more particular maritime regimes, such as those in the Mediterranean and Caribbean Seas, that provide relevant lessons. Second, only as a preface for extant arrangements between the

Association of Southeast Asian Nations and China, such as the Draft Code of Conduct. Notably, such an approach problematises cooperation at the level of actors' strategic choices.

In contrast, this chapter contributes by refocusing the analysis back to the textual and contextual issues within UNCLOS itself, and how these dovetail concerns in the South China Sea.[6] It discusses various types and interpretations of obligations embedded in the Convention. Although UNCLOS provides obligations to cooperate in enclosed and semi-enclosed seas under Article 123, the extent to which States are required to comply is still unresolved. The sources of this are multifarious: ambiguity between hortary and mandatory languages involved, lack of precise obligations to meaningfully make sense of a general duty to cooperate, and the variegated nature and application of the duty to cooperate depending on the maritime zone in question. Other concerns also include the Convention's silence regarding the manner of publicity and implicit nature of certain provisions.[7]

Different interpretations of obligations under UNCLOS seriously hamper its effectiveness. This chapter recommends to negotiate an amendment to the Convention in order to address ambiguity in interpretations of treaty obligations. The language of the extent of obligations and their very nature – whether as an obligation of conduct or result, an implicit or explicit duty – deserve further refinement. It draws attention to the technical and legal issues within UNCLOS itself, which have the potential to spillover relevant bilateral and multilateral arrangements. More attention should be given to the adoption of domestic legislation pursuant to UNCLOS provisions. The Asian States such as China and Japan do not directly apply international law in their courts, opting instead to pass parallel legislations which are then applied in courts.

In the final analysis, States must recognise that the obligation to cooperate is a continuing process which they are expected to display in amicable pursuit of diplomatic negotiations. Nonetheless, the duty to cooperate in Article 123 is exhortatory and preserves the careful balance of rights and obligations under the Convention. States which border a semi-enclosed sea, in the exercise of the rights and the performance of their duties under the Convention, are not granted any additional rights beyond those that they are entitled under UNCLOS.[8]

The duty to cooperate

The duty to cooperate is widely accepted as a customary principle of international environmental law.[9] The United Nations (UN) Charter in Article 1 embodies the notion of international cooperation, along with principles such as friendly relations among States, and the maintenance of international peace and security.[10] Nevertheless, these principles merely describe the purposes of the UN as an organisation and the duty to cooperate remains declaratory in nature and does not contain a general legal obligation to cooperate. No international treaty or resolution of the UN General Assembly or any other international organisation, has categorically defined the scope and extent of the term "cooperation" in international law.[11]

International cooperation is a common and underlying leitmotif of UNCLOS. However, UNCLOS is beset with issues related to the variegated nature and language of this obligation. One pertains to the duty to cooperate having different types and even mixtures of obligations, namely obligations of conduct and of result. Provisions such as "shall cooperate to make information available to all States" or "shall cooperate through the conclusion of agreements" embody a general duty to cooperate and a desired result through a particular modality. As will be shown in this chapter, obligations of result are sometimes implied rather than expressly stated, which whittles down the binding force of such provisions on State parties. In others, such as duties to cooperate in combatting piracy, the precise obligations that fall within the scope of the general duty to cooperate is not set out in UNCLOS.[12] This ambiguity exists despite the fact that Article 100 is the only provision in UNCLOS with the title "duty to cooperate," utilising the strongest language found in UNCLOS with regard to this obligation; namely, that all States shall cooperate "to the fullest possible extent."[13]

Another set of issues relates to the inconsistent shift from mandatory to hortatory language. Expressions of the former include those such as "shall publish,"[14] "shall notify,"[15] "shall communicate,"[16] "shall cooperate,"[17] "shall enter into negotiation,"[18] "should cooperate,"[19] "may cooperate,"[20] "shall seek to agree upon,"[21] and "shall promote international cooperation."[22] In other provisions, phrases such as "make every effort to" and "seek to" are more suggestive rather than mandatory. Article 123, which enshrines the duty to cooperate in semi-enclosed seas, is open to different interpretations as to whether it demands a legally binding obligation to cooperate or merely promotes a policy of cooperation:

> States bordering an enclosed or semi-enclosed sea *should cooperate* with each other in the exercise of their rights and in the performance of their duties under this Convention. To this end they *shall endeavour*, directly or through an appropriate regional organization… [emphasis added]

The nebulous nature of the "duty to cooperate" demonstrates intentional ambiguity in treaty drafting.[23] The centrality of State sovereignty as a fundamental principle of international law dictates that any constraints on the exercise of State sovereignty necessitate a conservative interpretation. In the *Wimbledon Case*, the Permanent Court of Justice said: "all restrictions or limitations upon the exercise of sovereignty… must be construed as restrictively as possible and confined within the narrowest limits."[24] This allows a competent tribunal to construe this term minimally to require a State to act consistently with its relevant treaty obligations.[25] This opens room for potential differences in interpretation regarding the extent of concrete obligations to cooperate by States, through cross-referencing or utilisation of contextual clues. One such example is the *MOX Plant Case* under the International Tribunal for the Law of the Sea (ITLOS) where the Tribunal stated that "the duty to cooperate is a fundamental principle in the prevention of pollution of the marine environment under Part XII of the Convention and general international law…"[26] This declaration was cited with approval in the 2015 ITLOS advisory opinion, *Request for an Advisory Opinion Submitted by the Sub-Regional Fisheries Commission (SRFC)*.[27] Nonetheless, more explicit provisions may be needed to resolve compliance issues surrounding the treaty obligations to the Convention.

In a broader context, the obligation of States to cooperate has near-universal coverage. There are 193 States parties to the UN Charter, which requires under Article 2(2) that members comply with international obligations in good faith. Furthermore, the Vienna Convention on the Law of Treaties (VCLT), widely regarded as representative of the foundational principles of international law, stipulates *pacta sunt servanda* as an elementary aspect of State relations.[28] States that have acceded to treaties and agreements are required by good faith to fulfill attendant obligations under such texts.

UNCLOS similarly provides in Article 300 that "States Parties shall fulfil in good faith the obligations assumed under this Convention". Since it opened for signature in 1982, it has been ratified or acceded by 168 States.[29] Asian countries were involved in one-third of the 29 contentious cases before the ITLOS, which was created under UNCLOS (cases 3&4, 9, 12, 14, 15, 16, 24, and 28) and submitted statements in two advisory proceedings (cases 17 and 21).[30]

The duty to cooperate is especially relevant for Asian countries. According to the Maritime Security Index of Stable Seas Programme,[31] even as Asian countries are parties to the eight global maritime legal agreements, such as UNCLOS, UN Convention on Transnational Organised Crime (Palermo Convention), and the UN Convention Against Illicit Trafficking in Narcotic Drugs and Psychotropic Substances (Vienna Convention), accession to agreements such as the Port State Measures Agreement, UN Fish Stocks Agreement, and the UN Convention for the Suppression of Unlawful Acts against the Safety of Maritime Navigation (SUA) remains much more limited. The South China Sea in particular is beset by problems of overfishing, marine environmental degradation, and contested territorial delimitation and militarisation. Furthermore, the International Maritime Bureau reported a total of 85 incidences of piracy and armed robbery against ships in South, East, and Southeast Asia in 2018, second only to Africa.[32]

The regional maritime environment is not merely about interstate territorial dispute – even as it bears heavily in public consciousness: littoral States in the South China Sea are also making strides in "practical maritime cooperation", or functional programs that address challenges at sea, such as the 2016 Trilateral Cooperative Arrangement (TCA) between Indonesia, Malaysia, and the Philippines to hold joint tri-border patrols in the Sulu-Celebes Seas.[33]

These underscore the relevance of international regimes for Asian countries. In the case of UNCLOS, the Convention in itself does not preclude cooperation by relevant parties with unresolved maritime disputes. International relations and diplomacy, by their very nature, demand cooperation from States. The principle of national sovereignty and the international duty to cooperate have to be balanced. As the *Lac Lanoux* arbitration case illustrates, France had a duty to cooperate by giving appropriate consideration to Spain's interests, even as France exercised sovereignty over the territory under customary law. The point here is that sovereign rights may be tempered by an international duty to cooperate.[34]

General duty to cooperate under UNCLOS

At a general level not limited to closed or semi-enclosed seas, the legal obligation to cooperate is established in UNCLOS by words such as "shall" or "should". A multitude of such provisions can be found throughout the Convention. They specify the material scope and forum of cooperation. The former refers to the specific topic where cooperate is mandated, e.g., "shall cooperate in", while the forum or particular modality or channel of cooperation is reflected in words such as "in consultation with,"[35] "through,"[36] "by way of,"[37] or "on a … regional or global basis."[38] More specifically, there are provisions dealing with the following:

> sea lanes and traffic separation schemes;[39] conservation and management of the living resources in EEZs and the high seas,[40] fishing rights;[41] inquiries into marine casualty or incidents of navigation;[42] repression of piracy;[43] suppression of substance trafficking;[44] marine scientific research;[45] transit of land-locked States;[46] protection and preservation of the marine environment;[47] the pollution of the marine environment;[48] and the protection of underwater cultural heritage.[49]

In sum, the obligation to cooperate under UNCLOS includes:

> an obligation to notify affected states of actual or imminent danger to the marine environment, to make contingency plans for dealing with such dangers, to research, to study and to exchange information and data in order to provide scientific criteria for the development of rules, standards, procedures and practices to reduce, prevent or control pollution.[50]

"Shall" and "should" cooperate

The obligation to cooperate under UNCLOS takes many forms and thus has been subject to varying interpretations, with some cases submitted for international adjudication before relevant international courts and tribunals. The following sections discuss the different variations and categories of the obligation to cooperate, as well as possible policy recommendations that would aid future compliance with the Convention's provisions.

Provisions related to unequivocal mandatory language use "shall cooperate" or equivalent variants. These are cases where the obligation to cooperate is clear, but the extent to which States are required to do so is the subject of debate.[51] There are three broad issues related to this.

First, the obligation to cooperate may be expressed as a general duty without further qualification or precision. Consequently, it is "difficult to instantiate it, i.e., to translate it into more specific obligations and standards of State conduct."[52] One such case is the application of UNCLOS in relation to anti-piracy efforts: "UNCLOS … did not set out the precise obligations that fall within the scope of the general duty to cooperate."[53] Article 100 stipulates that "States shall cooperate to the fullest possible extent in the repression of piracy on the high seas or in any other place outside the jurisdiction of any State". The lack of precision regarding the threshold for the "fullest possible extent" complicates any interpretation or attempt to impose an obligation. This is indicated by the fact that UNCLOS does not provide for an organ or arbiter which determines whether a State adequately fulfills its obligation to suppress piracy.[54]

Second, the concept of the duty to cooperate is not easily understood and applied in various ways depending on the subject matter or maritime zone under consideration. For maritime delimitation, the *North Sea Continental Shelf* and *Fisheries Jurisdiction* cases construe said duty as a duty to negotiate in good faith. The same is not true with respect to the *MOX Plant* and *Land Reclamation* cases, where the duty to cooperate involves an obligation to consult and possesses a higher standard for cooperation. The threshold to fulfill the duty to cooperate in maritime delimitation is therefore lower than for marine environment protection and resource conservation.[55]

From these two examples, we glean that the nature of the obligation to cooperate, on its own, is comprehensive. Aside from the general duty, specific provisions are in order, so as to promote uniformity in understanding, interpretation, application, and observance. The duty to cooperate demands clear and specific material scope and or terms of reference for the provisions to acquire unequivocal status as a legal obligation. For this reason, textual approaches to interpretation may supersede contextual and teleological approaches. However, precisely because of the procedural and substantive issues in the language of obligations to cooperate under the Convention, contentions arise when broad strokes provisions are applied on particular cases.

Third, there is an issue regarding the inherent inconsistency between "shall" and "should" in a single provision. The usage of "should" complicates the concept of a general duty to cooperate because it straddles between that of a guiding normative principle that simply encourages cooperation, and a language that mandates State behaviour to always cooperate. Article 123, which specifically deals with cooperation between States bordering an enclosed or semi-enclosed sea, contains a confusing mixture of hortatory and obligatory expressions:

> States bordering an enclosed or semi-enclosed sea *should cooperate* with each other in the exercise of their rights and in the performance of their duties under this

> Convention. To this end they *shall endeavour*, directly or through an appropriate regional organization:
>
> a to *coordinate* the management, conservation, exploration, and exploitation of the living resources of the sea …;
> b to *coordinate* the implementation of their rights and duties with respect to the protection and preservation of the marine environment;
> c to *coordinate* their scientific research policies and undertake where appropriate joint programmes …;
> d to invite, as appropriate, other interested States or international organisations to cooperate with them ….[56]

Attempts to reconcile the usage of "should" and "shall" have yielded different interpretations. The Arbitral Tribunal in the *OSPAR Convention* case described the duty to cooperate as an obligation of conduct by interpreting the language "shall cooperate" as mandatory in nature, which subsequently requires contracting parties to take some action.[57] In the *MOX Plant* case, both the United Kingdom and Ireland agreed that the nature of the duty to cooperate in Article 123 is hortatory, rather than mandatory.[58] It may be noted that the ITLOS fell short of touching on substantive issues in the *MOX Plant* Case when Ireland withdrew its claims against the United Kingdom.[59] Nonetheless, Ireland noted that they were of the opinion that the hortatory view of treaty obligations under Article 123 "may also have an effect upon the meaning of other provisions that are undoubtedly mandatory."[60] Similarly, Article 43 of UNCLOS stipulates that States "should by agreement cooperate" in matters regarding the prevention, reduction, and control of pollution and navigation and safety standards, even as Article 243 categorises the obligation as a mandatory "shall."[61]

An alternate approach is that Article 123 is a limited mandatory obligation to cooperate. Linebaugh[62] argues that the first sentence describes the general context of cooperation, whereas the second sentence more importantly supplies the operative part. The usage of "shall" in the second sentence generates a legal duty to cooperate, but is applicable only to items listed in subsections (a)–(d) since the list follows the word "shall." In effect, purely textual interpretation construes Article 123 as providing for a narrow duty to cooperate in matters relating to subsections (a)–(d).

However, Linebaugh also argued that a textual approach renders the very nature of Article 123 redundant in light of the fact that other provisions of UNCLOS already provide for cooperation over the same set of activities.[63] The *travaux* indicated two conflicting interpretations. On one hand, deliberations between the third and fourth sessions support a limited duty to cooperate in activities under subsections (a)–(d). There was disagreement whether the provision must be hortatory or mandatory, and thus the wording was changed from "shall" to a weaker "should". On the other hand, debates in the Second Committee signify an intention to create new legal duties on signatory States. A contextual interpretation unpacks Article 123 as a possible result of poorly worded drafting inconsistent with the intention of framers. Viewed in this light, the intention for Article 123 is to impose a duty to cooperate "in any exercise of rights or performance of dutied under the Convention."[64]

In sum, the tension between mandatory and hortatory language of treaty obligations has significance for the interpretation of the duty to cooperate.

Duty of publicity, notification, and other exchanges of information

This next section considers the duty to exchange information as a "particular obligation within the general duty to cooperate." The notion of "exchange" is construed as a reciprocal process, thereby creating a right to request information and a duty to respond. This point is especially important for scientific information in the conservation of living resources of exclusive economic zones (EEZs) (Art. 61(5)) and high seas, where States who provide information to another may also request information regarding action taken, which may imply a duty to respond based on the information received originally based on an obligation to cooperate.

The nomenclature of information exchanges distinguishes between publicity, notification, and other exchanges of information. Publicity and notification are parallel insofar as they both involve a "cascading standard of expression", a term used in the 2003 arbitral award over the dispute regarding Article 9 of the Convention for the Protection of the Marine Environment of the North-East Atlantic (OSPAR Convention).[65]

The concept derives from the notion that treaties impose different levels of particular obligations on contracting parties: there is a spectrum running between demands to perform an action and outcome mandated by a convention (e.g., "shall include," "introduce") and lesser forms of engagement such as those of information gathering and sharing which do not necessarily provide for requirements on how to make use of the data. This same logic applies to information exchange which has a hierarchy of obligations within its own class, which are meant to operationalise general and loose obligations in order to address disparate objectives.

Notification differs from publicity in that the particular intended or mandated recipient of the information or report is specified. Within their own umbrella, these two concepts also neatly produce distinctions.

For publicity, a distinction is held between "appropriate" and "due" publicity depending on whether information pertains to dangers or restrictions, and are applied, respectively. Appropriate publicity involves information related to dangers, such as those within or over straits (Art. 44), archipelagic sea lanes (Art. 54), and navigation of territorial seas (Art. 24(2)). In contrast, due publicity is applicable to navigation within territorial seas (Art. 24(2)), dangers within or over straits (Art. 44), and dangers within or over archipelagic sea lanes (Art. 54). The term "dangers" can also apply to situations where the depth, position, and dimensions of any installations or structures are not entirely removed in EEZ (Art. 60(3)).

However, it is important to highlight that there is no express guide for how "appropriate" and "due" publicity differ from each other; a contextual approach is often used to infer that "appropriate" publicity is a higher or stricter level of publicity in view of the immediacy required by dangers. Another silence of UNCLOS worth noting here is the manner of publicity with respect to the publication of reports and the submission of attendant information. Both are of concern in relation to limits of a "particular, clearly defined area" prescribed in Article 211(6) and the results obtained in risk monitoring of pollution as mentioned in Articles 204 and 205.

As for the latter, there is no mention of "due" and "appropriate" to qualify the nature of publicity. One conundrum here is that from a purely textual interpretation, it could be argued that the manner of publicity is the sole discretion of concerned States. The same is true for all cascading standards of publicity, namely, (1) appropriate, (2) due, and (3) simple. However, the case is not so straightforward when one considers that pollution and marine environment degradation in or by one State will likely affect others, which should make standards in Article 205 similar to those governing submission of information pertaining to restrictions. Another case is that the nature of the obligation considered in Article 205 is implicitly one of result and not merely conduct; Article 205 requires States to provide reports to international organisations, who in turn are expected to disseminate such reports to "all States".

In contrast, the particular modality of information exchange by notification is applicable to the following:

> the flag State of vessels subject to law enforcement within territorial seas (art. 27(3)); the flag State of vessels subject to law enforcement within EEZs (art. 73(4)); the flag State of vessels concerned with any enforcement measures taken against foreign vessels pursuant to section 6 of Part XII (art. 231); and the neighboring land-locked States, geographically disadvantaged States, and coastal States with regard to marine scientific research (arts. 246(3) and 254(1)).[66]

Notification too has a cascading standard of expression: (1) to notify immediately, (2) to give warning, (3) to give due notice, and (4) to give simple notice. This gradation is different from the characterisation by the International Court of Justice of a general duty to warn based on imminent risk with significant harm.[67] Such a foundational principle of international law is enshrined in the Convention through Articles 198 and 211(7), but with the usage of "prompt notification" and "shall immediately notify" as opposed to "warn". The practical application of this is that regulatory and enforcement measures applied by coastal States to foreign vessels would require immediate notification in light of possible actual and direct damage to vessels concerned,[68] whereas customary duty to warn applies for cases involving imminent danger to the navigation of vessels more generally.

As regards due notice, different types apply depending on whether the action of exchange refers to States' duties within the jurisdiction of coastal States or whether the information is for the lawful restriction of other States' interests. The second variant has been noted to concern the depth, position, and dimensions of artificial islands, installations, or structures within their EEZs.[69]

Before proceeding, it should be noted that the duty to exchange information is not without exceptions. Article 302 of UNCLOS permits non-disclosure of information "which is contrary to the *essential interests* of [state] security."[70] This rule appears to be "based on the fundamental principle under international law requiring States to fulfill their obligations in good faith."[71]

Obligation to enter into consultation or negotiation

Finally, there is an issue on the nature of the obligation to enter into consultation under Article 118 of the Convention. In brief, the nature of the obligation matters because it may be argued that legal obligations require an express provision in favour of prohibition of conduct and/or result. An alternative view is that a legal obligation can arise from an "implicit duty" to cooperate.

Article 118 instructs that

> States shall cooperate with each other in the conservation and management of living resources in the areas of high seas. States whose nationals exploit identical living resources, or different living resources in the same area, shall enter into negotiations with a view

> to taking the measures necessary for the conservation of the living resources concerned. They shall, as appropriate, cooperate to establish subregional or regional fisheries organizations to this end.

The phrase "for the purpose of" in a hypothetical text of "A for the purpose of B" supplies the conceptual foreground for such a case, given that the adjoining phrase relates A as a method of fulfilling B. The jurisprudence of ITLOS in the *MOX Plant* case seems to support the latter view, insofar as it ordered that Ireland and the United Kingdom "shall cooperate and shall, for this purpose, enter into consultations forwith in order to... devise, as appropriate, measures to prevent pollution of the marine environment".[72] The same was affirmed in the *Land Reclamation* case where Malaysia and Singapore "shall cooperate and shall, for this purpose, enter into consultations forthwith".[73] As such, the requirement to consult is a practical method of fulfilling the prescribed duty to cooperate.

However, in practical terms, the usage of consultation for the purpose of satisfying the duty to cooperate is paltry. Around 12 per cent of global fish catch is sourced from the South China Sea, but bleak predictions estimate a possible 50 per cent decline in key fish-stocks by 2045 has been reported by the United Nations Food and Agricultural Organisation (FAO).[74] Continued maritime delimitation disputes in the areas, which are subject to the dispute settlement provisions of UNCLOS as framework, conflict with the duty to cooperate in the management of fisheries which may also be served by the internationalisation. One such step is by "mapping out common fishing grounds where regional fishers can compete on equal footing for fish caught under agreed-upon rules."

Indeed, much is to be desired regarding compliance with Article 123 of UNCLOS. However, cooperation on marine living resources, environment protection, and marine scientific research may be more adequately settled at the regional level, as opposed to broader internationalisation under the United Nations system. Interestingly, Article 123 also imposes an obligation "to invite, as appropriate, *other interested States or international organizations* to cooperate with them..." (emphasis added). An equally meritorious case could also be made for a global rather than regional approach to the management of the abovementioned issues, especially since the South China Sea is of utmost importance to major non-littoral States such as the United States.

The absence for instance of a regional fisheries regime or organisation is indeed indicative of the real-life tension between sovereignty and international cooperation, even as these may not be necessarily mutually exclusive.[75] Indeed, there is scope, if not the necessity, for States bordering the South China Sea, to cooperate with each other in protecting and preserving the marine environment and conserving, managing, exploring, and exploiting the natural resources of the South China Sea. The littoral States need to consider the adoption of laws, regulation, and measures which are no less effective than international rules, standards, and recommended practices and procedures, and endeavour to harmonise their policies on these issues directly or through an appropriate regional organisation.[76]

Conclusion

The "duty to cooperate", notwithstanding the ambiguities presented above, is a theme that resonates in UNCLOS. This duty to cooperate is a fundamental principle of international environmental law and applies in particular to States bordering an enclosed or semi-enclosed sea. The duty to cooperate, despite its reverential place as a principle of customary international law is dependent on the precise context or "regime" upon which the duty operates.[77]

Within the context of UNCLOS, even the unilateral exercise of coastal States rights and obligations in areas under national jurisdiction implies some degree of cooperation. The duty to cooperate, in the words of Judge Wolfrum in his Separate Opinion in the *MOX Plant* case, "balances the principle of sovereignty of States and thus ensures that community interests are taken into account vis-a-vis individualistic State interests."[78]

This chapter raised three main concerns in the interpretation of UNCLOS obligations. First, there is confusion arising from the inconsistent use and shift between the mandatory and hortatory language of treaty obligations to cooperate. One example is that Article 123 deploys a mixture of both. In the *MOX Plant* arbitration case, it is worth remembering that Ireland noted that this places the provision in a situation where the hortatory aspect "may also have an effect upon the meaning of other provisions that are undoubtedly mandatory."[79] Whilst the Tribunal in the *Mox Plant* case did not provide much guidance or elaboration as to the content of the "duty to cooperate" principle, it did affirm its importance and provided an opportunity for the measures prescribed to serve as a guide in future cases with similar facts.

The reconciliation of hortatory and mandatory segments of a general duty to cooperate is of prime importance in order to achieve clarity within the particular provision in itself and in relation to others. The cause of this, of course, is bureaucratic in nature: conventions are negotiated piecemeal and inconsistencies arise, and as such, purely textual interpretations will have to be complemented by contextual analysis (e.g., of the *travaux preparatoires*) to better align interpretations with the intentions of drafters.

Second, interpretation of UNCLOS obligations can be affected by the fact that the Convention is silent with respect to the manner of publicity, and that some obligations to cooperate are of implicit nature. Another area explored above is the importance of a cascading standard of expression between particular obligations of notification, publicity, and other exchanges of information. This concept is relevant not only for UNCLOS interpretation itself but for broader negotiated texts regarding maritime regimes, such as a draft Code of Conduct in the South China Sea where the importance and gravity of certain obligations relative to each other must be properly reflected as an internally coherent hierarchy of duties.

The foregoing considered, the authors recommend a round of negotiations over an amendment to UNCLOS in order to clarify various obligations and conceptual-legal issues contained therein. However, it is also prudent to consider the negotiation not only out of pure technical necessity but in terms of broader geopolitical interests which could affect revisions if such an amendment takes place.

Third, as a practical measure, there needs to be a regional effort to thresh out a standard for obligations that better encourage State conduct to comply across a various range of topics, such as overfishing, degradation of the marine environment, innocent passage, and building of artificial installations. Instead of an amendment to UNCLOS itself, it may even perhaps be a more workable alternative to craft a particularistic regional approach with substantive buy-in of States bordering the semi-enclosed sea. Within ASEAN itself, there has been a trend toward so-called practical maritime cooperation activities, which sidestep issues of sovereignty and maritime delimitation under UNCLOS, in favour of negotiated ad hoc policy settlements. One such example is the tri-border patrol between Indonesia, Malaysia, and the Philippines which was created to respond to the ISIS threat in 2016, while shelving ongoing conflicting territorial claims amongst them.

However, even as practical maritime cooperation arrangements are easier to deploy on-the-ground, great caution must be exerted so they do not drift away from the legal framework created by UNCLOS and customary international law. Great powers may have the interest to undermine aspects of the Convention by negotiating practical mechanisms under the guise of an obligation to cooperate and amicably settle disputes. Great cognisance must be given to asymmetries in wealth, power, and diplomatic tools since resulting bilateral or multilateral agreements may potentially undermine international law.

Notes

1 United Nations Convention on the Law of the Sea, 1833 U.N.T.S. 397.
2 Satya N. Nandan and Shabtai Rosenne (eds.), *United Nations Convention on the Law of the Sea 1982: A Commentary* (Volume III, Martinus Nijhoff, 19995) at 343, 356, 365.
3 Permanent Court of Arbitration Case No. 2013–19, In the Matter of the South China Sea Arbitration before an Arbitral Tribunal Constituted Under Annex VII to the 1982 United Nations Convention on the Law of the Sea between the Republic of the Philippines and the People's Republic of China, Award, 12 July 2016. See, for example, Lowell Bautista, "The South China Sea Arbitral Award: Evolving Post-Arbitration Strategies, Implications, and Challenges," (2018) 10(2) *Asian Politics and Policy* 178–189.
4 Alfred Hu Nien-Tsu, "Semi-enclosed Troubled Waters: A New Thinking on the Application of the 1982 UNCLOS Article 123 to the South China Sea," (2010) 41 *Ocean Development & International Law* 281–314.
5 See for example, Vivian L. Forbes, *Conflict and Cooperation in Managing Maritime Space in Semi-enclosed Seas* (National University of Singapore Press, 2001); Jon M. Van Dyke and Sherry P. Broder, "Regional Maritime Cooperation in the South China Sea: COBSEA and PEMSEA," in Yann-huei Song and Keyuan Zou (eds.), *Major Law and Policy Issues in the South China Sea: European and American Perspectives* (Ashgate, 2014): 17–23; Hua Zhang, "The Duty of Cooperation in Semi-Enclosed Seas: Exploring the Way Forward for the South China Sea," in Keyuan Zou (ed.), *Maritime Cooperation in Semi-Enclosed Seas: Asian and European Experiences* (Brill, 2019) 30–49.
6 Seokwoo Lee and Jeong Woo Kim, 'UNCLOS and the Obligation to Cooperate: International Legal Framework for Semi-Enclosed Seas Cooperation', in Keyuan Zou (ed.), *Maritime Cooperation in Semi-Enclosed Seas: Asian and European Experiences* (Brill, 2019) 11–29.
7 Seokwoo Lee, "UNCLOS and the Obligation to Cooperate," NBR Special Report No. 37 (The National Bureau of Asian Research, 2012).
8 Nandan and Rosenne, *supra* note 2, at 345.
9 John O'Brien, *International Law* (Cavendish Publishing, 2001) at 625; P.W. Birnie and Alan Boyle, *International Law and the Environment* (Oxford University Press, 2001) at 126; Fisheries Jurisdiction Case (Federal Republic of Germany v Iceland) (1973) ICJ Rep 49; Elise Anne Clark, "Strengthening Regional Fisheries Management – An Analysis of the Duty to Cooperate," (2011) 9(2) *New Zealand Journal of Public and International Law* 223–246, at 234.
10 Article 1, United Nations, Charter of the United Nations, 24 October 1945, 1 UNTS XVI. [Hereinafter, UN Charter]. See also, Principle 24 of the Stockholm Declaration reads that: "International matters concerning the protection and improvement of the environment should be handled in a cooperative spirit by all countries big or small or on an even footing."
11 *See*, Resolution 2625 (XXV) Declaration on Principles of International Law concerning Friendly Relations and Co-operation among States in Accordance with the Charter of the United Nations, A/RES/25/2625, adopted on 24 October 1970, which proceeds from a preconceived terminology and also does not define the term "cooperation."
12 Yaron Gottlieb, "Combating Maritime Piracy: Inter-Disciplinary Cooperation and Information Sharing," (2014) 47 *Case Western Journal of International Law* 303–333, at 307.
13 Article 100, UNCLOS. Id.
14 See, e.g., Article 211(6)(b), UNCLOS.
15 See, e.g., Articles 73(4), 198, 211(6)(c), 217(7), 231, and 254(1), UNCLOS.
16 See, e.g., Articles 206, 211(3), and 250, UNCLOS.
17 See, e.g., Articles 41(3), 61(2), 64(1), 65, 66(3)(b), 66(4), 69(3), 70(4), 94(7), 98(2), 100, 108(1), 117, 118, 197, 199, 200, 201, 226(2), and 235(3), UNCLOS.
18 See, e.g., Articles 118 and 130(2), UNCLOS.
19 See, e.g., Articles 43 and 123, UNCLOS.
20 See, e.g., Article 129, UNCLOS.

21 See, e.g., Article 63(1) and (2), UNCLOS.
22 See, e.g., Article 143, UNCLOS.
23 Nandan and Rosenne, *supra* note 2, at 362–363.
24 Wimbledon Case, 1923 PCIJ Reports, Ser. A. No. 1.
25 See for example, Southern Bluefin Tuna Cases (New Zealand v. Japan; Australia v. Japan), Provisional Measures, ITLOS Cases Nos. 3 and 4, available at: https://www.itlos.org/cases/list-of-cases/case-no-3-4/
26 MOX Plant Case (Ireland v United Kingdom), ITLOS Case No. 10, available at: https://www.itlos.org/cases/list-of-cases/case-no-10/. (MOX Plant (Ireland v. United Kingdom), Provisional Measures, Order of 3 December 2001, ITLOS Reports 2001, p. 95, at p. 110, para. 82).
27 Request for an advisory opinion submitted by the Sub-Regional Fisheries Commission (SRFC), International Tribunal for the Law of the Sea, Case No. 21, 2 April 2015) [140], available at: https://www.itlos.org/affaires/role-des-affaires/affaire-no-21/. The Tribunal further held that "this obligation extends also to cases of alleged IUU fishing activities."
28 United Nations, Vienna Convention on the Law of Treaties, 23 May 1969, United Nations, Treaty Series, vol. 1155, p. 331. See Article 26.
29 Chronological lists of ratifications of, accessions and successions to the Convention and the related Agreements, available at: http://www.un.org/Depts/los/reference_files/chronological_lists_of_ratifications.htm
30 See International Tribunal for the Law of the Sea, List of Cases, available at: https://www.itlos.org/cases/list-of-cases/
31 Stable Seas Program. 2019. "Maritime Security Index." One Earth Future Foundation, available at: https://stableseas.org/issue-areas/international-cooperation
32 ICC International Maritime Bureau. 2019. "Piracy and Robbery Against Ships- 2018 Annual Report". London: ICC International Maritime Bureau.
33 See, for example, Ian Storey, "Trilateral Security Cooperation in the Sulu-Celebes Seas: A Work in Progress," (2018) 48 *ISEAS Perspective*, 27 August 2018.
34 Michail Risvas, "The Duty to Cooperate and the Protection of Underwater Cultural Heritage", (2013) 2(3) *Cambridge Journal of International & Comparative Law* 562, 569.
35 Article 41(5), UNCLOS.
36 Article 197, UNCLOS.
37 Article 98(2), UNCLOS.
38 Articles 69(3), 70(4), and 197, UNCLOS.
39 Article 41(5), UNCLOS.
40 Articles 61(2), 64(1), 65, 66(3)(b), and (4), 117, 118, UNCLOS.
41 Articles 69(3), 70(4), UNCLOS.
42 Article 94(7), UNCLOS.
43 Article 100, UNCLOS.
44 Article 108(1), UNCLOS.
45 Articles 200, 201, UNCLOS.
46 Article 130(2), UNCLOS.
47 Articles 197, 235(3), UNCLOS.
48 Article 226(2), UNCLOS.
49 Article 303(1), UNCLOS. See Article 149, UNCLOS (providing *lex specialis* with regard to the duty to cooperate under art. 303(1)). See also Risvas, *supra* note 34, at 572, arguing that reading

> Article 149 in the light of Article 303(1), it could be deduced that all states—and particularly the states of origin, either cultural origin or historical and archaeological origin—shall cooperate for the protection and preservation of UCH. Preferential rights (*in casu* those established in Article 149) do not imply the `extinction of concurrent rights of other states', which have to be determined through negotiations, and thus reinforce cooperation.
>
> (citing *Fisheries Jurisdiction* (U.K. v Iceland), Merits, 1974 ICJ Reports 3, 27–28, 32)

50 Moira L. McConnell and Edgar Gold, "The Modem Law of the Sea: Framework for the Protection and Preservation of the Marine Environment?", (1991) 23 *Case Western Reserve Journal of International Law* 83, 91.
51 Risvas, *supra* note 34, at 568.
52 Id., at 572.

53 Gottlieb, *supra* note 10, at 307.
54 Samuel Menefee, "Problems with Piracy, Maritime Terrorism, and the 1982 Convention on the Law of the Sea," (1990) 6 *Connecticut Journal of International Law* 6 (147).
55 Risvas, *supra* note 34, at 568–569 (internal citations omitted).
56 UNCLOS, art. 123 (emphases added).
57 *See* Final Award, Dispute Concerning Access to Information under Article 9 of the OSPAR Convention (Ireland v. UK), (PCA July 2, 2003), para. 129, available at: http://www.pcacases.com/web/sendAttach/121
58 Reply of Ireland, MOX Plant Case (Ireland v. UK), (PCA, Mar. 7, 2003), available at: http://www.pcacases.com/web/sendAttach/853, para. 7.17
59 Order No. 6, UNCLOS Arbitral Tribunal, June 6, 2008, available at: http://www.pca-cpa.org/MOX%20Plant%20Order%20No.%2061846.pdf?fil_id=1112
60 Reply of Ireland, *supra* note 54, para. 7.17.
61 Article 243 provides that "States and competent international organisations *shall cooperate, through the conclusion of bilateral and multilateral agreements*, to create favourable conditions for the conduct of marine scientific research…" (emphasis added).
62 Christopher Linebaugh, "Joint Development in a Semi-Enclosed Sea: China's Duty to Cooperate in Developing the Natural Resources of the South China Sea," (2014) 52 *Columbia Journal of Transnational Law* 542, 555 (2014).
63 Id., at 556. The author points out that, for example, with respect to Article 123(a), provisions such as Articles 61(2), 63, 117, and 118 already impose a duty to cooperate in the use and management of the living resources of the sea. With respect to Article 123(b), provisions such as Article 193 imposes a duty to cooperate with respect to the marine environment. And with respect to Article 123(c), Article 242 requires cooperation with respect to marine scientific research. Finally, with respect to Article 123(d), provisions such as Article 61(2), 197, and 242 requires cooperation with international organizations and one another.
64 Id., at 555 (emphasis in original).
65 See Final Award, *supra* note 57
66 Lee and Kim, *supra* note 6 at 25.
67 Phoebe N. Okowa, *State Responsibility for Transboundary Air Pollution in International Law* (Oxford University Press, 2000), 145, 165.
68 See, e.g., Article 231, UNCLOS; Article 61(5), UNCLOS.
69 Article 60(3), UNCLOS.
70 Article 302, UNCLOS (emphasis added).
71 Gottlieb, *supra* note 10, at 322.
72 Order of Dec. 3, 2001, *supra* note 26, para. 82.
73 Order of Oct. 8, 2003, Case concerning Land Reclamation by Singapore in and around the Straits of Johor (Malaysia v. Singapore), ITLOS case no. 12, paras. 92 and 106(1).
74 Marina Tsirbas. "Saving the South China Sea Fisher: Time to Internationalise." https://nsc.crawford.anu.edu.au/department-news/10725/saving-south-china-sea-fishery-time-internationalise
75 Nguyen Thanh Trung, "David and Goliath: Time for Southeast Asian Fishery Cooperation in the South China Sea," 20 June 2019, available at: https://amti.csis.org/davids-and-goliath-time-for-southeast-asian-fishery-cooperation-in-the-south-china-sea/
76 Robin M. Warner, "Stemming the Black Tide: Cooperation on Oil Pollution Preparedness and Response in the South China Sea and East Asian Seas," (2015) 18(2) *Journal of International Wildlife Law and Policy* 184–197, at 187.
77 Margaret A. Young and Sebastian Rioseco Sullivan, "Evolution through the Duty to Cooperate: Implications of the Whaling Case at the International Court of Justice," (2015) 16 *Melbourne Journal of International Law* 311–343, at 334.
78 Mox Plant Case, *supra* note 22. Separate opinion of Judge Wolfrum, at 135.
79 Reply of Ireland, *supra* note 54, para. 7.17.

18

ASEAN AND THE SOUTH CHINA SEA

*Robert Beckman and Vu Hai Dang**

Introduction

This chapter examines the role of the Association of Southeast Asia Nations (ASEAN) in the South China Sea disputes. It begins with a brief historical background of ASEAN, its institutions, and the principles the organization follows to achieve its objectives. Next, it provides a brief background on the sovereignty and maritime disputes in the South China Sea, and the role of ASEAN in those disputes. This chapter then gives an overview of the ASEAN and the ASEAN-led mechanisms which deal with the disputes in the South China Sea. It then examines the history of negotiations between ASEAN and China which led to the 2002 Declaration on the Conduct (DOC) of Parties in the South China Sea and the ongoing negotiations to agree on a Code of Conduct (COC) in the South China Sea. The relevant statements of the ASEAN Foreign Ministers relating to the disputes in the South China Sea are then summarized to determine the issues on which they have been able to reach a consensus. Finally, this chapter examines the possible impact of the ASEAN outlook on the Indo-Pacific on the ASEAN and the South China Sea disputes.

ASEAN: A brief historical background

Founding and treaty of amity and cooperation

ASEAN came into being at the height of the Cold War between the United States and the Soviet Union and during the fiercest days of the Viet Nam War. On 8 August 1967 in Bangkok, Thailand, Ministers of Foreign Affairs of five Southeast Asian countries (namely Indonesia, Malaysia, the Philippines, Singapore and Thailand) signed the ASEAN Declaration (Bangkok Declaration).[1] The Declaration formally established "an Association for Regional Cooperation among the countries of South-East Asia to be known as the Association

* The authors would like to acknowledge Mr. Tay Wei Xuan and Ms. Tasha Ng Chi En, students at the Faculty of Law, National University of Singapore, for their assistance in the completion of this chapter.

of South-East Asian Nations (ASEAN)".[2] According to the Bangkok Declaration, the aims and purposes of ASEAN were:

1 to accelerate the economic growth, social progress and cultural development in the region through joint endeavours in the spirit of equality and partnership in order to strengthen the foundation for a prosperous and peaceful community of South-East Asian Nations;
2 to promote regional peace and stability through abiding respect for justice and the rule of law in the relationship among countries of the region and adherence to the principles of the United Nations Charter;
3 to promote active collaboration and mutual assistance on matters of common interest in the economic, social, cultural, technical, scientific and administrative fields;
4 to provide assistance to each other in the form of training and research facilities in the educational, professional, technical and administrative spheres;
5 to collaborate more effectively for the greater utilization of their agriculture and industries, the expansion of their trade, including the study of the problems of international commodity trade, the improvement of their transportation and communications facilities and the raising of the living standards of their peoples;
6 to promote South-East Asian studies; and
7 to maintain close and beneficial cooperation with existing international and regional organizations with similar aims and purposes, and explore all avenues for even closer cooperation among themselves.[3]

In February 1976, at the first ASEAN Summit in Bali, Indonesia, the leaders of the five original members of ASEAN (Indonesian President Suharto, Malaysian Prime Minister Hussein Onn, Philippine President Ferdinand Marcos, Singaporean Prime Minister Lee Kuan Yew and Thai Prime Minister Kukrit Pramoj) signed the Treaty of Amity and Cooperation in Southeast Asia (TAC).[4] The purpose of TAC is to promote peace, amity and cooperation among its signing members.[5] It affirmed six fundamental principles which serve as guidance for the relations between them: (i) Mutual respect for the independence, sovereignty, equality, territorial integrity, and national identity of all nations; (ii) The right of every State to lead its national existence free from external interference, subversion or coercion; (iii) Non-interference in the internal affairs of the other; (iv) Settlement of differences or disputes by peaceful means; (v) Renunciation of the threat or use of force; and (vi) Effective cooperation among themselves.[6]

New members and the establishment of the ASEAN community

ASEAN has since doubled its membership, from its five founding member states in 1967 to ten. In 1984, Brunei became ASEAN's sixth member and in 1995, Viet Nam joined as its seventh member. Laos and Myanmar joined ASEAN in 1997. The last member was Cambodia, which joined ASEAN in 1999.

At the 9th ASEAN Summit in 2003, ASEAN leaders adopted the Declaration of ASEAN Concord II (Bali Concord II) which provided for the establishment of an ASEAN Community.[7] According to the Concord, the future ASEAN Community would comprise of three pillars: political and security cooperation, economic cooperation and socio-cultural cooperation. The ASEAN Security Community was established to bring ASEAN's political and security cooperation to a higher plane to ensure that countries in the region live at peace with one another and with the world at large in a just, democratic and harmonious environment. The ASEAN Economic Community is the realization of the end-goal of economic integration to create a stable, prosperous and highly competitive ASEAN economic region in which there is a free flow of goods, services, investment and a freer flow of capital, equitable economic development and reduced poverty. The ASEAN Socio-Cultural Community envisaged a Southeast Asia bonded together in partnership as a community of caring societies.[8]

ASEAN Charter

At the 13th ASEAN Summit in 2007, the ASEAN Charter was signed to serve as a foundation for building the ASEAN Community. The Charter provides the legal status and institutional framework for ASEAN. It codifies ASEAN norms, rules, and values and sets clear targets for ASEAN. It also contains provisions designed to increase the accountability of ASEAN Member States and to ensure their compliance with ASEAN decisions.[9] Pursuant to article 31 of the ASEAN Charter, the chairmanship of ASEAN rotates annually, based on the alphabetical order of the English names of Member States.[10]

The ASEAN way

ASEAN is well-known for its "ASEAN Way": the tradition of dealing with regional and international issues, especially the resolution of inter-State conflicts, in a manner strongly influenced by Asian traditions and values. It prefers consensus, consultation, informality, and non-confrontation, rather than the legally binding, high institutionalization and compliance-oriented approaches followed in regional groups such as the European Union.[11] The influence of the ASEAN Way may be observed in the ASEAN decision-making process, as enshrined in Article 20 of the ASEAN Charter, which states that "[a]s a basic principle, decision-making in ASEAN shall be based on consultation and consensus".[12]

ASEAN and the South China Sea: the background

ASEAN and the South China Sea in the 1990s

ASEAN began looking at the South China Sea issues in the late 1980s when China occupied six features in the Spratly Islands. In 1988, China used force to drive Viet Nam off Johnson Reef.[13] Tensions between China and Viet Nam increased in the early 1990s over oil concessions in Vanguard Bank, off the southern coast of Viet Nam.[14]

In January 1990, Indonesia convened the first Workshop on Managing Potential Conflicts in the South China Sea. This workshop process was headed by Ambassador Hasjim Djalal of Indonesia and Professor Ian Townsend-Gault of Canada, with funding from Canada, and became an important informal policy-oriented Track 2 forum for discussions on the South China Sea. The Workshops were attended by ASEAN Member States, China and Chinese Taipei.[15]

The first official ASEAN joint declaration on the South China Sea was issued in 1992.[16] This could have been a response to the adoption by China of the Law on the Territorial Sea and Contiguous Zone in February 1992,[17] which had prompted negative reactions from Indonesia, Malaysia and the Philippines.[18]

Tensions between China and the Philippines increased in 1995 after China occupied Mischief Reef in late 1994.[19] From the mid-1990s onward, there were regular incidents between China and Viet Nam, and between China and the Philippines. In 1997, tensions arose between the Philippines and China over Scarborough Shoal.[20] Tensions also continued between China and Viet Nam over exploration of oil and gas in Vanguard Bank.[21]

Malaysia had also occupied several of the Spratly Islands in the early 1980s, but there were no reported incidents between Malaysia and China in the 1990s.

Implications of ASEAN's policy of making decisions by consensus

ASEAN as a body takes decisions by consensus in order to further the purposes and principles of ASEAN as a regional institution. On some of the issues it faces, all ten Member States have a common interest. On others, however, their interests vary considerably.

The South China Sea is one of those issues on which the members have divergent interests. Four of its members – Brunei, Malaysia, the Philippines and Viet Nam – border the South China Sea and are "claimant States" in the sense that they claim sovereignty over some or all of the disputed features in the Spratly Islands, which are also claimed by China. In addition, Viet Nam claims sovereignty over the Paracel Islands, which are occupied and claimed by China. Indonesia is not a claimant State, but it borders the South China Sea and China's claim to sovereign rights and jurisdiction inside its nine-dash line map overlaps with Indonesia's claim to an exclusive economic zone from the Natuna Islands in the southern portion of the South China Sea. China's claim to rights and jurisdiction inside its nine-dash line also overlaps with the exclusive economic zone claims of Brunei, Malaysia, the Philippines, and Viet Nam. In addition, the maritime claims of the Philippines may also overlap with the maritime claims of Malaysia and Viet Nam. Consequently, five of the ten ASEAN Member States have a direct interest in the maritime and sovereignty disputes in the South China Sea.

On the other extreme, two of the ASEAN Member States have almost no interest in the South China Sea. Lao PDR is a land-locked State and Myanmar borders the Andaman Sea. While Cambodia and Thailand border the Gulf of Thailand rather than the South China Sea, they have an interest in the commercial shipping route connecting the Gulf of Thailand and the South China Sea. Singapore also has an interest in the South China Sea because the major shipping route between the Indian Ocean and East Asia passes through the Straits of Malacca and Singapore before entering the South China Sea.

Not only do the ASEAN Member States have divergent national interests in the maritime and sovereignty disputes in the South China Sea, but they also have different relationships with the major powers which have interests in the South China Sea, especially China. As a result, it is sometimes extremely difficult for the Member States to reach a consensus on statements concerning the South China Sea. To reach a consensus on some controversial issues, Member States must be willing to put their direct national interests aside and support what the group believes is in the interests of ASEAN as a whole. This is especially difficult when dealing with issues concerning China and the South China Sea, as some ASEAN Member States which have little or no national interests in the South China Sea have very close bilateral relations with China.

An example of the difficulties inherent in the ASEAN policy of decision-making by consensus is the failure of the ASEAN Foreign Ministers' Meeting to reach a consensus on the South China Sea paragraphs in the ASEAN Ministerial Meeting (AMM) Joint Communiqué, at the 45th AMM in July 2012 in Phnom Penh. Because of a deadlock on the wording relating to the South China Sea issue, the annual meeting of the ASEAN Foreign Ministers did not conclude with the customary Joint Communiqué for the first time. The Foreign Minister of Indonesia at the time, Marty Natalegawa, described this failure in his book on ASEAN as one of the lowest points of his experience of ASEAN cooperation.[22]

One of the most significant developments on the South China Sea was the decision by the Philippines in 2013 to institute arbitral proceedings against China under Annex VII of the 1982 United Nations Convention on the Law of the Sea (UNCLOS).[23] China refused to participate in the case and adopted a policy of non-participation and non-compliance. Nevertheless, the case proceeded, and the Arbitral Tribunal made its decision on the merits of the case in July 2016.[24] Although this case was obviously of great interest to the claimant States in the South China Sea, the ASEAN Foreign Ministers were never able to reach a consensus on any language about the arbitration case to be included in their annual statements on the South China Sea. In his book on ASEAN, the Foreign Minister of Indonesia, Marty Natalegawa made the following comments on this issue:

> ASEAN has regretfully thus far been incapable or unwilling to collectively and explicitly make reference to the award [...] the silence by ASEAN on the PCA Award is deafening. [...] For an organization that has incessantly emphasized the primacy of the rule of law and the efficacy of diplomacy, this is a position that is difficult to countenance.[25]

ASEAN mechanisms dealing with the South China Sea issues

ASEAN Summit

The ASEAN Summit comprises Heads of State or Government of ASEAN Member States. It is the supreme policy-making body of ASEAN which deliberates, provides policy guidance, and takes decisions on key issues pertaining to the realization of ASEAN objectives and important matters of interests to the Member States. The ASEAN Summit is usually held twice a year, hosted by the Member State holding ASEAN Chairmanship.[26] So far 35 ASEAN Summits have been held and the South China Sea issue has been on the agenda since the 4th ASEAN Summit in 1992.

During the latest 37th ASEAN Summit held on 12 November 2020 in Hanoi, Viet Nam, ASEAN Leaders discussed various issues, including the South China Sea.[27] On the South China Sea, ASEAN Leaders discussed some concerns on the land reclamations and activities in the area, which have eroded trust and confidence, increased tensions, and may undermine peace, security and stability in the region. They reaffirmed the need to enhance mutual trust and confidence, exercise self-restraint in the conduct of activities, avoid actions that may further complicate the situation and pursue peaceful resolution of disputes in accordance with international law, including the 1982 UNCLOS. They emphasized the importance of non-militarization and self-restraint in the conduct of all activities by claimants and all other states, including those mentioned in the DOC that could further complicate the situation and escalate tensions in the South China Sea.[28]

ASEAN Foreign Ministers Meeting

The ASEAN Foreign Ministers' Meeting (AMM), the first Ministerial Sectoral Body of ASEAN, met for the first time in Bangkok in 1967 during which they adopted the ASEAN Declaration (Bangkok Declaration).[29] According to the Bangkok Declaration, AMM should meet annually by rotation.[30] Since then, AMM has held 53 annual meetings to discuss the

ASEAN political-security cooperation and external relations. The AMM is assisted by the ASEAN Senior Officials' Meeting (ASEAN SOM) in the performance of its duty.[31]

The latest 53rd ASEAN Foreign Ministers Meeting was held on 31st July 2019 in Bangkok, Thailand. During this meeting, ASEAN Foreign Ministers discussed various issues including the ASEAN Outlook for the Indo-Pacific and the South China Sea.[32] On the South China Sea, ASEAN Foreign Ministers discussed the situation in the South China Sea, during which concerns were expressed by some Ministers on the land reclamations, activities and serious incidents in the area, which have eroded trust and confidence, increased tensions and may undermine peace, security and stability in the region. They reaffirmed the need to enhance mutual trust and confidence, exercise self-restraint in the conduct of activities, avoid actions that may further complicate the situation, and pursue peaceful resolution of disputes in accordance with international law, including the 1982 UNCLOS. They emphasized the importance of non-militarization and self-restraint in the conduct of all activities by claimants and all other states, including those mentioned in the DOC that could further complicate the situation and escalate tensions in the South China Sea.[33]

ASEAN Defence Ministers Meeting

The ASEAN Defence Ministers Meeting (ADMM) was established in 2006 with the objective of promoting regional peace and stability through dialogue and cooperation in defence and security; to give guidance to existing senior defence and military officials dialogue and cooperation in the field of defence and security within ASEAN and between ASEAN and dialogue partners; to promote mutual trust and confidence through a greater understanding of defence and security challenges as well as enhancement of transparency and openness; to contribute to the establishment of an ASEAN Security Community and to promote the implementation of the Vientiane Action Programme. The ADMM meets every year with the Agenda focusing on exchanging views on regional and international security and defence issues, voluntary briefings on defence and security policies, discussing related activities outside the ASEAN process, discussing interaction with external partners, and reviewing ASEAN defense cooperation. The ADMM is assisted by an ASEAN Defence Senior Officials Meeting (ADSOM).[34]

At the latest 14th annual meeting held on line on 9 December 2020 the ADMM discussed various issues including the South China Sea.[35] On the South China Sea, the Ministers emphasized the need to maintain and promote an environment conducive to the early conclusion of an effective and substantive Code of Conduct in the South China Sea in accordance with international law, including UNCLOS, while underlining the full and effective implementation of the Declaration of Conduct of the Parties in the South China Sea in its entirety. They also welcomed confidence building measures such as Code for Unplanned Encounters at Sea, Guidelines for Air Military Encounters, Guidelines for Maritime Interaction, and the ASEAN Direct Communications Infrastructure and other activities under the DOC framework to promote communication, mutual trust and confidence, and reduce tensions and the risk of accidents, misunderstandings and miscalculation in the air and at sea.[36]

ASEAN-led mechanisms that consider the South China Sea issues

East Asia Summit

The East Asia Summit (EAS) is a forum among Leaders of 18 countries of the Asia-Pacific region formed to further the objectives of regional peace, security and prosperity. EAS

Membership includes ten ASEAN Member States, Australia, China, India, Japan, New Zealand, Republic of Korea, Russia and the United States.[37] The first EAS was held on 14 December 2005 in Kuala Lumpur, Malaysia with the participation of Heads of States of ASEAN, Australia, China, India, Japan, Republic of Korea, New Zealand.[38] The United States and Russia formally became members at the 6th EAS in 2011.[39]

To date, 15 EAS have been organized. During the latest 15th EAS held on 14 November 2020 via videoconference the Leaders discussed various topics.[40] On the South China Sea, EAS leaders discussed some concerns on the land reclamations and activities in the area, which have eroded trust and confidence, increased tensions, and may undermine peace, security and stability in the region. They reaffirmed the need to enhance mutual trust and confidence, exercise self-restraint in the conduct of activities and avoid actions that may further complicate the situation, and pursue peaceful resolution of disputes in accordance with international law, including the 1982 UNCLOS. They emphasized the importance of non-militarization and self-restraint in the conduct of all activities by claimants and all other states, including those mentioned in the DOC that could further complicate the situation and escalate tensions in the South China Sea.[41]

Bilateral ASEAN + 1 Summits

ASEAN has maintained regular bilateral Summit-level meetings with a number of partners, such as Australia, China, Republic of Korea, Japan, India and the United States.

ASEAN Defence Ministers Meetings Plus (ADDM-Plus)

At the 2nd ASEAN Defence Minister Meeting in 2007, ASEAN Ministers of Defence adopted the concept paper to establish ADMM-Plus, which serves as a platform for ASEAN and its Dialogue Partners to strengthen security and defence cooperation for peace, stability and development in the region.[42] The objectives of ADMM-Plus are to benefit ASEAN member countries in building capacity to address shared security challenges, while cognisant of the differing capacities of various ASEAN countries; to promote mutual trust and confidence between defence establishments through greater dialogue and transparency; to enhance regional peace and stability through cooperation in defence and security, in view of the transnational security challenges the region faces; to contribute to the realization of an ASEAN Security Community and to facilitate the implementation of the Vientiane Action Programme.[43] Participants of ADMM Plus are Ministers of Defence from the ten ASEAN Member States and eight ASEAN Dialogue Partners, namely Australia, China, India, Japan, New Zealand, Republic of Korea, Russian Federation, and the United States. ADMM-Plus meets yearly, back-to-back with the ADMM.

ASEAN Regional Forum

The convening of the ASEAN Regional Forum (ARF) was agreed upon by ASEAN Ministers of Foreign Affairs at the 26th AMM in 1993[44] with objectives being to foster constructive dialogue and consultation on political and security issues of common interest and concern, and to make significant contributions to efforts towards confidence-building and preventive diplomacy in the Asia-Pacific region.[45] The first ARF was held in 1994 in Bangkok, Thailand. Participants of the ARF comprise the ASEAN member states, the observers, and consultative and dialogue partners of ASEAN.[46]

At the latest 27th ARF Meeting in 2020 in Hanoi Viet Nam, Ministers discussed the matters relating to the South China Sea and concerns were expressed on the land reclamations and activities in the area, which have eroded trust and confidence, increased tensions, and may undermine peace, security and stability in the region. They reaffirmed the need to enhance mutual trust and confidence, exercise self-restraint in the conduct of activities and avoid actions that may further complicate the situation, and pursue peaceful resolution of disputes in accordance with international law, including 1982 UNCLOS. The Ministers emphasized the importance of non-militarization and self-restraint in the conduct of all activities by claimants and all other states, including those mentioned in the DOC[47] that could further complicate the situation and escalate tensions in the South China Sea.[48]

China-ASEAN negotiations on a Code of Conduct

2002 Declaration on Conduct of Parties in the South China Sea

The establishment of a Code of Conduct for all relevant parties in the South China Sea was first suggested in the 1992 Declaration on the South China Sea by ASEAN Ministers of Foreign Affairs at the 25th AMM.[49]

The first codes of conduct on the South China Sea were adopted bilaterally between the Philippines and China, and the Philippines and Viet Nam in 1995.[50] These two codes of conduct demonstrated the willingness and determination of parties concerned to resolve their territorial and jurisdictional disputes by peaceful means, without resorting to the use or threat to use of force, through friendly consultations and negotiations by sovereign States directly concerned, in accordance with universally recognized principles of international law, including UNCLOS. They also undertook to promote suitable forms of bilateral and multilateral cooperation in environmental protection, safety of navigation, prevention of piracy, marine scientific research, disaster mitigation and control, search and rescue, meteorology, and maritime pollution control.[51]

The proposal for a regional Code of Conduct was then endorsed at the 29th AMM in Jakarta, Indonesia in 1995. The two bilateral codes of conduct were to serve as models.[52] The Philippines and Viet Nam were requested to prepare a draft of the Code of Conduct for ASEAN,[53] which was then recognized by the 32nd AMM[54] and ASEAN Third Informal Meeting in 1999.[55] The ASEAN Draft Code of Conduct was presented to China during the 6th ARF Meeting in 1999.[56] China was at first reluctant but later seemed to be quite interested in suggesting its own version of the draft code.[57] The 1st ASEAN-China Consultation on the Code of Conduct on the South China Sea was held in Hua Hin, Thailand in 2000.

During these negotiations between the ASEAN and China, important disagreements appeared. For instance, China rejected the mention of Paracels in the disputed areas and the commitments to refrain from occupying new islands, reefs, or shoals. ASEAN objected to China's proposal to ban multilateral military exercises and military patrols in the Spratlys. These differences seemed to be irreconcilable.

To resolve the deadlock in negotiations, Malaysia suggested at the 35th AMM in July 2002 in Brunei to have a "declaration on the conduct", which would be less binding than a "code of conduct".[58] This suggestion was endorsed by the AMM.[59] China also accepted the idea of a declaration of conduct. The result was the adoption of the 2002 DOC in the South China Sea by Ministers of Foreign Affairs of China and ASEAN in November 2002 in Phnom Penh, Cambodia.

The DOC has no provisions on the controversial issues that had been raised by the parties in the negotiations. It only refers to the South China Sea and does not state exactly where it applies. It does not ban military exercises and military patrols. In fact, most of the DOC's content is very similar to the 1992 ASEAN Declaration on the South China Sea and the two bilateral codes of conduct adopted in 1995.[60] Its provisions include respect for international law, peaceful resolution of disputes, respect for freedom of navigation and overflight, the exercise of self-restraint, confidence-building measures, and cooperative activities. However, the DOC also reaffirmed that the adoption of a code of conduct in the South China Sea would further promote peace and stability in the region, and reiterated the Parties' commitment to working, on the basis of consensus, towards the eventual attainment of this objective.[61]

2011 Guidelines for implementation of the 2002 DOC

In 2004, two years after the adoption of DOC, the 1st ASEAN-China Senior Officials Meeting for the implementation of the DOC (SOM-DOC) was convened in Kuala Lumpur, Malaysia to set up a Joint Working Group to implement the DOC (JWG-DOC).[62] Its Terms of Reference stated that the JWG would formulate recommendations in guidelines and action plans for the implementation of the DOC, specific cooperative activities in the South China Sea, a register of experts and eminent persons who may provide technical inputs, non-binding and professional views or policy recommendations to the JWC-DOC, and the convening of workshops, as the needs arose.[63]

Due to the disagreements between the two sides on the specific content of the guidelines for the implementation of the DOC, it took seven years for China and ASEAN to reach an agreement on the guidelines.[64] At the 44th ASEAN PMC+1 (Post Ministerial Conference) Session with China in July 2011, a set of Guidelines for Implementation of the DOC was adopted.[65] The objective of the Guidelines is to guide the implementation of possible joint cooperative activities, measures and projects as provided for in the DOC. As such, seven guiding principles were agreed:

1 The implementation of the DOC should be carried out in a step-by-step approach in line with the provisions of the DOC.
2 The Parties to the DOC will continue to promote dialogue and consultations in accordance with the spirit of the DOC.
3 The implementation of activities or projects as provided for in the DOC should be clearly identified.
4 The participation in the activities or projects should be carried out on a voluntary basis.
5 Initial activities to be undertaken under the ambit of the DOC should be confidence-building measures.
6 The decision to implement concrete measures or activities of the DOC should be based on consensus among parties concerned, and lead to the eventual realization of a Code of Conduct.
7 In the implementation of the agreed projects under the DOC, the services of the Experts and Eminent Persons, if deemed necessary, will be sought to provide specific inputs on the projects concerned.
8 Progress of the implementation of the agreed activities and projects under the DOC shall be reported annually to the ASEAN-China Ministerial Meeting (PMC).[66]

ASEAN-China confidence-building measures from 2014 to 2018

From 2014 to 2018, a series of confidence-building measures were adopted by China and ASEAN in order to build trust and confidence between the parties.

In 2014, at the 17th ASEAN-China Summit in Nay Pyi Taw, Myanmar, leaders of ASEAN and China agreed to support

> the adoption of the first list of commonalities on COC [Code of Conduct] consultation, the establishment of a hotline platform among search and rescue agencies, a hotline among foreign ministries on maritime emergencies, and a table-top exercise on search and rescue to promote and enhance trust and confidence in the region.[67]

These measures were considered "early harvest measures" to build trust and confidence among relevant parties and to avoid miscalculations and incidents on the ground in the South China Sea.[68] The details for the implementation of these measures were discussed in 2016 at the 11th SOM-DOC.[69]

At the 19th ASEAN-China Summit in 2016, leaders of both sides adopted the Joint Statement on the application of the Code for Unplanned Encounters at Sea (CUES)[70] in the South China Sea and the guidelines for hotline communications among senior officials of the Ministries of Foreign Affairs of the ASEAN Member States and China in response to maritime emergencies in the implementation of the DOC.[71] The joint statement on the application of the CUES reaffirms the commitments of China and ASEAN to the CUES, in order to improve the operational safety of naval ships and naval aircraft in the air and at sea, and contains the parties' agreement to use the safety and communication procedures for the safety of all their naval ships and naval aircraft, as set out in the CUES, when they encounter each other in the South China Sea.[72] The guidelines for hotline communications aim to ensure immediate and effective exchange of information and views, and coordination among the Ministries of Foreign Affairs of the ASEAN Member States and China regarding maritime emergencies that require immediate policy-level intervention. The guidelines provide for the designation of a contact point for the Ministries of Foreign Affairs' hotline communications, and procedures for undertaking actions.[73] The ASEAN Member States and China successfully conducted a hotline test exercise from 18 to 24 April 2017.[74]

In addition, a maritime exercise between ASEAN and China was organized in 2018 as another confidence-building measure. The maritime exercise took place in two phases. The first phase was a table-top exercise from 2 to 3 August 2018 in Changi Naval Base, Singapore in which navies from the ASEAN Member States and China developed plans to deal with maritime incidents such as search and rescue operations, and medical evacuation.[75] The second phase was a field training exercise taking place from 22 to 27 October 2018 in Ma Xie Naval Base, Zhejiang, China in which 1,000 personnel and eight ships from both sides undertook joint search and rescue operations, and medical evacuation drills with the use of helicopters. The CUES was used as the basis for activities in both exercises.[76] Although largely symbolic, these inaugural ASEAN-China maritime exercises were considered the first step forward in promoting practical measures for confidence-building and maritime safety in the South China Sea.[77]

The Declaration for a Decade of Coastal and Marine Environmental Protection in the South China Sea was adopted on 13 November 2017 at the 20th ASEAN-China Summit in Manila, Philippines, on the occasion of the 15th anniversary of the signing of the DOC.[78] The Declaration declared that 2017–2027 would be the "Decade for the Protection of Coastal and Marine Environment in the South China Sea". Governments of the ASEAN Member States and China are committed to taking action for the protection, preservation, and sustainable management of the coastal and marine environment of the South China Sea.[79]

Renewed negotiations on the Code of Conduct leading to Single Draft Negotiating Text

China expressed interest in renewing the negotiations for a COC with ASEAN in 2013. Some observers opine that this was probably linked to the fact that in January 2013 the Philippines had instituted arbitral proceedings against China under Annex VII of the 1982 UNCLOS.[80] At the 19th ASEAN-China Senior Officials' Consultation in Beijing, China in April 2013, Chinese officials announced their willingness to commence discussions with ASEAN on a COC later in the year.[81] In August 2013, at a press conference in Hanoi, Viet Nam, Chinese Minister of Foreign Affairs, Mr. Wang Yi, stated that China and ASEAN had "agreed to hold consultations [as distinct from negotiations] on moving forward the process on the Code of Conduct in the South China Sea under the framework of implementing the Declaration on the DOC in the South China Sea".[82] ASEAN and China held their first formal consultation on the COC at the 6th ASEAN-China SOM-DOC and the 9th ASEAN-China JWC-DOC in Suzhou, China, 14–15 September 2013. At the consultation, it was agreed that parties would adopt a step-by-step approach to reach consensus on the COC process through consultation, starting from identifying the consensus before gradually expanding it and narrowing differences.[83] At the 16th ASEAN-China Summit in October 2013, leaders of both sides welcomed the positive outcomes achieved at the first official consultation on the COC and agreed to maintain the momentum of regular official consultations, and work towards the adoption of the COC.[84]

After two rounds of consultations, both sides agreed on the first list of commonalities on COC consultation at the 8th SOM-DOC in August 2014.[85] At the 17th ASEAN-China Summit in 2014, China and ASEAN considered the adoption of the first list of commonalities on COC consultation an "early harvest measure" to promote and enhance trust and confidence in the region.[86] At the 9th SOM-DOC in July 2015, they concluded that by adopting the second list of commonalities, the COC consultation had entered a new stage.[87] At the 10th SOM-DOC in October 2015, two preliminary leaving documents were formulated, namely the list of crucial and complex issues and the list of elements for the outline of a COC.[88] At the ASEAN PMC 10 + 1 Session with China in August 2015, the Meeting welcomed the recent agreement between the ASEAN Member States and China to proceed to the next stage of consultations towards the establishment of the COC and looked forward to the expeditious negotiations on the framework, structure and elements of the COC.[89] At the same time, the Ministers of Foreign Affairs of ASEAN and China issued a joint statement on the full and effective implementation of the DOC, in which the Parties reaffirmed that the adoption of a code of conduct in the South China Sea would further promote peace and stability in the region, and agreed to work towards the eventual attainment of this objective on the basis of consensus.[90]

At the 14th SOM-DOC in May 2017, a draft framework was submitted to the ASEAN PMC 10+1 session with China in August 2017 in Manila, Philippines.[91] The Ministers of Foreign Affairs of China and ASEAN adopted the Framework and tasked their Senior Officials to start substantive consultations and negotiations on the COC. The Framework contains three parts: Preambular Provisions, General Provisions and Final Clauses. Most of the provisions and principles are similar to the DOC, but there are some notable differences. First, it is clearly stated that the COC is not an instrument to settle territorial disputes or maritime delimitation issues. Second, there is a clause States not parties to respect the principles contained in the COC. Third, there is a clause stating that it is necessary to include mechanisms to monitor the implementation of its provisions. There are no provisions on some of the more controversial issues, such as the geographic scope of the agreement and an enforcement mechanism.[92]

At the 15th SOM-DOC in June 2018, a Single Draft COC Negotiating Text (SDNT) was adopted by officials from ASEAN and China. The officials agreed that this would be a living document; it would serve as the basis for the negotiations and its content would be kept strictly confidential throughout the entire process. They further agreed that there would be at least three readings of the SDNT. Finally, they decided to submit the text to the ASEAN PMC 10+1 Session with China in August 2018, and leave the announcement that ASEAN and China had agreed on the SDNT for the ASEAN-China PMC.[93] At the ASEAN PMC 10 + 1 Session with China in August 2018 in Singapore, Ministers of Foreign Affairs of ASEAN and China

> noted that ASEAN Member States and China had agreed on a Single Draft Code of Conduct in the SCS (COC) Negotiating Text at the 15th ASEAN-China Senior Officials' Meeting on the Implementation of the Declaration on the Conduct of Parties in the SCS in Changsha, China on 27 June 2018, and encouraged further progress towards an effective COC.[94]

In that same year, Chinese Prime Minister Li Keqiang stated that China hoped the COC consultations would complete in three years.[95]

In 2019, ASEAN and China completed the first reading of the SDNT and exchanged views on the second reading at the SOM-DOC level.[96] At the ASEAN PMC 10+1 Session with China and 22nd ASEAN-China Summit, both sides welcomed the completion of the first reading of the SDNT and the commencement of the second reading of the SDNT. They also welcomed the aspiration to conclude the COC within a three-year timeline as proposed by China.[97]

Positions of ASEAN Foreign Ministers on issues in the South China Sea

This section summarizes the ASEAN position regarding the issues in South China Sea issue by examining the joint statements of the AMM on the South China Sea from the adoption of the ASEAN Declaration on the South China Sea in 1992. As seen in previous sections, the AMM is the main actor in ASEAN when dealing with the South China Sea. The AMM is also responsible for overseeing the negotiations with China on the COC. The main issues that have been repeated in the declarations and joint communiqués of AMMs are as follows:

1 *Resolution of all sovereignty and jurisdictional issues in the South China Sea by peaceful means without resort to force or threat of force in accordance with recognized principles of international law including 1982 UNCLOS*:

The ASEAN Declaration on the South China Sea in 1992 called for the resolution of all sovereignty and jurisdictional disputes in the South China Sea by peaceful means without resort to force.[98] At the 29th AMM in 1996, the expression was changed to "to resolve the problem by peaceful means in accordance with recognized international law in general and the UNCLOS of 1982 in particular".[99] Since 1999, it has become "in accordance with recognized principles of international law, including the 1982 United Nations Convention on the Law of the Sea".[100] At the latest meeting, 53rd AMM in 2020, ASEAN Foreign Ministers reaffirmed the need to "pursue peaceful resolution of disputes in accordance with international law, including the 1982 UNCLOS".[101]

2 *Exercise of self-restraint*

The 1992 ASEAN Declaration on the South China Sea urged all parties concerned to exercise restraint with a view to creating a positive climate for the eventual resolution of all disputes.[102] From 1995, the expression was changed to exercise of "self-restraint".[103] Since 2015, the expression used has been "to exercise self-restraint in the conduct of activities that would complicate or escalate the dispute".[104] In 2017, the call for self-restraint was clarified as being applicable to "claimants and all other states".[105] At the 53rd AMM, ASEAN Foreign Ministers emphasized the importance of self-restraint in the conduct of all activities by claimants and all other states, including those mentioned in the DOC, that could further complicate the situation and escalate tensions in the South China Sea.[106]

3 *Conclusion of the COC*

The 1992 ASEAN Declaration on the South China Sea commanded all parties concerned to apply the principles contained in the Treaty of Amity and Cooperation in Southeast Asia as the basis for establishing a code of international conduct over the South China Sea.[107] At the 29th AMM in 1996, ASEAN Foreign Ministers endorsed the idea of concluding a regional code of conduct in the South China Sea which will lay the foundation for long-term stability in the area and foster understanding among claimant countries.[108] At the 35th AMM in 2002, while agreeing to work towards a Declaration on the Conduct of Parties in the South China Sea, ASEAN Foreign Ministers reaffirmed that the adoption of a code of conduct in the South China Sea further would promote peace and stability in the region.[109] After the adoption of the DOC, ASEAN Ministers affirmed that the DOC was an important step towards a Code of Conduct in the South China Sea.[110] Since the process of consultations and negotiations between ASEAN and China on the COC began, ASEAN Foreign Ministers have been calling all parties to work expeditiously for the early adoption of an effective COC. At the 53rd AMM, the Ministers "were encouraged by the progress of substantive negotiations towards the early conclusion of an effective and substantive Code of Conduct in the South China Sea (COC) within a mutually-agreed timeline".[111]

4 *Confidence-building measures and cooperative activities*

The 1992 ASEAN Declaration on the South China Sea resolved, without prejudicing the sovereignty and jurisdiction of countries having direct interest in the area, to explore the possibility of cooperation in the South China Sea relating to the safety of maritime navigation and communication, protection against pollution of the marine environment, coordination of search and rescue operations, efforts towards combatting piracy and armed robbery, as well as collaboration in the campaign against illicit trafficking in drugs.[112] By 2001, ASEAN Foreign Ministers seemed to recognize the significance of confidence-building measures and cooperative measures within the framework of the Indonesian Informal Workshops Series on Managing Potential Conflicts in the South China Sea. For instance, at the 34th AMM in 2001, the Ministers were "satisfied with the on-going South China Sea Workshops on Managing Potential Conflict in the South China Sea through dialogue, confidence-building and cooperative measures".[113] At the 36th AMM in 2003, the Ministers urged all concerned parties to undertake the confidence-building and cooperative measures called for in accordance with the DOC.[114]

Since the 38th AMM in 2005, the Ministers have started to mention confidence-building in general as they "[encourage] all parties concerned to [...] continue to undertake confidence-building measures that would contribute to the maintenance of peace and stability in the region".[115] During the 53rd AMM, the Ministers stressed the importance of undertaking confidence-building and preventive measures to enhance, among others, trust and confidence amongst parties.[116]

4 *Implementation of the DOC*

After the DOC was adopted, at the 36th AMM in 2003, ASEAN Foreign Ministers stressed the need for observance of the provisions of the DOC and urged all concerned parties to undertake the confidence-building measures called for in accordance with the Declaration.[117] At the 37th AMM, the Ministers welcomed the stock-taking in the implementation of all provisions of the DOC.[118] At the 38th AMM in 2005, ASEAN Foreign Ministers endorsed the establishment of the ASEAN-China Joint Working Group to study and recommend measures to translate the provisions of the DOC into concrete cooperative activities. At the 39th AMM in 2006, the Ministers noted the convening of the 2nd ASEAN-China Senior Officials' Meeting on the Implementation of the DOC and the convening of the First and Second Meetings on the ASEAN-China Joint Working Group on the Implementation of the DOC as a concrete step towards the full implementation of the DOC.[119] During the period 2007–2009, the Ministers underscored the need to intensify efforts to move forward with the implementation of the DOC.[120] In 2012, the ASEAN Foreign Ministers agreed to the Six-Point Principles proposed by Indonesian Foreign Minister Marty Natalegawa and called for the full implementation of the DOC.[121] In 2014, the expression was changed to a call for "full and effective implementation of the DOC"[122] and since 2015, the phrase "in its entirety" has been added.[123] At the 53rd AMM in 2020, ASEAN Foreign Ministers underscored the importance of the full and effective implementation of the DOC in its entirety.[124]

5 *Supporting the Indonesian South China Sea Workshops on Managing the Potential Conflicts in the South China Sea*

During all AMM meetings in the 1990s and early 2000s, ASEAN Foreign Ministers expressed support for the Indonesian-led Workshops on Managing Potential Conflicts in the South China Sea. According to the Ministers, the Workshops promoted understanding, confidence-building among the countries concerned of the issues involved and cooperative activities.[125] This support was repeated again at the 44th AMM in 2011, during which the ASEAN Foreign Ministers stated that the Workshops had been able to encourage cooperation with a view to fostering trust and understanding among participants.[126]

6 *Respect for freedom of navigation and overflight*

Respect for freedom of navigation and overflight was mentioned for the first time by the 28th AMM in 1995, during which the ASEAN Foreign Ministers called for all parties to refrain from taking actions that could destabilize the region, including possibly undermining the freedom of navigation and aviation in the affected areas.[127] During the period 2000–2002, the Ministers welcomed all parties to ensure the freedom of navigation in the South China Sea.[128] Since 2010, the expression has changed to "respect the freedom of navigation in and over-flight above the South China Sea".[129] In 2016, the term "safety" was also added.[130] At the 53rd AMM, ASEAN Foreign Ministers reaffirmed the importance of maintaining and promoting, *inter alia*, safety and freedom of navigation in and overflight above the South China Sea.[131]

7 *Non-militarization*

Non-militarization was mentioned for the first time in the joint communiqué of the 49th AMM in 2016, which stated that ASEAN Foreign Ministers emphasized the importance of non-militarization in the conduct of all activities.[132] Since 2017, the principle has appeared in all of AMM's joint communiqués with the addition of "by claimants and all other states".[133] At the 53rd AMM, the Ministers emphasized the importance of non-militarization in the conduct of all activities of claimants and other states.[134]

8 *Concerns about incidents and land reclamation activities*

ASEAN Foreign Ministers expressed concerns over events in the South China Sea during the 28th, 29th and 30th AMMs from 1995 to 1997.[135] At the 44th AMM in 2011, the ASEAN Foreign Ministers expressed serious concern over the recent incidents.[136] In their statement on the current developments in the South China Sea in 2014 in Nay Pyi Taw, the ASEAN Foreign Ministers also expressed "serious concerns over the ongoing developments in the South China Sea, which have increased tensions in the area".[137] At the 48th AMM in 2015, the Ministers "took note of serious concerns expressed by some Ministers" on the land reclamations in the South China Sea, which have eroded trust and confidence, increased tensions, and may undermine peace, security and stability in the South China Sea.[138] At the 49th AMM in 2016, the Ministers "remain seriously concerned over recent developments" and took note of the concerns expressed by some Ministers on the land reclamations "and escalation of activities" in the area, which have eroded trust and confidence, increased tensions, and may undermine peace, security and stability in the region.[139] These expressions have been repeated during 53rd AMM Meeting in 2020.[140]

2019 ASEAN Outlook on the Indo-Pacific and the South China Sea

At the 34th ASEAN Summit in June 2019 in Bangkok, Thailand, the ASEAN leaders adopted the ASEAN Outlook on the Indo-Pacific to help guide ASEAN's engagement and cooperation in the wider Indo-Pacific region.[141]This was a result of lobbying efforts by Indonesia.[142] The Outlook envisages ASEAN centrality as the underlying principle for promoting cooperation in the Indo-Pacific region, with ASEAN-led mechanisms such as East Asian Summits as platforms for dialogue and cooperation. It also defines four broad range of areas in which ASEAN will undertake cooperation: maritime cooperation, connectivity, UN sustainable development goals 2030, and economic and other areas.[143]

The ASEAN Outlook on the Indo-Pacific is a response to the "Free and Open Indo-Pacific" strategy of the United States, the increased US-China competition, and the emergence of several Indo-Pacific initiatives. The objective of the Outlook is to preserve ASEAN autonomy against the intensifying competition between the United States and China in the Asia-Pacific region. ASEAN is concerned about regional polarization and a weakening of its central role. The ASEAN Outlook is more than a simple hedging move between two superpowers. It is a proactive approach designed to establish an inclusive multipolar regional architecture to promote confidence-building measures, preventive diplomacy, and cooperative security.[144]

The content of the ASEAN Outlook relating to maritime cooperation can shed some light on future ASEAN policy on the South China Sea. Pursuant to the Outlook, ASEAN will "prevent, manage and eventually resolve" maritime issues such as unresolved maritime disputes, unsustainable exploitation of maritime resources, and marine pollution in a more focused, peaceful and comprehensive way. The maritime cooperation will be carried out in accordance with universally recognized principles of international law including the 1982

UNCLOS. The areas of cooperation include the peaceful settlement of disputes, sustainable management of marine resources, marine pollution, and marine scientific research.[145]

The ASEAN Outlook does not signal a change in ASEAN policy towards the South China Sea. Rather, ASEAN policy towards the South China Sea will likely be a continuation of the current approach, with a renewed emphasis on ASEAN Centrality. First, ASEAN will continue to put greater emphasis on the prevention and peaceful management of the underlying sovereignty and maritime disputes, rather than their resolution. Second, ASEAN will continue to advocate for the peaceful settlement of disputes based on international law, in particular UNCLOS. Finally, ASEAN will continue its efforts to play the primary role as a facilitator by providing a forum for the relevant parties to discuss, agree and cooperate.

Conclusion

This chapter attempts to demonstrate that the role that ASEAN envisages it should play in Southeast Asia in general, and in the South China Sea in particular. The South China Sea disputes present a formidable challenge for ASEAN. ASEAN's policy has been to approach the issues by applying the fundamental principles it has applied since its founding. ASEAN will continue to apply the principles of inclusiveness and decision by consensus to maintain peace in the region, and the association will also continue to promote the principle of ASEAN Centrality when dealing with States that are not members of ASEAN.

The ASEAN Outlook may have implications for the current negotiations between ASEAN and China on the COC. It could mean that ASEAN does not consider the COC to be a solution for the South China Sea disputes which must be achieved by all costs, but rather, that ASEAN values the COC negotiation process as one of the mechanisms for conflict prevention in the South China Sea.

Notes

1 The ASEAN Declaration (ASEAN Declaration), 8 August 1967, Bangkok, Thailand.
2 *Ibid.*, Art. 1.
3 *Ibid.*, Art. 2.
4 Treaty of Amity and Cooperation in Southeast Asia, 24 February 1976, Bali, Indonesia.
5 *Ibid.*, Art. 1.
6 *Ibid.*, Art. 2.
7 Declaration of ASEAN Concord II (Bali Concord II) adopted at the 9th ASEAN Summit, 7–8 October 2003, Bali, Indonesia.
8 *Ibid.*
9 Charter of the Association of Southeast Asian Nations (ASEAN Charter), 20 November 2007, Singapore.
10 *Ibid.*, Art. 31.
11 A. Acharya, "Ideas, Identity and Institution-building: From 'ASEAN Way' to the 'Asia-Pacific Way'?", *The Pacific Review* 10 (1997): 319–346.
12 ASEAN Charter, supra note 9, Art. 20.
13 B. Hayton, *The South China Sea: The Struggle for Power in Asia* (London: Yale University Press, 2014), 81–84.
14 *Ibid.*,125.
15 H. Djalal and I. Townsend-Gault, "Preventive Diplomacy: Managing Potential Conflicts in the South China Sea", in C. A. Crocker, F. O. Hampson and P. Aall (eds), *Herding Cats: Multiparty Mediation in a Complex World* (Washington, DC: United States Institute of Peace Press, 1999), 107.
16 ASEAN Declaration on the South China Sea (1992 ASEAN Declaration on the South China Sea), 22 July 1992, Manila, Philippines. For a reproduction of the text, see: Nguyen Hong Thao, "Vietnam and the Code of Conduct for the South China Sea", *Ocean Development and International Law* 32 (2001): 105–130 at 124–125.

17 The Law claims sovereignty over China's mainland and offshore islands, including the Spratlys. See Law on the Territorial Sea and the Contiguous Zone of the People's Republic of China, 25 February 2020, online: UN DOALOS https://www.un.org/depts/los/LEGISLATIONANDTREATIES/PDFFILES/CHN_1992_Law.pdf, Art. 2.
18 L. Buszynski, "ASEAN, the Declaration on Conduct, and the South China Sea", *Contemporary Southeast Asia* 25 (2003): 343–362 at 348.
19 Hayton, supra note 13, at 84–89.
20 I. Storey, "Creeping Assertiveness: China, the Philippines and the South China Sea Dispute", *Contemporary Southeast Asia* 21 (1999): 95–118 at 98.
21 R. Amer, "The Sino-Vietnamese Approach to Managing Boundary Disputes", *IBRU Maritime Briefing* 3 (2002): 23–25.
22 M. Natalegawa, *Does ASEAN Matter? A View from Within* (Singapore: Institute for Southeast Asian Studies, 2018), 128–130.
23 Adopted in Montego Bay, Jamaica on 10 December 1982, UNTS 1833, at 397 (entered into force 16 November 1994). As of 30 May 2020, 167 States and the European Union are parties, including China and all ASEAN member States except Cambodia.
24 PCA Case No 2013–19, in the Matter of the South China Sea Arbitration, The Republic of the Philippines v. The People's Republic of China, Award of 12 July 2016, https://docs.pca-cpa.org/2016/07/PH-CN-20160712-Award.pdf.
25 *Ibid.*, at 135.
26 ASEAN Charter, supra note 9, Art. 7.
27 37th ASEAN Summit Chairman's Statement, 12 November 2020, Hanoi, Viet Nam.
28 *Ibid.*, paras. 84-85.
29 Joint Press Release of the 1st AMM, 8 August 1967.
30 ASEAN Declaration, supra note 1.
31 Overview, online: ASEAN Foreign Ministers' Meeting https://asean.org/asean-political-security-community/asean-foreign-ministers-meeting-amm/#12e7a83058760b4da.
32 Joint communiqué of the 53rd AMM, 9 September 2020, Videoconference.
33 *Ibid.*, para. 95.
34 "Concept Paper for the Establishment of an ASEAN Defence Ministers' Meeting" adopted at the Inaugural ASEAN Defence Ministers' Meeting, 9 May 2006, Kuala Lumpur, Malaysia. For details about the concept paper, see online: ASEAN https://admm.asean.org/dmdocuments/1.%20Concept%20Paper%20for%20the%20Establishment%20of%20an%20ASEAN%20Defence%20Ministers.pdf.
35 Joint Declaration of the 14th ADMM, 9 December 2020, videoconference.
36 *Ibid.*, paras 36 – 37.
37 India at the East Asia Summit (August 2018) online: Ministry of External Affairs of India http://mea.gov.in/aseanindia/about-eas.htm.
38 1st EAS Chairman's Statement, 14 December 2005, Kuala Lumpur, Malaysia.
39 6th EAS Chairman's Statement, 19 November 2011, Bali, Indonesia.
40 15th EAS Chairman's Statement, 14 November 2020, videoconference.
41 *Ibid.*, paras. 30–32.
42 Joint Declaration of the 2nd ADMM, 14 November 2017, Singapore, para. 3.
43 For details, see "Concept Paper for the Establishment of an ASEAN Defence Ministers' Meeting" online: ASEAN https://admm.asean.org/dmdocuments/1.%20Concept%20Paper%20for%20the%20Establishment%20of%20an%20ASEAN%20Defence%20Ministers.pdf.
44 Joint Communiqué of the 26th AMM, 23–24 July 1993, Singapore, para. 8.
45 Objectives, online: ASEAN Regional Forum http://aseanregionalforum.asean.org/about-arf/.
46 To date, participants to the ARF include ASEAN Member States and Australia, Bangladesh, Canada, China, Democratic People's Republic of Korea, EU, India, Japan, Mongolia, New Zealand, Pakistan, Papua New Guinea, Republic of Korea, Russia, Sri Lanka, Timor-Leste and United States.
47 For background information relating to the Declaration of Conduct of Parties the South China Sea, see below 2002 Declaration on Conduct of Parties in the South China Sea.
48 27th ARF Chairman's Statement, 12 September 2020, Hanoi, Viet Nam, para. 11.
49 1992 ASEAN Declaration on the South China Sea, supra note 16.
50 Joint Statement of the RP-PRC on the South China Sea and on Other Areas of Cooperation, 9–10 August 1995, and Joint Statement of the 4th Annual Bilateral Consultations between the Republic

of Philippines and the Socialist Republic of Viet Nam, Hanoi, 7 November 1995. For a reproduction of the text of these two codes of conduct see: Thao, supra note 16, at Appendixes 2 & 3.
51 *Ibid.*
52 Joint Communiqué of the 29th AMM, 20–21 July 1996, Jakarta, Indonesia, para. 11. See also Buszynski, supra note 18, at 354.
53 Buszynski, supra note 18, at 355.
54 Joint Communiqué of the 32nd AMM, 23–24 July 1999, Singapore, para. 39.
55 Chairman's Press Statement on ASEAN 3rd Informal Summit, Manila, Philippines, 28 November 1999.
56 R. Amer, "Ongoing Efforts in Conflict Management", in T. Kivimäki (ed.), *War or Peace in the South China Sea* (Copenhagen: NIAS Press, 2002), 117 at note 27. See also 6th ARF Chairman's Statement, 26 July 1999, Singapore, para. 11.
57 Nguyen Hong Thao, "The Declaration of Conduct of Parties in the South China Sea: A Vietnamese Perspective 2002–2007", in S. Bateman and R. Emmers (eds), *Security and International Politics in the South China Sea: Towards a Co-operative Management Regime* (London: Taylor and Francis, 2009), 207 at 209; and L. Buszynski, supra note 18, at 355.
58 Buszynski, supra note 18, at 356.
59 Joint Communiqué of the 35th AMM, 29–30 July 2002, Brunei, paras. 40–41.
60 See supra notes 16 and 50.
61 Declaration on the Conduct of Parties in the South China Sea, 4 November 2002, Phnom Penh, Cambodia.
62 Press Release of the 1st SOM-DOC, 7 December 2004, Kuala Lumpur, Malaysia.
63 Terms of Reference of the ASEAN-China Joint Working Group on the Implementation of the Declaration on the Conduct of Parties in the South China Sea, adopted by the ASEAN-China Senior Officials' Meeting on the implementation of the DOC, 07 December 2004, Kuala Lumpur, Malaysia. See also C. Thayer, "China-ASEAN and the South China Sea: Chinese Assertiveness and Southeast Asian Responses", in Y. H. Song and K. Zou (eds), *Major Law and Policy Issues in the South China Sea: European and American Perspectives* (London: Routledge, 2016), 25 at 44.
64 China objected to a clause which specified "ASEAN will continue its current practice of consulting among themselves before meeting with China". China insisted that that outstanding disputes should be resolved by bilateral consultations "among relevant parties" and not with ASEAN. See C. Thayer, "Chinese Assertiveness in the South China Sea and Southeast Asian Response", *Journal of Current Southeast Asian Affairs* 2 (2011): 77–104 at 91.
65 Chairman's Statement on the ASEAN PMC+1 Sessions, 21–22 July 2011, Bali, Indonesia.
66 Guidelines for the Implementation of the DOC, adopted at the ASEAN-China Senior Officials' Meeting at the 44th ASEAN PMC+1 Session with China, 21–22 July 2011, Bali, Indonesia.
67 17th ASEAN-China Summit Chairman's Statement, 13 November 2014, Nay Pyi Taw, Myanmar, paras. 9–11.
68 Joint Press Briefing on the 14th SOM-DOC, 18 May 2017, Guiyang, Guizhou Province, China.
69 "11th Senior Officials Meeting on the Implementation of the Declaration on the Conduct of the Parties in the South China Sea Held in Singapore" (29 April 2016) online: Ministry of Foreign Affairs of the People's Republic of China https://www.fmprc.gov.cn/nanhai/eng/wjbxw_1/t1360552.htm and "ASEAN and China Senior Officials in 12th Meeting" (10 June 2016) online: Vietnam News <https://vietnamnews.vn/politics-laws/297999/asean-and-china-senior-officials-in-12th-meeting.html>.
70 The CUES was adopted at the 2014 Western Pacific Naval Symposium in Qingdao, China by navies of 35 Pacific countries to provide communication and manoeuvring procedures among naval vessels and aircraft when they operate in close proximity, see Code for Unplanned Encounter at Sea, version 1, adopted at 24th Western Pacific Naval Symposium, 22 April 2014, Qingdao, China.
71 19th ASEAN-China Summit Chairman's Statement, 7 September 2016, Vientiane, Laos, paras. 20–21.
72 Joint Statement on the Application of the Code for Unplanned Encounters at Sea in the South China Sea, adopted at the 19th ASEAN-China Summit Chairman's Statement, 7 September 2016, Vientiane, Laos.
73 Guidelines for Hotline Communications among Senior Officials of the Ministries of Foreign Affairs of ASEAN Member States and China in Response to Maritime Emergencies in the

Implementation of the DOC, adopted at the 19th ASEAN-China Summit Chairman's Statement, 7 September 2016, Vientiane, Laos.

74 Joint Press Briefing on the 14th SOM-DOC, 18 May 2017, Guiyang, Guizhou Province, China.

75 "Singapore Navy Hosts Table-Top Exercise as part of Inaugural ASEAN-China Maritime Exercise" (3 August 2018) online: Ministry of Defence of Singapore https://www.mindef.gov.sg/web/portal/mindef/news-and-events/latest-releases/article-detail/2018/august/03aug18_nr2/!ut/p/z0/fY0xE8FAFIR_iyLlzbuEiDYoMEgT5lyTOTxxJC-SO8G_d6FR6XZ3vt0FCQIkqVb-nyuqKVOH8Tg6zKJlOZnwQrJMw9Xm8TdNlOF7PN9EQFiD_A25BX-paxiAPFVl8WhClpi-Oe2MeT9fi5KtHjhA_DFB0Zti41Hi-URWNZgwUqgy4IuD_yuLrnd-NavO-UP8qoCbqXoFl-NVjnIm7JnpulUgeh4EF8exC9_u8r96xH33p0VbGg!/.

76 "ASEAN and China Successfully Conclude ASEAN-China Maritime Exercise" (27 October 2018) online: Ministry of Defence of Singapore https://www.mindef.gov.sg/web/portal/mindef/news-and-events/latest-releases/article-detail/2018/october/27oct18_nr.

77 S. L. C. Koh, "Inaugural ASEAN-China Maritime Exercise: What To Expect" (3 August 2018) RSIS Commentary No.131.

78 20th ASEAN-China Summit Chairman's Statement, 13 November 2017, Manila, Philippines, paras. 12–14.

79 Declaration for a Decade of Coastal and Marine Environmental Protection in the South China Sea (2017–2027), adopted at the 20th ASEAN-China Summit, 13 November 2017, Manila, Philippines, paras. 12–14.

80 C. Thayer, "New Commitment to a Code of Conduct in the South China Sea?" (9 October 2013) The National Bureau of Asian Research. For details about the South China Sea arbitration, see Implications of ASEAN's Policy of Making Decisions by Consensus.

81 *Ibid.* See also "19th ASEAN-China Senior Officials' Consultation" (4 April 2013) online: ASEAN https://asean.org/19th-asean-china-senior-officials-consultation/.

82 "Foreign Minister Wang Yi on Process of "Code of Conduct in the South China Sea" (5 August 2013) online: Ministry of Foreign Affairs of the People's Republic of China https://www.fmprc.gov.cn/mfa_eng/wjb_663304/wjbz_663308/activities_663312/t1064869.shtml.

83 "The Sixth Senior Officials Meeting and the Ninth Joint Working Group Meeting on the Implementation of the "Declaration on Conduct of Parties in the South China Sea" Are Held in Suzhou" (15 September 2013) online: Ministry of Foreign Affairs of the People's Republic of China https://www.fmprc.gov.cn/mfa_eng/zxxx_662805/t1079289.shtml.

84 16th ASEAN-China Summit Chairman's Statement, 9 October 2013, Brunei, paras. 15–16.

85 "ASEAN-China Cooperation Moves Forward at the 8th ASEAN-China SOM" (24 October 2014) online: Ministry of Foreign Affairs of the Kingdom of Thailand http://www.mfa.go.th/main/en/media-center/28/50886-ASEAN-China-cooperation-moves-forward-at-the-8th-A.html.

86 17th ASEAN-China Summit Chairman's Statement, 13 November 2014, Nay Pyi Taw, Myanmar, paras. 9–11.

87 L. Li, *China's Policy towards the South China Sea: When Geopolitics Meet the Law of the Sea* (New York: Routledge, 2018), 192.

88 "Tenth Senior Officials Meeting on the Implementation of the Declaration On the Conduct of the Parties In the South China Sea Held in Chengdu" (20 October 2015) online: Ministry of Foreign Affairs of the People's Republic of China https://www.fmprc.gov.cn/mfa_eng/wjbxw/t1307573.shtml.

89 Chairman's Statement of the ASEAN PMC 10+1 Sessions with Dialogue Partners, 5 August 2015, Kuala Lumpur, Malaysia.

90 Joint Statement of Ministers of the Foreign Affairs of ASEAN and China on The Full and Effective Implementation of the Declaration on the Conduct of Parties in the South China Sea, 25 July 2016, Vientiane, Laos.

91 Joint Press Briefing on the 14th SOM-DOC, 18 May 2017, Guiyang, Guizhou Province, China.

92 Framework of a COC, adopted by at the ASEAN PMC 10+1 Session with China, 6 August 2017, Manila, Philippines. For a comprehensive assessment of the Framework of the COC, see Ian Storey, "Assessing the ASEAN-China Framework for the Code of Conduct for the South China Sea" (8 August 2017) ISEAS Perspective No.62/2017.

93 Carl Thayer, *ASEAN and China Set on Agree on Single Draft South China Sea Code of Conduct*, The Diplomat, June 27, 2018, https://thediplomat.com/2018/07/asean-and-china-set-to-agree-on-single-draft-south-china-sea-code-of-conduct/.

94 Chairman's Statement of the ASEAN PMC 10+1 Sessions with Dialogue Partners, 2–3 August 2018, Singapore.
95 Lee Chyen Yeen, *Chinese Premier Li Says Talks on South China Sea Code Should End in Three Years*, Reuters, November 13, 2018, https://www.reuters.com/article/us-asean-summit-china/chinese-premier-li-says-talks-on-south-china-sea-code-should-end-in-three-years-idUSKCN-1NI0B0.
96 "The 17th Senior Officials' Meeting on the Implementation of the Declaration on the Conduct of Parties in the South China Sea (DOC) Held Successfully in China" (19 May 2019) online: Ministry of Foreign Affairs of the People's Republic of China https://www.fmprc.gov.cn/nanhai/eng/wjbxw_1/t1665134.htm and "The 18th ASEAN-China Senior Officials' Meeting on the Implementation of the Declaration on the Conduct of Parties (DOC) in the South China Sea Successfully Held" (16 October 2019) online: Ministry of Foreign Affairs of the People's Republic of China https://www.fmprc.gov.cn/mfa_eng/wjbxw/t1708862.shtml.
97 Chairman' Statement of the ASEAN PMC 10+1 Sessions with Dialogue Partners, 31st July–1 August 2019, Bangkok, Thailand, and 22nd ASEAN-China Summit Chairman's Statement, 3 November 2019, Bangkok/Nonthaburi, Thailand, para. 18.
98 1992 ASEAN Declaration on the South China Sea, supra note 16.
99 Joint Communiqué of the 29th AMM, 20–21 July 1996, Jakarta, Indonesia, para. 11.
100 Joint Communiqué of the 32nd AMM, 23–24 July 1999, Singapore, para. 39.
101 Joint Communiqué of the 53rd AMM, 9 September 2020, videoconference, paras. 94–95.
102 1992 ASEAN Declaration on the South China Sea, supra note 16.
103 Joint Communiqué of the 28th AMM, 23–30 July 1995, Brunei, para. 9.
104 Joint Communiqué of the 48th AMM, 4 August 2015, Kuala Lumpur, Malaysia, paras. 150–156.
105 Joint Communiqué of the 50th AMM, 5 August 2017 Manila, Philippines, paras. 191–197.
106 Joint Communiqué of the 53rd AMM, 9 September 2020, videoconference, paras. 95–96.
107 1992 ASEAN Declaration on the South China Sea, supra note 16.
108 Joint Communiqué of the 29th AMM, 20–21 July 1996, Jakarta, Indonesia, para. 11.
109 Joint Communiqué of the 35th AMM, 29–30 July 2002, Brunei, paras. 40–41.
110 See, for instance, Joint Communiqué of the 36th AMM, 16–17 June 2003, Phnom Penh, Cambodia, para. 26; Joint Communiqué of the 37th AMM, 29–30 June 2004, Jakarta, Indonesia, paras. 22–23, and Joint Communiqué of the 38th AMM, 26 July 2005, Vientiane, Laos, paras. 13–15.
111 Joint Communiqué of the 53rd AMM, 9 September 2020, videoconference, paras. 95–96.
112 1992 ASEAN Declaration on the South China Sea, supra note 16.
113 Joint Communiqué of the 35th AMM, 29–30 July 2002, Brunei, paras. 40–41.
114 Joint Communiqué of the 36th AMM, 16–17 June 2003, Phnom Penh, Cambodia, para. 26.
115 Joint Communiqué of the 38th AMM, 26 July 2005, Vientiane, Laos, paras. 13–15.
116 Joint Communiqué of the 53rd AMM, 9 September 2020, videoconference, paras 95–96.
117 Joint Communiqué of the 36th AMM, 16–17 June 2003, Phnom Penh, Cambodia, para. 26.
118 Joint Communiqué of the 37th AMM, 29–30 June 2004, Jakarta, Indonesia, paras. 22–23.
119 Joint Communiqué of the 38th AMM, 25 July 2006, Kuala Lumpur, Malaysia, paras. 27–28.
120 See, for example, Joint Communiqué of the 42nd AMM, 20 July 2009 in Phuket, Thailand, paras. 21–22.
121 Thayer, supra note 80, https://www.nbr.org/publication/new-commitment-to-a-code-of-conduct-in-the-south-china-sea/.
122 ASEAN Foreign Ministers' Statement on the Current Developments in the South China Sea, 10th May 2014, Nay Pyi Taw, Myanmar.
123 Joint Communiqué of the 48th AMM, 4 August 2015, Kuala Lumpur, Malaysia, paras. 150–156.
124 Joint Communiqué of the 53rd AMM, 2 September 2020, videoconference, paras. 95–96.
125 See for example Joint Communiqué of the 26th AMM, 23–14 July 1993, Singapore, para. 6, and Joint Communiqué of the 27th AMM, 22–23 July 1994, Bangkok, Thailand, para. 8
126 Joint Communiqué of the 44th AMM, 19 July 2011, Bali, Indonesia, paras. 22–26.
127 Joint Communiqué of the 28th AMM, 23–30 July 1995, Brunei, para. 9.
128 Joint Communiqué of the 33rd AMM, 24–25 July 2000, Bangkok, Thailand, paras. 24–25; Joint Communiqué of the 34th AMM, 23–24 July 2001, Hanoi, Viet Nam, para. 20, and Joint Communiqué of the 35th AMM, 29–30 July 2002, Brunei, paras. 40–41.
129 Joint Communiqué of the 43rd AMM, 19–20 July 2010, Hanoi, Viet Nam, paras. 28–29.

130 Joint Communiqué of the 48th AMM, 4 August 2015, Kuala Lumpur, Malaysia, paras. 150–156.
131 Joint Communiqué of the 53rd AMM, 2 September 2020, videoconference, paras. 95–96.
132 Joint Communiqué of the 49th AMM, 24 July 2016, Vientiane, Laos, paras. 174–181.
133 Joint Communiqué of the 50th AMM, 5 August 2017, Manila, Philippines, paras. 191–197.
134 Joint Communiqué of the 53rd AMM, 2 September 2020, videoconference, paras. 95–96.
135 Joint Communiqué of the 28th AMM, 23–30 July 1995, Brunei, para. 9; Joint Communiqué of the 29th AMM, 20–21 July 1996, Jakarta, Indonesia, para. 11, and Joint Communiqué of the 30th AMM, 24–25 July 1997, Subang Jaya, Malaysia, para. 16.
136 Joint Communiqué of the 44th AMM, 19 July 2011, Bali, Indonesia, paras. 22–26.
137 ASEAN Foreign Ministers' Statement on the Current Developments in the South China Sea, 10th May 2014, Nay Pyi Taw, Myanmar.
138 Joint Communiqué of the 48th AMM, 4 August 2015, Kuala Lumpur, Malaysia, paras. 150–156.
139 Joint Communiqué of the 49th AMM, 24 July 2016, Vientiane, Laos, paras. 174–181.
140 Joint Communiqué of the 53rd AMM, 2 September 2020, videoconference, paras. 95–96.
141 Chairman's Statement of the 34th ASEAN Summit, 23 June 2019, Bangkok, Thailand, para. 56.
142 D. F. Anwar, "Indonesia and the ASEAN outlook on the Indo-Pacific", *International Affairs* 96 (2016): 111–129 at 125.
143 ASEAN Outlook on the Indo-Pacific, adopted at the 34th ASEAN Summit, 23 June 2019, Bangkok, Thailand.
144 Anwar, supra note 142, at 113. See also R. J. Heydarian, "At a Strategic Crossroads: ASEAN Centrality Amid Sino-American Rivalry and the Indo-Pacific" (April 2020) Brookings Report, and S. T. See, "Consigned to Hedge: South-east Asia and America's 'Free and Open Indo-Pacific' Strategy", *International Affairs* 96 (2020): 131–148.
145 ASEAN Outlook on the Indo-Pacific, adopted at the 34th ASEAN Summit, 23 June 2019, Bangkok, Thailand, para. 15.

19
FROM DOC TO COC
A regional rules-based order

Ramses Amer and Li Jianwei

Introduction

With the intervention of human activities (on behalf of individuals, institutions (organizations) or states) in or through the waters, the South China Sea benefits as well as divides countries in the region and beyond. On the one hand, activities including but not limited to maritime trade, exploitation of marine resources, marine environment protection, marine scientific research as well as safety and security of sea-lanes of communication not only benefit parties directly involved in the South China Sea disputes but also promote the prosperity of the region. On the other hand, conflict of interest exists among coastal countries of the South China Sea relating to their overlapping claims to insular features and exclusive sovereign rights generated from the mainland and these insular features. These disputes, if the behaviour of relevant countries is not regulated in relation to activities in the overlapping-claimed areas, will increase insecurity and distrust among the countries concerned.

A rule is considered a clear statement of a preference when it becomes compulsory[1] and rules are reached among interested parties to regulate their behaviour to uphold a rules-based order on their shared common values.[2] Countries tend to follow rules because rules reflect not only big powers' common interests, but also create to a certain extent an order that benefits the countries involved and makes inter-state affairs more predictable so as to constrain unacceptable or potentially destructive action from which all will suffer. Therefore, a rules-based order tends to be more stable than a political order based on naked power.[3] Maritime order is part of the international order and the basic international rules and principles which regulate interstate behaviour at sea are the United Nations Charter (UN Charter) and the United Nations Convention on the Law of Sea (UNCLOS) of 1982.

Due to the special circumstances and issues concerned, countries in various regions tend to establish rules based on internationally recognized rules and principles taking into consideration elements specific to the region and issues concerned. In this regard, members of the Association of Southeast Asian Nations (ASEAN) and China have made joint efforts to create rules in the South China Sea region to constrain behaviour that is detrimental to order while promoting others conducive to good order. The process leading to good order in the South China Sea is a process of negotiations and trade-offs of different interests among the 11 countries. Up till now, there are two processes at the regional level, one leading to the

Declaration on the Conduct of the Parties in the South China Sea (DOC) and the other ongoing one that aims to reach a higher-level code of conduct (COC).

This chapter elaborates on efforts in the South China Sea region to establish a rule-based order. Section II outlines the DOC process. It focuses on the analysis of the implications and contributions of the DOC to the regional order. Section III elaborates on the ongoing COC consultation process. After an overview of how it was re-initiated and the relevant mechanisms, the three phases of the process are presented. Section IV identifies who the key players are and what the major issues to address during the negotiations on substantive issues. This is followed by an elaboration of the positions of the key players on these issues. Section V is the conclusion.

The DOC: contributions and implications

The DOC is the first document signed between China and the ten ASEAN countries to control activities and actions in the South China Sea through a set of accepted norms. By having the mutually accepted norms included in the DOC, the signatory countries can better predict the activities and actions of other countries involved as well as constrain theirs to those which are considered in line with the DOC. In so doing it is expected that conflicts can be avoided and co-operative activities promoted.[4]

ASEAN, as a regional organization, was first involved in the South China Sea issues in 1992 when the ASEAN Declaration on the South China Sea was adopted at the 25th ASEAN Foreign Ministerial Meeting (AMM), calling on all parties concerned to "apply the principles contained in the Treaty of Amity and Cooperation in Southeast Asia (TAC) as the basis for establishing a code of international conduct over the South China Sea".[5] China responded positively on the same occasion by stating its position as "not willing to see the differences (over maritime issues) lead to conflicts affecting negatively friendly relations between relevant countries and regional peace and stability"[6] and subscribed to the declaration's "principles".[7] In 1995, two events pushed ASEAN to be more active in involving itself in the South China Sea issues, the Chinese-Filipino Mischief Reef incident in February and the admission of Vietnam into ASEAN in July. On 18 March the ASEAN foreign ministers issued the 1995 Statement on the Recent Developments in the South China Sea, expressing their "serious concern" and recalling the message spelt out in its 1992 Declaration.[8] At the same time encouraging developments occurred bilaterally. China and the Philippines signed an eight-point code of conduct in the Joint Statement of the Republic of Philippines and the People's Republic of China Consultations on the South China Sea and on Other Areas of Cooperation in August. The Philippines and Vietnam reached a nine-point code of conduct in the Joint Statement of the Fourth Annual Bilateral Consultations Between the Philippines and Vietnam in November.[9] They agreed to manage their bilateral maritime disputes by rules of behaviour. This was the first time that China started a bilateral discussion on a code of conduct in the South China Sea.[10] Through the joint communiqué at the 29th AMM in 1996, the ASEAN foreign ministers "endorsed the idea of concluding a regional code of conduct in the South China Sea which will lay the foundation for long-term stability in the area and foster understanding among claimant countries".[11] Both the Hanoi Plan of Action and Hanoi Declaration, issued at the 6th ASEAN Summit in 1998, emphasized the importance of continued efforts on "establish(ing) a regional code of conduct in the South China Sea among the parties directly concerned".[12] In November 1999 ASEAN adopted the draft Code of Conduct prepared by the Philippines and Vietnam and sent it to China. Earlier in October 1999, China proposed its draft code of conduct. After informal consultation, the

First Meeting of the Working Group of the ASEAN-China Senior Officials Consultations on the Code of Conduct was convened in Kuala Lumpur on 26 May 2000.[13] Through dialogues among ASEAN member states as well as between ASEAN and China, it was agreed that a joint document was to be reached as a first step and joint efforts would continue for the final adoption of a code of conduct in the South China Sea.[14] On 4 November 2002, the DOC was signed at the 8th ASEAN Summit.

The signing of the DOC was hailed as a milestone event in China-ASEAN relations over the South China Sea. The DOC upholds key principles of international law to manage their relations in the South China Sea, in particular the principle of peaceful settlement of disputes.[15] It has shown

> the collective commitment of the ASEAN Member States and China to promote peace, stability and mutual trust, as well as peaceful settlement of disputes in the South China Sea in accordance with the universally recognized principles of international law, including the 1982 UNCLOS.[16]

The DOC made important contributions to implementing the goal set in this commitment. Since it was signed claimant countries have neither occupied new insular features in any form nor used force to settle their territorial disputes over insular features. When tensions occurred, measures have been taken to reduce and diffuse them. Furthermore, attempts have been made to further promote practical co-operation projects. The DOC, together with the UNCLOS, was considered as the basis for the Tripartite Agreement for Joint Marine Seismic Undertaking in the Agreement Area in the South China Sea among national oil companies of China, the Philippines and Vietnam, which was signed on 14 March 2005. The Joint Oceanographic Marine Scientific Expedition in the South China Sea was launched jointly by the Philippines and Vietnam in 1994 and later joined by participants from China, the US and Canada. Four expeditions were carried out in April 1996, May 2000, April 2005 and April 2007, respectively.[17]

The ten years' process of ASEAN's efforts from initiating the concept of COC in its 1992 Declaration to the signing of a DOC in 2002 had several implications. First, ASEAN has a role to play in the affairs relating to the South China Sea issues. It has successfully drawn China into ASEAN-led mechanisms to discuss the issues and both sides reached an agreement on the DOC. However, such a role is limited. As a regional organization, ASEAN is not a sovereign state directly linked or involved in disputes over territorial sovereignty and maritime jurisdiction. Within ASEAN the claimant states have different interests from those who have no claims. Furthermore, all the ten members have different concerns and will take different approaches in their relations with China.[18] Second, the process has led China to adjust its approach to dealing with the issues. China had previously insisted on bilateral negotiations with the claimant states and had avoided multilateral approaches. The signing of the DOC indicated China's willingness to work with ASEAN member States to build trust and confidence through practical co-operation and to maintain peace and stability in the region.[19]

Third, the DOC has limitations. The DOC is not a legal instrument but a political declaration, thus it is technically not legally binding. As a political declaration, the DOC does not provide clear guidance for state action as a code[20] and it is not aimed at resolving territorial disputes and imposing legally binding obligations on the parties concerned.[21] As such, the provisions governing the conduct of parties are not prescribed in prohibitive but more positive language for the aim of reducing tensions over the territorial and jurisdictional disputes in the South China Sea[22] and creating an environment more conducive to their final resolution. The DOC sets out four confidence-building measures and five areas for voluntary cooperation including marine environmental protection (MEP); marine scientific research (MSR); safety of navigation and communication at sea; search and rescue operations; and combating transnational crime, including but not limited to trafficking in illicit drugs, piracy and armed robbery at sea and illegal traffic in arms.[23] Vagueness is another feature of the DOC in relation to provisions where conflict of interest may occur. As to "the scope of application," Thao has pointed out, the title of the DOC permits the understanding that the provisions are to apply beyond the Spratly Archipelago and allows for both narrow and broad interpretations depending on the interests of the signatories.[24] As to "self-restraint," there is no clear definition of what activities are considered to have the impact of complicating or escalating the situation.[25] It has also been observed that the DOC did not fully meet the expectations of some ASEAN members, including Vietnam, because it did not specify the applicable geographical scope and did not ban the construction of new structures on submerged features, two key provisions that Vietnam sought to include in the prospective COC.[26] Lack of monitoring mechanisms is also considered the reason for continuous activities not in line with the spirit of the DOC.[27]

The DOC fell short of what ASEAN had been seeking, which was a commitment to a code of conduct. However, when seen against the backdrop of prior developments, it indicated a trend towards the adoption of norms to regulate behaviour. Importantly, the parties reaffirmed their agreement on the eventual adoption of a code of conduct in the South China Sea on the basis of consensus of this objective.[28] Peace and stability in the South China Sea is the main objective of China and the member countries of ASEAN, which lays the foundation for future efforts towards drafting a COC.[29] When China and the member states of ASEAN are convinced that new developments may endanger regional peace and stability there will be a stronger sense of urgency to reach an agreement on a COC.

The COC consultation: re-initiation, mechanisms and process

Re-initiation

Despite the regional efforts on setting norms of behaviour for activities in the South China Sea through the DOC, tensions broke out now and then between the claimant countries. As mentioned in Part II, due to the vagueness in the DOC in the area of application and unclear definition of what activities should be under "self-restraint", the parties tended to interpret the provisions to their own advantages and carried out various activities which are not clearly banned by the DOC but have the potential for escalating tensions, such as exploitation of living and non-living resource, law enforcement, facility enhancement on occupied insular features in the overlapping-claimed area.[30] Tensions lingered throughout the 2000s and since 2009, old tensions over the South China Sea were rekindled by new disputes involving fishing activities, energy resources exploitation, law enforcement activities, expansion of control and presence, legal contestations and major power strategic rivalry.[31]

Before the deadline of 13 May 2009 for submission to the UN Commission on the Limit of Continental Shelf of the application for the outer limit of the continental shelf beyond 200 nautical miles from baselines, two submission cases aroused protests and counter-protests in the South China Sea region, the Malaysia-Vietnam joint submission relating to the southern part of the South China Sea on 6 May and Vietnam's partial submission relating to the northern part of the South China Sea on 7 May. Both China and the Philippines were involved in the legal spat over the territorial and maritime claims in the South China Sea.[32] In March 2009 the passage of the Philippines' new act on its archipelagic baselines also led to protest from China by reiterating its claims to Scarborough Shoal and the Spratly Islands as well as "their adjacent waters." While the verbal row over claims simmered by measures of passing domestic laws or lodging protests with the UN, tensions also intensified relating to marine resources exploitation and law enforcement in 2011 and 2012 between China and the Philippines as well as between China and Vietnam.[33] In March 2011, China sent marine surveillance vessels to an overlapping-claimed area in Reed Bank where the Philippines in early 2011 endowed the UK-based company Energy Forum with a two-year contract to explore oil and gas resources. The Philippines claimed that the Chinese vessels harassed the seismic survey vessels of Energy Forum. In June the Philippines listed 15 oil blocks for bidding, three of them were also claimed by China. Fishing also became a source of bilateral tension. While the Philippine fishing vessels in the Spratly Archipelago were warned off by Chinese law enforcement vessels in February, the Philippines arrested six Chinese fishermen in March and "harassed" a Chinese fishing vessel around the same area.[34] The most serious China-Philippines tension occurred during the bilateral standoff over Scarborough Shoal, which lasted over a month from April to May in 2012. Serious incidents between China and Vietnam occurred in late May and early June 2011 relating to Vietnamese oil exploration activities in areas which both China and Vietnam laid claims to. Both sides blamed the other for harassing their legitimate activities.

These incidents at sea occurred parallel with China's growing national power. The concerns over China's future assertive responses in the South China Sea, which are different from its previous "keeping a low profile" orientation, pushed both Vietnam and the Philippines to urge ASEAN to re-initiate the COC negotiation with China to restrain China's behaviour in the South China Sea.[35] Within ASEAN, its members started reconsidering a more robust agreement to manage the disputes. At the 44th AMM on 19 July 2011, the ASEAN foreign ministers initiated discussions on a regional COC in the South China Sea and endowed the ASEAN Senior Officials' Meeting (SOM) to work on "the development of the COC and submit a progress report to the 19th ASEAN Summit".[36] The day after, China and ASEAN members signed the Guidelines for the Implementation of the DOC, in which point 6 emphasized that the implementation of concrete measures or activities of the DOC should lead to the eventual realization of a Code of Conduct. At the 45th AMM on 9 July 2012, ASEAN foreign ministers adopted the "key elements" of the COC, which was finalized at the seventh meeting by ASEAN SOM earlier in June 2012. Meanwhile, the obvious division over the issues of the South China Sea unfolded within ASEAN which led to a failure to release a joint communiqué by their foreign ministers. To show ASEAN solidarity, after Indonesia's shuttle diplomacy among member states, ASEAN foreign ministers released a statement on ASEAN's six principles on the South China Sea, in which they reiterate their commitment to "the early conclusion of a Regional Code of Conduct in the South China Sea."[37] At the ASEAN summit later that year, the ASEAN leaders reached the consensus that it was time to discuss with China over the region's COC.[38] At the 46th AMM in June 2013, the ASEAN foreign ministers expressed their expectations for formal consultations between China and ASEAN at the SOM level on the COC.[39]

Meanwhile, China's new leadership which took office after the 18th National Congress of the Communist Party of China in early 2013 made adjustments to China's policies towards its neighbouring countries, which affected its approach to dealing with its maritime disputes in the South China Sea and the East China Sea. Under the new objectives of creating "harmonious neighbouring relations" and "harmonious Asia-Pacific," China attached more importance to its foreign policies with neighbouring countries.[40] In relation to managing the South China Sea issues, China became more active in promoting dialogues and communications with ASEAN countries. Furthermore, starting from 2009 with its implementation of the "Pivot to Asia" policy, the United States became more interested in the South China Sea issues. The extra-regional powers, in particular, the United States made stronger involvements in the South China Sea issues which seemed to have exerted pressure on various parties including China to accelerate the implementation of the DOC.[41] On 5 August 2013 China's Foreign Minister Wang Yi elaborated on China's position on the COC consultation and indicated that China would start COC consultation with ASEAN member states at the next Senior Officials Meeting on the implementation of the DOC (SOM-DOC).[42] At the 6th SOM-DOC in September 2013 the Joint Working Group on the Implementation of the DOC (JWG-DOC) was assigned by the SOM-DOC to negotiate the details of the COC.[43] The China-ASEAN COC consultations formally started.

Mechanisms

Three parallel mechanisms are involved in the China-ASEAN COC consultation process, one within ASEAN, one within China and the third is the China-ASEAN mechanisms functioning as negotiating platforms among key players relating to major issues. As half of its members are involved in the South China Sea disputes, ASEAN plays an important role in promoting peace and security in the South China Sea. In practice, ASEAN is a venue for the ten members to coordinate the positions before their meetings with China. Within ASEAN, three layers of mechanisms are involved in the COC consultation and they are, from high to low, the ASEAN summit, the AMM and the ASEAN SOM. The AMM is the key player. Through the joint communiqué of each AMM, the ASEAN foreign ministers announce their decisions in relation to the COC consultation such as assigning tasks to and adopting drafts by the ASEAN SOM, or by submitting agreements to the ASEAN Summit for endorsement by the political leaders of the member states. Relevant decisions are announced in the statements released after each AMM or ASEAN summit. Within China, the Foreign Ministry (MFA) is the key authority representing China in its COC consultations with the ASEAN Member States. The Chinese delegation to the SOM-DOC is headed by a Vice Minister and the JWG-DOC by a high-level officer from the Department of Boundary and Ocean Affairs of the Chinese MFA supported by officers from other divisions and experts.

The China-ASEAN mechanisms include, from top to low, China-ASEAN Summits, China-ASEAN Foreign Ministers Meetings, the SOM-DOC, the JWG-DOC and the Eminent Persons and Experts Group (EPEG). While the latter three mechanisms are in charge of the practical work of negotiations, the agreements adopted will be submitted for endorsement by the other two levels of mechanisms. The SOM-DOC was established on 29 November 2004 with the responsibilities to "provide guidance for and review the implementation of the DOC." The JWG-DOC was established on 7 December 2004 with the obligations to "draw up the guidelines for the implementation of the DOC and to provide recommendations to the SOM-DOC on policy and implementation issues" as well as to identify actions that caused tension. The members of the EPEG were to be nominated by the JWG-DOC to provide technical support and non-binding policy recommendations.[44] Up till the end of 2019, the SOM-DOC had met 18 times and the JWG-DOC 30 times. To assist the COC consultations a decision was made at the 9th SOM-DOC in July 2015 to set up an EPEG.[45]

Process

Since the China-ASEAN mechanisms are the venues for the ASEAN Member States and China to communicate and negotiate over issues in relation to the COC, the process and achievements of the SOM-DOC and JWG-DOC reflect the COC process. An overview of the published ASEAN documents and the news relating to the 18 SOM-DOCs plus 30 JWG-DOCs (Annex 1) indicates that the COC consultation process has gone through three phases, namely, ASEAN's internal preparation process and informal communications with China from July 2011 to September 2013 when China and ASEAN countries formally started their COC consultation; China-ASEAN initial consultation for procedural matters till November 2017 when at the 20th China-ASEAN Summit the Leaders announced the official commencement of negotiations on the text of the COC; and substantive negotiations on the content of COC since March 2018 when the 22nd JWG-DOC was held to kick off the work for this phase.

During the first phase, while China took a cautious position toward the timing for restarting the COC negotiations, ASEAN member states in particular the Philippines and Vietnam were pressing ahead. ASEAN's efforts were focused on two aspects: involving China in restarting the consultation process and drafting ASEAN's COC to pass on to China. As early as July 2011 at the 44th AMM, the ASEAN SOM was assigned to work on a draft COC. In January 2012, the Philippines circulated an informal working draft COC for the ASEAN SOM to work on. The internal SOM discussion was convened on 13 June and the agreed draft was submitted to the ASEAN foreign ministers at the 45th AMM on 9 July which led to the ASEAN's *Proposed Elements of a Regional Code of Conduct in the South China Sea*. Based on the Key Elements and ASEAN's *Six Principles on the South China Sea*, Indonesia drafted its *Zero Draft A Regional Code of Conduct in the South China Sea* and circulated among the ASEAN members in September.[46] Meanwhile efforts were made at a series of China-ASEAN meetings to involve China in restarting the COC negotiation. China responded positively with caution by stating that China "keeps an open attitude," and hoped that all parties "abide by the DOC strictly to create an environment conducive to COC consultations".[47] On 9 August 2013 at a press conference after the China ASEAN (10+1) Foreign Ministers' Meeting Wang Yi stated that China advocated the "dual-track" approach in resolving the South China Sea issue, which means disputes over sovereignty and maritime jurisdiction were to be resolved by countries directly concerned and peace and stability in the South China Sea were to be managed by China and the ASEAN countries. This indicated that China had gradually accepted or coordinated with ASEAN over the COC consultations,[48] but at this stage, China's focus was on promoting practical co-operation at sea to build confidence in the region through, for example, the establishment of the China-ASEAN Maritime Cooperation Fund in 2011 and hosting two seminars on Disaster Reduction in the South China Sea and Marine Biological Environment and Supervision Technologies in 2012.[49]

The consultations at the second phase started with discussions over approaches and principles to be followed through the process and possible technical mechanism to be established. It was agreed at the 6th SOM-DOC which was held in Suzhou, China that the consultation should follow a "step-by-step approach" and the principle of "consensus through negotiation". Also on this occasion, the JWG-DOC was endowed to negotiate the details of the COC and establish an EPEG for such a purpose.[50] During this period the frequency of the JWG-DOC and SOM-DOC meetings was increased. The JWG-DOC met three times a year and in 2017 four meetings were held, while the SOM-DOC met twice a year and in 2016, there were three such occasions. The achievements included the adoption of two consensus documents to sum up the common ground of the parties and two open lists of "Crucial and Complex Issues" and "Elements of the Possible Framework of the COC" which foresees the key issues and challenges to be faced in the future negotiations. At the 12th SOM-DOC in June 2016, the nature of the COC and the approaches to design it were covered. Finally, at the 14th SOM-DOC in May 2017 the draft COC framework was adopted for endorsement by the Foreign Ministers of China and the ASEAN member states in their August retreat. The adoption of the COC Framework was hailed by all participants as an important periodic achievement,[51] which "provides a basis for future consultation" and signifies a "positive momentum"[52] for "the conclusion of an effective COC on a mutually-agreed timeline".[53] On 13 November 2017 at the 20th China-ASEAN Summit in Manila, it was announced that as a next step, the ASEAN Member States and China will officially commence substantive negotiations on the text of the COC.[54] It is worthwhile to note that during this period progress was also made in practical co-operation, including the adoption of the *Guidelines for Hotline Communications among Senior Officials of the Ministers of Foreign Affairs of the ASEAN Member States and China in Response to Maritime Emergencies at Sea* and *Joint Statement on the Application of CUES in the South China Sea*.[55]

The work for the third phase is expected to be tough when the substantive issues are to be negotiated. While claimant parties intend to maximize their interests a compromise needs to be made. After the 23rd and 24th JWG-DOC meetings, a Single Draft COC Negotiating Text (SDNT) was agreed upon at the 15th SOM-DOC on 27 June 2018.[56] It was also agreed to conclude an effective COC within a mutually agreed timeline after at least three readings of the draft text. The adoption of the SDNT indicated that all 11 parties had become stakeholders in the SDNT process.[57] Over eight months and four JWG-DOCs elapsed before the first reading was completed, which indicated the difficulty in reaching a comprise among the parties and led the Chinese and ASEAN ministers to "urge their Senior Officials to make further progress in subsequent readings towards the early conclusion of an effective and substantive COC" within "a 3-year timeline as proposed by China or earlier."[58] The second reading was announced at the 22nd China-ASEAN Summit in November 2019[59] and is to be followed by further reading(s).

The COC future: major issues of debate, key players and their positions

Key players and major issues of debate

As the COC consultation process came to negotiations over substantive issues it was described as in the "deep sea" area.[60] The future of the COC depends on the policies of the key players in this process, in particular how much they are willing to compromise their positions on the major issues of debate. During the process from the re-initiation to the current consultations, several key players could be identified as taking into consideration the positions of other claimant countries, and their level of involvement in the consultation process. For the purpose of this chapter, the authors take China, Vietnam, the Philippines, Malaysia and Indonesia into this category because (1) they have overlapping claims to the insular features in the South China Sea in whole or in part and (or) overlapping claim to maritime zones with other countries in the South China Sea, (2) they have been involved in noticeable incidents relating to their maritime claims, and (3) they are actively involved in the re-initiation of and discussions in the process. The non-claimant ASEAN members have a role to play but their focus of attention is more on the common interests than issues of debates. ASEAN plays a key role in creating a platform for China and ASEAN member states to discuss and to work towards a consensus over issues of mutual concern, therefore ASEAN has to focus on the goal and common interests of its member states while taking into consideration China's legitimate concerns.

Although it was agreed at the 15th SOM-DOC that all parties shall keep the SDNT strictly confidential throughout the entire process of COC negotiations,[61] the text was leaked out,[62] which shows major issues of debate when coming into the first reading of the SDNT. The major issues of debate include the geographic area, the status of the COC, duty to cooperate, dispute settlement and the role of third parties. As a "living document" and "a work in progress" it is possible that new issues might emerge in future readings.[63]

Positions of the key players

China

Since the consultation started in 2013, China has gradually adjusted its positions and become more active in offering its proposals and suggestions on mechanisms, ways of consultations and roadmap. As to the process, in August 2013 Wang Yi elaborated China's four views on the COC negotiation. Wang stated that expectations for the COC consultation process should be reasonable and it could not be a "quick fix" because the COC involved multilateral interests of different parties, and its formulation would be a process of sophisticated and complex coordination. Meanwhile, Wang stated that reaching a COC is a part of the implementation of the DOC, therefore the promotion of maritime co-operation is the current top priority.[64] Wang's speech indicated that China took a cautious approach in the beginning. After one year of coordination, China adjusted its position. In 2014 the statement by Chinese Premier Li Keqiang that China and ASEAN countries had agreed to actively carry out consultations to reach a COC "on the basis of consensus and at an early date" indicated that China's position on the timing of the COC is close to the ASEAN's, i.e., to have a COC at an early stage. This position was reiterated in his speech at the 2015 East Asia Summit (EAS).[65] China became more proactive in the COC consultation in 2016 and 2017 by providing China's visions and roadmap. At the 2016 ASEAN series meetings, after expressing the vision of adopting with ASEAN countries a COC framework by mid-2017, Wang Yi specifically indicated that China was willing to push ahead with the COC process with ASEAN on a "quick track."[66] At the China-ASEAN foreign ministers' meeting in August, Wang Yi proposed China's roadmap from the adoption of the COC framework to the discussions on measures, principles and action plan by the SOM-DOC, then to the announcement of the substantive consultations on the text by the end of the year.[67] China also adjusted its position of prioritizing the implementation of the DOC to the position of pushing ahead the implementation of the DOC and the COC consultations hand in hand, which was elaborated in Li Keqiang's speech at the 2015 China-ASEAN Summit. At the 21st China-ASEAN Summit in 2018, Li further proposed China's vision of working together with ASEAN countries to reach a COC within three years from 2019 to 2021.[68] As to the approaches to the final COC, China supported "consensus through negotiations" and "elimination of interference," which means all parties should make efforts to create the necessary conditions and atmosphere conducive to the consultation and the process should observe maximum consensus and respect the comfort level of each claimant party.[69]

As to the content, in Li Keqiang's speech at the 2015 EAS, two of the five initiations can be considered as being related to the content of the COC. While the statement that countries outside the region should respect and support the efforts from countries in the region for maintaining peace and stability is related to behaviours of third parties, "all countries enjoy the freedom of navigation and overflight in the South China Sea" is in relation to the basic principles. In 2019, Chinese high officials further elaborated their positions at the ASEAN series meetings in July and the Summit in November. Regarding the actual effectiveness of the future COC, Wang Yi emphasized that the COC would be a more strengthened and upgraded version of the DOC, and when in place "it will be high-quality regional rules with more binding force and more concrete connotations that better meet the actual needs of the region." When referring to the third parties, Wang Yi commented that the freedom of navigation and overflight "will be further safeguarded, and the legitimate rights and interests of non-regional countries will be better protected."[70] At the 14th EAS and 22nd China-ASEAN summit, Li Keqiang shared his three comments on the COC:

- the COC is an upgraded version of the DOC, representing the same principles, spirits and key elements but more effective, with more substantive content and more operational.
- the COC represents important regional rules to be jointly formulated, observed and implemented by China and the ten ASEAN countries. As such, the COC reflects the common interests and concerns of the 11 parties.
- the purpose of the COC is to build trust and promote cooperation with differences properly managed.[71]

The points China proposed in the SDNT indicated that China's focus is on promoting maritime cooperation in six areas: conservation of fishing resources, maritime law and security cooperation, navigation and search and rescue, MSR and MEP, marine economy including aquaculture and oil and gas cooperation, and marine culture. It was observed that China was sensitive to involving companies from countries outside the region in economic cooperation and joint military exercises in the South China Sea.[72] China proposed that military activities must be "conducive to enhancing trust" and encourage military-to-military cooperation among the parties. China further proposed that military vessels and aircraft enjoy sovereign immunity.[73] The core of China's policy is to establish the image of a responsible power through the COC consultation process to create law and order in the South China Sea.[74]

Vietnam and the Philippines

Vietnam's positions relating to the COC consultation are elaborated at various DOC-SOM meetings. Vietnam supports the early conclusion of a COC from the re-initiation within ASEAN in 2011. In 2016 the Head of Vietnam Delegation stressed the need to promptly reach a COC and proposed increasing the frequency of meetings and discussions for drafting the COC.[75] Vietnam strongly supports a legally-binding COC which officially appeared in its joint statement with the US signed during President Trump's visit to Hanoi in November 2017 as both parties "called for …an early conclusion to an effective, legally binding Code of Conduct for the South China Sea (COC)."[76] For Vietnam, to have a legally-binding COC is to "regulate relevant parties' behaviours"[77] and "manage and prevent disputes" in the South China Sea.[78] Vietnam strongly supports under the "duty to cooperate" that self-restraint of Point 5 in the DOC should be elaborated in the COC by listing activities of "to-do" and "not-to-do".[79] Therefore in the SDNT, Vietnam listed 27 points, including: respect for maritime zones as provided for and established in accordance with the 1982 UNCLOS; 60 days notification of impending joint/combined military exercise/drill; no construction on any artificial island; no militarization of features; no blockade of vessels carrying provisions or personnel for rotation; no declaration of an Air Defense Identification Zone (ADIZ) in the South China Sea.[80] As to "geographic scope", Vietnam proposed that the COC "shall apply to all disputed features and overlapping maritime areas claimed under the 1982 UNCLOS in the South China Sea."[81] As Le pointed out that Vietnam holds the position that the COC should be applicable to both the Paracels and the Spratlys, as well as the disputed waters in the South China Sea. As to "dispute settlement", Vietnam proposed that parties settle their disputes "through friendly negotiations, enquiry, mediation, conciliation and other means as may be agreed by the disputing Contracting Parties." Vietnam further suggested that if the above measures failed, the parties should invoke the High Council offered in the TAC and nothing in the COC "shall prevent" the peaceful settlement of disputes under Article 33(1) of the UN Charter which may include arbitration, judicial settlement, resort to regional agencies or arrangements, or other peaceful means decided by the parties concerned.[82]

In 2011 and 2012 when the concept of COC was reinitiated within ASEAN, the Philippines were active in pushing forward and drafting the ASEAN COC, but for the next three and half years, it was pre-occupied by its initiated South China Sea Arbitration Case against China until Duterte took office as the Philippines' president on 30 June 2016. When the Philippines became the Chair of ASEAN in 2017 it set the COC consultation as a priority for the ASEAN agenda.[83] Duterte clarified his vision of the COC before his fifth working visit to China late August 2019. He would push for a binding COC at an early stage to reduce tension and minimize the risk of incidents and miscalculation.[84] At the SOM-DOC level, the Philippines' inputs in the SDNT focus more on "Duty to cooperate." The Philippines proposed five areas of cooperation including MEP, MSR, the safety of navigation and communication at sea and combating transnational crime. Together with China, it proposed a call for the "just and humane treatment of all persons who are either in danger or in distress in the South China Sea."[85]

Malaysia and Indonesia

Malaysia supports the regional efforts to reach a COC and recognizes the importance of dispute management for better broader relations. Although it still keeps silent on proposals for maritime crisis management, it is flexible on existing and new crisis-management and confidence-building initiatives in the South China Sea.[86] When Malaysia presented its proposals in the SDNT, it kept vague regarding the "geographic scope" and proposed that "depending on the operative elements/contents of the COC, the geographic scope/scope of application may have to be defined."[87] Malaysia did give support to the High Council of the TAC for dispute settlement. Malaysia tried to preserve its rights in choosing business partners in marine resources exploitation in the South China Sea by proposing that nothing in the COC "shall affect... rights or ability of the Parties to conduct activities with foreign countries or private entities of their own choosing."[88]

Indonesia was active in pushing ahead a regional COC from the beginning. In 2012 it circulated its zero draft document of the COC among ASEAN members. At that year's 45th AMM meeting in July, Indonesia's then Foreign Minister stressed the need to conclude a COC at an early stage, meanwhile the COC must be "prescriptive" to provide rules and means.[89] As to "dispute settlement," Indonesia continued to pursue its position in the zero draft. While proposing the High Council of TAC or other international dispute settlement mechanism, it emphasized the consent of the parties. Indonesia continued to support cooperation areas listed in the DOC and added illegal fishing to the DOC list on transnational crimes.[90]

Concluding remarks

Up till now China and ASEAN have experienced two attempts to establish regional rules to regulate the behaviour of relevant parties in the South China Sea. The first resulted in the DOC and the ongoing process is to reach an agreement on a more effective COC. The re-initiation of the COC consultation process is closely linked with the overall situation in the South China Sea. When incidents between competing claimants increase in frequency and intensity, tension follows and regional peace and stability are negatively impacted. Then there is a common urge and interest in reaching an agreement on a regional COC. The purpose is to have a regional rules-based order, in which China and the ten ASEAN countries are to constrain their behaviour within the set of rules. These rules are preventive for avoiding incidents and to constrain them from escalation if they do occur.

Up to the completion of the first reading of the SDNT, China and ASEAN countries, the key players in particular, had been trying to promote their own interests which may increase distrust among the parties. The gaps in trust need to be bridged before reaching the final COC. Other challenges include the Arbitration Case. China did not participate in the Arbitration Case and does not accept the awards, while the Philippines will not ignore them and the non-parties to the Case including Vietnam, Malaysia and Indonesia may invoke the Case, either explicitly or implicitly, to their advantage.

However, it is the consensus that for the long-term peace and stability in the South China Sea, it is important that the COC achieves effectiveness in ensuring that relevant parties exercise self-restraint, promote confidence-building measures and implement co-operative activities in non-sensitive areas. Since the start of the official consultations in 2013, all 11 countries have shown their commitment to reaching a COC through official statements and joint statements. Meanwhile, the consultation mechanisms have been set up and they had over nearly 20 years' experience of negotiation and compromises. With further readings to come, the key players have to be willing to comprise in order to make the COC a reality.

Appendix A2: SOM-DOC&JWG-DOC Meetings and Achievements on COC Consultations (2011-)

Date and Place	*SOM-DOC*	*JWG-DOC*
18 Apr. 2011 Medan, Indonesia		6th JWG-DOC Constructive consultation
20 Jul. 2011 Bali, Indonesia	3rd SOM-DOC Adoption of the Guidelines for the Implementation of the DOC and its point 6 reads: The decision to implement concrete measures or activities of the DOC should be based on consensus among parties concerned and lead to the eventual realization of a Code of Conduct.	

Date and Place	SOM-DOC	JWG-DOC
14 Jan. 2012 Beijing, China	4th SOM-DOC Consensus reached on making full use of the SOM-DOC and the JWG-DOC; setting up technical committees on MSR, MEP, S&R and combatting transnational crimes at sea; promoting practical cooperation in the SCS through the China-ASEAN Maritime Cooperation Fund. According to the Workplan 2012 adopted at the SOM-DOC, China hosted two seminars on Disaster Reduction in the South China Sea and Marine Biological Environment and Supervision Technologies.	
Jun. 2012 Hanoi, Vietnam	5th SOM-DOC Consensus reached on promotion of the implementation of the DOC and cooperation in the South China Sea	
14–15 Sep. 2013 Suzhou, China	6th SOM-DOC Agreement on consultations done by following "step-by-step approach and consensus through negotiation" and starting with finding out existing consensus; steadily pushing ahead COC process during full implementation of the DOC; endowment to the JWG-DOC on negotiating the details of the COC; decision to establish a EPEG for such a purpose.	9th JWG-DOC
18 Mar. 2014 Singapore		10th JWG-DOC
21 Apr. 2014 Pattaya, Thailand	7th SOM-DOC Discussion over cooperation projects and establishment of three technical committees and guiding views on the work by the JWG-DOC; agreement on steadily pushing ahead the COC consultation process.	
25 Jun. 2014 Bali, Indonesia		11th JWG-DOC
28–29 Oct. 2014 Bangkok, Thailand	8th SOM-DOC Confirmation of the consultation approach of "finding out a consensus, starting from the easier and consensus through negotiation"; adoption of the first consensus document.	12th JWG-DOC
29 Jul. 2015 Tianjin, China	9th SOM-DOC Adoption of the second consensus document and the Terms of Reference for the EPEG; endowment to the JWG-DOC on establishing the EPEG at an early stage; implementation of the "early harvest" projects; the decision to start the next phase of consultation to discuss "the important and complicated issues" for finding out the key elements for the COC framework; endowment to the JWG-DOC on drafting "working methods."	
20 Oct. 2015 Chengdu, China	10th SOM-DOC Conclusion of two open lists of "Crucial and Complex Issues" and "Elements of the Possible Outline of the COC," endowment to the JWG-DOC on continuous work on the two lists; agreement on the content of 2015 achievements: the second consensus document, the term of reference for the EPEG and the above two lists.	15th JWG-DOC

(*Continued*)

Date and Place	*SOM-DOC*	*JWG-DOC*
27 Apr. 2016 Singapore	11th SOM-DOC Agreement on enriching the content of the "List of Elements of the Possible Outline of a COC" and the "List of Crucial and Complex Issues" establishment of the EPEG at an early stage; Implementation of the "Early Harvest" projects including establishing a hotline in response to urgent contingencies at sea for Chinese and ASEAN foreign affairs senior officials and a China-ASEAN hotline for search and rescue at sea; discussion on the possibilities of application of CUES in the South China Sea.	16th JWG-DOC
9 Jun. 2016 Quảng Ninh, Vietnam	12th SOM-DOC First discussion on the nature of the COC and approaches to designing it; Agreement to draft "*Guidelines for Hotline Communications among Senior Officials of the Ministers of Foreign Affairs of the ASEAN Member States and China*; complete the ASEAN-China Joint Statement on the Implementation of the Code for Unplanned Encounters at Sea.	17th JWG-DOC
15–16 Aug. 2016 Manzhouli, China	13th SOM-DOC Commit to foster rules-based regional framework to manage differences, deepen practical maritime cooperation, advance COC consultation; adopt two outcome documents, i.e., *Guidelines for Hotline Communications among Senior Officials of the Ministers of Foreign Affairs of the ASEAN Member States and China in Response to Maritime Emergencies at Sea* and *Joint Statement on the Application of CUES in the South China Sea;* exchanged views on ways to achieve the "four visions" on COC consultation without interference.	18th JWG-DOC
27 Feb. 2017 Bali, Indonesia		19th JWG-DOC Agree on the basic outline of the draft framework
30 Mar. 2017 Siem Reap, Cambodia		20th JWG-DOC Discuss a longer version of the draft framework
17–18 May 2017 Guiyang, China	14th SOM-DOC Adoption of the draft COC framework; adoption of the Non-document on the Procedure to Set up the Three Technical Committees and the results of the testing operation of the China-ASEAN Senior Foreign Affairs Officials.	21st JWG-DOC
30 Aug. 2017 Manila, the Philippines		22nd JWG-DOC exchange views on implementing the DOC; boost maritime cooperation; consult on the COC

Date and Place	SOM-DOC	JWG-DOC
1–2 Mar. 2018 Nha Trang, Vietnam		23rd JWG-DOC Consult on the COC
27 June 2018 Changsha, China	15th SOM-DOC Agreement on a Single Draft COC Negotiating Text (SDNT); discussion on the content of COC and methods for negotiating this document; discussion on the next steps and content to be reported to the ASEAN-China PMC.	24th JWG-DOC (25–26 Jun. 2018) discuss details of the COC; clarify the principles and the next activities: agree to regular reports of the progress and outcomes to the SOM-DOC and (PMC). two ad hoc technical meetings on MEP and safety of navigation
1–2 Sep. 2018 Siem Reap, Cambodia		25th JWG-DOC Start the first reading of the SDNT
24–26 October 2018 Manila, the Philippines	16th SOM-DOC Joint emphasis on the importance of the full and effective implementation of the DOC and on greater efforts to build a practical and effective COC; agreement on extension of the action plan on the implementation of the DOC during 2016–2021; urging the JWG to step up exchanges and discussions to achieve effective negotiations	26th JWG-DOC (24–25 October)
27–28 February 2019 Nay Pyi Taw, Myanmar		27th JWG-DOC Discuss the SDNT; acknowledge the progress in the implementation of the DOC and the negotiations of the COC

(*Continued*)

Date and Place	*SOM-DOC*	*JWG-DOC*
18 May 2019 Hangzhou, China	17th SOM-DOC Conclusion of the first reading of the COC text; agreement on speeding up the negotiations in order to reach the COC at an early date; adoption of the DOC implementation plan for 2016–2021	28th JWG-DOC
1 July 2019 Malaysia		29th JWG-DOC
15 Oct. 2019 Da Lat, Vietnam	18th SOM-DOC Exchange view on the second review of the COC text; agree to redouble efforts to conclude an effective and result-oriented code; discuss new working methods	30th JWG-DOC (13–14 Oct.)

Note: Sources to each meeting listed here are from official websites of ASEAN and Ministry of Foreign Affairs of participating countries of the mechanisms, as well as news. Information on relevant links is available from the authors.

Notes

1 Leszek Buszynski, "ASEAN, the Declaration on Conduct, and the South China Sea," *Contemporary Southeast Asia* 25, no. 3 (2003): 343–362, at 344.

2 Zhou Shixin, "Code of Conduct for Constructing a Regional Order in South China Sea," *Asia-Pacific Security and Maritime Affairs* 5 (2018): 84–96, at 84.

3 Shirley V. Scott, "A Rules-Based Order for the Asia-Pacific: Identifying Opportunities for Australia-Japan Cooperation in Strengthening Rules-Based Order in the Asia-Pacific: Deepening Japan-Australia Cooperation to Promote Regional Order," *ASPI Special Report*, December 2014, at 16; Wu Shicun and Chen Xiangmiao, "Ocean Governance in the South China Sea from the Perspective of Ocean Order Evolution," *Pacific Journal* 26, no. 4 (2018): 25–36, at 27.

4 Supra note 1, at 350.

5 1992 ASEAN Declaration on the South China Sea, available at https://cil.nus.edu.sg/wp-content/uploads/2017/07/1992-ASEAN-Declaration-on-the-South-China-Sea.pdf (accessed on 3 November 2019).

6 Luo Yongkun, "COC: Initiation, Process and Prospects," *International Studies* 8 (2017): 2–11, at 6.

7 Rodolfo C. Severino, "ASEAN and the South China Sea," *Security Challenges* 6, no. 2 (2010): 37–47, at 42.

8 Ibid.

9 Nguyen Hong Thao and Ramses Amer, "A New Legal Arrangement for the South China Sea," *Ocean Development and International Law* 40, no. 4 (October–December 2009): 333–349, at 336–337.

10 Supra note 6 at 6.

11 Joint Communique of the 29th ASEAN Ministerial Meeting, available at https://cil.nus.edu.sg/wp-content/uploads/formidable/18/1996-29th-AMMJC.pdf (accessed on 1 December 2019).

12 Hanoi Plan of Action, available at http://www.asean.org/news/item/hanoi-plan-of-action (accessed on 15 January 2020).

13 Supra note 6 at 7.

14 Point 10 of "Declaration on the Conduct of Parties in the South China Sea", available at https://asean.org/?static_post=declaration-on-the-conduct-of-parties-in-the-south-china-sea-2 (accessed on 1 November 2019); Supra note 9 at 337.

15 Point 1 of the DOC, ibid.

16 Joint Statement of the 15th ASEAN-China Summit on the 10th Anniversary of the Declaration on the Conduct of Parties in the South China Sea, available at http://www.china.org.cn/world/2012-11/20/content_27167423.htm (accessed on 3 November 2019).

17 Supra note 9 at 337–339.

18 Ramses Amer, "The South China Sea: Challenge for ASEAN," *Policy Brief* 150 (2014), available at https://isdp.eu/content/uploads/publications/2014-amer-the-south-china-sea-challenge-for-asean.pdf (accessed on 1 October 2015).

19 Carlyle A. Thayer, "ASEAN, China and the Code of Conduct in the South China Sea," *SAIS Review of International Affairs* 33, no. 2 (2013): 75–84 at 77.
20 Nguyen Hong Thao, "The 2002 Declaration on the Conduct of Parties in the South China Sea: A Note," *Ocean Development and International Law* 34, no. 3–4 (2003): 279–286, at 281.
21 Wu Shicun and Ren Huaifeng, "More than a Declaration: A Commentary on the Background and Significance of the Declaration on the Conduct of the Parties in the South China Sea," *Chinese Journal of International Law* 2, no. 1 (2003): 311–320, at 311.
22 Supra note 20 at 280.
23 Supra note 9 at 337.
24 Supra note 20 at 280.
25 Supra note 9 at 338.
26 Le Hong Hiep, "Vietnam's Position on the South China Sea Code of Conduct," *Perspective* 22 (2019), Yusof Ishak Institute.
27 Li Mingjiang, "Managing Security in the South China Sea: from DOC to COC," available at https://kyotoreview.org/issue-15/managing-security-in-the-south-china-sea-from-doc-to-coc/ (accessed on 18 November 2019).
28 Supra note 19 at 77.
29 Supra note 21 at 311.
30 Supra note 9 at 338–339.
31 Lim Kheng Swe, Ju Hailong and Li Mingjiang, "China's Revisionist Aspirations in Southeast Asia and the Curse of the South China Sea Disputes," *China: An International Journal* 15, no. 1 (2017): 187–213, at 210.
32 For details of the verbal row, see Jianwei Li and Ramses Amer, "Managing Tensions in the South China Sea: Comparing China-Philippines and China-Vietnam Approaches," in *Power, Law, and Maritime Order in the South China Sea*, edited by Tran Truong Thuy and Le Hung Trang (Lanham, MD: Lexington Books, An imprint of Rowman & Littlefield, 2015): 243–265.
33 For details of dispute situation between China and the Philippines and China and Vietnam from 2009 to 2014, see ibid.; Ramses Amer, "China and Vietnam: Managing Tensions in Troubled Waters," *Policy Brief*, no. 141, 21 January 2014; Ramses Amer, "China-Vietnam Drilling Rig Incident: Reflections and Implications," *Policy Brief*, No. 158, 19 August 2014. Institute For Security and Development Policy.
34 Press Conference by Spokesperson Jiang Yu of 20 October 2012, available at http://www.fmprc.gov.cn/chn/gxh/tyb/fyrbt/jzhsl/t869317.htm (accessed on 26 October 2012).
35 Hoang Thi Ha, "From Declaration to Code: Continuity and Change in China's Engagement with ASEAN on the South China Sea," *Trends in Southeast Asia 5 (2019)*, ISEAS Yusof Ishak Institute, at 2; Carlyle A. Thayer, "ASEANS Code of Conduct in the South China Sea: A Litmus Test for Community-Building?," *The Asia-Pacific Journal* 10, no. 34, 4 (2012) at 3.
36 Joint Communiqué of the 44th ASEAN Foreign Ministers Meeting, available at https://asean.org/wp-content/uploads/images/archive/documents/44thAMM-PMC-18thARF/44thAMM-JC.pdf (accessed on 30 November 2019).
37 ASEAN's Six-Point Principles on the South China Sea, available at https://www.asean.org/storage/images/AFMs%20Statement%20on%206%20Principles%20on%20SCS.pdf (accessed on 10 December 2019).
38 Zhang Mingliang, "Compromise under the Principle: ASEAN and the Code of Conduct for the South China Sea," *Southeast Aslan Studies* 3 (2018): 58–80, at 73.
39 Joint Communiqué of the 46th ASEAN Foreign Ministers' Meeting, available at https://www.asean.org/wp-content/uploads/images/2013/news/joint%20communique%20of%20the%2046th%20asean%20foreign%20ministers%20meeting%2046th%20amm%20-%20final%20-%2030%20june%202013.pdf (accessed on 12 November 2019).
40 Lin Liming, "New Developments in China's Foreign Policies after the 18th Party Congress," available at http://www.banyuetan.org/chcontent/sz/hqkd/2014113/90915.shtml (accessed on 30 January 2010).
41 Supra note 27.
42 Liu Dongkai, "Push Ahead the COC Consultation with a Responsible and Pragmatic Attitude," *XinhuaNet*, available at http://www.gov.cn/jrzg/2013-08/05/content_2461618.htm (accessed on 25 December, 2019).
43 The 6 SOM-DOC and the 9 JWG-DOC were held in Suzhou, available at https://www.fmprc.gov.cn/web/wjb_673085/zzjg_673183/bjhysws_674671/xgxw_674673/t1099054.shtml (accessed on 3 October 2019).

44 Para. 1.5.2 of "Plan of Action to Implement the Joint Declaration on ASEAN-China Strategic Partnership for Peace and Prosperity", available at https://asean.org/?static_post=plan-of-action-to-implement-the-joint-declaration-on-asean-china-strategic-partnership-for-peace-and-prosperity (accessed on 22 January 2020); Huang Yao, "Drafting a Code of Conduct in the South China Sea: Developments, Issues and Prospects," *Law-based Society* 1 (2016): 23–36, at 26–28.
45 The 9th SOM-DOC was held in Tianjing, available at http://www.xinhuanet.com/politics/2015-07/29/c_1116082906.htm (accessed on 13 November 2019).
46 Thayer, Supra note 35 at 3; Mark J. Valencia, "What the Zero Draft Code of Conduct for the South China Sea Says (and Doesn't Say)," available at http://www.globalasia.org/v8no1/feature/what-the-zero-draft-code-of-conduct-for-the-south-china-sea-says-and-doesnt-say_mark-j-valencia (accessed on 30 November 2019).
47 Press Conference by Chinese Foreign Ministry Spokesperson Hong Lei in Regard to ASEAN's Six Principles on the South China Sea, available at http://www.gov.cn/xwfb/2012-07/21/content_2188719.htm (accessed on 16 December 2019).
48 Supra note 38 at 75.
49 China, ASEAN held a SOM-DOC, available at http://news.sina.com.cn/c/2012-01-14/213523801551.shtml (accessed on 21 January 2020).
50 Supra note 43.
51 The 14th SOM-DOC was held, available at https://www.fmprc.gov.cn/nanhai/chn/wjbxw/t1463132.htm (accessed on 8 October 2019).
52 Chee Wee Kion, "Joint Press Briefing on the 14th ASEAN-China Senior Officials' Meeting on the Implementation of the Declaration on the Conduct of Parties in the South China Sea(SOM-DOC)," available at https://asean.org/storage/2017/05/14th-SOM-DOC-Co-Chairs-Joint-Press-Briefing-Remarks-As-delivered-18-May-amen.pdf (accessed on 8 December 2019).
53 Chairman's Statement of the ASEAN Post Ministerial Conference (PMC) 10+1 Sessions with the Dialogue Partners, available at https://asean.org/wp-content/uploads/2017/08/ASEAN-PMC-Chairmans-Statement-FINAL1.pdf (accessed on 17 December 2019).
54 Chairman's Statement on the 20th China-ASEAN Summit, available at https://asean.org/wp-content/uploads/2017/11/FINAL-Chairmans-Statement-of-the-20th-ASEAN-China-Summit-13-Nov-2017-Manila1.pdf (accessed on 11 November 2019).
55 Ibid.
56 Chairman's Statement of the ASEAN Post Ministerial Conference (PMC) 10+1 Sessions with the Dialogue Partners, available at https://asean.org/wp-content/uploads/2018/08/Chairmans-Statement-of-the-ASEAN-PMCs-final1.pdf (accessed on 17 December 2019).
57 Carl Thayer, "ASEAN and China Set to Agree on Single South China Sea Code of Conduct," *The Diplomat*, available at https://thediplomat.com/2018/07/asean-and-china-set-to-agree-on-single-draft-south-china-sea-code-of-conduct/ (accessed on 10 December 2019).
58 Chairman's Statement of the PMC with dialogue Partners, available at https://asean.org/storage/2019/08/Chairmans-Statement-of-the-PMC-with-DP_FINAL.pdf (accessed on 17 December 2019).
59 Chairman's Statement of the 22nd ASEAN-China Summit, available at https://asean.org/storage/2019/11/Chairmans-Statement-of-the-22nd-ASEAN-China-Summit-final.pdf (accessed on 11 December 2019).
60 Yan Yan, "Review of the 'COC' and Prospects of the Consultation over the Text," *South China Sea Review* 2 (2017): 85–101, at 85.
61 Supra note 57.
62 For the discussion of the SDNT, see Carl Thayer, "A Closer Look at the ASEAN-China Single Draft South China Sea Code of Conduct," available at https://thediplomat.com/2018/08/a-closer-look-at-the-asean-china-single-draft-south-china-sea-code-of-conduct/ (accessed on 8 August 2018).
63 Ibid.
64 Foreign Minister Wang Yi On Process of "Code of Conduct in the South China Sea," available at http://www.chinaembassy.se/eng//xwdt/t1064869.htm (accessed on 25 December 2019).
65 Speech by Li Keqing at 10th East Asia Summit, available at http://www.gov.cn/guowuyuan/2015-11/23/content_5015797.htm (accessed on 3 November 2019).
66 China proposed "four visions" to ASEAN, available at http://m.international.caixin.com/m/2016-07-25/100970512.html (accessed on 18 December 2019).

67 Wang Yi proposed the roadmap over the COC consultation at China-ASEAN Foreign Ministers' Meeting, available at http://m.news.cctv.com/2017/08/06/ARTI0WcJ4nb7tRGUf5sSc-cIU170806.shtml (accessed on 20 December 2019).
68 Speech by Li Keqiang at the 21 China-ASEAN Summit, available at http://www.gov.cn/guowuyuan/2018-11/15/content_5340502.htm (accessed on 20 December 2019).
69 Supra note 64.
70 Chinese state councilor says consultations on COC in South China Sea can be concluded in time, available at http://www.xinhuanet.com/english/2019-08/01/c_138275052.htm (accessed on 28 January 2020).
71 Speech by H.E. Li Keqiang Premier of the State Council of The People's Republic of China At the 22nd China-ASEAN Summit, available at https://www.fmprc.gov.cn/mfa_eng/wjdt_665385/zyjh_665391/t1713324.shtml (accessed on 20 December 2019).
72 Supra note 62.
73 Ibid.
74 Chen Cihang and Kong Lingjie, "Sino-American Cognitive Differences and Policy Interaction on the Code of Conduct in the South China Sea," *Southeast Asia Studies* 3 (2018): 81–107, at 105.
75 ASEAN and China senior officials in 12th meeting, available at https://vietnamnews.vn/politics-laws/297999/asean-and-china-senior-officials-in-12th-meeting.html (accessed on 31 January 2020).
76 Joint Statement between the United States of America and the Socialist Republic of Vietnam, available at https://www.whitehouse.gov/briefings-statements/joint-statement-united-states-america-socialist-republic-vietnam/ (accessed on 15 November 2017).
77 ASEAN, China urge trust building measures in DOC implementation, available at https://en.vietnamplus.vn/asean-china-urge-trust-building-measures-in-doc-implementation/133633.vnp (accessed on 10 February 2020).
78 Supra note 75.
79 Ibid.
80 Supra note 26; supra note 62.
81 Ibid.
82 Ibid.
83 Supra note 38 at 77.
84 Renato Cruz De Castro, "The Philippines' Complicity in Creating China's Vision of Regional Order," available at https://www.philstar.com/other-sections/news-feature/2019/11/09/1967327/commentary-philippines-complicity-creating-chinas-vision-regional-order#XK81Uwe2Far-MxgSz.99 (accessed on 3 December 2019).
85 Supra note 62.
86 Prashanth Parameswaran, "Malaysia's Approach to the South China Sea Dispute after the Arbitral Tribunal's Ruling," *Contemporary Southeast Asia* 38, no. 3 (2016): 375–381, at 377–378.
87 Supra note 62.
88 Ibid.
89 Supra note 35.
90 Supra note 62.

20

MAINLAND CHINA-TAIWAN INTERPLAY IN THE SOUTH CHINA SEA

Fu-Kuo Liu

Introduction

The nature of South China Sea (SCS) claims by mainland China (People's Republic of China, PRC) and Taiwan (Republic of China, ROC) was clearly originated from the same historical and political foundation. Right after the end of the Second World War, ROC's Ministry of Interior made it clear to publish *The Location Map of the South China Sea Islands* in 1947 on which the "11-dashed line" is based, as a way of preventing others from encroaching its territorial integrity of sovereignty.[1] In 1951, after PRC was established, the communist government in Beijing gave up two-dashed lines within the Gulf of Tonkin (also named Beibu Bay) to its communist brother – Vietnam. Thus, it became a "9-dashed line." Although for political reasons Taiwan may have gradually tended to take an ambiguous position on territorial claims as a process of democratization and differentiation away from the relevance of "China," it does not change any historical links with China's sovereignty per se. The unsettledness of the cross-strait political relation would determine any possibilities of cooperation or hindrance on policy issues, especially the SCS issue. Many may wonder if they both have confidentially conducted policy coordination for the same position. In all counts, the same position China and Taiwan have taken in the SCS issue does not mean that there has been a clear coordination on policy between Beijing and Taipei. Rather, based on reckoning of respective policy interests, over the last few decades, it came up mostly to be parallel with, if not contradicted to, each other.

Although PRC and ROC have not been able to conduct policy coordination, their SCS policies have over time proven to be mostly paralleled with each other. Politically, both PRC and ROC are still at the status of civil war. However, in protecting sovereign integrity in the SCS, they have been firm on keeping policy line against the intrusion of the rest of the claimants. In spite of political estrangement, PRC and ROC may often come up with a more compatible policy on the SCS. It is always interesting to see what both adversaries based on the same territorial claims present as quite opposite approaches to protecting sovereignty. This chapter examines cross-strait interplay on the SCS issues and envisages future development under the circumstance of worsening cross-strait relations today. When both Beijing and Taipei follow their constitutional courses, the SCS issue would be of similarity in policy presentation. However, if Taipei considers that a new political course may tend to revolutionize the existing constitution, common grounds in the SCS would be eliminated dramatically with Beijing. As the US-China strategic competition intensifies further, Taiwan risks strategic uncertainty in the SCS and the Taiwan Strait.

Political antagonism with coherence of "One China" conviction

China's civil war between PRC and ROC has not officially ended as of today. During President Chiang Kai-Shek's duration (five terms of presidency, 1950–1975) in power, PRC fought against ROC several battles along the Chinese mainland coastal areas. Over the last few decades, there were three crises across the Taiwan Strait: the first in 1954–1955, the second in 1958, and the third in 1995–1996, which defined deep antagonism between ROC and PRC along the line of the Cold War.

Immediately after the end of the Second World War, ROC established political and military domination in the entire SCS areas within the 11-dashed line, while PRC was mostly preoccupied with the inward-looking of the nation-building process. Until the 1970s, ROC's jurisdiction over the SCS was fully recognized by the international community and with no objection from neighbouring states. Although PRC did not have much liberty to be actively involved in managing the SCS matters then, it did not challenge ROC's control over the SCS. On 19 January 1974, the Battle of the Paracels (Xisha Islands) broke out between the Republic of Vietnam (South Vietnam) Navy and the Chinese People's Liberation Army Navy (PLAN). In consideration of naval disadvantage in the SCS, Beijing quickly dispatched three missile frigates of the East Sea fleet to reinforce the contingency. ROC had military superiority over the Taiwan Strait, but the flotilla went by the strait safely without having been inflicted from the ROC navy's challenge. It is said that the late President Chiang Kai-shek understandably admitted PLAN vessels to sail across because the Battle of the Paracels was considered protecting China's sovereign integrity, which was equally shared by Beijing and Taipei then.[2]

The historical example shows that protecting the territorial sovereign integrity of the SCS is fully shared by ROC and PRC, though their political difference and even prolonged hostility remain. Much of what they have claimed is almost parallel with the national interest of each other. ROC in 1947 made the territory in the SCS clear by regulating the "11-dashed line" (or the U-shaped Line), while PRC in 1953 on the foundation of the 11-dashed line removed two dashed lines inside the Beibu Bay, which became the known "9-dashed line." No matter what the 11-dashed line or 9-dashed line goes until today, this is what the international community identifies the bases of ROC and PRC's position in the SCS, as well as the prevailing definition of SCS geography and geopolitical landscape.

Basically, on the SCS sovereign issues and territorial disputes, ROC and PRC do not have any different claims and insistence, as they both are originated from the same historic sources of evidence and practical involvement. From the aspect of a common origin, the SCS serves as a political adhesion to tie ROC and PRC together regardless of political estrangement. With "One China" conviction in politics across the Taiwan Strait, ROC and PRC will of course uphold the right to protect their sovereignty according to their definition of national interest respectively.

Watershed of different perceptions to the SCS

For long, Beijing's desire for national unification with Taiwan defines the path of engagement with Taipei. When PRC's overall national strength increases, it boosts confidence in employing comprehensive means to facilitate the process of peaceful unification vis-à-vis

Taiwan, i.e. united front strategy. For Taipei and Beijing, their SCS policy may have the same story to tell, but their approaches towards the SCS are rather different. During the eras of President Chiang Kai-Shek and Chiang Ching-Kuo (1978–1988), ROC's commitment to maintaining the sovereign integrity of the SCS was unquestionably affirmative. From the 1950s to the 1980s, ROC resorted to political and military means to guard against external attempts to infringe on its territorial sovereignty. Quite frequently, ROC's government dispatched contingent troops to dispel illegal occupation of the Paracels by France and of the Spratlys (Nansha Islands) by the Philippines. ROC's policy toward the SCS continues to be very firm and complete.

Over the last three decades, the democratization process taking place in Taiwan does gradually change the relevance of the SCS to its national policy and general perception of territorial sovereignty. Many have wondered why Taiwan declines its involvement in the SCS issues. Even, elites in Taiwan are worrying about ROC being marginalized in the SCS issues. Although generation transformations and regime changes in Taiwan signal a new tendency of different perceptions to the SCS, Democratic Progressive Party's (DPP) main political intention of pushing for independence and driving away from China matters the most. Almost since 1995 when ROC maritime police (the then coast guard force) abruptly failed a regular patrol mission to the Spratly Islands, the intensity and strength of territorial claim have been weakened as a result of political intrigue played up by President Lee Teng-hui and deteriorating cross-strait relation then. Immediately after the incident, in order to manage contingencies in the SCS, the Ministry of Interior assembled a task force on "Contingent Response to Emergencies in the South China Sea". However, two years later the original "SCS Task Force" was put on hold till 2003.[3] The political transformation taking place in Taiwan which led to the process of democratization deeply influences political perception and redirects Taipei's political agenda on the SCS.

From the 1950s to the 1960s, newly independent countries such as the Philippines became interested in exploring control of land features in the SCS, mainly the Spratly Islands. The Philippine government did not make any formal sovereign claim in the SCS then until the late 1970s, but it was skilful to reserve the rights of its citizens to exploit resources and allowed them to settle there.[4] However, PRC did not respond harshly against the Philippines. Instead, with geopolitical consideration of the Sino-America rapprochement and containing Vietnam's influence further into the region then, PRC made a more conciliatory approach to the Philippines and Malaysia on the SCS disputes.[5] From the 1950s to the 1970s, when PRC was preoccupied with domestic political reestablishment and power struggle, the SCS issue caught little attention on the political agenda. There were only a few strong irredentist statements on the SCS but not much practical engagement.

In the 1970s, the SCS situation began to turn into a challenging course, as the Philippines and Vietnam (South Vietnam or the Republic of Vietnam, ROV) took actions to occupy some features in the Spratly Islands and Paracel Islands, which ROC and PRC regarded as illegal and offensive moves against their national interest. Due to the profound impacts of the Cultural Revolution (1966–1976), China was bogged down by the ten-year catastrophe and did not act much in the SCS situation. Until 1974, in order to protect sovereign integrity, PRC engaged in a battle against ROV Navy in the Paracels (Xisha Islands). As a result of winning the battle, PRC has since stepped up its strength to materialize control of the Paracel Islands. The Republic of Vietnam lost the Battle of the Paracels and quickly redirected its troops to occupy six islets of the Spratly Islands. In this particular episode, ROC, the Philippines, and PRC condemned the Vietnamese government's action. Because of other claimants' blunt advance into the SCS, PRC was alerted and became paying since then, greater attention to the SCS.[6]

In 1982, the United Nations Convention on the Law of Sea (UNCLOS) was signed and brought about a profound implication for the international community and PRC's claims to the SCS. Under the new ocean regime of UNCLOS, individual coastal states will have to promulgate their domestic laws to bring an update of their legal system in accord with the main trend. The process of internalizing UNCLOS in the region has led to new efforts of legitimizing their claims among the SCS claimants. For instance, PRC promulgated a few new laws: e.g. in 1992 "Law of the People's Republic of China on the Territorial Sea and contiguous Zone," and in 1998 "Law of People's Republic of China on the Exclusive Economic Zone and Continental Shelf." Encouraged by the UNCLOS regime, the Philippines, Vietnam, Malaysia and even Brunei manage to legalize related national laws of sea and legitimize their territorial claims in the SCS. The legitimate process taking place in all claimant states has brought about tremendous impacts on the stability of the SCS. First, the traditional China-driven system that existed for decades is directly challenged by the UNCLOS regime, which causes immediate controversy in the SCS. Second, based on UNCLOS and newly promulgated domestic laws of the sea, other claimants advance further to occupy more land features in the Spratly Islands and challenge the system of Chinese domination. Third, when claimants try to legislate territorial disputes into national laws, it has not only tied up diplomatic flexibility among claimants but also stirred up confrontational interest in territorial disputes by national laws. As a result, legal, political and military conflicts in the SCS become almost inevitable.

Throughout the past decades, ROC has been quite firm about sovereignty over most parts of the SCS and maintained its position unchanged, though it has gradually taken much softer approaches toward other claimants. During the last three decades or so, ROC's SCS involvement has been on the declining trend. It is closely related to the changing political perception of China shaped by political campaigns between the two major parties, KMT and DPP, in Taiwan. Before the 1970s, while ROC was committed to the protection of the sovereignty over the SCS more seriously, PRC defined its policy on the basis of international political accounts.

Waxing and waning of power in the SCS

China's emerging role

After PRC was established in 1949, the diplomatic contest continues between Taipei and Beijing. Although PRC and ROC have the same claim for the SCS sovereignty and share a common interest in retaining the sovereign integrity of China, they do not ease down the degree of the overall diplomatic contest, even in the context of the SCS. What Beijing is concerned with is Taipei may take advantage of involvement in the SCS occasion to expand its diplomatic effort and Taipei's inescapable claimant status in the SCS would be wrongly identified by others as the involvement of a "normal state." Politically, China and Taiwan interplay in the SCS depends on the atmosphere of the cross-strait relation and the progress of bilateral rapprochement. Since the late 1970s, PRC has stepped up its presence and strength in coping with Southeast Asian claimants' encroachment into the SCS. Three important factors played out Beijing's increasing role. First, the signing of UNCLOS to some extent accelerated regional strategic contest among claimants, as each claimant would be legally supported by the new ocean regime. Under the new legal regime, new efforts by claimants to redistribute and reinforce their "legitimate rights" in wider areas of the SCS. It resulted in claimants' expansion of claimed territories and of course overlapping claims with China. Such an action taken by other claimants heightened the need for China to defend its national interest.

Second, the universal ocean regime of UNCLOS entitles all coastal states to follow up on regulation and practice on the ground. PRC signed UNCLOS in 1982, ratified in 1996, and adapted into its legal system and national policy. Since China came pretty late in the SCS legal claim campaign, the desperation of claiming what it should have in the SCS may have thereafter determined the policy course in the following years. During the 1990s, based on UNCLOS, China defined its territorial sea, contiguous zone, exclusive economic zone, and continental shelf, and drew baselines except for the areas in the Spratly Islands. Relevant to UNCLOS, China has confronted with two sets of legal and historic claims. It is still in the process of developing a new effort to confirm whether China's historic claim (9-dashed line) would prevail and whether there would be any contradiction between historic claim and legal claim. In fact, most of the claimants in the SCS except Brunei have complicated sorts of claims. In the policy discourse, most of them emphasise their legal rights under UNCLOS, which would allow them to argue against China expanding much further into the U-shaped line.

Third, geostrategic significance in the SCS increasingly propels China's strategic ambition and security alert over territorial disputes. Passing through the early stage of the turbulent nation-building process, China has since 1979 opened out to the outside world and entered into the world system with a consistent policy. It was around the time China was in involving the debates on a number of new rules, such as the continental shelf, exclusive economic zone, and delimitation during the Third United Nations Conference on the Law of Sea. According to the Deputy Representative of China Delegation to the Conference, though there was a discussion between Vietnamese and Chinese delegations on the status of Paracels and Spratlys in a 1974s session, the SCS was not made an issue throughout the conference. Even then, none of the neighbouring countries raised any different opinions on the 9-dashed line in the SCS.[7] Following the guideline given by the 18th Chinese Communist Party Congress, China reinstated its overall maritime strategy for the new era. In order to protect its territorial sea and the rights of islands, what China needs is to define clear goals of overall maritime strategy.[8] As China in 2010 became the second-largest economy in the world and would be the number one by 2030, it considers comprehensive national power to reach a comfortable level to build a maritime power.[9] For economic, energy, transportation, geopolitical reasons, the SCS is at the centre of developing its maritime power. Then, in 2010, the US Secretary of State Hillary Clinton made a stunning announcement indicating that the United States has a "national interest in freedom of navigation, open access to Asia's maritime commons, and respect for international law in the South China Sea" in Hanoi during the ASEAN Regional Forum (ARF) annual ministerial meeting.[10] The US's new move entangling itself in the SCS disputes has triggered Beijing's active response, as China reckons that its geostrategic interest may be threatened by the United States and its allies in the region. Accompanying the grand strategy of the Belt and Road Initiative, China definitely needs to secure a geostrategic advantage in the SCS. It is almost envisaged that China would want to expand and consolidate its sovereign claim in the SCS.

Decline of a most active claimant: Taiwan

While PRC has dramatically increased its engagement and presence in the SCS over the last three decades, ROC losing out the diplomatic battle to represent the seat of "China" and forced to walk out of the United Nations in 1971, which has significantly reduced its legitimate effort of securing sovereign rights in the SCS. Fundamentally, this sea change occurred in the early 1970s as a result of a fierce diplomatic contest between PRC and ROC as well as between the United States and the Soviet Union. The diplomatic contest between PRC and ROC reflects exactly the mark of the Cold War. On the geopolitical context in East Asia in the 1970s and the 1980s, ROC's international status was shaken and resulted in diplomatic feebleness of holding on to Chinese U-shaped line in the SCS vis-à-vis other claimants. When the original dominant of the SCS, ROC stepped back, the Philippines and Vietnam took that opportunity to quickly occupy more land features and establish their outposts in the Spratly Islands.

Taiwan's overall presence and influence in the SCS is dramatically decreasing over time. Some presume that the ROC's formal representation of China in the UN was replaced by PRC, which resulted in losing political and legitimate foundation to guard against its sovereign rights in the SCS. In sum, there are six complicated factors crippling ROC's leading role in the SCS. First, the emerging trend of supporting Taiwan independence and new political trend of de-sinicisation advocated by the DPP governments. Based on this developing perception towards the SCS in the Taiwanese society, whatever the situation happens on the ground, Taipei's response would generally be ambiguous and try to toe the American policy line, particularly during the DPP's reign. As the political trend drifting from traditional wisdom gradually emerges in the Taiwan society, among the general public political belief in the SCS becomes weaker and much vaguer. For now, the most critical factor keeping politicians in Taipei engaged in the SCS is not nationalism or any national glory, but very much with protecting existing territories, i.e. the Taiping Island (Itu Aba) and Tongsa Islands (Pratas Islands).

Second, the "US factor" matters a lot in the process of decision-making in Taipei regarding the SCS. Whenever the ruling party in Taipei is pressing on the SCS policy, the priority becomes clearer that it would not contradict with the US policy line. In some cases, for geopolitical and political consideration, Taipei would quietly admit the US policy at the expense of its national interest in the SCS. During the SCS arbitration case proceedings, Taipei was frequently demanded by Americans through both official and non-official ways to clarify the real meaning of "the 11-dashed line" and not to put forth any substantial pieces of evidence to boost Beijing's position in the SCS. One of the obvious examples was that the US government denied ROC President Ma Ying-jeou's intended visit to the Taiping Island in December 2015, while the government in Taipei originally planned to celebrate the 70th anniversary of the memorial day when a ROC Navy contingent led by the *Taiping* Ship arrived at the island and named the island as the "Taiping" in 1945. Later, President Ma finally managed to make the trip to the Taiping Island in January 2016. Surprisingly, the US openly criticised the trip as "disappointing" and "unhelpful."[11] It had stirred up a serious debate among policy thinkers in Taipei as to whether there may be a way around other than following the American interest at the expense of asserting sovereignty in the SCS. To some extent, it has significantly constrained Taipei's flexibility in shaping its own SCS policy, especially any effort made to strengthen its traditional position in the SCS could be regarded as contradicting with US policy.

Third, complicated domestic politics and democratisation shifting traditional political perception to links with Mainland China have further constrained the government's policy in the SCS. However, whenever the DPP is in power (President Chen Shui-bian 2000–2008; President Tsai Ing-Wen 2016-present) the SCS policy is completely inactive. For instance, in 2005, the "South China Sea Task Force" under the auspice of the Ministry of Interior was dismantled and the mission on the SCS has since then shifted to the "Maritime Situation Briefing" at the National Security Council (NSC). Although it looks as if the SCS issue has been upgraded on the policy agenda to the management of the higher political level at the NSC, the mechanism became on a provisional basis and leaning much more to responsive and passive nature, crisis management, and problem-solving approach. Unlike the original legal framework, the task force was designated to manage all related development including policy coordination among different agencies and planning policy ahead. All related agencies inside the government organisational framework would be assigned for specific tasks. Its institutional mechanism took proactive approaches to cope with situation change in the SCS. During Chen Shui-bian's presidency, the SCS policy began clearly inactive except for filing diplomatic protests to other claimants' excessive actions. On the SCS issue, President Chen ended his presidency by paying a visit to the Taiping Island inaugurating the completion of the airstrip and issuing "the Nansha Initiative." It shows that there has not been enough political will from the decision-making level to support strong actions in the SCS.

The SCS arbitral tribunal gave the final award in July 2016, when President Tsai went into her second month in the office. She immediately rejected the award. The statement went: "The ROC government does not accept any decisions that undermine the rights of the ROC, and declares that they have no legally binding force on the ROC."[12] Checking the words on the statements by both the Presidential Office and the Ministry of Foreign Affairs, it implies certain policy shift from traditional policy position. As both statements purposely dropped the focus of "history" and "historic use" from the previous government's statements.[13] In addition, the official stance of Tsai's administration on the SCS emphasises Taiwan's entitlement of all rights in accordance with international law and the law of the sea (referring to UNCLOS), which was significantly different from previous governments.[14] It is ever clear that Tsai's administration intends to act differently from China. Based on political hostility against China, the SCS policy stand of Tsai's administration is contradicted with itself and denies Taiwan's connection with the recent history of ROC. However, her political gesture is interpreted at home and abroad as strategically siding with the United States against China and drifting further away from China.

Fourth, the complicated cross-strait relation has been the cause of Taiwan's feebleness to the SCS. Driven by Taiwan's independence ideology and perhaps new Taiwan identity, the DPP government would try any possible ways to go around direct engagements with China. As the political deadlock on the definition of the "1992 consensus" between DPP and the Communist Party of China (CPC) for now seems insurmountable, Beijing's political formula of unification is based on the concept of the "one country, two systems," which DPP rejects it outright. The broader implication of differences between Taipei and Beijing for the cross-strait future and the involvement in the SCS becomes worrisome. It has significantly diminished Taiwan's credibility in the SCS claims if there was no understanding across the Taiwan Strait and no domestic consensus supporting the policy to move on. While DPP governments continue to appeal to the world that Taiwan should be included in all "multilateral mechanisms aimed at resolving disputes,"[15] without warm relation with China, it is absolutely impossible for Taiwan to be included. Worsening relations with China has made Taiwan even more difficult to be marginalised from almost all official regional fora. The key for Taiwan now is whether there would be a way to improve relations with Beijing, which happens to be the Achilles' heel of DPP.

Fifth, in the prolonged political antagonism across the Taiwan Strait, Taiwan suffers badly from diplomatic disadvantage in the international community. After formally winning the right of representation in the United Nations in 1971, China gains an upper hand in all possible regional mechanisms on the SCS. Since 1979 the United States formally severed diplomatic relations with ROC, it has substantially compromised Taiwan's overall efforts of involvement in the SCS issues. Subsequently, the change of international political supports weakened the political will of defending sovereignty in Taipei.

As always, China would try either to get rid of Taiwan's representation or significantly press down Taiwan's role, even including the Informal SCS Workshop, which is defined as a track II establishment.[16] Since both PRC (China) and ROC's (Taiwan or Chinese Taipei) representative delegations attended the Informal Workshop in Bandung in 1991, they for most of the time fought against each other except for the period from 2008 to 2016, when the cross-strait relation was much improved. Completely losing diplomatic advantage, ROC (Taiwan) has been kept out of most of the official multilateral fora in the region. In 2002, when China and ASEAN signed the Declaration on the Conduct of the Parties in the South China Sea (DOC) to regulate order in the SCS, only could Taiwan watch and protest to the outside world from the sideline.[17] Moreover, China and ASEAN have begun to regenerate consultation momentum for the Code of Conducts (COC) in the SCS since 2016. The progressive course of the negotiation is a reflection of international politics and increasingly intensified US-China strategic competition. Throughout the process of the negotiation for COC, Taiwan's role is further marginalised and made irrelevant, because of the Chinese diplomatic boycott.

Since 2009, the territorial disputes in the SCS entered into a more complicated legal realm, as all claimants try to redefine their rights of maritime space in accordance with the specification of UNCLOS by submitting their national scientific survey reports on the extended continental shelf to the UN Commission on the Limits of the Continental Shelf (CLCS). In reality, UNCLOS and CLCS have granted legitimate rights to claimants for claiming legal rights against others in the SCS breaking through the conventional claims of historical rights. Now, PRC is driving the direction of the SCS disputes toward clear control of territorial jurisdiction and away from the traditional course of ambiguity, while ROC is declining further in the process of managing regional order.

Contribution of track two diplomacy across the Taiwan Strait

Over the last three decades, ROC's and PRC's delegations including officials and experts met annually on the occasion of the Workshop on Managing Potential Conflicts in the SCS taking place in Indonesia. Although from the onset the full agenda of the workshop was easily crippled by quarrels on the insistence of the "One China" Principle and the name ROC's delegation should take in the workshop. On those occasions, the workshop was pretty much overwhelmed by the cross-strait political debates. Not much could real agenda be pushed forward. The process taking place in the informal workshops reflected a critical moment to the SCS issue, for China's emerging role became to take charge of the course and Taiwan's significance in the SCS relatively diminished. The workshop establishment originally began with an ambitious aspiration of introducing the concept and practice of preventive diplomacy to the region. For China and Taiwan sharing a similar interest in the SCS but maintaining political antagonism, the establishment serves as a useful and beneficial platform to engage with each other. Those who attended the workshops from the both sides would be able to know their counterparts and began the preliminary step of confidence building.

The most contributory function of this workshop is practicing the processes of confidence-building and preventive diplomacy for Taipei and Beijing. On the SCS issue, the workshop provides an important arena for all delegates to share different views on SCS policy and cultivate general common interest. Although delegates from the both sides based on their political stands argued for their best interest against other claimants on the territorial dispute, confidence and mutual trust were gradually built and personal networks expanded as a result. Delegates from China and Taiwan who attended the series of workshops and met with their counterparts helped pave a way for the future practice of track II diplomacy on the SCS across the Taiwan Strait.

Informal multilateral workshop: beginning of interplay

Track II diplomacy on the SCS across the Taiwan Strait began to take place almost around the beginning of the Informal Workshop on the SCS in 1990. There were several rounds of cross-strait bilateral workshops taking place. During the 1990s, the main topics of the workshops were mostly on international legal development of UNCLOS and traditional claims China had alleged in the SCS. It was a preliminary attempt to connect think tanks from the both sides. In spite of political antagonism, those workshops were held in mainland China and Taiwan, respectively. In the historical context of UNCLOS taking effect in 1994, all claimants tried to introduce domestic legal frameworks to adapt to the new UNCLOS maritime regime. ROC promulgated the Law on the Exclusive Economic Zone and Continental Shelf of the Republic of China in 1998.[18] Together, the Law on the Territorial Sea and the Contiguous Zone of the Republic of China was also promulgated at the same time.[19] In order to strengthen its claim and make the position clear to other claimants in the SCS, ROC went further in 1999 to promulgate the baselines including the Tongsa Islands and Huanyan Island (Macclesfield Bank – Scarborough Shoal).[20]

The series of workshops which took place during the 1990s reflected political demands for the both sides to consult with each other on new terms of maritime territorial management under UNCLOS. Before then, China and Taiwan did not have any proper discussion on their different elaboration and claim in the SCS. Especially, after UNCLOS becomes universal norms in the seas, China and Taiwan in different statuses came up with a separate arrangement of application.[21] Under different definitions of "One China," both China and Taiwan "recognize there is only one China, but agree to differ on its definition."[22] They both promulgated related law, but carefully circumvented direct legislation over the overlapping jurisdiction for now. Due to the complicated nature of the cross-strait relation, they need extensive consultation to be sure of avoiding miscalculation and standing firm on the conventional claim in the SCS.

Bilateral dialogue across the Taiwan Strait

During the 1990s, many individual players facilitated the cross-strait track II engagement. The practice was considered an important part of cross-strait confidence-building measures, though politically and legally track II diplomacy may not as useful as expected. Presumably, the effort was encouraged by the United States as a way to reduce tension and avoid conflict in the Taiwan Strait. Since 2001, the cross-strait workshop series on the SCS has become more institutionalised and organised. The series would annually take a turn to be held in mainland China and Taiwan. The main organisers are the Hainan Research Institute of South China Sea (In 2004, the Centre transformed to become the National Institute of the South China Sea Studies) for the China side and the Institute of International Relations at the National Chengchi University for the Taiwan side. Over the years, the SCS studies community across the Taiwan Strait is steadily enlarging. The nature of dialogues has been dramatically shifted from debates and quarrels in the early stage to exchanging analyses, sharing information, and encouraging potential cooperation lately.

Thereafter, the workshop series continues to meet annually, no matter what political difficulty presented by different ruling parties in Taiwan would be. According to the SCS immediate situation, the key issues were selected and discussed on the occasion of the workshop. Since 2010, the workshop has further generated a joint research publication: annual assessment of the SCS situation, which is the first and only well received and widely circulated publication contributed by experts from mainland China and Taiwan.[23] Based on the mutual benefit of China and Taiwan and seeking possible ways of cooperation, the workshop has focused on issues, such as management of natural resources, the challenge of law enforcement, implementation of challenging legal perspectives, and exploration of cross-strait cooperation. The key issues identified over the workshops carry broader implications of territorial disputes for their SCS policies. First, throughout the first decade of the 21st Century and after the DOC was signed between China and ASEAN members in 2002, exploration of natural resources was highlighted as one of the most important issues to be discussed and recognized between China and Taiwan. It was understandable that both China and Taiwan did not make substantial efforts to explore oil and natural gas in the SCS, while other claimants had started to explore and enjoy fruits of energy from the surrounding areas of the SCS.

Second, since 1999, the Chinese authority has implemented an annual fishing ban in the northern part (up to 12th degree north latitude) of the SCS covering most waters of the Beibu Bay and the Paracel Islands from 1 May to 16 August every year. It is part of China's effort to "promote sustainable marine fishery development and improve marine ecology."[24] Due to contested territorial claims among claimants, the imposition of the Chinese fishing ban is considered an exercise of jurisdiction in the SCS, which some claimants oppose this unilateral exercise of the fishing ban. The Vietnamese government openly opposes it and even encourages the fishing community to challenge it.[25] Every May, the beginning of fishing ban season, Vietnamese fishing boats would disregard restrictions and challenge Chinese law enforcement agencies on purpose. As China takes this occasion to further strengthen its law enforcement in cracking down on illegal and unlawful acts in the SCS, it may imply expanding national jurisdiction and materializing real control. Taiwan will also have to guard its sovereignty by imposing law enforcement in the SCS, though it has not done much in the past two decades.

By the SCS policy stand standpoint, China and Taiwan would have a similar responsibility to protect and secure sovereignty. During those workshops, experts from the both sides could exchange their perspectives on the practice of law enforcement, share difficulties in the SCS realities and learn from each other. From 2008 to 2016, under President Ma Ying-jeou the cross-strait interactions were completely changed to a much more benign stage. Focuses of dialogue would then be able to tackle common challenges in the SCS and explore possible ways of cooperation across the Taiwan Strait to strengthen the policy stand. At the peak of these cosy relations, China and Taiwan on the occasion of the 2nd Chiang-Chen Dialogue signed the Cross-Strait Sea Transport Agreement in which Article 7 addresses search and rescue at sea.[26] Based on the agreement, the coast guard agencies from the both sides moved forward to organise the Cross-Strait Joint Maritime Search and Rescue Exercise in 2010, 2012, and 2014.[27] With successful progress made to secure the safety of shipping and navigation in the Taiwan Strait, this positive progress inspired experts attending the workshops to explore a possible joint mechanism for coordinating search and rescue (SAR) missions as part of law enforcement in the SCS. Although there was a high hope to develop a course of cooperation, Taipei's political concern with regional complication and the US factor compromised the attempt.

Third, one of the continuous issues presented in the workshop series is the legal contest in the SCS. After the completion of the negotiation in the UN Conference on the Law of the

Sea in 1982, a new maritime regime was introduced thereafter. Once UNCLOS took effect in 1994, SCS claimants measured up their legal obligation and rights to legislate relevant national laws. During much of the 1990s and 2000s, territorial contest gradually shifted toward the legal dimension, as most of the claimants completed their law of the sea, baseline law, etc. On territorial dispute, the legal argument will have to be based on UNCLOS and historical inheritance. For the elaboration of China's long history with the relevance of the SCS, it is critical to detail the historical possession of the territory in parallel with UNCLOS. The legal contest continues to be kept on the agenda of the workshops because Taiwan and China hope to generate an integrated and convincing legal argument vis-à-vis other claimants.

Politically, Kuomintang (KMT, referring to Nationalist Party of China) and Communist Party of China (CPC) may have a certain understanding of common ground and thus be willing to dialogue and exchange policy orientation with each other. Unfortunately, there is no common political basis between DPP and CPC at all. Neither would the both concede any common policy on the SCS for now and in the near future. In this particular political circumstance, official contacts were not made available and possible. Thus, the track II channels gradually taking shape made certain policy communication on behalf of the two governments. On the Taipei side, the government took an encouraging attitude but was not directly involved in the process of coordination and dialogue. To the least, different government branches in Taipei may sometimes provide limited financial support to these events. Up to today, Taipei has not officially designated or allocated a fixed budget supporting these events to take place, which reflected that the democratic governments in Taipei do not have long-term planning to the policy dialogue across the strait. It becomes even more difficult, as Taiwan has entered into the full democratic era and a lot of policy planning only aims for the short-term perspective. In all circumstances, only will DPP try to bolster any proposal encouraging independent political identity away from China. The SCS has presented a historical link with ROC's legacy and the history of China, which DPP would definitely try to deviate from its traditional course. In sum, when DPP is in power, the SCS issue will not be placed as a critical issue as it should be on the policy agenda. Rather, cooling down from within the policy community.

The efforts made to contribute to the success of track II diplomacy across the Taiwan Strait mostly depended on institutional support and personal commitments. The effectiveness of the track II process depends mostly on continuity of engagement and mutual trust among all participants and good faith of the representative institutions. While Beijing has a long-term political agenda for peaceful unification vis-à-vis Taipei, continuity of engagement is characterised by its delicacy and sophistication of policy on the process. Nevertheless, it becomes quite difficult to organise it on the Taiwan side, as some DPP Legislators view the confidence-building process across the Strait very differently, which always blends with clear animosity to Beijing and clandestine accusation to those who would work with Beijing. Without sufficient political mutual trust built inside Taiwan's politics, the promotion of the track II effort with China could be politically blamed and discredited. So far, the most difficult obstacle to continue the track II diplomacy on the SCS is not from Beijing, but rather from Taipei's domestic politics.

China's expectation vs. Taiwan's retreat

Both ROC and PRC over time have gradually developed similar articulation of the historical claim of the SCS. Before formal dialogues between China and Taiwan were conducted by the occasions of multilateral platforms or bilateral workshops, they claim their sovereign rights respectively. Nevertheless, hardly would Taipei and Beijing criticise each other's SCS policy. Even though they both may not have ever expressed comfortable notes on the SCS to each other, each works through its own approaches and tries to safeguard self-defined national interest. Rather, in the diplomatic campaign, PRC maintains its consistent course of pressurisation against ROC's role in the SCS. As Beijing tries all along to deny the existence and block the presence of ROC/Taiwan in the international community after it was established in 1949, the effort of exclusion was mainly driven by uncertainty through nation-building process and thus consolidation of legitimate government in Beijing. Regardless of political continuity and regime transition in China, PRC engaged with ASEAN in the process of negotiation on DOC and later COC without considering ROC's constructive role in the process. In Beijing's stern political stand, exclusion of ROC from all possible international fora fits well with its prolonged political struggle against its existence. It is clear whether ROC/Taiwan would involve itself in the SCS settlement process is not an immediate concern to Beijing, unless it comes to a whole rapprochement between ROC and PRC. It is obvious whether ROC would be included in the process of SCS peaceful settlement depends mostly on the definition of the cross-strait relation.

After the San Francisco Peace Treaty was signed in 1951, which mandated Japan's renunciation of illegally occupied territories during the wartime including the SCS, the transformation of the whole region began to take place. The general situation of the SCS could be roughly divided into five phases: (1). the 1950s–1970s: ROC domination, (2). 1970s: the beginning of claimants' excursion, (3). 1980s–1990s: territorial contending campaign, (4). 2000s: diplomatic challenge, and (5). 2010 onwards: lawfare and PRC emerging domination. Up until the SCS situation moves into the fifth phase of lawfare, PRC realises that to make a strong case and a convincing historical argument about the compelling link between China and the SCS, the part of early China's history regarding ROC should not be disconnected. Otherwise, it is almost impossible that PRC would be able to stand alone rebutting legal challenges from others. Reflecting the larger context of political rapprochement across the Taiwan Strait from 2008 to 2016, Beijing would seriously consider to connect the history of ROC with the birth of PRC and formally acknowledge the whole effort ROC has contributed to the sovereign dignity of the SCS, though it was a tough job to define what ROC may mean today. Especially, in May 2016, when the government-linked Chinese (Taiwan) Society of International Law in Taipei submitted a position paper on the SCS to the Permanent Court of Arbitration in a hope to influence tribunal's final decision before it concluded the arbitration case, Beijing's response was favourable as suggesting "Chinese people on both sides of the Taiwan Strait all have a responsibility to jointly protect the ancestral property of the Chinese people."[28]

Into the stage of lawfare, PRC raised a high hope that ROC would reinforce its strong position of protecting sovereign rights in the SCS, which would be in accordance with PRC's line of the traditional claim and help indirectly strengthen PRC's policy articulation, though politically Beijing did not lower the bar of blocking Taipei. In parallel with the cosy cross-strait relation during President Ma's terms, Beijing's expectation that Taipei would utilize its rich historical documentation to argue against the objection of Chinese historic titles in the SCS and in a way to help boost Chinese legitimate claim prior to the manifestation of UNCLOS regime was comparable to Taipei's optimism to deepen a better relation thereafter. The truth of Beijing's expectation is inevitably fraught with political intention, as suggested that Chinese people living on both Taiwan and mainland China would guard against the loss of inheritance of territorial integrity. However, it becomes clear that Taiwan has been put in a dilemma, as it wants to continue to strengthen its claim of sovereignty in the SCS, but is reluctant to simply respond to what PRC may wish for. Because a political consensus across the Taiwan Strait is fundamental and presently remains to be developed either between CPC and KMT or CPC and DPP, it would not be feasible to advocate policy coordination and cooperation on the SCS. Unless the relationship between Taipei and Beijing could be properly advanced and Beijing would tolerantly open a larger room for Taiwan to play in the future process of SCS settlement, the engagement will bring about a possible feedback to Beijing's expectation.

In addition, political pressure from the US becomes blunt and clear. Although different US administrations may imply for some policy issues publicly, they would easily go through private channels, e.g. think tanks analyses and private talks, to encourage Taiwan to take a certain position in favour of the United States.[29] When the US-China strategic competition fiercely escalates during President Trump's era, then Secretary of State, Michael Pompeo openly denied China's legal rights in the SCS on 13 July 2020.[30] Consequently, it has put Taiwan in an even more difficult position, as American denial of PRC's legality in the SCS may also imply for refuting effect to ROC's claim. For Taiwan's democratic administrations, the SCS issue has become so challenging, as other claimants aggressively expand areas of control and encroach into ROC's claim of sovereignty and the US tries to push China out of the game. Basically, there are three fronts of contention testing Taipei's governing credibility in the SCS and Taiwan's diminishing role: first, the domestic front – conventional school vs. revolutionary school; second, the cross-strait front – the China factor; third, the diplomatic front – the US factor.

Conclusion

On the "One China" concept, ROC and PRC developed a concurrent course of the policy in the SCS without communication and consultation at all. Literally, they both share the same definition of inheriting assets including all land features and historic title within the U-shaped line. They have fought for their national interest and protecting sovereign integrity. It is natural that under one China concept with different interpretations, their claim of sovereignty comes exactly similar. In the later stage, PRC takes a more assertive approach, while ROC maintains a peaceful appeal to the region.

Over the last four decades, ROC's dominant role declines further, mainly because PRC has replaced ROC's representation in the UN and international community, the introduction of UNCLOS in the 1980s gave rise to redefining maritime rights among littoral states in the SCS, and Taipei is lacking clear political will to engage in this affair. Based on UNCLOS, new claimants attempt to expand their "legitimate" rights in the SCS and further complicate the situation. As a result of the rising China, the PRC that enhances its overall national power and critical capabilities becomes a dominant player in contesting territorial rights and strategic interest in the SCS. By far, the biggest security issue between ASEAN and China has been territorial disputes in the SCS. In order to settle territorial and maritime disputes, China and ASEAN have gone through diplomatic efforts to reach DOC in 2002. Presently, the COC negotiation is still undergoing. Although both important, it is likely that these regimes would not solve sovereign disputes among all claimants, both DOC and COC after completion of negotiation focus on maritime disputes and would lead to a possible regime regulating regional order. However, China and ASEAN would go ahead with the negotiation process without Taiwan. For the unsolved question of Taiwan's involvement, it may have to wait until the cross-strait interplay moves in a favourable direction.

Track II diplomacy's contribution to the cross-strait interplay in the SCS is significant. Although the workshop experiences have not been known outside of the policy community in Taipei and Beijing, they are contributive to facilitating understanding of ROC and PRC's policy orientation. The groundwork made by the track II channels would be hopeful to develop future policy consultation and possibly coordination for Taipei and Beijing, should the political situation allow.

The cross-strait interplay in the SCS is tremendously constrained by a number of factors. First, once Taiwan's domestic politics is reigned by DPP, the hopeful scenario of interplay in the SCS will shift to the negative side. From the experiences of two DPP governments, the SCS was significantly played down on the policy agenda, as it intends to avoid diplomatic embarrassment when engaging in regional disputes through non-official channels. Second, the cross-strait relation is critical at play. Without warmer relations with Beijing, Taipei's appeal to be part of SCS settlement will only become wishful thinking. Even if the cross-strait relation may turn to a positive one, both Taipei and Beijing will have to solve numerous political terms first, which would remain to be open questions. Third, the US factor seriously impacts Taipei's political will. As the United States and China are intensifying its strategic competition, Taiwan is included in the expansion of the free and open Indo-Pacific region advocated since the Trump administration.[31] When the US government openly denounces China's unlawful rights in the SCS, the DPP government toes the American policy line, which would further deviate from the hopeful cross-strait interplay. It has become a tough choice for Taipei.

With the US-China strategic competition intensifying and the COC negotiation undergoing, the cross-strait interplay following through the current negative tendency in play may somewhat add on the tempo of the SCS complication. Now, Taiwan is clearly siding with the United States in this comprehensive strategic competition and has been dragged to the brink of conflict against China. On 23 July 2020, accelerating the campaign against China, Michael Pompeo appealed to build "a new alliance of democracies."[32] The clear effect of it is to tear the cross-strait interplay in the SCS further apart.

Notes

1 "Peace in the South China Sea, National Territory Secure Forever: Position Paper on ROC South China Sea Policy," Ministry of Foreign Affairs, ROC, May 2016, https://www.mofa.gov.tw/en/Upload/WebArchive/1989/Position%20Paper%20on%20ROC%20South%20China%20Sea%20Policy%20(illustrated%20pamphlet%20PDF).pdf.
2 "In 1974, the Truth of PLAN Fleet Went Pass the Taiwan Strait," Meire Toutiao, 17 November 2015, https://kknews.cc/zh-tw/military/y66eoma.html.
3 "Quiet Down for Six Years, the South China Sea Task Force Reemerges," *Liberty Times*, 20 August 2003, http://old.ltn.com.tw/2003/new/aug/20/today-p8.htm.
4 Chi-kin Lo, *China's Policy towards Territorial Disputes: The Case of the South China Sea Islands* (London and New York: Routledge, 1989), p. 141.
5 Ibid., Chapter 6.
6 Jian Zhang, "China's South China Sea Policy: Evolution, Claims and Challenges," in Leszek Buszynski, and Christopher Roberts (eds.), *The South China Sea Maritime Dispute: Political, Legal and Regional Perspective* (London and New York: Routledge, 2015), p. 62.
7 San Xu, "The Whole Story of China's Participation in the UN Conference on the Law of Sea Negotiation," *Oriental Outlook*, issue 47, 9 December 2012, http:/dailynews.sina.com/bg/chn/chnpolitics/sinacn/c/sd/2012-12-10/141125774618.html.
8 *China's Ocean Development Report (2014),* State Oceanic Administration, Ministry of Land and Resources (Beijing: Ocean Press, 2014), p. 334.
9 Ibid., p. 330.
10 "Remarks at Press Availability," Hillary Rodham Clinton, US Secretary of State, National Convention Center, Hanoi, Vietnam. 23 July 2010, https://2009-2017.state.gov/secretary/20092013clinton/rm/2010/07/145095.htm
11 J.R.Wu, "U.S. Slams Taiwan President's Planned Visit to Contested South China Sea Island," Reuter, 27 January 2016, https://www.reuters.com/article/us-taiwan-southchinasea-idUSKCN0V502V

12 "ROC Government Position on the South China Sea Arbitration," Presidential Office of Republic of China, 12 July 2016, https://english.president.gov.tw/NEWS/4939
13 "ROC Position on the South China Sea Arbitration," Ministry of Foreign Affairs, Republic of China, 12 July 2016, https://www.mofa.gov.tw/en/News_Content.aspx?n=1EADDCFD4C6EC567&s=5B5A9134709EB875
14 Chih-Tin Tsai, "Taiwan's South China Sea Evolution," Asia Maritime Transparency Initiative, CSIS, 12 April 2018, https://amti.csis.org/taiwan-scs-policy-evolution/.
15 "The Ministry of Foreign Affairs of the Republic of China (Taiwan) states the following position related to ROC sovereignty over the South China Sea Islands," Ministry of Foreign Affairs, Republic of China. 14 July 2020, https://www.mofa.gov.tw/en/News_Content_M_2.aspx?n=1EADDCFD4C6EC567&s=C36D37156BF4FB62.
16 The Informal South China Sea Workshop which is a series of Workshops on Managing Potential Conflicts in the South China Sea coordinated by the Indonesian Government has since 1990 continued the process of building confidence among claimants. Hasjim Djalal, *Preventive Diplomacy in Southeast Asia: Lessons Learned* (Jakarta: Habibie Center, 2002), pp. 49–96.
17 "Statement of the Ministry of Foreign Affairs concerning the Declaration on the Conduct of Parties in the South China Sea signed by the Association of Southeast Asian Nations (ASEAN) and the People`s Republic of China (PRC) in Cambodia on November 4, 2002," Ministry of Foreign Affairs, Republic of China, https://www.mofa.gov.tw/En/News_Content.aspx?n=0E7B91A8FBEC4A94&sms=220E98D761D34A9A&s=90E8913405634AB8.
18 "Law on the Exclusive Economic Zone and the Continental Shelf of the Republic of China," Department of Land Administration, Ministry of Interior, 21 January 1998, https://www.land.moi.gov.tw/enhtml/enlawdet/29?elid=77.
19 "Law on the Territorial Sea and the Contiguous Zone of the Republic of China," https://www.land.moi.gov.tw/law/Resultdet1/105?LCID=212&lawname=中華民國領海及鄰接區法.
20 "First Set of the Baselines and Outer Limits of the Territorial Sea and the Contiguous Zone of the Republic of China" Department of Land Administration, Ministry of Interior, 10 February 1999, https://www.land.moi.gov.tw/upload/d-20190731175018.pdf and see https://www.land.moi.gov.tw/upload/d-20180906120151.pdf; also see J. Ashley Roach and Robert W. Smith, "Limits in the Seas: Taiwan's Maritime Claims," No. 127, Bureau of Oceans and International Environmental and Scientific Affairs, US Department of State.
21 China is a formal contracting state of UNCLOS, while Taiwan is completely out of the picture and unilaterally declares to attach to it.
22 "Chinese, U.S. Presidents Hold Telephone Talks on Taiwan, Tibet, (03/26/08)," Embassy of the People's Republic of China in the United States, 27 April 2008, http://www.china-embassy.org/eng/zt/twwt/t418675.htm
23 Co-edited by Liu Fu-Kuo and Wu Shichun, the annual published book is jointly sponsored by the National Institute of South China Sea Studies at Haikou and Institute of International Relations/Taiwan Centre for Security Studies, National Chengchi University at Taipei, and formally published in Taipei.
24 "Summer Fishing Ban Starts in South China Sea," Xinhua, 1 May 2020, http://www.xinhuanet.com/english/2020-05/01/c_139024157.htm.
25 Vu Hai, "China's East Sea 'Fishing Ban' Invalid: Agriculture Ministry," *VN Express*, 11 May 2020, https://e.vnexpress.net/news/news/china-s-east-sea-fishing-ban-invalid-agriculture-ministry-4097870.html
26 "Cross-Strait Sea Transport Agreement," Mainland Affairs Council, ROC, 4 November 2008, https://ws.mac.gov.tw/001/Upload/OldWeb/www.mac.gov.tw/public/Data/963010362171.pdf.
27 Wang Li-jen, and Lee Kai-jen, "Interview with Cheng Chang-hsiung, Commander-in-Chief of the 2012 Cross-Strait Joint Maritime Search and Rescue Exercise" *Coast Guard*, no. 59, October 2012, p. 62, https://www.cga.gov.tw/bookcase/CoastGuardBC/NO59/CoastGuard59/files/assets/basic-html/page64.html.
28 Greg Torode and J. R. Wu, "Taiwan Enters South China Sea Legal Fray, as Group Seeks to Sway International Court," Reuters, 10 May 2020, https://www.reuters.com/article/us-southchinasea-taiwan-idUSKCN0Y02LD.
29 Lynn Kuok, "Taiwan and the South China Sea: More Steps in the Right Direction," op-ed, the Brookings Institution, 24 August 2015, https://www.brookings.edu/opinions/taiwan-and-the-south-china-sea-more-steps-in-the-right-direction/.

30 "U.S. Position on Maritime Claims in the South China Sea," Press Statement, Secretary of State, Michael Pompeo, US Department of State, 13 July 2020, https://www.state.gov/u-s-position-on-maritime-claims-in-the-south-china-sea/.

31 "Remarks by AIT Director W. Brent Christensen at Forum on Deepening Economic Ties in the Indo-Pacific," American Institute in Taiwan, 18 June 2019, https://www.ait.org.tw/sp-06182019/.

32 "Communist China and the Free World's Future," Speech by Secretary of State, Michael Pompeo, Yorba Linda, California, Richard Nixon's Presidential Library and Museum, 23 July 2020, https://www.state.gov/communist-china-and-the-free-worlds-future/.

21
COOPERATION THROUGH TRACK II MECHANISMS

Rommel C. Banlaoi

Introduction

To contribute to the overall efforts to promote international peace and regional stability, a new type of diplomacy has become prominent in the 21st-century international relations beset by complex and dynamic traditional and non-traditional security threats. Called Track II diplomacy, it is powered not by governmental processes (Track I) but by non-governmental initiatives. Track II diplomacy champions a new type of international cooperation that articulates informal voices and unofficial positions to grapple with the current and the future world security order. This type of diplomacy has played a critical role in seeking solutions to global and regional security issues that remain in the official agenda of governmental players. Issues covered by Track II diplomacy pertain to a myriad of concerns from inter-state conflicts and internal armed conflict to social and economic threats, climate change and environmental security, transnational crimes, international terrorism, pandemic (international terrorism, pandemic, and proliferation of weapons of mass destructions, among others) and proliferation of weapons of mass destruction, among others.

In the Asia-Pacific region, Track II diplomacy has demonstrated exemplary practices in encouraging dialogues and consultations on important security issues confronting the region. Track II diplomacy in the Asia-Pacific not only promotes confidence-building measures but also advances the idea of preventive diplomacy and the prospect for the adoption of a common approach to regional conflict resolution. One of the issues that loom large in the agenda of Track II diplomacy in the Asia-Pacific region is the South China Sea (SCS).

This chapter examines the role of Track II diplomacy in promoting cooperation in the SCS. This chapter takes stock of the contributions of Track II diplomacy in advancing confidence-building measures, promoting peaceful consultations, and pursuing pragmatic cooperation in the SCS. Specifically, this chapter describes the role of Track II diplomacy in the adoption of the 2002 Declaration on the Conduct of Parties in the South China Sea (DOC), the on-going negotiation on the Code of Conduct in the South China Sea (COC), and the current bilateral mechanisms among claimants to peacefully manage the SCS dispute.

Conceptual background and framework of analysis

Track II diplomacy is an innovative practice that encourages unofficial and non-state processes in addressing the official problems of the state. It is an informal and non-governmental process that aims to assist government officials in solving state problems or resolving inter-state or intra-state conflicts. Because of its informal nature, Track II diplomacy is also known as "backchannel diplomacy" as it uses the backdoor as an innovative way to tackle state issues that are still sensitive or deemed premature to discuss officially. Though it is unofficial, it aids the official process in finding alternative and effective ways to solve state problems through non-governmental mechanisms. It also provides creative avenues for parties in conflict to converse with each other in an informal manner despite the adversarial nature of their relationship. In other words, Track II diplomacy allows enemies to talk to one another in order to explore ways to improve their relationship and find measures to resolve their conflicts through non-governmental initiatives.[1]

Track II diplomacy dates back to 1981 when American diplomat, Joseph Montville, has coined the term to refer to the "unofficial, informal interaction between members of adversarial groups or nations with the goals of developing strategies, influencing public opinion, and organizing human and material resources in ways that might help resolve the conflict."[2] Track I refers to "official diplomacy" while Track II pertains to "unofficial diplomacy." In Monville's concept, officials perform Track II diplomacy on their unofficial, private and personal capacities to build confidence, encourage discussions and explore solutions to state problems. A high level of informalities makes Track II diplomacy an effective mechanism to encourage frank and candid discussions on sensitive issues that officials are reluctant or constraint to address during formal deliberations.

The initiative of an Australian diplomat, John Burton indicates an earlier case of the successful use of Track II diplomacy.[3] To peacefully manage boundary conflicts between Indonesia, Malaysia, and Singapore, Burton has utilized the "workshop method" of mediation and facilitation as an informal problem-solving mechanism. A "non-partisan" third-party player serves as the moderator and facilitator of the workshop. The success of this method has become the classic framework for cooperation in Track II mechanisms.

Since then, the theory and practice of Track II diplomacy have evolved to include various players and stakeholders. Track II diplomacy now includes representatives of the conflicting parties facilitated by an impartial third-party composed of academics, scholars, experts, analysts, and practitioners as well as learned participants who have access to officials or can whisper to the ears of decision-makers. A very important feature of Track II diplomacy is the strict application of the Chatham House rule of non-attribution.[4] The use of this disclaimer encourages free and open discussions of issues not usually articulated during official conversations.

In the Asia-Pacific region, the post-cold war has seen the rise of the Track II mechanism with the "burgeoning of non-governmental activities and institutional linkages concerning security cooperation in the Asia-Pacific region, in which government officials were greatly involved but in their private or non-official capacities."[5] Policy think tanks and academic institutions initiate these non-governmental activities in order to promote confidence-building, dialogues, consultations, and various forms of cooperation on the panoply of security issues confronting the region. In fact, Track II processes have been closely associated with activities of think tanks. Four types of think tanks have been identified pursuing Track II initiatives in the region: (1) Academic think tanks associated with universities; (2) Contract research think tanks commissioned by governments and international agencies; (3) Advocacy think tanks engaged in policy debates and lobbies; and (4) Government-linked think tanks.[6] These think tanks contributed immensely to the promotion of regional cooperation through Track II mechanisms.

Track II cooperation in the SCS: past initiatives

The Indonesia workshop

Track II diplomacy has also been applied to peacefully manage the SCS dispute. The most cited example of Track II diplomacy in the SCS is the Indonesia Workshop on Managing Potential Disputes in the SCS. Otherwise known as the South China Sea Workshop (SCSW), the Indonesia Workshop began in 1990 to provide a platform for informal discussions on technical rather than political aspects of the SCS for purposes of confidence building, the major building block for regional cooperation.[7] Guided by the principle of consensus as practiced by the Association of Southeast Asian Nations (ASEAN), the Indonesia Workshop became the major platform for participants from claimants and many user States to deeply examine the many ramifications of the SCS in order to advance functional cooperation in marine scientific research, marine environmental protection, sustainable management of marine resources, the safety of navigation, protection of the sea lanes of communications, sharing of hydrographic data, combatting transnational crimes at sea, and regional legal cooperation, among others. Discussions on these areas aim to build trust among stakeholders in order to promote peace and avoid armed conflicts in the SCS through practical cooperation in functional, technical, and nonpolitical areas.

During its first workshop in Bali, Indonesia in 1990, only six ASEAN members attended: Brunei Darussalam, Indonesia, Malaysia, the Philippines, Singapore, and Thailand. Because of the nonpolitical nature of the process, one innovative feature of the Indonesia Workshop was the inclusion of both the People's Republic of China (PRC) and Taiwan in its informal dialogue activities. Initially, there were difficulties involving China in the process because of China's aversion against the "internationalization" of the SCS disputes.[8] The inclusion of Taiwan also made China uncomfortable. Moreover, China preferred bilateral discussions rather than multilateral discussions on the SCS. China finally agreed to join the process because of the unofficial nature of the Indonesian Workshop. Eventually, Cambodia, Laos, Vietnam, and other countries joined the Track II processes.

The Indonesia Workshop has become the only regular platform where scholars, experts, and officials from ASEAN countries closely engage their counterparts in China and Taiwan on SCS issues.[9] Participants collaborate to conduct joint research on the many ramifications of the SCS disputes in order to manage potential conflicts.[10] The Indonesian Workshop has established five Technical Working Groups (TWGs) where participants seriously pursue cooperation on the following research areas of mutual interests not only to claimants but also to other stakeholders in the SCS: (1) Marine Scientific Research; (2) Resource Assessment; (3) Marine Environmental Protection; (4) Safety of Navigation, Shipping, and Communication; and (5) Legal Matters. During its first 20 years of Track II activities covering the period from 1990 to 2010, the following lessons have been learned:

- The parties of the disputes must realize that the outbreak of the conflict, especially armed conflict, will not settle the disputes and will not bring benefits to either party; in fact, they may only bring mutual damage or loss to the parties.
- The existence of political will to settle the disputes peacefully, and to take measures so that the continuation of the disputes would not escalate into armed conflict. The parties must realize that the solution of the disputes would be more in their interest than in their continued prolongation.
- The parties should not legislate any territorial claims and should not involve as much a public opinion as possible, especially in the area where the claims are clearly disputed.

Legislating territorial claims and seeking support through public opinion tends to harden the position of all sides, making it more difficult to seek solutions or compromises or even temporary solutions like "joint developments."

- The need to increase "transparency" in national policy, legislation, and documentation, and more frequent meetings among the legal officers of the various regional countries in order to exchange their documentation and information as well as their legislative planning. Successful efforts often begin by informal efforts, either through the Track-II process or through the informal Track-I process. After those efforts indicate some possible success, a more formal "Track I" approach can be attempted. This was the case with the Cambodian issue, which started with informal "cocktail parties", the Southern Philippines issue, and the South China Sea Workshops. Preventive diplomacy requires patience, tenacity, and consistent efforts.
- Preventive diplomacy should be undertaken by all parties who have interests in the solution of the problems, either regionally or internationally. Solutions that take into account only national as well as regional interests but ignore the interests of states outside the region would not be an effective long-term solution.[11]

To date, in almost 30 years of Track II activities, the Indonesia Workshop has been persistent in championing functional cooperation in the SCS that has contributed to the SCS agenda of the ARF and China-ASEAN relations.[12] The scope of functional cooperation has broadened to other fields like marine information technology, ocean governance, law enforcement cooperation, and blue economy.

On 11–12 September 2019, Indonesia hosted the 29th Workshop in Batam. Attended by 54 participants from China, Indonesia, Lao PDR, Malaysia, Chinese Taipei, Vietnam, and the Philippines, the 29th Indonesia Workshop highlighted the need to pursue functional cooperation in the SCS, particularly in the area of business and maritime trade. The Ministry of Foreign Affairs of the Republic of Indonesia and the Center for Southeast Asian Studies jointly organized the 29th Workshop to support the negotiation effort in the (intergovernmental) first-track, by building trust (confidence-building measures) among parties in the region.[13]

Though Indonesia is not strictly a claimant state in the SCS, it has high stakes on the issue because of the Natuna Islands and the scope of its exclusive economic zone (EEZ) in this maritime domain. Thus, Indonesia is playing an honest broker in order to promote peace in the SCS.

Initially, the Canadian International Development Agency (CIDA) financed the Indonesia Workshop for 12 continuous years to promote confidence building in the SCS. CIDA's participation in Track II cooperation in the SCS received support from claimants and stakeholders because of Canada's reputation of being non-partisan. Moreover, participants to the Indonesia Workshop regarded Canadian scholars as honest brokers to the disputes with the expertise to contribute to maritime conflicts, to wit:

> Canada's perceived impartiality on regional security issues allowed the Canadian International Development Agency (CIDA), in conjunction with Canadian scholars, to support the Indonesian-hosted South China Sea dialogues in the 1990s. These were an important confidence-building measure at a time of escalating tension over disputed maritime space and the only meeting where all South China Sea claimants, including Taiwan, were present. Canada's role as an honest broker was evidenced by the fact that the Chinese were on record as preferring Canadian funding to US or Japanese funding

> for future South China Sea workshops. This role was possible because Canada then, as now, was not seen as a party to the disputes and had substantial expertise to contribute.[14]

When CIDA concluded the funding, the Indonesia Workshop has diversified its funding sources to include China, Taiwan, Vietnam, and other participants in recent years. For almost three decades, the Indonesia Workshop has not only contributed to the promotion of confidence-building in the SCS, it has also added important value to the production of new knowledge on the scientific, legal, technical, and other aspects of the SCS. Moreover, the Indonesia Workshop has also strengthened institutional networks and interpersonal relationships of participants, particularly those coming from the official sectors. These institutional networks and interpersonal relationships have created a more nuanced view of the SCS that informs the position of officials and policymakers during formal discussions.

CSCAP Workshops on SCS

The Council for Security Cooperation in the Asia-Pacific (CSCAP) has become the leading organization in the region pursuing Track II diplomacy. Since its establishment in 1993, CSCAP has organized various activities through workshops, conferences, and meetings that aim to promote regional security cooperation through a variety of confidence-building measures. CSCAP has also proposed ideas on the adoption of preventive diplomacy and the development of a common approach to conflict resolution in the Asia-Pacific that have become the objectives of the ASEAN Regional Forum (ARF), an official institution upholding regional security cooperation in the Asia-Pacific.

Like the Indonesian Workshop, CSCAP has also contributed to Track II cooperation in the SCS.[15] Since 1993, CSCAP has been complementing the Track II activities of the Indonesian Workshop from small meetings of less than 20 participants to large conferences of more than 300 participants. The annual Asia-Pacific Roundtable (APR) organized by the ASEAN Institutes of Strategic and International Studies (ASEAN-ISIS) provides CSCAP the largest venue for pursuing Track II cooperation in the Asia-Pacific. All think tanks, academic institutions, and policy-oriented non-governmental organizations involved in CSCAP activities also reinforce the complex network of Track II processes in the Asia-Pacific covering the SCS.

CSCAP seriously tackles SCS issues in its Working Group on Maritime Cooperation.[16] Though this Working Group covers broad issues of maritime security from the Pacific Ocean to the Indian Ocean and from the East China Sea to the Malacca Straits, as well as Sulu and Sulawesi Seas, SCS has taken focused attention because of its economic, geopolitical and strategic importance. Moreover, rising tensions in the SCS at the turn of the 21st century have attracted many scholars in the Asia-Pacific to pay greater attention to the SCS. The following objectives of this Working Group have immensely contributed to frank discussions to promote the calming of the security situation in the SCS:

- To foster maritime cooperation and dialogue among the states of the Asia-Pacific region and enhance theft ability to manage and use the maritime environment without prejudicing the interests of each other;
- To develop an understanding of regional maritime issues and the scope they provide for cooperation and dialogue;
- To contribute to a stable maritime regime in the Asia-Pacific region which will reduce the risk of regional conflict;

- To undertake policy-oriented studies on specific regional maritime security problems;
- To promote particular maritime confidence and security-building measures (MCSBMs); and,
- To promote adherence to the principles of the 1982 UN Convention on the Law of the Sea (UNCLOS)[17]

Other Working Groups such as on Confidence and Security Building Measures (CSBMs), Concepts of Comprehensive and Cooperative Security, and Transnational Crimes also inevitably cover serious discussions on SCS along with security issues in the Taiwan Straits, Korean Peninsula, and the East China Sea.[18] However, Working Groups deliberately avoided issues encroaching on national sensitivities of participants, particularly on sovereignty matters. Nonetheless, some participants to these Working Groups, particularly on Maritime Cooperation, have become informal advisers to officials handling the SCS at ARF meetings and even China-ASEAN summits. As aptly described by one participant:

> To its credit, the Maritime Cooperation WG [Working Group] has not demurred from discussing politically controversial issues, including the South China Sea. Although CSCAP's governing Steering Committee has avoided taking any position on the Spratly Islands because of China's strenuous objections, the Maritime WG has commissioned papers on the topic. At its 1997 meeting in Kuala Lumpur, a paper by the East-West Center's South China Sea specialist, Mark Valencia, identified several scenarios for resolution of the Spratly Islands dispute based on a multilateral management authority. The ensuing discussion clarified a number of issues that would have to be resolved in overlapping maritime zones. Among the obstacles were military objections to sharing marine data that could compromise naval deployments; the fact that country capabilities to meet various obligations under a multilateral regime vary; and the tendency of Spratly claimants to devote their attentions exclusively to territorial claims, ignoring the larger issues of ocean governance, which include resource management, environmental protection, and security implications.[19]

A useful product of CSCAP activities is the issuance of a Memorandum on burning security issues facing the Asia-Pacific region. To date, CSCAP has issued 33 Memoranda published on its official website.[20] Many of these Memorandums have maritime security agendas prepared by known experts and scholars not only from the Asia-Pacific region but also from Europe. Although all CSCAP Memoranda are useful for SCS discussions, the following Memoranda have a direct significance to the SCS Track II cooperation mechanisms:

- Memorandum 4 – Guidelines for Regional Maritime Cooperation
- Memorandum 5 – Cooperation for Law and Order at Sea
- Memorandum 5 – Practice of the Law of the Sea in the Asia Pacific
- Memorandum 8 – The Weakest Link? Seaborne Trade and Maritime Regime in the Asia Pacific
- Memorandum 12 – Maritime Knowledge and Awareness: Basic Foundations of Maritime Security
- Memorandum 13 – Guidelines for Maritime Cooperation in Enclosed and Semi-Enclosed Seas and Similar Sea Areas of the Asia Pacific
- Memorandum 15 – Security Implications of Climate Change
- Memorandum 16 – Safety and Security of Offshore Oil and Gas Installations

- Memorandum 21 – Implications of Naval Enhancement in the Asia Pacific
- Memorandum 24 – Safety and Security of Vital Undersea Communications Infrastructure
- Memorandum 25 – Maritime CBMs. Trust, and Managing Incidents at Sea
- Memorandum 29 – Harmonization of Aeronautical and Maritime Search and Rescue (SAR)
- Memorandum 30 – Preventive Diplomacy: Promoting Prospects for Mediation and Peaceful Settlement of Disputes in the Asia Pacific
- Memorandum 31 – Enhancing Marine Environment Protection in the Asia Pacific

DAV SCS international conference

The annual SCS International Conference organized by the Diplomatic Academy of Vietnam (DAV) and the Vietnam Lawyers' Association (VLA) also contributes to the Track II process in the SCS. This annual international conference aims "to review latest developments, identify the drivers behind relevant dynamics, and explore different avenues for conflict management and resolution in the SCS region, as well as for greater cooperation on a number of maritime issues."[21]

Like other Track II activities on the SCS, DAV's annual international conference upholds the tradition "of candid and open exchange" on various issues surrounding the SCS. Most of the participants in this annual event are also participants in the Indonesian Workshops and CSCAP meetings on the SCS. Thus, many participants are familiar with each other and have already established the habit of research cooperation with each other. DAV publishes the annual proceedings of this event containing scholarly works of participants on various issues of the SCS: claimants' positions, stakeholders' analysis, maritime delimitations, conflict resolution, functional cooperation, marine environmental protection, dispute resolution, international arbitration, oil and gas development, and fisheries management, among others. These publications provide scholarly analyses and recommendations that promote various forms of cooperation in the SCS.[22]

As of this writing, DAV had conducted 11 conferences held mostly in Hanoi and Danang. However, DAV's hosting of this annual conference is open to criticism because Vietnam is a party to the SCS disputes. There is a view that Vietnam is using this annual conference to have a platform to internationalize the disputes and to create an opportunity for Hanoi to promote its official national positions. Nonetheless, the DAV SCS International Conference still serves as a venue to advance Track II cooperation. It complements other Track II activities on the SCS. It also sustains academic exchanges and inter-personal relationships of participants from governmental and non-governmental sectors. Like other Track II activities, this annual activity reinforces the socialization and familiarization of participants on SCS issues that help inform officials during formal activities.

Manila Conference on the South China Sea

In cooperation with DAV, the National Defense College of the Philippines (NDCP) and the Foreign Service Institute (FSI) of the Philippines organized the Manila Conference on the South China Sea on 5–6 July 2011. This conference took place just a year before the 2012 Scarborough Standoff between the Philippines and China. It also happened against the backdrop of renewed security tensions in the SCS. With a theme, "Toward a Region of Peace, Cooperation, and Progress," the Manila Conference aimed to intensify the academic discussion on the SCS with the expectation that it would "contribute meaningfully to the peaceful and harmonious interactions among parties and relevant stakeholders."[23] The conference contained academic papers describing the SCS situation, China's behavior in the area, ASEAN response, and the role of extra-regional powers, particularly the United States. The conference also discussed options on how to peacefully manage the SCS disputes. Key observations and recommendations of the Manila Conference were the following[24]:

1. There is no shortage of good ideas, only a lack of political will. All parties need to compromise and abide by all agreements. Regional interest must be seen to be in the national interests;
2. To improve the climate of dialogue, there is a need to continue confidence-building measures such as exchange of information, including notifications of activities, and efforts to reduce border tensions by demilitarizing sensitive areas;
3. All SCS claimant states should clarify their claims in accordance with UNCLOS. China, in particular, should clarify its U-shaped claims. Other claimants' adherence to international law and other internationally recognized frameworks may encourage the rest to do the same;
4. Some cooperative activities under DOC-SCS worth pushing for include joint fisheries and human treatment of fishermen. China is likely to continue its assertive approach, and the DOC-SCS may not be enough to dissipate current tensions. Some speakers considered the necessity of a code of conduct (COC) that should contain conflict avoidance measures, principles for functional cooperation, and rights of coastal and user states, among others. Under international law, even a non-binding COC has its merits. A COC should reflect agreement on a normative framework and should not be vague in wording, as the DOC-SCS has been; a COC should have clear compliance rules and mechanisms.
5. Some proposals that were raised on how ASEAN and could move forward should a diplomatic stalemate persist:

    a. An ASEAN's Treaty of Conduct in the SCS that may be opened for accession to other countries.
    b. Voluntary guidelines regarding military and intelligence gathering activities in foreign EEZ s, where the goal is to avoid untoward incidents from happening. Such voluntary guidelines may also have provisions on the rights and duties of coastal states or other states in EEZ.
    c. A 6-4-2 formula, whereby the six ASEAN non-claimants persuade the four ASEAN claimants to engage in two non-ASEAN claimants. Any multilateral engagement should be agreeable to all claimants.

6. On the role of the United States:

    a. On freedom of navigation, the United States and other countries (Japan, Korea, etc.), major users of routes traversing the SCS and therefore legitimate stakeholders, must be included in the process of managing the disputes.
    b. On the military activities in the EEZ, regional countries and the United States would need to continue dialogue on maritime security and freedom of navigation at various forums to clarify the issue. A Chinese-US bilateral agreement regarding military activities in the EEZ would also be useful in reaching a regional agreement on the matter.
    c. The United States must accede to UNCLOS, as it has become the acceptable legal framework of the claimants and other coastal states.

Most of the speakers to this conference were regular speakers of the DAV SCS International Conference indicating the apparent bilateral cooperation between Vietnam and the Philippines at the Track II level. Even at the Track I level, Vietnam and the Philippines just leveled up their bilateral cooperation by forging an agreement on Bilateral Strategic Partnership, the first one that the Philippines entered into with Southeast Asian countries.

CSIS Annual South China Sea Conference

The annual conference organized by the Center for Strategic and International Studies (CSIS) through its Asian Maritime Transparency Initiative (AMTI) in Washington DC adds to the overlapping and even redundant Track II discussions on the SCS. Inaugurated in 2011, this annual conference largely showcases the geopolitical, military, and legal aspects of the SCS disputes. Though previous conferences covered marine environment, joint development, and law enforcement, the "state of play," "recent developments," and "rules-based order" have been prominent topics in this annual event.

However, this annual conference has been observed to be articulating American if not anti-China perspectives on SCS disputes. Most, if not all, participants in this annual conference are known scholars and experts who are arguably thinking alike with the US or are critical of China's positions and activities in the SCS. Many speakers in this conference denounced China's land reclamation activities and Beijing's rejection of the international arbitration decision on the SCS. Thus, China felt being singled out in this Track II process. Nonetheless, this annual conference still offered peaceful solutions to the disputes. For example, during its 9th conference on 24 July 2019, CSIS covered a panel on dispute management, which provided some options for peaceful actions in this contested body of water through the rule of law.

Recent initiative: the China-Southeast Asia Research Center on the South China Sea

To encourage robust engagement between China and ASEAN members in addressing the SCS disputes, another Track II mechanism took the center stage in recent years in order to promote peaceful cooperation in the SCS. Capitalizing on the official China-ASEAN dialogue partnership arrangement, this Track II mechanism led to the establishment of the China-Southeast Asia Research Center on the South China Sea (CSARC) in 2014. Think tanks in China and Southeast Asia tackling SCS issues formed CSARC to promote Track II cooperation with a serious intention to inform Track I cooperation between China and ASEAN.

CSARC had its embryonic stage on 14–15 September 2015 when the Jakarta-based CSIS and China's National Institute for South China Sea Studies (NISCSS) assisted by Singapore's S. Rajaratnam School of International Studies (RSIS) conducted the China-ASEAN Workshop on the SCS in Jakarta. With a theme, "Partnership for Regional Peace: Operationalizing ASEAN-China Strategic Partnership in Southeast Asia" this workshop pursued a Track II cooperation project in the SCS called "Finding A Resolution to the Issues on the South China Sea." This project aimed to achieve the following objectives:

- To provide a Track 1.5 venue, led by Indonesia and China, to forge a common understanding between China and ASEAN on the importance of maritime security and good order at sea; and,

- To generate ideas on how maritime challenges could be managed through the effective implementation of cooperation agenda between China and ASEAN, especially in managing the SCS.[25]

The CSIS-Indonesia paper served as the background material to steer the discussions of the first China-ASEAN workshop. The paper describes some gains of the China-ASEAN Track I efforts on the SCS.[26] It argues that a peaceful resolution of the SCS dispute will also be "the guarantee for the future relations between China and ASEAN that will keep peace, stability, and development in Southeast Asia."[27] To institutionalize the process of cooperation between China and ASEAN on the SCS, China and ASEAN have established the Joint-Working Group (JWG), and the Senior Officials Meetings (SOM). These two institutions are deliberating on the implementation of the DOC and the conclusion of the COC.

Although results of China-ASEAN Track I activities on the SCS are confidential, understanding the activities of these two institutions is essential in informing the agenda of the China-ASEAN Track II cooperation in the SCS. So far, Track I activities have focused on three major topics: promoting confidence, preventing accidents and managing accidents (if they occur).[28] Track I activities have also pursued the following areas of cooperation: Satellite Survey of Physical Features of the SCS, Safety of Navigations and Communications at Sea, and Marine Environmental Protection. With the CSIS paper as the background material, the first China-ASEAN workshop created four working groups to discuss the various facets of the SCS:

- ASEAN-China Working Group on Joint Cooperation/Activities and Sustainability in the South China Sea
- ASEAN-China Working Group on the COC
- ASEAN-China Working Group on Maritime Safety and Security
- ASEAN-China Working Group on UN Convention on the Law of the Sea vis a vis the Historic Right of China

On 3 November 2015, the organizers held a meeting in Bali, Indonesia to assess the outcome of the first workshop. Based on their assessment of the first China-ASEAN workshop, the organizers held the second China-ASEAN workshop on 18–19 January 2016 in Haikou, Hainan. The second workshop was a milestone as it included established and rising scholars working on SCS issues. Established scholars were veterans of the Indonesian and CSCAP Workshops while emerging scholars were younger participants from DAV conferences and other recent conferences on SCS organized by NISCSS. The second workshop formed four working groups to discuss important areas of cooperation in the SCS:

- ASEAN-China Working Group on Legal Principles on the Maritime Domain
- ASEAN-China Working Group on Confidence-Building Measures
- ASEAN-China Working Group on Preventive Diplomacy
- ASEAN-China Working Group on Crisis Management

Around 70 participants from China and ASEAN countries attended each workshop with around 20 experts coming from China. Since some officials from China and ASEAN countries in charge of SCS issues attended these workshops in their own private capacities, the organizers deliberately avoided discussions on overlapping territorial and maritime claims. Participants attended these workshops with the assumption that "the peaceful resolution and stability of the South China Sea is critical to assure the establishment of a peaceful region."[29]

Participants also accepted the view that "A peaceful resolution will also be the guarantee for a positive and conducive future relation between China and Southeast Asia."[30] Given these assumptions, participants covered the following topics during the two workshops:

- Latest developments in the SCS
- Dispute and Settlement Mechanisms
- Legal Issues
- Role of Extra-regional Powers
- Joint Cooperation
- Confidence-Building Measures
- Preventive Diplomacy
- Crisis Management
- Code of Conduct

The knowledge produced during these two workshops encouraged participants to establish the CSARC as a pioneering China-Southeast Asia research center dedicated to pursuing scholarly research and academic studies on the many aspects of the SCS. Launched on 25 March 2016 at the sideline of the Bo'ao Forum for Asia, CSARC aims to promote maritime cooperation in the SCS within the framework of the 2002 China-ASEAN Declaration on the Conduct of Parties in the SCS (DOC).[31] Seven leading think tanks and research institutes of China and Southeast Asian countries became CSARC's founding member organizations. Members of the Board of CSARC elected Dr. Wu Shicun of NISCSS as Chairman on 22 July 2016 during its first board meeting in Haikou. CSARC holds its office at the NISCSS building in Haikou.

Because of its intention to implement the DOC by conducting research and organizing conferences, CSARC received a grant from ASEAN-China Maritime Cooperation Fund. Though endorsed and supported by government officials from China and ASEAN countries as a result of the two China-ASEAN workshops on the SCS, CSARC remains an independent, non-government academic institution that intends to promote maritime cooperation in the SCS by conducting research, organizing workshops, and holding conferences and meetings within the Track II cooperation mechanism. CSARC is also a non-profit organization that aims to enhance cooperation and mutual trust among relevant countries.

CSARC, together with NISCSS, CSIS (Indonesia), and RSIS, organized the third and final China-ASEAN workshop on the SCS in Singapore on 21–22 July 2016. The third workshop presented results of discussions from the four working groups formed during the second workshop: legal principles on the maritime domain, confidence-building measure, preventive diplomacy, and crisis management. The third workshop included not only China-ASEAN experts but also international observers from Australia, Europe, India, Japan, and the United States. It was also during the third workshop when CSARC formed its members of the Board of Directors to represent China and ASEAN members.

These three recent China-ASEAN workshops were so valuable as they produced up-to-date policy papers that offered important inputs and useful feedbacks to governments in China and ASEAN countries on SCS issues. These three workshops also immensely facilitated trust-building among China and Southeast Asian participants, particularly among officials who seldom discuss SCS issues in an open, frank, and non-confidential setting. As observed,

> Even the officials representing the Track One has learned a lot about the different perspectives among states. The project takes pride in the openness and transparency of its processes. Such process is an effective catalyst for trust and confidence in conflict resolution.[32]

Though participants held the third workshop just a few days after the International Arbitral Tribunal rendered its decisions on the case filed by the Philippines against China, officials who attended remained candid, open, and cooperative during the meeting. These three workshops highlighted the need for China and Southeast Asian countries to cooperate in the SCS in the post-arbitration period. The workshops also encouraged other stakeholders to cooperate with China and ASEAN in order to maintain peace and stability in the SCS.

To sustain its efforts in pursuing cooperation in the SCS through Track II mechanisms, CSARC conducted its Workshop on Regional Cooperation on Marine Environmental Protection in the South China Sea in Bali, Indonesia on 29–30 November 2019. Supported by NISCSS and CSIS-Indonesia, this first CSARC Workshop on Regional Cooperation covered important topics that can implement the DOC in the area of marine scientific research and marine environmental protection, to wit:

- Existing Regional Cooperative Projects on Marine Environmental Protection
- Best Practices in Collaborative Marine Protected Area Management
- National Policies on Marine Protected Areas
- Perspectives of Illegal, Unregulated and Unreported (IUU) Fishing
- Cooperative Project on Environmental Protection in the South China Sea

Since its establishment in 2016, CSARC has organized several activities promoting cooperation in the SCS through Track II mechanisms. In March 2017, CSARC co-organized a sub-forum on the SCS at the sideline of the Bo'ao Forum for Asia International Conference. Since then, CSARC has been co-organizing sub-forums on the SCS at the Boao Forum in order to discuss important issues of the SCS. These sub-forums have been providing platforms for officials, experts, and scholars to face-off on recent developments in the SCS.

On 7–8 December 2017, CSARC held the First Annual CSARC Conference in Haikou coinciding with the International Symposium on "Belt and Road Initiative (BRI) and Common Development of the Greater South China Sea Region" co organized with NISCSS. At least 70 participants attended the symposium with guest speakers coming from various government agencies as well as distinguished think tanks and research institutes of China, Indonesia, Malaysia, the Philippines, Singapore, Thailand, Vietnam, Belgium, Italy, Portugal, and the United Kingdom.

CSARC co-organizes with NISCSS the program of China-ASEAN Academy on Ocean Law and Governance being held annually in Haikou. With NISCSS and the Australia-based National Centre for Ocean Resources and Security (ANCORS) of the University of Wollongong, CSARC also conducts the annual Maritime Law Enforcement (MLE) of China-ASEAN Academy on Ocean Law and Governance launched in Haikou on 21 October 2019. These two main training programs not only aim to build knowledge and capacities of participants on issues surrounding the SCS. They also build deeper interpersonal relationships among participants, which are essential for regional cooperation.

During the COVID-19 pandemic, CSARC co-organized in November 2020 the Inaugural Symposium on Maritime Cooperation and Ocean Governance with NISCSS, Institute for China-America Studies (ICAS), and China Institute of the University of Alberta to discuss the global ocean governance and regional practices, recent development and hotspot issues in the SCS. This demonstrated that even during the time of the pandemic, CSARC continued its Track II initiatives in the SCS.

Achievements of Track II mechanisms: Role in the DOC and COC

Track II processes have enormously contributed to the implementation of the DOC and to the discussions, and eventually, to the negotiation on the COC. When ASEAN got its first involvement in SCS issues in 1992, Track II processes helped ASEAN officials to think through. Think tanks from ASEAN countries, especially those associated with the CSCAP network and ASEAN Institutes of Strategic and International Studies (ASEAN-ISIS), provided vital input to officials on how ASEAN should address the SCS problem. Scholars, academics, and experts covering SCS issues also produced several policy papers and scholarly journal articles to serve as references of officials in their Track I activities. ASEAN-ISIS, for instance, has received formal recognition at annual ASEAN ministerial meetings for its contributions to regional diplomacy and peaceful management of disputes in the SCS.[33]

Prior to the official signing of the DOC in 2002, Track II efforts recommended measures on how parties should behave in order to promote peace and maintain stability in the SCS. For example, knowledge produced during the first ten years of the Indonesian Workshop provided vital inputs to the formulation of the DOC. The DOC's commitment to "the freedom of navigation in and over-flight above the SCS as provided for by the universally recognized principles of international law, including the 1982 UN Convention on the Law of the Sea" has been discussed and championed by various Track II activities in the SCS.[34] Many principles of regional cooperation found in the DOC have already been articulated in the various reports of Track II activities. Many innovative ideas generated through Track II efforts, particularly that of the Indonesia Workshop, enormously helped officials in China and ASEAN to finalize the contents of the DOC.[35] The following areas of cooperation enumerated in the DOC have, in fact, been on the agenda of the Indonesian Workshop and other Track II workshops in the SCS:

- Marine Environmental Protection
- Marine Scientific Research
- Safety of Navigation and Communication at Sea
- Search and Rescue Operations
- Combatting Transnational Crimes (including International Terrorism)

To implement the DOC, Track II initiatives provided China-ASEAN officials creative ideas to engage in maritime cooperation. During the ASEAN-ISIS 17th Asia Pacific Roundtable in Kuala Lumpur on 6–9 August 2003, some papers hailed the official adoption of the DOC as an important step towards confidence building and conflict reduction in the SCS. Though the issue of international terrorism loomed large in the agenda of many Track II activities in the Asia-Pacific region following the 9/11 terrorist attacks on the US, the DOC was a big thing between ASEAN and China. Thus, the implementation of the DOC continued to be in the agenda of China-ASEAN Track II activities.

With inputs coming from Track II sources, the ASEAN-China Senior Officials' Meeting (SOM) convened in 2003 in order to oversee the implementation of the DOC and to set up a joint working group to cover the details of implementation.[36] Parties created the SOM on the DOC in November 2004 in Kuala Lumpur to focus on how the DOC should be implemented. On 4–5 August 2005, the first China-ASEAN Joint Working Group on the Implementation of the DOC held its first meeting in Manila. It was during this meeting when ASEAN proposed a draft document of seven-point guidelines for the implementation of the DOC. Track II institutions commented on and analyzed these guidelines in various meetings, workshops, and conferences. But it was only in 2011 when China and ASEAN approved the Guidelines for the Implementation of the DOC. These Guidelines are based on eight principles:

1 The implementation of the DOC should be carried out in a step-by-step approach in line with the provisions of the DOC.
2 The Parties to the DOC will continue to promote dialogue and consultations in accordance with the spirit of the DOC.
3 The implementation of activities or projects as provided for in the DOC should be clearly identified.
4 The participation in the activities or projects should be carried out on a voluntary basis.
5 Initial activities to be undertaken under the ambit of the DOC should be confidence-building measures.
6 The decision to implement concrete measures or activities of the DOC should be based on consensus among parties concerned, and lead to the eventual realization of a Code of Conduct.
7 In the implementation of the agreed projects under the DOC, the services of the Experts and Eminent Persons, if deemed necessary, will be sought to provide specific inputs on the projects concerned.
8 Progress of the implementation of the agreed activities and projects under the DOC shall be reported annually to the ASEAN-China Ministerial Meeting (PMC).[37]

Track II activities have also provided useful ideas for the Track I discussions on the COC. When Manila lobbied for a COC to constrain China's assertive actions in the aftermath of the Mischief controversy in 1995, the Philippine government consulted some academics and experts for inputs and ideas. The Indonesian Workshop and CSCAP conferences have also produced several reports in the 1990s and at the turn of the 21st century calling for the need to adopt a regional code of conduct in the SCS in order to peacefully manage the SCS disputes. Though Track II activities do not expect a regional code of conduct to settle sovereignty claims, they, however, produce knowledge about the necessity of having a regional code in the SCS promoting good order at sea by compelling all parties to behave responsibly, lawfully, and peacefully.

Calls for the adoption of a COC became stronger in the aftermath of the 2012 Scarborough Standoff between the Philippines and China. Various think tanks not only in Southeast Asia but also in Europe and America produced various studies, analyses, and commentaries urging for the adoption of the COC. The Philippine government, after filing an international arbitration case against China in 2013, also lobbied officially with other ASEAN members for the "most expeditious conclusion" of the COC. It was also in 2013 when China started its land reclamation activities in the Spratlys. All these developments convinced ASEAN to seriously discuss with China on the conclusion of the COC.

During the 27th Asia Pacific Roundtable in Kuala Lumpur on 3–5 June 2013, most experts and academics and other scholars involved in Track II activities conveyed the need for the conclusion of the COC in the light of recent developments in the SCS. On 15 September 2013, China and ASEAN participants held the first China-ASEAN Senior Officials' Meeting (SOM) on the COC in Suzhou, China. Participants agreed to proceed with the COC discussions on the principles of observing consensus and adopting a gradual and incremental approach.

At the China-ASEAN meeting in Brunei Darussalam in October 2013, China agreed to start talks with ASEAN on the eventual conclusion of the COC. During the ASEAN Summit in Myanmar on 11 May 2014, the Philippine government pushed for the "immediate conclusion" of the COC. But the ASEAN released a softer position calling for an "early conclusion" of the COC. Rising security tensions in the SCS in 2015 prompted think tanks and academics in ASEAN, particularly from the Philippines, to expedite talks on the COC.[38] When the International Arbitral Tribunal rendered the historic ruling on 12 July 2016 in favor of Philippine positions, China agreed to officially accelerate discussions on the COC, especially when the Philippine government under President Rodrigo Roa Duterte decided to set aside the ruling in order to rebuild friendlier ties with China.

When President Duterte visited China in October 2016 and met President XI Jinping, Philippines-China relations reached its newest heights resulting in the reduction of the overall security tension in the SCS.[39] It should be noted that prior to Duterte's visit to China, experts and officials from China and the Philippines conducted a landmark Track II effort "to break the ice." On 10–11 August 2016, former Philippine President Fidel V. Ramos met in Hong Kong former Chinese Ambassador to the Philippines, Madam Fu Ying, who at that time was the Chair of the Foreign Affairs Committee of the National Peoples' Congress. Ramos was accompanied by former Secretary Rafael Alunan and Mr. Chito Santa Romana, former President of the Philippine Association for Chinese Studies (PACS) who would later be appointed as Philippine Ambassador to China. Joining Madam Fu Ying was Dr. Wu Shicun, President of NISCSS. This "meeting of friends" in Hong Kong was informal in nature with the primordial goal to reinvigorate Philippines-China relations and to explore areas of cooperation between the two countries in the SCS.[40]

With Duterte's paradigm shift to China, the SCS enjoyed a calm moment when the Philippine government hosted the ASEAN Summit in 2017. During this summit, which marked the 50th anniversary of ASEAN, China and ASEAN endorsed the Framework on the COC on 6 August 2017, which the China-ASEAN SOM-COC earlier approved in Guiyang, China on 19 May 2017. The easing of security tensions between the Philippines and China provided a conducive regional security environment for China and ASEAN to discuss the adoption of the COC. Philippines-China friendly relations under Duterte tremendously contributed "to better atmospherics in ASEAN-China relations" that effectively facilitated positive discussions on the COC.[41] Positive discussions between China and ASEAN on the COC Framework led to the final adoption a Single Draft South China Sea Code of Conduct Negotiating Text (SDNT) on 3 August 2018 in Singapore.[42] With the adoption of the SDNT, which was also discussed heavily on various Track II activities on the SCS, China expressed optimism to conclude the COC within three years. The SDNT had its first reading in Bangkok, Thailand on 31 July 2019. China and ASEAN approved the first draft of the COC in September 2019.

Amidst official activities towards the conclusion of the COC was the constructive, and sometimes critical, the role played by Track II initiatives. As stated earlier, CSARC conducted in 2016–2019 several Track II activities involving China and ASEAN officials, think tanks and academic institutions to discuss issues being covered by the COC. The Indonesian Workshops in 2016–2019 also covered issues being tackled in the official negotiations of the COC. DAV workshops during this period also contained discussions on the COC. The CSIS-AMTI workshops also heavily tackled the need to adopt a COC in order to establish a rules-based regime in the SCS.

In other words, Track II mechanisms contributed positively to the adoption and even implementation of the DOC as well as in the discussions and negotiations on the conclusion of the COC. Track II activities handled difficult issues that governments found them difficult to deliberate officially. Through Track II activities, ASEAN members were able to engage

China bilaterally and multilaterally on SCS issues. Track II initiatives allowed China and ASEAN members to socialize with pertinent players covering SCS issues. Track II efforts also facilitated China and ASEAN members to be familiarized with each other's outlooks and perspectives on the implementation of the DOC and the conclusion of the COC. Track II innovations created comfort levels for officials to squarely face SCS issues at the formal setting.

Challenges and limitations of Track II mechanisms

There is no doubt that Track II processes champion many ideas to promote cooperation among parties in conflict. However, there are some limitations that pose challenges to Track II efforts to achieve its desired objectives. While Track II activities have become essential features of China-ASEAN cooperation in the SCS, there have also been issues associated with the "autonomy dilemma" of Track II mechanisms involving China and ASEAN members.[43]

In the Asia-Pacific region, in general, Track II is "almost synonymous with the entire spectrum of non-official diplomatic activities. Yet, these distinctions and their implications for foreign policy processes show the increasing complexity of the world of non-official diplomatic activities."[44] Furthermore, the "dichotomy between Tracks 1 and 2 no longer suffices to cover the extent of these activities."[45] Even in the process called Track 1.5 where officials meet informally with the presence of non-official participants, its distinction with Track II is blurred.[46] Though Track II encourages governments to interact with experts and academics in their personal capacities, the nature of their participation, however, is being viewed to be just a "polite fiction" as the line demarcating between officials and non-officials really lacks clarity.[47]

In theory, Track II mechanisms intend to engage officials in their private capacities in order to allow governments to think outside their official boxes for purposes of confidence-building and exploration of creative ideas that are sensitive for official discussions. In practice, however, "the prospect of engaging governments and officials in spontaneous and unrestricted dialogue is inherently problematic" as some governments regard Track II as an opportunity to promote official positions.[48] Thus, the idea of official parties participating in Track II in a private capacity is a "polite fiction at best and discount the promise of Track II security dialogues for innovation and path-breaking initiatives."[49]

In China and Southeast Asia, the autonomy dilemma is exacerbated by the fact that most participants from the academe and think tanks are too connected to their governments. This situation finds it difficult for Track II to really break ground leading to "status quo thinking" that can delay, if not, prohibit cooperation.[50] There is also a perceived danger for experts to be co-opted by their governments in order to justify official positions taken by states prior to Track II processes.[51] Under these circumstances, Track II efforts "may be used to lend prestige to official decisions reached independently of outside expert inputs."[52] A serious question posed to Track II is its effectiveness to influencing government policies. As one expert argues:

> In order to answer this question, one needs to examine the relationship between the Track 1 and Track 2 groups. Does one group mainly affect the other, or do they influence each other? In theory, Track 2 groups were created to influence their government counterparts by providing studies on issues that officials had neither the time nor the expertise to address, or that were too sensitive to be raised in official meetings. The idea was that non-official specialists would influence the deliberations of government policy. In reality, however, government officials may ask for Track 2 studies that would provide the data and analysis to justify decisions already reached by governments. Additionally, governments may discourage Track 2 counterparts from embarking on certain topics by

> implying that Track 1 officials will pay no attention to the resulting studies. Therefore, the influence flows both ways between the two groups.
>
> Another issue that needs to be addressed is the independence of the Track 2 groups. In theory, Track 2 groups are independent of governments. They are composed of non-governmental experts who are beholden to no particular political group, who speak out independently on issues. In reality, some Track 2 groups are extensions of governments, particularly in communist states where the idea of independent specialists on security issues does not prevail, such as China, Vietnam and Laos. One way of determining independence is to see how Track 2 members are chosen. Are they appointed or elected? How long do the specialists serve on the group? Is there a hierarchy within the Track 2 group? Who determines the agenda of study? By addressing these questions, one can assess the independence of Track 2 groups.[53]

However, the closeness of participants to their governments can actually facilitate pragmatic cooperation as difficult issues are already threshed out in Track II processes. While Track II cannot set the official agenda, it can propose agenda for official discussions. Track II can also lay the groundwork for Track I processes to occur. Ideas generated during Track II activities can facilitate official negotiations for clearing the cobwebs. Track II can also provide early warning signs to officials to prevent misunderstanding and avoid further conflicts.

Conclusion

In the SCS, organizations and personalities in China and ASEAN involved in Track II activities have facilitated the adoption of DOC in 2002. China-ASEAN Track II mechanisms have also encouraged parties to implement the DOC. In the negotiation on the conclusion of the COC, China-ASEAN Track II initiatives provide important inputs to the official processes. In the Indonesia Workshops, the CSCAP Workshops, the DAV Conferences, and the CSIS-AMTI Conferences, among others, are known Track II mechanisms covering SCS issues.

The most recent initiative pursuing Track II activities in the SCS involving China and ASEAN participants is the CSARC. It is currently the leading Track II mechanism covering SCS issues between China and ASEAN countries. Though CSARC members can be viewed to be too close to their governments, their Track II activities contribute to confidence-building and fruitful conversations between China and ASEAN on the SCS. While CSARC may be used by China and ASEAN countries to propagate national positions of concerned parties, its Track II activities, however, facilitate governments to pursue pragmatic cooperation between China-ASEAN to peacefully manage the SCS disputes.

Notes

1 D. S. Kaye, *Talking to the Enemy: Track Two Diplomacy in the Middle East and South Asia* (Santa Monica, CA: RAND Corporation, 2007).

2 J. V. Montville, "The Arrow and the Olive Branch: A Case for Track Two Diplomacy," in J. W. McDonald and D. Dendahmane (eds.), *Conflict Resolution: Track Two Diplomacy* (Washington, DC: Foreign Service Institute, US Department of State, 1987), 5–20.

3 Robin Fraser, "Track Two Diplomacy: A Distinct Conflict Intervention Category" (Thesis submitted to the University of Victoria for the Master of Arts in Dispute Resolution, 20 June 2012), 3.

4 Ibid., 4.

5 Desmond Ball and Kwa Chong Guan, eds., *Assessing Track 2 Diplomacy in the Asia Pacific Region: A CSCAP Reader* (Singapore: S. Rajaratnam School of International Studies, 2010).

6 Barry Desker, "The Role of Think Tanks in East Asia," in Amitav Acharya and Lee Lai To (eds.), *Asia in the New Millennium: APISA First Congress Proceedings, 27–30 November 2003* (Singapore: Marshall Cavendish Academic, 2004), 248–254.

7 Scott Snyder, Brad Glosserman, and Ralph A. Cossa, "Confidence Building Measures in the South China Sea," *Issues and Insights, 2-01* (Honolulu: Pacific Forum CSIS, August 2001). Available at https://csis-website-prod.s3.amazonaws.com/s3fs-public/legacy_files/files/publication/issuesinsightsv01n02.pdf.

8 Hashim Djalal, "South China Sea – 2nd Track Diplomacy," in Tran Truong Thuy (ed.), *The South China Sea: Cooperation for Regional Security and Development* (Hanoi: Diplomatic Academy of Vietnam, 2009), 274.

9 For an analysis on the participation of Taiwan in the dialogue process, see Yann-Huei Song, "The South China Sea Workshop Process and Taiwan Participation," *Ocean Development and International Law*, Volume 41, Number 3 (2010), 253–269.

10 Hasijm Djalal and Ian Townsend-Gault, "Managing Potential Conflicts in the South China Sea: Informal Diplomacy for Conflict Prevention," in C. A. Crocker, F. O. Hampson, and P. Aall (eds.), *Herding Cats: Multiparty Media on in a Complex World* (Washington, DC: United States Institute of Peace Press, 1999), 107–133.

11 Hashim Djalal, "Lessons Learned from Various Conflicts and Potential Conflicts Management in Southeast Asia," in *The South China Sea Reader* (Papers and Proceedings of the Manila Conference on the South China Sea: Toward a Region of Peace, Cooperation and Progress, Manila, Philippines, 5–6 July 2011), 166–167.

12 Rommel C. Banlaoi, *The ASEAN Regional Forum, the South China Sea Disputes and the Functionalist Option* (Quezon City: National Defense College of the Philippines, 2001).

13 Ministry of Foreign Affairs of the Republic of Indonesia, "Batam Hosts Workshop on Managing Potential Conflict in the South China Sea" (11 September 2019).

14 James Manicom, "Canada and the South China Sea Dispute: Challenges for Re-engagement in East Asia," *Canada-Asia Agenda*, Issue 26 (31 May 2012), 6.

15 Ball and Guan, op cit.

16 See Sam Bateman and Stephen Bates (eds.), *The Seas Unite: Maritime Cooperation in the Asia Pacific Region,* Canberra Papers on Strategy and Defence No. 118 (Canberra: Strategic and Defence Studies Centre, Australian National University, 1996).

17 Sam Bateman and Stephen Bates (eds.), *Calming the Waters: Initiatives for Asia Pacific Maritime Cooperation*, Canberra Papers on Strategy and Defence No. 114 (Canberra: Strategic and Defence Studies Centre, Australian National University, 1996).

18 Bunn Nagara and Cheah Siew Ean (eds.), *Managing Security and Peace in the Asia- Pacific* (Kuala Lumpur: Institute of Strategic and International Studies, Malaysia, 1996).

19 Sheldon W. Simon, "Evaluating Track 2 Approaches to Security Dialogue in the Asia Pacific Region," in Ball and Guan, 93.

20 See Council for Security Cooperation in the Asia Pacific, *CSCAP Official Website* at http://www.cscap.org/index.php?page=memoranda.

21 Diplomatic Academy of Vietnam, "SCS Annual International Conference" at https://dav.edu.vn/en/first-announcement-the-11th-south-china-sea-international-conference-cooperation-for-regional-security-development/.

22 See for example Tran Truong Thuy (ed.), *The South China Sea: Towards a Region of Peace, Security and Cooperation* (Hanoi: Diplomatic Academy of Vietnam, 2011).

23 *The South China Sea Reader: Papers and Proceedings of the Manila Conference on the South China Sea – Toward a Region of Peace, Cooperation and Progress* (Manila: National Defense College of the Philippines, Foreign Service Institute and Diplomatic Academy of Vietnam, 5–6 July 2011).

24 Ibid., 9–11.

25 *Final Report and Policy Recommendations* (Partnership for Regional Peace: Operationalizing ASEAN-China Strategic Partnership in Southeast Asia, Finding A Resolution to the Issues on the South China Sea, Center for Strategic and International Studies, National Institute for South China Sea Studies and S. Rajaratnam School of International Studies: Bali, Indonesia, 14–15 September 2015).

26 Jusuf Wanandi, "General Outline on the Results of the First Track Efforts on the South China Sea between ASEAN and China" (Paper circulated during the First Conference of the "Partnership for Regional Peace: Operationalizing China-ASEAN Strategic Partnership – A Project on

Finding a Resolution to the Issues in the South China Sea organized by the Indonesia Center for Strategic and International Studies and National Institute for South China Sea Studies, 13–16 September 2015).

27 Ibid.

28 Ibid.

29 *Final Report and Policy Recommendations*, op cit.

30 Ibid.

31 "*China establishes joint research center on S. China Sea", Global Times, 25 March 2016.*

32 Ibid.

33 Joint Communiqués of the Twenty-sixth ASEAN Ministerial Meeting, Singapore, 23–24 July 1993 and the Twenty-eighth ASEAN Ministerial Meeting, Bandar Seri Begawan, 29–30 July 1995. Also cited in See Seng Tan, "Courting China: Track 2 Diplomacy and the Engagement of the People's Republic" (Paper presented at the ASEAN 40th Anniversary Conference, "Ideas and Institutions: Building an ASEAN Community?" jointly organized by the Friedrich Ebert Stiftung and the S. Rajaratnam School of International Studies held in Singapore on 31 July – 1 August 2007).

34 *Declaration on the Conduct of Parties in the South China Sea*, 4 November 2002.

35 Ignatius Agung Satyawan, "The Deployment of Track II Diplomacy in Indonesian-led Workshop on Managing Conflict in the South China Sea, 1990–2002" (Doctoral Dissertation: Universiti Utara Malaysia, 2015).

36 Li Mingjiang, "Managing Security in the South China Sea: From DOC to COC," *Kyoto Review of Southeast Asia*, Issue 15 (March 2014).

37 "Guidelines for the Implementation of DOC" at https://www.asean.org/wp-content/uploads/images/archive/documents/20185-DOC.pdf accessed on 13 December 2019.

38 Rommel C. Banlaoi, "Renewed Tensions and Continuing Maritime Security Dilemma in the South China Sea: A Philippine Perspective" in Tran Truong Thuy (ed.), *The South China Sea: Cooperation for Regional Security and Development* (Hanoi: Diplomatic Academy of Vietnam, 2009), 143–159.

39 Rommel C. Banlaoi, "Philippines' Security Policy Options and Future Prospects," in Fu-Kuo Liu, Keyuan Zou, Schicun Wu and Jonathan Spangler (eds.), *South China Sea Lawfare: Post-Arbitration Policy Options and Future Prospects* (Taipei: South China Sea Think and Taiwan Center for Security Studies, 2017), 99–110.

40 Lucio Blanco Pitlo III, "Breaking the Ice to Warm Relations: Ramos-Fu Track II Meeting and Beyond," *China-US Focus*, 17 October 2016.

41 Ian Storey, "Assessing the ASEAN-China Framework for the Code of Conduct for the South China Sea," *ISEAS Perspective*, Issue 2017, Number 62 (8 August 2017).

42 Carl Thayer, "A Closer Look at ASEAN-China Single Draft South China Sea Code of Conduct," *The Diplomat*, 3 August 2018.

43 Hermann Kraft, "The Autonomy Dilemma of Track Two Diplomacy in Southeast Asia," *Security Dialogue*, Volume 31, Number 3 (2000), 343–356.

44 Ibid.

45 Ibid.

46 Ibid.

47 Diane Stone, "Networks, Second Track Diplomacy and Regional Cooperation: The Role of Southeast Asian Think Tanks" (Paper delivered at the 38th Annual Convention of the International Studies Association held in Toronto, Canada on 22–26 March 1997), 19.

48 Brian L. Job. "Track 2 Diplomacy: Ideational Contribution to the Evolving Asia Security Order," in Muthiah Alagappa (ed.), *Asian Security Order* (Stanford, CA: Stanford University Press, 2003), 241–279.

49 Ibid.

50 See regional cases in Dalia Dassa Kaye, "Rethinking Track II Diplomacy: The Middle East and South Asia," *Cligendael Diplomacy Papers*, Number 3 (June 2005).

51 Sheldon W. Simon, "Evaluating Track II Approaches to Security Diplomacy in the Asia Pacific The CSCAP Experience," *NBR Special Report* (1 September 2001).

52 Ibid.

53 Ibid. Also cited in Ball and Guan, op cit. 82.

PART VI

Challenges and prospects

22

DISPUTE SETTLEMENT MECHANISMS FOR SOUTH CHINA SEA ISSUES

J. Ashley Roach

Introduction

Under general principles of international law, States may not be compelled to participate in dispute settlement without their consent. All of the South China Sea littoral States – China, the Philippines, Vietnam, and Malaysia – are parties to the 1982 UN Convention on the Law of the Sea (the Convention).[1] They have thereby consented – in advance – to be bound by the Convention's provisions on the settlement of disputes contained in Part XV.[2]

That is not the situation with the International Court of Justice (ICJ). State Parties to the Statute of the ICJ have the option to declare at any time unconditionally or on condition of reciprocity that they recognize as compulsory ipso facto and without a special agreement the jurisdiction of the Court in specified circumstances.[3] Otherwise, the jurisdiction of the Court comprises all cases which the parties refer to it and all matters specially provided for in the Charter of the United Nations or in treaties and conventions in force and depends on the form in which the State's consent is expressed.[4]

The general provisions for settlement of disputes under the Convention are contained in Section 1, Articles 279–285, of Part XV, as summarized next.

Obligation to settle disputes by peaceful means of their choice

Types of disputes

Article 279 of Section 1 of Part XV of the Convention provides that State Parties are required to settle any "dispute" between them "concerning the interpretation or application" of the Convention.

A "dispute" has been defined as a "disagreement on a point of law or fact, a conflict of legal views or of interests between two persons."[5]

The jurisdiction of the ICJ is broader.[6]

Peaceful means of their choice

Article 279 also requires these disputes be settled by peaceful means in accordance with Article 2, paragraph 3, of the United Nations (UN) Charter which provides "All Members shall settle their international disputes by peaceful means in such a manner that international peace and security, and justice, are not endangered."[7]

Article 279 further provides that State Parties shall seek a solution to their dispute by the means indicated in Article 33, paragraph 1, of the Charter, which provides

> The parties to any dispute, the continuance of which is likely to endanger the maintenance of international peace and security, shall, first of all, seek a solution by negotiation, enquiry, mediation, conciliation, arbitration, judicial settlement, resort to regional agencies or arrangements, or other peaceful means of their own choice.

Article 280 preserves the right of State Parties to agree "at any time" to settle a dispute between them concerning the interpretation or application of this Convention "by any peaceful means of their own choice."

Procedure where no settlement has been reached by the parties

Under Article 281 the procedures in Part XV only apply when no settlement has been reached by recourse to peaceful means of their choice and no other procedure has been agreed by the parties, including expiration of an agreed time limit.

Article 282 requires that obligations under general, regional or bilateral agreements apply in lieu of Part XV, unless the parties to the dispute agree otherwise.[8]

Obligation to exchange views

Article 283 requires parties to a dispute concerning the interpretation or application of the Convention to proceed expeditiously to an exchange of views on settling the dispute. In other words, there is an obligation to negotiate ("exchange of views"), but there is no obligation to reach an agreement or a settlement. Whether this requirement is met in any particular dispute depends on the facts and circumstances; there is no fixed minimum standard.

Settlement of seabed disputes

Article 285 provides that settlement of disputes concerning Part XI by the Seabed Disputes Chamber of the International Tribunal for the Law of the Sea are governed by Section 1 of Part XV.

Because of the broader scope of disputes under Part XI, Part XV, Section 1, applies to disputes between

- a State Parties;
- b a State Party and the International Seabed Authority; and
- c parties to a seabed mining contract, including State Parties, the Authority, States not a party to the Convention, the seabed mining Enterprise, State enterprises, and natural or juridical persons.[9]

Compulsory procedures entailing binding decisions

Section 2 of Part XV provides for compulsory procedures entailing binding decisions where no settlement has been reached by recourse to Section 1.

Application of procedures under Section 2

Article 286 provides that in the circumstances where no settlement has been reached by recourse to Section 1, the dispute *shall* be submitted at the request of *any* party to the dispute to the court or tribunal having jurisdiction under Section 2, without having to obtain consent from the other party or parties.

Thus unilateral action is sufficient to provide the court or tribunal with jurisdiction. That court or tribunal may render a decision, whether or not the other party participates in the process.[10]

Choice of procedure

Pursuant to Article 287, a State is free to choose one or more of these four fora for the settlement of disputes:

a the International Tribunal for the Law of the Sea (ITLOS),
b ICJ,
c an arbitral tribunal constituted in accordance with Annex VII to the Convention (Arbitration), or
d a special tribunal constituted in accordance with Article VIII (Special Arbitration) for one or more of the categories of disputes specified therein, that is, fisheries, protection and preservation of the marine environment, marine scientific research, or navigation including dumping.

To date, none of the South China Sea littoral States has formally made a choice of forum by written declaration.

Article 287, paragraph 3, provides that in such a situation the default forum is Annex VII Arbitration, as was the situation in the South China Sea arbitration.

Article 287, paragraph 2, provides that a choice under paragraph 1 does not divest the Seabed Disputes Chamber of jurisdiction per Part XI, Section 5.

Jurisdiction

The following courts and tribunals have jurisdiction pursuant to Article 288 over any dispute concerning the interpretation or application of the Convention submitted to it:

1 the four fora identified in Article 287 submitted pursuant to Part XV;
2 those four fora over any dispute concerning the interpretation or application of an international agreement *related to* the purpose of the Convention and *submitted* to it in accordance with that agreement;[11] and
3 the Seabed Disputes Chamber of ITLOS, and any other chamber or tribunal referred to in Part XI, Section 5, submitted to it in accordance with it.

In the event of a dispute as to whether the court or tribunal has jurisdiction, the matter is to be settled by the decision of the court or tribunal.[12] There can be no appeal from that decision.

Because of this jurisdictional limitation to interpretation or application of the Convention, which does not address sovereignty, disputes involving sovereignty may not be heard under Part XV unless the Parties agree.

The jurisdiction of the ICJ is based on different factors.[13]

Experts

Article 289 provides that two or more scientific experts may sit with a court or tribunal without the right to vote where desired in cases involving scientific or technical matters.

A list of such experts is to be prepared in accordance with Annex VIII, Article 2, by the relevant specialized UN agencies, such as the International Maritime Organisation (IMO), Food and Agriculture Organization (FAO), Intergovernmental Oceanographic Commission/United Nations Educational, Scientific and Cultural Organization (IOC/UNESCO), and UN Environment Programme (UNEP). The lists of experts are available on the Division for Ocean Affairs and the Law of the Sea (DOALOS) website.[14]

Their role is similar to that of "assessors" appointed under Article 30, paragraph 2, of the ICJ Statute.

Provisional measures

Article 290 permits a court or tribunal to prescribe any provisional measure which it considers appropriate under the circumstances to:

a preserve the respective rights of the parties to the dispute, or
b prevent serious harm to the environment,

pending the final decision.

Provisional measures may be prescribed only if the court or tribunal considers that *prima facie* it has jurisdiction.

Article 290 contains detailed provisions for the prescription of provisional measures in various situations.[15]

Article 41, paragraph 1, of the ICJ Statute has a narrower authorization, reflecting the mid-20th century in which it was adopted when concern for the environment was not so prominent: "The Court shall have the power to indicate, if it considers that circumstances so require, any provisional measures which ought to be taken to preserve the respective rights of either party."

Access

Article 291 provides that all the dispute settlement procedures specified in Part XV are open to all State Parties, but to entities other than State Parties only as specified in the Convention, i.e., in Article 2 and Part XI.

Only States may be parties in cases before the ICJ.[16]

Prompt release of vessels and crews

The Convention contains four provisions on the prompt release of vessels and crews, one applying to fishing vessels and their crews, and the others to all vessels and their crews.

Article 73 addresses the rights and duties of coastal States in their exclusive economic zone regarding their sovereign rights to explore, exploit, conserve and manage the living resources in their EEZ. Paragraph 2 requires that vessels and their crews arrested for violating EEZ laws and regulations be promptly released upon the posting of reasonable bond or other security.

Article 292 provides procedures for the prompt release of a vessel and its crew, where the detaining State has not complied with the provisions of the Convention for their prompt release upon the positing of a reasonable bond or other financial security.[17] It is not limited to fishing vessels.[18]

Paragraph 2 of Article 292 permits the application for release to be made only "by or on behalf of" the flag State of the vessel.

Two other provisions provide for prompt release in the case of environmental offenses: Articles 220, paragraph 7, and 226, paragraph (1)(b).[19]

In four cases provisional measures applications have sought release of detained vessels.[20]

Applicable law

Article 293 requires a court or tribunal having jurisdiction to apply the Convention and other rules of international law "not incompatible" with the Convention.

The court or tribunal may also decide the case *ex aequo et bono* only if the parties so agree. A similar provision appears in Article 38, paragraph 2, of the ICJ Statute.

Preliminary proceedings

Article 294 provides that a court or tribunal, or conciliation commission formed under Article 297, upon request or *proprio motu*, can determine if a claim constitutes an abuse of legal process or whether *prima facie* is well founded.

If so found no further action is to be taken in the case.

This provision was added to reduce the fear that the burden in defending against frivolous or vexatious claims would be too burdensome.[21]

Exhaustion of local remedies

Article 295 requires, as a prerequisite for a court or tribunal to exercise jurisdiction, local remedies have been exhausted where this is required by international law.

This last phrase was added in recognition that the exhaustion principle of international law had several limitations.[22]

Final and binding force of decisions

Article 296 provides that any decision rendered by a court or tribunal having jurisdiction under Part XV Section 2 is "final and binding" only on the parties to the dispute and only as to that particular dispute.

Article 33 of the ITLOS statute, Article 11 of Annex VII on arbitration, and Article 4 of Annex VIII on special arbitration provide for the final and binding force of their decisions, and require the decisions to be complied with by all parties to the dispute.

The latter rule also applies to decisions of the ICJ as stated in Article 94, paragraph 1, of the UN Charter.

The reasoning in such decisions is, however, often persuasive in subsequent cases involving other parties.

Limitations and exceptions to the applicability of compulsory procedures entailing binding decisions

Limitations

Part XV circumscribes several categories of disputes subject to compulsory dispute settlement. Article 297, paragraph 1, provides that, when the dispute concerns the interpretation or application of the Convention with regard to the exercise by a coastal State of its sovereign rights or jurisdiction provided in Article 56 of the Convention, the application of compulsory procedures to these categories of disputes is limited when it is alleged that:

a a coastal State has acted in contravention of the provisions of the Convention in regard to the freedoms and rights of navigation, overflight or the laying of submarine cables and pipelines, or in regard to other internationally lawful uses of the sea specified in Article 58;
b a State in exercising its freedoms, rights or uses has acted in contravention of the Convention or of laws or regulations adopted by the coastal State in conformity with the Convention and other rules of international law not incompatible with the Convention; or
c a coastal State has acted in contravention of specified international rules and standards for the protection and preservation of the marine environment which are applicable to the coastal State and which have been established by the Convention or through a competent international organization or diplomatic conference in accordance with the Convention.

Procedures

Article 297, paragraph 2, provides the procedures for the settlement of such disputes, as follows.

Marine scientific research

a Disputes concerning the interpretation or application of the provisions of the Convention with regard to marine scientific research shall be settled in accordance with Section 2, except that the coastal State is not obliged to accept the submission to such settlement of any dispute arising out of:

  i the exercise by the coastal State of a right or discretion in accordance with Article 246; or
  ii a decision by the coastal State to order suspension or cessation of a research project in accordance with Article 253 of the Convention.

b A dispute arising from an allegation by the researching State that, with respect to a specific project, the coastal State is not exercising its rights under Articles 246 and 253 in a manner compatible with the Convention shall be submitted, at the request of either party, to conciliation under Annex V, Section 2, provided that the conciliation commission shall not call in question the exercise by the coastal State of its discretion to designate specific areas as referred to in Article 246, paragraph 6, or of its discretion to withhold consent in accordance with Article 246, paragraph 5.

Paragraph 3 provides limitations in disputes involving fisheries:

a Disputes concerning the interpretation or application of the provisions of the Convention with regard to fisheries shall be settled in accordance with Section 2, except that the coastal State is not obliged to accept the submission to such settlement of any dispute relating to its sovereign rights with respect to the living resources in its exclusive economic zone or their exercise, including its discretionary powers for determining the allowable catch, its harvesting capacity, the allocation of surpluses to other States, and the terms and conditions established in its conservation and management laws and regulations.

b Where no settlement has been reached by recourse to Section 1 of Part XV, a dispute shall be submitted to conciliation under Annex V, Section 2, at the request of any party to the dispute, when it is alleged that:

 i a coastal State has manifestly failed to comply with its obligations to ensure through proper conservation and management measures that the maintenance of the living resources in the exclusive economic zone is not seriously endangered;
 ii a coastal State has arbitrarily refused to determine, at the request of another State, the allowable catch and its capacity to harvest living resources with respect to stocks which that other State is interested in fishing; or
 iii a coastal State has arbitrarily refused to allocate to any State, under Articles 62, 69, and 70 and under the terms and conditions established by the coastal State consistent with the Convention, the whole or part of the surplus it has declared to exist.

c In no case shall the conciliation commission substitute its discretion for that of the coastal State.
d The report of the conciliation commission shall be communicated to the appropriate international organizations.
e In negotiating agreements pursuant to Articles 69 and 70, States Parties, unless they otherwise agree, shall include a clause on measures which they shall take in order to minimize the possibility of a disagreement concerning the interpretation or application of the agreement, and on how they should proceed if a disagreement nevertheless arises.

These complex provisions sought to balance the interests of coastal States, those of other States with navigational interests, and those of the landlocked and geographically disadvantaged States.[23]

Optional exceptions to compulsory procedures

In recognition that certain categories of disputes were too sensitive to be subject to compulsory dispute settlement, Article 298 provides for optional exceptions to the application of Section 2. Paragraph 1 provides that a State may declare in writing that it does not accept any one or more of the procedures set out in Section 2 with respect to one or more of the following categories of disputes:

Maritime delimitation and historic bays or titles

a (i) disputes concerning the interpretation or application of Articles 15, 74, and 83 relating to sea boundary delimitations, or those involving historic bays or titles,[24] provided that a State having made such a declaration shall, when such a dispute arises subsequent to the entry into force of the Convention and where no agreement within a reasonable period of time is reached in negotiations between the parties, at the request of any party to the dispute, accept submission of the matter to conciliation under Annex V, Section 2;[25] and provided further that any dispute that necessarily involves the concurrent consideration of any unsettled dispute concerning sovereignty or other rights over continental or insular land territory shall be excluded from such submission;

ii after the conciliation commission has presented its report, which shall state the reasons on which it is based, the parties shall negotiate an agreement on the basis of that report; if these negotiations do not result in an agreement, the parties shall, *by mutual consent*,[26] submit the question to one of the procedures provided for in Section 2, unless the parties otherwise agree;

iii this subparagraph does not apply to any sea boundary dispute finally settled by an arrangement between the parties, or to any such dispute which is to be settled in accordance with a bilateral or multilateral agreement binding upon those parties;

Military activities and law enforcement activities

b disputes concerning military activities, including military activities by government vessels and aircraft engaged in non-commercial service, and disputes concerning law enforcement activities in regard to the exercise of sovereign rights or jurisdiction excluded from the jurisdiction of a court or tribunal under Article 297, paragraph 2 or 3;[27]

UN Security Council action

c disputes in respect of which the UN Security Council is exercising the functions assigned to it by the UN Charter unless the Security Council decides to remove the matter from its agenda or calls upon the parties to settle it by the means provided for in the Convention.[28]

Any or all of these optional exceptions may be made when consenting to be bound by the Convention, or at any time thereafter. Any such declaration may be withdrawn at any time by a State Party, or agreement to compulsory dispute settlement in a particular dispute.

South China Sea littoral States

Of the South China Sea littoral States, only China has exercised its right to invoke the optional exceptions. It has chosen to exclude all disputes described in paragraphs (a), (b), and (c). It did so well before the Philippines instituted its Annex VII arbitration. Disputes in categories (a) and (b) were considered in the South China Sea arbitration, and are discussed in the next chapter.

Right of the parties to agree upon a procedure

Article 299 provides that only by agreement of the parties to a dispute excluded under Article 297 or excepted by a declaration made under Article 298, may the dispute be submitted to the procedures in Section 2.[29]

Effect of failure to appear

The failure of a party to a case to appear or defend its case does not deprive the court or tribunal of its jurisdiction.[30]

A cost to the non-appearing party is the loss of its right to participate in the selection of arbitrators or a judge (if none of their nationality is already sitting as a member of the court).

Article 53, paragraph 1, of the ICJ Statute provides that whenever one of the parties does not appear before the Court or fails to defend its case, the other party may call upon the Court to decide in favor of its claim.

Both the ITLOS Statute, Article 28, and the ICJ Statute, Article 53 paragraph 2, stipulate that, before making a decision in a case where a party does not appear or fails to defend its case, it must satisfy itself, not only that it has jurisdiction, but also that the claim is well-founded in fact and law.

Factors in choice of forum

There are major differences in the cost and speed of cases before the ICJ, ITLOS, or arbitration.

As the ICJ and ITLOS are standing bodies, costs to parties are generally limited to paying counsel. However, in arbitration, as the tribunal is ad hoc, the parties bear the cost equally of the tribunal, registrar as well as counsel.

In the South China Sea arbitration, the Philippines paid the full costs of the proceedings which took 42 months to complete, having begun on 27 January 2013 with the final award issued on 12 July 2016.

Cases before the ICJ and arbitration normally take considerably longer than cases heard by ITLOS.

On the other hand, conciliation offers advantages not available in compulsory dispute settlement.

First, it is not a binary win-lose outcome resulting from adjudication.

Second, parties engaging in conciliation enjoy discretion, confidentiality, reputation management, and relationship preservation.

Third, the non-adversarial nature of conciliation helps to preserve goodwill between disputing parties that may otherwise be difficult in an adversarial process where there will be a clear winner and loser.

Fourth, the outcome is consensual and win-win.[31]

Fifth, conciliation allows a holistic approach to disputes, for example considering both legal and non-legal factors that support or impede progress.

Sixth, conciliation allows outcomes not likely to result from an adversarial process.

Seventh, the flexibility of conciliation permits States to tailor the proceedings to their own circumstances, therefore allowing greater control of the process and perhaps greater ownership of the outcome.[32]

Advisory opinions

The Convention specifically authorizes the Seabed Disputes Chamber to give advisory opinions at the request of the Assembly or Council on legal questions arising within the scope of their activities.[33] The Chamber has done so in one case.[34]

ITLOS has claimed the right to issue advisory opinions on a legal question if this is provided for by "an international agreement related to the purposes of the Convention"[35] and has done so in one case.[36]

The ICJ is authorized to give advisory opinions on any legal question upon request of the General Assembly or Security Council.[37] Other organs of the United Nations and specialized agencies, which may at any time be so authorized by the General Assembly, may also request advisory opinions of the Court on legal questions arising within the scope of their activities.[38] The ICJ has issued advisory opinions in 27 cases between 1948 and 2019.[39]

Conciliation, arbitration and special arbitration

Annexes V, VII and VIII provide more details for the conduct of voluntary and compulsory conciliation (Annex V, Sections 1 and 2), arbitration (Annex VII) and special arbitration concerning the interpretation or application of the Convention relating to (1) fisheries, (2) protection and preservation of the marine environment, (3) marine scientific research, or (4) navigation (Annex VIII).

Conciliation

It should be recalled that conciliation is not a means of settlement with a binding effect, as in the other forms of dispute settlement. The results can be binding only after the parties to the dispute have agreed that the proposed or recommended solutions will be binding on them.

As noted previously, the Convention's system for dispute settlement using conciliation involves two different processes, voluntary described in Section 1 of Annex V, and compulsory in certain circumstances as the process is described in Section 2 of Annex V.

Voluntary conciliation

The process for voluntary conciliation is set out in some detail in Section 1 of Annex V. It includes 10 articles: on the institution of proceedings (Article 1), list of conciliators (Article 2),[40] the constitution of the conciliation commission (Article 3), procedure (Article 4), amicable settlement (Article 5), functions of the commission (Article 6), report (Article 7), termination (Article 8), fees and expenses (Article 9), and right of the parties to modify procedure (Article 10).

Compulsory conciliation

The process for compulsory conciliation appears in the four articles of Section 2 of Annex V: the institution of proceedings (Article 11), failure to reply or to submit to conciliation (Article 12), competence (Article 13), and application of Section 1 (Article 14).

Arbitration

The practical aspects of arbitration proceedings are set out in Annex VII to the Convention. As the *Virginia Commentary* notes, Annex VII has, in essence, three fundamental rules:

1 the tribunal is to consist of five members, two of whom are nationals (one of each party) and of three others (of whom one presides) who are not nationals of either party;
2 a list of potential arbitrators is to be drawn up and maintained by the UN Secretary-General (i.e., DOALOS); and
3 the refusal or negligence of one party in appointing its member of the tribunal, as well as any difficulty over the appointment of the other three members, can be overcome by their appointment *ex officio* by the ITLOS President.[41]

The procedure of Annex VII arbitration is flexible and not wholly unique. It is set out in 13 articles. Many of its prescribed procedures follow the format if not the substance of the conciliation procedures described above. Article 1 addresses the institution of procedures;

Article 2 provides for a list of arbitrators; Article 3 describes how the arbitral tribunal is to be constituted; Article 4 prescribes the functions of an arbitral tribunal; Article 5 briefly provides that the tribunal determines its procedures; Article 6 sets out the duties of parties to a dispute; Article 7 provides that the expenses of the tribunal are to be borne equally by the parties; Article 8 prescribes that decisions of the tribunal must be by majority vote; Article 9 addresses the consequences of default of appearance by a party — the arbitration may continue if requested by the other party; Article 10 addresses the content of the award of the tribunal; Article 11 provides for the finality of the award; Article 12 permits the arbitral tribunal to interpret or manner of implementation of its award; and Article 13 provides that the Annex applies *mutatis mutandis* to any dispute involving entities other than State Parties.

Notes

1 The text of the Convention is available at https://www.un.org/Depts/los/convention_agreements/texts/unclos/closindx.htm. A list of the parties to the Convention is available at https://www.un.org/Depts/los/reference_files/status2019.pdf.

2 *Virginia Commentary* para 286.2. A comprehensive history of the negotiations on Part XV and relevant annexes are contained in Shabtai Rosenne and Louis B. Sohn (eds), *United Nations Convention on the Law of the Sea 1982: A Commentary*, volume V (Dordrecht/Boston/London: Martinus Nijhoff, 1989) (*Virginia Commentary*). For another summary of the compulsory dispute settlement provisions in the Convention, see S. Jayakumar, "Compulsory Dispute Settlement and Conciliation Under UNCLOS," in *The Timor-Leste/Australia Conciliation, infra* note 25, at 1–29. For a list of ICJ and related cases regarding Part XV through 2009, *see* Barbara Kwiatkowska, *Decisions of the World Court Relevant to the UN Convention on the Law of the Sea: A Reference* Guide (2nd rev. ed.) 269–303 (Leiden/Boston: Martinus Nijhoff, 2010).

3 ICJ Statute article 36, paragraphs 2 and 3. Of the South China Sea littoral States only the Philippines has made such a declaration. See https://www.icj-cij.org/en/declarations and https://www.icj-cij.org/en/declarations/ph.

4 ICJ Statute article 36, paragraph 1. In addition to the optional declaration, consent may be expressed by special agreement or treaties.

5 The Mavrommatis Palestine Concession case (*Greece v. UK*), PCIJ, Series A, No. 2, at 11 (1924) https://www.icj-cij.org/files/permanent-court-of-international-justice/serie_A/A_02/06_Mavrommatis_en_Palestine_Arret.pdf, cited in *Virginia Commentary* 18–19. Factors to be considered in determining whether there is a dispute have been examined by the ICJ in a number of cases, such as Obligations concerning Negotiations relating to Cessation of the Nuclear Arms Race and to Nuclear Disarmament *(Marshall Islands* v. *Pakistan),* Jurisdiction and Admissibility, Judgment, [2016] ICJ Rep. 552, at paras 25–55.

6 ICJ Statute article 36, paragraph 1.

7 The text of the UN Charter is available at https://www.un.org/en/charter-united-nations/index.html.

8 For example, the 1948 American Treaty on Pacific Settlement "Pact of Bogotá" http://www.oas.org/en/sla/dil/inter_american_treaties_A-42_pacific_settlement_pact_bogota.asp.

9 *Virginia Commentary* para 285.4 and Convention article 187.

10 *Virginia Commentary* para 286.6.

11 Article 288(2) was invoked in the Request for Advisory Opinion submitted by the Sub-Regional Fisheries Commission, Advisory Opinion, 2 April 2015, Case No. 21, [2015] ITLOS Rep. 4.

12 A similar provision is contained in Article 36, paragraph 6, of the Statute of the ICJ.

13 *See* "Basis of the Court's Jurisdiction," https://www.icj-cij.org/en/basis-of-jurisdiction. An extensive list of the treaties governing the ICJ's jurisdiction in contentious cases is provided in https://www.icj-cij.org/en/treaties.

14 https://www.un.org/Depts/los/settlement_of_disputes/experts_special_arb.htm.

15 ITLOS has decided ten provisional measures cases: Nos. 3&4, 10, 12, 18, 20, 22, 24, 26, and 27 https://www.itlos.org/cases/list-of-cases/: Southern Bluefin Tuna Cases (*New Zealand v. Japan; Australia v. Japan*) (Nos. 3 & 4) (order 27 August 1999); The MOX Plant Case (*Ireland v. United Kingdom*) (No. 10) (order 3 December 2001); Case concerning Land Reclamation by Singapore

in and around the Straits of Johor (*Malaysia v. Singapore*) (No. 12) (order 8 October 2003); The M/V "*Louisa*" Case (*Saint Vincent and the Grenadines v. Spain*) (No. 18) (judgment 28 May 2013); The "ARA *Libertad*" Case (*Argentina v. Ghana*) (No. 20) (order 15 December 2012); The "*Arctic Sunrise*" Case (*Kingdom of the Netherlands v. Russian Federation*) (No. 22) (order 22 November 2013); The "*Enrica Lexie*" Incident (*Italy v. India*) (No. 24) (order 24 August 2015); Case concerning the detention of three Ukrainian naval vessels (*Ukraine v. Russian Federation*) (No. 26) (order 25 May 2019); and The M/T "*San Padre Pio*" Case (*Switzerland v. Nigeria*) (No. 27) (order 6 July 2019).

16 ICJ Statute article 34, paragraph 1.

17 ITLOS has decided nine prompt release cases: Nos. 1, 5, 6, 8, 9, 11, 13, 14, and 15. The scope of "reasonable bond or other financial security" was discussed in Cases Nos. 14, 13, 11, 6, and 5. The Court provided guidance on this standard in the *Hoshinmaru* case (No. 14); to be reasonable the bond must be proportional to the gravity of the offense (para 88). In this case the Court found that a bond for false reporting of the catch was one half of that set by Russia that was based on the value of the ship and cargo (para 93).

18 Of the nine prompt release cases, all but two did not involve fishing vessels. The two cases involved the refrigerated cargo vessel *Juno Trader* (the "*Juno Trader*" Case No. 13 (*Saint Vincent and the Grenadines v. Guinea-Bissau*) (judgment 18 December 2004); and the M/V *Saiga*, a bunkering vessel supplying fuel oil to fishing vessels and other vessels operating off the coast of Guinea (the M/V "*SAIGA*" Case (*Saint Vincent and the Grenadines v. Guinea*) (No. 1) (judgment 4 December 1997).

The seven cases involving fishing vessels were the *53rd Tomimaru* (the *"Tomimaru"* Case *(Japan v. Russian Federation)* (No. 15) (judgment 6 August 2007); the *88th Hoshinmaru* (the "*Hoshinmaru*" Case (*Japan v. Russian Federation*) (No. 14) (judgment 6 August 2007); the *Volga*, a long-line fishing vessel (the "*Volga*" Case (*Russian Federation v. Australia*) (No. 11) (judgment 23 December 2002); the M/V "*Chaisiri Reefer 2*" (the "*Chaisiri Reefer 2*" Case (*Panama v. Yemen*) (No. 9) (order removing case from list 13 July 2001 as the vessel had been released); the *Grand Prince* (the *"Grand Prince"* Case *(Belize* v. *France)* (No. 8) (judgment 20 April 2001); the *Monte Confurco* (the "*Monte Confurco*" Case (*Seychelles v. France*) (No. 6) (judgment 18 December 2000); and the *Camouco (the "Camouco"* Case *(Panama* v. *France*) (No. 5) (judgment 7 February 2000).

19 See the discussion in James Harrison, "Safeguards against Excessive Enforcement Measures in the Exclusive Economic Zone," in Henrik Ringbom (ed), *Jurisdiction over Ships: Post-UNCLOS Developments in the Law of the Sea* 231–238 (Leiden/Boston: Brill Nijhoff, 2015).

20 M/V *Louisa* (*Saint Vincent and the Grenadines v. Spain*) (No. 18) (judgment 23 May 2013); The "*Arctic Sunrise*" Case (*Kingdom of the Netherlands v. Russian Federation*) (No. 22) (order 22 November 2013); Case concerning the detention of three Ukrainian naval vessels (*Ukraine v. Russian Federation*) (No. 26) (order 25 May 2019); and The M/T "*San Padre Pio*" Case (*Switzerland v. Nigeria*) (No. 27) (order 6 July 2019). See the discussion in Harrison 239–241.

21 *Virginia Commentary* para 294.5.

22 For details of these limitations see *Virginia Commentary* para 295.5.

23 For details see *Virginia Commentary* para 297.19.

24 The following State Parties have exercised one or more of these options: Algeria, Angola, Australia, Canada, Chile, China, Democratic Republic of the Congo, Ecuador, Egypt, Equatorial Guinea, France, Gabon, Greece, Italy, Kenya, Mexico, Montenegro, Palau (delimitation), Portugal, Republic of Korea, Russia, Saudi Arabia, Singapore, Spain, Thailand, Trinidad and Tobago, Tunisia and Ukraine https://treaties.un.org/Pages/ViewDetailsIII.aspx?src=TREATY&mtdsg_no=XXI-6&chapter=21&-Temp=mtdsg3&clang=_en.

25 This option was first exercised in 2017 by Timor-Leste against Australia in its dispute over seabed resources in the Timor Sea. The conciliation is explored in depth in Hao Duy Phan, Tara Davenport and Robert Beckman (eds), *The Timor-Leste/Australia Conciliation: A Victory for UNCLOS and Peaceful Settlement of Disputes* (Singapore: World Scientific Publishers, 2019) (*The Timor-Leste/Australia Conciliation*).

As neither the Convention nor Annex V provides rules of procedure for the conduct of a compulsory conciliation, as noted in that book on page 185, the Rules of Procedure adopted in this case are publicly available, having been attached to the report of the Conciliation Commission https://pcacases.com/web/sendAttach/2336.

Iceland has expressly accepted conciliation for any interpretation of Article 83 (continental shelf delimitation).

26 The ambiguity of the term "by mutual consent" has not been clarified by a Part XV court or tribunal.

27 The scope of this optional exception has been explored in the Case concerning the detention of three Ukrainian naval vessels (*Ukraine v. Russian Federation*), Provisional Measures (ITLOS Case No. 26) (25 May 2019) and in the Annex VII arbitration Dispute Concerning Coastal State Rights in the Black Sea, Sea of Azov, and Kerch Strait (*Ukraine v. the Russian Federation*), PCA Case 2017-06 https://pca-cpa.org/en/cases/149/.

The following State Parties have exercised one or more of these optional exclusions: Algeria, Belarus, Cabo Verde, Canada, Chile, China, Ecuador, Egypt, France, Greece, Mexico, Portugal, Republic of Korea, Russia, Saudi Arabia, Thailand, Togo, Tunisia, Ukraine, United Kingdom, and Uruguay (law enforcement activities).

28 This optional exception has been exercised by the following State Parties: Algeria, Belarus, Canada, Chile, China, Ecuador, Egypt, France, Greece, Portugal, Republic of Korea, Russia, Thailand, Togo, Tunisia, Ukraine, and United Kingdom. For the duties of the Security Council, see UN Charter, Chapter V.

29 *See further Virginia Commentary* para 299.5.

30 Annex VI article 28, Default; Annex VII Arbitration article 9, Default of appearance. China did not appear in the South China Sea arbitration brought by the Philippines in 2013. In the Kerch Strait cases, Russia did not appear in ITLOS provisional measures case brought by Ukraine in 2019, but did appear in the Annex VII arbitration which commenced 16 September 2016. Previously Russia did not appear in the *Arctic Sunrise* provisional measures case before ITLOS in 2013 or in the arbitration which commenced in 2013 and concluded with the final award on 10 July 2017.

31 Jayakumar, "Compulsory Dispute Settlement," in *The Timor-Leste/Australia Conciliation, supra* note 25, at 27.

32 Quinlan, "Perspective of Australia," in *The Timor-Leste/Australia Conciliation, supra* note 25, at 195.

33 Article 191.

34 *Responsibilities and obligations of States sponsoring persons and entities with respect to activities in the Area* (Case No. 17) (Advisory Opinion of 1 February 2011).

35 Rules of the Tribunal, article 138.

36 *Request for an advisory opinion submitted by the Sub-Regional Fisheries Commission (SRFC)* (Case No. 21) (Advisory Opinion of 2 April 2015).

37 UN Charter, article 96, paragraph 1; ICJ Statute, article 65, paragraph 1.

38 UN Charter, article 96, paragraph 2.

39 For a list of those cases see https://www.icj-cij.org/en/advisory-proceedings.

40 It is not required to choose the conciliators from the list. None of the conciliators in the Timor-Leste/Australia conciliation was on the list at the time they were chosen.

41 *Virginia Commentary* para A.VII.2 at 422–423. It is not required to draw the arbitrators from this list.

23

THE SOUTH CHINA SEA ARBITRATION AND ITS IMPLICATIONS[1]

Christopher Whomersley

Introduction

The arbitration was commenced by the Philippines, under Part XV of the United Nations Convention on the Law of the Sea (UNCLOS), on 22 January 2013. In outline, the Philippines sought decisions, first that the rights and obligations of the Philippines and China in the South China Sea are governed by UNCLOS and that "China's claims based on its 'nine-dash line' are inconsistent with the Convention and therefore invalid", second as to the status of certain features in the South China Sea, and third that "the Philippines [is enabled] to exercise and enjoy the rights within and beyond its economic zone and continental shelf that are established in" UNCLOS.[2] It is important to note here that the Philippines expressly stated that "it does not seek in this arbitration a determination of which Party enjoys sovereignty over the islands claimed by both of them. Nor does it request a delimitation of any maritime boundaries".[3] This is a significant statement which needs to be borne in mind in considering the subsequent reasoning of the Arbitral Tribunal, as well as the reaction to the Tribunal's Award.

The Arbitral Tribunal was constituted under Annex VII of UNCLOS,[4] and the Philippines nominated Judge Wolfrum of Germany as its arbitrator. As China took the view that the Tribunal had no jurisdiction over the dispute raised by the Philippines, China refused to nominate an arbitrator; as a result, the Japanese President of the International Tribunal for the Law of the Sea nominated Judge Pawlak of Poland as an arbitrator, and then, because there could be no agreement between China and the Philippines as to the remaining arbitrators, the President nominated Professor Soons of the Netherlands and Judge Cot of France as arbitrators, and Judge Mensah of Ghana to be the President. As will be seen, four out of five arbitrators were therefore from European countries, and it was obviously a shame that, for example, no jurist from Asia was nominated as arbitrator.

The consistent position of China was that "at the core of the disputes between China and the Philippines in the South China Sea are the territorial disputes over some islands and reefs" in the South China Sea, that the two States have overlapping maritime claims in the South China Sea, which are excluded from the Tribunal's jurisdiction, and that the two sides had agreed to settle any disputes through bilateral negotiations.[5] China therefore declined to appear in the proceedings. The Tribunal concluded that this did not prevent it from proceeding with the arbitration, but the Tribunal noted that under Article 9 of Annex VII to

UNCLOS, "before making its award, the arbitral tribunal must satisfy itself not only that it has jurisdiction over the dispute but also that the claim is well founded in fact and law".[6]

The dispute and its proper characterization

The Tribunal, being constituted under Part XV of UNCLOS, only has a limited jurisdiction, namely, to decide disputes "concerning the interpretation or application" of UNCLOS, as required by Articles 286 and 288. The Tribunal accepts that there is a dispute between the parties, but that "it is further necessary that it be identified and characterised"[7] to decide whether that dispute falls within the Tribunal's jurisdiction; quoting earlier case-law from the International Court of Justice, the Tribunal states that it is required to "isolate the real issue in the case and to identify the object of the claim".[8] The Tribunal notes that China's position is that the issues raised by the Philippines relate to territorial sovereignty, but in an important statement the Tribunal says that

> the Philippines has not asked the Tribunal to rule on sovereignty and, indeed, has expressly and repeatedly requested that the Tribunal refrain from so doing. The Tribunal likewise does not see that any of the Philippines' Submissions require an implicit determination of sovereignty. The Tribunal is of the view that it is entirely possible to approach the Philippines' Submissions from the premise – as the Philippines suggests – that China is correct in its assertion of sovereignty over Scarborough Shoal and the Spratlys.[9]

The Tribunal nevertheless concludes that it is

> satisfied that disputes between the Parties concerning the interpretation and application of the Convention exist with respect to the matters raised by the Philippines in all of its Submissions in these proceedings.[10]

In addition, China has exercised the option available under Article 298(1)(a)(i) of UNCLOS to exclude "sea boundary delimitations" from the requirement that disputes be settled compulsorily. The Tribunal, however, takes the view that whilst "the Philippines has challenged the existence and extent of the maritime entitlements claimed by China in the South China Sea … [t]his is not a dispute over maritime boundaries".[11] The Tribunal indicates that the exclusion of sea boundary delimitations would not apply where "a State claims maritime zones in an area understood by other States to form part of the high seas"[12] – thus presumably opening up the possibility that a State might wish to challenge a declaration of maritime zones by another State anywhere in the world, however remote geographically from the first State. The Tribunal refers to the fact that several of the Philippines' submissions seek a decision from the Tribunal about the "status" of certain features in the South China Sea[13] (i.e. whether they are "islands", "rocks", or low-tide elevations, as explained below), and that therefore there is a dispute about "maritime entitlements".[14] As I have said elsewhere, given that the Tribunal accepts that it cannot decide questions of territorial sovereignty, this is a case of "putting the status cart before the sovereignty horse".[15]

Is the dispute excluded from the Tribunal's jurisdiction?

Next, the Tribunal considers China's claim that they and the Philippines are bound to resolve their differences through bilateral negotiations. In particular, under the Declaration on the Conduct of Parties in the South China Sea,[16] signed by the Governments of China and the Association of Southeast Asian Nations (ASEAN) countries, including the Philippines, "the Parties concerned undertake to resolve their territorial and jurisdictional disputes by peaceful means, without resorting to the threat of force, through friendly consultations and negotiations by sovereign states directly concerned".[17] This might seem clear enough, but the Tribunal refers to Article 281 which excludes the dispute settlement procedures in Part XV of UNCLOS only in certain, limited circumstances: this Article applies where the parties "have agreed to seek settlement of the dispute by a peaceful means of their own choice". The Tribunal considers that this Article requires an "agreement" and thus looks to see whether there is an "agreement" for the purposes of the Article.[18] The Tribunal then analyses the legal status of the Declaration, noting that it has some characteristics of a legally binding agreement,[19] but concludes that the Declaration was intended to be "an aspirational political document", and thus "it becomes apparent to this Tribunal that the [Declaration] was not intended to be a legally binding agreement with respect to dispute resolution".[20]

That would be sufficient in the Tribunal's view to mean that Article 281 is inapplicable; however, that Article also requires that "the procedures provided for in this Part [i.e. Part XV] apply only where … the agreement between the parties does not exclude any further procedure". So the question is whether the Declaration excludes "any further procedure". There has been a difference of opinion between judicial bodies as to whether an express exclusion is required, and the Tribunal sides with those who consider that it is, in other words, that it is necessary to say specifically that no other procedure is available and that it is insufficient to imply this by setting out alternative arrangements.[21] It follows in the Tribunal's view that the Declaration would not in any event have excluded the operation of the dispute settlement provisions in UNCLOS.

China also quoted a number of bilateral statements between the Philippines and China, in all of which the two sides suggested that they would settle any disputes bilaterally.[22] However, the Tribunal finds that none of them meets the requirements of Article 281.[23] The Tribunal goes on to consider whether the statements constitute an estoppel, i.e. that they were representations which could be, and indeed were, relied upon to its detriment by the Philippines.[24] In the Tribunal's view, however, the statements did not involve a representation by the Philippines that it would not resort to the procedures in UNCLOS,[25] although the basis for this conclusion is not very clear. The Tribunal then examines other regional and multilateral treaties and concludes that none of them excludes the operation of Part XV of UNCLOS, for the purposes of Articles 281 or 282 (which make similar provisions in relation to regional agreements).[26]

A more serious objection might be thought to arise from Article 283, which requires as a pre-condition to recourse to the settlement procedures in Part XV that the parties to the dispute should have first engaged in "an exchange of views regarding its settlement by negotiation or other peaceful means", given that China denied that any such exchange of views had taken place.[27] The Tribunal, however, "is convinced the Parties have unequivocally exchanged views regarding the possible means of settling the disputes between them that the Philippines has presented in these proceedings";[28] it concludes that

> the extensive record of communications between the Parties, including frequent bilateral consultations, establishes that China was aware of the issues in respect of which the Parties disagreed and cannot have been taken by surprise when the Philippines decided to proceed with arbitration.[29]

This seems to reduce the pre-condition in Article 283 to a very scanty one.[30]

Finally, the Tribunal considers the various limitations and exceptions to its jurisdiction, as set out in Article 297 (automatic limitations) and Article 298 (optional exceptions, all of which have been exercised by China, including in particular that relating to maritime delimitation).[31] However, the Tribunal reaches the view that, in relation to a number of the submissions made by the Philippines, the question of whether the Tribunal has jurisdiction is not "exclusively preliminary in character"[32] but is intimately bound up with the merits of the dispute.[33] Thus the Tribunal concludes at this stage that, in relation to only three of the Philippines' 15 submissions, it does have jurisdiction;[34] that, in relation to two more, it does have jurisdiction, provided that the events in question took place in the territorial sea of Scarborough Shoal;[35] that, in relation to two more, it does have jurisdiction, provided, apparently, that on consideration of the merits it does not appear that there might be overlapping entitlements between China and the Philippines, which would affect the evidence relating to the status of the features;[36] and that, in relation to the remaining eight submissions, it should reserve a decision on jurisdiction until it has considered the merits.[37] The result therefore of this first phase of the arbitration was that none of the Philippines' submissions were ruled outside the jurisdiction of the Tribunal, as China had argued; on the other hand, the Tribunal decided definitively that it only had jurisdiction in relation to three submissions, plus two more where its jurisdiction was geographically limited; and that its jurisdiction in relation to the remaining ten submissions depended to a greater or lesser extent upon the results of its consideration of the merits.

The merits phase of the arbitration

The Tribunal begins the Award on the Merits by rehearsing the history of the arbitration so far and referring to the various communications from the Government of China.[38] The Tribunal does, however, reiterate two significant points. The first is that

> the Convention ... does not address the sovereignty of States over land territory. Accordingly, this Tribunal has not been asked to, and does not purport to, make any ruling as to which State enjoys sovereignty over any land territory in the South China Sea, in particular with respect to the disputes concerning sovereignty over the Spratly Islands or Scarborough Shoal. None of the Tribunal's decisions in this Award are dependent on a finding of sovereignty, nor should anything in this Award be understood to imply a view with respect to questions of land sovereignty.[39]

Likewise, the Tribunal, noting that China has exercised the right under UNCLOS to exclude questions of maritime delimitation from the provisions about the compulsory settlement of disputes, states that "the Tribunal has not been asked to, and does not purport to, delimit any maritime boundary between the Parties or involving any other State bordering on the South China Sea".[40] The Tribunal then recounts the steps it has taken to deal with the fact that China has chosen not to participate in the proceedings,[41] and summarizes its Award on Jurisdiction.[42]

"The nine-dash line"

The Tribunal thereafter gets on to one of the meaty allegations made by the Philippines, and this concerns what the Tribunal calls "The 'Nine-Dash Line' and China's Claim to Historic Rights in the Maritime Areas of the South China Sea".[43] The Tribunal explains that by the 'nine-dash line' it is referring to the line drawn on a map dating from 1948,[44] and repeated in a map submitted to the Secretary-General of the United Nations in 2009.[45] In its *Note Verbale* to the Secretary-General dated 7 May 2009, China states that it "has indisputable sovereignty over the islands in the South China Sea and the adjacent waters, and enjoys sovereign rights and jurisdiction over the relevant waters as well as the seabed and subsoil thereof (see attached map)".[46] Neither in that *Note Verbale* nor in a subsequent one dated 14 April 2011[47] does China mention "historic rights" as such.[48] It is important to note therefore that the issue of "historic rights" was not raised by China, but only by the Philippines in its arguments to the Tribunal.[49]

The Tribunal takes the view that "it necessarily falls to the Tribunal to ascertain, on the basis of conduct, whether China's claim amounts to 'historic title'",[50] and that "where … China has asserted rights in areas beyond the maximum entitlements that could be claimed under [UNCLOS], the Tribunal considers that such assertions indicate a claim to rights arising independently of" UNCLOS.[51] Basing itself upon three instances where China is alleged to have asserted claims to jurisdiction going beyond UNCLOS,[52] and relying on a commitment by the Chinese Government to "freedom of navigation and over-flight" in the South China Sea – which the Tribunal points out does not apply in internal waters and the territorial sea[53]

> the Tribunal understands that China claims rights to the living and non-living resources within the 'nine-dash line', but (apart from the territorial sea generated by any islands) does not consider that those waters form part of its territorial sea or internal waters.[54]

The Tribunal then turns to the question of whether the exception to its jurisdiction in Article 298(1)(a)(i) of UNCLOS, relating to "disputes … involving historic … titles", is applicable in this case. The Tribunal traces the history of this provision and concludes that "the reference to 'historic titles' in Article 298(1)(a)(i) of [UNCLOS] is accordingly a reference to claims of sovereignty over maritime areas derived from historical circumstances", and that "this usage was understood by the drafters of" UNCLOS.[55] The Tribunal concludes that "China does not claim historic title to the waters of South China Sea, but rather a constellation of historic rights short of the title"[56]; thus, the exception to jurisdiction in Article 298(1)(a)(i) does not apply.

The next following question for the Tribunal is whether this "constellation of historic rights" remains in place despite the adoption of UNCLOS.[57] The Tribunal concludes that UNCLOS

> does not include any express provisions preserving or protecting historic rights that are at variance with [UNCLOS]. On the contrary, [UNCLOS] supersedes earlier rights and agreements to the extent of any incompatibility. [UNCLOS] is comprehensive in setting out the nature of the exclusive economic zone and continental shelf and the rights of other States within those zones. China's claim to historic rights is not compatible with these provisions.[58]

The Tribunal seeks to bolster this conclusion by examining the negotiating record of UNCLOS[59] and other case-law.[60] The Tribunal thus states that

> upon China's accession to [UNCLOS] and its entry into force, any historic rights that China may have had to the living and non-living resources within the 'nine-dash line'

> were superseded, as a matter of law and as between the Philippines and China, by the limits of the maritime zones provided for by [UNCLOS].[61]

However, it goes on to say that "the Tribunal considers that, in ratifying [UNCLOS], China has, in fact, relinquished far less in terms of its claim to historic rights than the foregoing conclusion might initially suggest".[62] In an important reiteration of its position, the Tribunal says that

> certain claims remain unaffected by this decision. In particular, the Tribunal emphasises that nothing in this Award should be understood to comment in any way on China's historic claim to the islands of the South China Sea. Nor does the Tribunal's decision that a claim of historic rights to living and non-living resources is not compatible with [UNCLOS] limit China's ability to claim maritime zones in accordance with [UNCLOS], on the basis of such islands.[63]

The Tribunal therefore concludes that China's maritime entitlements in the South China Sea are exclusively determined by UNCLOS.[64]

The status of features in the South China Sea

The Tribunal then turns to one of the key questions put to it, namely the status of certain features in the South China Sea. By way of background, Article 121(1) of UNCLOS provides that "an island is a naturally formed area of land, surrounded by water, which is above water at high tide"; in principle, an island can generate the same maritime zones as any other land territory; however, in a key provision, paragraph 3 of Article 121 states that "rocks which cannot sustain human habitation or economic life of their own shall have no exclusive economic zone or continental shelf": the interpretation and implications of paragraph 3 take up a large section of the Award on Merits.[65] UNCLOS also mentions "low-tide elevations", although only in the context of the drawing of baselines; Article 7(4) generally prohibits the drawing of straight baselines from such elevations, as does Article 47(4) for archipelagic baselines, whereas under Article 13 such an elevation may be used as a baseline where it is situated within the territorial sea. The Tribunal notes that that latter Article defines a low-tide elevation as "a naturally formed area of land which is surrounded by and above water at low tide but submerged at high tide", and seems to treat that as a provision generally applicable, although whether that was the intention, or rather whether it was intended that that definition should only apply for the purposes of the drawing of baselines, is not explored by the Tribunal.[66] Furthermore, the Tribunal takes the position that low-tide elevations cannot be appropriated in the same way as land territory,[67] although the decisions of the International Court of Justice which are relied upon do not seem to support so definitive a conclusion.[68] Rather confusingly, the Tribunal terms features which are covered by paragraphs 1 and/or 3 of Article 121 as "high-tide features".[69]

The Tribunal repeats again that the issues here are about status, not sovereignty,[70] notes that the Philippines has argued that ten features are low-tide elevations,[71] and goes on to describe these ten features.[72] It turns to the interpretation of Article 13, and in particular how to interpret the terms "naturally formed" and "high tide" in that Article;[73] and then considers the available evidence from satellite imagery[74] and from nautical charts, records of surveys, and sailing directions,[75] to decide whether the various features meet the requirements of Article 13. It concludes that five features are "low-tide elevations" but six are not.[76]

The Tribunal's next task is to consider whether these six features, as well as the six other largest features in the Spratly Group,[77] fall within paragraph 3 of Article 121, i.e. are rocks which do not generate an exclusive economic zone or a continental shelf, or fall within paragraph 1 of that Article and therefore do generate those maritime zones.[78] For this purpose, the Tribunal identifies what it perceives to be six relevant elements in the text of Article 121(3), namely "rocks", "cannot", "sustain", "human habitation", "or", and "economic life of their own",[79] and engages in a detailed analysis of each of these elements.

The Tribunal then considers the "object and purpose" of Article 121,[80] and in particular emphasizes its view that the "natural condition" of the feature is decisive;[81] the Tribunal also sees a link with the purpose of the exclusive economic zone established in UNCLOS, which is designed to benefit the coastal State, and in the view of the Tribunal this strengthens the argument that under Article 121(3) an exclusive economic zone should only be generated where there is "the habitation of a feature by a settled group or community for whom the feature is a home".[82] The Tribunal continues by looking at the history of Article 121 and of the discussions about it at the conference which adopted UNCLOS,[83] and notes in particular that attempts to define "islands" and "rocks" by reference to size were not accepted.[84]

Some of the Tribunal's key conclusions on the interpretation of Article 121(3) are as follows. First, "'rocks' for the purposes of Article 121(3) will not necessarily be composed of rock".[85] Second, "'cannot' in Article 121(3) indicates a concept of capacity ... the fact that a feature is currently not inhabited does not prove that it is uninhabitable... the fact that it has no economic life does not prove that it cannot sustain an economic life".[86] Next, "the Tribunal considers that the ordinary meaning of 'sustain' has three components. The first is the concept of the support and provision of essentials. The second is a temporal concept: the support and provision must be over a period of time and not one-off or short-lived. The third is a qualitative concept, entailing at least a minimal 'proper standard'".[87] As to "human habitation", this "would require that a feature be able to support, maintain, and provide food, drink, and shelter to some humans to enable them to reside there permanently or habitually over an extended period of time";[88] the term also implies habitation "by a group or community of persons".[89] The Tribunal goes on to interpret the word "or" as in effect meaning "and" in this context.[90] On the term "economic life of their own", the Tribunal says that a feature "must have the ability to support an independent economic life, without relying predominantly on the infusion of outside resources or serving purely as an object for extractive activities, without the involvement of a local population";[91] in addition, "economic activity derived from a possible exclusive economic zone or continental shelf must necessarily be excluded".[92]

The Tribunal adds that an assessment of whether the feature falls within Article 121(3) must be carried out on a case-by-case basis, and lists some of the factors which will need to be taken into account, including the presence of water, food, and shelter, the climate, the proximity to other population centers, and the potential for livelihoods; the Tribunal distinguishes "mere survival" from "human habitation" for the purposes of Article 121(3).[93] Furthermore, in the Tribunal's view, "the most reliable evidence of the capacity of a feature will usually be the historical use to which it has been put".[94] The Tribunal then goes on to discount "outside support [if it] is so significant that it constitutes a necessary condition for the inhabitation of a feature"; it "notes that a purely official or military population, serviced from the outside, does not constitute evidence that a feature is capable of sustaining human habitation", because, apparently, this might be a device "to stake a claim to the territory and the maritime zones generated by it".[95] The Tribunal finally dismisses the relevance of State practice in one paragraph.[96]

Applying its interpretation of Article 121(3) to the six features which it has already decided are not low-tide elevations,[97] the Tribunal concludes that all are "rocks" within the meaning of Article 121(3).[98] The Tribunal then turns to the six largest features in the Spratly Group[99] and examines what it calls "a substantial volume of evidence"[100] relating to their status; it organizes its consideration of this evidence under five headings, as follows: the presence of potable fresh water,[101] vegetation and biology,[102] soil and agricultural potential,[103] presence of fishermen,[104] and commercial operations.[105] The conclusion of the Tribunal is that these six features "are capable of enabling the survival of small groups of people"; there is evidence of potable water, as well as "naturally occurring vegetation capable of providing shelter and the possibility of at least limited agriculture".[106] Thus, "the principal features of the Spratly Islands are not barren rocks or sand cays, devoid of fresh water, that can be dismissed as uninhabitable on the basis of their physical characteristics alone"; the Tribunal therefore goes on to say that it "is called upon to consider the historical evidence of human habitation and economic life".[107] The Tribunal dismisses the presence of fishermen or miners as temporary,[108] and also discounts the presence of military or other government personnel, who are not there of "their own volition", would leave once their official functions are over, and are only there because of the disputed sovereignty claims to the features.[109] Thus, in the Tribunal's view, none of these six features are capable of sustaining human habitation.[110] As to whether any of these six features is capable of sustaining an economic life of its own, the Tribunal believes that any economic activity was "extractive" and thus is to be ignored.[111] Thus, the Tribunal concludes that all of the features in the Spratly Group whose status was questioned in the proceedings by the Philippines are either low-tide elevations[112] or are "rocks" within the meaning of Article 121(3) of UNCLOS;[113] thus, in the Tribunal's view, none of these features generate an exclusive economic zone or a continental shelf.

As an excursus, the Tribunal picks up on a reference by China to treating the Spratly Islands "as a whole",[114] and seems to have drawn the conclusion that this represents an attempt to justify the drawing of straight baselines around the Spratly Group.[115] Without explaining its reasoning, and referring only in a very general manner to the practice of "some States",[116] the Tribunal dismisses this possibility.[117]

"Chinese Activities in the South China Sea"

The next heading in the Tribunal's Award is "Chinese Activities in the South China Sea".[118] Under this heading the Tribunal deals with a disparate group of allegations made by the Philippines against China, namely "Interference with the Philippines' Sovereign Rights in its EEZ and Continental Shelf",[119] "Failure to Prevent Chinese Nationals from Exploiting the Philippines' Living Resources",[120] "China's Actions in respect of Traditional Fishing at Scarborough Shoal",[121] "Failure to Protect and Preserve the Marine Environment",[122] "Occupation and Construction Activities on Mischief Reef",[123] and "Operation of Law Enforcement Vessels in a Dangerous Manner".[124]

'Interference with the Philippines' sovereign rights in its EEZ and Continental Shelf', 'Failure to prevent Chinese nationals from exploiting the Philippines' living resources', 'China's actions in respect of traditional fishing at Scarborough Shoal'

As regards the first set of allegations, the Tribunal recounts the complaints made by the Philippines about attempts by China to discourage the exploitation of non-living resources on what the Philippines claims to be its continental shelf,[125] as well as China's assertion of jurisdiction over fisheries in the South China Sea,[126] including a moratorium on fishing in parts of the South China Sea "to rehabilitate the area's marine resources".[127] The Tribunal states that "it is apparent that the Philippines and China have each proceeded on the basis that it, and not the other, has exclusive rights to resources and have acted accordingly",[128] but in the light of the Tribunal's view that none of the features in the Spratly Group may generate an exclusive economic zone or a continental shelf,[129] it is inevitable that the Tribunal should conclude that "the relevant areas can only constitute the exclusive economic zone and continental shelf of the Philippines … accordingly, the Philippines—and not China—possesses sovereign rights with respect to resources in these areas".[130] It follows that the Tribunal upholds the Philippines' complaints in this respect.[131]

The next complaint is that "China has unlawfully failed to prevent its nationals and vessels from exploiting the living resources in the exclusive economic zone of the Philippines";[132] it is in particular noted that Chinese fishing vessels in the vicinity of Second Thomas Shoal and Mischief Reef have been accompanied by Chinese government vessels,[133] although apparently only during a single period;[134] likewise for defined periods, such vessels were present at Scarborough Shoal and Subi Reef.[135] The Tribunal follows the International Tribunal for the Law of the Sea in saying that "anything less than due diligence by a State in preventing its nationals from unlawfully fishing in the exclusive economic zone of another would fall short of the regard due pursuant to" UNCLOS;[136] thus, China is, according to the Tribunal, required to take all necessary measures to ensure that fishing vessels flying its flag do not fish in what the Tribunal has now held the exclusive economic zone of the Philippines, without the consent of the latter. Since Chinese government vessels were present, and thus any fishing could not be said to be covert,[137] the Tribunal concludes that China has breached the obligation to take these necessary measures.

The Tribunal turns to the Philippines' complaint about Chinese interference with traditional fishing activities at Scarborough Shoal. The important point here is that, having found that Scarborough Shoal is not a low-tide elevation, the Tribunal accepts that it must have at the least a 12-mile territorial sea.[138] The Tribunal reviews the evidence for traditional fishing by Filipino fishermen at Scarborough Shoal[139] and for Chinese actions to prevent fishing there.[140] Yet again the Tribunal states that it will not rule on the sovereignty over Scarborough Shoal, which is disputed between China and the Philippines, but that its conclusions will apply to whichever has sovereignty.[141] The Tribunal reaches the conclusion that "within that zone (sc. the territorial sea)—in contrast to the exclusive economic zone—established traditional fishing rights remain protected by international law".[142] Thus, the Tribunal upholds the Philippines' complaint.[143]

"Failure to protect and preserve the marine environment"

The Tribunal now turns to a different issue, namely the allegation that by its activities China has breached its obligation under UNCLOS to protect and preserve the marine environment.[144] The Award on the Merits lists a number of incidents of "Harmful Fishing Practices and Harvesting of Endangered Species";[145] these seem to relate to the taking of corals, turtles, and giant clams, and the use of explosives and cyanide. Ten of these incidents took place in the eight-year period between 1998 and 2006 in the waters of Scarborough Shoal;[146] there seem to have been two further incidents there in April 2012,[147] as well as two incidents in February 2012[148] and May 2013[149] at Second Thomas Shoal; in other words, there appear to have been a total of 14 incidents over a period of 15 years.

The Tribunal then discusses a different set of complaints, namely about the environmental impact of China's construction activities on seven features in the South China

Sea.[150] Evidence was adduced by the Philippines as to the large scale of these activities, which the Philippines alleges was in breach of China's "obligation to protect and preserve the marine environment" under Article 192 of UNCLOS; China, on the other hand, states that it "had gone through science-based evaluation and assessment with equal importance given to construction and protection" and that it had taken "full account of issues of ecological preservation and fishery protection" and "followed strict environmental protection standards".[151]

Citing earlier case-law, the Tribunal states Article 192 requires that States "ensure that activities within their jurisdiction and control respect the environment of other States or of areas beyond national control"; thus, States have a positive "'duty to prevent, or at least mitigate' significant harm to the environment when pursuing large-scale construction activities".[152] However, this obligation is one of "due diligence", i.e. it requires States to adopt appropriate legislation, but also to show vigilance in enforcing it and where appropriate to investigate breaches of the legislation and to take remedial action.[153] South China Sea is said to be a "rare or fragile ecosystem", as specifically highlighted in Article 194(5) of UNCLOS.[154] The Tribunal then notes that Article 197 requires States to cooperate in the environmental field, especially, in accordance with Article 123, in enclosed or semi-enclosed seas,[155] and that Articles 204 and 206 place an obligation on States to monitor the risks or effects of pollution and to assess the potential effects of planned activities.[156]

As regards the complaints about fishing, the Tribunal "considers that the general obligation to 'protect and preserve the marine environment' in Article 192 includes a due diligence obligation to prevent the harvesting of species that are recognised internationally as being at risk of extinction and requiring international protection";[157] this includes prevention of indirect harm through the destruction of habitats.[158] On this basis, the harvesting of turtles, clams, and coral could potentially involve a breach of Articles 192 and 194 of UNCLOS.[159] As to China's responsibility under international law for these potential breaches, the Tribunal says that China was aware by 2005 of these activities,[160] and although China has adopted legislation on these issues, there is no evidence that China has taken steps to enforce these rules; the Tribunal therefore finds China in breach of its obligations under UNCLOS.[161] The Tribunal is particularly concerned about the practice of using propellers to harvest clams[162] and finds this to be a breach of UNCLOS.[163] It is to be noted that these conclusions seem to be based upon the occurrence of 14 incidents over a 15-year period, i.e. less than one a year. However, having reviewed the evidence brought by the Philippines about the use of explosives and cyanide, the Tribunal finds that this does not suffice to justify a holding of breach of UNCLOS by China.[164]

The Tribunal then looks at the construction activities of China on features in South China, and summarises the evidence as follows: "since the end of 2013, China has created on top of the coral reefs approximately 12.8 million square metres of land, from millions of tons of dredged coral, rocks and sand".[165] The Tribunal appointed a team led by Dr. Ferse to consider the impact of these activities on the environment and describes the team's views, contrasting them with those of Chinese scientists, but preferring those of the Ferse team.[166] The Tribunal therefore "has no doubt that China's artificial island-building activities on the seven reefs in the Spratly Islands have caused devastating and long-lasting damage to the marine environment", and thus it concludes that China is in breach of its obligations under UNCLOS.[167] It furthermore chides China for failure to cooperate with other regional States,[168] and not for failing to monitor and assess the impact of its construction activities, but rather for failing to communicate the assessment.[169]

"Occupation and construction activities on Mischief Reef"

This complaint is based upon rather different legal principles than the preceding one and deals with an argument that Chinese activities on Mischief Reef involve either a breach of the provisions in UNCLOS about artificial islands or an illegitimate attempt to appropriate territory.[170] The Tribunal notes that both sides have here acted on the basis that it has sovereign rights over Mischief Reef;[171] nevertheless,

> however much these beliefs have been held in good faith, the Tribunal has found that Mischief Reef is a low-tide elevation that falls within an area where only the Philippines possesses possible entitlements to maritime zones under the Convention. Mischief Reef, therefore, can only constitute part of the exclusive economic zone and continental shelf of the Philippines; it does not lie within any entitlement that could be generated by any feature claimed by China (or another State).[172]

Proceeding on that basis, the Tribunal, noting that under Articles 56, 60, and 80 of UNCLOS only the coastal State has the right to establish artificial islands and installations,[173] finds that China is in breach of those Articles.[174] As to the question of appropriation, the Tribunal reiterates its view that as a low-tide elevation Mischief Reef is not capable of appropriation.[175]

"Operation of law enforcement vessels in a dangerous manner"

The Philippines' complaint is that in two incidents in April and May 2012 where Chinese law enforcement vessels allegedly acted in a manner contrary to the Convention on the International Regulations for Preventing Collisions at Sea, adopted by the International Maritime Organisation in 1972,[176] normally known as the International Regulations for Preventing Collisions at Sea (COLREGS). Both incidents took place in the territorial sea of Scarborough Shoal,[177] and the Tribunal is acting on the basis that this is under Chinese sovereignty.[178] Nevertheless, the Tribunal holds that the COLREGS apply on the basis of Article 94 of UNCLOS[179] (even though that Article is situated in the Part of UNCLOS relating to the high seas), and that the Chinese vessels acted contrary to them.[180]

Aggravation or extension of the dispute between the parties

The next section of the Award deals with the Philippines' argument that by its actions China has aggravated and extended the dispute between the two States.[181] The Philippines' complaints relate, first, to Chinese activities at Second Thomas Shoal, especially by interfering in the rotation and resupply of Philippine personnel there,[182] and second, to Chinese construction activities at the seven features in the South China Sea about which complaint was made on environmental grounds;[183] the Philippines argues that, as a result of these activities undertaken after the commencement of the arbitration, China has aggravated and extended the dispute.[184] However, as regards the first set of complaints, namely those about Chinese activities at Second Thomas Shoal, the Tribunal finds that it has no jurisdiction to consider these, since "this represents a quintessentially military situation, involving the military forces of one side and a combination of military and paramilitary forces on the other, arrayed in opposition to one another",[185] and China has, in accordance with UNCLOS, excluded "disputes concerning military activities"[186] from the compulsory dispute settlement procedures in UNCLOS.[187]

As to the more general Philippines' complaint, the Tribunal states

> that there exists a duty on parties engaged in a dispute settlement procedure to refrain from aggravating or extending the dispute or disputes at issue during the pendency of the settlement process. This duty exists independently of any order from a court or tribunal to refrain from aggravating or extending the dispute and stems from the purpose of dispute settlement and the status of the States in question as parties in such a proceeding.[188]

The Tribunal considers "that China's intensified construction of artificial islands on seven features in the Spratly Islands during the course of these proceedings has unequivocally aggravated the disputes between the Parties".[189]

Future conduct of the parties

Finally, the Philippines asked for an order requiring China to comply with UNCLOS,[190] but the Tribunal considers it neither necessary nor appropriate to make such an order.[191]

The Tribunal's holdings (the "Dispositif")

The Tribunal finally sets out a summary of its findings (what the lawyers call the "Dispositif"). It begins by recalling its findings in the Award on Jurisdiction,[192] but because it did not hold definitively in that Award that it had jurisdiction in relation to a number of the submissions made by the Philippines,[193] the Tribunal has to state its final conclusions on the question of jurisdiction. It holds[194] that it has jurisdiction over all of the Philippines' submissions except 14(a) to (c), which are excluded from its jurisdiction by the Chinese invocation of the "military activities" exception,[195] and 15, on which the Tribunal sees no need to rule.[196]

Turning then to the substantive issues, the Tribunal sets out a summary of its decision.[197] It begins by confirming that UNCLOS applies,[198] and then goes on to reiterate its findings as to whether Scarborough Shoal and the 11 features in the Spratly Group are low-tide elevations or not[199] and whether the other features in the Spratly Group are or are not "rocks".[200] It then confirms its view that certain Chinese activities in the South China Sea involve a breach of the Philippines' exclusive economic zone,[201] and that Chinese actions against traditional fishermen at Scarborough Shoal were unlawful.[202] It makes findings that China has breached the provisions of UNCLOS relating to the marine environment[203] and that Chinese activities at Mischief Reef infringe the Philippines' rights in its exclusive economic zone.[204] Finally, the Tribunal finds that China has breached the COLREGS,[205] and that it has aggravated the dispute.[206]

China's attitude to the arbitration

China rejected the Philippines' request to initiate the arbitration and maintained that any tribunal established to decide the issues raised by the Philippines would have no jurisdiction,[207] arguing that the essence of the dispute concerned territorial sovereignty, that China and the Philippines had agreed to settle their bilateral disputes by arbitration and that in any case the subject-matter of the arbitration raised questions of maritime delimitation.

China therefore declined to participate in the arbitration proceedings, a situation which is however foreseen in UNCLOS, which provides that in such circumstances an "arbitral tribunal must satisfy itself not only that it has jurisdiction over the dispute, but also that the claim is well founded in fact and law".[208] The day following the issue of the Tribunal's Award on Jurisdiction, the Ministry of Foreign Affairs of China made a statement, rejecting that Award,[209] and likewise made a statement rejecting the Award on Merits on the day it was issued.[210] In these various statements, China takes the position that the Arbitration Award is "null and void", and is not binding.

The implications of the Arbitration Award: the stance of the Tribunal

The implications of the Award can be roughly divided into those relating to the Tribunal's processes, those relating specifically to the South China Sea dispute, and those of a more general character.

The first issue is whether the Tribunal correctly identified the "real issue" in the proceedings.[211] The Tribunal seems to have accepted that the "real issue" did not relate to the disputed sovereignty over the various features in the South China Sea, but as one learned commentator has said:

> it is obvious, and should have been so to the Tribunal as well, that ... the Philippines ... real purpose and main objective [was] to get a direction from it against the claims of China based on historic titles and associated maritime entitlements or at least seek to limit them using the Convention as the sole applicable law, knowing full well that the Convention does not encompass in its object and purpose or scope issues of sovereignty, historic titles or bays.[212]

In other words, was not the "real issue" which the Philippines wished to resolve one which, despite its protestations, was outside the jurisdiction of a tribunal established to decide disputes about the interpretation or application of UNCLOS?

Furthermore, there is a question whether the Tribunal might perhaps have declined, in its discretion, to proceed with the proceedings. As indicated below, the Tribunal could only deal with one small part of the overall dispute, namely the status of certain features in the South China Sea, and not the perhaps more important, but certainly antecedent, issues, namely the territorial sovereignty over those features and the maritime delimitation between them and the Philippine archipelago. In these circumstances, should the Tribunal, as a judicial body, have considered whether it was appropriate for it to proceed with the case? Thus, the International Court of Justice has referred to the importance attached by it and its predecessors to the need to "maintain their integrity as judicial bodies".[213] Interestingly, since the Award was given, the International Court of Justice has stated that in exceptional circumstances the Court may decline to exercise its jurisdiction over a dispute where the applicant's conduct amounts to an abuse of process,[214] and in one of those cases, one judge held that such an argument had been made out.[215] It is therefore not at all unprecedented to say that an international court or tribunal has the discretion to refuse to exercise jurisdiction in a particular case. If such an argument had been put to the Tribunal, one wonders what their reaction would, or should, have been?[216]

The implications of the Arbitration Award specific to the South China Sea

In this connection, it is important to note that the Tribunal expressly disavowed on several occasions that it could, or would, rule on the question of sovereignty.[217] Thus, this of course leaves unresolved the underlying dispute between China and the Philippines, and indeed between China and the other claimant States, especially Vietnam, but also Malaysia and Brunei. Thus, any final resolution of the dispute in the South China Sea must still lie in the future. This would require first a decision as to the territorial sovereignty over the various features, and then a delimitation of the maritime zones between each of the States, in which connection there would need to be a consideration of the status of the various features (i.e. whether they are "islands", "rocks", or low-tide elevations).

As to the status of the features, I have said before that for the Tribunal to make decisions on status without being able to decide on sovereignty is a case of putting the status cart before the sovereignty horse.[218] There seems to be no precedent for an international court or tribunal deciding on the status of a feature when it could not decide upon where sovereignty over the feature lies; on closer inspection, the four cases quoted by the Philippines as being precedents for this were all ones where the court or tribunal had power to decide upon the territorial sovereignty in question.[219] Indeed, on the contrary, the precedents suggest that an international court or tribunal will wish to decide upon the territorial sovereignty of offshore features before considering the question of their status and therefore the extent of maritime zones. This is the basis of the oft-quoted maxim that "the land dominates the sea". As the International Court of Justice said in one case, "it is … the terrestrial territorial situation that must be taken as starting point for the determination of the maritime rights of a coastal State".[220]

Furthermore, China had utilized the option in UNCLOS to exclude "disputes concerning the interpretation or application of articles 15, 74 and 83 relating to sea boundary delimitations".[221] The Tribunal throughout uses the shorthand "maritime boundary delimitation" to describe this exception, but this might be thought misleading; in particular, there is no doubt that there is an intimate connection between the status of features and the process of maritime delimitation, as indeed the Tribunal seems to recognize.[222] In this connection, it is to be noted that in another case, the International Tribunal for the Law of the Sea equated the word "concerning" with the phrase "having a bearing on",[223] and the status of a feature will certainly have a significant bearing upon how it is treated for the purposes of any maritime delimitation; thus, it can be argued that "disputes concerning … sea boundary delimitations", which are excluded from the Tribunal's jurisdiction, should encompass disputes about the status of features which would be relevant to a subsequent delimitation.

Another point, perhaps an oddity, is this. The Philippines has a territorial claim to all of the features whose status was raised in the proceedings. Thus, by submitting that none of them is entitled to a full set of maritime zones, the Philippines has in effect reduced the value of those features if its claim to them were eventually to prevail. Furthermore, the effect of the Award is that, in the Tribunal's view, there is a strip of high seas in the middle of the South China Sea, in which it could be open to non-regional States to exploit the natural resources, especially fish; it would seem difficult for the Philippines, having initiated the arbitration, to claim the right to exercise jurisdiction in that strip of waters, nor indeed to cooperate with other States in exercising jurisdiction there.

Finally, much ink has been spilled over the question of China's claim to historic rights in the South China Sea. In fact, in the diplomatic notes on the matter which began the latest round of disputation about the South China Sea, namely the Chinese objections to the joint Malaysia-Vietnam submission to the Commission on the Limits of the Continental Shelf, that term is not used;[224] rather, the focus of those objections seems to relate to the question of sovereignty over the land features in the South China Sea. Furthermore, the Tribunal expressly disclaims any intention "to comment in any way on China's historic claim to the islands of the South China Sea".[225] In fact, all that the Tribunal says about "historic rights" is that in its view China is limited to claiming the maritime zones provided for in UNCLOS.[226]

The implications of the Arbitration Award: other disputes in the South China Sea

It is important to stress that the Award only relates to Scarborough Shoal and the Spratly Group; it does not cover any of the other features in the South China Sea, in particular, the more northerly Paracel Islands, which are disputed between China and Vietnam, nor Vaughan Bank, where lately there has been a stand-off between those two States. In relation to the latter, there have been hints that Vietnam might consider legal proceedings under UNCLOS; if so, it would be interesting to see whether a differently constituted tribunal would follow the lead of the Tribunal in the South China Sea Arbitration, and consider the status of Vaughan Bank when it would be debarred from deciding upon the sovereignty over the feature. But clearly Vietnam would have to accept that any legal proceedings under UNCLOS could not resolve the dispute over the territorial sovereignty of Vaughan Bank as it, according to China, is an integral part of the Spratly Islands.

There have also recently been issues between China and Indonesia in the area off the Natuna Islands in the southern South China Sea. The Chinese position is that "China and Indonesia don't have disputes over territorial sovereignty. We have overlapping claims of maritime rights and interests in some areas in the South China Sea".[227] Indonesia however has disputed the latter point, referring to the South China Sea Arbitration Award.[228]

Finally, Malaysia has submitted to the Commission on the Limits of the Continental Shelf a claim for a continental shelf beyond 200 nautical miles from baselines drawn from East Malaysia;[229] it is reported that, as one would expect, China intends to object to this submission, and one assumes that the Commission will follow its Rules of Procedure and decline to consider the submission because there is a "dispute".

The implications of the Arbitration Award: Article 281

Article 281(1) of UNCLOS provides that:

> if the States Parties which are parties to a dispute concerning the interpretation or application of [UNCLOS] have agreed to seek settlement of the dispute by a peaceful means of their own choice, the procedures provided for in this Part [i.e. Part XV] apply only where no settlement has been reached by recourse to such means and the agreement between the parties does not exclude any further procedure.

China's view was that, since in the Declaration on the Conduct of Parties in the South China Sea, signed by China and the ASEAN States, including the Philippines,[230] as well as in other bilateral statements, the two States had committed themselves to resolve any disputes through bilateral discussions, Article 281 applied, and the Philippines were therefore precluded from having recourse to the procedures in Part XV of UNCLOS. This argument was rejected by the Tribunal:[231] it considered whether there was "a binding 'agreement' within the meaning of Article 281",[232] and concluded that the Declaration was not.[233]

However, there is a question of whether a binding agreement is indeed required for the purposes of Article 281. In its Draft Conclusions on Subsequent Agreements and Subsequent Practice in relation to the Interpretation of Treaties,[234] the International Law Commission concluded that an "agreement" for the purposes of Article 31(3)(a) and (b) of the Vienna Convention on the Law of Treaties "may, but need not, be legally binding";[235] in the same context, the Commission also quotes a judgment of the International Court of Justice which refers to a "tacit agreement".[236] One must therefore wonder whether the word "agreed" in Article 281 necessarily involves the existence of a binding and/or explicit agreement.[237]

Furthermore, it is submitted that the Tribunal dismisses too lightly the possibility that the Philippines was estopped from pursuing the dispute settlement procedures in UNCLOS. In brief, an estoppel arises if one State has made a representation which another State has relied upon. The Tribunal says that it "would first have to find that the Philippines had made clear and consistent representations that it would not resort to the Part XV compulsory dispute settlement procedures. The Tribunal finds no evidence of such representations".[238] It is difficult, however, to see that the Declaration does not involve a representation, and given that in other cases the reliance necessary to found an estoppel has been accepted as being quite slight, it would be reasonable to say that China has indeed relied upon what was said in the Declaration.

But perhaps more importantly, whatever the detailed legal arguments, it is suggested that the Tribunal's interpretation of Article 281 seems to defeat, rather than give effect to, what was clearly the intention of the parties. As one commentator has said,

> in defeating the original purpose [of] Article 281(1) and incentivizing this rush to litigation, the Tribunal has also called into question in the South China Sea and beyond the value of political undertakings, such as the proposed Code of Conduct, that are solemnly arrived at and seek to resolve differences by mutual consensus.[239]

The implications of the Arbitration Award: the interpretation of Article 121(3) and Itu Aba (Taiping) Island

A key question concerns the Tribunal's interpretation of the terms "island" and "rock" in Article 121 of UNCLOS. There is no doubt that the wording of Article 121 is far from ideal; Nordquist and Phalen describe it as "imperfect wording with deliberate ambiguities… imperfect solutions [being] better than no solutions at all".[240] So, it is not surprising that the proper interpretation of Article 121 has long been recognized as a difficult and controversial question in UNCLOS, nor that on two occasions the International Court of Justice has declined to give its view on the point.[241] The Tribunal, however, was clearly very keen to give guidance on the issue, and devotes considerable space to do so – some 28 pages; whether as an ad hoc tribunal this was appropriate is a question to be asked. Be that as it may, the Tribunal proceeds to a detailed, disaggregated analysis of Article 121(3), looking at each element in turn. But in doing so, it is submitted, the Tribunal fails to look at the provision as a whole; it does not see the wood for the trees, as the English expression goes. Furthermore, even on the level of detailed interpretation, the Tribunal fails to account for why the word "rock", and not "island", was included in paragraph 3 of Article 121;[242] as Sean Murphy says: "the Tribunal seems to ascribe no significance whatsoever to the use of the word 'rock' rather than 'island' in paragraph 3".[243] The implications of this flawed interpretation of Article 121 are exemplified by its treatment of the Itu Aba, as discussed below.

In addition, in its interpretation of Article 121(3), the Tribunal introduces a number of new elements, which are certainly not expressly referred to in that Article, and which to the writer's knowledge had not previously been mentioned in the academic literature. In particular, the Tribunal says that the presence of military personnel does not count in deciding whether the feature can sustain human habitation;[244] that an "infusion of outside resources or purely … extractive activities"[245] are to be ignored when deciding whether the feature can sustain an economic life of its own; and that economic activity derived from a possible exclusive economic zone or continental shelf must also be excluded from consideration.[246] All of these propositions are apparently novel and seem to involve significant extrapolations from the text.

As suggested above, the Tribunal's treatment of the status of Itu Aba indicates the shortcomings of its interpretation of Article 121(3). The Tribunal's conclusion that Itu Aba is a "rock" is key because, if it had held that Itu Aba was an island falling within Article 121(1), the Tribunal would clearly have had no jurisdiction since there would then have been, on any view, potentially overlapping entitlements between the Philippines and China, requiring a maritime delimitation – which would have been covered by China's exclusionary declaration under Article 298(1)(a)(i) of UNCLOS.[247] The Philippines' legal team seems to have conceded as much in their arguments to the Tribunal and indeed urged the Tribunal on these grounds to find that Itu Aba was a "rock" so that it would have jurisdiction.[248]

In fact, Itu Aba is 430,000 square meters in size (more than 100 acres), has been inhabited continuously since the 1950s, and now has a population of several hundred people (admittedly largely, and maybe entirely, military personnel from Taiwan, who of course in the Tribunal's view have to be ignored); it has potable water,[249] extensive vegetation,[250] and soil capable of sustaining agriculture;[251] fishermen were reported to be present in the 1930s;[252] and Japanese nationals were engaged in commercial and industrial activities there before the Second World War.[253] Despite all of this, the Tribunal reaches what seems on the face of it to be the remarkable conclusion that Itu Aba is a "rock"; Nordquist and Phalen are blunt in asserting that "the … Award is factually flawed in its holding that the island of Itu Aba … is merely a 'rock'".[254]

This finding by the Tribunal has a further knock-on effect in that four of the findings against China of breaches of UNCLOS[255] are directly dependent upon the Tribunal's conclusion that Itu Aba is a "rock" and therefore does not generate its own exclusive economic zone and continental shelf. This connection seems to be accepted by the Tribunal,[256] and there is a suggestion that the Tribunal did not doubt the good faith of China in taking at least some of the actions complained about.[257]

Finally, in considering Article 121(3), the Tribunal dismisses the relevance of State practice in two paragraphs.[258] This is a shame as in the Law of the Sea field the evidence of State practice is unusually extensive and easily available, through the United Nations Law of the Sea Bulletin and the International Maritime Boundaries volumes published by the American Society of International Law. Where, as here, the provision in UNCLOS is admittedly not straightforward to interpret, one would think that any international tribunal would want to look carefully at how States had in practice interpreted that provision. Thus in one case, the International Court of Justice approved a statement by the International Law Commission that

> the importance of … subsequent practice in the application of the treaty, as an element of interpretation, is obvious; for it constitutes objective evidence of the understanding of the parties as to the meaning of the treaty. Recourse to it as a means of interpretation is well-established in the jurisprudence of international tribunals.[259]

The Court went on to say that "indeed in the past, when called upon to interpret the provisions of a treaty, the Court has itself frequently examined the subsequent practice of the parties in the application of that treaty".[260] And the International Law Commission has just produced a draft set of Conclusions on Subsequent Agreements and Subsequent Practice in relation to the Interpretation of Treaties,[261] which discusses the issue in considerable depth, with copious references to jurisprudence.

As it is, it seems clear that the interpretation of Article 121(3) which the Tribunal espouses is significantly at variance with State practice.[262] Nor is the interpretation consistent with other decisions of international and national courts.[263] The result could thus be destabilizing; as Joanna Mossop says, when discussing the extent to which the decision of the Tribunal is consistent with the practice of New Zealand, whose exclusive economic zone was established in 1977, "the up-ending of maritime zones that have stood unchallenged for 40 years or more as the result of one tribunal decision would not be a positive contribution to the order of the seas".[264]

The implications of the Award more generally: other issues

Obviously, an extensive Award such as this one raises a lot of more general issues for the lawyers. But the following seems the most important.

The finding that China is in breach of Article 192 of UNCLOS concerning the protection and preservation of the marine environment raises some difficult issues. The Tribunal admits that this Article is "phrased in general terms",[265] and accepts that the requirement is only that States should exercise "due diligence".[266] In other words, one might see Article 192 as articulating an objective or an aspiration, rather than an absolute obligation, with subsequent provisions of UNCLOS, and indeed of other related instruments, making concrete the terms of Article 192.[267] One wonders whether the drafters of UNCLOS really intended that a single failure, or even several individual failures, to protect or preserve the marine environment, as opposed to a conscious policy to harm the environment, would lead to the State concerned being regarded as in breach of UNCLOS. In this case, the Tribunal identifies a number of incidents which it considers to have involved a failure to protect and preserve the marine environment; given that in fact there appear to be 14 such incidents, occurring over a 15-year period,[268] by a Chinese population of around 1.4 billion, one must question whether it is right for the Tribunal to hold that China has failed to exercise "due diligence", and has thus breached the general obligations in UNCLOS about the marine environment. Indeed, it is interesting to speculate whether a lot of other States might, on the basis of the approach taken by the Tribunal, be at risk of being held to be in breach of those obligations.

There are two other instances where the Tribunal's interpretation of UNCLOS seems open to serious doubt. First, there is the proposition that foreign fishermen may have a "vested right" to engage in "traditional fishing" in the territorial sea of another State.[269] No precedent for this view is given and it seems inconsistent with the provision in UNCLOS which states that vessels undertaking passage through the territorial sea may not engage in "any fishing activities".[270] Furthermore, the Tribunal itself takes the view that any such fishing rights in coastal States' exclusive economic zones have not survived the adoption of UNCLOS;[271] it seems odd that foreign fishermen should continue to enjoy such rights in the zone adjoining the coast, but not in the zone beyond that. The Tribunal's view flies in the face of the conventional, and well-established, wisdom that under UNCLOS the coastal State has the absolute right to decide whether or not to allow foreigners to engage in fishing in its territorial waters.[272]

Second, the Tribunal finds that China is in breach of the COLREGS because of the actions by its law enforcement vessels in the territorial sea of Scarborough Shoal (which on the assumptions adopted by the Tribunal is to be regarded as China's own territorial waters).[273]

There are two problems with the Tribunal's conclusion:[274] as far as UNCLOS is concerned, it only places an obligation upon "foreign ships" in another State's territorial waters to comply with the COLREGS,[275] and there is nothing in it to require that a State's own vessels should comply with the COLREGS in its territorial waters;[276] and as far as the COLREGS are concerned, it is not at all clear that they were intended to apply to vessels exercising law enforcement functions when it is obvious that they may need to carry out maneuvers which would not normally be permissible.

Finally, the Tribunal says that States are under a general obligation to avoid aggravating a dispute.[277] On the face of it, this seems to be a very broad proposition, for which the Tribunal cites no precedent, except for cases where a court or tribunal has made an appropriate order, or where there is a specific provision in a treaty; the UN General Assembly Friendly Relations Declaration, which is also referred to, is limited to action which might "endanger the maintenance of international peace and security". It must be questioned whether it was therefore right, or indeed helpful, for the Tribunal to articulate such a general principle.[278]

Conclusion

The conventional question which is always asked about legal proceedings is: who won? And the conventional answer in the case of the *South China Sea Arbitration* would be: the Philippines. As justification for this answer one could point to the fact that the *dispositif* of the Award lists nine breaches of UNCLOS by China, although four of these are a direct result of the finding that Itu Aba is a "rock".[279] But of course, this does not tell anything like the full story. Most importantly, the Award does not, indeed could not, address the key underlying issue in the South China Sea, namely the sovereignty over the various features there. Nor does it, nor could it, deal with the question of the delimitation of the maritime zones belonging to the States with coasts bordering on the South China Sea. In addition, the Tribunal adopted an entirely novel and unprecedented approach by seeking to rule on the status of features without their sovereignty being first established. Furthermore, the cogency of the Award will be undermined by the doubts over the key factual finding, namely that on the status of Itu Aba.

More generally, a number of the Tribunal's interpretations of UNCLOS seem to be open to doubt. In particular, the Tribunal has suggested that a number of new, and previously unthought of, elements are relevant to the question of whether a feature is an island or a rock for the purposes of Article 121(3) of UNCLOS. In that respect, as well as in relation to the drawing of baselines around offshore archipelagos, the Tribunal has ignored the relevant State practice. In addition, the Tribunal's statements about the right to conduct traditional fishing activities in another State's territorial sea and the application of the COLREGS to law enforcement operations in a State's own territorial waters appear to be dubious. And in its interpretation of the procedural requirements of Articles 281 and 283 (the obligation to exchange views),[280] the Tribunal does not seem to have given effect to the reasonable expectations of the States parties to UNCLOS. The Tribunal's pronouncements are not binding upon other international judicial bodies, and indeed it will be interesting to see what weight they are accorded in future cases.[281]

Finally, what is ultimately the most important question: has the Arbitration Award advanced the cause of international peace and security in general and the resolution of the disputes in the South China Sea in particular? As to the latter, as indicated above, the Award does not even begin to resolve the underlying disputes in the South China Sea about sovereignty and maritime delimitation. As to the more general issue, Sam Bateman, a seasoned observer of the region, concludes that

> the longer-term implications for regional maritime security of the Philippines instituting international arbitration need to be balanced against the shorter-term implications. In the short-term, the action has increased tensions in the South China Sea and delayed both co-operation and progress towards an agreed Code of Conduct. In the longer-term, it may clarify some legal issues, but this is at the risk of undermining the international dispute settlement process.[282]

Finally, lawyers always tend to assume that it is best to seek the resolution of disputes and to do so through litigation, but Abraham Sofaer, the former Legal Adviser in the US State Department, points out that this assumption is not always sound, and goes on to say that:

> whether the rule of law is advanced through a given adjudication depends on the real-world consequences of the litigation and of the decision issued as a result. Judged by that standard, the Philippine case has already adversely affected the interests of all parties, and the consequences are likely to get even worse after the tribunal's decision unless a way is found to break the cycle of challenges.[283]

Notes

1 See https://pca-cpa.org/en/cases/7/; there are two Awards, one on Jurisdiction and Admissibility, and the other on Merits, just called the Award on the PCA website. In this chapter, for the sake of convenience, the names used for the various features in the South China Sea are those which the Tribunal terms the English names, although in one important instance, namely that of Itu Aba, the name so termed by the Tribunal is clearly not derived from the English language. For full surveys of the Awards, see Yoshifumi Tanaka, The South China Sea Arbitration: Toward an International Legal Order in the Oceans (Hart, 2019) [broadly favorable] and the Chinese Society of International Law, "The South China Sea Awards: A Critical Study", *Chinese Journal of International Law*, Volume 17, Issue 2, June 2018, pp.207–748 [unfavorable]. See also the shorter, but also critical survey by Michael Sheng-ti Gau, "The Sino-Philippine Arbitration on the South China Sea Disputes: A Preliminary Assessment of the Merits Award", in Gordon Houlden and Nong Hong (eds.), *Maritime Order and the Law in East Asia* (Routledge 2018).
2 Award on Jurisdiction, paragraph 26.
3 Ibid.
4 This was because neither the Philippines nor China had expressly chosen any of the fora for the settlement of disputes set out in Article 287(1) of UNCLOS (i.e. the International Court of Justice, the International Tribunal for the Law of the Sea, arbitration under Annex VII or a special arbitral tribunal under Annex VIII), and therefore under Article 287(3) China was deemed to have accepted arbitration under Annex VII.
5 Award on Jurisdiction, paragraph 27.
6 Award on Jurisdiction, paragraphs 11–12 and 112–123.
7 Award on Jurisdiction, paragraph 150.
8 Ibid.
9 Award on Jurisdiction, paragraph 153.
10 Award on Jurisdiction, paragraph 178.
11 Award on Jurisdiction, paragraph 157.
12 Award on Jurisdiction, paragraph 156.
13 Award on Jurisdiction, paragraph 169.
14 Award on Jurisdiction, paragraph 170.
15 http://chinaus-icas.org/materials/philippines-v-china-putting-status-cart-sovereignty-horse/.

16 The China–ASEAN Declaration on the Conduct of Parties in the South China Sea, dated 4 November 2002.
17 Award on Jurisdiction, paragraph 198.
18 Award on Jurisdiction, paragraph 195.
19 Award on Jurisdiction, paragraphs 213–216.
20 Award on Jurisdiction, paragraph 217.
21 Award on Jurisdiction, paragraphs 223–225; the Tribunal does, however, go on to say that the Declaration does not in any event imply an exclusion of other procedures, even if that were permissible under Article 281: Award on Jurisdiction, paragraphs 226–228.
22 Award on Jurisdiction, paragraphs 231–232.
23 Award on Jurisdiction, paragraph 248.
24 Award on Jurisdiction, paragraph 250.
25 Award on Jurisdiction, paragraph 251.
26 Award on Jurisdiction, paragraphs 252–321; the Tribunal here seems to be acting out of an abundance of caution, since it was not seriously suggested that any of these treaties would be relevant for the purposes of Article 281 or 282.
27 Award on Jurisdiction, paragraph 324.
28 Award on Jurisdiction, paragraph 342.
29 Award on Jurisdiction, paragraph 343.
30 Christopher Whomersley, "The South China Sea: The Award of the Tribunal in the Case Brought by Philippines against China – A Critique", *Chinese Journal of International Law*, Volume 15, Issue 2, June 2016, pp. 239–264, paragraphs 51–55.
31 Award on Jurisdiction, paragraph 354.
32 Award on Jurisdiction, paragraph 390.
33 Award on Jurisdiction, paragraphs 393–396.
34 Award on Jurisdiction, paragraphs 400, 404 and 408.
35 Award on Jurisdiction, paragraphs 407 and 410.
36 Award on Jurisdiction, paragraphs 401 and 403.
37 Award on Jurisdiction, paragraphs 398, 399, 402, 405, 406, 409, 411, and 412.
38 Award on Merits, paragraphs 1–115.
39 Award on Merits, paragraph 5.
40 Award on Merits, paragraph 6.
41 Award on Merits, paragraphs 116–144.
42 Award on Merits, paragraphs 145–168.
43 Award on Merits, heading V, before paragraph 169.
44 Award on Merits, paragraph 181; the map is reproduced on page 75 of the Award on Merits; this line is often called the U-Shaped Line: see Keyuan Zou and Xinchang Liu, 'Historic Rights and the Philippines v. China Arbitration Case' and Ted McDorman, 'The Law of the Sea Convention and the U-Shaped Line: Some Comments', in Shicun Wu and Keyuan Zou (eds.), *Arbitration Concerning the South China Sea: Philippines versus China* (Routledge, 2016): 127–155.
45 Award on Merits, paragraph 183, the map is reproduced on page 77 of the Award on Merits.
46 Annex 191 to the Philippines Memorial dated 30 March 2014.
47 Annex 201 to the Philippines Memorial dated 30 March 2014.
48 At most there are references to "historical … evidence" in the latter *Note Verbale*, and elsewhere to China's claims being "formed over a long course of history": Award on Merits, paragraphs 186 and 200.
49 Award on Merits, paragraphs 192 and following.
50 Award on Merits, paragraph 206.
51 Award on Merits, paragraph 207.
52 Award on Merits, paragraphs 208–211.
53 Award on Merits, paragraphs 212–213.
54 Award on Merits, paragraph 214; however, given that the Chinese statements were not made in a legal context, one might query whether such a legalistic conclusion is justified.
55 Award on Merits, paragraph 226; the latter assertion does not seem to be supported by the evidence: see Christopher Whomersley, "The Award on the Merits in the Case Brought by the Philippines against China Relating to the South China Sea: A Critique", *Chinese Journal of International Law*, Volume 16, Issue 3, September 2017, paragraph 6.

56 Award on Merits, paragraph 229; in ibid., paragraph 228, the Tribunal again relies upon the Chinese statements referred to above: see footnote 54 above.
57 Award on Merits, paragraph 235.
58 Award on Merits, paragraph 246.
59 Award on Merits, paragraphs 248 and following.
60 Award on Merits, paragraphs 255 and following.
61 Award on Merits, paragraph 262.
62 Award on Merits, paragraph 263.
63 Award on Merits, paragraph 272.
64 Award on Merits, paragraphs 277–278.
65 Part V of the Award on Merits on this subject comprises some 364 paragraphs.
66 In Award on Merits, paragraph 304, the Tribunal states that "this definition [sc: in Article 13] operates in parallel with that of an island in Article 121", although how that conclusion was reached, and how its implications, are not further explained.
67 Award on Merits, paragraph 309.
68 See Whomersley, supra note 30, paragraph 12.
69 Award on Merits, paragraph 280.
70 Award on Merits, paragraph 283.
71 Award on Merits, paragraphs 281–282; the Tribunal's subsequent conclusions on this point relate to 11 features as it divides Gaven Reefs into North and South and reaches different conclusions about each.
72 Scarborough Shoal (Award on Merits, paragraph 284), Cuarteron Reef (ibid., paragraph 285), Fiery Cross Reef (ibid., paragraph 286), Johnson Reef, McKennan Reef, and Hughes Reef (ibid., paragraph 287), the Gaven Reefs (ibid., paragraph 288), Subi Reef (ibid., paragraph 289) and Mischief Reef and Second Thomas Shoal (ibid., paragraph 290).
73 Award on Merits, paragraphs 303 and following.
74 Award on Merits, paragraphs 322 and following.
75 Award on Merits, paragraphs 327 and following.
76 Low-tide elevations: Hughes Reef (Award on Merits, paragraph 358), Gaven Reef (South) (ibid., paragraph 366), Subi Reef (ibid., paragraph 368), Mischief Reef (ibid., paragraph 378) and Second Thomas Shoal (ibid., paragraph 381).

Not low-tide elevations: Scarborough Shoal (ibid., paragraph 334), Cuarteron Reef (ibid., paragraph 339), Fiery Cross Reef (ibid., paragraph 343), Johnson Reef (ibid., paragraph 351), McKennan Reef (ibid., paragraph 354) and Gaven Reef (North) (ibid., paragraph 365).

77 Itu Aba Island (Award on Merits, paragraph 401), Thitu Island (ibid., paragraph 402), West York Island (ibid., paragraph 403), Spratly Island (ibid., paragraph 404), North-East Cay (ibid., paragraph 405) and South-West Cay (ibid., paragraph 406). Note that the first of these is under the control of Taiwan, the fourth and sixth under the control of Vietnam, and the second, third and fifth under the control of the Philippines. The Tribunal states that it

> considers that if the six largest features described above are all to be classified as rocks for purposes of Article 121(3) of the Convention, the same conclusion would also hold true for all other high-tide features in the Spratly Islands.

Award on Merits, paragraph 407.

78 Award on Merits, paragraph 385.
79 Award on Merits, paragraph 478.
80 Award on Merits, paragraphs 507 and following.
81 Award on Merits, paragraph 511; see also ibid., paragraph 541; but as Nordquist and Phalen point out "there is not even a hint in [UNCLOS] to prevent the owners of islands from making improvements on their territory" (MH Nordquist and WG Phalen, 'Interpretation of UNCLOS Article 121 and Itu Aba (Taiping) in the South China Sea Arbitration Award', in MH Nordquist, J. Norton Moore and R. Long (eds), *International Marine Economy: Law and Policy* (Brill, 2017), at p.64); Nordquist and Phalen also argue persuasively that "the only legitimate starting point for determining the time of whether a feature is a 'rock' or an 'island' in a lawsuit is at the time the case was filed" (ibid., at p.5; also at pp.39–40).
82 Award on Merits, paragraph 520.
83 Award on Merits, paragraphs 521 and following; note the much more extensive analysis by Nordquist and Phalen, supra note 81, pp.10–28 and 41–61.

84 Award on Merits, paragraph 538.
85 Award on Merits, paragraph 482; see also ibid., paragraph 540.
86 Award on Merits, paragraph 484; see also ibid., paragraph 545.
87 Award on Merits, paragraph 487.
88 Award on Merits, paragraph 490.
89 Award on Merits, paragraph 491; see also ibid., paragraph 542.
90 Award on Merits, paragraph 496; see also ibid., paragraph 544.
91 Award on Merits, paragraph 500; see also ibid., paragraph 543.
92 Award on Merits, paragraph 502.
93 Award on Merits, paragraph 546.
94 Award on Merits, paragraph 549.
95 Award on Merits, paragraph 550.
96 Award on Merits, paragraph 553.
97 See footnote 76 above.
98 Scarborough Shoal (Award on Merits, paragraph 554), Johnson Reef (ibid., paragraph 557), Cuarteron Reef (ibid., paragraph 560), Fiery Cross Reef (ibid., paragraph 563), Gaven Reef (North) (ibid., paragraph 566), and McKennan Reef (ibid., paragraph 569).
99 See footnote 77 above.
100 Award on Merits, paragraph 577.
101 Award on Merits, paragraphs 580 and following.
102 Award on Merits, paragraphs 585 and following.
103 Award on Merits, paragraphs 594 and following.
104 Award on Merits, paragraphs 597 and following.
105 Award on Merits, paragraphs 602 and following.
106 Award on Merits, paragraph 615.
107 Award on Merits, paragraph 616.
108 Award on Merits, paragraphs 618–619.
109 Award on Merits, paragraph 620.
110 Award on Merits, paragraph 622.
111 Award on Merits, paragraph 623.
112 Five features: Hughes Reef, Gaven Reef (South), Subi Reef, Mischief Reef and Second Thomas Shoal.
113 Twelve features: Scarborough Shoal, Cuarteron Reef, Fiery Cross Reef, Johnson Reef, McKennan Reef, Gaven Reef (North), Itu Aba Island, Thitu Island, West York Island, Spratly Island, North-East Cay and South-East Cay.
114 Award on Merits, paragraph 571.
115 Award on Merits, paragraph 573.
116 Award on Merits, paragraphs 575–576.
117 Award on Merits, paragraph 576; in fact, the State practice is relatively extensive and uniform, and the Tribunal's conclusion seems dubious: see C. Whomersley, "Offshore Archipelagos Enclosed By Straight Baselines: A Reply to J. Ashley Roach", *Ocean Development & International Law*, Volume 49, Issue 3, 2018, pp.203–207.
118 Heading before Award on Merits, paragraph 649.
119 Award on Merits, paragraphs 649 and following.
120 Award on Merits, paragraphs 717 and following.
121 Award on Merits, paragraphs 758 and following.
122 Award on Merits, paragraphs 815 and following.
123 Award on Merits, paragraphs 994 and following.
124 Award on Merits, paragraphs 1044 and following.
125 Award on Merits, paragraphs 651 and following.
126 Award on Merits, paragraphs 668 and following.
127 Award on Merits, paragraphs 671–672.
128 Award on Merits, paragraph 696.
129 Footnotes 112 and 113 above.
130 Award on Merits, paragraph 697.
131 Award on Merits, paragraph 716; this conclusion follows logically from, and is contingent upon, the Tribunal's view that none of the features in the Spratly Group generates an exclusive economic zone.

132 Award on Merits, paragraph 717.
133 Award on Merits, paragraphs 719–721.
134 Award on Merits, paragraph 745.
135 Award on Merits, paragraphs 748–749; the Tribunal again disclaims any intention to rule on the sovereignty of any feature: ibid., paragraph 750.
136 Award on Merits, paragraph 744.
137 Award on Merits, paragraphs 753–756; again, this conclusion follows logically from, and is contingent upon, the Tribunal's view that none of the features in the Spratly Group generates an exclusive economic zone.
138 Compare Award on Merits, paragraph 759.
139 Award on Merits, paragraphs 761 and following.
140 Award on Merits, paragraphs 764 and following.
141 Award on Merits, paragraph 793; see also ibid., paragraph 814.
142 Award on Merits, paragraph 804(c); this conclusion is an entirely novel one and is very difficult to accept: see Whomersley, supra note 55, paragraphs 69–79.
143 Award on Merits, paragraph 814.
144 Award on Merits, paragraph 815; under this heading, the Tribunal deals with complaints about both fishing issues and construction activities.
145 Award on Merits, paragraphs 826 and following. As will be apparent from the succeeding footnotes, the Tribunal duplicates the lists of the incidents about which complaints were made.
146 Award on Merits, paragraphs 827–834; see also the list at ibid., paragraph 968, of incidents involving cyanide and dynamite, all of which are covered in the listing at ibid., paragraphs 827–834, but with the addition of an incident in the Spratly Islands in 1995.
147 Award on Merits, paragraphs 835 and 838; see also the list at ibid., paragraph 950, which covers the incidents at Scarborough Shoal listed at ibid., paragraphs 827–834, 835 and 838.
148 Award on Merits, paragraph 845.
149 Award on Merits, paragraph 846; also listed at ibid., paragraph 951.
150 Award on Merits, paragraph 852; Cuarteron Reef, (ibid., paragraphs 863 and following); Fiery Cross Reef, (ibid., paragraphs 867 and following); Gaven Reef (North), (ibid., paragraphs 871 and following); Johnson Reef, (ibid., paragraphs 875 and following); Hughes Reef, (ibid., paragraphs 879 and following); Subi Reef, (ibid., paragraphs 883 and following); Mischief Reef, (ibid., paragraphs 887 and following).
151 Award on Merits, paragraph 862.
152 Award on Merits, paragraph 941; footnotes in the original omitted.
153 Award on Merits, paragraph 944.
154 Award on Merits, paragraph 945.
155 Award on Merits, paragraph 946.
156 Award on Merits, paragraphs 947–948.
157 Award on Merits, paragraph 956.
158 Award on Merits, paragraph 959.
159 Award on Merits, paragraph 960.
160 Award on Merits, paragraph 963.
161 Award on Merits, paragraph 964.
162 Award on Merits, paragraph 965.
163 Award on Merits, paragraph 966.
164 Award on Merits, paragraph 975.
165 Award on Merits, paragraph 976; although note the view of Norquist and Phalen at footnote 81 above.
166 Award on Merits, paragraphs 977 and following; note that the Ferse team were not able to make a site visit: ibid., paragraph 142.
167 Award on Merits, paragraph 983.
168 Award on Merits, paragraph 986.
169 Award on Merits, paragraph 991.
170 Award on Merits, paragraph 994.
171 Award on Merits, paragraph 1029.
172 Award on Merits, paragraph 1030.
173 Award on Merits, paragraphs 1032–1034.

174 Award on Merits, paragraphs 1035–1038; this is another case where the Tribunal's conclusion follows logically from, and is contingent upon, the Tribunal's view that none of the features in the Spratly Group generates an exclusive economic zone.
175 Award on Merits, paragraph 1040; although note footnote 68 above.
176 1050 UNTS 1976.
177 Award on Merits, paragraphs 1047 and 1050.
178 Award on Jurisdiction, paragraph 153.
179 Award on Merits, paragraph 1109.
180 Award on Merits, paragraph 1109; this conclusion fails to take account of a number of salient points and must therefore be treated with some caution: Whomersley, supra note 30, paragraphs 60–68.
181 Award on Merits, paragraph 1110.
182 Award on Merits, paragraphs 1113 and following.
183 Award on Merits, paragraphs 1128–1129; see footnote 150 above.
184 Award on Merits, paragraph 1134.
185 Award on Merits, paragraph 1161.
186 Article 298(1)(b) of UNCLOS.
187 Award on Merits, paragraph 1162.
188 Award on Merits, paragraph 1169;
189 Award on Merits, paragraph 1177; also ibid., paragraph 1181.
190 Award on Merits, paragraph 1182.
191 Award on Merits, paragraph 1201.
192 Award on Merits, paragraph 1202.
193 See footnotes 32–37 above.
194 Award on Merits, paragraph 1203A; note that the Tribunal reiterates here that its decision is "without prejudice to any questions of sovereignty or maritime boundary delimitation".
195 Footnote 187 above.
196 Footnote 191 above.
197 Award on Merits, paragraph 1203B.
198 Points (1) and (2); footnote 64 above.
199 Points (3), (4), (5) and (6); footnotes 76 and 112 above.
200 Point (7); footnotes 76, 97 and 112 above.
201 Points (8), (9) and (10); footnotes 131 and 137 above.
202 Point (11); footnote 143 above.
203 Points (12) and (13); footnotes 161, 167 and 168 above.
204 Point (14); footnote 174 above.
205 Point (15); footnote 180 above.
206 Point (16); footnote 189 above.
207 See the Position Paper of the Government of the People's Republic of China on the Matter of Jurisdiction in the South China Sea Arbitration Initiated by the Republic of the Philippines, dated 7 December 2014, *Chinese Journal of International Law*, Volume 17, Issue 2, June 2108, at p.655.
208 Article 9, Annex VII, of UNCLOS.
209 Statement of the Ministry of Foreign Affairs of the People's Republic of China on the Award on Jurisdiction and Admissibility of the South China Sea Arbitration by the Arbitral Tribunal Established at the Request of the Republic of the Philippines, dated 30 October 2015, ibid., at p.679.
210 Statement of the Ministry of Foreign Affairs of the People's Republic of China on the Award of 12 July 2016 of the Arbitral Tribunal in the South China Sea Arbitration Established at the Request of the Republic of the Philippines, dated 12 July 2016, ibid., at p.681.
211 Footnotes 7–10 above.
212 Sreenivasa Rao Pemmaraju, "The South China Sea Arbitration (The Philippines v. China): Assessment of the Award on Jurisdiction and Admissibility", *Chinese Journal of International Law*, Volume 15, Issue 2, June 2016, pp.265–307, at paragraph 78.
213 *Judgment No. 2867 of the Administrative Tribunal of the International Labour Organisation*, ICJ Reports 2012, page 10, at p.19, paragraph 34.
214 *Equatorial Guinea v. France (Preliminary Objections)*, ICJ Reports 2018, paragraph 150; *Iran v. United States (Preliminary Objections)*, ICJ Reports 2019, paragraph 114.

215 Dissenting Opinion of Judge Donoghue in *Equatorial Guinea v. France (Preliminary Objections)*; note that at paragraph 19 she states that the Court should decline jurisdiction because of the need "to preserve the integrity of [the Court's] judicial function".
216 Compare Anthony Carty, "The South China Sea Disputes Are Not Justiciable", who, writing before the Award was made, took the view, mainly because of the difficult evidential issues, that "it is arguable that, despite the fact that the Tribunal would normally have jurisdiction to interpret authoritatively the meaning of Article 121 of UNCLOS, the juridical policy of non-justiciability would argue against it", in Shicun Wu and Keyuan Zou (eds.), *Arbitration Concerning the South China Sea: Philippines versus China* (Routledge, 2016), p.27.
217 See, for example, footnotes 3, 9, 39, 63, 70, 135, 141 and 194 above.
218 See footnote 15 above. See also Sreenivasa Rao Pemmaraju, footnote 212 above, at paragraph 79.
219 Whomersley, supra note 30, paragraph 33.
220 *Qatar v. Bahrain*, ICJ Reports 2001, page 40, paragraph 185.
221 Article 298(1)(a)(i) of UNCLOS; my emphasis.
222 Award on Jurisdiction, paragraph 155. See also the surveys by Tullio Treves "Maritime Delimitation and Offshore Features", in S. Jayakumar, T. Koh and R. Beckman (eds.), *The South China Sea Disputes and Law of the Sea* (Edward Elgar Publishing, 2014), p.121, especially pp.134–142; Michael Sheng-ti Gau, "The Legal Status of Maritime Features in the Sino-Philippine South China Sea Arbitration: Admissibility and Jurisdiction", in Shicun Wu and Keyuan Zou (eds.), *Arbitration Concerning the South China Sea: Philippines versus China* (Routledge, 2016), pp.82–84; and Robert Beckman and Leonardo Bernard, "The Significance of Offshore Geographic Features to Maritime Claims", ibid., at pp.192–196.
223 *M/V Louisa Case,* ITLOS Case No. 18, Judgment, paragraph 83. See also Michael Sheng-ti Gau, ibid., at pages 79–81.
224 Footnotes 46–48 above.
225 Footnote 63 above.
226 Footnote 64 above.
227 Foreign Ministry Spokesperson Geng Shuang's Regular Press Conference on January 8, 2020 (https://www.fmprc.gov.cn/mfa_eng/xwfw_665399/s2510_665401/t1730335.shtml). See also the Press Conferences on 31 December 2019 (https://www.fmprc.gov.cn/mfa_eng/xwfw_665399/s2510_665401/2511_665403/t1729013.shtml) and on 2 January 2020 (https://www.fmprc.gov.cn/mfa_eng/xwfw_665399/s2510_665401/2511_665403/t1729272.shtml).
228 There seems to have been a statement by the Indonesian Ministry of Foreign Affairs on 1 January 2020, but this seems no longer to be on the Ministry's website (but see the press report at https://www.rfa.org/english/news/china/indonesia-natuna-01022020165115.html).
229 https://www.un.org/Depts/los/clcs_new/submissions_files/submission_mys_12_12_2019.html.
230 Footnote 16 above.
231 Footnotes 17–20 above.
232 Award on Jurisdiction, paragraph 212.
233 Award on Jurisdiction, paragraphs 217–218.
234 https://legal.un.org/docs/?path=../ilc/texts/instruments/english/commentaries/1_11_2018.pdf&lang=EF
235 Conclusion 10, paragraph 1, at ibid., page 75.
236 *Dispute regarding Navigational and Related Rights*, ICJ Reports 2009, page 213 at paragraph 64, cited at ibid., page 60.
237 However, the Commission in the *Conciliation between The Democratic Republic of Timor-Leste and The Commonwealth of Australia* has since held that a binding agreement is required: Decision on Competence of 19 September 2016, paragraph 56 (https://pcacases.com/web/sendAttach/1921).
238 Award on Jurisdiction, paragraph 251.
239 Sourabh Gupta, "China-ASEAN Relations in the South China Sea: Persistent Features and Obstacles to Cooperation", in Gordon Houlden and Nong Hong (eds.), *Maritime Order and the Law in East Asia* (Routledge, 2018), Chapter 1; the writer makes the same argument about the Decision of the Commission in the *Conciliation between The Democratic Republic of Timor-Leste and The Commonwealth of Australia* (see footnote 237 above). See also Whomersley, supra note 30, pp.239–264, paragraphs 39–50.
240 Footnote 81 above, p.77.

241 *Romania v. Ukraine*, ICJ Reports 2009, 61, at paragraph 187; *Nicaragua v. Colombia*, ICJ Reports 2012, 624, at paragraph 180.
242 Whomersley, supra note 55, pp.387–423, at paragraph 34.
243 Sean D. Murphy, "International Law Relating to Islands", *Hague Recueil: Collected Courses of the Hague Academy of International Law*, Volume 386 (2016), at p.74.
244 Footnote 95 above.
245 Footnote 91 above.
246 Footnote 92 above.
247 Footnote 221 above. The same conclusion is reached by Nordquist and Phalen, footnote 81 above, at p.72 and following, and by J. Mossop, "The South China Sea Arbitration and New Zealand's Maritime Claims", *New Zealand Journal of Public and International Law*, Volume 15, 2017, p.265, at p.291.
248 Permanent Court of Arbitration, Day 2 Transcript of Hearing on Merits, pp.127–129; available at https://pca-cpa.org/en/cases/7/. As Professor Gewirtz says, this is a remarkable submission: P. Gewirtz, "Limits of Law in the South China Sea", Brookings Center for East Asia Policy Studies, East Asia Policy Paper 8 (May 2016), at pp.9–10.
249 Award on Merits, paragraphs 580–583.
250 Award on Merits, paragraphs 585–592.
251 Award on Merits, paragraphs 594–596.
252 Award on Merits, paragraph 599.
253 Award on Merits, paragraphs 602–603 and 606–611.
254 Footnote 81 above, at p.66; commentators writing before the issuance of the Award also took the view that Itu Aba was not a "rock": see Sam Bateman, "The Impact of the Arbitration Case on Regional Maritime Security" in Shicun Wu and Keyuan Zou (eds.), *Arbitration Concerning the South China Sea: Philippines versus China* (Routledge, 2016), p.238, and Professor P. Gewirtz, who stated that to find that Itu Aba was a rock would defy "what ordinary human beings would conclude and common sense would suggest", footnote 248 above, at p.9.
255 Points (8), (9), (10) and (14) in the Dispositif in Award on Merits, paragraph 1203B.
256 Footnote 128 above.
257 Footnote 172 above.
258 Award on Merits, paragraphs 552–553; the Tribunal is equally dismissive of the State practice of drawing straight baselines around offshore archipelagos: see footnote 117 above.
259 *Kasikili/Sedudu Island Case* [1999] ICJ Reports 1999, page 1045, at paragraph 49.
260 Ibid., paragraph 50.
261 Footnote 234 above.
262 See the comments of the very knowledgeable Alex Oude Elferink: "The South China Sea Arbitration's Interpretation of Article 121(3) of the LOSC: A Disquieting First" (September 7, 2016), on-line: http://site.uit.no/jclos/files/2016/09/The-South-China-Sea-Arbitrations-Interpretation-of-Article-1213-of-the-LOSC-A-Disquieting-First.pdf: "there is an abyss between the Tribunal's approach and the practice of many States". See also Stefan Talmon, "The South China Sea Arbitration and the Finality of 'Final' Awards", *Journal of International Dispute Settlement*, Volume 8, Issue 2, May 2017, at paragraph 23.
263 Talmon, ibid., at paragraph 22.
264 Mossop, (2017) 15 NZJPIL, page 265, at page 281; a similar point about stability is made by Alex Oude Elferink at ibid.
265 Award on Merits, paragraph 941.
266 Footnote 153 above.
267 Whomersley, supra note 55, pp.387–423, at paragraph 82. Compare the conclusion of the International Court of Justice in the *Oil Platforms Case (Iran v. United States)* ICJ Reports 1996, page 803, paragraphs 25–28, where it held that Article 1 of the Treaty in issue, which provided for "firm and enduring peace and sincere friendship between the United States … and Iran", "must be regarded as fixing an objective, in the light of which the other Treaty provisions are to be interpreted and applied".
268 Footnotes 160–163 above.
269 Footnotes 138–143 above.
270 Article 19(2)(i) of UNCLOS.
271 Paragraphs 803 and 804(b) of Award on Merits.

272 Whomersley, supra note 55, paragraphs 69–79.
273 Footnotes 177–180 above.
274 Whomersley, supra note 55, paragraphs 60–68.
275 Article 24(1) of UNCLOS.
276 The Tribunal seeks to rely upon Article 94 of UNCLOS, but this provision is in the Part of UNCLOS which relates to the high seas.
277 Footnotes 188–189 above.
278 Whomersley, supra note 55, paragraphs 95–100.
279 See footnote 255 above.
280 Footnote 30 above.
281 Talmon, footnote 262 above, at paragraph 21.
282 Bateman, footnote 254 above at p.239.
283 Abraham Sofaer, "The Philippine Law of the Sea Action against China: Relearning the Limits of International Adjudication", *Chinese Journal of International Law*, Volume 15, Issue 2, 2016, pp.393–402, at paragraph 22.

24
US-CHINA RIVALRY IN THE SOUTH CHINA SEA

Mingjiang Li and Archana Atmakuri

Introduction

The South China Sea disputes are multi-dimensional. One particular dimension that has had a profound impact on peace and stability in this maritime area, as well as the future trajectory of the disputes, is the strategic rivalry between China and the United States. US-China strategic rivalry has affected the positions and policies of various claimant countries, the role of the Association of Southeast Asian Nations (ASEAN) in regional security management, and the involvement of other external players in the South China Sea. US-China interactions in the South China Sea may have a significant impact on the management of various non-traditional security challenges in the area as well.

While many analysts would take the US current interventions in the South China Sea for granted, it is not the case that Washington has always wanted to play an important role in this dispute. Before the Second World War, the United States had very little interest in getting involved in the conflicts in the South China Sea. Even during the Cold War era, the US involvement in the dispute demonstrated different patterns at different times. It is in the post-Cold War era, particularly after the 2010s, that Washington began to play a much more interventionist role in the South China Sea. And, of course, the US interventions in the area were mainly targeted at China. Beijing believes that the South China Sea issue is used as a major platform by the United States as part of its containment strategy against China. US-China rivalry has become a regional geopolitical backdrop that significantly shapes the dynamics of disputes and security in the South China Sea.

This chapter addresses these questions: How did China and the United States interact in the South China Sea in historical times? What are the major sources of rivalry between the two countries in the region in the contemporary era? What major policy tools do the two powers employ to secure their respective strategic interests? What are the implications of US-China strategic rivalry for the South China Sea disputes?

Historical evolution of US-China interactions in the South China Sea

To understand the US policy in the South China Sea in the contemporary era, it is important to have a historical review of Washington's involvement in the dispute. A brief historical overview from the 1930s to the 1980s reveals that the US policy in the South China Sea has been closely linked to its geopolitical interests in East Asia and in the South China Sea in particular.

US indifference towards France-China dispute in the 1930s

In the early 1930s, China protested when the French colonial authorities in Vietnam began to occupy some islands in the South China Sea. When France consulted the American government on its annexation of these islands, the US State Department officials reportedly noted that they first heard of these islands through press reports on the French claim.[1] The United States remained indifferent and did not make any statement in favour of either France or China.[2]

During the Sino-French conflict, the then Filipino Senator Isabelo de los Reyes claimed that the islands occupied by France should belong to the Philippines because of geographic proximity and urged William Francis Murphy, the then American Governor-General of the Philippine Islands, to negotiate with France on this issue. Murphy requested Washington's opinion, but he did not receive any response from the Roosevelt administration. Subsequently, in reply to Reyes, the American colonial authorities claimed that the islands were excluded in the Treaty of Paris of 1898, which ended the Spanish-American war and enabled the United States to take over the colonial rule of the Philippines from Spain. The American colonial government in Manila concluded that the French occupation in the South China Sea had nothing to do with the Philippines and thus it was not a concern for the United States.[3]

US weak response to Japanese occupation 1938–1939

A bigger challenge for the United States came when the Japanese began to use forceful means to expel the French forces from the Paracels and occupied those islands in November 1938 and later the Hainan Island. After the occupation, the Japanese government claimed the Paracels to be part of Japanese territory. The Japanese activities made France and Great Britain uneasy. Fearful that the Japanese occupation of the Paracels and Hainan Island may pose a threat to their colonial presence in Southeast Asia, the two countries lodged a joint protest against the Japanese government. They demanded explanations for the purposes, nature, and duration of Japanese occupation. Japan did not give them any substantive reply.[4]

While the United States was watching closely Japan's invasion of China at that time, the Roosevelt government failed to react strongly to Japan's activities at the Paracels and Hainan Island. On 15 February 1939, the then US Secretary of State Cordell Hull asked the American ambassador in Tokyo to deliver a verbal inquiry from the US government to Japan to remind the Japanese government of the many American missionaries and other Americans working in the educational sector in Hainan. The verbal inquiry also urged Japan to inform the United States of the purposes of Japan's occupation activities because the United States and other powers had important interests in the West Pacific.[5] In response to the moderately-toned US message, Japan explained that its occupation of the Paracels and Hainan Island was aimed at blockading mainland China and did not make any promise to protect American nationals in Hainan.[6]

While continuing to keep an eye on Japan's moves, the United States sent a warship from Hong Kong to Hainan to inspect the situation of American nationals in Hainan. France, under the wrong assumption that Washington was going to take a tough position on Japan, took the opportunity to propose to the United States and Great Britain that the three countries could send warships to Hainan at the same time to exert pressure on Japan. France failed to gain support from both Washington and London.[7]

In March 1939, Japan continued to advance its military occupation to the Spratlys and declared the area to be Japan's territory. Japan informed American, British, and French ambassadors in Tokyo that it annexed these islands on the basis of Japanese nationals' first utilisation of these land features. Both France and Great Britain were very concerned about the possibility of Japan using these Spratly islands as a springboard for military actions against their colonial possessions in Southeast Asia. Senior American officials were also worried about this new round of Japanese aggression in the South China Sea. The American ambassador to Japan noted in a cable to the State Department that Japan's occupation of the Spratlys was a brazen forceful annexation of territory.[8] The US ambassador to France also noted that Japan's move in the Spratlys was aimed at further military expansion in Southeast Asia.[9] Despite these negative assessments provided by America's senior diplomats, the Roosevelt government did not take any concrete action to counter Japan's occupation of the Spratlys. Even when France twice urged Washington to put pressure on Japan, the US State Department claimed that it was still undertaking an investigation of the issue and refused to make any public statement. The State Department attempted to justify its reticence on the ground that the Spratlys, unlike Hong Kong or Indo-China, were territories under dispute.[10]

Later, Washington's position changed slightly. On 17 May 1939, the Roosevelt government sent a diplomatic note to Japan, which emphasised that the Spratlys were disputed between France and Japan and that the legal ground for Japan's incorporation of these islands as Japanese territory was questionable. The diplomatic note suggested that Japan and France resolve the dispute through bilateral negotiations or international arbitration.[11] The United States made this position change largely because of serious warnings from France, Britain, and the Netherlands about Japan's upcoming military campaigns in Southeast Asia, which would also harm American interest in the region.[12] Washington did not take any further action to help curb Japan's expanding ambition. The American mild response to Japan's occupation of the islands in the South China Sea in the late 1930s was mainly a result of the neutrality policy that the United States pursued in Asia before Japan's surprise attack on Pearl Harbour in 1941.

US changing postures in the South China Sea during the Cold War era

After the end of the Second World War, the Republic of China's government sent warships to the Paracels and Spratlys to occupy a few major islands in the South China Sea. Because of the close relations between the United States and the Chiang Kai-shek government during the Second World War, Washington did not oppose China's actions. The founding of the People's Republic of China under the rule of the Chinese Communist Party marked a significant turning point in America's policy towards the South China Sea. In 1951, the United States successfully managed to block any wording in the San Francisco Peace Treaty with Japan that would allow Beijing to infer any sovereignty over the islands in the South China Sea, despite the then Soviet Union foreign minister's strong efforts to help China during the drafting of the treaty.[13] The peace treaty proclaimed that Japan should give up all the islands in the South China Sea that it had occupied during the Second World War, but it did not mention which country should take sovereignty over these islands. In the 1950s and 1960s, the South China Sea played an important part in America's strategy to contain China. The US military presence and activities in the South China Sea served to block the expansion of Chinese and Vietnamese communism in Southeast Asia and beyond. On a number of occasions when China and South Vietnam had frictions over the Paracels, the the US naval ships and planes were sent to the vicinity to help South Vietnam conduct surveillance and to deter China's military actions.[14]

Washington's policy in the South China Sea dispute significantly changed again after the US-China rapprochement in the early 1970s. Soon after Nixon's visit to China in February 1972, Winston Lord, a senior member of the National Security Council, informed Chinese Ambassador to the United Nations Huang Hua that the US Department of Defense had ordered the Seventh Fleet not to get into the waters within 12 nautical miles of the Paracels.[15] During the military conflict between China and South Vietnam in January 1974, the United States followed a policy of diplomatic and military non-intervention. Before the conflict broke out, Washington openly stated that the dispute should be resolved by the claimant parties themselves.[16] Amid the South Vietnamese government's repeated requests for help, the Seventh Fleet was told by the US Department of Defense not to get close to the conflict area.[17] The Americans did not even support South Vietnam's request for the United Nations Security Council to discuss the issue.[18] While Washington did not want to get directly involved, the Seventh Fleet did provide intelligence support to South Vietnam behind the scene. Some American officials expressed regret that the dispute was resolved through military means.[19]

In the 1980s, in the context of US-China quasi alliance relationship, Washington's policy in the South China Sea could be characterised as strict neutrality. America's neutral position can be seen in the case of the Sino-Vietnamese conflict in March 1988 in the Spratlys area. Both officials at the State Department and the US Pacific Command leaders stated that the United States would not take any position and had no interest to intervene in the conflict.[20] It is commonly believed that the US neutral policy in the South China Sea in the 1970s and 1980s was driven by the Soviet factor, in particular Moscow's interests in Cam Ranh Bay and Danang ports, which may complicate the security of sea lines of communication in the South China Sea.[21]

It can be seen from this brief historical account that the US policy in the South China Sea has indeed been heavily shaped by its strategic interest in East Asia. Different from the US motivations, China's policy and activities in the South China Sea from the 1930s to the 1980s have perhaps been primarily driven by its understanding of sovereignty claims and nationalistic impulses.

Intensifying US-China strategic rivalry in the contemporary era

After the end of the Cold War and at the beginning of the 21st century, US-China geopolitical rivalry in the South China Sea dramatically increased. Such escalation of tensions can be seen in various aspects: tit-for-tat diplomatic tussle of war between the two sides, clearer and more critical views of the United States on China's claims, increased military presence and activities of both countries in the South China Sea, and both powers' political pressures on many regional states. The intensification of US-China strategic rivalry can be attributed to many factors. The most important factor is China's rising power and all the accompanying repercussions. A stronger China finds itself increasingly less tolerable of the existence of the US geopolitical and military supremacy in East Asia, a region which many Chinese elites may consciously or unconsciously regard as China's backyard. From the Chinese perspective, the US military supremacy in the region poses a daunting challenge to China, along with many regional territorial and maritime disputes related to the East China Sea, Taiwan, and the South China Sea. The US's strong presence in the region also significantly constrains

China's ambition to expand its political and security influence in the region. As a result, Beijing has many reasons to change the geopolitical status quo in the region, while the United States appears to be determined to sustain the existing US-led regional security order.

The South China Sea issue is thus placed in the centre of US-China strategic rivalry in East Asia. If Washington does not play an active interventionist role in the South China Sea, it is almost certain that the developments in this dispute will strengthen Beijing's position, given the much weaker power of all other claimant countries in comparison to China. American inaction to the dispute or regional perception of the US's weak response would significantly undermine the US regional security leadership role. The latter is largely buttressed by US alliances and close security partnerships with a number of regional states, strong American military deployment in the region, and the rules and norms that are advocated by Washington.

Such rivalry has been played out between the two major powers in the past two decades. The competition is most evident in the rapid catch-up of Chinese hard power versus that of the United States. To begin with, China's defence spending increased drastically over the last two decades. Moreover, China has enhanced informatisation of its military power, defined as a force's ability to use advanced information technology and communications systems to gain an operational advantage over an adversary. It continues to regularly restructure the armed forces by reorganising personnel, creating new institutions, and developing new weaponry including precision-guided cruise and ballistic missile systems.[22] Going by China's grand strategic naval vision, China would become a global sea power and hence be on par with the US military power in the region in the coming decades.

The military competition in the South China Sea is also related to the strategic nuclear deterrence between the two powers. The US Department of Defense is wary that China's nuclear forces are undergoing major reform: expanding and diversifying its nuclear arsenal by developing nuclear theatre-range precision-strike systems capable of reaching US territory, allies, and partners as well as the US forces and bases in the region.[23] China's naval and air projection in the South China Sea, in the words of one analyst, is part of its bastion strategy, whereby a safe 'bastion' is constructed for hiding its nuclear deterrent.[24] Through this strategy, China requires near-exclusive control of the central South China Sea, and therefore it pursues regular rejection of other claimants and outside navies. Some view this strategy as a temporary solution to combat the rivals until the People's Liberation Army (PLA) succeeds in establishing a permanent primacy in the region.

US-China rivalry can also be easily observed in Washington's views and actions whenever there are conflicts between China and other claimant states. From the Chinese perspective, American statements and activities in response to these conflicts all reflect the US inclination to take sides in the South China Sea dispute in favour of other claimant countries. We can take a look at a few examples. In 2012, the Philippines and China were involved in a maritime dispute for nearly two months over the Scarborough Shoal. America did not take a position on the sovereignty issue. However, the US officials maintained that the issue was of America's national interest in peace and international law and freedom of navigation in the South China Sea.[25] In 2014, China and Vietnam had a serious conflict over energy resources in the waters near the Paracels. A crisis situation between China and Vietnam continued for a few months after China deployed an oil rig Haiyang Shiyou 981 for exploratory drilling approximately 120 nautical miles east of Vietnam's Ly Son Island. The United States encouraged Hanoi to pursue international arbitration. The then US Secretary of State John Kerry told his Chinese counterpart that China's deployment of the oil rig was 'provocative'.[26]

Such skirmishes and conflicts between China and Southeast Asian claimant countries over energy resources and fishery activities were frequent in the past years. And Washington has consistently criticised China each time that China interfered in other claimant states' energy exploitation activities in areas that Beijing claimed to enjoy certain rights.[27] There are very significant legal differences between the two powers in the South China Sea. In fact, international law in the context of the South China Sea has become another battleground between Washington and Beijing. The United Nations Convention on the Law of the Sea (UNCLOS), in particular, has been used by Washington to criticise and undermine China's claims in the region. The main target of American contestation has been the nine-dash line map that was promulgated by the Republic of China government in 1947 and accepted by the People's Republic of China after 1949. A popular view of the nine-dash line is that it is too expansive as it overlaps with an extensive area of other regional littoral states' exclusive economic zones.[28] At the core of the US criticism of China's claim is the historic rights within the nine-dash line that Beijing is determined to claim. Although China has not officially clarified the actual historic rights it claims in the South China Sea, many analysts believe that the claims would include fishing, navigation, and resources.[29]

While Chinese analysts contend that China can legally enjoy historic rights in the nine-dash line area,[30] the United States has argued that international law, particularly UNCLOS, does not allow China to claim historic rights in the South China Sea. In December 2014, the US Department of State issued a report that concluded that any maritime boundary claim or historic waters/rights claim on the basis of the nine-dash line would not be supported by UNCLOS.[31] Senior US political and military leaders repeatedly criticised China's historic claims in the South China Sea.[32] The United States also opposed China's straight baseline around the Paracels.[33] In the past few years, US naval ships conducted freedom of navigation operations within the baseline of the Paracels.[34] Washington is worried that China may announce straight baseline claims around the Spratlys in the future.

In the past years, US officials took every opportunity to challenge China's claim and some activities in the South China Sea from a legal perspective. The verdict by an arbitral tribunal in July 2016, a legal move launched by the Philippines under the former President Aquino III, may have now provided a powerful legal weapon for the United States to attack Beijing's positions on the South China Sea disputes. The ruling concluded that China's historic rights claim from the nine-dash line is not supported by UNCLOS. The verdict also stated that none of the land features in the South China Sea can be regarded as an island that is capable of generating an exclusive economic zone, and continental shelf. It is no surprise that Washington unequivocally called for all parties concerned, especially China, to respect the tribunal's ruling.[35] Beijing announced that it would not recognise, accept, and execute the ruling. Furthermore, China reaffirmed its position that it will continue to claim historic rights in the South China Sea after the tribunal's ruling.[36] The legal contention between Washington and Beijing is expected to last for decades to come.

Another major development in the South China Sea that has significantly heightened Sino-American rivalry in the region was China's massive land reclamation activities and deployment of various military assets on the artificial islands in the Spratlys since 2014. A Pentagon report claimed that China had reclaimed about 3,200 acres of land in the South China Sea by 2016.[37] China deployed paramilitary forces such as anti-ship cruise missiles and long-range surface-to-air missiles on three features of Spratly islands. In doing so, China could detect the rival claimants' activities in the area. China's intention to reclaim land is evident in its effort to strengthen its operational capabilities within the nine-dash line to discourage rivals from challenging its territorial claims. For China, the land construction on its South China Sea islands and reefs is a 'legitimate right and is purely defensive in nature'.[38] But the United States has reacted to China's construction activities in the South China Sea with outrage. The then US Defense Secretary Jim Mattis criticised China's construction activities on the islands and stated that America 'cannot and will not accept unilateral, coercive changes to the status quo' at the Shangri-La Dialogue in 2017.[39]

US-China rivalry in the South China Sea is likely to remain unabated in the future as strategic competition has now become a more prominent feature in the overall bilateral relations. Many political leaders, policy analysts, and opinion leaders in the United States believe that it is now the time for Washington to pursue a tougher policy towards China on potential disagreements concerning trade and investment, intellectual property rights, hi-tech industry, human rights, political influence, military power, among others. With this competitive mode set in motion in the US's China policy, the South China Sea is likely to continue to be a focal point in US-China strategic rivalry in Asia. The two countries will continue to engage in a balance of military power game, legal contestations, and diplomatic bickering concerning the South China Sea.

Strategic policy tools for the two titans

Both the United States and China have employed various strategic policy tools to compete with each other in the South China Sea. These policies include regional strategic realignment, security cooperation with regional states, political engagement with ASEAN, and economic statecraft.

Shaping regional strategic realignments

Given the strategic, political, and economic importance of the South China Sea, Washington and Beijing sought to compete for regional geopolitical influence by employing their own bilateral and multilateral strategies to engage with regional countries. One of America's major moves is the Indo-Pacific strategy, which is said to be President Donald Trump's 'Pivot to Asia' strategy. The fact that President Trump unveiled the 'free and open Indo-Pacific' in Da Nang, Vietnam, at the Asia Pacific Economic Cooperation (APEC) Summit, is not a coincidence, given China's disputes in the South China Sea, particularly with Vietnam and the Philippines. The official document of the Indo-Pacific Strategy report reassures the Asian partners the following:

> The United States, our allies, and our partners are at the forefront of preserving the free and open regional order. All nations have a shared responsibility to uphold the rules and values that underpin a free and open Indo-Pacific. We are increasing the tempo and scope of our work with allies, partners, and regional institutions such as the Association of Southeast Asian Nations (ASEAN), the Mekong states, the Pacific Island countries, and our strategic partner India to address shared challenges and advance a shared vision.[40]

China's strategy to reshape the regional order has been characterised by President Xi Jinping as a community with a shared future. Chinese leader Xi has utilised bilateral meetings with leaders of regional countries and various multilateral occasions to promote his vision of an Asian community of shared future. The Chinese vision of regional order emphasises the principles of mutual respect and equality and all countries, the balance between short- and long-term issues, coordinated governance to address regional problems, multilateralism in opposition to unilateralism and protectionism, the realisation of mutual benefit and common development of Asian countries, and common security in the region.[41] Official Chinese media highlighted that significant progress has been made in building a regional community of shared future in trade, regional connectivity, regional multilateralism, and the establishment of regional rules.[42]

In this competition for regional strategic realignment, Washington may have gained an upper hand marginally. The four core countries, the United States, Japan, Australia, and India, have further deepened their military and security cooperation to some extent. The idea of the Indo-Pacific has been widely accepted by many other regional states and even other external powers such as France and Great Britain.[43] One significant development is the ASEAN's adoption of an Outlook on the Indo-Pacific (AOIP).[44] In contrast, China's vision for an Asian community of shared future has not been notably accepted by political leaders in other regional countries. On the other hand, the AOIP document is carefully phrased to avoid annoying China. The document downplayed the military and security dimensions in regional cooperation across the Indo-Pacific. ASEAN, instead, emphasised economic integration in the region and the imperative of utilising existing multilateral institutions with ASEAN as the central player. The AOIP did not mention the South China Sea disputes at all.

Contentions over freedom of navigation

In retaliation for China's land reclamation and intelligence survey activities, Washington began to intensify its Freedom of Navigation Operations (FONOPs) in the South China Sea in 2015. The US ships conducted six in 2017, five in 2018, and nine FONOPs in 2019 in the area.[45] These FONOPs were aimed at challenging China's requirement that ships provide notification or obtain permission before transiting through another state's territorial sea under innocent passage. More importantly, from the US perspective, the objective of FONOPs is to oppose excessive maritime claims and conduct comprehensive, regular, and routine execution to advance the longstanding American national interest in maintaining the freedom of the seas.

In response to US FONOPs, Beijing's statement is that it respects the freedom of navigation in the South China Sea, that it considers the US actions 'provocative', and vows to protect China's sovereignty and security interests in the South China Sea.[46] Beijing has been cautious to avoid military collision with American forces. Occasionally, Chinese countermeasures could be a challenge for America. Washington claims that on at least six occasions between 2001 and 2014, the US warships were harassed by Chinese vessels during surveillance operations in international waters in the region.[47] In 2014 alone, People's Liberation Army Air Forces (PLAAF) fighters performed at least five high-risk interceptions of the US surveillance aircraft around Hainan Island to prevent the US pilots from collecting intelligence.[48] In the backdrop of a heightened trade war, in 2018, the USS Decatur ship while conducting a FONOP in the Spratlys, was forced to manoeuvre out of the way to prevent collision with a Chinese warship.[49]

Washington's security cooperation with regional States

Another major tool for the United States is to further enhance its security cooperation with its allies and partners in the region. The United States and the Philippines signed the Enhanced Defense Cooperation Agreement (EDCA), which was envisioned to advance the implementation of the existing Mutual Defense Treaty (MDT) first signed in 1951. The EDCA was designed to promote interoperability, maritime capacity building, and strengthening the Philippine military for better external defence and maritime security. Washington reaffirmed its commitment to the MDT with the Philippines, providing assurances that 'as the South China Sea is part of the Pacific, any armed attack on Philippine forces, aircraft, or public vessels in the South China Sea will trigger mutual defense obligations of MDT'.[50]

Washington continues to engage with Vietnam to improve its defence capabilities by providing security assistance, including unmanned aerial vehicles, T-6 trainer aircraft, a former US coast guard high endurance cutter, and small patrol boats.[51] Although there are no defence treaties with Vietnam similar to that of the Philippines, the US military engages with Hanoi from time to time to advance their security cooperation. The United States held numerous annual training exchanges and activities to enhance bilateral cooperation and interoperability with the Vietnamese army and navy over the years. For instance, the United States transferred a major piece of defence equipment to Vietnam – the Coast Guard's Hamilton-class cutter US CGC Morgenthau – in 2018 to help improve Vietnam's security and law enforcement capabilities. That ship is now active in maritime security missions for Vietnam. America and Vietnam have begun holding joint naval exercises frequently since 2010 and have boosted their maritime ties since 2018. For the first time after the war between the two countries, a US Navy aircraft carrier arrived in the Danang, signifying the importance of Vietnam's relationship and the US resolve to develop strong maritime and defence ties.[52]

The United States maintains numerous engagements with ASEAN countries, such as Thailand, Malaysia, and Singapore to enhance defence relations as well. Washington had two major maritime exercises with ASEAN: the Cooperation Readiness and Afloat (CARAT) and the Southeast Asia Cooperation Training (SEACAT) exercises. In addition to existing exercises, Washington held a multilateral maritime exercise for the first time with ASEAN countries in the Gulf of Thailand and the South China Sea in 2019. According to media sources, America issued a statement that the purpose of the five-day maritime drill was to 'maintain maritime security, focus on prevention and pre-empt wrongdoing in the sea'.[53] Additionally, to promote dialogue and strengthen cooperation to address regional security challenges facing the region, the plan of action was to implement the ASEAN-US Strategic Partnership 2016–2020.

US security strategy dovetails with regional countries' interests. ASEAN needs to expand its military might to strengthen sovereignty and to oppose China's land reclamation activities in the South China Sea. China claims that the projects are mainly for marine scientific research, navigation safety, and improving the living and working conditions of the stationed troops on the outposts. However, some analysts believe that China is attempting to bolster its de facto control in the U-dash line by improving its military and civilian infrastructure in the South China Sea. Militarising the islands with airfields, berthing areas, and resupply facilities would improve China's ability to detect and challenge activities by rival claimants and also give China an advantage to maintain a more flexible coast guard presence.

China's security engagements with regional players

China has engaged with ASEAN through various regional forums such as the ASEAN plus China, ASEAN Defense Ministerial Meeting-Plus, ASEAN Regional Forum (ARF), Shangri-La Dialogue, and Jakarta International Defense Dialogue. China also holds informal defence ministers' meetings with ASEAN.

While increasing its assertiveness in the South China Sea in recent years, China also attempted to reassure littoral claimant ASEAN states. For example, immediately after the Scarborough Incident in April 2012, China agreed to implement the Declaration on the Conduct of Parties (DOC) in the South China Sea after 18 years of negotiations. The DOC guidelines were seen as mechanisms for conflict management but not for conflict resolution. Consequently, DOC failed to set guidelines to resolve the territorial claims or the maritime boundary claims related to the Scarborough Incident in 2012, for example. When the Philippines was successful in its appeal to the international tribunal to address the Scarborough Incident, China was criticised for openly rejecting the verdict. Two years later, Beijing agreed to hold consultations to accelerate the process of establishing the 'Code of Conduct in the South China Sea (COC)' under the framework of implementing the DOC and showing its commitment to multilateralism.

As the COC is considered a mechanism for security management and stability building in the South China Sea, it is expected to serve as a rules-based framework to promote confidence-building. Taking a step further, China set a timeline of three years to conclude the COC. The COC, unlike the previous kind of negotiations, will be China's proposal against the 11 proposals from Southeast Asian countries. The DOC does not stipulate a non-compliance policy for unilateral actions at sea and it also lacked a legal entitlement; in contrast, the COC is designed to restrain the actions of claimant parties and to increase confidence-building measures to prevent major military conflicts that would jeopardise security environment in the South China Sea.

China believes that ASEAN would lend support to the Philippines and Vietnam in times of dispute. However, individual countries in ASEAN tend to fail to take a stronger stand against China and Beijing has taken advantage of the divides among ASEAN countries on the South China Sea issue. This divide-and-rule strategy works well for China. Through the Belt and Road Initiative (BRI) projects and infrastructure development, China managed to garner the support of Laos, Cambodia, and other ASEAN countries. While the United States explicitly aims to contain China through its Indo-Pacific strategy, China has pushed for its own strategies through the DOC. Since the 2000s, China's key condition throughout the COC process has been the exclusion of external interference.[54]

Economic statecraft

Although Washington has considerable influence over ASEAN through defence and security cooperation and economic assistance, Beijing has experienced greater success by using economic assistance, foreign aid, loans and assistance, and debt relief policies. China also has a geographical and diaspora advantage in ASEAN. Since the early 2010s, China's state-owned companies have funded dam, road, and other infrastructure projects in Southeast Asia. Moreover, China's BRI, unveiled in 2013 by President Xi Jinping, funds huge connectivity projects that bring ASEAN closer to mainland China.

Under the broader BRI spectrum, China initiated sub-regional infrastructure initiatives such as the Lancang-Mekong Cooperation (LMC) mechanism. The LMC ropes in six Southeast Asian countries, namely Cambodia, China, Laos, Myanmar, Thailand, and Vietnam, to work closely on regional infrastructure projects. The vast economic influence is a combination of economic inducements and coercion to advance Beijing's strategic objectives in Southeast Asia. Furthermore, the Regional Comprehensive Economic Partnership (RCEP) conclusion in 2019 reaffirmed China's commitment to work with ASEAN to achieve a comprehensive, and mutually beneficial economic partnership agreement.

Washington has been under significant pressure to cope with China's economic influence in Asia.[55] The United States has come up with a number of economic engagement proposals in the region.[56] In October 2018, the US Congress passed the Better Utilisation of Investment Leading to Development (BUILD) Act, which allowed the government to provide US$60 billion for the newly-established US International Development Finance Corp (IDFC) to support infrastructure development in Asia and Africa. American leaders and senior officials frequently mention that the new BUILD Act can be a tool to counter China's BRI in the Indo-Pacific region.[57] With strong support from Washington, the US Chamber of Commerce's US-India Business Council (USIBC), together with the US-Japan Business Council, launched the Indo-Pacific Infrastructure Trilateral Forum to encourage the private sector in India, the United States, and Japan to invest in regional infrastructure and connectivity.[58] The US government has also taken the lead to form the Blue Dot Network, which aims to 'promote quality infrastructure investment that is open and inclusive, transparent, economically viable, financially, environmentally and socially sustainable, and compliant with international standards, laws, and regulations'.[59]

The regional economic power competition between China and the United States will have a significant impact on the security dynamics in the South China Sea. Some regional states, such as Cambodia and Laos, are becoming increasingly dependent on China's economic support. It is no surprise that these countries would diplomatically support China to benefit from the latter's security management of the South China Sea. China has become the largest trade partner for almost all regional states, making it almost impossible for ASEAN as a grouping to adopt a confrontational posture towards China. Clearly, Beijing has gotten an upper hand in the economic statecraft rivalry between China and the United States.

Conclusion

The United States, as a non-claimant party in the South China Sea, has been involved in this regional dispute mainly because of its geopolitical interests since the 1930s. Today, the strategic drive for Washington's involvement in the South China Sea is perhaps stronger than ever. This is mainly because of the rise of China, an emerging regional hegemon that is keen to pursue its territorial and maritime interests in Asia. The South China Sea has thus become an unfortunate battleground for US-China strategic rivalry. Washington will have high stakes for its regional security leadership role and its geopolitical presence in Asia if it appears to be weak in response to China's activities in the South China Sea. Beijing, likewise, will also have high stakes not only for its national interests but also for its domestic politics. The two countries are locked in this great-power rivalry over supremacy in the South China Sea and the whole Asian region.

Intensified strategic competition between the two major powers has further complicated the resolution of the South China Sea disputes. Facing strategic pressures from Washington, Beijing will have a greater incentive to increase its military power in the South China Sea and to change the status quo in the dispute and expand its presence in the region in order to gain a more favourable position versus the United States. China will have less incentive to significantly amend some of its claims and positions that have been criticised as legally invalid. These Chinese policies and activities will not only further prompt the US push-back but also complicate China's interactions with other claimant states and even non-claimant states in Southeast Asia. Trust and mutual confidence between China and Southeast Asian states could be weakened, which in turn undermines China-ASEAN security management in the South China Sea.

There are very few signs that US-China strategic rivalry in the South China Sea will decline in the future. Currently, neither Beijing nor Washington is prepared to engage in an outright military confrontation in the region. Very likely, the two powers will continue to use the same strategic policy tools against each other in the coming years. And there is unlikely to be a clear winner or loser in this strategic contestation in the coming decades.

Notes

1 Kathleen Barnes, "Spratlys Seizure Revives Conflicting Claims," (1930) 8 *Far Eastern Survey* 9, at 109.
2 Li Guang, "Yi jiu san ling niandai meiguo dui nanhai zhengduan de lichang Pingxi," [US Attitudes towards the South China Sea Dispute in the 1930s] (2016) 24 *Taipingyang xuebao* [Pacific Journal] 7, 64–72.
3 Han Zhenhua, ed., *Woguo nanhai zhudao shiliao huibian,* [A Compilation of Historical Materials about China's South China Sea Islands] (Beijing: Dongfang Publishing), 261.
4 "The Ambassador in Japan (Grew) to the Secretary of State," Tokyo (Feb. 14, 1939) in *Foreign Relations of the United States: Diplomatic Papers*, 1939, The Far East, vol. III (US Government Printing Office, 1955) at 108.
5 "The Secretary of State to the Ambassador in Japan (Grew)," Washington (Feb. 15, 1939), in *Foreign Relations of the United States: Diplomatic Papers*, 1939, The Far East, vol. III, (US Government Printing Office, 1955) at 109.
6 "The Ambassador in Japan (Grew) to the Secretary of State," Tokyo (Feb. 17, 1939), in *Foreign Relations of the United States: Diplomatic Papers*, 1939, The Far East, vol. III, (US Government Printing Office, 1955) 110–111.
7 The Ambassador in France (Bullitt) to the Secretary of State, Paris (Feb. 16, 1939, in *Foreign Relations of the United States: Diplomatic Papers*, 1939, The Far East, vol. III, (US Government Printing Office, 1955) at 110.
8 "The Ambassador in Japan (Grew) to the Secretary of State," Tokyo (Mar. 31, 1939), in *Foreign Relations of the United States: Diplomatic Papers*, 1939, The Far East, vol. III, (US Government Printing Office, 1955) 111–112.
9 The Ambassador in France (Bullitt) to the Secretary of State, Paris (Apr. 1, 1939), in *Foreign Relations of the United States: Diplomatic Papers*, 1939, The Far East, vol. III, (US Government Printing Office, 1955) at 114.
10 "Memorandum of Conversation, by the Chief of the Division of Far Eastern Affairs (Hamilton)," Washington (Apr. 11, 1939), in *Foreign Relations of the United States: Diplomatic Papers*, 1939, *The Far East*, vol. III (US Government Printing Office, 1955) 115–116.
11 "The Secretary of State to the Japanese Ambassador (Horin-ouchi)," Washington, May 17, 1939, in Papers relating to the Foreign Relations of the United States, Japan: 1931–1941 (in two volumes), vol. II (U.S. Government Printing Office, 1943) 280–281.
12 Guang, supra note 2.
13 Qiu Qingjun, "Ershi shiji wushi niandai meiguo nanhai zhengce lunshu," [Analysis of US South China Sea Policy in the 1950s] (2018) 1 *Shehui kexue dongtai* [Social Sciences Studies], 66–71.
14 Ibid.
15 Henry Kissinger, *The White House Years,* (Boston, MA: Little, Brown and Company, 1979).
16 Michael Morrow, 'Today Hsisha, Tomorrow...?', *Far Eastern Economic Review*, Jan. 28, 1974.
17 'U.S. Cautioned 7th Feet to Shun Paracel Clash', *The New York Times*, Jan. 22, 1974.
18 Bernard Gwertzman, 'Peking Reports Holding U.S. Aide', *The New York Times*, Jan. 26, 1974.
19 Qiu, supra note 13.
20 Jia Qingjun, "Yi jiu wu ling-yi jiu jiu ling nian meiguo nanhai zhengce zhuyao tedian lunshu," [Main Features in US Policy towards the South China Sea from 1950 to 1990], (2018) 2 *Yatai anquan yu haiyang yanjiu* [Asia-Pacific Security and Maritime Studies] 59–72.
21 Ang Cheng Guan, "The South China Sea Dispute Re-visited," Institute of Defense and Strategic Studies (Singapore) Working Paper No. 4 (Aug. 1999).
22 China Defence White Paper 2019.
23 Mary Beth Morgan, "A 'World-Class' Military: Assessing China's Global Military Ambitions" (Testimony delivered before the U.S.-China Economic and Security Review Commission),

Jun. 20, 2019, available at https://www.uscc.gov/sites/default/files/Morgan_USCC%20Testimony_Final.pdf.

24 Bill Hayton, The South China Sea – "The Status Quo is not the Worst Situation," CEIAS Insights, Oct. 29 2019; available at https://ceias.eu/the-south-china-sea-the-status-quo-is-not-the-worst-situation/.

25 US Department of State, "Press Statements, South China Sea," Aug. 3, 2012, available at https://2009-2017.state.gov/r/pa/prs/ps/2012/08/196022.htm.

26 Reuters, 'United States' John Kerry Says China Action in Seas Dispute 'Provocative', May 13, 2014, available at https://uk.reuters.com/article/usa-kerry-china/kerry-says-china-action-in-s-china-sea-dispute-provocative-idUKL3N0NZ32420140513.

27 See for instance, Department of State, "Chinese Coercion on Oil and Gas Activity in the South China Sea," Press Statement, Jul. 20, 2019, available at https://www.state.gov/chinese-coercion-on-oil-and-gas-activity-in-the-south-china-sea/.

28 Antonio Carpio, *The South China Sea Dispute: Philippine Sovereign Rights and Jurisdiction in the West Philippine Sea*, (Manila: Institute for Maritime and Ocean Affairs, 2017).

29 Bill Hayton, 'China's 'Historic Rights' in the South China Sea: Made in America?', *The Diplomat*, Jun. 21, 2016.

30 Zhiguo Gao and Bingbing Jia, "The Nine-Dash Line in the South China Sea: History, Status, and Implications," (2013) 107 *American Journal of International Law* 1, 98–124.

31 Office of Ocean and Polar Affairs Bureau of Oceans and International Environmental and Scientific Affairs, U.S. Department of State, "Limits in the Seas, No. 143, China: Maritime Claims in the South China Sea," Dec. 5, 2014, available at https://www.state.gov/wp-content/uploads/2019/10/LIS-143.pdf.

32 See for instance, BBC, 'US Presses Beijing over South China Sea Dispute', Feb. 6, 2014, available at https://www.bbc.com/news/world-asia-china-26062033; The Associated Press, 'Pacific Fleet's 4-Star Warns of Chinese Intimidation', Dec. 13, 2019, available at https://www.navytimes.com/news/your-navy/2019/12/13/pacific-fleets-4-star-warns-of-chinese-intimidation/; Ankit Panda, 'US Secretary of State Criticizes China's South China Sea Practices', *The Diplomat*, Mar. 14, 2019, available at https://thediplomat.com/2019/03/us-secretary-of-state-criticizes-chinas-south-china-sea-practices/.

33 J. Ashley Roach, "Offshore Archipelagos Enclosed by Straight Baselines: An Excessive Claim?," (2018) 49 *Ocean Development & International Law* 2, 176–202.

34 Lynn Kuok, 'Challenging China's Illegal Maritime Baselines', *The Wall Street Journal*, Oct. 26, 2016.

35 Jeremy Au Yong, 'The Hague Ruling: US Officials Urge China to Respect Decision', *The Straits Times*, Jul. 14, 2016, available at https://www.straitstimes.com/world/united-states/us-officials-urge-china-to-respect-decision.

36 "Statement of the Ministry of Foreign Affairs of the People's Republic of China on the Award of 12 July 2016 of the Arbitral Tribunal in the South China Sea Arbitration Established at the Request of the Republic of the Philippines," Jul. 12, 2016, available at https://www.fmprc.gov.cn/nanhai/eng/snhwtlcwj_1/t1379492.htm.

37 U.S. Office of the Secretary Defense, "Annual Report to Congress: Military and Security Developments Involving the People's Republic of China 2019," at 75.

38 Xinhuanet, 'Where There Are Threats, There Are Defenses: Chinese Defense Minister on South China Sea', Jun. 2, 2019, available at http://www.xinhuanet.com/english/2019-06/02/c_138110712.htm (accessed 11 Jan. 2020).

39 U.S. Department of Defense, "Remarks by Secretary Mattis at Shangri-La Dialogue," Transcript, Jun. 3, 2017.

40 U.S. Department of State, *Bureau of East Asian and Pacific Affairs Report: A Free and Open Indo-Pacific: Advancing a Shared Vision*, Nov. 3, 2019, available at https://www.state.gov/a-free-and-open-indo-pacific-advancing-a-shared-vision/.

41 Shi Xiaohu, 'Building an Asian Community with a Shared Future', *Khmer Times*, Dec. 9, 2019, available at https://www.khmertimeskh.com/50668114/building-an-asian-community-with-a-shared-future

42 China Daily, 'China, ASEAN Make Great Strides in Building Community with Shared Future', Dec. 15, 2019.

43 James Rogers, "European (British and French) Geostrategy in the Indo–Pacific," (2013) 9 *Journal of the Indian Ocean Region* 1, 69–89.

44 Statements and Communiques, Association of Southeast Asian Nations, "ASEAN's Outlook on the Indo-Pacific," Jun. 23, 2019, available at https://asean.org/storage/2019/06/ASEAN-Outlook-on-the-Indo-Pacific_FINAL_22062019.pdf.

45 David B. Larter, 'In Challenging China's Claims in the South China Sea, the US Navy Is Getting More Assertive', *Defense News*, Feb. 5, 2020, available at https://www.defensenews.com/naval/2020/02/05/in-challenging-chinas-claims-in-the-south-china-sea-the-us-navy-is-getting-more-assertive/.

46 The Straits Times, 'China Condemns US for South China Sea Freedom of Navigation Operation', Oct. 2, 2018, available at https://www.straitstimes.com/asia/east-asia/china-condemns-us-for-south-china-sea-freedom-of-navigation-operation; China Daily, 'China Voices Resolute Opposition to Provocations in South China Sea', Feb. 28, 2019, available at http://www.chinadaily.com.cn/a/201902/28/WS5c77e9c1a3106c65c34ec0a9.html.

47 Ronald O'Rourke, *Maritime Territorial and Exclusive Economic Zone (EEZ) Disputes Involving China: Issues for Congress* (Washington, DC: Congressional Research Service, 22 December 2015), 12–13, available at http://fas.org/sgp/crs/row/R42784.pdf.

48 Greg Torode and Megha Rajagopalan, 'Chinese Interceptions of US Military Planes Could Intensify Due to Submarine Base', Reuters, Aug. 28, 2014, available at http://www.reuters.com/article/2014/08/28/us-china-usa-militaryidUSKBN0GS2MZ20140828.

49 Teddy Ng and Kristin Huang, 'America Accuses Chinese Warship of Unsafe Maneuvers after Near Collision with USS Decatur in South China Sea', *South China Morning Post*, Oct. 2, 2018, available at https://www.scmp.com/news/china/military/article/2166565/chinese-destroyer-nearly-collided-uss-decatur-after-trying-drive.

50 Raissa Robles, 'US promises to Defend the Philippines from 'Armed Attack' in South China Sea, as Manila Mulls Review of Defence Treaty', *South China Morning Post*, Mar. 1, 2019, available at https://www.scmp.com/week-asia/geopolitics/article/2188305/us-promises-come-philippines-defence-south-china-sea-event.

51 For details, see US Department of State, "U.S. Security Cooperation with Vietnam," May 21, 2019, available at https://www.state.gov/u-s-security-cooperation-with-vietnam-2/

52 U.S. Department of Defense, "Aircraft Carrier USS Carl Vinson Makes Vietnam Port Call," Mar. 5, 2018, available at https://www.defense.gov/Explore/News/Article/Article/1458238/aircraft-carrier-uss-carl-vinson-makes-vietnam-port-call/.

53 The Straits Times, 'US, ASEAN to Hold First Joint Maritime Exercise', Aug. 25, 2019, available at https://www.straitstimes.com/asia/us-asean-to-hold-first-joint-maritime-exercises.

54 Li Xiaokun and Zhang Ting, 'Foreign Minister Warns of South China Sea Issue', *China Daily*, Jul. 26, 2010, available at http://www.chinadaily.com.cn/china/2010-07/26/content_11046544.htm.

55 Naná de Graaff and Bastiaan van Apeldoorn, "US–China Relations and the Liberal World Order: Contending Elites, Colliding Visions?," (2018) 94 *International Affairs* 1, 113–131.

56 Joel Wuthnow, "From Friend to Foe-Ish: Washington's Negative Turn on the Belt and Road Initiative," The Asan Forum, May 21, 2018, available at http://www.theasanforum.org/from-friend-to-foe-ish-washingtons-negative-turn-on-the-belt-and-road-initiative/.

57 For an explanation of the BUILD Act, see Daniel F. Runde and Romina Bandura, "The BUILD Act Has Passed: What's Next?," *CSIS*, Oct. 12, 2018, available at https://www.csis.org/analysis/build-act-has-passed-whats-next; See also then Acting Secretary of Defense Patrick M. Shanahan's speech at the Shangri-la Dialogue in Singapore on Jun. 1, 2019, available at https://dod.defense.gov/News/Transcripts/Transcript-View/Article/1871584/acting-secretary-shanahans-remarks-at-the-iiss-shangri-la-dialogue-2019/.

58 The Economic Times, 'Indo–Pacific Infrastructure Forum Launched to Tap Private Sector in India, United States And Japan', May 15, 2018, available at https://economictimes.indiatimes.com/news/economy/infrastructure/indo-pacific-infrastructure-forum-launched-to-tap-private-sector-in-india-us-japan/articleshow/64171805.cms.

59 State Department, "Blue Dot Network," available at https://www.state.gov/blue-dot-network/.

25

STRUGGLES FOR PRESTIGE AND POWER, 960–2020

C. J. Jenner

Introduction

"Prestige means the recognition by other people of your strength." Historian and diplomat E. H. Carr said, "Prestige (which some people scoff at) is enormously important; for if your strength is recognised, you can generally achieve your aims without having to use it."[1] Wealth and power steered global prestige from East to West and back to Asia. History's serial relocations of economic growth and corollary power changed the character of the South China Sea into a conflictual conduit for Eastern and then Western colonialism, a strategic sea space in a worldwide war, and now a cockpit of contest to maintain or revise the rules-based international order. For the first time in several centuries, China's blue water navy is projecting power across the Indo-Pacific and prosecuting a national maritime security strategy to transform the South China Sea into a "Chinese lake."[2] In large part, the winner of the Sino-American struggle for preponderance in the South China Sea will steer the course of the 21st century in the Indo-Pacific.[3]

The South China Sea is rich in marine resources, geopolitical influence, and simultaneously generates globally significant regional conflict and cooperation.[4] Seven of its coastal countries are contesting ownership of geographic features therein to gain sovereignty rights over the seas' marine resources.[5] More than 95 percent of all regional voice and data transmission, half of worldwide annual merchant fleet tonnage, and a third of all maritime traffic worldwide traverse the South China Sea's lines of communication and undersea cables.[6] Approximately two-thirds of the Republic of Korea's energy supplies, 60 percent of Japan's and Taiwan's energy supplies, and 90 percent of the People's Republic of China's (PRC) crude oil are imported via the South China Sea.[7] Some of the world's biggest fisheries and significant reserves of oil, gas, and minerals are under its surface. Per-capita fish consumption in the PRC was 35.1 kg in 2010, nearly double the global average of 18.9 kg. Feeding its people requires the PRC to take more than 30 percent of the total catch in the South China Sea, the next largest take is that of Indonesia at 11 percent.[8] The PRC's fishing fleet is by far the largest in the South China Sea. In support of Beijing's illegal claim to the South China Sea, Chinese fishing fleets conduct coercive sub-war influence operations in coordination with the Coast Guard and maritime China Militia under the People's Liberation Army (PLA) Navy's communication network and chain of command.[9]

In the 1980s, the founding fathers of Beijing's present-day maritime security strategy launched a farsighted renaissance in Chinese sea power. Paramount leader Deng Xiaoping and Admiral-General Liu Huaqing understood the fundamental role of the South China Sea in the PRC's economic development and national security.[10] Rising uniquely to General and Admiral, Liu Huaqing's command of China's maritime strategy and military modernisation was second to none except his friend and patron, Deng Xiaoping. Deng and Liu conceived and sought a strategic objective of nothing less than China's return to regional primacy.[11] Beijing now aims to manoeuvre Washington into a position where the United States of America (USA)'s prestige and power stand on its ability to defend the rules-based order in the South China Sea in concert with its allies, partners, and the Association of Southeast Asian Nations (ASEAN).[12]

In 2019, Xi Jinping's now limitless termed administration published a national security strategy stating the USA "provoked and intensified competition among major countries, significantly increased its defence expenditure, pushed for additional capacity in nuclear, outer space, cyber and missile defence, and undermined global strategic stability." Moreover, China has "the firm resolve and the ability to safeguard national sovereignty and territorial integrity, and will never allow the secession of any part of its territory by anyone, any organization, or any political party by any means at any time." Beijing will use of force in defence of the PRC's perceived national interest, and reserves "the option of taking all necessary measures."[13] If the other claimant states do not change or acquiesce to Beijing's unlawful sovereignty rights claim to the South China Sea, then we are sailing towards rather than away from military conflict.[14]

Still blessed by robust American democracy and a term-limited presidency, Washington now perceives both China and Russia as "strategic competitors" and "revisionist powers." Although manifest worldwide, the Sino-American rivalry is contested most in the Indo-Pacific region. Beijing has deliberately transformed the South China Sea into the strategic cockpit of this epochal contest. According to the U.S. National Security Strategy, "China seeks to displace the United States in the Indo-Pacific region, expand the reaches of its state-driven economic model, and reorder the region in its favour."[15]

The South China Sea is an integral part of the First Island Chain, the prime geography in the PRC's national maritime security strategy:

> The South China Sea islands and Diaoyu Islands are inalienable parts of the Chinese territory. China exercises its national sovereignty to build infrastructure and deploy necessary defensive capabilities on the islands and reefs in the South China Sea, and to conduct patrols in the waters of Diaoyu Islands in the East China Sea.[16]

Command of the South China Sea is an indispensable prerequisite to the realisation Xi Jinping's vaunted rejuvenation of China.

Command, strategic contest, and confidence-building among the disputing territorial claimants in the South China Sea are governing theatres of influence in the epochal Sino-American struggle for prestige and power. To better understand the struggle's regional geopolitical origins, present-day manifestations, and likely trajectories this chapter exam ines the agency of these three influential operational dimensions in the semi-enclosed sea where General Secretary Xi Jinping's Communist Party dictatorship is strategically posturing China as the preponderant power and ASEAN, the USA, and their allies and partners are concerting to maintain the rules-based international order.

Command

Maritime power is the ability to apply maritime capabilities at and from the sea to influence the behaviour of policy executives and military commanders and the course of international relations. Maritime diplomacy is the use of maritime power to support, persuade, deter, or compel.[17] East-West seaborne trade generates global wealth. A nation's maritime power reflects its economic power and prestige. Consequently, a preponderant power will strive to command the East-West joining South China Sea and its Malacca, Sunda, Lombok, and Makassar straits: Chinese (Sung 960–1279, Yuan 1279–1368, and Ming 1368–1644), Iberian (1511–1640), Dutch (1640–1780), British (1780–1942), and American (1945–).[18] Albeit temporarily, the country holding the prestige of command in the South China Sea has often steered the course of history in the Indo-Pacific. Since the era of John Selden (1584–1654) and Huig de Groot (1583–1645), preponderant and rising sea powers have struggled via maritime diplomacy, cartographic competition, and juridical lawfare to realise perceived sovereignty rights.[19] D. P. O'Connell described the constant international competition for command:

> The history of the Law of the Sea has been dominated by a central and persistent theme – the competition between the exercise of governmental authority over the sea and the idea of the freedom of the seas. The tension between these has waxed and waned through the centuries, and has reflected the political, strategic, and economic circumstances of each particular age. When one or two great commercial powers have been dominant or have achieved parity of power, the emphasis in practice has lain upon the liberty of navigation and the immunity of shipping from local control; in such cases the seas have been viewed more as strategic than as economic areas of competition. When, on the other hand, great powers have been in decline or have been unable to impose their wills on smaller states, or when an equilibrium of power has been attained between a multiplicity of states, the emphasis has lain upon the protection and preservation of maritime resources, and consequently upon the assertion of local authority over the sea.[20]

British Maritime Doctrine defines command as a perceived or actual "ability to use the sea in its entirety for one's own purposes at any time and deny its use to an adversary."[21] Indeed, the "object of naval warfare must always be directly or indirectly to secure the command of the sea or to prevent the enemy from securing it." Regarding the South China Sea, the second part of Julian Corbett's trenchant proposition

> should be noted with special care in order to exclude a habit of thought, which is one of the commonest sources of error in naval speculation. That error is the very general assumption that if one belligerent loses the command of the sea it passes at once to the other belligerent.[22]

The PLA Navy aims to revise the U.S. Navy's 75-year-old preponderance but that does not necessarily mean that Beijing will thus take command of the South China Sea. Combined with the USA and its allies, the evolving "poison shrimp" strategies of China's concerted smaller neighbours aim to give Beijing a momentous stomach-ache should it resort to war to regain regional command. If the geographically acquisitive Chinese "cow's tongue" laps up the South China Sea by force, it will likely be militarily and politically too poisonous for the PRC to hold down and digest.[23]

Thus Beijing's optimal means of taking command of the South China Sea is via "Three Warfares" (*San Zhong Zhanfa*) operations in the grey zone.[24] Since 2013, in pursuit of its unlawful maritime sovereignty rights claims Beijing has undertaken massive dredging to construct more than 3,000 acres across the South China Sea, destroying coral reefs and fisheries in the process. The PRC has continued to deploy military capabilities on these constructed and internationally disputed features, including by adding sensor arrays, bunkers, ports, and anti-ship and air defence missiles. Beijing has used these outposts as staging grounds for the maritime militia, civilian law enforcement, and PLA Navy joint operations to deter South-East Asian states from accessing offshore resources. The PRC's campaign of coercion to command the South China Sea is threatening regional security and blocking South-East Asian coastal states from accessing a potential $2.5 trillion in oil and natural gas and some of the world's richest fishing grounds.[25]

Command of the South China Sea is among the most prestigious of geographic objectives in the history of global maritime power. Following the Second World War, its strategic significance increased steadily in tandem with ballistic nuclear missile submarines' deterrent power during the Cold War's three proxy wars in Indochina (1946–1954, 1959–1975, and 1978–1991). "To some degree," Warren Cote wrote, "undersea geography is destiny when it comes to hiding and finding nuclear submarines."[26] Chinese naval analysts have long since noted President Dwight Eisenhower's stark warning to Congress during the First Taiwan Strait Crisis (1954–1955). On 24 January 1955, Eisenhower wrote that a loss of the U.S. Navy's primacy in the South China Sea or the East China Sea would severe "the island chain of the Western Pacific that constitutes, for the United States and other free nations, the geographic backbone of their security in that ocean."[27] PLA Navy strategists perceive the USA's command of the First Island Chain as a geostrategic threat to "China's reach to the sea."[28] PLA Navy Senior Captain and Professor, Fang Liang has explicated command's primacy in China's maritime worldview:

> [Command of] China's ocean geography determines its status as a global maritime power. For more than 30 years since the reform and opening-up [initiated by paramount leader Deng Xiaoping], with China's rapid development and substantial increase in its comprehensive strength, other global sea powers' hostility and containment of China have deepened and become tighter and tighter. Moreover, with the rapid growth of China's economy and the increase in its foreign trade, China's dependence on maritime strategic access security has become greater and greater. *Command of the sea has become the focus of the big powers' contest to realise their respective national interests as well as an important bargaining chip to balance and restrain China in the Asia-Pacific region. Therefore, command of the sea has increasingly become an important factor impacting China's security and development.*[29]

During the Sung Dynasty, the Chinese deployed the world's most powerful and technologically advanced navy for a period of more than 500 years. The Sung established China's first permanent national navy as an independent armed service and administered it via a central government agency. Starting in 1132, China's inaugural period of command in the South China Sea was directed by the "Imperial Commissioner's Office for the Control and Organisation of the Coastal Areas," which prosecuted the Sung's regional primacy via a navy of 52,000 men.[30] As a comparison of relative sea power, Nicholas Rodger reckons that Great Britain did not properly centralise the administration of the Royal Navy until 1545.[31] China's command of the South China Sea continued through the Yuan Dynasty (1279–1368).

The Ming Dynasty (1368–1644) achieved the acme of Chinese global sea power but eventually deliberately withdrew its prestigious battle fleets from the ocean with a self-defeating national isolation strategy. Before China's temporary turn to autarkic isolationism, the Ming undertook seven trans-oceanic voyages between 1405 and 1433. Emperor Yong-Le appointed grand imperial eunuch, Admiral Zheng He as commander of the world's most powerful navy. Admiral He's first expeditionary fleet was comprised of 317 ships and 27,870 men.[32] Burnished by the Middle Kingdom's magnificent culture and the putative political righteousness of the Emperor, the Ming Dynasty deployed the preponderant sea power of its blue-water battle fleet to realise China's imperial interests across the Indo-Pacific.[33] "On arriving in the outlying countries," the Admiral wrote,

> those among the barbarian kings who obstructed the transforming influence [of China's command of the sea] and were disrespectful, we captured alive. We exterminated the brigands who indulged in violence and plunder. Consequently, the sea-route [through the South China Sea] was purified and tranquilised.[34]

And thus Admiral Zheng He re-asserted China's prestigious command of the sea.

The early maritime imperialism of the Ming dynasty had its equivalent in the subsequent colonial projections of European sea powers. Commencing with Portugal's capture of Melaka in 1511, Spain, the Netherlands, Great Britain, and France all took partial command of the South China Sea via colonial maritime territories in East and South-East Asia. Following the Ming's Dynasty's decision to withdraw its command of the South China Sea and a corollary flourishing of Persian and Arab merchant seafarers, the leading European maritime nations established colonies in South-East Asia by imposing the "modern" concept of sovereign rights via overwhelming sea power.[35] European colonial maritime power was, however, insufficient to challenge China's command of the South China Sea until the 19th century.[36] All European and South-East Asia envoys underwent the formalities of obeisance to the emperor of China, the "tributary system," and the Chinese elite's hegemonic worldview. The Middle Kingdom's perceived command of the South China Sea stood unchallenged until 1793 when the Royal Navy's preponderant power projection enabled Lord Macartney to refuse the symbolic kowtow of "three kneeling and nine prostrations."[37] Until Lord Macartney, Britain's first ambassador to China no European or Asian country had publicly questioned the emperor-state's imperial belief in Chinese global superiority.

Command of the South China Sea enabled Britain to build the port city of Singapore, seize Melaka from the Dutch in 1795, prosecute the Opium Wars (1839–1842, 1856–1860) against China, and establish the colonial dominion of Hong Kong as well as protectorates in Malaya and Borneo. Britain's rampant maritime colonialism spurred the Dutch to cluster their colonies in the Netherlands East Indies, known now as Indonesia. Spain followed with a consolidation of its colonial interests in the Philippines. In 1858, the *Marine Nationale* began France's colonisation of Indochina. French sea power enabled France to lease territory on China's Liaozhou peninsula from the late 19th century until the Second World War. Through most of the colonial period, no sovereignty disputes occurred over the Paracel or Spratly Islands. South China Sea islands stood salient in Asian, American, and European minds mainly as dangers to navigation. Britain formally claimed the Spratly Islands in 1877, but no substantive exercise of sovereignty followed its claim. The Qing Dynasty (1644–1911) was equally negligent of a claim that it made in 1909 to sovereignty over the Paracel Islands.

Japan's victory in the First Sino-Japanese War (1894–1895) thwarted the Qing's attempts to re-establish China as a sea power. Tokyo took possession of Taiwan and the Pescadores

Islands through the Treaty of Shimonoseki and forced the Qing elite to renounce the Korean peninsula. Signed on 17 April 1895, the Treaty ended the warfighting but sowed resilient seeds of enmity and irredentism in Chinese minds. During the Treaty's negotiations, Ambassador Li Jingfang pointedly informed his Japanese interlocutors, "Nothing will so arouse the indignation of the people of China and create in them a spirit of hostility and hatred, as to wrest from their country important portions of their territory."[38] Ambassador Li's observation exerts powerful agency in the First Island Chain today, especially amongst the countries contesting Beijing's illegal claim to sovereignty rights over nearly all the South China Sea. Like other international law-based agreements between imperial China and colonial maritime powers, the Treaty of Shimonoseki is perceived by the Chinese as a manifestation of colonialism, exploitation, and national humiliation; China's imperious sovereignty rights claims in the South China Sea today are perceived similarly by the other claimant countries. In meetings with Chinese military commanders, President Xi Jinping often remarks that he

> cannot help thinking of China's modern history when the country was so weak and destitute that it was for everyone to bully. Foreign aggressors broke China's land and sea defences hundreds of times, plunging the Chinese nation into the abyss of calamity.[39]

Until Xi Jinping's dictatorship over the Chinese Communist Party, East and South-East Asian policymakers had been more concerned with domestic politics, economic growth, and developing post-colonial regional command than juridical rulings from the United Nations Convention on the Law of the Sea (UNCLOS) arbitral tribunal.[40] Nearly half of China's elite now perceive the agency of international historical grievance regarding command in the South China Sea and colonial-era exploitation as the most probable catalyst to conflict in the First Island Chain.[41] The 2016 UNCLOS arbitral tribunal ruling against the PRC's unlawful sovereignty rights claims in the South China Sea is concerting the other claimant countries with ASEAN, the USA, and their allies and partners in opposition to the Chinese Communist Party's perceived imperialism in the First Island Chain.[42]

Strategic contest

Today's international flux and strategic contest are in part born of the post-Cold War decline in the USA's maritime power relative to the PRC's. According to the best-informed primary source-based report in the public domain,

> The PRC has the largest navy in the world, with an overall battle force of approximately 350 ships and submarines including over 130 major surface combatants. In comparison, the U.S. Navy's battle force is approximately 293 ships as of early 2020.[43]

The potential for the epochal Sino-American struggle to devolve into direct or proxy conflict is greatest in the South China Sea, but dangerous corollary belligerent dynamics are apparent in Russia's and Iran's respective maritime areas of influence.[44] For good or bad in war or peace, nature fills strategic vacuums in power, politics, trade, and geography. In 1975, Indonesia's foreign minister Adam Malik observed,

> South-East Asia is one region in which the presence and interests of most major powers converge, politically as well as physically. The frequency and intensity of policy interactions among them, as well as their dominant influence on the countries in the region,

> cannot but have a direct bearing on political realities. In face of this, the smaller nations of the region have no hope of ever making any impact on this pattern of dominant influence of the big powers, unless they act collectively and until they develop the capacity to forge among themselves an area of internal cohesion, stability, and common purpose.[45]

Geopolitical strategic contest at sea fuses the practice of politics and maritime diplomacy with the command of geography. A process now manifest in the international struggle for prestige and power in the South China Sea, the global ocean's most contested territory.[46] Politics exert relatively little influence at the tactical level of warfighting but are a governing agent of influence at the strategic level of planning and positioning for war. In peacetime, sentient states build effective deterrence by planning for war and pre-positioning armed services in strategic geography to maximise opportunities for victory in the most likely future conflicts. Effective deterrence convinces "a potential aggressor that the consequences of coercion or armed conflict would outweigh the potential gains. This requires the maintenance of a credible military capability and strategy with the clear political will to act."[47] Under Xi Jinping's dictatorial rule over the Chinese Communist Party, the PRC's perceived relative military capability and political will to act has surpassed the USA's in the South China Sea.

Deng Xiaoping and Liu Huaqing, the founding fathers of the PRC's whole-of-state national maritime security strategy grasped the strategic opportunity created by U.S. Navy's withdrawal from the South China Sea at the end of the Second Indochina War.[48] In January 1974, Minister of Defence and Vice-Chair of the Central Military Commission General Ye Jianying and Deng Xiaoping jointly commanded the PLA Navy's occupation of the Paracel Islands; the operation's success empowered Deng during his political resurrection in the Chinese Communist Party.[49] From Beijing's standpoint, the extent of Chinese territory encroached upon by other claimant states in the South China Sea includes Vietnam, 1,170,000 square kilometres; the Philippines, 620,000 square kilometres; Malaysia, 170,000 square kilometres; Brunei, 50,000 square kilometres; and Indonesia, 35,000 square kilometres.[50]

The ratification of UNCLOS in 1982 appeared to weaken Beijing's campaign for command in the South China Sea. According to the Convention, the only basis for a lawful claim to the continental shelf at the South China Sea's centre is legitimate possession of one of the Spratly Islands. Of the six claimants, only Bandar Seri Begawan and Beijing did not occupy any features in the Spratly Islands. Chinese naval and scientific vessels began probing surveys of the Spratly Islands in 1987. The surveying operations increased after General Secretary Gorbachev's momentous speech in Vladivostok on 28 July 1986 announcing the Soviet Union's strategic disengagement from South-East Asia. Corollary reductions in Soviet military and economic support precluded Hanoi from continuing its war against the ASEAN-USA-PRC supported Khmer Rouge.[51] Following the withdrawal of Soviet support, Hanoi was dangerously isolated in face of the tacit alliance between Beijing, Washington, and ASEAN. In March 1988, the Soviet Union's disengagement enabled the PLA Navy's occupation of several features in the Spratly Islands. One of the features was close to an island occupied by Vietnamese maritime forces. In the ensuing sea battle, three PLA Navy frigates sunk three Vietnam People's Navy transport vessels and killed 74 Vietnamese sailors and soldiers.

Beijing's ratification of the PRC Territorial Waters Law on 25 February 1992 reiterated its claim to the South China Sea and mandated China's armed forces to fiercely defend all claimed Chinese maritime territory. Article 2 of this legislation specifically identifies both the Paracel and Spratly Island archipelagos as PRC territory.[52] The dissonance between UNCLOS and the PRC's Territorial Waters Law produced widespread international alarm. Concern at Beijing's unlawful breach of UNCLOS grew on 8 February 1995 when Chinese maritime forces ousted a Philippines Marine Corps unit from their base on Mischief Reef in the Spratly Islands. Beijing's forceful intervention had a direct bearing on the 1951 Mutual Defence Treaty between the USA and the Philippines.

Three decades after the West squandered the opportunity created by the Cold War's negotiated conclusion, Beijing, Moscow, and Tehran are now concerted strategic rivals of liberal democracy, deliberately divergent from the USA-led rules-based international order that heretofore prevented the outbreak of a third world war.[53] In 2019, the *Worldwide Threat Assessment of the U.S. Intelligence Community* found that

> China and Russia are more aligned than at any point since the mid-1950s and the relationship is likely to strengthen in the coming year... As China and Russia seek to expand their global influence, they are eroding once well-established security norms and increasing the risk of regional conflicts.[54]

Inaugural Sino-Russian naval exercises took place in the East China Sea in 1999 and the first in the South China Sea occurred in 2016.[55] In 2019, the PRC and Russia began joint air operations in and around Taiwan's airspace.[56] The Iranian Navy joined its Chinese and Russian counterparts in trilateral naval exercises in the Mediterranean in 2015, the Baltic Sea in 2017, and the Persian Gulf and the Indian Ocean in 2019. Security in the South China Sea, "the geographic backbone" of the Indo-Pacific's 75-year-old rules-based international system is clearly undermined by the decline in the USA's sea power relative to the PRC's.[57] According to Admiral Philip Davidson, today's commander of U.S. forces in the Indo-Pacific, "China is now capable of controlling the South China Sea in all scenarios short of war with the United States."[58] In July 2020, the Indo-Pacific Command reported, "The greatest danger for the United States is the erosion of conventional deterrence. Without a valid and convincing conventional deterrent, China and Russia will be emboldened to take action in the region to supplant U.S. interests."[59]

Leaders in China, Russia, and Iran aspire to secure their respective sea and land frontiers within spheres of influence and to crush perceived domestic threats to their putative political mandates via dictatorship and unlimited authoritarianism.[60] In rejuvenating the regional maritime imperialism of the Sung, Yuan, and Ming dynasties, Xi Jinping's signature One Belt, One Road campaign is laying strategic logistical foundations for the PRC's sphere of influence. Beijing aspires to extend its influence in the South China Sea through the Malacca Strait and into the Indian Ocean.[61] Gargantuan in its geopolitical ambition, One Belt, One Road is unprecedented in history. Command in the South China Sea is an indispensable prerequisite to realising Beijing's governing objective of gaining global prestige and influence via regional preponderance.[62] One Belt, One Road's massive overseas investments maximise Beijing's power via its correlate influence in participating economies and geostrategic economic corridors. The USA's belated implementation of the "Asia Reassurance Initiative Act" (4 December 2018) and the Defence Department's associated "Indo-Pacific Strategy" (1 June 2019) are manifestations of Washington's reaction to One Belt, One Road. Having announced his regional courtship campaign in September and October 2013 in respective twin speeches in Nur-Sultan, Kazakhstan, and Jakarta, Indonesia, President Xi's regional policy is at least six years ahead of Washington's. Beijing claims that Xi's $1.3 trillion multi-year strategic courtship has now engaged more than 60 countries, including to varying degrees all ten ASEAN members; in comparison, when Secretary of State Mike Pompeo announced that Washington would increase its own investments in the Indo-Pacific he offered a relatively meagre $113 million.[63] A widespread regional backlash followed the exposure of One Belt and One Road's "debt-trap diplomacy" after Sri Lanka's chastening experience with the ports of Hambantota and Colombo.[64] But in accord with widespread "hedging" policies, Huong Le Thu found that most regional governments "remain open to Chinese investment, albeit with a heightened degree of caution."[65]

For a brief period in the aftermath of the ideology rooted Cold War and its attendant regional proxy conflicts, global commerce seemed to supersede geopolitics as the governing dimension of the strategic contest in the South China Sea. But exactly three months after *al-Qaeda*'s 9/11 terrorist attacks, China joining the World Trade Organisation on 11 December 2001 marked the zenith in the delightful vision of an increasingly open Chinese economy steering the PRC incrementally towards integration into a liberal international order. In 1992, Indonesia's Foreign Minister, Ali Alatas presciently voiced the ASEAN member states' common concern at the "security disequilibrium" that would follow if the USA's maritime power was subject to a relative decline in the South China Sea.[66] Singapore led the subsequent public and private strategic policy efforts to facilitate the U.S. Navy's continuing command in the South China Sea. "If the [USA] packs up," Le Kuan Yew observed,

> then all the ancient suspicions and animosities between Japan and China, Japan and Korea, Korea and Japan, and the fears of ASEAN for China and Japan will shift the focus from the positive we've achieved to defence and security, which is a zero-sum game.[67]

As foreseen by sentient South-East Asian statesmen, a rampant Sino-American strategic contest is now the most dangerous agent of influence on the regional competition for command and sovereignty rights in the South China Sea.

Building confidence and trust

Contemporary confidence-building initiatives are rooted in the international and supranational efforts to prevent the transformation of the Cold War into the Third World War. In 1982, a comprehensive study by the United Nations found

> the goal of confidence-building measures is to contribute to, reduce, or in some cases even eliminate the causes for mistrust, fear, tensions, and hostilities, all of which are significant factors in the continuation of the international arms build-up in various regions and, ultimately, also on a world-wide scale.[68]

Framed by the Sino-American strategic contest, Brunei, the PRC, the Republic of China, Indonesia, Malaysia, the Philippines, and Vietnam are contesting territory and sovereignty rights in the South China Sea and spurring a corollary arms build-up. To offset Beijing's "unilateral actions, power-based coercion, violation of international law, militarisation, change in the status quo, and infringement upon Vietnam's sovereignty, sovereign rights, and jurisdiction as provided in international law," Hanoi is forging impressive strategic partnerships with old and new friends including Australia, India, France, Japan, the United Kingdom, and the USA.[69]

Nonetheless, the potential is growing rapidly for sub-war engagement in the grey zone to spark a military conflict. All the contestant nations publicly support the common objectives of avoiding conflict and preventing war. Yet 30 years' worth of intra-regional and bilateral confidence-building measures failed to correct the conflict-making dynamic created by "China's occupation and militarisation as well as related activities in the South China Sea, along with the U.S. Freedom of Navigation Operations and other powers' similar actions."[70]

In July 2010, an extraordinarily acrimonious ASEAN Regional Forum meeting revealed the dangerous dearth in confidence and trust among the claimant states and a rising potential for conflict. In the preceding year, Beijing had declared to the United Nations via a *note verbale* the PRC's "indisputable sovereignty over the islands in the South China Sea and adjacent waters," and that it "enjoys sovereign rights and jurisdiction over the relevant waters as well as the seabed and subsoil thereof."[71] Neither "adjacent waters" nor "relevant waters" are terms found in the UNCLOS, nor does either term have meaning in international law. In July 2012, disagreement over how to constructively militate against the PRC's imperious regional posture prevented ASEAN's annual forum from issuing a post-meeting joint communiqué for the first time in its 45-year history.

After Xi Jinping assumed office as General Secretary in November 2012, Beijing began building forward military bases in the South China Sea. Through 2015, China transformed various reefs into manmade islands, thereby causing massive marine pollution and environmental damage.[72] Subsequently, the Chinese army, marine, and naval forces constructed more military facilities on the proliferating manmade islands, with several bases including hangars, barracks, underground fuel, and water storage facilities, and bunkers to house offensive and defensive systems.[73] These actions are clearly discordant with the unequivocal commitment President Xi Jinping made on 25 September 2015 in the Rose Garden of the White House when he said that the PRC would not "pursue militarization" in the South China Sea.[74] Moreover, Beijing continued its campaign to command the South China Sea despite the UNCLOS Permanent Court of Arbitration's judgement on 12 July 2016 against the PRC's territorial claim, which voided its governing concept of "historic" maritime sovereignty rights.[75]

A conflictual legacy from Eastern and Western colonialism, Beijing's illegal claim to sovereignty rights in the South China Sea is a primary generator of struggles for command, territory, and freedom of navigation in the First Island Chain.[76] In 2010, at the acrimonious ASEAN Regional Forum meeting in Hanoi, 12 foreign ministers asked their Chinese colleague to justify Beijing's unlawful claim to the South China Sea. Glaring across the table at his concerted counterparts, Yang Jiechi bluntly responded, "China is a big country and other countries are small countries and that is just a fact." Moreover, Yang imperiously warned China's regional neighbours to refrain from joining "a cabal organised by an outside power."[77] Reviewing the Obama Administration's regionally well-received rebalancing of the USA's maritime power in the Indo-Pacific, Secretary of State Hillary Clinton emphasised that freedom of navigation is a vital American national interest. Washington opposed the use of force to settle disputes over sovereignty rights and stood ready to facilitate talks on implementing the "Declaration on the Conduct of Parties in the South China Sea;" the agreement drawn up by ASEAN and Beijing in 2002 to manage the sovereignty rights disputes, which the two sides have singularly failed to implement for the past 18 years. The Declaration contains various practical confidence-building measures developed during a series of track 1.5 workshops that started in 1990.[78] Outputs from this constructive work and future confidence-building fora have been undermined severely by the South China Sea's transformation into the primary maritime theatre of Sino-American strategic contest.

Lee Kuan Yew observed that the rancorous Forum in 2010 marked the beginning of a "decades-long" struggle between Washington and Beijing for preponderance in the South China Sea and across the Indo-Pacific region. Regrettably, the subsequent decade proved the veracity of Mr. Lee's formidable foresight. "Unipolarity is over," according to Graham Allison,

> and with it the illusion that other nations would simply take their assigned place in a U.S.-led international order. For the United States [and its allies and partners in the

South China Sea], that will require accepting the reality that there are spheres of influence in the world today—and that not all of them are American spheres.[79]

Beijing presaged this new global balance when it informed Washington in 2010 via Admiral Thomas Keating, then commander of U.S. armed forces in the Indo-Pacific that the two sea powers should divide the Indo-Pacific into spheres of influence following the first deployments of PLA Navy aircraft carrier battle groups.[80]

Building intra-regional confidence and trust sufficient to deter the proliferation of threats to peace in the world's most contested sea is an urgent and globally significant objective.[81] But deterrence of conflict during the PRC's destabilising ascent to regional preponderance requires conception and conduct of effective policies for confidence-building, deterrence, and maritime diplomacy. Hard questions arise from a survey of the well-intended but serially breached outputs from the past three decades' extensive regional confidence-building efforts. Beijing and Washington and their respective allies and partners are today in fierce contest over different perceptions of freedom of navigation, sovereignty rights, and other fundamental provisions in UNCLOS. Led by the USA, Western maritime powers are struggling to defend freedoms of navigation whereas many Asian countries are simultaneously hedging and seeking restrictions on these freedoms within their littoral waters.[82]

This challenging situation prompts various questions and concomitant observations:

- firstly, can conflict in the South China Sea be deterred absent common understanding or at least agreement on practical measures to mitigate the risks of flashpoint incidents?[83]
- UNCLOS (1982), ASEAN Declaration on the Conduct of Parties in the South China Sea (2002), Code for Unplanned Encounters at Sea (2014), as well as the Sino-American bilateral Military Maritime Consultative Agreement (1998), Rules of Behaviour for Safety of Air and Maritime Encounters (2013), and the Notification of Major Military Activities (2014) are all significant maritime confidence-building measures. Yet having ratified UNCLOS and agreed to uphold the above agreements, why is Beijing repeatedly violating the letter and spirit of them in the Spratly, Paracel, and Natuna Island archipelagos? Since December 2019, Indonesia, Malaysia, the Philippines, and Vietnam each submitted *notes verbale* to the United Nations rejecting the PRC's nine-dash line and attendant claims to "historic rights" in the South China Sea as breaching UNCLOS.[84]
- The Sino-American agreements on the conduct of ships and aircraft are aspirational rather than obligatory, and subjective rather than explicit. Why are non-naval assets overlooked by the unplanned encounters code as well as other agreements?
- In support of Beijing's campaign to command the South China Sea, Chinese fishing fleets have conducted multiple coercive sub-war influence operations in coordination with the Chinese People's Armed Police Force Coast Guard Corps and maritime China Militia under the People's Liberation Army (PLA) Navy's communication network and chain of command.[85] On 22 June 2020, the PRC adopted a revised law to centralise the Communist Party of China Central Committee's and Central Military Commission's command over the military including the Coast Guard's and China Militia's maritime law enforcement and grey zone operations in the South China Sea.[86]
- Washington postures itself as the world-leading defender of the rules-based international order; why then is the USA not a party to UNCLOS, the primary legal instrument for preserving the freedom of the seas?

- If the USA and the PRC seek to realise regional peace, prosperity, and security in reality as well as rhetoric why do they both not ratify and uphold UNCLOS, and refrain from acts that endanger ships and aircraft of other nations operating in the South China Sea's various Exclusive Economic Zones?
- During the past three decades, Beijing has effectively imposed its command over one of the world's most important strategic waterways. Are ASEAN, the USA, and their allies and partners capable of conceiving and prosecuting a concerted maritime strategy to counter Beijing's command in the South China Sea and deter further Chinese geostrategic acquisitiveness?[87]

To be practical and effective, confidence-building measures and deterrence operations must engage directly the governing threats in a specific situation and thereby reduce the situation's primary security problems.[88]

Conclusion

The USA, China's neighbours in the South China Sea, and many other countries are now acutely alarmed at the steep increase in Beijing's relative maritime power and increasingly imperial regional posture.[89] In a joint *note verbale* submitted to the United Nations on 16 September 2020, France, Germany, and the United Kingdom stated that China's claims to "'historic rights' over the South China Sea waters do not comply with international law and UNCLOS provisions and recall[ed] that the arbitral award in the Philippines v. China case dating to 12 July 2016 clearly confirms this point."[90] A median of 79 percent of people surveyed by the Pew Research Centre in 2019 said that China's growing sea power is bad for their country. In each country surveyed in the First Island Chain, more people named the USA as their most dependable ally in an open-ended question, including around two-thirds in Japan and the Philippines. The opinion of the USA remained positive across the South China Sea despite Donald Trump's maladroit presidency. In general, a lack of confidence in Xi or Trump came with a lack of confidence in the other; relative to many of their less powerful peers, neither leader engendered international prestige.[91]

Nonetheless, despite widespread disenchantment with Beijing's regional bullying, sentient governments know that since the end of the Cold War no country has contributed more to global economic growth than the PRC. "The size of China's displacement of the world balance is such that the world must find a new balance," observed Lee Kuan Yew presciently in 1993. "It is not possible to pretend that this is just another big player. This is the biggest player in the history of the world."[92] The founding fathers of the PRC's maritime security strategy prioritised command of the First Island Chain as a governing national interest.[93] Xi Jinping's vaunted One Belt, One Road campaign and the realisation of the nation-binding China Dream are contingent on the command of the South China Sea. From Beijing's standpoint,

> Offshore defence is the fundamental guarantee of national maritime security. In the 1970s, Deng Xiaoping promulgated [China's] strategy of preparation for combat in the offshore area, since the range of [China's] maritime strategic defence was until then coastal. This was done for the purpose of designating a practical set of strategic guidelines for China's navy and includes the range of sovereignty across China's territorial waters and islands. It also covers all maritime areas over which China has jurisdiction under international sea law. The distinguishing feature of the maritime strategy put forward on this offshore defence basis is the realisation of national unification, giving a

> prominent position to the safeguarding of maritime rights and interests. [The strategy] emphasises that the navy must be able to respond to a regional war at sea, [as well as] to neutralize enemy encroachments. According to the requirements of national interests and the development of naval battle operations capability, the range of naval strategic defence should progressively expand.[94]

Rampant sea power and international status anxiety are concerting the authoritarian worldviews of dictatorships in Beijing, Moscow, and Tehran in common pursuit of their respective maritime spheres of influence.[95] Beijing's early mismanagement of the Covid-19 outbreak, the subsequent global pandemic, and the imposition of draconian security law for Hong Kong that deliberately breaks Deng Xiaoping's nuanced one country two systems agreement with the United Kingdom have magnified the destabilising dynamics of strategic competition in the maritime domain.[96] From Australian Minister for Defence Linda Reynold's well-informed standpoint, the Indo-Pacific region "is now facing the most consequential strategic realignment since the end of World War Two."[97]

This interdisciplinary examination of struggles for prestige and power in the South China Sea has revealed multiple economic, environmental, political, social, and strategic outcomes from the ongoing regional realignment in the balance of maritime power. An empirical analysis of command, strategic contest, and confidence-building shows that the imperfect rule of international law and UNCLOS backed by open alliances of law upholding nations are now the optimal means to realise security, prosperity, and peace.[98] If the ASEAN member countries, PRC, USA, and their allies and partners fail to uphold international law and UNCLOS the regional order will unravel, vitiating the prospects of peace in favour of war.[99]

A careful student of China's and America's prestige and power, Zou Enlai explained to Henry Kissinger

> the objective fact of the largeness of the Chinese nation and Chinese area easily create a tendency to nationalistic sentiments and big-nation chauvinism. Because if there are too strong nationalist feelings, then one will cease to learn from others; one will seal oneself in and believe one is the best or will cease to learn from the strong points of others.[100]

In the conflictual history of the South China Sea, countries with an embarrassment of power but a relatively small amount of prestige are repeatedly myopic regarding equitable policies aimed at building regional security, prosperity, and peace.

Notes

1 Carr, E. H., "Great Britain as a Mediterranean Power," The Gust Foundation Lecture (Nottingham, 1937), p. 10.

2 U.S. Department of Defence (DoD), Secret, "Tran Quang Co's Pentagon Meeting on 26 May 1992," 9 June 1992, Reel 363, pp. 16–18, POW-MIA Document Collection, Library of Congress.

3 U.S. Department of State (DoS), "Maritime Disputes in East Asia," Testimony of Assistant Secretary Daniel R. Russel, Bureau of East Asian and Pacific Affairs before the House Committee on Foreign Affairs Subcommittee on Asia and the Pacific, Washington, DC (2 May 2014); Jenner, C. J., "International Threat-Making in a Semi-enclosed Sea: A Survey of Challenges to Cooperation in the South China Sea, 1949–2014," in Zou, K. ed., *Maritime Cooperation in Semi-enclosed Seas: Asian and European Experiences* (Leiden, 2019), pp. 220–221.

4 Jenner, C. J., and Tran, T. T., "Introduction," in Jenner, C. J. ed., *The South China Sea: A Crucible of Regional Cooperation or Conflict-Making Sovereignty Claims?* (Cambridge, 2018), p. 2.

5 "Indonesia Lodges Strong Protest against China over 'Violation of Sovereignty,'" *Jakarta Post* (1 January 2020).
6 There is a common misconception that most international communications are routed via satellites. In fact, well over 95 percent of this traffic is routed via submarine fibre-optic cables. Data and voice transmission via these cables is cheaper and far quicker than via satellite. Carter, L. et al., *Submarine Cables and the Oceans: Connecting Our World* (Cambridge, 2009), p. 3.
7 U.S. Energy Information Administration, "More Than 30% of Global Maritime Crude Oil Trade Moves through the South China Sea," *Today in Energy* (27 August 2018); United Nations Conference on Trade and Development, *Review of Maritime Transport, 2016* (New York, 2016).
8 Asia-Pacific Fishery Commission, *Regional Overview of Fisheries and Aquaculture in Asia and the Pacific 2012,* (Bangkok, 2013), p. 2.
9 Yang, S. and Geng, Y., "Strategic Thinking on Strengthening Low-Intensity Maritime Rights Defence and National Defence Mobilization," *National Defence* (in Chinese), vol. 1 (2017); Reuters, "Satellites and Seafood: China Keeps Fishing Fleet Connected in Disputed Waters," (27 July 2014).
10 Liu, H., *Memoir of Liu Huaqing* [*Liu Huaqing Huiyilu*] (Beijing, 2004); Defence Intelligence Agency (DIA), Secret, *Biographic Sketch: General Liu Huaqing* (May 1993), National Security Archive.
11 Wang C. ed., *Deng Xiaoping's Modern Military Theory and Practice* [Deng Xiaoping Xiandai Junshi Lilun Yu Shijian], (Nanchang, 1991), pp. 211–222.
12 UK Mission to the UN, *Note Verbale*, UK NV No. 162/20 (16 September 2020); U.S. Department of State, "U.S. Position on Maritime Claims in the South China Sea," Press Statement (13 July 2020); Indonesia Joins Neighbours in Protesting Beijing's Claims in South China Sea," *Jakarta Post* (1 June 2020); Foreign and Commonwealth Office, "Statement by United Kingdom, France, and Germany on the Situation in the South China Sea" (29 August 2019).
13 The State Council Information Office of the PRC, *China's National Defence in the New Era* (Beijing, 2019), pp. 3, 7.
14 "In the Matter of the South China Sea Arbitration" (Phil.-China), PCA Case No. 2013-19, Award (12 July 2016).
15 White House, *The National Security Strategy of the United States of America* (Washington, 2017), p. 25.
16 The State Council Information Office of the PRC, Ibid., p. 7
17 Ministry of Defence, Joint Doctrine Publication 0-10, *UK Maritime Power* (Swindon, 2017), p. 69; Royal Navy, BR 1806, *British Maritime Doctrine* (Norwich, 2004), p. 277.
18 Lo, J. P., *China as a Sea Power, 1127–1368: A Preliminary Survey of the Maritime Expansion and Naval Exploits of the Chinese People During the Southern Sung and Yuan Periods*, ed., B. A. Elleman (Singapore, 2012), pp. 342–343; Mahan, A. T., *The Influence of Sea Power Upon History, 1660–1783* (Louisiana, [1890] 2003).
19 Kittrie, O., *Lawfare: Law as a Weapon of War* (Oxford, 2016); Bederman, D., "The Sea," in Fassbender, B., and Peters, A. eds., *The Oxford Handbook of the History of International Law* (Oxford, 2012), pp. 359–378; Kratoska, P. H., R. Raben, and H. S. Nordholt, *Locating Southeast Asia: Geographies of Knowledge and Politics of Space* (Singapore, 2005); Zou, K., "The Chinese Traditional Boundary Line in the South China Sea and Its Legal Consequences for the Resolution of Boundary Disputes over the Spratly Islands," *International Journal for Marine and Coastal Law*, 14:1 (1999), pp. 27–55.
20 O'Connell, D. P., *The International Law of the Sea*, vol. 1 (Oxford, 1987), p. 1.
21 Royal Navy, B.R. 1806, *British Maritime Doctrine* (Norwich, 2004), p. 246.
22 Corbett, J., *Some Principles of Maritime Strategy* (London, 1911), p. 87.
23 The PRC's Dashed Line claim resembles a giant cow's tongue on maps of the South China Sea.
24 Jenner, C. J., "History, Strategy, and the South China Sea," in Jenner, C. J., ibid. (Cambridge, 2018), pp. 313–14.
25 Rutnam, E., "Sri Lanka Should Engage with China in Ways That Protect Its Sovereignty – [Ambassador] Alaina B. Teplitz," *Daily Mirror* (5 October 2020); Zhang, K., "Cautious Bully: Reputation, Resolve, and Beijing's Use of Coercion in the South China Sea," *International Security*, 44:1 (Summer 2019).
26 Cote, O. R., "Invisible Nuclear-Armed Submarines, or Transparent Oceans? Are Ballistic Missile Submarines Still the Best Deterrent for the United States?" *Bulletin of Atomic Scientists*, 75:1 (January 2019), p. 30.

27 DoS, *Foreign Relations of the United States, 1955–1957*, China, vol. II (Washington, D.C., 1986), document 34; Chen, C. G. and Jiang, S. H., "Taiwan: the Basis of U.S. Geostrategy in the Asia-Pacific Region," *Journal of Jiangxi Institute of Education*, 23 (August 2004), p. 24.
28 Fang, L. and Duan, T. Z., "Characteristics of China's Sea Geostrategic Security and Sea Security Strategy in the New Century," *China Military Science*, (in Chinese) (January 2007), pp. 22, 27, 29.
29 Italics added by translator. Fang, L., *On Maritime Strategic Access* (in Chinese) (Beijing, 2011), p. 10.
30 Lo, J. P., "The Emergence of China as a Sea Power During the Late Sung and Early Yuan Periods," *The Far Eastern Quarterly*, vol. XIV (August 1955), p. 491.
31 Rodger, N. A. M., *The Safeguard of the Sea: A Naval History of Britain, 660–1649* (London, 1997), p. 225.
32 Dreyer, E. L., *Zheng He: China and the Oceans in the Early Ming Dynasty, 1405–1433* (New York, 2006).
33 Wade, G., "The Zheng He Voyages: A Reassessment," ARI WP Series no 31 (October 2004), p. 19.
34 Xiang Da, ed., *History of the Western Regions* (in Chinese) (Beijing, 1961), p. 55; Duyvendak, J. J. L., "The True Dates of the Chinese Maritime Expeditions in the Early Fifteenth Century," *T'oung Pao*, 34:5 (1939), pp. 345–346.
35 Pearson, M. N., "Merchants and States" in Tracy, J. D. ed., *The Political Economy of Merchant Empires: State Power and World Trade 1350–1750* (Cambridge, 1991), pp. 41–116; Churchill, R. R., and Lowe, A. V., *The Law of the Sea* (Manchester, 1999), pp. 3–4.
36 Wang, G., "Early Ming Relations with Southeast Asia: A Background Essay" in Fairbank, J. K. ed., *The Chinese World Order: Traditional China's Foreign Relations* (Cambridge, 1968).
37 Blussé, L., "Chinese Century: The Eighteenth Century in the China Sea Region," *Archipel* 58 (1999).
38 "'Memorandum of the Ambassador Plenipotentiary His Imperial Majesty the Emperor of China in Reply to the Draft of Treaty Proposed by the Plenipotentiaries of His Imperial Majesty the Emperor of Japan,' Shimonoseki, 5 April 1895," in Kajima, M. ed., *The Diplomacy of Japan 1894–1922*, vol. I, *The Sino-Japanese War and Triple Intervention* (Tokyo, 1976), p. 224.
39 "Build Strong Border Defences, Xi Jinping Tells Chinese Military," *The Times of India* (28 June 2014).
40 Jenner, C. J. and Nguyen, H. S., "Domestic Politics: The Overlooked Under-Current in the South China Sea," in Jenner, C. J., ibid. (Cambridge, 2018), pp. 133–148.
41 Green, M. J. et al., *Power and Order in Asia: A Survey of Regional Expectations* (Washington, D.C., 2014), p. 13; Miller, M. C., *Wronged by Empire: Post-imperial Ideology and Foreign Policy in India and China* (Stanford, 2013), pp. 133–134.
42 UK Mission to the UN, Note Verbale, UK NV No. 162/20 (16 September 2020); Storey, I., "As U.S.-China Tensions Rise, What Is the Outlook on the South China Sea Dispute in 2020–21?" *South China Morning Post* (5 September 2020); "Indonesia Joins Neighbours in Protesting Beijing's Claims in South China Sea," *Jakarta Post* (1 June 2020).
43 DoD, *Military and Security Developments Involving the People's Republic of China 2020* (Washington, D.C., 2020), pp. ii, vii, 44–49.
44 Islamic Republic News Agency website in Persian via BBC Monitoring (BBCM), "Iran 'Formulates Important' Military Document with China, Says Commander," (3 December 2019); Mashregh News website in Persian via BBCM, "Senior Islamic Revolutionary Guard Corps Commander Interviewed on Iran, China, Russia Cooperation," (21 September 2019); Esfandiary, D. and Tabatabai, A., *Triple-Axis: China, Russia, Iran and Power Politics* (London, 2018).
45 Malik, A., "Regional Cooperation in International Politics," *Regionalism in South-East Asia* (Jakarta, 1975), pp. 162–163.
46 Mathews, R., and Lozano, A., "Evaluating Motivation and Performance in ASEAN Naval Acquisition Strategy," in Chan, J., and Till, G. ed., *Naval Modernisation in South-East Asia: Nature, Causes and Consequences* (Abingdon, 2014), pp. 57–59; Dzurek, D. J., "The Spratly Islands Dispute: Who's on First?" *Maritime Briefing*, 2:1 (1996), p. 1.
47 Royal Navy, ibid. (Norwich, 2004), p. 253.
48 Jenner, C. J., ibid., (Cambridge, 2018), pp. 308–316.
49 Fan, Y., *Ye Jianying in 1976* (in Chinese) (Beijing, 1990), p. 48.
50 Ni, J. ed. *China Ocean* (Beijing, 1997), p. 368; Liu, H., *Selected Military Writings of Liu Huaqing* (in Chinese) (Beijing, 2008), p. 528. Chen, S., ed., *Collection of Names and Materials on the South China Sea Islands* (Guangzhou, 1987), p. 381.

51 White House, MemCon, Secret, President's meeting with Ambassador Morton Abramowitz, 1 February 1979, Declassified Document Reference System (DDRS); White House, Memcon, Top Secret/Sensitive/Eyes Only, Vice President Walter Mondale's meeting with PRC Vice Premier Deng Xiaoping, 28 August 1979, DDRS.
52 "Law of the People's Republic of China on the Territorial Sea and Contiguous Zone," *People's Daily* (26 February 1992), p. 4, reprinted in *UN Law of the Sea Bulletin*, 21 (1992), pp. 24–27.
53 "Russia, China, Iran Sought to Influence U.S. 2018 Elections: U.S. Spy Chief," *Reuters* (21 December 2018); Esfandiary, D. and Tabatabai, A., *Triple-Axis: China, Russia, Iran and Power Politics* (London, 2018).
54 Office of the Director of National Intelligence, *Worldwide Threat Assessment of the U.S. Intelligence Community* (29 January 2019), p. 4.
55 *Segodnya* newspaper in Russian via BBCM, "First Sino-Russian Naval Exercises" (7 October 1999).
56 Van Oudenaren, J., "Why Are Russian Military Planes Flying Around Taiwan?" *The Diplomat* (16 January 2020).
57 FRUS, 1955–1957, China, vol. II, ibid.
58 Senate Armed Services Committee, Unclassified, "Advance Policy Questions for Admiral Philip Davidson, USN Expected Nominee for Commander, U.S. Pacific Command" (17 April 2018), p. 18.
59 USINDOPACOM, NDAA 202 Section 1253 Assessment (Unclassified version), "Investment Plan for Implementing the National Defense Strategy, Fiscal Years 2022-2026," (Hawaii, 2020) p. 10.
60 Islamic Republic News Agency website in Persian via BBCM, "Iran 'Formulates Important' Military Document with China, Says Commander," (03 December 2019); *Mashregh News* website in Persian via BBCM, "Senior Islamic Revolutionary Guard Corps Commander Interviewed on Iran, China, Russia Cooperation," (21 September 2019).
61 Duchâtel, M., "Overseas Military Operations in Belt and Road Countries: The Normative Constraints and Legal Framework," in N. Rolland ed., *Securing the Belt and Road Initiative: China's Evolving Military Engagement Along the Silk Roads* (Washington, 2019), pp. 7–17.
62 Shambaugh, D., "U.S.-China Rivalry in Southeast Asia: Power Shift or Competitive Coexistence?" *International Security*, 42:4 (Spring 2018), p. 96.
63 "Pompeo Announces $113 Million in New US Initiatives in 'Indo-Pacific,'" *Reuters* (30 July 2018).
64 Lo, K., "Sri Lanka Wants Its 'Debt Trap' Hambantota Port Back. But Will China Listen?" *South China Morning Post* (7 December 2019).
65 Le, T. H., "Southeast Asian Narratives about US–China Competition (Part 1): Choice and Necessity," *The Strategist* (13 November 2019).
66 "ASEAN Member States Agree on U.S. Presence in Region – Alatas," *Business Times* (29 October 1992).
67 "U.S. Holds Key to Asian Security – Lee," *Reuters News Service* (16 May 1993).
68 Department of Political and Security Council Affairs, UN Centre for Disarmament, Report of the Secretary General, *Comprehensive Study on Confidence-Building Measures* (New York, 1982), p. 6.
69 Ministry of National Defence, *2019 Viet Nam National Defence* (Hanoi, 2019), p. 7.
70 Ministry of Defence, *Defence White Paper* (Kuala Lumpur, 2020), p. 21; *Sinar Harian* newspaper website in Malay via BBCM, "Maritime Power Is a Tool to Showcase Strength" (14 January 2020).
71 "People's Republic of China *note verbal*, April 13, 2009, concerning the Republic Act No. 9522: An Act to Amend certain Provisions of Republic Act No. 3046, as amended by Republic Act No. 5446, to Define Archipelagic Baselines of the Philippines, and for Other Purposes, Deposited by the Republic of the Philippines with the Secretary General, May 9, 2009" *Law of the Sea Bulletin*, 70 (New York, 2009), p. 58.
72 Smith L. et al., "Evidence of Environmental Changes Caused by Chinese Island-Building," *Scientific Reports*, 9, article 5295 (2019).
73 "Pentagon Calls Chinese Anti-ship Missile Test in South China Sea 'Disturbing,'" *The Japan Times* (3 July 2019).
74 The White House, Office of the Press Secretary, "Remarks by President Obama and President Xi of the People's Republic of China in Joint Press Conference," Rose Garden (25 September 2015).
75 "In the Matter of the South China Sea Arbitration" (Phil.-China), PCA Case No. 2013-19, Award (12 July 2016), para. 1158.
76 Green, M. J., et al., ibid., p. 13.

77 Bader, J. A., *Obama and China's Rise: An Insider's Account of America's Asia Strategy* (Washington, DC, 2012), p. 105; Pomfret, J., "U.S. Takes a Tougher Tone with China," *Washington Post* (30 July 2010).
78 Shoji, T., "Vietnam, ASEAN, and the South China Sea: Unity or Diverseness?," NIDS *Journal of Defense and Security*, 13 (December 2012), p. 5, fn. 3.
79 Lee, K. Y., "Battle for Pre-eminence," *Forbes* (23 September 2010); Allison, G., "The New Spheres of Influence: Sharing the Globe With Other Great Powers," *Foreign Affairs* (10 February 2020).
80 Kraska, J., ibid. (Oxford, 2011), pp. 325–326.
81 Flournoy, M., "How to Prevent a War in Asia: The Erosion of American Deterrence Raises the Risk of Chinese Miscalculation," *Foreign Affairs* (18 June 2020); Lampton, D. and Wang J., "How to Prevent US-China Rivalry from Turning Southeast Asia into a Conflict Zone," *South China Morning Post* (30 January 2020).
82 Kuik, C. C., "Hedging in Post-Pandemic Asia: What, How, and Why?" The Asan Forum (6 June 2020). Maritime Institute of Malaysia, "Seminar on Foreign Military Activities in Malaysia's EEZ: Issues and Challenges," (14 October 2008); Zou, K., *China's Marine Legal System and the Law of the Sea* (London, 2005), pp. 23–98, 92–95; U.S. DoS, Bureau of Research & Intelligence, "Straight Baselines: Vietnam, Limits in the Seas," 99:9 (12 December 1982).
83 Bateman, W. S., *Freedoms of Navigation in the Asia-Pacific Region: Strategic, Political, and Legal Factors* (London, 2019), p. 78.
84 Storey, I., "As U.S.-China Tensions Rise, What Is the Outlook on the South China Sea Dispute in 2020-21?" *South China Morning Post* (5 September 2020); "Indonesia Joins Neighbours in Protesting Beijing's Claims in South China Sea," *Jakarta Post* (1 June 2020); Kyodo News Service, "Indonesia Steps Up Sea Patrols over Border Intrusion by China" (4 January 2020); Pedrozo, P., "The U.S.-China Incidents at Sea Agreement: A Recipe for Disaster," *Journal of National Security and Law Policy*, 6:207 (2012), pp. 221–223.
85 Japan Ministry of Defence, "China's Activities in the South China Sea" (October 2020), pp. 37–38; Kroodsma, D. A. et al., "Tracking the Global Footprint of Fisheries," *Science*, 359:6378 (23 February 2018), pp. 904–908; Yang S. and Geng Y., supra note 11; Reuters, "Satellites and Seafood: China Keeps Fishing Fleet Connected in Disputed Waters," (27 July 2014).
86 China Global Television Network via BBCM "China Adopts Revised Law Calling for Party's Unified Leadership over Military" (21 June 2020).
87 U.S. Pacific Fleet Public Affairs, "People's Liberation Army Navy lased a U.S. Navy P-8A in Unsafe, Unprofessional Manner," (27 February 2020); "PLA Navy Drill in Pacific Ocean Challenges US Hegemony," *Global Times* (26 February 2020); "Malaysia, China, and Vietnam in 'Dangerous, Ongoing Game of Chicken' in South China Sea," *South China Morning Post* (22 February 2020); Kim, J., and Druckman, D., "Shelved Sovereignty or Invalid Sovereignty? The South China Sea Negotiations, 1992–2016," *The Pacific Review*, 33:1 (2020).
88 Department of Political and Security Council Affairs, ibid., p. 25.
89 Pew Research Centre, *Unfavourable Views of China Reach Historic Highs in Many Countries: Majorities Say China Has Handled COVID-19 Outbreak Poorly* (6 October 2020); U.S. Department of State, "U.S. Position on Maritime Claims in the South China Sea," Press Statement (13 July 2020); "ASEAN Takes Position Versus China's Vast Historical Sea Claims," *Associated Press* (27 June 2020); "ASEAN Reaffirms International Law as Basis for Sovereignty in South China Sea," *The Jakarta Post* (18 January 2020); "Beijing Must Not Be Allowed to Bully Southeast Asian Nations in the South China Sea," *South China Morning Post* (13 January 2020); "China's Drive for Hegemony Meets Resistance: Diplomatic Failure in the Indo-Pacific," *Asia Times* (14 June 2020).
90 UK Mission to the UN, ibid.
91 Pew Research Centre, Spring 2019 ibid; Pew Research Center, "Around the World, More See the U.S. Positively Than China, But little confidence in Trump or Xi" (10 January 2020).
92 Kristof, N. D., "The Rise of China," *Foreign Affairs* (November/December 1993).
93 Xu Qi, supra note 3, pp. 76–77.
94 Xu Qi, ibid.
95 Press Trust of India, "Indo-Pacific Concept a Rejection of Spheres of Influence: UN External Affairs Minister S. Jaishankar" (20 November 2020); Watkins, S., "PRC Aims to Build Intelligence Hub in Iran Under 25-Year Deal," OilPrice.com (8 September 2020); Islamic Republic News Agency website in Persian via BBCM, "Iran 'Formulates Important' Military Document with China, Says Commander," (03 December 2019); Mashregh News website in Persian via BBCM,

"Senior Islamic Revolutionary Guard Corps Commander Interviewed on Iran, China, Russia Cooperation," (21 September 2019); Esfandiary, D. and Tabatabai, A., *Triple-Axis: China, Russia, Iran and Power Politics* (London, 2018).

96 "China's Draconian Security Law for Hong Kong Buries One Country, Two Systems," *The Economist* (2 June 2020); BBCM, "Covid-19 Analysis: Beijing Dials Up South China Sea Assertiveness Amid Pandemic" (1 May 2020); "Leaked Five Eye Report Lays Out Case Against China Bat Virus Program," *The Daily Telegraph* (4 May 2020); "Covid-19 Geopolitics: Russian, Chinese Defence Chiefs Discuss Cooperation," *Ria Novosti* in Russian via BBCM (8 May 2020); USNI News, "U.S. Sends Warships on Patrol Near South China Sea Standoff," (8 May 2020): "Autocrats Denounce America: China, Russia, and Iran Exult at America's Turmoil," *The Economist* (13 June 2020).

97 Australian Government, Department of Defence, Minister for Defence Linda Reynolds, "Speech - Australian Strategic Policy Institute" (2 June 2020).

98 Lee, H. L., "The Endangered Asian Century: America, China, and the Perils of Confrontation," *Foreign Affairs* (July/August 2020).

99 Clauset, A., "Trends and Fluctuations in the Severity of Interstate Wars," *Science Advances*, 4:2 (February 2018); Vasquez, J., "Mapping the Probability of War and Analysing the Prospects of Peace: The Role of Territorial Disputes," *Conflict Management and Peace Science*, 18:2 (2001), pp. 145–174; Vasquez, J. and Henehan, M. T., ibid.

100 Foreign Relations of the United States, 1969–1976, Volume XVIII, *China, 1973–1976*, Memorandum of Conversation, 2:43–7:15 p.m., Beijing (18 February 1973), Zhou Enlai, Premier, PRC State Council; Dr Henry Kissinger, Assistant to the President for National Security Affairs, et al., p. 139.

APPENDIX

A chronology of contest in the South China Sea, 1877–2019

- **1877**

  For centuries fishermen from all the littoral states, including China, operated in the South China Sea, and some camped periodically on a few of the islands. During the nineteenth century, several countries conducted hydrographic surveys of the area and published maps and charts. Great Britain made the first modern legal claim to the Spratly Islands in 1877.
- **1946**

  In 1946, the Republic of China (ROC) established a garrison on Woody Island in the Paracels and Taiping Island (Itu Aba) in the Spratlys. Then in 1947, the Chinese Government drew up The South China Sea Islands Location Map *that marked out a large U-shaped claim to nearly all the South China Sea with an eleven-dash line.*
- **1949**

  Following the Chinese Communist Party's victory over the Kuomintang and the establishment of the People's Republic of China (PRC) in 1949, Chinese Premier Zhou Enlai reduced the ROC's eleven-dash line to a nine-dash line that encompassed essentially the same area.
- **1950**

  After the People's Liberation Army drove the ROC's forces out of Hainan, the National Revolutionary Army garrisons in the Paracels and Spratlys withdrew to Taiwan.
- **30 August 1951**

  The US and the Philippines sign a mutual defence treaty.
- **June 1952**

  Taiwan reoccupies Taiping, the biggest of the Spratly Islands archipelago.
- **1953**

  The PRC drops its claims in the Gulf of Tonkin, revising the eleven dashed line to nine.
- **1956**

  In 1956, the Democratic Republic of Vietnam formally accepted that the Paracel and Spratly Island groups were historically Chinese. However, in that same year, the Republic of Vietnam announced that it had annexed the Paracel and Spratly archipelagos and garrisoned Prattle Island (Shanhu) in the Paracels. The PRC concurrently established a garrison on Woody Island (Yongxing) in the Paracels, and Taiwan again deployed troops to Taiping Island in the Spratlys.

- **1970**
  In 1970, the PRC extended its presence in the South China Sea by establishing a garrison in the Amphitrite Group in the Paracel Islands.
- **1970–1971**
  The Philippines occupied five of the Spratly Islands and claimed the western part of the group.
- **19 January 1974**
  Nearly a year after the US ends its involvement in the Vietnam War, PRC forces occupy the western portion of the Paracel Islands. South Vietnamese troops retreat south and establish their first permanent station on the Spratly Islands. Beijing builds military facilities on Woody Island (Yongxing), the largest of the Paracel Islands.
- **11 March 1976**
  The Philippines makes its first oil discovery in the Northwest Palawan Basin in the Nido oilfield off the Palawan Islands. The discovery follows Manila passing the Philippines Oil Exploration and Development Act in 1972.
- **14 March 1988**
  China and Vietnam clash on the Johnson Reef in the first such armed conflict over the Spratlys. The PLA Navy sinks three Vietnamese vessels, killing 74 sailors. The incident follows Beijing's establishment of a physical presence on Fiery Cross Reef in the Spratly Islands in January 1987. Vietnam occupies several other reefs to monitor Chinese activity.
- **25 February 1992**
  China passes the Law on the Territorial Sea and the Contiguous Zone.
- **January 1996**
  In China's first military conflict with any Association of Southeast Asian Nations (ASEAN) member other than Vietnam, three PLA Navy vessels fight a Philippine Navy gunboat near Capones Island in the Mischief Reef. Part of the Spratly Islands, it is claimed by Manila. The Mischief Reef incident revives US-Philippine military ties. In mid-1996, Manila and Beijing sign a non-binding code of conduct that calls for peaceful resolution of their territorial dispute.
- **1996**
  China, Malaysia, and Brunei join the United Nations Convention on the Law of the Sea (UNCLOS).
- **19 January 1998**
  The PRC and the USA sign the first-ever bilateral military deal between the two countries in the form of a Military Maritime Consultative Agreement. The accord aims to promote defence dialogue between the two navies.
- **1 April 2001**
  A US Navy EP-3 surveillance plane collides with a PLA Navy F-8 fighter jet over the South China Sea. The USN crew makes an emergency landing with their damaged plane onto the PLA's Lingshui airfield on Hainan Island. The PRC detains the 24 crew members for 11 days and asks the USA to "apologise." The US expresses "regret" at the loss of the life of the PLA Airforce pilot.
- **4 November 2002**
  The PRC and the 10 ASEAN countries agree in Phnom Penh on the Declaration on the Conduct of Parties in the South China Sea. The non-binding code of conduct follows six years of negotiations and aspires to create practical guidelines for conflict resolution. China's signing marks the first time that it has accepted a multilateral approach to resolving the South China Sea disputes.
- **6 May 2009**
  Malaysia and Vietnam file a joint submission to the UN Commission on the Limits of the Continental Shelf to extend their continental shelves, creating disputes over maritime sovereignty in

the South China Sea. The PRC terms it an infringement upon its "indisputable sovereignty" over the islands in the South China Sea.

- **23 July 2010**
  US Secretary of State Hillary Clinton reiterates Washington's neutrality on sovereignty in the South China Sea in a speech at an acrimonious Asian Regional Forum meeting in Hanoi. Amid Vietnam's attempts to internationalise the dispute PRC Foreign Minister Yang Jiechi imperiously warns his regional neighbours to refrain from joining "a cabal organised by an outside power."
- **17 November 2011**
  US President Barack Obama says in a speech to the Australian parliament that his country will "pivot" its strategic attention to the Asia-Pacific. The Obama administration announces that reductions in US defence spending would not affect commitments to the region. Simultaneous negotiations for a Trans-Pacific Partnership exclude the PRC.
- **February 2012**
  Chinese Foreign Ministry spokesman Hong Lei states that "no country including China has claimed sovereignty over the entire South China Sea," putatively moderating the nine-dash line claim.
- **21 June 2012**
  Vietnam's National Assembly approves a new maritime law claiming sovereignty over the Spratly and Paracel Islands. China terms the law null and void and raises the administrative status of the disputed islands to prefecture level.
- **12 July 2012**
  Disagreement over how to deal with the PRC's claim to the South China Sea prevented the ASEAN Regional Forum from issuing a post-meeting joint communiqué for the first time in its 45-year history.
- **22 January 2013**
  Beijing refuses to participate in the Philippines-initiated formal arbitration of China's maritime claims in the South China Sea. The arbitration goes on under the UNCLOS with an Annex VII Arbitral Tribunal at The Hague.
- **September 2013**
  President Xi Jinping unveils the $1.3 trillion One Belt, One Road Campaign.
- **23 November 2013**
  China announces an air defence identification zone in the East China Sea surrounding the Diaoyu/Senkaku Islands. It claims the right to monitor and intercept aircraft in the zone.
- **5 December 2013**
  The USS Cowpens is forced to take emergency evasive manoeuvres to avoid a collision with a PLA ship. The US missile-carrying cruiser was observing China's aircraft carrier, the Liaoning, which was on its first voyage in the South China Sea.
- **28 April 2014**
  Barack Obama visits Manila to sign a 10-year US-Philippines Enhanced Defence Cooperation Agreement, which provides for rotation of more US troops and ships.
- **May-July 2014**
  State-owned energy firm China National Petroleum Corporation moves an oil rig near the Paracel Islands on 2 May. The drilling operation, known as the Zhongjiannan Project, prompts anti-Chinese protests in Vietnam and a series of face-offs between Chinese and Vietnamese vessels in the area. Chinese ships remove the rig from the area on 15 July after completing the drilling operation.

- **19 August 2014**
  A PLA Airforce fighter jet intercepts a US Navy P-8 Poseidon anti-submarine and reconnaissance plane about 135 miles east of the PRC island of Hainan.
- **September 2015**
  China completes a 3,125m runway on Fiery Cross Reef.
- **2 October 2014**
  The US State Department eases its embargo on selling arms to Vietnam.
- **November 2015**
  The PRC accuses the Philippines of breaching the 2002 code of conduct between China and ASEAN nations. Arguments commence against the PRC's claims to the South China Sea in its absence from the arbitration tribunal at The Hague.
- **2016**
  Inaugural Sino-Russian naval exercises take place in the South China Sea.
- **19 May 2016**
  Days before US President Obama's trip to Asia from 21–28 May, which included a G-7 summit in Japan and his first trip to Vietnam, Pentagon reports an "unsafe" interception of a US surveillance aircraft by PLA Airforce jets over the South China Sea. Obama announces lifting of the 50-year arms embargo on Vietnam.
- **14 June 2016**
  The ASEAN countries fail to agree to express "serious concerns" over developments in the South China Sea.
- **12 July 2016**
  The Annex VII Arbitral Tribunal at The Hague rules in favour of the Philippines and declares China's historic rights within the "nine-dash line" to be inconsistent with the UNCLOS. China says it "neither accepts nor recognises" the ruling.
- **20 October 2018**
  The ASEAN defence ministers ink the world's first multilateral air guidelines aimed at ensuring safe passage for military aircraft and for ships over the high seas. The countries hope to persuade others including the US and China to subscribe to the new non-binding air code.
- **22 27 October 2018**
  The navies of PRC and ASEAN countries hold their first-ever maritime exercise off the coast of China's Guangdong Province in an effort to widen cooperation amid negotiations over a South China Sea code of conduct. This is also the first time ASEAN holds such an exercise with any other country.
- **18 November 2018**
  At the APEC summit held in Port Moresby, as a result of deep divisions between the USA and PRC over trade and other issues, regional leaders fail to agree on a final communique for the first time in the summit's history. US Vice-President Mike Pence says that differences between Beijing and Washington go "beyond that to freedom of navigation in the seas."
- **20 November 2018**
  President Xi Jinping pays the first state visit by a Chinese head of state to the Philippines in 13 years, two years after his Philippine counterpart Rodrigo Duterte visited Beijing and promised to set aside the 2016 international tribunal ruling that ruled against China's expansive claim over the South China Sea. Beijing and Manila agree to maintain "freedom of navigation in and over-flight above the South China Sea... by peaceful means... in accordance with universally recognised principles of international law, including the Charter of the United Nations and the 1982 UNCLOS."

- **2019**
  The PRC and Russia begin joint air operations in and around Taiwan's airspace.
- **23 April 2019**
  A Philippine Navy vessel participates in an international fleet review in China marking the 70th anniversary of the founding of the PLA Navy. In January, three Chinese navy ships visited the Philippines. Port calls resumed between the two countries in July 2017, seven years after stopping in 2010 amid worsening disputes over South China Sea islands.
- **18 November 2019**
  ASEAN Defence Ministers issue joint statement warning against big power rivalry and growing threats to security in Southeast Asia.
- **30 December 2019**
  Indonesia lodges strong protest against PRC over "violation of sovereignty."

Source: Prepared by J.C. Jenner.

INDEX

Note: **Bold** page numbers refer to tables; *italic* page numbers refer to figures and page numbers followed by "n" denote endnotes.

For Product Safety Concerns and Information please contact our EU representative GPSR@taylorandfrancis.com
Taylor & Francis Verlag GmbH, Kaufingerstraße 24, 80331 München, Germany

www.ingramcontent.com/pod-product-compliance
Lightning Source LLC
LaVergne TN
LVHW080801011026
849160LV00015B/1506
* 9 7 8 1 0 3 2 0 1 3 2 3 7 *